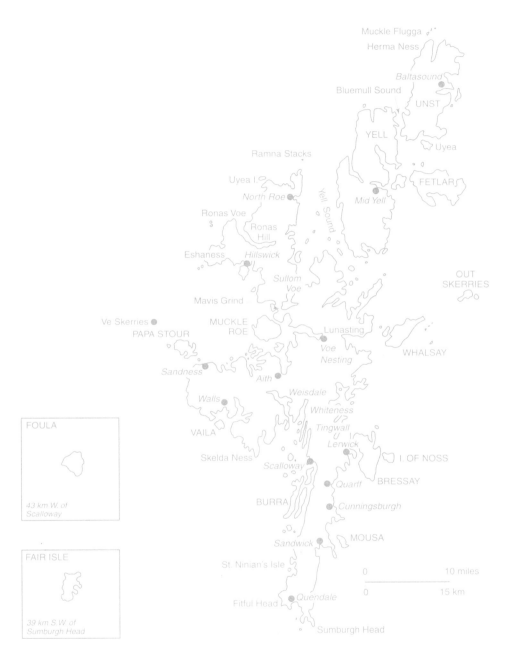

Muckle Flugga

Herma Ness

Baltasound

Bluemull Sound

UNST

YELL

Uyea

Ramna Stacks

Uyea I.

North Roe

FETLAR

Ronas Voe

Ronas Hill

Yell Sound

Mid Yell

Eshaness

Hillswick

Sullom Voe

OUT SKERRIES

Mavis Grind

Ve Skerries

MUCKLE ROE

PAPA STOUR

Lunasting

Voe

Nesting

WHALSAY

Sandness

Aith

Weisdale

Walls

Whiteness

VAILA

Tingwall

Lerwick

Skelda Ness

Scalloway

I. OF NOSS

Quarff

BRESSAY

BURRA

Cunningsburgh

Sandwick

MOUSA

St. Ninian's Isle

0   10 miles

0   15 km

Fitful Head

Quendale

Sumburgh Head

Map of Shetland.

D1612699

A Naturalist's Shetland

For Patricia

And strangely, the rose
clinging between the grass and the tangles,
its fragile bloom basking on the south-facing cliffs
in the unexpected company of campion and lovage,
thrift and plantain,
a tiny piece of porcelain in the focstle at Snarraness

Snapshots from a year at Snarraness

A Naturalist's Shetland

by J Laughton Johnston

Red throated divers

Illustrations by John Busby

T & A D
POYSER
NATURAL
HISTORY

Illustrations © John Busby
Text © 1999 by ACADEMIC PRESS

First published in 1999 by T & A D Poyser Ltd
24–28 Oval Road, London NW1 7DX

This book is printed on acid-free paper

Typeset by Paston Press Ltd, Loddon, Norfolk
Printed and bound in Singapore by Kyodo

A CIP record for this book is available
from the British Library

ISBN 0-85661-105-0

Contents

Cover illustration shows Arctic tern and phalarope.

Foreword

You don't need me to tell you that Shetland is a very special place. It certainly is to me – I like to think of it as one of my 'special subjects': the farther north I go, the closer I feel to my native homeland of Iceland. And this book by Laughton Johnston about his own ancestral homeland shows how special it is to him, too.

Laughton, who used to be a teacher, is a former colleague from Scottish Natural Heritage; he has now taken early retirement from SNH after 28 years with us and our predecessor bodies (the Nature Conservancy and the Nature Conservancy Council). Latterly he was the SNH Area Manager for Tayside and the Project Manager for the Cairngorms Management Project; before that he had been Chief Warden on the island of Rum (our flagship National Nature Reserve) for five years, and before *that* he had worked in Shetland for 13 years – indeed, it was while he was in Shetland that he made the career switch from teaching to the NCC.

Nearly 20 years ago he wrote *The Natural History of Shetland*, with Sam Berry, for the Collins New Naturalist series (1980). But time moves on, especially in the field of nature conservation and biological diversity. New research and surveys are always extending our knowledge and understanding, and have greatly increased the numbers of species recorded on Shetland. So this is not so much a revised version of that pioneering 1980 volume as a new book on the same topic.

Shetland is the marine Crewe Junction of the North. For my ancestors, the Vikings, it was the stepping stone from Scandinavia to the newly discovered territory of Iceland in the ninth century, and then part of the great Norse earldom of the Northern Isles that dominated large parts of Scotland for half a millennium.

For migrant birds and land mammals it has always been a happy landfall; those which settled became, like the Shetlanders themselves, isolated and specialized (the house mice, for instance, are among the largest recorded in the world) and in their own way unique, chiselled and honed by circumstance and survival.

As befits a former teacher who has also written and published a great deal of poetry, there is not only scientific precision but also a sweetly lyrical quality about his story of the long and sometimes stormy marriage between mankind and Nature in this northern outpost of the British Isles. The natural history of a place can never be separated from its cultural history. Laughton takes us from Shetland's geological origins through the Holocene period (the end of the Ice Ages, 12 000 years ago), through the arrival of the first human settlers to all the busy-ness of the oil industry that has so transformed the lives of today's islanders.

In between those significant brackets we read of the Neolithic farmers and the Picts and the Norsemen and how they harvested the bounty of land and sea. We read of the mosaic of habitats and their inhabitants, feathered and four-footed. We read of the astonishing biological diversity of the island and their surrounding seas, and of the effects of our efforts to exploit them, like the fish farming that has replaced deep-sea fishing, the agricultural support systems which have radically altered the face of the islands, and the impact of nature conservation to cope with changing social and economic imperatives.

It is an enthralling tale, told by an expert with expert help – a well-rounded and profoundly well-informed account of an archipelago of islands whose past and whose future are of crucial interest to all who have at heart the care of our natural and cultural heritage, and a care for Shetland itself.

Magnus Magnusson KBE
January 1998

Preface

S hetland is probably best known among naturalists for its teeming bird life, and for many years ornithologists have flocked to the islands from all parts of the world. There have been a number of excellent accounts of Shetland birds, notably Saxby's *The Birds of Shetland* (1874), Venables and Venables' *Birds and Mammals of Shetland* (1955) and Williamson's *Fair Isle and its Birds* (1965). For botanists there has been Thomas Edmondston's *A Flora of Shetland* (1854), the *Flora Zetlandica* by Druce (1922) and *The Flowering Plants and Ferns of the Shetland Islands* compiled by Palmer and Scott (1987). In 1974 the Nature Conservancy Council (NCC) organized a meeting on the natural environment of Shetland, and the proceedings thereof (edited by R. Goodier) were the first general, if abbreviated, account of the biology and geology of the islands. In 1980 *The Natural History of Shetland* by Berry and Johnston, which included a compilation of all the known species lists for the islands, was the first complete and systematic account of the biology and geology of Shetland. That book was particularly designed to meet the needs of the well-informed and interested naturalist.

I have undertaken this book in an attempt to make these works more available to a general readership and to summarize much of the other fascinating information about Shetland's natural history, as well as complementing more general accounts of the islands. Furthermore much information is hidden in theses and specialized journals, and there are many scientists who have worked in Shetland but never published their results. I have tried to record the sources of these data, so that they will be accessible to future workers; hence the extensive bibliography.

The last account of Shetland's natural heritage, *The Natural History of Shetland* (1980), of which I was co-author, is now out of print. Over the last 18 years an immense amount of research, survey and monitoring has been carried out that shed new light on the islands' geological and biological resources and on their histories. In addition, the species lists have been added to immeasurably and nowhere are they gathered together in one place and easily available.

Since the last account appeared there have also been huge changes to Shetland's industries and to the structure of Shetland's economy. An immense oil industry has come to dominate the local economy; fish farming has come to replace deep-sea fishing as the most important fisheries industry; while agricultural support systems are changing the landscape. To one extent or another these developments are having both direct and indirect effects on Shetland's wildlife.

Shetland has a biological significance as an isolated series of communities exposed to the stressful rigours of the North Atlantic. This outweighs any purely local importance it has as, for example, the principal breeding site in the Northern Hemisphere of the *bonxie* (great skua), or the possessor of some of the highest cliffs in the British Isles (on Foula). I believe, as does Professor R. J. Berry (co-author of the previous book), that Shetland should stand alongside the Galapagos, Hawaiian and Seychelles Islands as a gigantic field laboratory giving fundamental information about the reaction and resistance of living organisms to their environments.

There is also a renewed interest in our natural environment, and specifically that of Shetland, indicated by the increasing number of visitors who come to Shetland to view its wildlife, and among Shetlanders themselves, demonstrated by the local establishment of several natural history clubs and 'environmental' trusts, and the increasing role of environmental education in local schools.

This book necessarily builds on and summarizes the work of very many naturalists. Two chapters have been written by people who have made special contributions to our knowledge of Shetland: Chapter 2 by Professor Derek Flinn of the Geology Department of Liverpool University, who also contributed to Chapter 10, particularly on the geologists; and Chapter 9 by Mr David Okill, Chairman of the Fair Isle Bird Observatory Trust and Dr Roger Riddington the Warden. Professor Sam Berry contributed to Chapter 1 and to Chapters 5 and 10. Chapter 4 is based on the contribution of the late Professor David Spence of St Andrews University to *The Natural History of Shetland* (1980) and I am particularly indebted to Dorothy Spence for permission to use much of that material. Finally Dr Ian Napier of the North Atlantic Fisheries College, Scalloway, contributed the introductory marine section and the material on fish and fishing to Chapter 5. I am responsible for the rest of the text.

I hope this book will be of interest and use to the first-time visitor to Shetland, to the specialist concerned with particular groups or habitats, and to Shetlanders. To make the book more readable, I have been very selective with references within the text, although there is a full bibliography. The bibliography cannot include *all* the references for Shetland, but I hope it is reasonably comprehensive. I have also included as many lists of different plant and animal groups as I could in Appendix 3. Some of these lists (such as the birds and the flowering plants and ferns) will, I believe, be widely used; others (such as the lower plants and invertebrates) will be understandable and relevant to fewer people. Notwithstanding, it has seemed right to include all the lists as a summary of available facts about Shetland natural history to date, an indication of what has been achieved by dedicated naturalists and a pointer to where there are major gaps. I am very grateful to all those who compiled or helped to compile these lists: D. H. Dalby (lichens); Dr M. E. Newton (bryophytes and liverworts); W. Scott and R. Palmer for revising and abbreviating their published flora of Shetland; Dr B. R. Laurence (Diptera); J. E. D. Milner (spiders); the late R. M. Tallack (non-marine molluscs). I wish to thank the Royal Botanic Garden, Edinburgh, for allowing me to extract the list of fungi; this was originally published in *The Fungus Flora of Shetland* by Professor Roy Watling in 1992. I am particularly grateful to M. E. Pennington for contributing all the other insect lists and to K. Osborn of the Shetland Bird Club (and to all the members who have contributed over the years) for the very comprehensive list of the birds breeding and visiting Shetland.

I have also included an annotated list of places to visit (Appendix 1). I hope this will help tourist and professional alike to share the diversity and excitement that I find in the topography and natural history of Shetland and to find many of the places mentioned in the text.

Without the encouragement and support of several organizations and their staff and several others, who freely contributed information and gave constructive criticism, this book would have been quite incomplete and inaccurate in detail. I am especially grateful to: Scottish Natural Heritage and their staff, for the contribution of photographs and the map of protected areas and for access to their library and records, both at Edinburgh and Lerwick; Shetland Oil Terminal Environmental Advisory Group and their staff at Sumburgh, particularly Martin Heubeck; the Royal Society for the Protection of Birds and their staff at Sumburgh, particularly Pete Ellis; Centre for Continuing Education, Aberdeen University; BP Exploration, Aberdeen; Seabird and Cetacean Branch (Joint Nature Conservation Committee); Sea Mammal Research Unit; various departments of Shetland Islands Council; Shetland Islands Tourism; Shetland Amenity Trust; Shetland Environmental Education Trust; Shetland Bird Club, particularly Kevin Osborn; Shetland Entomological Group; Shetland Cetacean Group; Shetland Field Studies Group; Shetland Museum and Library; Shetland Meteorological Office; North Atlantic Fisheries College, Scalloway; and the Wildfowl and Wetland Trust.

Among those who read and commented on drafts or who provided other assistance and advice and to whom I am particularly indebted are Professor Sam Berry (University College London), Ruth Briggs (SNH), Keith Bennett (Cambridge University), Alan Blain (Shetland Amenity Trust), Ed Brown, Simon Butler, Professor Bob and Barbara Crawford (St Andrews University), Dennis Coutts, Callan Duck (Sea Mammal Research Unit), Pete Ellis (RSPB), Pete Evans, Noel Fojut (Historic Scotland), Bob Furness (Glasgow University), John Goodland (Shetland Fishermens Association), John Graham, Lolly Graham, Andrew Harmsworth (SIC), Paul Harvey (SNH), Jens-Keld Jensen (Faroe), James Mackenzie (Shetland Amenity Trust), Martin Heubeck (SOTEAG), Tony

Martin (SMRU), Eric Meek (RSPB, Orkney), Ian Napier (North Atlantic Fisheries College), Dave Okill (Fair Isle Bird Observatory Trust), Kevin Osborn (Shetland Bird Club), Richard Palmer, George Petrie (SOAFD), David Pottinger, John Scott, Walter Scott, Brian Smith (SIC), Jonathan Swale (SNH), Kate Thompson (JNCC, Aberdeen), Val Turner (Shetland Amenity Trust), John Uttley (SNH), Dave Wheeler (Fair Isle), Professor Graeme Whittington (St Andrews University), Jonathan Wills.

In addition to the many photographs contributed by SNH and several individuals, Derek Flinn provided several of the photographs for Chapter 2, while Bill Jackson kindly allowed me to use his award-winning photographs. I am grateful to Mary-Ellen Odie for permission to use a number of photographs taken by the late Bobby Tulloch and to David Edmondston of Buness and Joy Sandison who kindly allowed the reproduction of pictures of their famous antecedents.

Several people have contributed, or allowed me to use, tables and diagrams and to them I am most grateful. I consider myself very fortunate that John Busby agreed to contribute illustrations to the book that have enhanced it immeasurably and to him I am also particularly indebted.

To Alistair Clarke who rescued my manuscript and data from the maw of the computer on more than one occasion, and to Bob and Elaine Templeman who allowed free use of their photocopier and fax, many thanks. Additionally I must thank Shetland Amenity Trust for a loan towards the costs of an extended stay in Shetland, and P & O Ferries, Margaret Robertson, Betty and Dudley Annand and Elizabeth Balneaves for generous help in kind.

There are many gaps in our knowledge about Shetland's natural history. It is my hope that some may be stimulated by this book to fill them. Readers will no doubt find blemishes and for these I must take the blame. Notwithstanding, I shall feel my labours worth while if the volume helps amateur, professional and Shetlander alike to further understand, appreciate and care for Shetland's unique natural environment.

There are many old Shetland names and expressions, particularly for birds, and where I have felt they are still in common use, and indeed in use outwith Shetland, I have used them in the text. To make this account more accessible to the general reader I have omitted Latin names from the text (except in the case of subspecies) and have tried to avoid references in the text except for quotations.

I must point out that my pleasurable task in writing this book has been possible only because of an enormous amount of field and ground work carried out by many 'Shetland' naturalists, only some of whom I have been able to name. To them all I am very grateful.

Finally my biggest debt of gratitude is to my wife, Patricia Johnston, who earned the bread to allow me to indulge in the great pleasure of putting this book together.

CHAPTER 1

Between the North Sea and the Atlantic

Scene of houses and boats

The Zoology of Archipelagoes will be well worth examination.

Charles Darwin, after visiting the Galapagos Islands in 1835

Islands have a glamour – usually greater to outsiders than to the native islanders – that attracts visitors, whether they stay for a day or a decade; while islanders themselves usually have a great love of their home, fierce pride in their identity and a strong self-belief in their ability to manage the island's resources. Islands are also used to illustrate common and often complex political and social issues in a more simplistic form; one just has to think of the fictions based on islands, from *Gulliver's Travels* to *Lord of the Flies*. Even the smallest are often pawns in political machinations: witness the Falklands (Malvinas), Malta in the Second World War and Shetland from the ninth century to its impignoration as part of a dowry from Norway to Scotland in the fifteenth century. But supremely and perhaps surprisingly, they have played a significant part in the development of modern humans.

LINKS WITH GALAPAGOS

Until the latter half of the nineteenth century, the populations of the Western and Christian nations, who dominated the globe, assumed the world to be unassailably

1

stable and species to be immutable; the world created by God as it stood, regulated by rational laws. All this changed dramatically and painfully with the radical revolution effected by Charles Darwin and his advocacy of evolution, set out in *On the Origin of Species by Means of Natural Selection* in 1859. This book was published after years of agonizing, following his voyage and visit in 1835 to a small and remote group of islands in the Pacific, the Galapagos Islands, little more than twice the size of Shetland.

As a result of Darwin's theory of evolution, we are now conditioned to think of cause and the inevitability of change rather than continuous advance; intellectual and spiritual rootlessness has replaced the often fearful self-confidence and security of early Western society. It is a far cry from the relative peace of the islands to the turmoils of our urban society (although island societies seem to be catching up in today's world of instant communications), but there is a direct link, because islands are biological testing grounds for new processes, new possibilities. Many island forms are extreme developments of their mainland relatives and highlight the possibilities latent in more conservative fauna and flora. Indeed, islands prove the lie to dogmatic changelessness more effectively than any philosophy or history, Shetland no less than any other.

Darwin began to realize this on his journey around the world as naturalist on the *Beagle*. He first became suspicious about current biological ideas of the origin and relationships of living beings when he saw the variations of mammals in time and space in South America; he was then impressed by the tame and peculiar creatures of the Falkland Islands; but above all he was influenced by the unique forms existing on the Galapagos. In the same period, Alfred Russel Wallace, an English contemporary, was having his eyes opened by the unevenness of animal distribution, particularly in the Malayan archipelago and the East Indies. He too made a visit to South America, to the Amazon in 1848, and in 1858 presented a joint paper on natural selection with Darwin to the Linnean Society. Just 2 years before Wallace's South American trip and 10 years after Darwin's crucial visit to the Galapagos, a Shetland naturalist, Thomas Edmondston from Unst, stepped ashore on these same islands, perhaps asking himself the same questions. Tragically, as he landed on mainland South America at Ecuador on his return from the islands in 1846, he was killed in a careless accident.

Naturalists who saw rather than theorized were convinced of the rapid and therefore spectacular genetic changes that can occur in isolated conditions; and as the idea of biological change was accepted, so the naive and peculiarly Victorian doctrine of progress was taken over by economists, educationalists, sociologists, industrialists, politicians and even (though they are usually loath to acknowledge their academic pedigree) physical scientists.

These exotic sources of inspiration, however, have deflected us from the importance of our own offshore islands: the Channel Isles and Scillies to the south, the Hebrides to the west, Orkney, Fair Isle and Shetland to the north. We revel in, or retreat in exhaustion from, the romance, inconvenience and unpredictability of island life, but often do not appreciate the unique characteristics of their flora and fauna. This is not to belittle the achievements of the many individual naturalists and geologists who have pursued their interests in these islands, but merely to point out the gaps in our understanding of those parts of the British Isles where isolation

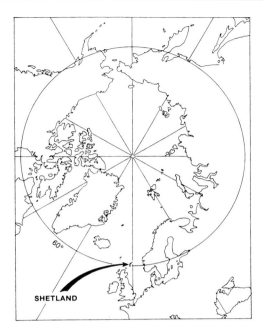

FIGURE 1 *Shetland in relation to other parts of the Northern Hemisphere* (from Berry & Johnston, 1980).

and environmental constraints often mean that pressures for adaptation are at their greatest.

The group of islands known as Shetland occupy a particular place here (Fig. 1): the northernmost and most isolated parts of the British Isles, lying in the track of the depressions that sweep eastward across the North Atlantic, yet on the same latitude as the southern part of Greenland, and as far north as the permanently snow-covered South Shetland Islands lie south in the Southern Hemisphere. At the coldest part of the last Ice Age, Shetland was covered by an ice sheet and was connected neither to continental Europe nor, for very long, to mainland Britain (see Chapter 2) as the ice melted. Consequently the present animals and plants have colonized the islands within the past 10 000–12 000 years, and hence provide information about the extent and efficiency of their transport and rate of evolution.

ISOLATION AND ADAPTATION

One of the most interesting biological discoveries this century has been the amount of genetic variation possessed by virtually all organisms. Sexually reproducing individuals receive sets of genes from both their parents; a number of techniques (most important, the electrophoretic separation of proteins) show that each individual receives slightly different forms (*alleles*) of about 1 in 10 of these genes from each parent. This means that there is a tremendous amount of inherited variation present in all populations. Now a small number of individuals is very unlikely to carry the same alleles in the same proportions as in the population from which they came: if a small group of individuals enters a habitat unoccupied by their species they will form the nucleus of a population that will almost inevitably differ in many ways from the ancestral population. The descendant population is therefore likely to have a unique set of allele frequencies, and these will form the basis of the population as the colonizers reproduce to fill the available territory. Thus island forms will immediately differ from their nearest relatives, and any further immigrants will have little impact on the gene frequencies established 'by mistake' in this way. The new form will thus depend to a large extent on the chance genetic constitution of its founders; this is known as the *founder effect* (Fig. 2).

Once a species has survived the initial establishment and dispersion phase of colonization, predators and parasites become important, and intraspecific pressures on space and fertility begin to operate. In other words, the species becomes exposed again to the checks that operated on its ancestors. However there will be differences.

1. The newly introduced form will have a paucity of genetic variation as a result of the founder effect, and possibly suffer a lack of adaptability.
2. Diseases and competitors will be less common than in a continental area.
3. The range of niches available for colonization is likely to be less than in the ancestral area.
4. Lack of gene flow from the same species living under slightly different conditions makes local adaptation easier and more precise. For example, flightless insects and seeds with reduced dispersal potential are far commoner on oceanic islands than elsewhere.

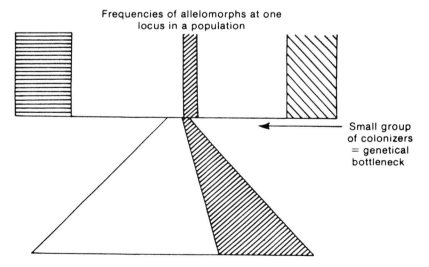

FIGURE 2   *The founder effect: a drastic influence on gene frequencies, which also results in a reduction of variation* (from Berry & Johnston, 1980).

5. The presence of few competing species provides more opportunities for adaptation to a wider variety of environmental opportunities (the radiation of Darwin's *Geospiza* finches on the Galapagos Islands is a well-known example of this).

All these facets indicate that the intensity of natural selection will be strong, and will not necessarily lead to convergence with the ancestral form. Almost certainly, however, the selective pressures will mean that the random changes of genetic drift will be far less common than is suggested in the literature. In time, the local island races will diverge so far from their nearest relatives as to become recognizable species. This last stage has, arguably, not been reached yet in Shetland, although some forms have been separated as true species by older taxonomists, such as the Shetland field mouse, *Apodemus sylvaticus fridariensis*; some modern taxonomists still consider Shetland's unique chickweed *Cerastium nigrescens nigrescens* to be a full species. There are also a number of other subspecies and microspecies.

One last point needs to be borne in mind: the evolutionary results of a 'founder event' followed by adaptation are likely to be much more marked than the effects of simple isolation on animals and plants, which leaves them as *relicts* on part of a previously continuous species range. Biogeographers tend to be overfond of invoking land-bridges to account for unusual distributions. Geologists believe the biogeographers' assertions and suggest evidence for the existence of these hypothetical stretches of land, which in turn is believed by biologists. Let it be explicitly repeated: the living animals and plants of Shetland are post-Ice Age colonizers. The islands have a vast intrinsic interest, but they have worldwide importance as representing, in microcosm and (because of their isolation) relative simplicity, the biological pressures of the last 10 000 years.

PHYSICAL CONTEXT

Tacitus records that a Roman fleet circumnavigated Scotland, and from its northernmost foray saw the edge of the world (*Dispecta est et Thule*). From the north of the Orkneys, on a clear day, it is possible to see three points of land: Fair Isle, Fitful Head at the south end of Shetland Mainland, and the furthermost, Foula. However it is probable that the Romans sailed no further; the violent currents of the 'roosts' between Orkney and Shetland and the changeable weather were unlikely to tempt early sailors further northwards towards the theological uncertainties of the *ultima thule*. However, a very different view of Shetland's geographical position occurs when looked at from another perspective, as we shall see.

Shetland lies in the so-called 'Gulf of Winter Warmth' produced by the North Atlantic and Shelf Currents. Only in very exceptional winters does any ice form on the sea. These currents, which bring relatively warm water from the south, cause the mean sea temperatures to be higher than the average for 60° N; there is not much difference in winter from the temperatures further south in Britain, although the northern summers are much cooler (Table 1). Rainfall is not excessive (Table 2), but there is frequent 'precipitation' due to the commonness of light rain or mist. The average monthly figures for relative humidity (80–85%) are the highest in

TABLE 1   *Temperature (°C): long-term monthly average, 1931–60 dataset (except Bergen 1951–60)* (reproduced with permission of the Meteorological Office)

	Tórshavn, Faroe	Lerwick, Shetland	Kirkwall, Orkney	Stornoway, Hebrides	Bergen, Norway	Kew, London
Jan.	3.0	2.7	3.1	3.1	0.9	3.7
Feb.	2.3	2.4	3.1	3.2	0.7	4.2
Mar.	3.3	3.5	4.7	4.8	3.7	6.6
Apr.	4.3	5.1	6.4	6.3	6.9	9.4
May	7.2	6.9	9.0	9.3	11.7	10.0
June	9.3	10.2	11.6	11.8	14.7	16.4
July	11.3	12.2	13.1	13.0	17.2	18.1
Aug.	11.1	11.9	13.1	12.6	16.5	17.3
Sep.	9.1	9.9	11.4	10.9	12.7	14.4
Oct.	6.5	7.4	8.4	8.1	8.3	9.5
Nov.	5.1	5.3	6.0	5.6	5.2	6.5
Dec.	3.8	3.8	4.4	4.5	2.7	4.5
Range	9	9.8	10	9.9	16.4	14.4

TABLE 2   *Precipitation (mm): monthly average, 1931–60 dataset (except Bergen 1951–60)* (reproduced with permission of the Meteorological Office)

	Tórshavn, Faroe	Lerwick, Shetland	Kirkwall, Orkney	Stornoway, Hebrides	Bergen, Norway	Kew, London
Jan.	149	109	105	152	143	54
Feb.	136	87	79	104	142	40
Mar.	114	69	65	80	109	37
Apr.	106	68	51	86	139	37
May	67	52	46	61	83	46
June	74	55	48	74	126	45
July	79	72	71	93	142	57
Aug.	96	71	75	104	168	59
Sep.	132	87	78	121	228	49
Oct.	157	104	113	142	235	57
Nov.	156	111	107	131	211	64
Dec.	167	118	112	149	204	48
Total	1433	1003	950	1297	1930	593

Britain. Indeed, an early writer accurately described the situation: 'the vapour of the sea tempers the air'. Sea mists are more common in summer than winter; temperatures are often too low to disperse low-lying fog in the summer months. Snow is not often a problem even though the winter is the wettest part of the year: it snows on about 40 days a year, but the snow rarely lies for more than a total of about 20 days and very often less.

The frequent low-lying cloud reduces the amount of sunshine (Table 3) and this means that the ground is slow to dry in the spring and the crops slow to ripen in the summer. This mist may be very local: Hamnavoe on the west coast of

1.   *Rainfall on the hill: rainfall tends to be light and often, clothing the hill and its blanket bog in dampness.*
(Courtesy of L. Johnston.)

2.   Pionersk *(klondyker) wrecked at Gulberwick 1994: shipwrecks are almost an annual event in Shetland's
winter storms.* (Courtesy of B. Jackson.)

Shetland has 13% more sunshine than Lerwick 13 km away on the east, and only
29 days of frost compared with an average of 51 in Lerwick. Notwithstanding the
frequency of low cloud, which indicates still conditions in other parts, Shetland is
one of the windiest places in Britain (Table 4). The mean wind speed throughout
the year is $7.1\,\mathrm{m\,s}^{-1}$ (15–17 m.p.h.), and gales occur on an average of 58 days a
year (a gale is defined as a wind exceeding $22.6\,\mathrm{m\,s}^{-1}$ for more than 1 hour).

TABLE 3   *Bright sunshine (hours): monthly average, 1931–60 dataset (except Bergen 1951–60)* (reproduced with permission of the Meteorological Office)

	Tórshavn, Faroe	Lerwick, Shetland	Kirkwall, Orkney	Stornoway, Hebrides	Bergen, Norway	Kew, London
Jan.	15	25	34	35	21	46
Feb.	41	51	60	62	63	64
Mar.	76	90	99	108	91	113
Apr.	113	132	150	142	156	160
May	137	165	169	195	182	199
June	140	158	170	173	182	213
July	109	125	135	128	179	198
Aug.	102	117	129	133	186	188
Sep.	82	105	114	111	98	142
Oct.	58	67	79	76	55	98
Nov.	22	33	40	45	33	53
Dec.	7	14	25	26	13	40
Total	902	1082	1204	1234	1259	1514

TABLE 4   *Wind speed (m s^{-1}): monthly average, 1961–90 dataset* (reproduced with permission of the World Meteorological Office)

	Tórshavn, Faroe	Lerwick, Shetland	Stornoway, Hebrides	Gatwick, London
Jan.	6.9	8.6	7.7	4.4
Feb.	6.6	7.8	7.2	4.3
Mar.	6.7	8.2	7.3	4.3
Apr.	5.7	6.7	6.1	4.1
May	4.9	6.3	5.9	3.9
June	4.6	5.8	5.6	3.5
July	4.7	5.8	5.4	3.4
Aug.	4.5	5.5	5.1	3.3
Sep.	5.7	6.9	6.3	3.3
Oct.	6.5	7.7	6.7	3.3
Nov.	6.5	7.8	6.7	3.9
Dec.	7.1	8.5	7.5	4.1
Year	5.9	7.1	6.5	3.8

1 m s^{-1} ≈ 2.26 m.p.h.
3.5–5.4 m s^{-1}, gentle breeze.
5.5–7.9 m s^{-1}, moderate breeze.
8.0–10.7 m s^{-1}, fresh breeze.

Some of the highest wind speeds in Britain have been measured at the top of Saxavord (285 m) in Unst: in early 1979 a gust of 118.7 m s^{-1} (202 m.p.h.) was recorded before the anemometer blew away. Shetland has a mean of 236 hours of gale a year, less only than the Bell Rock (255 hours) and the Butt of Lewis (378 hours), while Kirkwall in Orkney has a mere 52 hours. The highest average monthly wind speed at Gatwick (4.4 m s^{-1} in January) is still below the minimum average wind speed in Shetland $(5.5\,\text{m}\,\text{s}^{-1}$ in August). In January 1993 when the *Braer* went ashore at the south end of Shetland there were 25 gale days recorded in that month alone. Wind directions display two maxima: a wet southerly in winter due to Icelandic low pressure and a dry northerly in summer due to low pressure over Central Asia. High pressure over Scandinavia brings dry bright weather with winds from the east or south-east. Overall, the prevailing wind is from the south-west (Fig. 3). Shetlanders have an expression for 'good' days that aptly sums up the rigours of the climate: 'a day atween weathers'.

In midsummer the altitude of the sun at noon in Shetland is 53.5°; in midwinter it is 6.5°. The sun is above the horizon for 18 hours 52 minutes in midsummer, the *simmer dim* (when it is possible to read a newspaper at midnight by natural light), but for only 5 hours 30 minutes in midwinter. In south-west England the altitudes are 63.5° and 16.5° respectively. The extra hours of daylight in the northern summer are not very useful for plant growth because the angle of the sun is low and the sun's energy is not absorbed as readily as when the sun is higher in the sky. Additional daylight does not necessarily translate into sunshine; even in June Shetland still has 55 hours less sunshine than London (Table 3). However it extends the activity of the day by another third for Shetlanders and somewhat compensates for the short winter days.

Climatic change is normally a very slow process; global warming has not yet made any difference to long-term averages, but there are anecdotal and observable changes in Shetland over the last decades, similar to those reported from other parts of the British Isles, which may or may not be connected to global warming. It has

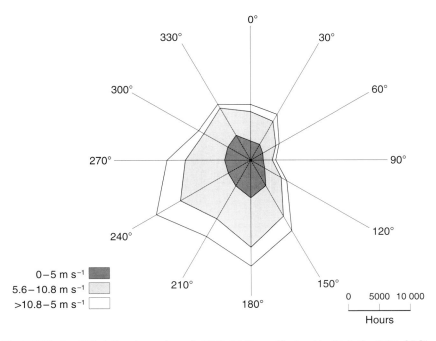

FIGURE 3   *Wind direction and speed, 1970–86* (from *Shetland in Statistics 1989*, SIC).

been noticed, for example, that there is almost a shift in the seasons. Cattle are presently let out in the spring a month or so later than in the past and, conversely, are out a month longer in the autumn before being taken in. It is also noticeable that harvest weather has not been as reliable as in the past and it is increasingly difficult to dry hay. Finally it is also becoming more difficult to grow grain crops as they are not ripening. Changes have also been recorded in sea temperatures in the north-east Atlantic, possibly causing a delay in the spring phytoplankton bloom with repercussions that may be affecting the timing and availability of food for fish and seabirds. We will have to wait another few decades to know if these climatic and oceanographic changes are simply short-term fluctuations or the beginning of something longer term.

GEOGRAPHICAL CONTEXT

Although we are accustomed, from our usual British mainland perspective, in regarding Shetland as the *ultima thule* for travellers moving north, if we look at the islands' position from another angle it becomes apparent that Shetland is an equally obvious landfall and stepping stone for all travellers from Scandinavia and from Iceland who are moving west and south (Fig. 4). Migrating peoples and animals usually choose their route intentionally, but in the natural world many

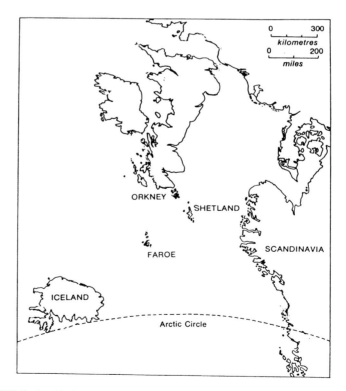

FIGURE 4   *Shetland's geographical position* (from Berry & Johnston, 1980).

animals and plants also travel unintentionally, subject to the natural agencies of the wind and the sea.

In human history Shetland was the most northerly point of the British Isles reached by Neolithic, Bronze Age and Iron Age peoples, and later also the first step for Vikings travelling west. However, a few thousand years before then, and ever since, spores of primitive plants, seeds of higher plants, insects and birds have dropped on to Shetland from all points of the compass (though relatively few from the open spaces of the North Atlantic to the west). The majority have undoubtedly come from the nearest landfalls of Orkney and the Scottish mainland, but many, like the later Vikings, have come from the next nearest landfall, Scandinavia.

Where climate and habitat have been similar to the point of origin, many of these travellers have settled and become part of Shetland's natural ecology. Shetland, we will see again and again in almost all groups, is a place where arctic, Scandinavian and southerly races and species overlap. For the natural world Shetland is a toe-hold only for a number of species whose main populations lie to the north, east or south.

Shetland's geographically isolated position as an island in the North Atlantic is, of course, relative and there are a number of differences in the composition of its flora and fauna when compared with those islands both more isolated to the north and less isolated to the south.

BIOLOGICAL CONTEXT

The natural history of Shetland then has been moulded by the caprices of colonization and the disciplines of adaptation. The same factors apply to an even greater degree to the Faroe archipelago (61° 20′ N, 6° 15′ W to 62° 24′ N, 7° 41′ W) lying to the north-west of Shetland, and even more remote from continental landmasses. The climate of Faroe, although a little wetter, is not strikingly different from Shetland (see Tables 1–4), but the appearance of the islands is very different, consisting of unwelcoming Miocene trap and basalt, with a number of vertical cliffs of 400–500 m. The highest sea cliffs in the world are at Enniberg on the Island of Vidov. There is very little cultivable land and the human economy depends heavily on fishing. Fewer species exist in Faroe than Shetland: for example there are about 50 regularly breeding birds in Faroe compared with about 70 in Shetland; the field mouse has never established itself in Faroe, despite being common in both Shetland and Iceland, and its place is taken by the house mouse; rabbits survive in only two places in Faroe. The 'native flora' (flowering plants and ferns excluding introductions) of Shetland is 393 species, while Faroe has only around 283. Such lists could be continued for a long time. A detailed comparison between Shetland and Faroe would be of considerable interest.

In contrast, Shetland's other island neighbour, Orkney (58° 42′ N, 3° 25′ W to 59° 23′ N, 2° 20′ W), is both more fertile and biologically diverse. Geologically it is composed of Old Red Sandstones, which also comprise the productive plain of Caithness. The landscape is more rolling and is extensively cultivated, especially for beef cattle production. Sand-dune formation is common. However the

Seals and tysties

climate is very similar: Kirkwall is only slightly warmer and drier than Lerwick. The big difference between the island groups is the close proximity of Orkney to the large island of Great Britain: the Pentland Firth is only 9.6 km across at its narrowest point. This means that Orkney shares most of its flora and fauna with the mainland, and although its natural history has many points of interest, the extent of gene flow from the south makes it essentially an outlier of north Britain.

The influence of the North Atlantic Current is most apparent when the North Atlantic islands are compared with localities elsewhere at the same latitude. Nanortalik on the east coast of Greenland lies on almost exactly the same latitude as Lerwick, yet the mean temperature in 5 months of the year is below freezing point, and the yearly mean is 5.5° C lower than in Lerwick. There is an extensive snow cover and frequent sea ice.

Even more extreme are islands in the Southern Hemisphere. In 1819, William Smith of Blyth in Northumberland was driven off course when sailing round Cape Horn and discovered the South Shetland Islands, so named because they lie on latitude 62° S. They were, he wrote 'a land condemned to everlasting rigidity by Nature'. Their biological history has been one of seal and later of whale exploitation. The South Shetlands are mountainous and actively volcanic. Only two species of vascular plant occur in the Antarctic, *Deschampsia antarctica* and *Colobanthus crassifolius*, although mosses and lichens may grow on snow-free ground and rock. There is no soil. The only land animals are less than 100 species of invertebrates: tardigrades, mites, ticks and representatives of five insect

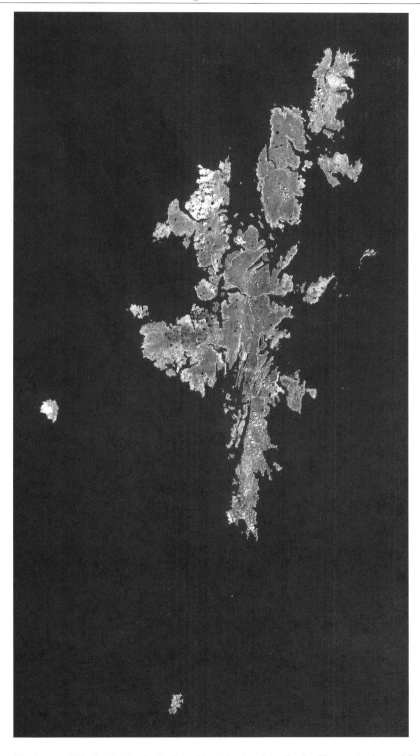

3. *Satellite image of Shetland: islands dominated by upland and peatland with an extensive and fragmented coastline.* (Courtesy of MSAT.)

orders. The climate in the South Orkneys (60° S) is only slightly less extreme. The British Antarctic Survey maintain a biological base on Signy Island in the South Orkneys.

The Falkland Islands are ecologically closer to Shetland than the South Shetland group, although they lie nearer to the equator (51° S, about the latitude of London in the north) and are somewhat cooler; no month is entirely frost-free. They are windy, with a mean wind speed of about $7.7 \, m \, s^{-1}$ (17 m.p.h.), and like Shetland are treeless. This means that the climax vegetation is heath and dwarf shrub grassland. There is up to 4.5 m depth of peat. Sheep farming is the main land use. Albatrosses replace gannets and penguins replace auks, but the general ambience of Falkland and Shetland is similar. Unfortunately, Falkland natural history (with the exception of birds: 63 breeding species, with 17 Falkland races recognized) is relatively poorly known.

Finally, Macquarie Island (58° 31′ S, 158° E) can be mentioned as a truly oceanic island. It lies about halfway between Australia and the Antarctic continent, and is swept by the prevailing westerly winds at all seasons. However the most noticeable feature of its climate is its uniformity, the coldest and warmest months having a mean temperature difference of only 4° C. Although it is a damp island like Shetland, the number of days with precipitation (317) is more marked than the total amount of rainfall (90 cm). Macquarie is treeless but well grassed and overrun with rabbits, which cause severe overgrazing in parts. Like Shetland it has its own biogeographical and evolutionary successes, but only 46 bird species and 38 vascular plant species.

HUMAN CONTEXT

People in Shetland faced the same opportunities and vicissitudes that faced other life that colonized the islands, including isolation, food shortage on occasion, competition from new colonizers, but above all the unreliability of the climate. The chief conclusions from a study of their character are, firstly, the extraordinarily constant pattern of life in Shetland over many centuries, as we shall see in Chapter 3; and, secondly, the pure Viking origin of the bulk of the population, although an analysis of the surnames of the inhabitants of South Mainland indicates that about one-third of the population in this region is of lowland Scottish origin, incomers in the years following the pledging of Shetland to Scotland by the King of Denmark in 1469.

The population has varied substantially over time. Prior to the Vikings it is very difficult to put a figure to it, but it is apparent that the fertile landscape was well filled by the Iron Age and perhaps earlier, with maybe several thousand inhabitants. By the twelfth century the population is estimated to have been around 10 000–12 000. It appears to have risen gradually through the medieval period and then grew rapidly in the nineteenth century, reaching an unsustainable peak of 31 000 towards the mid–late part of that century. It then fell rapidly towards the end of the century with large emigration. Thereafter a slow fall continued through both world wars and the slump of the 1930s as livelihoods were difficult to find, right up to the early 1980s and the arrival of oil. With the oil came many direct and ancillary jobs that attracted a return of Shetlanders and many newcomers. The population rose again to its present level of around 23 000. Shetland's method of dealing with the oil industry in obtaining the best controls and return to the community has become a model for other small isolated communities facing up to potentially overwhelming external industrial and commercial pressures.

The new and unprecedented oil wealth has coincided with dramatic changes in the crofting landscape and in the voes and sounds. Only a few years ago the crofting townships were composed of traditional single-storey crofthouses, with their black tarred roofs, surrounded by a patchwork of small fields, or *rigs*, of grain and root crops and hay, with tethered milk cows and sheep. Oil money has brought improved housing in the form of much larger and brighter modern and non-traditional buildings, which in some places form suburbs or dormitory villages for the capital Lerwick (Fig. 5), and in others sit incongruously, with no softening dykes or shrubs, on the edge of the hill land half surrounded by peaty moorland. At the same time the agricultural support system has encouraged the keeping of ever-increasing numbers of sheep. Reseeding of the hill land, which has been occurring for some 40 years, is now slowing. Within the hill dyke, fields are being 'improved' and turned over to permanent pasture or silage. The ancient contrast between the varied patterns of the green and yellow arable ground within the hill dyke and the grazed brown outwith has become blurred and in some places has disappeared altogether. There is still a strong connection to the land for many, but their numbers as a proportion of the population are dwindling. Meanwhile, in the sheltered voes and sounds has sprung up one of the most successful fish-farm industries in Britain. If the connection with the land is slipping, the love of the sea and use of the traditional Shetland boat has certainly not. Variants have been used for sailing and handline fishing for a 1000 years and today traditional designs are being built again purely for the pleasure of inter-community rowing competitions.

The new wealth has brought wonderful opportunities for Shetlanders and their children, which they have taken up with their usual vigour and imagination. The schoolchildren of Shetland today are as sophisticated as their mainland cousins, probably even more travelled and supported by educational, sporting, recreational and cultural facilities that are second to none. Although wild fishing is no longer as important as it was, Shetland (the island of Whalsay particularly) still has some of the most modern deep-sea fishing boats. Inshore, where local fishermen have traditionally harvested shellfish and where some species are now few in number, a new era of local control and conservation is dawning, supported by Shetland's own North Atlantic Fisheries College. Shetland today is thriving with industry and culture as it never has before.

NATURALISTS AND VISITORS

The usual approach to Shetland is either by plane to Sumburgh Airport at the southern end of Mainland or by the P & O ferry from Aberdeen to Lerwick. Both

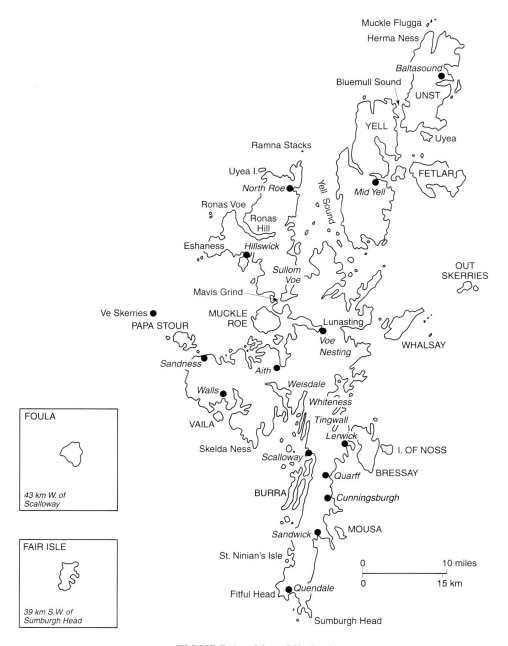

FIGURE 5 *Map of Shetland.*

introductions to Shetland give an impression of a stark and dull topography, of rolling, dark, peat-covered hills bordered by a largely rocky coast. As will become clear in the rest of the book, this apparent uniformity of the islands is very superficial, and conceals a wealth of geological and ecological variety.

4. *The P&O ferry* St Clair *passing the Bressay Lighthouse: the founder of the Pacific and Orient Shipping Company was a Shetlander, Arthur Anderson, and the main link to Shetland is still by sea, although there are daily flights for those in a hurry!* (Courtesy of L. Johnston.)

This is not the place to recapitulate the ways that ornithologists, botanists, geologists, pedologists, archaeologists and others, have recognized the complexity of Shetland's natural history and its evolution. However, a glance at the bibliography indicates the immense amount of investigation that has been carried out by scientists and naturalists over many years. In the chapters following the description of Shetland's geology, we look at the history of colonization and environmental change over the 12 000 years since the last Ice Age and at Shetland's wonderful range of habitats and wildlife, both marine and terrestrial, from its flora to its birds and mammals. We look at Fair Isle and the work of the Bird Observatory on migration and then say something about the many individual 'Shetland' naturalists who have contributed so much to our knowledge over the past 200 years and more. In the penultimate chapter we look at the oil industry and its operations over almost 20 years. Finally, in the closing chapter we look at the conservation of Shetland's natural history, the contribution of Shetlanders to it, at the island's industries and their impact on it, and at some of the lessons we must learn for the future.

Herring gulls and puffins

CHAPTER 2

The Making of Shetland

Foula on horizon

All is lithogenesis ....

On a Raised Beach, Hugh MacDiarmid

The Shetland Islands are a partially drowned range of hills rising above the flat continental shelf to the north of Scotland. The history of their development may be divided into two phases. During the first phase, beginning at least 3000 million years ago, the rocks forming the islands were made in all their diverse varieties and complicated relationships. Then in the period from about 350 million years ago to the present time the islands were carved by erosion from this complex mass of rocks.

Over most of Shetland the rocks belong to the deeply eroded ancient Caledonian mountain chain (Fig. 6), which extended from Norway and Greenland through Scotland and the northern part of Ireland to North America. A part of the basement on which this mountain chain was built can be seen in the extreme north-west of Shetland in the cliffs of Uyea, North Roe and the Ve Skerries to the north-west of Papa Stour.

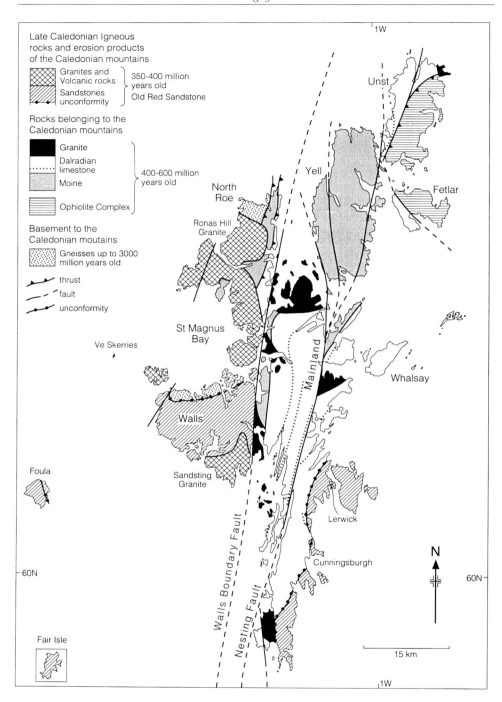

FIGURE 6   *Geology of Shetland* (courtesy of D. Flinn).

THE BASEMENT

The rocks of the basement in Shetland have ages ranging from more than 2900 million years to 1600 million years, and are composed predominantly of quartz and feldspar. They are similar to the Lewisian gneisses of north-west Scotland and the Outer Hebrides. They were already in existence in very much the same state as now long before the Caledonian mountains started to form. Even farther back, several thousand million years ago, they were granites intruded by small bodies of gabbro. Later, during the building of mountain chains much older than the Caledonian, they were recrystallized and deformed at high temperature deep in the earth's crust and thereby transformed into the gneisses now exposed in North Roe.

In the cliffs on either side of the entrance to Sand Voe in North Roe, these extremely old rocks forming the basement can be seen in direct contact with the younger, but still very old, rocks of the Caledonian chain to the east. The contact results from the rocks to the east being thrust westwards against the basement during the building of the mountains and is seen in the cliffs as a hair-sharp line. This contact or thrust is called the Wester Keolka Shear and is generally considered to be a continuation of the Moine Thrust, which in the North-west Highlands of Scotland separates the Lewisian basement to the west from the Caledonian rocks to the east. In the seas between Shetland and Orkney, oil prospectors have traced the thrust on seismic sections some 30 km or more down through the crust of the earth to the Moho or base of the crust.

THE CALEDONIAN MOUNTAIN CHAIN

The rocks of Shetland to the east of the Wester Keolka Shear form the roots of the now-eroded Caledonian mountain chain and are of four types: *metamorphic rocks*, which formed originally as sedimentary rocks accumulating on a continuously subsiding sea floor until they reached depths at which the temperature was so high that they were recrystallized to schists and gneisses; *sedimentary rocks*, the Old Red Sandstones, which were never heated to a sufficiently high temperature to recrystallize them into metamorphic rocks; *igneous rocks*, which rose in a molten state from the base of the crust or deeper into the metamorphic and sedimentary rocks; and subcrustal rocks from the *mantle*, the layer immediately below the crust, which have been thrust up to their present position above the crust as a solid mass.

Most of Shetland between the north of Yell and Fitful Head in the extreme south is formed of metamorphic schists and gneisses. In them the sedimentary layering, originally parallel to the sea floor on which they were deposited, is now nearly vertical. This layering runs parallel to the length of Shetland and the layers get progressively younger to the east. Thus the oldest of these rocks are those seen on the north-west coast of Yell and the youngest are those on the shores of Aith Voe, Cunningsburgh.

The rocks forming Yell were originally a rather monotonous succession of sandstones. After their deposition as sediments they were depressed to such a depth in the crust that the high temperature there caused their recrystallization.

They became schists, varying in mica content and rich in garnet. In many places they were so coarsely recrystallized as to become gneisses. They are equivalent to the Moine rocks that form most of the Highlands of Scotland north of the Great Glen.

The metamorphic rocks forming the west coasts of Unst and Fetlar to the east of Yell and in Mainland to the south of Yell are younger than those of Yell and equivalent to the Dalradian rocks of Scotland forming the Highlands south of the Great Glen. Many were originally sandstones as in Yell, but they accumulated in layers several kilometres thick, alternating with thick layers of limestone and volcanic lavas and ashes. Limestones, now metamorphosed to marbles, are well exposed north and south of Voe and in the Whiteness area. Volcanic rocks can be seen in the Scalloway quarry, in the cliffs of Hawks Ness north of Lerwick, and on the hillside and coast south of Mail, Cunningsburgh.

All these rocks accumulated on the sea floor in a trough caused by subsidence. The subsidence resulted from the stretching, thinning and fracturing of the crust as the continental plate below it was split and drawn apart. The thinning and fracturing of the crust led to the eruption of the volcanic rocks interlayered with the sediments. The final fracturing of the crust, when the two parts of the continental plate separated, was probably accompanied by the eruption of the kilometre-thick layer of volcanic rocks and pillow lavas occurring in the Mail, Cunningsburgh area. The pillow lavas formed when basaltic magma from below the crust erupted on to the sea floor and was chilled by the cold sea water as it erupted, so that it formed a mass of pillow-like bodies instead of forming a lava flow. Once the two parts of the continental plate had separated they moved apart, creating between them an ocean with a floor formed of gabbro and basalt.

About 100 million years later the two parts of the old continental plate came together again and their collision created the Caledonian mountain chain. The pile of sediments and volcanic rocks that had accumulated on the old subsiding sea floor was compressed and deformed between the colliding plates, so that it was forced down to great depths and regions of high temperatures and at the same time forced upwards to form mountains. The compression folded the layering of the sedimentary pile in Shetland into the upright attitude it now has, sheared it into discontinuous parts and thrust it westward on to the basement. At the same time the sediments deep in the crust were heated and recrystallized to schists and gneisses, and those uplifted above sea level to form mountains started to be eroded.

About 500 million years ago, during the collision of the two continental plates, slices of the ocean floor that had separated them with underlying mantle many kilometres in thickness were thrust up on to the metamorphic rocks. Thus, they too became exposed to the atmosphere and began to be eroded. The sediments created by this erosion accumulated in front of the advancing slices or nappes, were overridden, deeply buried and metamorphosed. During the metamorphism a variety of new minerals formed depending on the composition of the rocks and the temperatures reached. These minerals include biotite, chlorite, garnet, staurolite, kyanite, sillimanite, chloritoid, hornblende, epidote, diopside, microcline, talc and serpentine.

The remains of these slices or nappes of ocean crust and mantle (called ophiolite) can be seen forming the eastern halves of Unst and Fetlar. The Hill of Clibberswick, the Nikka Vord ridge north of Balta Sound in Unst and Vord Hill in Fetlar are slices of subcrustal mantle made prominent by the bright ochrous colour to which they weather. The hilly part of Unst south-east of Balta Sound is gabbro, which formed the oceanic crust overlying the mantle. On the north coast of Fetlar, north and east of Urie Ness, are conglomerates composed in part of pebbles of this gabbro, which were eroded from the gabbro as it was thrust into place and were then deformed and metamorphosed as the nappe overran them.

As a result of the collision of the two continental plates the roots of the mountain chain were forced down to regions of such high temperatures that rocks melted and rose as magma, which consolidated in cooler regions above as granite intrusions. The Sullom Voe area is occupied by such a granite, called the Graven Complex. It is about 9.6 km in diameter and was emplaced about 400 million years ago. It penetrated the metamorphic rocks in a very pervasive manner so that it is rich in xenoliths or fragments of metamorphic rocks up to 500 m across. In the region between Aith and Spiggie in south-east Shetland and extending under the sea to the west of Burra Isle are parts of another large mass of coarse granite intruded at about the same time.

THE EROSION OF THE MOUNTAIN CHAIN

By the time the Graven Complex had been emplaced, the buckling, folding, thrusting and metamorphism in the mountain chain had ended and erosion had become the dominant process. This had started much earlier, as soon as the rocks had risen above sea level. The higher the mountains were uplifted, the more rapidly they were eroded. For a time the mountains rose as fast as the erosion cut them down. This resulted in rocks that previously had been at great depth reaching the surface. In Middle Devonian times, 350 million years ago, erosion had already cut down to rocks in the Shetland area that, 50 million years before, had been 16 km or more deep. In the Spiggie and Quarff areas, Old Red Sandstones of this age can be seen resting unconformably on such rocks.

The material eroded from the mountains was deposited as sandstone in nearby low-lying areas. In the area between Shetland and Scotland the mountain chain had not only been breached by erosion but, by about 350 million years ago, had been buried again beneath a great thickness of Old Red Sandstones. It is possible that at one time the whole of Shetland was buried under Old Red Sandstones and that between Norway and Scotland none of the old mountain chain was left exposed.

During the deposition of the Old Red Sandstones molten granite continued to rise from the base of the crust. In places it penetrated not only the metamorphic rocks of the mountain chain but also their overlying erosion products. The Sandsting Granite in the Walls area cuts and metamorphoses the Old Red Sandstones. The Ronas Hill Granite very nearly reached the surface before it crystallized about 355 million years ago. Magma did reach the surface about that

5. *Sea stacks, The Drongs, Hillswick: on the Atlantic coast especially, the erosive power of the seas has exploited differential weaknesses in the rocks to create enormous natural sculptures.* (Courtesy of SNH, Lerwick.)

time and formed volcanoes. Considerable amounts of volcanic ashes and lavas can be seen interbanded with the Old Red Sandstones of the Walls area, while the cliffs of Esha Ness are a section through the side of a volcano. In these cliffs can be seen basaltic and andesitic lavas and layers of rock fragments produced during eruptions. Nearby, at Grind of the Navir, there is a sheet of ignimbrite formed from a nuée ardente, an incandescent cloud of drops of liquid rock explosively ejected by the volcano.

The sides of the old Caledonian mountains with their schists and gneisses enveloped in Devonian screes and sandstones can be seen all along the coast of Shetland, from Rova Head near Lerwick to Little Holm just west of the airport runway at Sumburgh and from Aith to Melby on the west side. To the north of Lerwick, at Rova Head, and extending eastwards into Bressay are great masses of conglomerate composed of large rounded boulders of granite and quartzite. These boulders are erosional fragments that were broken from the bedrock and washed along steep-sided rocky canyons through the mountains to the west of Lerwick during Devonian times. By the time the fragments had reached the Lerwick area they had become rounded, but there the canyon ended and the water that had carried the boulders along the canyon floor through the mountains spread out thinly over the Old Red Sandstone plain to the east leaving the boulders behind as an alluvial cone.

Sandy material washed along with the boulders was carried farther out by the streams and formed beds of sandstones that become progressively finer grained to the east. The sandstones were deposited by braided streams and distributaries flowing over the flat plains beyond the mountains. They are well exposed in the cliffs to the south of Lerwick. Characteristic of them are ripple marks on bedding planes and associated current bedding.

At times large freshwater lakes formed on the sandstone plains, in which fish and primitive vascular plants lived. Their fossilized remains can be found in several places. The plants of those times were too primitive to be able to live away from water so that the hillsides were bare of vegetation and erosion proceeded at a faster rate than at present.

THE SHAPING OF THE ISLANDS

From Middle Devonian times, about 350 million years ago, until about 50 000 years ago, towards the end of the Pleistocene, the period of Ice Ages, no rocks were formed in Shetland that have survived until the present day. There is, therefore, little direct evidence of what happened in Shetland area during that period, and the next phase in the history of the islands, during which they were carved by erosion from the remnants of the mountain chain into their present shape, has to be based on evidence from rocks found elsewhere. Much of this evidence has been obtained as a by-product of the search for oil under the seas around Shetland.

Nearly 300 million years ago the continental plate started to split again down the middle of what is now the North Sea. The land there started to subside to form a sea-filled trough once again. In this trough, the Viking Graben, sandstones eroded from the surrounding area including Shetland began to accumulate during Permo-Triassic times. The sandstones, then and later, periodically filled the Graben and spread beyond towards Shetland. Remnants are found at the foot of some of the present-day cliffs of Shetland, showing that at that time the islands were already taking shape.

Also at about that time movement took place on the Walls Boundary Fault and the Nesting Fault due to crustal compression. On the Nesting Fault the crust on the west side of the fault moved northwards about 16 km relative to the crust on the east side, as shown by the displacement on rock boundaries intersected by the fault. On the Walls Boundary Fault the movement was many times greater and more complex. The Walls Boundary Fault is probably a continuation of the Great Glen Fault in Scotland and its west side first moved southwards relative to the east side. Later it moved northwards, leaving a displacement of about 60 km on the Old Red Sandstones and a larger displacement on the older Caledonian rocks. The displacement across the faults is the result of a series of small movements each accompanied by an earthquake. The sliding movement of the two sides of the fault against each other crushed and sheared the rocks on either side. Along the Walls Boundary Fault the zone of broken rock is generally more than 0.8 km wide. In Calback Ness in the Graven Complex, the rocks are so shattered by the movements on the nearby Walls Boundary Fault that the area was found to be unsuitable for underground oil storage.

Subsidence and deposition continued in the Viking Graben area with little interruption until recently. During this time the oil and gas fields were formed there. However, the crust did not split and separate as it had done at the beginning of the formation of the Caledonian mountains; instead about 65 million years ago, at the end of the Cretaceous Period; the continental plate split to the west of Shetland and a new ocean, the Atlantic Ocean, formed as the two sides moved apart.

Sedimentation continued around Shetland until recently, with the sea level periodically rising and falling. One of the greatest rises took place during the Cretaceous Period. If at this, or any other, time Shetland subsided beneath the sea and was covered by sediments, when sea level fell again the cover was eroded leaving Shetland as an island mass or a range of hills rising above the surrounding younger sediments, as it appears today.

THE ICE AGE

Between 1 and 2 million years ago the climate became colder; since then ice sheets have formed in the Northern Hemisphere, extending at times over Europe and Shetland. Only a little is known about the history of Shetland during this time, the Pleistocene. The islands must have been covered by ice a number of times, but only the last ice sheet left much evidence of its presence. However it did not destroy all evidence of earlier glaciations.

At Uyea in North Roe and at Sel Ayre to the south of Melby small patches of peat can be seen, in the cliffs, underlying till or boulder clay deposited by the last ice sheet. This peat was formed at least several tens of thousands of years ago during one or more of the warm intervals that separated successive glaciations. The peat overlies till deposited by an earlier ice sheet that had covered Shetland prior to the warm period. There is other evidence for the existence of an earlier ice sheet: 5 km north of Sumburgh Airport is a boulder of rock from Tønsberg, just south of Oslo in Norway; it is called the Dalsetter erratic (Fig. 7) and weighs about 1.5 tonnes. Since Norwegian ice did not reach Shetland in the last glaciation, this boulder must have been carried from Norway to Shetland by an earlier ice sheet, when Shetland was covered by ice that crossed the North Sea from Norway.

The last glaciation started about 25 000 years ago and was over by 12 000 years ago. For part of this time the islands were covered by a local ice cap, which flowed to the west on the west side of Shetland and to the east on the east side (Fig. 7). In the south it flowed southward over Fair Isle and westward over Foula. Flow to the south-west may have been blocked by ice over Orkney. The northern edge of the Shetland ice cap lay over the northern tips of Unst and Yell (see Fig. 8), which were ice-free.

As the ice in the ice cap flowed it picked up loose rock and soil and nearly all the till left by the previous glaciation. Armed with this material embedded in its lower surface the ice attacked the bedrock, scouring and grinding the rock surface where the flow impinged on it and plucking away blocks of rock from the lee sides of protuberances. All this loose material was carried radially outwards and deposited

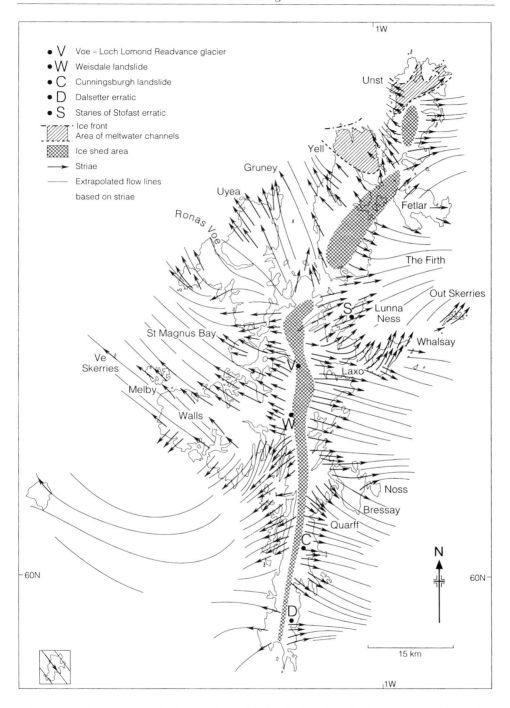

FIGURE 7   *Patterns of ice flow on Shetland during the last glaciation* (courtesy of D. Flinn).

6.   Glacial erratic, Stanes of Stofast, Lunna Ness: an illustration of the power of ice in lifting and transporting this 2000-tonne rock, now weathered into fragments. (Courtesy of D. Flinn.)

on low ground as till when the ice melted. The direction in which the ice flowed can be determined from a study of the scratches or striae on the ice-scoured surfaces and from a study of the distribution of erratics, blocks of rock carried along by the flowing ice. The largest erratic can be seen on Lunna Ness, broken into several parts by weathering. This erratic is called the Stanes of Stofast (Fig. 7) and weighs about 2000 tonnes, but most erratics are very much smaller.

By 12 000 years ago the ice had melted. As it melted the meltwater escaped from beneath the ice through tunnels within the ice and at its contact with the bedrock. Where the meltwater tunnels met the bedrock they eroded it, so that when the ice melted round-bottomed or U-shaped channels were left on the hillsides marking the sites of the tunnels. These channels, now usually lacking streams, run up, down and along the contours, unlike the V-shaped channels formed by subaerial streams flowing across the contours under gravity. In the tunnels in the ice the water moved under pressure, as it does in household plumbing, and so flowed uphill as well as down. There are many examples of subglacially eroded channels in the north of Yell and Unst (Fig. 8). The car park at the lighthouse station at Herma Ness is in a particularly good example. On a much larger scale are the subglacial valleys cutting through watersheds. These include the valleys in Unst leading to Wood Wick from the east and to Nor Wick from Haroldswick and the valley in Yell leading northwards to Gloup Voe. Immediately south of Tonga, on the west side of Unst, is a deeply incised gorge eroded by meltwater dammed by the ice cap to the east escaping over the cliffs.

The melting ice left a discontinuous layer of till in some of the lower-lying areas. If it left any moraines, these are now beneath the sea. In several places hillsides were over-steepened by glacial erosion under the ice. When the ice melted the hillside collapsed. On the west side of the valley of Weisdale (at map reference HU 385524) is a giant landslide scar. In the Cunningsburgh area is another similar landslide (at map reference HU 424291), the slid mass of which, below the road, can be mistaken for hummocky moraine.

After the ice had melted the climate became better than it is at present; the islands were repopulated by plants and peat started to form in the bottoms of the

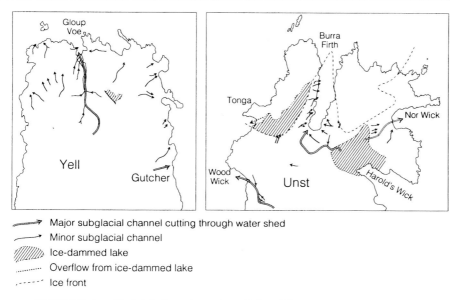

Major subglacial channel cutting through water shed

Minor subglacial channel

Ice-dammed lake

Overflow from ice-dammed lake

Ice front

FIGURE 8   *Glacial drainage in northern Yell and Unst* (courtesy of D. Flinn).

lochs. Then, about 10 000 years ago the climate worsened again during a period called the Loch Lomond Readvance in Scotland. This resulted in the formation of a small ice cap in the western Highlands of Scotland. In Shetland a small glacier formed in the Loch of Voe area (Fig. 7), which overflowed westward into Olna Firth at Voe. It left very slight traces of moraine in the Wethersta area and a barely discernible but perfectly formed terminal moraine south of Loch of Voe, both of which have been largely destroyed by road and agricultural improvement but can still be seen on old aerial photos.

7.   *Glacial overflow channel, Tonga, Unst: a valley enlarged by the flow from the ice shed on Unst during the last glaciation.* (Courtesy of D. Flinn.)

THE LANDSCAPE

The weight of an ice cap causes the land beneath it to be depressed and in compensation a ring of land around the ice cap to be uplifted. The ice over Scotland depressed Scotland, but the ice cap over Shetland may have lain within the zone of uplift caused by the Scottish ice cap being too small to have affected the uplift. When the ice melted the sea level rose, but the depressed land only recovered slowly. As Scotland rose a series of shorelines were cut into the hillsides by the sea. These raised shorelines occur at lower and lower levels to the north in northern Scotland and die out in Orkney. At that time Shetland was sinking instead of rising so that any early shorelines there are now below sea level.

It is not yet clear whether, when the ice melted, it left a dry-land connection to Scotland or whether the sea level had already risen sufficiently to drown the land. The sea level is thought to have fallen 130 m relative to the land during the glaciation and the deepest point between Shetland and Scotland is 93 m below present sea level about 14 km north of Fair Isle. However, the sea seems to have risen relatively slowly as the ice melted so that the land-bridge to Scotland was only drowned about 11 000 years ago, after all the ice had melted and before colonization by plants and animals.

Since the ice melted Shetland has been invaded by a continuously rising sea, which now dominates the landscape. The inland landscape of Shetland is one of hills and of valleys invaded by the sea. These reflect the underlying geology in a remarkably faithful manner. The large-scale layering of the metamorphic rocks underlying Mainland from Delting to Fitful Head is exactly reflected in the ridge and valley topography. Aerial photos can reveal in extraordinary detail the finer layering of these rocks and the offsets in them caused by small faults. Some of the larger granite masses cause topographic highs and some lows according to their resistance to erosion. The Graven Complex in the Sullom Voe area causes a topographic low, while the Ronas Hill Granite forms the highest hill in the islands. The Walls Boundary Fault, the Nesting Fault and the thrust marking the western edge of the serpentinite in Unst all lie in topographic depressions.

This topography seems to have been etched out of the rocks by a uniformly acting atmospherically controlled process. The topographic features do not cut across geological lines in the way that they would if, for example, rivers had been the dominant eroding agent. Even glacially formed features are all on a small scale. Aerial photos reveal patches of ice-formed fluting on the hills too weakly incised to be detectable on land. Topographic moulding by ice erosion occurs only on a small scale, as for example on the craggy topography of Lunna Ness and Lunnasting. If the dominant mechanism of erosion has, indeed, been atmospheric then the landscape has been forming very slowly, especially since plants evolved that could cover the hills with a protective layer.

However, there are several topographic features that are unrelated to geology. The most spectacular of these is the gap through the Clift Hills at Quarff. Less well-developed east–west gaps through the north–south trending and geologically controlled ridge-like hills occur at Voe, Yell Sound and Mid Yell. These may possibly be remnants of deep valleys cut by rivers when Shetland was part of a much larger group of hills, as it was in Middle Devonian times.

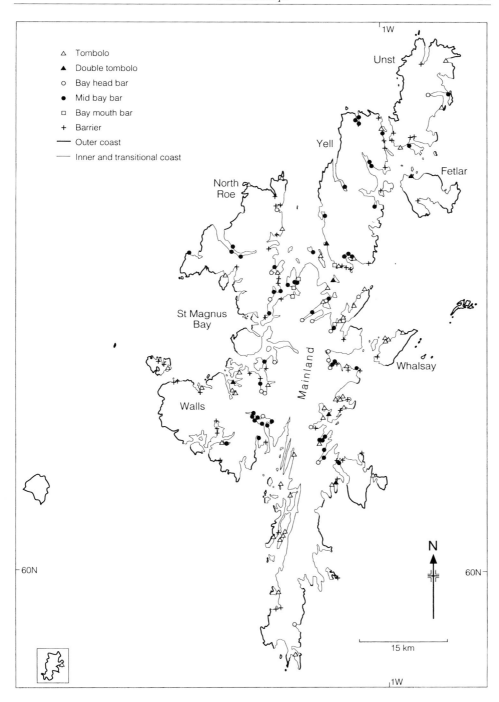

FIGURE 9 *Bars, spits and tombolos on the inner coast* (courtesy of D. Flinn).

8.   *Inner coast, White Ness and Strom Ness: typical of the long sheltered voes created by the drowning of valleys. Note the green limestone grassland of White Ness on the left contrasting with the brown moorland on the schists of Strom Ness.* (Courtesy of L. Johnston.)

The invasion of Shetland by the rising sea has given rise to two different forms of coastline: the *inner coast* and the *outer coast*. The inner coastline, composed of voes, firths and sounds, penetrates the islands so deeply that it is not possible to be much more than 5 km from the sea anywhere in Shetland. As the sea rose it turned hills into islands separated by sounds, and river valleys and even whole drainage basins into voes and firths. The waters of the inner coast are so sheltered from the waves of the open sea that little erosion took place in them as the sea flooded the valleys. Usually the sea was only able to erode the layer of peat and till to form a small cliff, a metre or two high, at the back of a rocky beach, but was unable to cut into the bedrock. At the heads of many of the voes the sea has been unable to erode even the peat, which now forms the beach. On the more exposed parts of the inner coast, where the rocks have been weakened by faults and groups of closely spaced joints, the sea has been able to cut into the bedrock to produce caves and long, narrow, rocky-sided inlets called *geos*, a characteristic feature of the Shetland coastline. In places the cave roof has collapsed, wholly or partially, thus giving rise to some of the *geos* and to inland holes such as the Holes of Scraada at Eshawick and similar holes on Papa Stour and, on a smaller scale, to blow-holes.

The till and loose fragments of bedrock stripped from the valley sides as the sea rose produced much gravel and sand, which has accumulated at sea level in a series of beaches, spits, bars and tombolos along the coastline (Fig. 9). Many of these are features that jut out into the sea, in a manner characteristic of very recently drowned coastlines. Spits tend to form at the head, in the middle and at the mouth of narrow inlets or voes. A particularly interesting example occurs at Swinister in Dales Voe, Delting, where a tombolo or bar connecting the island of Fora Ness to Mainland has thereby given rise to a small voe to the east, which has

9.   *Voe bars, Dales Voe: the sinking coast provides material for an enormous number and variety of coastal bars, often resulting in the formation of brackish and sometimes freshwater lochs.* (Courtesy of D. Flinn.)

developed a typical bay-head bar and a mid-bay bar. Continued accumulation of beach material can lead to the voe behind a spit being cut off from the sea by the spit extending right across the voe to become a barrier. The water behind the barrier then becomes a freshwater loch. Many freshwater lochs on Shetland, including Loch of Spiggie at the south end of Shetland, Loch of Cliff in Unst and Loch of Tresta in Fetlar, owe their existence to this process.

10.   *Tombolo, St Ninian's Isle: one of the most beautiful and symmetrical sand bars in Europe, connecting the island to Mainland.* (Courtesy of L. Johnston.)

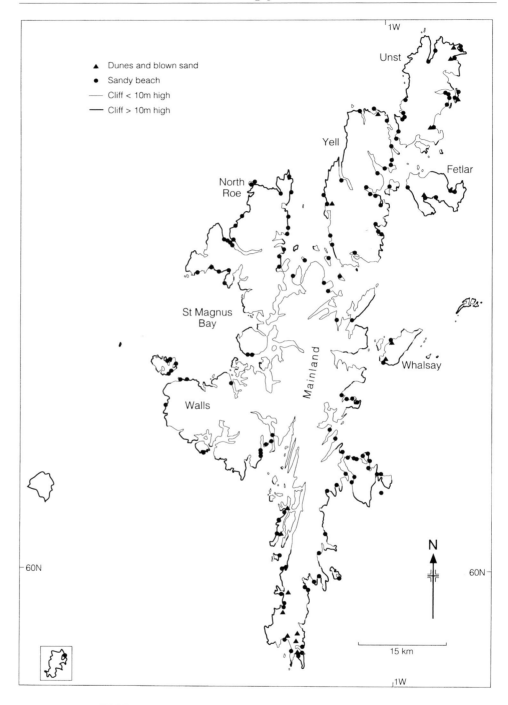

FIGURE 10   *Sandy beaches and cliffs* (courtesy of D. Flinn).

There are about 50 tombolos or bars joining islands to nearby shores in Shetland. The biggest and most beautiful of these is St Ninian's Ayre, a perfectly formed sand tombolo about 0.5 km long. The sand is probably a layer a few metres thick overlying pebbles. The tombolo was formed by waves from the Atlantic to the west being bent (refracted and diffracted) round the island on either side and meeting behind the island. In the meeting zone sand and pebbles on the sea floor, swept along by the waves, accumulated to form the tombolo.

Sandy beaches are prominent features of the Shetland coastline (Fig. 10). There are about 100 of them, varying from little more than a few metres up to 1 km in length. The sand on Shetland beaches is very variable in composition. The beaches vary from zero to 100% shell sand, but most commonly contain about 50%. The rest of the sand is made of siliceous minerals, dominantly grains washed out of the local till or obtained from local smashed or deeply weathered rocks. The local origin of the sand is made obvious by the occurrence of the same minerals in the sand, the local till and the local bedrock. The rocks of Yell are particularly rich in garnet, and the sand beaches there are commonly marked by streaks of red-garnet sand. The sandy beaches in the Wick of Gruting, Fetlar, are rich in magnetite. The beach at the head of Burra Firth in Unst is rich in muscovite, while small patches very rich in magnetite and garnet occur in the eastern part of the beach.

Drongs

The outer coast has a very different appearance from the inner coast, although it is usually separated from it by less than 1 km of transitional coastline. The outer coast faces the open sea and is formed of cliffs cut into the hard rocks. They vary in height from a few metres to 350 m (in Foula). The lower cliffs are swept by the sea

11.   *Outer coast, Silwick from Skelda Ness: typical cliff scenery exposed to the full force of the North Atlantic.*
      (Courtesy of L. Johnston.)

so that bare rock extends from sea level for several tens of metres inland and usually
is partly covered by boulder beaches. While the inner coastline follows the
contours, the outer coastline cuts across them, truncating hills and valleys. In
consequence the outer coast is interrupted by drowned valleys or voes and
truncates other valleys so that the streams in them reach the sea by falling over a
cliff.

On the inner coast the land surface passes without deflection beneath the surface
of the sea, while on the outer coast the cliffs truncating the land surface plunge
steeply beneath the sea to reach the surrounding sea floor of the continental shelf at
a depth of 82 m within 0.8 km of the shoreline, Shetland being surrounded by
deeper seas than any other part of the British Isles.

Shetland thus has two erosion surfaces (Fig. 11). The inland landscape of hills
and valleys is a subaerial erosion surface, while the cliffs, subaerial and
submarine, are a marine erosion surface. Both are extremely old. The inland
landscape has been little influenced by the glaciation so that it is much older than
the whole Pleistocene Ice Age. The same applies to the cliffs of the outer coast.
The depth of water at their feet is far less than the height of the great cliffs of Hill
of Clibberswick, Noss, Fitful Head, Foula and Ronas Hill, so that quite a small
retreat of these cliffs since the end of the Ice Age would have filled the sea at their
feet with erosional debris. Therefore, like the inland landscape the erosion surface
forming the outer coast must have been in existence before the Pleistocene Ice Age
very much as at present and the cliffs must be far older than the present rise in sea
level.

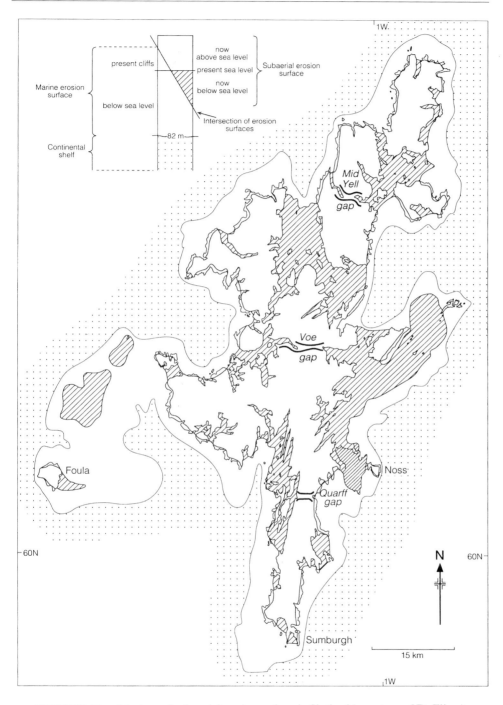

FIGURE 11 *Marine and sub-aerial erosion surfaces in Shetland* (courtesy of D. Flinn).

12. *Foula cliffs: the highest cliffs in Shetland, plunging at The Kame over 350 m to the sea.* (Courtesy of L. Johnston.)

GEOLOGY AND THE ENVIRONMENT

The nature of the rocks underlying the landscape exercises a strong influence on the plant cover, especially in the absence of agricultural intervention. This is considered in detail in Chapter 4. Most of Shetland, like much of Scotland, is covered by a layer of hill peat, or was until it was removed for fuel or cultivated. This peat accumulated on till or on siliceous rocks such as Old Red Sandstones, granites and metamorphic schists and gneisses for the last 7000 years or so. However, several types of rock created environments inimical to the accumulation of peat.

In particular, the large areas of serpentinite in Unst and Fetlar produce a very poor soil due to the lack of potassium, calcium, phosphorus and other elements in the rock. As a result the plant cover on the serpentinite was insufficient to give rise to a peat cover. The adjacent gabbro areas are similarly devoid of peat, though it is possible that in this case it has been completely removed by the inhabitants. Areas where sand has been blown inland from beaches and areas underlain by limestone and Old Red Sandstones are all more fertile than those underlain by siliceous schists and gneisses because of their calcium content.

Another area that owes a special appearance to the nature of the underlying rock is the Keen of Hamar in Unst. Here the serpentinite bedrock became crackled during the mountain building. Alternate freeze and thaw in a damp climate acting

13.   *Blockfield, Ronas Hill and the North Roe plateau: an arctic–alpine landscape shaped firstly by ice and then by the regular freezing and thawing of water in the thin soils.* (Courtesy of SNH, Lerwick.)

on the minute cracks has broken the exposed surface layer into a mass of tiny angular fragments. This layer, or regolith, is constantly churned by the freeze and thaw so that on steeper slopes stone stripes have developed due to fragments moving downhill. The effects of this environment on the plant community is considered in detail in Chapter 4. The summit of Ronas Hill is similar in some ways. The Ronas Hill Granite has been intensely shattered on its west side as seen in the cliffs at the back of the Lang Ayre and extending east to include the summit. Frost action there breaks down the exposed rock into a layer of fine angular debris that resists weathering into a soil, and is churned by freeze and thaw action. Both these areas have been considered to be the result of arctic conditions, but the nature of the rock is the controlling factor as both are matched by areas of unshattered rock where the regolith does not form. The summit of Foula, formed of Old Red Sandstones, is the same height as Ronas Hill but is insulated from frost by an unbroken cover of vegetation that is able to grow because of the more fertile nature of Old Red Sandstones. In Unst large areas of unshattered or uncracked serpentinite of the same type as that at Keen of Hamar are exposed to the atmosphere and fail to break down into a similar regolith.

EXPLOITATION

The rocks of Shetland have been exploited by humans from the earliest times. Some dykes of felsite in North Roe were used by early inhabitants to make polished stone axes of the finest quality, many of which can be seen in the Shetland Museum. In Norse times many deposits of steatite were worked for the manufacture of cooking utensils and fishing weights. The resultant quarries are particularly well preserved in Fetlar and Cunningsburgh. In the present century steatite has been quarried for industrial use in Unst. Schists and sandstones have been used in different parts of Shetland for the production of millstones for horizontal water mills and hand mills and earlier for knocking stones and trough querns.

As well as the production of steatite for its talc content, other minerals have been worked. A number of small copper veins are scattered over the area between Fitful

Head, Wadbister Ness and Noss. The copper occurs in the form of the mineral chalcopyrite. At Sandlodge the chalcopyrite is sparsely disseminated in a thick vein of ankerite. Attempts were made to mine this vein around 1800 and again in the 1870s and the 1920s, but more money was spent on sinking shafts than was gained from the sale of ore. In 1802 a steam engine built by Trevithick was installed to help work the mine. This particular engine was the world's first purpose-built high-pressure steam engine, the type of engine that powered the nineteenth-century industrial revolution until internal combustion and electric motors took over. Thus for the 2–3 years until it was replaced by an old-fashioned atmospheric steam engine, Shetland can be said to have led the world technologically.

Chromite was discovered at Baltasound in Unst by Samuel Hibbert in 1817. It was mined intermittently in the last century for the manufacture of yellow lead chromate pigment and in this century for use as a refractory. This activity had a greater impact on the environment than the copper mining as it involved quarrying and so left a series of pits and spoil heaps on the hills around Baltasound.

During the 1930s, D. Haldane, a Geological Survey officer, discovered some scarn-magnetite masses in the Sullom area. One was opened up by a Canadian army unit during the Second World War. After the war the magnetite was taken out and used for coal cleaning. Later the scarn was quarried for road metal.

Sand beaches have been used until recently for building sand and to a lesser extent for agricultural use. This has led in the past to the destruction or partial destruction of several fine beaches. This form of exploitation has stopped, but quarrying for stone for construction purposes takes place at a number of sites throughout the islands on both a large and a small scale for local needs and for export. In the Lang Kames, a granite, which has been so intensely and deeply weathered that it has the consistency of sand, has been quarried for this purpose. Kaolinite occurs in Unst, Fetlar and Weisdale and has been used in the past for whitewashing buildings.

Outer coast with seabirds

CHAPTER 3

The Holocene and the Shetlander

Broch with ponies

The breakers battered
our boats, cracked
in sleet-storm our two
sisters, our ships.
Curling, the killer-wave
crushed lives, the crew
endured; the undaunted
Earl's story won't die

Earl Rognvald's words on being wrecked at Gulberwick in 1148.
(From the *Orkneyinga Saga*)

H uman immigration to Shetland must have been always fraught with difficulties, but of course much happened long before the first people set foot on the land.

THE GREEN COLONIZATION

The 'interglacial' peat deposit at Fugla Ness (see previous chapter), which somehow survived the immense and destructive force of thousands of years of ice cover, gives evidence of the vegetation in 'Shetland' prior to the last Ice Age. Then, Shetland was dominated by heathers, but also supported pine trees: Shetland covered by a boreal forest! How different it must have been. It is sobering to think that at that time in human history Neanderthals were living in Europe and Asia, and that another 50 000 years would have to pass until our *Homo sapiens sapiens* ancestors would appear to displace them. Although the period we shall be looking at in detail in this chapter is very much shorter, from *c.* 12 000 before present (BP) until today, it should be central to our present reflections on the events of this period that biological 'change' is the norm and that 'change' can be beneficial or destructive, reversible or irreversible.

As the land of Shetland stood at last free of the ice sheet, the overall outline would have been not unlike that of today. There may have been a land-bridge with the British mainland at that point, but if there was it must have become submerged very early as sea level rose with climatic amelioration and occurred before terrestrial mammals reached the north Scottish mainland, since there is no biological evidence for the colonization of Shetland by mammals or by other flightless terrestrial animals such as amphibians or reptiles. It was the original theorist of the evolution of island fauna, Darwin himself who, by soaking various seeds in brine for different lengths of time, even sticking some on ducks' feet, and then successfully germinating them, showed that many seeds can survive immersion in the sea for long periods and that therefore land-bridges are not necessary to explain how islands become colonized and vegetated.

The first information we have of the plant communities that developed in Shetland through the Holocene (the time from the end of the last Ice Age, *c.* 10 000 years ago to the present) was published by Lewis early in 1907, but the first complete picture of the Holocene period comes from pollen profiles taken from Murraster near the Bridge of Walls only 20 years ago. Subsequent examination of other sediments and peat by several archaeological teams at a number of other sites since then, particularly at the Scord of Brouster, Dallican, Kebister and Papa Stour in association with archaeological excavations, have given us a detailed, fascinating and sometimes puzzling picture of the development of today's plant communities and the part played by the early human settlers, both within the field systems and on the hill. The evidence varies from site to site, so the extrapolation of the results for the whole of Shetland must be treated with caution.

The initial sediments that were laid down in the freshwater lochs from 12 000 BP were derived from the very first raw soils formed from the bare fragmenting rocks recently emerged from the ice. Only gradually, as the climate ameliorated, did these sediments begin to contain organic remains such as pollen and it is the presence of these today that tell us something about the plants that were present at that time. To catch a glimpse of that early environment of Shetland we do not have to visit the Arctic or the edge of a glacier in the mountains of Europe, but simply visit the top of Ronas Hill or the Keen of Hamar in Unst, where various concurrences of altitude, exposure, climate, soil and particularly geology have perpetuated a fellfield scene by inhibiting the development of more temperate plant communities. On to these bare, skeletal soils, carried by wind, sea and perhaps the feet of birds, arrived the spores of lichens, liverworts and mosses, such as the woolly hair-moss; also the seeds of arctic–alpine or montane plants, such as the arctic sandwort, arctic mouse-eared chickweed and northern rock-cress, alpine lady's-mantle, moss campion, purple saxifrage and a number of other less showy plants, such as the tiny three-leaved rush or the spiked woodrush, all of which are still to be found in Shetland. In addition there were probably a number of species now extinct, such as the mountain sandwort, for which there have been no certain records for almost 100 years.

With a mean annual temperature still below freezing the lower fellfield was gradually replaced (Fig. 12) before 9500 BP by montane grassland with herbaceous plants and shrubs, such as the montane downy willow, one specimen of which still survives in Shetland; dwarf birch, now extinct; and prostrate juniper, still frequent in North Mainland and on Fair Isle. There then followed a rapid improvement in the climate throughout north-west Europe, with temperatures rising to those of today by around 9000 BP, allowing the northern spread of temperate deciduous woodland.

In Shetland the evidence suggests that this woodland was not as dense or as widespread as on the Scottish mainland. At first it was composed of birch, hazel, rowan and most probably aspen. Today there are still a number of native rowan, particularly in North and West Mainland, a few birch in the vicinity of Ronas Hill, but only two hazel bushes survive, one of which can be seen along with a rowan and a rose clinging to the banks of the burn at Catfirth; the other, like so many of Shetland's native trees, survives only on an island in a loch.

Climatic improvement continued as the sea level rose, until by at least 8000 BP temperatures had risen to above those of today by up to 3°C – 'Bliss was it in that dawn to be alive' – but alas there is no conclusive evidence that people were present on Shetland at that time to enjoy it. The mixture of woodland and scrub diversified even beyond that sustainable in today's climate, with oak, alder and possibly even elm and ash on favoured sites. Pollen of pine has also been recorded but it is considered to have been conveyed to Shetland by long-distance wind transport. This was the climatic optimum, the zenith, of Shetland's environment since the last Ice Age, with scattered woodland up to an altitude of 200 m, or almost halfway up Ronas Hill, and rich brown soils in favourable sites.

Sufficient work on the pollen composition of that time has been done on a spread of sites throughout Shetland to indicate that there was some geographical and altitudinal variation in the nature of the woodland, although birch appears to have been the most common tree. This is not at all surprising when we remember that the backbone of Shetland is composed of acidic schists, gneisses and granites, the drift material from which forms poor soils only suitable for supporting pioneering

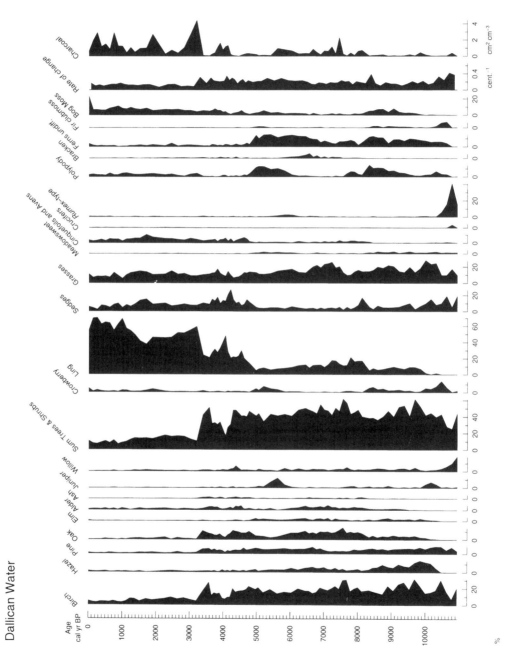

Dallican Water

FIGURE 12 *Variation in frequencies of selected pollen and spore types, palynological richness, rate of change and charcoal record for Dallican Water, Cattaness* (adapted from Bennett *et al.*, in press).

tree species such as birch. However, where the soil was derived from more basic rocks, and particularly limestone, hazel may have dominated along with oak and perhaps ash and elm. Above this broken woodland, which would have reached its greatest growth in the shelter of valleys and ravines, would have been montane grasslands, heathlands and willow communities with open fellfield on the highest slopes. Around freshwater bodies and in wet ground would have been willow carr. The ground flora of the woodland at that time, in the absence of grazing and again particularly on the more basic soils, would have been lush with ferns and tall herbs, such as meadow sweet, nettle, willowherb and umbellifers such as angelica. A shadow of those communities still exists on some isolated islands in lochs (see Chapter 4). The scene was a mosaic, of course, also composed of fens and flushes, grassland and heathland communities on the areas of sand-blow, and even at this time wet heaths of peat were forming in areas of impeded drainage on the upper slopes, while leached and acid soils with acid grasslands and dry heaths possibly covered the summits of the lower hills.

This climatic optimum lasted for at least 1000 years and then there was a decline in the climate accompanied by a slow change in the vegetation pattern, particularly marked by the gradual reduction in tree cover. This change was brought on by an inevitable slow acidification of the soils as the cooler climate with increased rainfall, over a long period of time, inexorably leached out the limited amount of basic minerals in the soils derived from Shetland's mainly acidic rocks. In higher areas grasslands would have imperceptibly given way to an increasing cover of heather. Then, *c.* 4600 BP, there came another but this time abrupt and dramatic change in the vegetation (Fig. 12). This change is characterized by the further decline of hazel and birch and tall herbs and ferns, the loss of juniper, an increase in heather and the appearance in quantity of ribwort plantain. This is the tell-tale sign of intervention in the natural vegetation by burning and clearing for arable and pastoral farming.

THE NEOLITHIC AND BRONZE AGES

At present there is no archaeological evidence for the presence of people in Shetland prior to 5500 BP, which is the earliest confirmed date we have for the first Neolithic Shetlander, at Sumburgh. Analysis of the lake sediments, between 7500 and 5400 BP, at Dallican Water in Lunnasting (Fig. 12) in 1992, while it indicates a continuation of the woodland, also points to a loss of the tall herb and fern community and an increase in charcoal at various times, usually associated with the presence of people and their grazing animals. It has been suggested that this demonstrates the presence of Mesolithic hunter-gatherers, possibly accompanied by red deer, their favourite herbivore and supplier of skin, bone and meat. To put this hypothesis in perspective, the earliest record we have at present for people in Scotland is on the island of Rum on the west coast around 8500 BP. These people came from the south, but it is possible that Mesolithic people from northern Europe could have used Shetland as a stepping stone to enter Scotland from the north.

There is limited evidence for these changes to the ground flora elsewhere, such as at the Loch of Brunatwatt, although these are very local changes and there is no direct evidence for the presence of people or red deer, and no convincing explanation as to why, after 5400 BP, the vegetation at Dallican returned to its earlier tall herb pattern. It has been suggested that the deer became extinct and that the Mesolithic people left the islands, but it is surely unlikely that red deer, once established in the Shetland of that time, could have been exterminated and there are no parallels elsewhere that would support a crash of the red deer population. There is no hard evidence for red deer in the Shetland of that time and indeed the only evidence for red deer in Shetland is a piece of antler and possibly a piece of bone at the Scord of Brouster some 3000 years later. The search for corroborative evidence is hindered by the fact that bone tends to decay in Shetland's soils and that the sea level was around 10 m lower at that time and therefore any traces of Mesolithic presence near the shore, where there was likely to have been settlements, have long since sunk beneath the waves. However, there are signs of earlier occupation under the stone walls of the earliest homes of Neolithic people in Shetland. So we cannot rule out Mesolithic occupation.

Although past its warmest around 5000 BP, the climate was still good by today's standards. This period coincides with a time of human expansion in Britain as a whole, of which the Shetland shores were their northern limit. The scene these Neolithic settlers found, however, was probably much better than they expected. There was vacant low ground, probably without continuous tree cover and therefore easy to cultivate, and ample food available from the sea, both fish and bird. And they must have been delighted to have found no predators, such as the wolf, bear or lynx, to attack them or their domestic stock. Maybe not an island paradise, but a good prospect none the less. At the Scord of Brouster by the Bridge of Walls the earliest evidence for Neolithic clearance of the woodland and tall herb communities for agricultural purposes is 4650 BP (Table 5). At Kebister near Lerwick it is 4540 BP, at Dallican in Lunnasting 4000 BP, while at Gunnister near Nibon it is much later at 3000 BP. These were not isolated one-off settlements. Over

14.   *Neolithic site, Scord of Brouster: one of the earliest recorded homes of Shetland's first farmers, now a degraded landscape of poor soils and peat.* (Courtesy of Shetland Museum.)

TABLE 5   *Holocene summary for Shetland* (from Butler 1992)

Years BP	Climate	Landscape ecology	Culture
1000	20th century warming Deterioration from *c.* AD 1500 leading to Little Ice Age of 17th and 18th centuries Notable warm phase of Little Optimum *c.* AD 1000–1300	Expansion of pasture Contraction of arable land Continued spread of moorland and blanket peat	18th and 19th century emphasis on livestock farming Intensificaion of fishing and trade Arable expansion?
2000	Cooler phase *c.* AD 550–800 Milder phase in early centuries AD	Continued spread of moorland and blanket peat	Norse immigrations *c.* AD 800 Pictish period mixed farming
3000	Marked deterioration More frequent storms	Litle remaining wood-land Contraction of arable land Sea levels similar to today	Concentration of settle-ments and arable land on lower slopes during Iron Age
4000	Cyclical deterioration	Declining soil productiv-ity Spread of podsols, heather moorland and blanket peat	Widespread upland heath farming during Bronze Age
5000	Fluctuating climatic conditions	Beginnings of woodland decline	Neolithic colonization and woodland clear-ance for mixed farming from *c.* 4700 BP
6000	Climatic optimum con-tinues	Sea level *c.* 10 m below present OD Extinction of red deer?	Mesolithic occupation?
7000	Climatic optimum con-tinues	Low rates of soil and vegetation change	Mesolithic occupation?
8000	Climatic optimum *c.* 8000–4500 BP. Tem-peratures 1–3°C higher than today. Low inci-dence of storms	Maximum development of woodland, tall herbs and ferns up to *c.* 200 m OD Widespread formation of stable brown-earth soils	Mesolithic occupation?
9000	Temperatures similar to today	Immigration of *Alnus* *c.* 8500 BP Diversification of wood-land	
10 000	Rapid amelioration Temperatures below freezing	Immigration of *Quercus* *c.* 9200 BP. Immigration of *Betula* and *Corylus* *c.* 9500 BP Sea level *c.* 65 m below present OD Fellfield and montane grassland and dwarf shrubs	

OD, Ordnance Datum.

this relatively short period Shetland changed from an uninhabited and untouched Eden to islands widely settled by communities who not only built distinctive chambered cairns but also created small field systems that were cleared of stone and substantial stone dykes that wandered far across the hill, dividing the land into pastoral or territorial units where they grazed the sheep and cattle they had brought with them. This was a system of mixed farming, possibly with arable fields adjacent to the homes, although as the 'field' walls do not look particularly stockproof it may be that domestic animals were tethered, as they still are today occasionally in the inbye, or shepherded. What we do not know is what the grazing pressure was outwith any 'hill dyke' that separated the arable and better pasture from the hill ground. That framework of *innadaeks–ootadaeks* (within–outwith the hill dyke) pattern of land use in Shetland, established then, is still in evidence today.

House sites from this period are still being uncovered in Shetland and the evidence from Orkney, and the Hebrides also, suggests that settlements, such as that at Brouster, were part of a well-filled and stable local landscape. At Brouster (and elsewhere in Shetland), which appears to have been a marginal site for agriculture even at that period, the accumulation of soil (lynchets) against the downslope field dykes suggests that even this marginal site was occupied over quite a long period of time. This could mean that the population was large and successful enough to have filled all the better land and still need more. Around the Bridge of Walls area there are remains of a whole succession of 'farmsteads'. Assuming other areas were similarly occupied and taking into consideration that around 180 Neolithic/Bronze Age houses have been recorded to date, some commentators have suggested an overall Shetland population of 8000–12 000 at that time.

Islands, insularity and the development of distinct characters and species was discussed briefly in Chapter 1. One of the fascinating elements of the earliest evidence for human settlement in Shetland is the long-recognized distinctiveness of its chambered cairns compared with those of Orkney and the mainland to the south. Recent excavations at the Scord of Brouster has also uncovered a style of decorated pottery previously only recorded at the Ness of Gruting and unknown outwith Shetland. This suggests a period of insularity, with little communication outside the islands following the first immigrants, which allowed a unique local culture to evolve. Where did these people come from? The very detailed report on the Scord of Brouster excavations (Whittle, 1986) states that these artefacts 'give no clue to the origins of the first settlers' of Shetland. We do not yet know and can only assume that they came either from the Scottish mainland via Orkney or direct from the west coast and islands where there are the earliest records for people in Scotland.

At least some of these earlier buildings so far excavated used exotic timber for roofing, such as driftwood of balsam fir, spruce and larch, probably from North America. Was there not sufficient, or perhaps sizeable, native material good enough even then? Was Shetland's native woodland, even in its heyday, of too limited stature for building use, or was there simply plenty of suitable driftwood available that had accumulated over hundreds of years and which, unlike the native trees, did not require felling, distant transportation and preparation? One only needs to visit remote beaches and *geos* today, such as Woodwick in Unst, to see how much flotsam and jetsam can accumulate if not regularly harvested. Even in

Norse days in Shetland natural driftwood may have been a significant phenomenon. The name 'Woodwick' itself derives from the Old Norse *vior* for driftwood and there are Treawicks (Old Norse for tree) in Lunnasting and Whalsay.

From *c.* 5600 BP to 4000 BP, while the farmers cultivated *innadaeks* for *bere* and possibly corn spurrey (or *meldie* as it was known locally) as a food or fodder plant, and grazed their cattle and sheep *ootadaeks*, the climate deteriorated dramatically. From the palynological and archaeological work at Kebister near Lerwick, it appears that during this period pastoralism increased and crop production declined. It has been suggested that early agriculture in oceanic climates such as Shetland, because of its dependency on manure as a fertilizer, sometimes fell into a *nutrient-flow trap*. As the human population expanded, the need for more arable ground to feed it reduced the good pasture *innadaeks* available for the domestic herbivores and therefore the supply of manure necessary for the fields. In a wet climate this resulted in a net loss of fertility, as the nutrients in the soil lost by leaching were not replaced. The soil gradually became so acid it could no longer support crops and became susceptible to peat formation. Gradually too, much of 'the hill' was changing from woodland and shrub, into grassland and then into heathland and eventually blanket peat, principally due to the deteriorating climate or to land management, or a combination of both.

Peat develops when the rate of decomposition of vegetation is sufficiently depressed for it to accumulate and this occurs primarily when acid soils become waterlogged. The loss of a woodland canopy in a wet, cool climate like Shetland was probably inevitable, particularly with its predominantly acidic soils. The loss of tree cover results in the loss of interception and transpiration back into the atmosphere of over 10% of rainfall and therefore an inevitable rise in the ground water table. This increases waterlogging and therefore exacerbates the formation of peat. Where soils are basic, on limestones for example, soil acidification and peat development may be held in check.

The spread of moorland and the all-encompassing formation of blanket peat that occurred over Shetland at this time, at about 1 cm per 25 years, also occurred over parts of the uplands of England, the Highlands and the west and north of Scotland. In fact the increasing wetness and coolness around 3000 BP (see Table 5), during the Bronze Age, persisted right across Europe for 1000 years, with temperatures on average 2°C lower than they had been at the climatic optimum.

Did the early Shetlanders (and other peoples elsewhere), by the progressive clearance of woodland and unsustainable land management (overburning and overgrazing of the pasture land and exhaustion of the arable land) probably with the best of intentions, initiate or at least exacerbate the rapid development of blanket peat? Are there areas of Shetland now under peat where, if soil fertility had been maintained by good management, blanket peat would not have become established and where broad-leaved woodland, arable fields and herb-rich pastures could still have survived? Possibly, but there is evidence that the formation of peat took place in some parts of Scotland before people were established in any numbers. We will come back to this topic later. Whatever the primary cause, we know today that Shetland's familiar moorland and peatland landscape was formed during this period, several thousand years ago. It must have been at this period also that the displacement of Shetland's woodland and scrub birds (of which there are very few today) by moorland waders, and the loss of woodland plants and invertebrates, accelerated.

These settlements scattered around Shetland were not the only focus of activity. From the many archaeological excavations we know that the earliest Shetlanders made use of all the natural resources available to them, quite apart from their domestic stock, and that there must have been regular communication between the settlements. Wooden implements have not survived the years but tools made of local split pebbles and quartz are common. Four specific Shetland rocks provided very special utensils and weapons. Firstly, steatite or soapstone, a soft rock that can be carved by stone tools, was cut from the bedrock, for example at Catpund near Cunningsburgh, and made into pots. Secondly, its near relative serpentinite, a highly coloured and easily polished stone, was made into axes and ornaments. Thirdly, reibeckite felsite, peculiar to a small outcrop to the north of Ronas Hill, a fine-grained, hard and distinctively patterned stone recognizable anywhere, was made into a number of implements. Fojut (1996) has described the felsite 'quarry' as 'one of the best-preserved artefact-working areas in Britain'. Examples of axes from there have been found on the Scottish mainland and even in northern England, while some tools originating in England have been found in Shetland, an indication of some level of maritime communication at that time. The fourth stone is schist, which because of its fine texture was used to make quern stones and hones, and it may be that these too were exported.

By the end of the Bronze Age, *c.* 2500 BP in Shetland, much of the hill land was dominated by heather, and blanket peat growth was widespread and would continue to develop right up to the present day. The settlements and arable land on the upper hill were being abandoned and buried under peat and therefore forced a contraction of settlements to the remaining good land on the middle hill and nearer the shore. Ironically it is partly because of the extensive and all-embracing nature of the blanket peat development that both the record of surrounding vegetation changes and so many of the buildings, enclosures and dykes of the Neolithic, Bronze and Iron Age people have been preserved. The early archaeological record in Shetland is in fact among the most comprehensive in Europe and still largely unexplored.

The several changes to the vegetation that we have briefly touched on from the end of the Ice Age up to the commencement of the first millennium AD, over a period of 8000–10 000 years, had a major effect on the land. From a scene of bare rock and glacial drift there followed, in sequence, fellfield, grassland and woodland and tall herb. Then there was a phase when the landscape gradually became dominated by blanket peat and heather moorland fringed by coastal plant communities, such as maritime grasslands; small areas of fen and tall herbs; scraps of woodland clinging to ravine, sheltered cliff and freshwater islands; and pockets of arable and pasture land associated with small settlements. It is humbling to realize that this 'final' phase is still easily recognizable some 2000 years later.

In addition to the vegetation change over this period there were of course changes due to active geomorphological coastal processes initiated by the slow rising of the sea level (discussed in the preceding chapter). Ayres, spits and bars evolved, the Loch of Spiggie and several other small water bodies became blocked off from the sea, while St Ninian's Isle became connected to Mainland.

THE IRON AGE AND THE PICTS

The deteriorating climate (see Table 5) forced the Bronze Age Shetlanders down the hill and had the effect of concentrating them into compact settlements and, for perhaps the first time, forced them into competition for the now much more limited arable land. It is quite possible too that the gradual increase in population also exacerbated the problem. New cultural influences from the south, in the shape of the making and use of iron, arrived at this point, around 2500 BP. This was the Iron Age, the age of the monumental defensive structures, the brochs and forts of the north and west of Scotland. Noel Fojut (1993) has listed 75 brochs or broch sites out of a possible original 100 plus. These are located right around the coasts of Shetland, but are particularly clustered on the fertile sandstones and sandy soils of South Mainland. There is also evidence of many settlements of the period, some of which are still being discovered today. The best remaining example of a broch in Scotland stands on Mousa, successfully used as a defensive retreat by an errant lady, Margaret the mother of Earl Harold, and her lover, Erland, in the twelfth century, perhaps 1000 years after it was built. Today, another 1000 years later, it is still virtually complete, a magnificent testimony to the stone-working skills of the time; only now, its intricate stonework is home to a colony of the 'swallows' of the seas, the storm petrel.

Towards the end of this period, from around 2500 BP to 1500 BP (500 BC to AD 500), the climate may have stabilized and even slightly improved, for there is evidence of increased cultivation, particularly of barley, and the beginnings of a settled farming structure. There is also evidence of the wide use of other resources for food, clothing and implements, such as seabirds, seals and shellfish, commenced 2000 years previously by the Neolithic people.

15.   *Broch of Mousa: one of the outstanding Iron Age monuments of Europe, perhaps more than 2000 years old.* (Courtesy of L. Johnston.)

Shetland today lies in the path of depressions tracking across the Atlantic, which can bring rain and wind one day, sunshine and calm the next, followed by rain and wind again from the opposite quarter on the third day. Over the 5000 years of human occupation of Shetland the climate has been no less fickle. Following a brief respite in the early part of the first millennium AD, which was taken advantage of by the Iron Age inhabitants, the climate deteriorated between 1500 and 1200 BP (AD 500–800). Blanket peat once again began its remorseless smothering of formerly cultivated fields and once again it is possible that the inhabitants unknowingly exacerbated the process.

This is the period of the Picts, when Christianity was introduced to Shetland by immigrants, the Papae, from the south, bringing a new culture to the islands. The archaeological records from this period, the Bressay and Papil and St Ninian's Christian stones and the incised stones from Cunningsburgh (King's Broch), indicate a vibrant society that all but disappeared under the next wave of immigrants, the Norse, probably the largest influx since the original Neolithic colonization 3000 years before.

THE NORSE

There is no evidence that there was human immigration from the east until around 1200 BP, turning Shetland from a backwater of civilization, the *ultima thule*, to the pivot of the Viking, later Norse, world. In fact, turning the northern world upside down (see Fig. 4), the north of (present) Scotland became Sutherland (South Land) and the Western Isles the Hebrides (Southern Islands). Coinciding with their arrival the Shetland climate once again improved (see Table 5) and this time it remained relatively good for 300–500 years, until the fourteenth century AD (600–700 BP). This period is known as the 'Little Optimum' as it is the period of the most favourable climate following the end of the first climatic optimum around 6000 BP.

From linguistic evidence, Jakobsen (1928) claimed that

> the character of the word-material in the Shetland Norn (i.e. old Norse) points so decisively to the south-west of Norway, that one can conclude that the Shetland islands were peopled to an altogether preponderating extent from . . . the stretch of country from Bergen down to Lister and Mandal, with its focal point in south Rogaland.

More recent archaeological evidence suggests that the whole west coast from Trondheim southwards probably provided the bulk of the men and women who sailed 'west over the sea' to Shetland.

Other evidence pointing to south Norway as the origin of the immigrants to Shetland comes from non-metrical variations of the skull. These are small variants of the bones where two or more alternatives exist: the presence or absence of a sutural bone, one or two foramina, the existence or not of small ridges, and so on. The alternatives are all 'normal' and are recognized by their presence or absence rather than by measurement (hence 'non-metrical'). The frequency with which any variant occurs in a population is a genetic characteristic of that population. Since each variant is based on a number of different genes, a multivariate statistic based on the frequencies of many variants will describe variations in a substantial part of the genetic constitution and be a valuable indicator of the degree of relationship between population samples. The frequency of 30 non-metrical variants in skulls excavated from St Ninian's Isle has been determined. Most of the skulls are probably of medieval date, when St Ninian's Chapel served as an ecclesiastical focal point for much of South Mainland. The last burials were in the mid-nineteenth century.

The St Ninian's skulls are much more like those in a sample from southern Norway (Jaeren) than elsewhere (Fig. 13). This affinity suggests that the Shetland sample represents the old population of the island and not the medieval incomers; and that the origin of the Shetland population (or at least that of South Mainland) was in southern Norway. If the measure of divergence shown by the skull characters is a valid measure of genetic similarity, the next closest relatives of the Shetlanders are in Orkney and the Viking settled area of the Outer Hebrides.

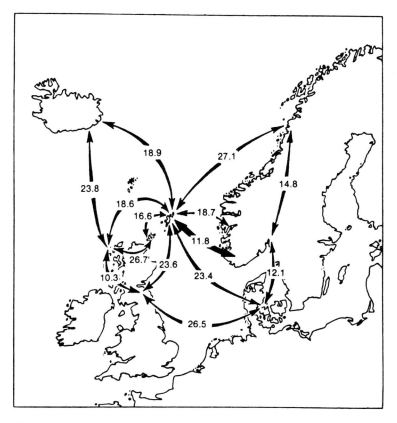

FIGURE 13 *Relationships between Shetlanders and other peoples. The figures are measures of divergence between population samples of skulls where low figures indicate close relationships* (from Berry & Muir, 1975).

What drove large numbers of Norsemen across the North Sea in the decades either side of AD 800? It has been suggested that in a country of limited arable land and an expanding population, the *udal* system of land tenure (where a family holding was inherited and divided between all the sons) may have been a factor, particularly if the limits of new land suitable for improvement had been reached. It has also been suggested that the imposition of unification of Norway by King Harold Finehair, in the late ninth century, pushed some recalcitrant local chiefs into a search for new territories for themselves. Behind this also was a successful 'European' trading nation expanding its markets that, with improving ship design, might naturally have looked westward across the North Sea. Whatever drove or attracted them, like the Neolithic people well before, the Vikings found agricultural advantages in Shetland. In their case, in contrast to coastal Norway, milder, more oceanic, winters that allowed them to keep their cattle out of doors through the winter.

The differences in the amount and quality of arable land, and possibly the climate, between Orkney and Shetland even at this date are illustrated by their different staple diets and the taxes paid by both groups of islands to Norway. Fish and shellfish became a more important part of the Shetland diet than in Orkney as the population increased; while the latter paid its taxes in butter and barley, Shetland paid its taxes in butter and *wadmel* (a coarse woollen cloth). Presumably Shetland was incapable of growing as much barley.

The nature of the Norse colonization of Shetland is unrecorded and therefore remains a mystery. Although there was, as far as we know, an extant Pictish population of unknown size in residence at the time of their arrival, for example analysis of the pollen at Dallican Water does not indicate that Catta Ness was deserted for a period before the arrival of the Norse, there is no evidence for a forceful take-over. It seems that the first Viking raiders only established bases for themselves in Shetland and Orkney, in order to make attacks on the Western Isles, the mainland of Britain and Ireland. Later settlements of farming immigrants then became established among the indigenous Pictish population and these settlers gradually came to dominate the latter, overwhelming them politically, socially, culturally and linguistically.

Relatively speaking, few Pictish place name survives from that period. Apart from the names for the islands of Yell, Fetlar and Unst perhaps, only in the more remote corners are there still places named by the Norse after their Pictish (*Pettr*) inhabitants or connections, such as Pettadale in Central Mainland in what is now a peat-covered valley, Pettifirth in Bressay, Pettadale Water in North Roe, Petester in Unst and Pettigarth's Fields in Whalsay. That settlements of Christian priests were still in existence is evident from place names such as Papa Stour, Papil Water in Fetlar, Papil in West Burra and Papil Geo on Noss, from Old Norse *papae* (priest). In Shetland, in contrast to Orkney, it seems that the Vikings did not immediately suppress the Papae, as both the Papil and Bressay (Christian) stones were carved after Norse establishment. The Iron Age forts and brochs were given Norse names derived from *borg* (a fortified place): Brough on Yell, Whalsay, Bressay and in South Nesting, East and West Burrafirth, Brough Skerries and Burga Water in West Mainland, and Ness of Burgi at Sumburgh, to mention but a few. Even pre-Iron Age sites, thought to be the homes of the *peerie folk* or *trows* who lived under the ground, were given Norse names, such as Trolligarts and Trouligarth near Walls and Trolla Water in Unst.

The improving climate allowed an expansion of agriculture and the development of Norse-type homesteads and farms, particularly on the fertile land with good sheltered access to the sea. The existing (Pictish) circular or cellular shape of house was replaced by the familiar rectangular shape of the crofthouse that still exists today. These 'new' farm sites with their Norse names, nearly all now submerged under their modern successors, with their barns and byres and sometimes corn-drying kilns, are ubiquitous in Shetland. Many of them, probably settled much later, are well inland, which suggests that the farmers took advantage of the improving climate and expanded the area of land under arable and pasture management over a long period of time. There is evidence of this at Kebister, where both hill dykes and dykes within the arable land, perhaps dividing it into smaller units, were constructed at this time. This might also reflect the Norse hereditary system of *udal* land tenure which resulted, as the population grew, in repeated subdivisions of the land. There is evidence at Sandwick in Unst indicative of the importance of keeping cattle (the peculiar shape of a doorway to a building with its greatest width halfway up) and also the large number of loom weights and spindle whorls, indicative of the importance of sheep. At the end of this period it is estimated that the population might have been around 10 000–12 000.

An indication of the original pattern of Norse settlement can be seen in the *scattalds* or common grazing divisions covering the whole of Shetland, each of which was originally named after one farm, e.g. Collafirth. This is hill land, within which each associated community to which it belonged had (and continue to have) numerous rights, of grazing and peat cutting for example.

If there was ever an Arcadia in the history of people in Shetland, apart from the period of the earliest Neolithic settlers, it must have been during that early Norse period following their immigration, when the climate was the most favourable it had been for over 2000 years and when there was a stable culture that allowed the development of a period of successful small-scale farming and fishing for fully half a millennium. During the twelfth century the strong cultural differences between Shetland and Orkney (and the north Scottish mainland) became established. Orkney became the seat of the Scandinavian Earls while Shetland was taken directly under the rule of the Norwegian crown, retaining very much closer links with Norway for several hundred years; in fact until well after the islands became politically part of Scotland.

There is probably little doubt that the Norse settlers, bringing their boats and sea-faring skills with them, introduced a great deal more sophistication into the exploitation of inshore fish. They also developed the exploitation and use of steatite, with which they were familiar from Norway, at a number of sites and for an extended range of uses, from containers to net, fishing line and loom weights to personal adornments such as pendants. Recent excavations at Catpund near Cunningsburgh revealed that exploitation of steatite from this period on was very extensive. It has been suggested that Shetland steatite was widely exported and that in fact it was the origin of much of the steatite that has been found in connection with Norse settlements throughout Britain and Ireland.

16. *Stone of Comba*, scattald *marker between Whiteness and Weisdale: the division of the hill into common grazings has been in place for over 1000 years.* (Courtesy of L. Johnston.)

The renaming of artificial and natural features by the Norse settlers also tells us something of the general environment at this time, particularly the status of woodland and scrub, and there is no doubt that a more systematic study of Shetland's Old Norse place names could tell us a great deal more about the environment. For example there are very few place names for birch, i.e. Birka Water in North Roe, Birka Vird at Gunnister, or place names associated with trees, such as Timriegarth from Old Norse *timbr* (tree), which suggests their relative rarity at that time. Lund, in Unst, is from the Old Norse for a grove and Tresta may be derived from Old Norse *tre* (tree), but as there are so few of such place names it would suggest that there was very little woodland remaining by the time the Norse arrived. However, the evidence from Dallican (see Fig. 12) indicates a drop in the presence of birch in that area just before 1200 BP. This was perhaps the culmination of the continuous loss from the earliest days, representing the final disappearance of birch from accessible steep slopes and scree. If this is so, then it adds to the evidence of the presence of farmers in Shetland carrying out pastoralism when the Vikings arrived.

Bird remains in the Norse archaeological record (cormorant, gannet and gulls for example), places named by the Norse after birds, and Norse bird names that have persisted until today also tell us a little about the species of bird present at the time. For example, places named after birds include Ramna Stacks, Ramna Geo, from *ramn* (raven), Old Norse *rafn*; *loomieshun* (diver loch) from the Old Norse *lomr* (red-throated diver), which must have been as common as it is today judging by the number of small lochs called *loomieshun*; Smerla Water from Old Norse *smyrill* (merlin; Shetland dialect *smirl*); and Erne Stack from *erne* (white-tailed eagle). Breeding birds with local names that are very similar to the Old Norse names include the *steynshekker* (wheatear) from the Old Norse *steinn-kalla*, stone-caller; the *shalder* (oystercatcher) from Old Norse *tjalder*; and the *bonxie* (great skua) from Old Norse *bunksi*, a thick-set person, to name only a few.

Otherwise we can only infer what species may have occurred then, and previously, from the present distribution of birds at Shetland's latitude in Scandinavia. However it is probably safe to say that those species which have always been associated with crofting agriculture, such as the corncrake and those passerine species that became virtual pests in the eighteenth and nineteenth centuries, were common in the Norse heyday. Such birds included the house sparrow, twite, corn bunting and starling. Prior to the loss of woodland and scrub there may also have been species such as the fieldfare and redwing, both of which breed irregularly today.

THE MEDIEVAL PERIOD, THE LITTLE ICE AGE AND THE CLEARANCES

From *c.* 500 BP (see Table 5) the climate deteriorated once again. And once again we have to ask: was the further loss of arable and pasture land due to waterlogging and peat formation inevitable, or could it have been sustained by better management? Whatever the answer, there is ample evidence of an intensification of fishing effort, as people turned for survival from the failures of cultivation and stock management to the sea. This turned out to be one of the most important changes to the Shetland economy, for not only did the marine fish resource come to the rescue of a struggling population, but it gradually became the major source of income from export, until today, when oil and even fish farming have overtaken it.

Like the previous climatic deterioration, that of 500 BP was widespread, resulting in the contraction of agriculture in Scotland and Iceland and the eventual abandonment of the Norse Greenland settlements, culminating in the Little Ice Age of the seventeenth and eighteenth centuries. Along with an increasingly harsh political regime it also resulted in one of the most unhappy and impoverished periods for the bulk of Shetland's population, only exceeded in its misery, for some, by the clearances of the nineteenth century.

However, to return to Shetland in the fifteenth century. In 1469 Shetland was transferred from Norwegian to Scottish rule with the marriage of Princess Margaret of Denmark to the future James III of Scotland. At this period in Shetland's human history there was an influx of Scots, not sufficient to significantly dilute the Norse ancestry of the Shetlanders, even though an analysis of surnames of the inhabitants of South Mainland has shown that about one-third of the population in this region is of lowland Scottish origin, but of sufficient rank and power to change its political structure and set up new lines of landownership. At about the same time the German (Hanseatic) merchants arrived in Shetland and set up a fishing industry with strong links with the Continent that were to dominate the Shetland economy for almost 300 years (see Chapter 7).

In the late-seventeenth century the economic health of Shetland failed due to the continental wars and to famine. The link with the German traders was broken and many local lairds were bankrupted. This resulted in a new land-holding and fishing system in the eighteenth century, with tenancies for the bulk of the small Shetland 'tenant farmers' becoming virtually 'fishing' tenures, with absolutely no security. Without this security tenants had no motivation to improve their land or even manage it sustainably. Increasingly they became fishermen, for ling, saithe and cod with which they paid their rent, along with butter and salt meat, the last of which they also cured for their winter food. Nearly all their equipment for fishing was 'loaned' from the laird to whom they also had to sell their catch. This was the notorious 'Truck' system that tied these tenants to their landlord as inextricably as slaves to their master, when the men were forced to the *haaf* fishing far offshore, pushing them into dangerous and sometimes fatal situations.

> Da snyrk an gronn o da gunnel
> Whaar da haaf-man poos at da oer
> An da timmers swirten an trimble
> As if very wid felt faer;
> Da face o da sea at da boo-haid
> As steep as a barrel's chine
> An da Laird's respects to da weedow,
> Wi a bill for a boucht o line

Da Ill Wind, William Tait

To survive, the tenants were forced into greater fishing efforts, often far offshore, resulting in a further neglect of agriculture. To expand his 'workforce' of fishermen and increase his financial return, the landowner encouraged the population to expand and holdings were continually being subdivided until many Shetlanders were living below subsistence level. It is a sad irony that the bulk of the Shetland population was not able to benefit directly from the marine wealth on their doorsteps until at least the great herring boom of the late-nineteenth century or the twentieth century and the beginning of North Sea fisheries decline.

The lairds however had some problems keeping their tenants at the fishing, especially the young men who were attracted to the Arctic whaling industry.

17. *Fethaland* haaf *station, nineteenth century: one of the many fishing bases from which the men sailed and rowed their sixerns 48–64 km offshore and to which many did not return.* (Courtesy of Shetland Museum.)

Whether they were at the fishing, the whaling or in the Navy, this meant that by and large the agricultural work fell on the women who struggled to keep it going at a subsistence level. The whaling industry, on the other hand, was a mini-boom for the Shetlander bringing much needed cash into the local economy, not just to the agents and merchants but to the common man and his family helping them to survive in difficult times.

If the post-glacial climatic optimum of 8000 BP was the zenith for Shetland's environment, the period from the middle of the eighteenth century to the end of the nineteenth century was its nadir. A growing population, doubling between 1755 and 1860 from approximately 15 000 to 31 000, put almost intolerable uncontrolled pressure on the hill land. Townships were expanded and many new *ootsets* created. Stewart (1987) gives 1075 *ootset* names in the 1860s. Tudor (1883) says 'the carrying capacity [of the hill] controlled the number of animals', going on to say that during the winter of 1784–85 the parish of Delting lost 500 sheep and 427 cattle and that the *scattald* was a place for

> pasturing cattle, sheep, horses and others (pigs and geese) thereon; by casting peats, feals, divots and pones and of quarrying stones thereon; digging and taking away heather and floss from the solum; rivving flaas and cutting, gathering and carrying away heather and floss from the surface of the scattald.

The *pones* and *feals* were dug up for roofing and walling, the *floss* was rush, used in making ropes, and the heather along with peaty material was used for bedding for the cattle in winter. This bedding, trampled and mixed with dung, was then taken out and spread on the fields in the spring. The practice of *scalping*, taking divots from the hill to fertilize the fields, was common and resulted in the stripping of the soil from many areas. In Papa Stour peat and soil was removed from two-thirds of the hill land and taken *innadaeks*, leaving the hill badly eroded and much reduced in value for grazing. As well as soil from the hill, tangles from the shore were used for fertilizing the fields and kelp was also burned for making potash during the last half of the eighteenth century. The result of all the additional material added to the fields *innadaeks* was a substantial improvement in its depth and fertility. *Planticrubs*, small walled enclosures, were also constructed *ootadaeks* to raise kale plants, and on the burns simple horizontal mills were built to grind the corn.

From the onset of the poorer weather at the end of the Norse period, Shetland never produced enough food to feed itself and had to rely on the income from exports, mainly fish, to purchase imported food. Every resource was used to survive in those days. Eggs and feathers and the young of seabirds were exploited, and the oil extracted for lighting from the blubber of seals, the livers of fish and the occasional *caain'* or pilot whale when there was a good 'drive'. Fish, such as *piltock* (coal fish), haddock, whiting and mackerel at certain seasons, was abundant and depended upon.

Here and there in this bare land there was a kind of privileged oasis, built by the landlord from the profits of the fish trade and rent. For example, as early as 1744 Symbister House on Whalsay had a thriving garden, while Low commented on the well laid-out gardens of Busta in 1774. By the 1840s travellers were commenting on

18. *Scalped moorland, Papa Stour: in some places where peat cover was thin it has been almost completely removed over time for fuel, agricultural or building purposes.* (Courtesy of SNH, Lerwick.)

the trouble, labour and expense some proprietors had gone to in trying to cultivate trees and gardens. Many of these plantings survive today, for example the sycamores at Halligarth in Unst. Accompanying the usurpation, division and control of the *scattald* by the landlords, commencing around 1815 and ending about 50 years later with much of it in their hands, came control of the grazing on the *scattald* and much-needed agricultural improvements on the new farms, such as those created at Veensgarth, Kergord and in Dunrossness from the clearances. Fields were enclosed and drainage, fertilization and rotation instigated.

A dreadful picture of the island scene at the beginning of the nineteenth century is given by Hibbert (1821). Quoting Patrick Neil, he described the exhausted and poorly managed land as 'the skeleton of a departed country'. Hibbert went on to comment on the poor management of the peat banks, the destruction wreaked by pigs on the hill, the sheep 'in a state of nature, almost wild, little tended, fed or shepherded'. Hibbert also described a scene of desolation in South Mainland, originally described by George Low in 1774 as 'now a mere wilderness', where poor land management, exploited by bad weather, had allowed extensive erosion of the sandy soils of the Brow Estate. Here, a huge area of first-class arable land, from Quendale north-eastwards, was devastated by blown sand, remaining in this state for many years, inundating the old House of Brow and the church, exposing the dead in the cemetery and ruining the once prosperous and fertile estate. Sir Walter Scott used the event in his novel *The Pirate*. Mertoun, the hero, searches out the seer Norna and as he approaches the church Scott describes the scene thus

> The ground rising steeply from the sea-beach [Quendale], permitted no view into the interior of the country, and seemed a scene of irretrievable barrenness, where scrubby and stunted heath, intermixed with the long bent, or coarse grass, which first covers sandy soils, were the only vegetables [vegetation] that could be seen.

This was not the first, nor was it to be the last, sand-blow in Shetland, but it was probably the most spectacular. Vegetation has only a tenuous hold on sand in such a windy and unsettled climate, particularly where the sea is gradually encroaching on the land. There are records in the stratigraphy of the archaeological site at Jarlshof of several sand-blow events and of course it was the storms of the 1890s that finally revealed that famous site. There are also more recent records of sand-blow, notably at Sandwick, Unst, where prior to 1900 the shoreline was estimated to be 30 m to seaward backed by a sand-dune system. The laird apparently drained a loch behind the dunes and subsequent erosion removed them all together, coincidentally uncovering three Norse houses from the sand (one now lost to the sea) and a Pictish grave that had previously been buried.

The Shetland clearances were much later and more protracted than those on the Scottish mainland, taking place from the 1830s through to 1886 and the Crofters Act. Arthur Nicolson of Fetlar, a typical Shetland laird of the time, dependent on the supply of tenants for his summer line fishing, virtually threatened his tenants with eviction if they went to the whaling. Many tenants ignored him and so he went ahead with one of the first clearances and established a sheep farm. In the long term, however, service in the Arctic whaling and in the Merchant Navy was only the continuation of the long sea-going tradition of the native Shetlander. During this period it provided steady employment, outwith the islands and outwith the control of the laird or merchant, bringing much needed wages back to support the family and croft right into the middle of the twentieth century and the demise of the British merchant fleet.

The clearances were predominantly intended to create farms, first arable and then for sheep, as improving transport to the mainland from the middle of the nineteenth century made sheep farming increasingly profitable. For example, Veensgarth was cleared in the 1850s and 1860s and made into a 1620-ha sheep farm; on the Symbister Estate in Whalsay much of the *scattald* was confiscated in 1865 and made into a 526-ha sheep farm; on Unst, the Buness Estate was cleared at Burrafirth, Cliff, Ordale and Rue during the 1860s and 1870s to create sheep farms. Between 1850 and 1900 the sheep population doubled from 56 000 to 110 000, pigs peaked at 4700 in the 1870s, ponies at 5000–6000 between 1870 and 1900, while cattle numbers varied at around 18 000–20 000.

During the middle of the nineteenth century the weather was particularly poor and there were crop and fishing failures, creating a starving population. The government was forced to set up the Board for the Relief of Highland Destitution; between 1849 and 1851, 188 km of roads were constructed in Shetland by the people, in return for a minimum payment or food. Thus were formed the backbone of the Shetland roads of today.

In the first half of the nineteenth century the amount of new land taken in for arable increased as the population rose; in the second half of the century there was increasing cultivation of potatoes, cabbage (kale) and turnip while natural grass increased by one-third as new farms were created. There was increased production of hay and turnips for feeding cattle and sheep through the winter months. During this period there was an associated increase in house building and in raising the walls of existing houses to create attic bedrooms to accommodate an increasing population. The pattern of housing created then has lasted 100 years. Ironically,

19.   *Township of Garth, Quendale, early 1870s: a typical nineteenth century township of huddled, thatched cottages with their yards and stacks, surrounded by arable fields.* (Courtesy of Shetland Museum.)

20.   *Garth 1880s, after clearance: the cottages have collapsed or been pulled down and the arable land is reverting to grassland and heath. Note the new sheep fence on the hill behind.* (Courtesy of Shetland Museum.)

this difficult period for Shetlanders, which must have seen the greatest area of land under intensive cultivation, must have supported the greatest number and variety of those bird species associated with 'crofting' expansion since the Norse period. For example, Saxby (1874) says of the sparrow 'doing great damage to ripening oats and barley and gooseberries . . . a pest . . . assembling to attack ripening corn'; of the twite 'the cruel attempts to slaughter the mountain linnet by thousands during the

21. *Garth 1996: only the lower walls of the buildings remain, the once-arable land is now 'improved' pasture and grassland and, with modern agricultural input, is capable of supporting many more sheep and cattle.* (Courtesy of L. Johnston.)

winter is useless!'; and of the corncrake '[they] arrive in considerable numbers about the end of May, and may then be heard in every cultivated district throughout the islands' and all night! It was not just the summer feeding and nesting habitat that was responsible for these numbers, but for resident species, such as the sparrow and possibly the twite, it was the availability of food in the winter, the cornyards in every *toonship*.

Thankfully this horrendous period for the Shetland population came to an end towards the turn of the century, particularly with the passing of the Crofters

22. *Early 1900s agriculture, Mary Inkster, Haa of Tangwick, Eshaness: 100 years ago on the croft, with poor soils and primitive equipment, life could be hard.* (Courtesy of Shetland Museum.)

Holdings (Scotland) Act 1886, which at long last gave security of tenure to the crofter, and as the human population, following the clearances, began to fall, with over 3500 people emigrating from Shetland between 1871 and the end of the century. Many emigrated to Leith and much further afield, for example Canada and New Zealand. It must be remembered of course that the Act came too late for the cottars who had already been evicted and no longer held any land. An indication of the plight and privations of a cottar family, in the early 1870s on Out Skerries, is given by the Rev. John Russell (1887):

> I found their dwelling to be an outhouse of the most wretched description. There was not a single article of furniture or domestic utensil except an iron pot in which to boil fish or potatoes. There was a little straw in a corner of the place where they huddled together at night. The parents were absent. Except for a shirt, one or two of the children were literally naked, cowering about the fire. I have seen misery in various places – tinkers camping outside in winter among snow for instance – but such utter wretchedness as this I never saw.

THE TWENTIETH CENTURY

By 1900 the emphasis in agriculture had changed from a subsistence economy to a stock economy supported by the cultivation of fodder crops. Security of tenure encouraged tenants to investment in and care for their croft land and buildings. The population continued to fall in the early years of the twentieth century to about 24 000 in 1921 and then more slowly right up to the oil boom of the 1980s. More men became full-time fishermen and part-time crofters. Money at last came back to the crofts, from the Shetland men who went away to the fishing, whaling (both Antarctic and local) and the Merchant Navy, from those who took on other part-time work and from the Fair Isle knitting by the women, which was becoming increasingly popular outwith Shetland. Times were not easy, particularly during the depression of the 1920s and 1930s, but living conditions were a lot better than those of the last century. Crofts became individual productive units, diverse in their crops with sheep on the hill and a few cows *innadaeks*, with much of the work carried out communally. At this time there were approximately 133 182 ha of *scattald*, 20 000 ha of permanent pasture and 7360 ha of arable. The scene remained that way, by and large, right up to the 1970s, until encouragement of further agricultural 'improvements' and a new source of real wealth from the developing oil industry brought new cultural influences.

In the last third of this century there has been an accelerating change in the economy and in the agriculture of Shetland, which by the 1990s had dramatically changed the landscape. Only on the periphery, West and North Mainland, on the islands and in a few corners does the crofting scene superficially resemble the diverse and intensive scene that had predominated for most of this century and before.

23. *Township of Fogrigarth, West Burrafirth, in the 1940s: crofting at its zenith? A diverse and well-managed mid-twentieth century crofting township within its hill dyke. Its crops of winter feed for cattle and sheep also provide food and shelter for breeding and wintering birds.* (Courtesy of Shetland Museum.)

24. *Fogrigarth 1996: modernized buildings and all the arable now down to permanent grassland for sheep.* (Courtesy of L. Johnston.)

A combination of events and pressures – well-paid and apparently secure jobs with the oil industry and related council activity and in fish farming; and the grants available under the Common Agricultural Policy (CAP), from the Department of Agriculture, Forestry and the Environment (SOAFED) and from Shetland Island Council (SIC) – has led to some dramatic changes in the crofting and farming scene, a loss of people from the croft and an almost completely part-time crofting system. There has also been an enormous expansion of the main town of Lerwick, the construction of new houses and the growth of villages, particularly within commuting distance of Lerwick, which together with agricultural developments has transformed the landscape over a very short period of time.

In this chapter we have briefly traced the evolution of Shetland's landscape through climatic change and the influence of humans since the last Ice Age over a period of 10 000–12 000 years. In succeeding chapters and particularly in the final chapter we return to those extinct and surviving species and habitats, and the overall Shetland landscape, in an effort to gain further perspective on today's situation. There are several topics we need to remember from the story of the Holocene: firstly, the fact of continual change, sometimes over millennia, but sometimes over much shorter time periods; secondly, the comings and goings of species; thirdly, the stark evidence of the effect of a small deterioration in climate on the vegetation generally and on cultivation, and linked to this, the retraction of small mixed agricultural units over two periods, from the Neolithic into the Bronze Age and from the Little Optimum to today; finally, in summation, the immense impact of people on Shetland's natural resources in their struggle to survive and raise their standard of living.

Sheep inbye

CHAPTER 4

A Fragile Skin

Quarff meadows

Affords no prepossessing appearance, the whole vista consisting of ranges of dreary wilds, black and dismal mountains, whose tops are covered with almost perpetual fogs, their sides swampy bogs, without either good heath or shrubs; the rocks in most places being the only support the eye has under the general dusk, which sticking thro' the sides of the hills is a sort of variety in this wretched prospect.

Those were the rather depressing observations of the Rev. George Low, one of the earliest contributors to our knowledge of the natural history of Shetland as, in 1774, his ship came abreast of Sumburgh Head. Similar observations have been made by numerous visitors over the years, and by not a few Shetlanders after a poor summer! However, just like many others, George Low repudiated his initial impressions as he became more familiar with the islands. Of Sound and Gulberwick he later wrote on that visit 'two small but beautiful spots' and of Sandness 'a beautiful flat of Corn, Grass and Meadow ground'.

There is no doubt that the backbone of Shetland is considered by many as not very 'prepossessing', but it has its own kind of wild and desolate beauty and it is a resource of international importance. From the Ward of Scousburgh in the south, through the length of Mainland to Sullom, over the most part of the island of Yell, and on to Herma Ness the northernmost headland on Unst there is a blanket of peat. Brown rolling hills of heather, moss, lochs and lochans, unrelieved by tree or shrub. However, just as George Low found, on further investigation there is a great deal more diversity, uniqueness, colour and beauty in the vegetation of Shetland than first meets the eye. In early spring warm, grassy banks can be covered in yellow primroses, which along with the laverock (lark) are the harbingers of summer days yet to come. On coastal pastures in June the ubiquitous spring squill (*grice-onions*, pig onions) can light a gentle blue haze above the green; on bright summer days in the meadows and ditches around the crofts, the yellow flowers of marsh marigold, monkey flower and autumn hawkbit can blaze as bright as Van Gogh's sunflowers, never mind the individual intensity of flowers such as the large 'Shetland' red campion or the brilliant blue of sheep's bit scabious.

> 'Grice Ingans'. Dat wis what da aald folk caaed dem.
> Da peerie flooers at growes ower every broo;
> As Voar gengs by you see dem ida Norland
> Sae tick dey're laek a mist o warm blue.

Grice Ingans, T. A. Robertson

In this chapter we will look at the environmental constraints on Shetland's vegetation at the plants and communities and, concentrating particularly on those that are of special 'Shetland' interest, at their phytogeographical relationships; and we will touch again on the enormous influence of people, which we have already covered historically in the previous chapter.

ENVIRONMENTAL CONSTRAINTS

Isolation and geographical position were initially responsible for the restricted number of early plant colonists. The communities that then developed, before the arrival of people, were shaped by the soils and the climate. As discussed in Chapter 1, Shetland has a very windy, damp, cool but relatively mild climate. Perhaps the climatic feature that most constrains plant growth is exposure. Even with long summer days the effect of low summer temperatures, regular cloud cover and wind effectively means that Shetland has a late spring and a short growing season, making the islands marginal for grain crops, trees and even heather. In fact the growing season at sea level in Shetland is equivalent to that at Dalwhinnie in the Scottish Highlands at an altitude of 350 m, while the wind speed on the summit of Shetland's highest point (Ronas Hill, 450 m) is probably higher than that on the summit of Britain's highest mountain (Ben Nevis, 1343 m). It is no surprise therefore that 'upland' heaths occur at sea level. This severe picture, however, belies the fact that in sheltered situations on good soils a surprising range of plants and trees can be grown, and that under glass the effects of the long summer days and evenings, the *simmer dim*, can be harnessed to grow even exotic vegetables and fruit.

After isolation and climate the next principal constraint on the types of plant communities that occur is the soil. In Chapter 2 we pointed out that the bulk of the rocks of Shetland – the siliceous sandstones of West and South Mainland and Bressay, the metamorphic schists and gneisses of the backbone of Mainland and of Yell, and the granites of North Mainland – are acidic. The effect of glaciation on this base was to leave a till, derived from these rocks, thin on the harder rocks and deeper in the dales; in the latter even covering much of the slim bands of limestone. This impervious and acidic till, exacerbated by the deteriorating climate from 3500 BP and possibly by the effects of management (see Chapter 3), has given rise to a waterlogged soil that has allowed the widespread development of the *blanket bog* that dominates so much of the Shetland landscape.

The dales contain two types of waterlogged peats, depending on the quality of nutrients reaching the soil surface: *nutrient-rich fens* or mires occur particularly in limestone areas, while those in valleys receiving drainage from blanket bog are *nutrient-poor*. Blanket bog and nutrient-poor valley peats are soils of low growth potential and bear the commonest vegetation in Shetland, mixtures dominated by mat grass, heath rush, cotton grass, deer grass and ling with prominent woolly hair-moss. Nutrient-rich fens are usually heavily grazed, but a few ungrazed examples with tall ferns and meadows exist that indicate the great botanical potential of such sites.

On the granites and serpentinites there are extensive *debris soils*, composed of small fragments of rock that form a flat and often unstable surface. This is a subarctic mountain–tundra soil that supports *fellfield* (areas with sparse plant cover) and woolly hair-moss heath. On parts of the limestone, serpentinite and some sandstone outcrops there are *brown soils*, and on links behind calcareous sand dunes there is a related sandy loam. However these soils are almost always cultivated in Shetland and comprise the main agricultural areas: Tingwall, Weisdale, Whiteness and Dunrossness, along with parts of Baltasound, Melby, Reawick, Breckon, Catfirth, etc. Even without cultivation, brown soils are well mixed by earthworms and such soils are therefore intrinsically fertile. In their 'unimproved' state, these soils at present mainly support grazed, species-rich grass heaths or grassland. The very few examples of ungrazed tall grassland and tall meadow on this soil type are enough to confirm the considerable growth potential its natural fertility would suggest.

The last soil of the well-drained group is *podsol*, derived from rocks low in calcium. Here a surface layer of organic matter or raw humus up to 23 cm deep overlies the mineral soil rather than being mixed up with it and earthworms are absent. Generally these soils support grazed and/or burnt heather-moor and appear to be of low growth potential, but this soil in rare ungrazed, unburnt places can support tall vegetation of greater woodrush and buckler fern with scattered scrub, again demonstrating the suppression of the land's real botanical potential by past and present management.

Any attempt to understand Shetland's present vegetation must take into account 5000 years of the presence of people, particularly the impact of their grazing stock, from which few Shetland plant communities have escaped. On both well-drained and waterlogged sites, there are scattered fragments of ungrazed vegetation composed of species quite different from their counterparts on grazed sites. Land use and not soil accounts primarily for these differences. In addition, the enclosed land within townships often contains patches of marshy or drained ground that are uncultivated, although commonly, until relatively recently, cut for hay. There are also ungrazed ditches between fields or alongside roads and ungrazed road banks themselves. All these sites frequently bear tall grasses and herbs, including many uncommon Shetland plants, in what is really rich fen or tall herb meadow. Furthermore, we must remember that soils and vegetation generally form a mosaic on the hills, which may, in some areas, like that on the serpentinites and metagabbro south of Baltasound in Unst, become complex and consist of five or six quite distinct types of vegetation. The descriptions of distinct communities that follow should therefore be taken as the ideal and do not conform to every situation.

THE VEGETATION

We will begin with the least managed, therefore most natural and oldest, and also, as it happens, the most unusual of the Shetland plant communities. We will then look at the rest of the grazing land, the moorland and grassland, before looking at the coast, wetland and, finally, planted woodland and croftland. In the following descriptions, plant communities are identified by one or two dominant species, using English names that are italicized. The description is based on selected, uniform patches or stands of vegetation (Spence, 1979). The English and botanical names of all the higher plants follow Scott and Palmer (1987) (Appendix 3). Fern descriptions and keys, and fuller accounts of the species of flowering plants, are given in the standard work by Stace (1997).

Fellfield and woolly hair-moss heath

As we saw in Chapter 3, following the retreat of the ice some 10 000 years ago, plant communities slowly developed on the bare rocks, fragments and till that became uncovered. The 'soils' derived from these, chiefly composed of small and angular fragments of the underlying rock and lacking organic matter, have persisted in some places in Shetland because of the climate and the physical and chemical nature of the fragments themselves. Due to regular 'frost-heave', the freezing and thawing of moisture in the soil in the winter that puffs up the soil and splits already fragmented rock, it is a very unstable environment. On slopes these fragments of rock become sorted into *stripes* of large and small stones running at right angles to the contours, while on level ground the stones may sort themselves into *polygons*, patterning the ground. The wind may also cause some of these rock fragments, which naturally and inexorably move downhill, to be blown back up again. The sparsely distributed plants that have developed on these raw soils survive as they are specially adapted to cope with the unstable nature of the environment.

Such open fellfield communities occur also on the British, and especially the Scottish, mountains and are widespread in Norway, Faroe and Iceland (of which the Shetland examples should be seen as an extension), descending in altitude

25. *Fellfield, Keen of Hamar, Unst: the arctic–alpine terrain on the serpentinite debris at sea level on which grow several of Shetland's rare and beautiful flowers.* (Courtesy of SNH, Lerwick.)

northwards as the climate deteriorates. In Shetland they occur at their lowest level in the British Isles in two forms. In the first, the debris is poorly colonized, mainly by flowering plants, particularly on sites like ridges or summits that are snow-free in winter. The most extensive distribution in Shetland of this form is on the granite of North Roe, particularly on Ronas (Old Norse *rön*, scree or rubble) Hill, whose rounded top dominates the North Roe skyline.

> Nortlaand, I see dy
> Lang stem o red ert
> Creepin laek a finger
> Ower da watter o Saint Magnus
> Swallin in da curlin ocean bent
> An stickin up da muckle croonin
> Knuckle kep o Rønas.

Fourteen Observations, Robert Alan Jamieson

Fellfield also occurs on the bare and brown serpentinite of the Keen of Hamar on Unst, in small patches on the sandstone of Sandness Hill and The Sneug on Foula and some granitic cliff tops in the south-west of Mainland. In the second form, the debris becomes colonized by woolly hair-moss with a thin black layer of organic matter between the base of the moss mat and the debris surface.

From a distance, and even from as close as the south side of Ronas Voe looking across to the almost vertical granite slopes of Ronas Hill, the uppermost dome of the hill appears almost devoid of vegetation. What catches one's eye is the stone *blockfield* of the summit with its large boulders, the extensive and apparently bare stony areas, and the *solifluction terraces*. Ronas Hill is actually one of the best sites in the British Isles to see some of these features and is thus a Site of Special Scientific Interest (SSSI), as described in the SSSI citation:

> Ronas Hill provides a fine range of periglacial features with solifluction terraces and ablation surfaces well developed at a lower altitude than on the British mainland. The effects of frost and wind are seen more clearly on Ronas Hill than on any other upland area in Britain. The sub-arctic oceanic climate has produced ground-pattern features, the most important of which are turf-bank terraces, wind stripes and composite stripe-terrace features. Hill dunes and small incipient polygons also occur. These active features result from wind and frost. Large-scale relict frost action phenomena including stone-banked terraces and blockfields are also present.
>
> Scottish Natural Heritage

The terraces mostly run parallel to the contours and occur above about 200 m. While the blockfield is a relic of the end of the last Ice Age, the turf-bank terraces are active features, common at two or three times this altitude on the British mainland. These terraces are caused by frost-heave and the subsequent movement of material downslope; they appear to be moving, extremely slowly, as units, each step or terrace remaining intact.

Once on the upper slopes of Ronas Hill it becomes apparent that the bare ground, above 300 m, does in fact support some vegetation, particularly in the lee of boulders. At this altitude viviparous fescue and three-leaved rush typify the fellfield, the latter at its only site in Shetland. They are accompanied on the granite gravel by the smallest native willow, least willow, heath bedstraw, the only Shetland plants of alpine lady's mantle, the very occasional and rarely flowering alpine saussurea (not seen there since the 1960s), and spiked mountain woodrush. Of the 25 arctic–alpine flowering plants that occur in Shetland, 15 are to be found on Ronas Hill while six are confined to the area. Least willow also occurs in the small fellfield areas on Sandness Hill and The Sneug, on Foula, accompanied by a few plants of filmy fern, and on some other high hills.

Woolly hair-moss heath covers the metagabbro on the summit of Sobul, east Unst, at 120 m, and with bell-heather and stiff sedge also occurs below the summit down to about 80 m. The heath is absent from the serpentinite (Unst and Fetlar), although the moss species itself is a common subordinate forming large tussocks in damp flush areas. Woolly hair-moss heath also occurs on the *risers* of the terraces of Ronas Hill, while a similar heath occurs on the undulating granite of North Roe. On Ronas Hill there is occasional bearberry and, as exposure increases on the upper slopes, fellfield is interspersed with crescents of woolly hair-moss and heather, which are dynamic features caused by continuous exposure to high winds predominantly from one particular direction. Woolly hair-moss reaches its highest altitude in Shetland on Ronas Hill, being confined near the summit to *wind shadows* behind granite boulders. Besides stiff sedge, alpine club-moss and the lichen *Cladonia uncialis*, there are several ericoid species including bearberry, alpine bearberry, cowberry, bilberry, crowberry and ling, and if a visit is made early enough in the summer one may find the beautiful tiny pink and red flower of prostrate azalea growing at the lowest altitude in the British Isles.

'In many places totally divested of vegetation, presenting to the wearied eye a naked waste of an iron-brown colour'. So T. S. Traill (1806) described the site of the most unique, and perhaps the oldest, plant community in Shetland, the Keen of Hamar (Old Norse for rocky outcrop on a hillside), in Unst. The bedrock here is serpentinite, and this is the largest area and the best example of 'serpentine-debris' vegetation anywhere in Britain and northern Europe, one of only a handful of such sites scattered across the globe, in Norway, North America, New Zealand and Africa, all of which support unique floras. Astonishingly, this barren-looking hill has one of the richest assemblages of rare plant species in Shetland and a very special resonance for Shetland botanists. Not surprisingly almost more botanical research has been done on the Keen of Hamar, commencing (with Spence) in the late 1950s, than on all the other Shetland plant communities put together, and for those familiar with research, again not surprisingly, there are many questions still left to answer.

At the Keen of Hamar, as on Ronas Hill, fellfield has probably persisted since the retreat of the last ice sheets. On the latter, at 430 m, it has persisted because of a combination of the acidic granite bedrock, exposure, climate and therefore soil instability. The Keen of Hamar, on the other hand, lies almost at sea level (its highest point is only 89 m above sea level) and it is no more exposed than any other well-vegetated ground at similar height in Shetland. Although there are small debris areas all over the Unst and Fetlar serpentinite, the Keen of Hamar is the only relatively large area of serpentinite fellfield exhibiting active stone striping.

The botanical importance of the Keen of Hamar was first recognized in 1837, when the 12-year-old (!) Thomas Edmondston of Buness, Baltasound, found a new arctic chickweed now known as the Shetland mouse-ear or Edmondston's chickweed (*Cerastium nigrescens* subsp. *nigrescens*). Along with its close Scottish relative, the arctic mouse-ear (*Cerastium nigrescens* subsp. *arcticum*), it is at present considered as a subspecies of a circumpolar species, although some think it should be a full species. This beautiful chickweed, with its large and white-petalled flowers, dark and almost purple leaves, occurs only on the Keen of Hamar, except for a very few colonies of a narrow-leaved variant (rediscovered by the author in 1969 after an absence of 75 years) nearby on the Muckle Heog, and on Crussa Field in 1981. The dark colouring of the leaves and one or two other unique features are considered to be adaptations of the plant to the specific soil conditions on the Keen of Hamar, as are the forms of scurvy grass, stone bramble, sea pink, sea plantain and black spleenwort.

Young Thomas Edmondston also discovered the mountain rockcress, which occurs on the serpentinite debris of both Unst and Fetlar, and is credited with discovering the arctic sandwort, found again on the Keen of Hamar and also sparingly on other parts of the Unst serpentinite. In Britain it occurs in only a very few other Scottish sites. Inadvertently on the same site he also discovered another

26.   *Shetland mouse-ear (Edmondston's) chickweed: the unique and handsome chickweed discovered by the young Thomas Edmondston.* (Courtesy of R. J. Tulloch.)

27. *Arctic sandwort: another of Shetland's subarctic flowers on the serpentinite debris on Unst, found in the British Isles in only a very few other places all in the west and north of Scotland.* (Courtesy of R. J. Tulloch.)

small and white-petalled member of the Caryophyllaceae, the mountain sandwort. This he sent, unbeknowing, along with specimens of the arctic sandwort in 1840 to the Botanical Society of Edinburgh. Scott and Palmer credit Beeby with its identification. Alas the species is now extinct in Shetland and it may be that

28.   *Moss campion: a more widespread arctic–alpine plant, also found on the Keen of Hamar and on limestone.*
(Courtesy of R. J. Tulloch.)

Beeby's later over-enthusiastic collection of specimens, all uprooted, could be responsible!

Not all of the Keen of Hamar is fellfield. There are areas of herb-rich heath, dominated by ling, bell heather, grasses, and rich in basicolous (base-loving as opposed to acidic-loving) species such as the tiny and fragile fairy flax, and mountain everlasting with its delicate blush of pink flowers. In addition there are other notable Shetland species such as fragrant orchid at its only known Shetland station, hoary whitlow grass, the difficult-to-spot frog orchid and even more elusive moonwort.

These are by no means all the plants that grow on the Keen of Hamar, but I hope the list conveys the richness and diversity of the site, which is hardly equalled in any other Shetland habitat. So why do so many arctic and subarctic rarities and specially adapted plants grow on the sparsely covered serpentine debris of this site, and why does one subspecies grow nowhere else at all?

The first ecological studies suggested that a combination of nutrient imbalance, exposure and the continuous fragmentation of the exposed serpentinite bedrock was responsible for the barren nature of the site and its special flora. It was noted that the soil derived from the bedrock has an excess of nickel and chromium, which can be toxic to plants, much magnesium and little calcium (the reverse of the usual situation) and low levels of nitrogen, potassium and phosphorus. Experimental evidence indicated that phosphorus deficiency was a main causal factor and that improvements in plant cover occurred when nitrogen and potassium were added. This was supported by the very successful pasture reseeding of half the site following the application of these three nutrients. Finally the rate of weathering of the serpentinite on the Keen was shown to be very much higher than on the serpentinite outcrops elsewhere on Unst and Fetlar.

However, subsequent work from the early 1970s has pointed out that high levels of nickel are not confined to the fellfield serpentinite of the Keen of Hamar and that the soil underlying the closed vegetation areas on the Keen itself is in fact serpentinite-derived drift material from the end of the last Ice Age and quite different from the fellfield soil. It now appears that closed vegetation might have covered a larger area of the Keen of Hamar than we see now and that at least some of the fellfield has been derived from this cover following its erosion. This might explain why so few early travellers to Unst commented on the unusual physical appearance of the site as it appears today. Two other pieces of evidence suggest the likely major causal factor of the barrenness.

Firstly, many of the plants on the Keen of Hamar show adaptations to living in very dry conditions, such as succulence, excessive hairiness and extensive root systems. Secondly, the fellfield soil, on the slopes of the Keen of Hamar, is very open textured, constantly fed with rock fragments from the shattered exposures of serpentinite. The major factor, therefore, may well be the physical nature of the debris itself, with constant frost-heave and movement, making it very freely draining and therefore susceptible to drought, which may possibly be exacerbated by toxicity and lack of nutrients. A word of caution to visitors to the Keen of Hamar: the site is a National Nature Reserve and many of the plants are very susceptible to trampling damage so tread carefully.

Relict woodland, tall herb and fern

The woolly hair-moss heath and two fellfield habitats that we have just discussed are remnants of habitats widespread in Shetland long ago. The only other habitat, apart possibly from the shore and coastal cliff, that is a relict of the vegetation prior to the arrival of people are ungrazed *holms* (islets) in freshwater lochs and ungrazed ledges on inland crags, streamsides and sheltered coastline. It is these sites that give us just the shadow of an impression of the woodland, scrub and tall herb and fern communities that dominated the Shetland landscape before the immigration of people and their domestic stock.

29.   *Freshwater holm with scrub vegetation, Vementry: safe from grazing stock, remnants of the original scrub and tree cover have survived only on holms and crags.* (Courtesy of Shetland Amenity Trust.)

On the siliceous rock covered by thin raw humus greater woodrush and broad buckler fern often dominate the ungrazed, sheltered sea cliff and inland ledges. Significantly, greater woodrush is a widespread dominant in ungrazed or lightly grazed birch woodlands on the Scottish mainland and is absent from woods grazed by cattle or sheep. An associated shrub layer, which is very limited and scattered, has prominent honeysuckle, with dog rose and eared willow. Less common is rowan, although there are a surprising number, often old and stunted. In six localities there is aspen, in one hazel and in a couple of localities birch.

As these ledges are often small, widely scattered and remote, the diversity and importance of their flora is often missed. However, even a casual glance at some of the ungrazed holms in freshwater lochs is enough to see that the vegetation can be spectacularly different from that of the loch shore. Spence (1979) listed 18 species that are common or dominant on the relatively few ungrazed freshwater holms, almost all of which are rare or absent on adjacent moorland. At least where there are no gulls nesting, the peat slope on holms (which on adjacent moorland carries a dry heath, or is eroded and lacks plant cover) is often dominated by dense growth of a *greater woodrush–wavy hair-grass* community, with buckler fern and polypody and with hay rattle, golden rod and devil's bit scabious all flowering freely, forming a field layer to occasional rowan, eared willow, rose and honeysuckle.

Nutrient-poor holms in lochs provide most examples of ungrazed fens in Shetland. Their shores are usually boulders or rocks covered to the water's edge with a layer of raw humus and roots, and bearing also a dense growth of greater woodrush, but this time with meadowsweet and angelica and up to 35 species of flowering plants: a luxuriant vegetation that once again contrasts with the sparse and low cover of most loch shores. At a very few localities on this ungrazed fen occurs Britain's tallest fern, the royal fern. It is unlikely that woodrush ever

30.   *Freshwater holm with royal fern: our tallest native fern, once probably a common fern of wet places that now survives in only a very few ungrazed places.* (Courtesy of L. Johnston.)

predominated in normal fen soils; instead royal fern and willow scrub may once have been the common vegetation.

On Fair Isle, where sheep grazing pressures have traditionally been lower than other parts of Shetland, another low-growing shrub, prostrate juniper, is still relatively common. Elsewhere in Shetland prostrate juniper occurs very occasionally, but is regularly found on freshwater holms and occurs in dense stands in a small area on the banks of a burn north of Ronas Hill. In one locality occurs one of two hazel shrubs in Shetland, at another common sallow. At yet another a downy willow survives at its lowest altitude in Britain, and at two further sites, stunted, and probably ancient, birch survive. These individual 'trees' are all that remains of Shetland's woodland.

Most of these ungrazed communities have survived because the holms are too small and not worth the effort of putting on grazing sheep or they are remote, and also because Shetland lochs rarely freeze hard enough in winter to allow accidental access by sheep. One of most accessible of the ungrazed shrubby holms is at the Loch of Clousta, while at the bridge over the burn at Catfirth, on the limestone ravine, hazel can be seen along with other ungrazed scrub species, now fenced off and protected from grazing.

Like tall grassland and herb meadow, this community-type is fragmentary but remarkably consistent in its make-up and bears witness to both the soil and climatic potential for growth, in the absence of grazing and burning. The sites are too small and fragmentary to support woodland birds – gardens and shelter belts now provide that habitat – but they are important as reservoirs for very restricted Shetland species and as a sheltered habitat for invertebrates; the willow species, specifically, are known as an important microhabitat for nearly 60 species of fungi. It is still also possible to find traces of what may once have been a *Lobarion* community from earlier scrub woodland, but these relicts are no longer only associated with trees and shrubs. For example, several lichen species with affinities to those of trees elsewhere in northern Britain can be found on fence posts. The germ of the flora and fauna once associated with woodland and scrub in Shetland is therefore still available and with increased broad-leaved planting could flourish again relatively quickly.

After surviving so long one might think that this unique Shetland habitat was fairly secure; unfortunately one of the last few remaining birch sites, near Birka Water, was destroyed when sheep gained access in the 1950s, while another ungrazed island with a tall herb and fern community was similarly destroyed in 1972. Recently the Shetland Amenity Trust has carried out protective work to several sites.

As a footnote to this section on Shetland's native 'trees', it is heartening to know (for the botanical explorer) that even on a relatively small group of islands such as Shetland recent surveys have added new sites for several of the species discussed, as well as new species themselves. The most recent curious discovery has been of individuals of crab apple on two sites, 14 km apart, on ledges on the east coast of Mainland, growing with other shrubs and woodrush on one of the sites. Although crab apple is a native of Britain and Europe, it is not a species normally associated with the other Shetland 'trees' and shrubs. In fact it is not known where in Europe it was originally native.

Blanket bog

Bit far ayont da dæk,
da laand's annider lækly,
belangin no t'maps,
bit t'da fit dat claims it
in da act o passin.
Quhedder hill or daal,
it's empty t'da ee dat's
seekin fir hit's aaner.

Ootadæks, Robert Alan Jamieson

Beyond the hill dyke (*ootadaeks*), on the *scattald*, is the hill, which we saw in Chapter 3 became covered in peat from *c.* 3500 BP. Today peat covers approximately 53% of Shetland and the commonest vegetation in Shetland is that growing on it or on soils derived from it. Common in Shetland, maybe, but these low-level oceanic blanket-bog communities of Shetland are transitional in species composition between the lowland oceanic mires of western Scotland and those of more extreme northerly latitudes in Faroe and Scandinavia, with plant associations very much their own, reflecting Shetland's geographical position.

One of the commonest community-types of high altitude, relatively undisturbed blanket bog on, for example, Weisdale Hill and Herma Ness, is dominated by deer grass and cotton grass. Poorly growing heather is frequent but *Sphagnum* species only dominate in a few places on this undisturbed peat and are more typical of bog pools and drainage channels. In a closely related community-type of deep peat, heather co-dominates with cotton grass while deer grass and hare's-tail are subordinate and crowberry is constant. Cross-leaved heath and the sweet-smelling bog asphodel are restricted to deep peats. The least common community-type on peat is confined to parts of the summit of Saxa Vord, Herma Ness, Sandness Hill and Fitful Head. Here blaeberry is dominant, crowberry subdominant, and bog whortleberry and greater woodrush locally dominant.

A further community-type of deep peat, but on well-drained slopes, is one where heather is dominant, with sweet vernal-grass as a constant. It appears to be intermediate floristically and ecologically between *heather–bog cotton* and acid *mat grass–heath rush* grasslands. The latter is the characteristic dominant on naturally or artificially drained peat, on redistributed peat (i.e. eroded and spread on fresh ground by rainwash, landslip or deliberate clearance for development) or formerly cut-over and deeper peat, with tormentil and heath bedstraw very common.

An extreme example of *mat grass–heath rush* development is on the wet heath of thin humus on shallow, badly drained soils, typical of surfaces where peat has been almost entirely removed, and of some overgrazed *scattalds* and outfields; it is particularly widespread near townships on a range of acid, non-calcareous rocks, such as at Muness, Belmont, Garderhouse and south of Sandness. Woolly hair-moss is frequent, along with heather and cross-leaved heath, bog asphodel, crowberry, purple moor-grass and deer grass and total cover rarely reaches 100%. Spence (1979) carried out an experiment on an example of this wet heath at Belmont where he fenced off an area from grazing and trampling. After 20 years both mat grass and heath rush have gone and have been replaced by a sweeter grassland dominated by bent and meadow grass. His experiment showed two things very relevant to the present and potential vegetation of these areas, which are of little grazing or wildlife value. Firstly, given time, unpalatable grass and rush can be eliminated and replaced by something of grazing value. Secondly, by excluding grazing altogether most of the herbs are lost and overall diversity is reduced. And the moral of these situations: reduce and control grazing and Shetland could have something of grazing *and* wildlife value *and* attractive to look at.

With increasingly milder winters (possibly due to the effects of global warming) already evident in Shetland and in other areas of western Europe, some moorland plant communities are going to suffer at the expense of others. Woody plants of blanket bog and moorland, including the dwarf shrubs such as cowberry, crowberry and heather, may remain active rather than dormant in the winter months and hence use up their stored energy. Come the spring they may then suffer dieback. On the other hand, deer grass, cotton grass and dwarf shrubs adapted to wet soil conditions, such as cross-leaved heath, may flourish. The implications of this for Shetland's blanket bog is discussed further in the last chapter.

Moorlands and grasslands of acidic soils

More commonly on the raw humus of well-drained sandstones and, locally, on steep free-draining peats over siliceous rocks such as the granites of North Mainland is a *ling–bell heather* 'dry' heath. This differs from the herb-rich heath on nutrient-rich soils in having a prominent mat of moss and only about half the number of flowering plants and ferns. The last large remnant of this heath in South Mainland can be found at Dalsetter where it is especially rich in lichens, in some

31. *Moorland, Houlma Water, West Mainland: the predominantly heather moorlands on the Old Red Sandstones of West and South-east Mainland tend to be less wet than that on the siliceous backbone of Shetland.* (Courtesy of L. Johnston.)

32. *Lichen-rich heath, Dalsetter, Dunrossness: one of the last remaining areas of short, dry moorland in South Mainland, in some areas dominated by lichens and a typical nesting habitat for whimbrel.* (Courtesy of SNH, Lerwick.)

places dominated by *Cladonia* species. Spence (1979) has suggested that the heath on acid peaty soils is more closely related to the herb-rich type on basic soils in Faroe and west Norway than to those found typically in eastern Scotland. Bracken, which is local in Shetland, is confined to this type of heath. It is generally stunted in growth, which suggests that it is reaching its climatic limit. However there are dense and healthy stands on the warm south-facing slopes of Ronas Voe. On similar soils, on open grazed hill land, brown bent and viviparous or red fescue dominate with mat grass, heath rush and heath bedstraw where ling and bell heather have probably been removed by burning and grazing.

Whimbrel

Moorlands and grasslands of somewhat organic soils

Herb-rich heath occurs on the Unst serpentinite and metagabbro, and also on parts of the limestone in Weisdale, Tingwall and pockets elsewhere where outcrops have not been subject to heavy grazing. In Unst the heath is very diverse, containing at least 36 species of flowering plant, fern and clubmoss and at least 15 species of moss and liverwort. Fairy flax, slender St John's wort, common and dog violets, common and heath milkworts, the ubiquitous heath spotted orchid, tormentil and thyme all flower abundantly. On the Unst herb-rich heath, alpine saussurea occurs in one of only two places in Shetland, while three-flowered rush occurs in its only Shetland station. Above an altitude of about 90 m, however, the heath becomes dominated by woolly hair-moss heath, while in the south-west there is a large area of impoverished wet heath. The dry heath contains thyme, violet, flea sedge and alpine meadow rue, as well as the more acid-loving cross-leaved heath, bog asphodel and mat grass; it is thus intermediate between heaths on base-rich soils and those found on rocks producing a more acid soil. Unst, in fact, has a very wide range of plant communities easily related to the underlying geology and the topography, well illustrated by Figs 14 and 15.

Herb-rich grasslands occur on the limestone of Weisdale, White Ness, Skellister (Nesting), Fladdabister, Voe, Loch of Cliff in Unst and Out Skerries. A striking example of the contrast between these herb-rich pastures and dry acid moors can be seen from the road above Wormadale (map reference HU 404461) looking west towards the *green* limestone peninsula of White Ness and beyond to the parallel *brown* Strom Ness peninsula of acid schist (Plate 8). Such herb-rich grasslands also occur on the serpentinite of Unst, Fetlar and at Hoo Field just south of Cunningsburgh, and, perhaps with a slightly more limited flora, in one or two small areas of calcareous schist such as at Ollaberry. We discuss both together here, although as Dalby (1989) has indicated the grassland floras of serpentinite

33.   *Dry grassland, Aith, Cunningsburgh: grassland on good soils that is lightly grazed can support a great variety of flowers, benefiting also insects, other invertebrates and birds.* (Courtesy of L. Johnston.)

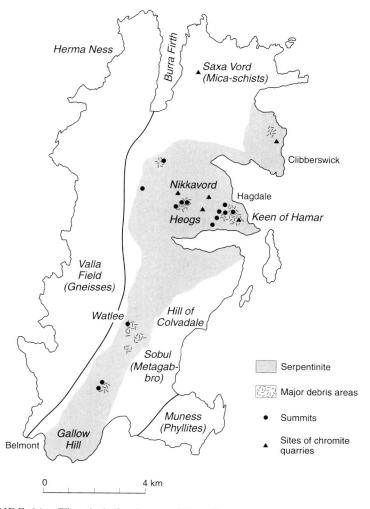

FIGURE 14 *The principal rock types of Unst* (from Spence, 1979).

and limestone may be similar but they are not identical, while Watling (1992) has also suggested that the herb-rich grass-sedge heath on the serpentinite of Fetlar has a unique fungus flora.

Floristically, the Shetland limestone grasslands are relatively poor in species compared with their Scottish mainland equivalents; nevertheless they represent an extreme northern variant of the north Scottish calcicolous grasslands. In fact there is no strictly calcicole element of flowering plants or ferns in Shetland, with most of the rarities on limestone occurring elsewhere. One of the features of the limestone outcrops themselves, due to their vertical dip, is the occurrence of one or two attractive and uncommon plants that either are species of dry rocky pasture, such as downy oat-grass, hoary whitlow-grass and stone bramble, or would otherwise be vulnerable to grazing, such as moss campion and the ferns maidenhair spleenwort

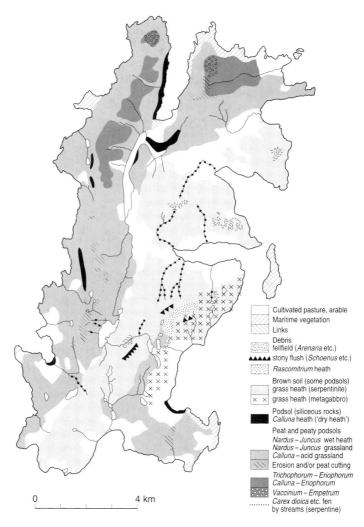

Cultivated pasture, arable
Maritime vegetation
Links
Debris
fellfield (*Arenaria* etc.)
stony flush (*Schoenus* etc.)
Rascomitrium heath
Brown soil (some podsols)
grass heath (serpentinite)
× × grass heath (metagabbro)
Podsol (siliceous rocks)
Calluna heath ('dry heath')
Peat and peaty podsols
Nardus – Juncus wet heath
Nardus – Juncus grassland
Calluna – acid grassland
Erosion and/or peat cutting
Trichophorum – Eriophorum
Calluna – Eriophorum
Vaccinium – Empetrum
Carex dioica etc. fen
by streams (serpentine)

0   4 km

FIGURE 15   *The vegetation of Unst, based on ground survey and Air Ministry aerial photographs* (from Spence, 1979).

and brittle bladder-fern. These limestone outcrops also support a most character-istic and diverse lichen flora.

The commonest limestone grassland species include the grasses red fescue, common bent and crested dog's-tail, sedges such as glaucous sedge, carnation sedge and flea sedge, and also many herbs including field gentian, frog orchid, moonwort, alpine meadow rue and, in damp areas, meadowsweet. Both limestone pastures and the Hoo Field serpentinite also support abundant primrose and lady's bedstraw and, in addition, in damper areas flea sedge and lesser celandine. Infrequent arctic–alpine species like alpine meadow rue, alpine bistort, hoary whitlow-grass and moss campion indicate the submontane affinities of this grass-land. It is most likely that much of these herb-rich grasslands, of both serpentinite

34.   *Herb-rich heath and grassland, Fladdabister: the latter, on the right of the fence, has probably been created from the former, on the left, by long-term grazing.* (Courtesy of L. Johnston.)

35.   *Links grassland (ungrazed), Sumburgh: on the sandy grassland around the airport vetches flourish in the absence of grazing.* (Courtesy of SNH, Battleby.)

and limestone, have been derived from herb-rich heaths by pasture management over a very long period of time, leaving only one or two remants of tall (ungrazed) grassland. Overgrazing and 'improvement' are now serious threats to the survival of these grasslands.

Arriving in Shetland by air on to the Sumburgh links in the summer, although they have been much modified by airport construction, the visitor has a colourful introduction to the potentially rich flora on soils formed from sand-blow. At Sumburgh the dominant plant on this (presently) ungrazed grassland is bird's-foot trefoil. This plant seems to be very attractive to grazers and otherwise only grows in this luxuriance, with its bright orange or red and orange colouring, by roadsides, on cliffs or in other sand dunes where it is protected from grazing. Behind sand dunes at Quendale, Spiggie, Norwick, Burrafirth, West Sandwick, etc., there are fairly level links, similar to the machair of the Western Isles of Scotland, although alas the first site mentioned has been modified by heavy grazing. They contain some of the species already mentioned for limestone grassland, along with grass of Parnassus, eyebright (as *Euphrasia arctica*) at Spiggie, curved sedge at Quendale, sheep's bit scabious, thrift and common spotted orchid.

A rare and beautiful example of the Shetland flora, and yet another indication of the islands' northerly position, that occurs only locally on dune pasture and on the limestone grassland at the Loch of Cliff is the northern subspecies of the autumn gentian (*Gentianella amarella* subsp. *septentrionalis*). This subspecies is known elsewhere only from Orkney and Iceland and has been lost from several of its Shetland localities since its first discovery, by whom else but Thomas Edmondston in 1837 on Balta Island. These herb-rich grazed grasslands, like the herb-rich heaths and the maritime grasslands (see Maritime communities), are the most delightful places in which to walk on a Shetland spring or summer day, so short is the vegetation and so full are they of colour, variety of form and beauty.

As mentioned earlier, one of Shetland's two surviving hazel bushes grows on an ungrazed ledge on limestone at Catfirth. It is accompanied here by rowan, dog rose, stone bramble, brittle bladder-fern, an as yet undescribed hawkweed, moss campion, lady's-mantle and primrose. Palynological evidence (see Chapter 3) suggests that hazel was once dominant in Shetland on these nutrient-rich grasslands, perhaps rather like the scrub it still forms on some limestones in Sutherland. Similarly, fragments of scrub and tall fern, tall grassland and tall herb communities are once again a reminder of how diverse and rich the field layer of Shetland must have been prior to the arrival of people and the introduction of grazing animals. False oat-grass is a conspicuous dominant of this grassland that is absent from grazed sites. It is typical of limestone meadows in northern Britain. Reedgrass often accompanies oat-grass, while ungrazed ledges and banks sometimes carry tufted hair-grass.

Ungrazed grasslands on nutrient-rich soils of cliff ledges, roadside and field edges, and sea banks are usually dominated by red fescue, sometimes by viviparous fescue. Common associates are bird's-foot trefoil as *forma grandiflora*, the large Shetland campion, tufted vetch, bush vetch, meadow vetchling and angelica that is often over a metre in height. All these species flower freely in these conditions. Cow parsnip, sheep's bit and the yellow lady's bedstraw, formerly used as a dye, also occur and are tall in contrast to their dwarf forms in links pasture. Roseroot and Scots lovage are common in these sheltered sea-cliff communities, which are among the most luxuriant and most colourful of all the Shetland plant communities.

This composite list represents tall grassland and herb meadow of nutrient-rich soils. On damper sites these grasslands grade into wet hay meadow (see Croftland), which used to be regularly cut or grazed annually, and fen, with yellow flag and meadowsweet. One of the best meadow sites in Shetland is at Aith (Cunningsburgh), but there are also good examples by the Loch of Asta at Tingwall, at Walls, Sandness, Fladdabister and at Nor Wick in Unst.

36. Damp grassland, Fladdabister: grassland merging into wet meadow also has its own distinctive character. (Courtesy of L. Johnston.)

Lochs

Before we look at the flora of Shetland lochs we need to look at their physical and chemical characteristics, which have a profound effect on the species and communities present.

The distinctiveness of the Shetland landscape is its absence of trees, its mosaic of water surfaces and smooth, rounded hills. The relatively high rainfall, low evaporation, mainly impermeable rocks and drift, large areas of peat, plus glacially eroded plateaux, drowned valleys and coastal deposition processes, have given rise to a large number of lochs and lochans (Table 6). Maitland and Britton (1985) estimated that there are 1596 water bodies, ranging from approximately 0.01 ha to the largest loch, the Loch of Strom, at 1.35 km^2. As many lochans under 0.2 ha were probably missed, this must be an underestimate. Overall, lochs account for less than 3% of the total land area, although in some areas, for example the glacially eroded plateau of North Roe and in parts of West Mainland, 30% of the

TABLE 6 *Classification of Shetland lochs into trophic categories based on the geology of the catchment* (after Britton, 1974).

	Number	Per cent of lochs
Dystrophic	547	34.7
Oligotrophic	661	41.9
Mesotrophic	212	13.4
Eutrophic (excluding serpentine)	39	2.4
Serpentine	72	4.6
Brackish	45	2.8
Marl	1	0.1

land surface is open water. There are also locally dense aggregations of peaty pools on areas of deep blanket peat, particularly on the island of Yell. Only a few lochs occupy valley troughs and these are generally the larger lochs, such as Girlsta, Tingwall and Cliff. The narrow dales give shape to these lochs, while the sinking of the land since the last glaciation has meant that many of these dales have been drowned and become arms of the sea, in the shape of voes. Occasionally silt or sand has blocked off these inlets (for example at the Loch of Spiggie) and fresh water has accumulated on the landward side.

The greatest concentration of lochs lies between 120 and 160 m, with very few over 180 m. The highest is on Ronas Hill at 250 m. Because of the complex geology (see Chapter 2) there is a greater variety of freshwater types in Shetland than in any comparable area on the Scottish mainland, although there are few nutrient-rich lochs. However, there are only 65 species and hybrids of aquatic vascular plants (including both submerged and emergent types) that have been recorded from Shetland; these include 27 highly adaptable species with a widespread British distribution, which occur in both nutrient-rich and nutrient-poor lochs (eutrophic and oligotrophic respectively). There are three principal reasons why the aquatic flora (and fauna) are impoverished and fairly uniform in Shetland.

Firstly, as we have already discussed, the isolation of Shetland hinders the immigration of many groups and species (including aquatic invertebrates). However, species with the most effective means of long-distance dispersal are well represented, for example there are 10 species of stonewort (*Chara* and *Nitella*). Secondly, since Shetland has relatively few nutrient-rich lochs there are numerous absentees among those species with a preference for the more productive habitats. On the other hand, with many nutrient-poor lochs, 12 of the 13 acid water-specific plants of Scotland are present. Thirdly, the combination of wind and the close proximity of the surrounding sea means that all freshwater lochs are to some extent affected by salt spray, and have a higher concentration of sodium and chlorine ions than lochs a similar distance from the sea on mainland Scotland. In fact virtually all lochs in Shetland up to 90 m from the sea and less than 9 m above sea level are brackish. This raised salt content in the more acidic lochs reduces the biological distinction between them and the more productive lochs by allowing colonization of the former by organisms normally restricted to the latter and by permitting some organisms characteristic of acid waters to replace absent species in the nutrient-rich lochs, giving a relative uniformity of species across many lochs. For example, water milfoil and shoreweed occur in both fairly peaty waters and those that are quite productive, while the stoneworts (*Chara aspera* and *C. delicatula*) also extend into much more acidic waters than on the Scottish mainland.

The maritime influence also has a distorting effect on freshwater phytoplankton populations. Of 58 lochs studied for their phytoplankton, all were different to some extent in their species composition and diversity; 400 phytoplankton species have been recorded and some of these seem to be new to science. Certain general features are extremely interesting, for example in nearly every loch two groups predominate, the Chlorococcales (green algae) and the Chrysophyceae (brown algae), with the latter of more importance. There is also a relative paucity of desmids and diatoms. The predominance of the Chrysophyceae, which thrive in nutrient-poor

37. Loch of Spiggie, Dunrossness: one of the few large, moderately rich lochs, which in addition to supporting a varied flora supports also breeding and wintering wildfowl. (Courtesy of SNH, Battleby.)

conditions, is a common feature in the Fenno-Scandia region but is rare in Britain, although a few similar areas to Shetland have been studied. The strong maritime influence may have something to do with this situation.

Phytoplankton abundance decreases with an increase in depth and size; an exception is Loch of Spiggie, which is one of the richest lochs, while another rich loch is the tiny Kirk Loch on the edge of the shell sand at Breckon, north Yell. In these *eutrophic* lochs, particularly those least influenced by sea spray, the phyto-plankton are mainly of the blue-green euglenoid type (Kirk Loch supporting a unique association) in contrast to the predominance of brown algae in more acidic lochs.

Aquatic species diversity of the higher plants in Shetland is not directly related to loch size. Some small peaty lochs have a comparatively rich flora, while some large productive lochs influenced by sea spray have only a very few species. Generally, the blurring of distinction between lochs, the general paucity of species diversity and the fact that the microclimate varies little between lochs means that there is an overall simplification of the ecology involving all groups. The most diverse and varied floras are found in a few of the large productive lochs, such as the lochs of Cliff and Tingwall, but also in the tiny machair-loch at Hillwell and some medium-sized *mesotrophic* lochs, such as the lochs of Kirkigarth and Bardister at Walls.

Aquatic vegetation occurs along a gradient from deep water to seasonally dry land. Under the best conditions a water-depth gradient is accompanied by submerged, then floating-leaved and, finally, emergent vegetation. However, the ever-present wind also contributes to the biology of the Shetland lochs (except in very sheltered situations or in small, shallow lochs) in more ways than as a vehicle for salt spray. The water surface is rarely still and continual wave action hinders the development of emergent plants so that their overall importance in the biology of the lochs is much less than that of the submerged species. This effect is exacerbated by the prevalence of a rocky substrata in many Shetland lochs that is not conducive to the growth of emergent plants. Very often the only emergent species on the more acidic lochs is the bottle sedge and in the more productive lochs quillwort and spikerush.

The wind also creates a certain amount of vertical water movement and even in the deepest loch (Girlsta, 22 m) there is no obvious thermal stratification as there is with eutrophic lochs on the Scottish mainland. Thus lochs classified as 'eutrophic' are designated with a peculiarly Shetland definition of the term, indicating a relatively high nutrient content with an associated relatively diverse flora and fauna. In contrast to the less nutrient-rich *oligotrophic* and the peaty *dystrophic* lochs, it does not indicate that these lochs are eutrophic in the classical sense, i.e. there is no deep layer, or *hypolimnion*, of organic material to reinvigorate these lochs in spring.

Lochan, bog cotton and divers

Large areas of Shetland on the most acidic and impermeable rocks have a covering of blanket peat with numerous lochs and *shuns* (lochans). These dystrophic water bodies, particularly those of 0.2 ha and less, are very numerous (see Table 6) and form a quite distinctive group. Generally they are shallow with dark-brown peaty water, low in nutrients, alkaline and have a high concentration of iron and phosphorus. In these peat-stained waters light penetration is extremely limited even a couple of centimetres below the surface, and submerged aquatics are found to a depth of only 1 m; in the clearer acidic lochs (oligotrophic) they may be found down to about 3 m. Typically these peaty lochs have soft edges and are the habitat of nesting *raingeese* (red-throated divers), which, because of their limited manoeuvrability on land, construct their nests just above the waterline where they can slip easily in and out of the dark protecting water (see Chapter 6).

Submerged, floating-leaved and reedswamp vegetation occur in the relative shallows of these water bodies and in some are found bladderwort and floating bur-reed or dense growths of submerged bog-moss. In the rocky, ice-scoured lochs of Flatpunds Loch and Lunga Water in West Mainland, floating-leaved and emergent plants are confined to small inlets about 0.5 m deep that are isolated from exposed open water. These inlets have a floor of soft mud and carry reedswamp. Bogbean is common, while white water lily, the largest flowered plant in Shetland, is confined to a few sheltered but nutrient-poor lochs in West Mainland, into a few of which it may have been introduced.

The other abundant loch-type are the oligotrophic lochs, which are usually larger and deeper than the dystrophic lochs; together they make up more than 75% of all Shetland lochs. Oligotrophic lochs are particularly common in North Roe where they lie in ice-scoured basins, surrounded by small smooth hills with much exposed rock. Imprisoned in the hard granitic rocks, lacking suspended peat particles generally, they are sparklingly clear. Because of their clarity these can be the most attractive lochs in Shetland. On still days, the rugged landscape of the North Roe plateau, viewed from the summit of Ronas Hill, can seem to lie in a multitude of broken pieces.

All the oligotrophic lochs have a rather similar flora. The cover of aquatics, except in very shallow sites, is extremely small and even in the large, typically stony-edged, lochs the vegetation is restricted to a narrow peripheral band up to a couple of metres from the shore. In the largest lochs this may occur only in sheltered bays and on sheltered shores. Two species that occur, in sparse pockets of gravel, and which are absent from the dystrophic lochs are water lobelia and quillwort. Sheltered edges may carry water horsetail and the common spike-rush. These lochs are generally poor in their phytoplankton and invertebrate populations, although many of them carry appreciable numbers of brown trout.

Improved nutrient status and smaller area (reducing fetch) allow better growth of floating-leaved and submerged plants. Thus Stanevatsoe Water (West Mainland) has a dense stand of broad-leaved pondweed and floating bur-reed in 1–2 m of water, along with various-leaved pondweed. Sand Water (Central Mainland) and Grasswater (West Mainland) have extensive stands of bulrush, which appears to be a recent immigrant to the islands. A lochan at West Burrafirth provides a rare example in Shetland of a reedswamp of common reed. Interestingly, the only site in Shetland with a large pure stand of common reed is at Rerwick (from Old Norse *röyrr*, reed), Dunrossness.

Mesotrophic lochs occur only on comparatively basic rocks, such as the crystal-line limestones and the relatively insoluble sandstones of West Mainland. Examples are Girlsta, Cliff, Tingwall, Asta, Kirkigarth and Bardister. These lochs have many species in common with the more extreme types, such as the alternate-leaved water milfoil, shoreweed and some of the stoneworts. The mesotrophic lochs with the most varied floras are the lochs of Kirkigarth and Bardister at Walls and the lochs of Asta and Tingwall. In all four occurs the rare Shetland pondweed (*Potamogeton rutilus*), known elsewhere in Britain only at a few sites in the Hebrides and on the Scottish mainland. One of the more interesting mesotrophic lochs is the Loch of Girlsta, the deepest loch and the only Shetland site for the arctic char.

With the exception of the Loch of Spiggie in South Mainland, the most productive, or eutrophic, lochs are generally small. These lochs lie on and within the catchments of the more basic and relatively soluble sandstones (such as

Bressay), on limestone and areas of blown shell sand (at Quendale and Breckon), and on the serpentinites of Unst and Fetlar, although the last are very different from the other eutrophic lochs.

Loch of Spiggie is a 'moderately rich' eutrophic loch in nutrient terms, cut off from the sea by a sand bar at its north end. There, its relatively shallow, calcareous sand floor is occupied by an open *stonewort–water milfoil* community, which is common in shallow nutrient-rich or calcareous sediments in Scottish lochs and in Shetland is a favourite feeding area for the flocks of wintering whooper swan and other wildfowl such as pochard, golden eye and tufted duck. Submerged vegetation in the loch comprises stands of various-leaved pondweed, *starwort–lesser pondweed*, quillwort, the moss *Fontinalis antipyretica* and the stonewort (*Nitella flexilis*).

With so little limestone it is not surprising that there is only one marl loch in Shetland, a tiny lochan on White Ness, which typically supports dense beds of common spike-rush, slender-leaved pondweed and stonewort. There is also only one loch wholly on calcareous shell sand, the Loch of Hillwell. For its size this is probably the most productive loch on Shetland and it is extremely important for wildfowl, both breeding and wintering. This loch used to contain the only few plants of spiked milfoil in Shetland, but since effluent, mainly agricultural, was piped into it in the 1970s this plant has disappeared and is now thought to be extinct. Hillwell is also one of only two sites for the flat-stalked pondweed, which appears to be a recent arrival, presumably by courtesy of migrant wildfowl. Although this very special Shetland loch has suffered the indignity of *eutrophication* from the effluent, it still supports a very diverse aquatic flora and a dense and luxuriant marginal swamp with bottle sedge, marsh horsetail, common spike-rush and water forget-me-not. Also occurring on the shore here is mare's tail which, although at the edge of its European range in Shetland, has spread in recent years at Hillwell and become a dominate plant there.

Generally, the eutrophic lochs are those with the highest alkalinity, indicating a high proportion of $CaCO_3$. The serpentinite lochs also have a high alkalinity, but it is caused by the presence of magnesium rather than calcium salts. In addition they have exceptionally high concentrations of nickel and chromium salts and low concentrations of potassium, phosphorus and nitrogen. As lochs on serpentinite are not particularly nutrient-rich, they should not properly be classified with the other eutrophic lochs. In fact, serpentinite lochs are very poor botanically and may have only one or two eutrophic species to the exclusion of all others. Very little is known of their biology, since there are very few lochs of this type in the British Isles, but since the chemical nature of their environment is very distinctive it is quite possible that their biology may also be unique.

Like the eutrophic lochs, the brackish lochs are usually small, but again with one exception, the Loch of Strom at Whiteness. They have usually been formed by coastal deposition processes, so common in the islands (see Chapter 2). There are very many lochs of this type, Easter Loch at Uyeasound in Unst being a good example of one of the more productive. Brackish lochs differ from eutrophic ones by the absence of the almost ubiquitous freshwater species shoreweed and bulbous rush, but share with them the stonewort (*Chara aspera*). They are characterized by the presence of sea arrow-grass, slender spike-rush and occasionally tassel pond-weed. As these sites grade into a more marine situation there is an increase in the seaweeds, typically the wracks (bladder and serrated) but also the red seaweeds. These brackish sites are also important for wintering wildfowl, but only where they are reasonably productive, as at Easter Loch.

Burns and ditches

Shetland has a much higher density of burns than most other areas in Britain due to the rugged terrain, wet climate and impermeable nature of most of the rocks. However they are mostly steep and short with a stony, gravelly or peaty base. They also tend to be irregular or 'flashy' in their flow and can dry up in the summer months, between May and June, when evapotranspiration exceeds rainfall. At other times of the year when the soil or peat is saturated, run-off can be almost immediate after heavy rain. The upper reaches of burns, especially where they are in reality peaty drainage channels, are often full of bog-moss (*Sphagnum subsecundum*), with bog pondweed, lesser spearwort and bulbous rush, merging into sphagnum moss mires with common cotton grass, round-leaved sundew and up to 16 other associated species, mainly mosses and leafy liverworts such as *Scapania undulata* which are typical of wetter blanket bog. Some peaty channels have no macrophytic vegetation at all.

It is only in the lowest reaches where burn flow is slow that the range of large vascular plants becomes more diverse. With a relative paucity of slow-moving burns, some emergents, more common on the mainland of Scotland, are fairly rare in Shetland, for example brooklime and mare's-tail. In the sluggish ditches and burns, usually in low-lying agricultural land, species are similar to those that are common in ungrazed fens, notably the emergents marsh marigold, the naturalized monkey flower, water cress, mint, amphibious bistort and blue water-speedwell.

Swamps and fens

Swamps occur where the summer water table lies above the soil surface and support predominantly sedges, horsetails or reed-like grasses. They lack a moss carpet but may have submerged bog-moss (*Sphagnum*) species. All vegetated sites that are flooded in winter, but where in summer the water lies at or under the soil surface, are called *fens* and here a moss carpet is frequent.

Fens are influenced by ground water chemistry and by the activities of people. In Shetland this means that, almost without exception, fens of uncultivated hill land are all heavily grazed while fens on reasonably nutrient-rich soils, sometimes bordering cultivated ground, were traditionally grazed, mown for hay or cut for sedge peat; ungrazed and unmown examples are very rare. Small examples of ungrazed fen occur on a few freshwater holms. However a rare and extensive example of ungrazed rich (eutrophic) fen occurs at Gulberwick, dominated by marsh horsetail and yellow flag. Apart from the lack of common reed, which occurs in a few other places, this tall vegetation contains at least 18 of the species that make up the many fen fragments in roadside ditches and drains at Tingwall and Whiteness for example. A second good example occurs at Culswick. Here meadows of iris, marsh marigold and white bent are mown or lightly grazed versions of the Gulberwick fen, sharing many of the potentially tall plants, like ragged robin, marsh marigold, water mint, yellow monkey flower and its many colourful hybrids, spotted orchid, water and creeping forget-me-nots, lady's smock and angelica. These ungrazed fens, like the tall-herb communities on cliff ledges, are amongst the most colourful and diverse plant communities in Shetland and contrast vividly with the brown of the hill and the humdrum green of improved grassland.

> Da Daal o Norwick is a lovely valley,
> Da girse sae green below da Joolie sky,
> Aa filled wi flooers over bank an brae an mödow
> Alang da burn at rins sae saftly by.
>
> *Norwick*, T. A. Robertson

Grazed fen can be found predominantly on limestone and serpentinite where open flushes are occupied by a *black bog-rush–moor grass* community with long-stalked yellow sedge; this often grades into a dioecious sedge and few-flowered spike-rush mire. Both these communities may be replaced in less rich sites by a carnation sedge–yellow sedge mire. The commonest grazed fen is dominated by common sedge, jointed rush and purple moor-grass; marsh thistle is frequent and there are often large clumps of yellow flag and soft rush.

Maritime communities

As pointed out in the first chapter, the Shetland coastline is extremely long and a great deal of it is also extremely exposed. On this outer coast, shelter for plants is only to be found in crevices, although this is the habitat where some of Shetland's lichens flourish, with the base of rocky cliffs and the rocky shore above the high-tide line dominated by the hardy yellow-orange lichen *Xanthoria parietina*. Where there is only minimal shelter and a mineral soil on these sea cliffs exposed to continuous

38.   *Lichen Caloplaca: a very common lichen of coastal cliffs and rocks.* (Courtesy of D. H. Dalby.)

salt spray, colonization is often limited to thrift and the dark-coloured moss *Grimmia maritima*. Oddly, this is also the only habitat in Shetland for the sea aster (normally a plant of salt marsh), looking strangely exotic on ledges in *geos*, in its only two recorded stations. Less frequently, moss campion and roseroot occur and, very occasionally, sea spleenwort. With increasing shelter occur sea campion, lovage, common sorrel and northern dock. With the addition of a few other species this can become a rich tall-herb meadow. Both the open and sheltered communities grade beyond the cliff tops into sea plantain swards or, ungrazed but still rather exposed, into a continuous sward of red fescue. The coastal or maritime grasslands, because of the enormous length of the Shetland coastline, cover a large area and are the typical green pastures of cliff tops, sea banks and many offshore holms.

True coastal swards lack mat grass and contain thrift, buck's-horn plantain and, often abundantly, spring squill, which also occurs in base-rich grassland and even on serpentinite debris and which is only locally distributed around the coast of Britain. Meadow grass and Yorkshire fog are common along with about 15 other species. The sward is always close-cropped, often the result of heavy grazing of fescue pastures. It is only a couple of centimetres high, almost as short as a bowling green, but as colourful as a tapestry. Thrift–sea plantain open communities occupy unstable ground to seaward of the plantain–fescue swards, often on top of stacks etc., where there are puffin burrows but no rabbits or sheep.

Coastal screes, which occur as gravel slides on crumbling cliffs, are unstable, exposed to salt spray and often mineral-rich, with or without the addition of guano from seabird colonies. Typical plants are sea campion, scurvy grass, thrift, sea plantain, sea pearlwort, buck's-horn plantain and scentless mayweed. The last species, scurvy grass, nettle, curled dock and mouse-ear chickweed are common on scree below seabird nests or roosts, and may also grow on shingle beaches; most are capable of rapid growth and appear to have a requirement for high amounts of phosphorus and nitrogen, here supplied by the guano input from seabirds.

39. *Sea-pinks and Muckle Flugga: a ubiquitous plant of the coast, flowering freely and in carpets where grazing is low. Beyond Muckle Flugga is only Out Stack and then the Faroe Islands and Iceland.* (Courtesy of R. J. Tulloch.)

On shingle beaches, bars and spits, of which there are many around the more sheltered coast of Shetland, plant cover is quite sparse with colonizing species establishing their roots on the remains of seaweed beneath a stony or pebbly surface. On sand and shingle foreshores characteristic species are the annuals sea rocket and orache species, the perennial curled dock and sea purslane.

One of the most beautiful maritime plants, alas with an increasingly precarious hold in Shetland, is the oyster plant, with its sea-green fleshy leaves and small blue and mauve flowers and which occurs on a very few shingly beaches. Like a bouquet cast up from the sea its clustered bunch of flowers lie prostrate on the shore. Studies have shown that the overwintering roots of some northern species, such as the oyster plant, respond to increased temperatures in winter by using up the carbohydrates normally stored for spring growth needs. Faced with a lack of this energy in spring the plants may die. The oyster plant is thus an example of those species near the edge of their range in Shetland and which react relatively rapidly to small changes in climate, illustrating the fact of continuous natural change in the environment of Shetland.

Orache may extend as far as the shingle crest, where it is often accompanied by scentless mayweed, sowthistle, spear thistle, curled dock, sea campion, chickweed and notably silver weed with its soft and floppy, yellow flower. Goosegrass is almost confined to this habitat. A shingle ridge at the head of Boddam Voe in Dunrossness supports the only wild population of herb Robert in Shetland. All these species are typical of shingle species in Scotland. Taking the list of shingle plants as a whole, many of them are species well known as weeds in fields and gardens, another set of often nutrient-rich habitats colonized by these opportunist plants.

Shetland salt marshes are very limited in extent and confined to areas at the head of some sheltered voes such as Baltasound or Whiteness or the edges of brackish lochs such as the Loch of Strom. The most diverse and largest example is at Dales Voe (Delting). The closed-sward communities of marshes near the sea are typical of

40. *Oysterplant: a beautiful northern shore plant alas declining in Shetland, possibly due to climatic change, but also vulnerable when shingle is removed for building purposes.* (Courtesy of R. J. Tulloch.)

the most widespread salt-marsh communities in the British Isles, dominated by common salt-marsh grass and greater sea spurrey, although Dalby (1985) suggests that the Shetland communities show great affinity with those from parts of the coasts of Norway. Salt-marsh rush dominates in swards above the *Puccinellia* zone with sea milkwort and sea arrow-grass. Seablite and sea (eel) grass are very rare. Another name for sea grass is *marlie*; hence the name given to Marlee Loch at the head of Brindister Voe. This species used to be very much more common in Shetland (as in Britain as a whole) and was so abundant that it was harvested at the head of Weisdale Voe as bedding for cattle until the 1920s.

Sand-dune systems in Shetland, which were discussed in Chapter 3, are regularly subject to erosion and wind blow, are nowhere common and rarely of any size. Outwith South Mainland, where a number of good examples occur, particularly Quendale which is the most extensive dune system in Shetland, the most interesting sand-dune system is probably the large shell sand site at Breckon in Yell. Here, on the dune pasture is one of the few Shetland sites for both the autumn gentian and the bog orchid. At Nor Wick, Unst, sea pea occurs in its only Shetland station. Nor Wick and Burrafirth on Unst, Spiggie and St Ninian's Isle in South Mainland, and West Sandwick in Yell have small dunes with mobile and early-fixed stages, although lyme grass replaces marram in some of them. In every case there is a fairly abrupt transition to dune pasture, which is not confined to sand hillocks as at Quendale but covers instead notably level links. Rabbits are common and contribute to overgrazing, loss of species diversity and often severe erosion in several dune systems. Regrettably most of the larger dune systems and links, for example Quendale, St Ninian's Isle, Spiggie and West Sandwick, have been physically damaged or their flora impoverished by either sand extraction or agricultural improvement.

Policies, shelter belts and gardens

We now direct our attention from the more exposed habitats of the islands to those that can provide the most shelter. In 'treeless' Shetland woodland is a rare habitat. Up until relatively recently it was the typical *policy* species of the big houses of the Scottish mainland that were planted by the Shetland lairds, rather than species native to the islands. One of the earliest of these may have been at Scalloway where Hibbert (1822) records a sycamore of 80 years of age. Sycamore has in fact proved to be one of the hardiest and most successful tree introductions to Shetland. The most northerly 'woodland' in Britain is that planted by Laurence Edmondston, father of Thomas, in the first half of the nineteenth century at Halligarth in Unst. In addition to Scalloway, other successful groups of sycamore and other species, such as wych elm, horse chestnut, ash and common whitebeam, can be found at Tresta, Kergord, Busta, Voe, Swinning and Veensgarth.

Just after the beginning of this century, between 1913 and 1920, a Shetland landowner turned to conifers and with a great deal of effort and patience established what is still the largest plantation on fertile soils at Kergord. These consisted of several shelterbelts, to which another two were added in the 1950s. The trees at Kergord include those broad-leaved species already mentioned above and conifer species in large numbers, of which Japanese larch and Sitka spruce have

41.   Kergord Plantations, Weisdale: the most successful shelterbelts to date, planted in the early part of the twentieth century and demonstrating what can be achieved on good soils and sheltered situations. (Courtesy of L. Johnston.)

been the most successful. At Kergord particularly, a number of introduced woodland plants are well established, such as bluebell, wood sorrel and foxglove, along with the native primrose. The plantations are particularly important for fungi and epiphytes, but there are few lichens. They also provide habitat for some of the woodland bird species that periodically attempt to breed in Shetland, support a rookery, and provide much-needed shelter for many woodland migrants (see Chapter 6).

In the 1950s and 1960s further trials of shelterbelts were carried out with Sitka spruce, lodgepole pine and mountain pine at Sullom and elsewhere. Sitka spruce has proved to be the most successful species, although lodgepole of Alaskan provenance has also fared reasonably well. More recently there has been a revival of interest in shelterbelts and in the use of broad-leaved and native Shetland species, which has sprung from the work of the Shetland Amenity Trust, and a number of shelterbelts and amenity woods with an increasing proportion of broad-leaved species have been planted in the late 1980s and early 1990s.

The Shetland Amenity Trust is now affiliated to the Nordic Arboretum Committee, which includes the Faroese and Icelandic forestry services; this should allow an increasing exchange of valuable information in woodland establishment. The Amenity Trust, set up by the Shetland Islands Council, is building up a bank of native tree material (cuttings from willow, root cuttings from aspen, seed from birch, etc.) to be used in Shetland. It is also looking more closely at the provenance of tree seedlings being purchased from Scotland and is carrying out trials in conjunction with the Forestry Commission on new exotic species to Shetland, such as Sitka alder from south-east Alaska and red alder also from Alaska. There are undoubtedly interesting times ahead for Shetland's woodlands.

In some of the plantations, in Lerwick and in a surprising number of croft gardens, other successful smaller trees include elder, rowan and several willow species such as goat willow, purple willow and hybrids of grey sallow. More

42. *Crofts with shrubs, Cuckron, Stromfirth: in the absence of native trees and shrubs those planted around crofts and houses (including shelterbelts) provide a nesting habitat for several Shetland birds and a sheltered haven for many migrants.* (Courtesy of L. Johnston.)

common in Shetland gardens are smaller shrubs, of which the most successful include the native honeysuckle, as well as fuchsia, flowering currant, cultivated rose species, New Zealand holly, cotoneaster, escallonia and laburnum. All these species, particularly when grown in sufficient numbers and close together, form a very important habitat for small breeding birds such as the house sparrow and blackbird, for migrants and wintering birds, and a microhabitat for invertebrates. They can also soften the impact of new houses in the landscape.

Croftland

Innadæks, quhar rigs ir rutted be tradition.

Ootadæks, Robert Alan Jamieson

We have now completed our tour of the Shetland plant communities and are back at the 'beautiful flat of Corn, Grass and Meadow ground' described by the Rev. George Low (1774). Even though it is not quite as diverse as it was due to changing agricultural practices, such as reseeding and fertilizing and the conversion of much arable land to grassland, the fields and *rigs* around the crofting townships still support a varied flora, particularly the ungrazed fens and hayfields that we have already discussed. Near the houses and byres themselves, perhaps the most striking native plant is the Shetland red campion, its large deep-red flowers blooming as magnificently as a prized garden plant. Two other very striking plants of unusual size, around some crofthouses, are the introduced *tussi girse* (*Poa flabellata*), a very large tussock-forming grass from the southern tip of South America and adjacent islands, and the equally impressive Magellan ragwort (*Senecio smithii*), also from the southern mainland of South America and Tierra del Fuego. Both are magnificent

43.   Red campion: the handsome Shetland form, frequently found around the croft, is large and deeply coloured.
(Courtesy of L. Johnston.)

plants and tradition has it that the seeds of these plants were brought back from the whaling by Shetland men. However, it has recently been suggested that both may have been introduced by more prosaic horticultural channels, the former in the middle of the last century and the latter towards its close.

The earliest plant introductions by people to Shetland would undoubtedly have been for agricultural land, brought in deliberately and/or accidentally as seed, perhaps as long as 5000 years ago. For example, along with the carbonized remains of *bere* or barley (*Hordeum vulgare*) seed found at the Scord of Brouster – a food crop, incidentally, used right up to this century – were other plant remains, possibly of corn spurrey and common chickweed, common weeds of cultivated ground even today. Other colonists of crofting areas that may have been brought in with seed or feeding are pignut and soft brome. Along with the other common weeds of cultivated ground they are important in supporting Shetland's native and visiting butterflies.

We cannot leave the plant communities without discussing the community that is the most colourful and still the most characteristic feature of many Shetland crofting areas, the hayfield. Shetland hayfields tend to be mostly at the wet end of the spectrum and can even merge into fen. Thus it is very difficult to give a 'typical' species list for a hayfield. In fact we have covered some of the communities and species already under tall grassland and tall herb meadow and under ungrazed fen. However if we look at both ends of the spectrum we might just get a picture of the great range of species involved.

The drier end tends to be characterized by grasses such as Yorkshire fog, sweet vernal-grass, rye-grass, oat-grass, common bent, red fescue and crested dog's-tail; with herbs such as common sorrel, curled dock, common mouse-ear, meadow buttercup, red and white clover, eyebright and the taller and more eye-catching devil's bit scabious and autumn hawkbit, to name but a very few. The wet end is characterized by stands of ragged robin, marsh marigold, marsh cinquefoil and

44.   *Wet meadows, Aith, Cunningsburgh: one of the most diverse and colourful plant communities of Shetland and like others created by traditional agriculture requires sensitive management if it is to survive.* (Courtesy of SNH, Battleby.)

meadow orchids and hybrids. Both ends of the hayfield spectrum can be seen at the Shetland hayfield *par excellence*, Aith Meadows, where 80 different species of flowering plants have been recorded!

ANALYSIS AND PHYTOGEOGRAPHY OF SHETLAND'S FLOWERING PLANTS

From the introduction to the list of flowering plants in Appendix 3, it can be seen that, excluding plants believed to be extinct, casuals and plants of garden or agricultural origin that have not become naturalized, the established flora of Shetland may be put at 568 taxa. This includes colonists that have by and large arrived courtesy of people, agricultural weeds for example. If we exclude the colonists, their hybrids and the few naturalized species, the native flora comprises about 400 species, which compares with just over 2000 for Britain as a whole. The only phytogeographical analysis of the Shetland flora has been carried out by Goode (1974) when he compared it with Skye and Faroe. To put the relatively small size of Shetland's flora in perspective, the floras for Skye and Faroe are of the order of 600 and 283 species respectively. The former is farther south, very much closer to the Scottish mainland and has an impressive mountain range far exceeding that of Shetland; the latter is further north, similar in size to Shetland and also has impressive mountains, but is very much more isolated.

A number of Shetland species are unrecorded in Faroe, while the latter has some 55 species unrecorded in Shetland, a number of which, due to the volcanic geology and more mountainous landform of Faroe, are alpines. Comparisons with Orkney are difficult as its flora much more closely resembles that of the adjacent northern mainland of Scotland, whose geology is similar to that of Orkney. Some 97 native or established species in Orkney are unrecorded for Shetland. Similarly, and surprisingly, some 98 Shetland species are unrecorded in Orkney; however, two-thirds of these are microspecies of dandelion (*Taraxacum*) and hawkweeds (*Hieracium* and *Pilosella*).

The most obvious feature of the Shetland flora is that widespread species (156) form almost 40% of the total. On the other hand, it is perhaps not surprising that Shetland is intermediary between Skye and Faroe in the number of its Atlantic (40), sub-Atlantic (75), continental (74) and northern montane (13) representatives; or that it has the same number of arctic–subarctic species as Skye (13) but slightly fewer than Faroe (19) and fewer arctic–alpine (22) than either (39 and 43 respectively). However, taking the last two elements together Shetland has a total of 35 arctic–subarctic and arctic–alpine species, which, significantly, is almost 10% of its native flora. Although several of the arctic–alpine species occur on the higher slopes of Ronas Hill, for example alpine saussurea, spiked mountain woodrush, three-leaved rush and mountain azalea, the majority in fact are frequent at lower levels and some (moss campion, roseroot, purple saxifrage and curved sedge) either favour, or are found only at, sea level. This analysis gives a fair indication of the effect of Shetland's relatively northerly position and climate, and of course its unique area of serpentinite fellfield.

It is typical of all floras that most species are rare or uncommon and that such rarity has several causes. An outstanding cause of rarity is endemism, which follows from total genetic isolation of a population for a long period of time, typical of island populations. Shetland in fact has few endemic plants, which is partly a reflection of the relativity of its isolation and partly the relatively short period between initial colonization by plants and today. Although the majority of the Shetland dandelions (*Taraxacum*) are colonists, one especially worthy of note is *Taraxacum geirhildae*, one of Shetland's recognized endemic microspecies, known only from a few remote parts of Shetland.

Further evolution due to isolation is demonstrated by the Shetland hawkweed (*Hieracium*) flora, which incidentally also throws a little more light on the diverse origins of Shetland plants: from the east as well as the south, just like some of its birds and human population. Of the 24 or so microspecies of hawkweed recorded from Shetland, no less than 15 are believed to be endemic and all belong to the mainly Scandinavian section Alpestria, which has its British stronghold in Shetland. Similarly, the Shetland mouse-ear hawkweed (*Pilosella flagellaris* subsp. *bicapitata*), another endemic, appears to be a subspecies of a Scandinavian and continental plant.

The surviving hawkweeds in Shetland are predominantly found on ungrazed grassy ledges, but can also occur on grassland where grazing is low, indicating that they were probably much more widespread and numerous in the past. The high number of hawkweed endemics is mostly due to the fact that they reproduce apomictically, or without fertilization by pollen (i.e. sexual reproduction of the normal type). Perpetuation of individual differences by mutation and other means therefore occurs and a whole series of small populations of similar plants arises, many of these being very rare. As a group hawkweeds, which are sensitive to grazing, are a showy feature of Shetland ledges. Another conspicuously flowered genus are the eyebrights, often found as beautiful miniatures in grazed herb-rich grassland and heath, which freely produce hybrid and hybrid swarms.

Shetland's best-known endemic plant (sadly not recognized as a full species), the mouse-ear chickweed, *Cerastium nigrescens* subsp. *nigrescens*, is confined to the fellfield of the Keen of Hamar. Visualize it as evolving from a plant that was once widespread in Shetland, just as similar vegetation occurs today in central Iceland. However, when the climate improved with the retreat of the ice, heath or grass-like vegetation eliminated its fellfield habitat with the exception of that on Ronas Hill and the Keen of Hamar. In the latter area, nutrient imbalance, deficiencies and the drought-inducing physical nature of the substratum kept the plant cover sparse and, over some 10 000 years, allowed this arctic chickweed to evolve in geographical isolation as a subspecies recognizably distinct from all other subspecies. On the Keen of Hamar fellfield thrift is another species that has evolved a distinct physiological race in response to the unusual soil, although different-*looking* plants have not yet evolved. Thrift is not so isolated as the mouse-ear chickweed since it also occurs on serpentinite in nearby grazed grassland and sea cliffs. In addition to thrift there are a number of other 'forms' and 'adaptations' of other common species that have no currently accepted taxonomic status; in other words, as with thrift, they are still adapting to a unique situation and evolving, though *we* will never know if they will become new subspecies or species.

CHAPTER 5

By Sea and by Air

Shetland sheep on the hill

There are no weasels [stoats] in all the Northern Isles of Zetland, as I am informed, tho' numerous in the Mainland, which they report thus came to pass: The [King's] Falconer having a power given to him, to get a Hen out of every House, once in the Year: but one year they refusing, or not be so willing to give, the Falconer out of Revenge, brought the next year two Weasels with him, which did generate and spread, so that now they are became very destructive to several goods of the Inhabitants, whereof a Gentleman, our Informer, told us he had killed several half an Ell long.

Brand, 1701

All of Shetland's terrestrial vertebrates (not including birds) have been introduced at one time or another, some for positive reasons, some accidentally,
most in ignorance of the effect they might have on Shetland's native fauna, but
luckily few, like the stoat, for malicious reasons.

Our knowledge of Shetland's terrestrial vertebrates is very good, but our
knowledge of most of its invertebrates is surprisingly limited. There are few
mammals and only the otter and the field mouse have been in the islands longer
than written history. Of the invertebrates, the Lepidoptera have been the most
studied because many local forms exist in Shetland. There has been a recent revival
in interest and recording of this group that has succeeded in doubling the number
of species recorded since 1980. The spiders and flies have also received some
attention; however, other invertebrates have been studied only piecemeal. A list of
all the land animals can be found in Appendix 3.

MAMMALS

The land mammals illustrate particularly well the limitations and fascinations of
the Shetland fauna. For some we have fairly definitive dates for introduction, for
others we can only hazard a guess. Once ashore all the animals have had to adapt
to the Shetland environment to some extent in order to survive. Unfortunately,
since the genotypes of the original colonizers is inevitably unknown, the amount of
this adaptive change is impossible to determine unless specimens are available from
different times during the history of the animals in Shetland. Only for sheep is
anything known about the differences between the breed in past centuries and
today. All other species have to be compared with their relatives in other areas.
Differences between the Shetland form and the typical form elsewhere can be
established in this way, but they may have arisen either by an initial genetic
difference in the colonizing group (the founder effect, see Chapter 1) or by
subsequent adaptation.

The hedgehog was introduced in the middle of the last century and is now
widespread throughout Mainland and most of the inhabited islands. A little earlier,
about 1830, the brown hare was introduced into both Orkney and Shetland by
their Member of Parliament, Samuel Laing. By the 1890s the brown hare was very
common in parts of Mainland and crofters were having to shoot large numbers to
protect their crops. In 1882 brown hares were released at Windhouse at Reafirth on
Yell, but they soon died out; after the turn of the century, the species began to
decline on Mainland, becoming extinct about 1937. In contrast the blue, or
mountain, hare was introduced from Scotland to the Kergord estate about 1907
and survives now in moderate numbers on heather moorland throughout Mainland. In recent years some animals were introduced on Ronas Hill and their
descendants now flourish in Northmavine. It is still abundant on Vaila where two
pairs from Perthshire were released about 1900. The Shetland hares share the
characteristic of the Scottish race of not turning completely white in winter, and
individuals with only their ears remaining brown are frequently seen in May. In
Shetland, of course, snow rarely lies for more than a few days at a time. A study of

two areas in north-east Mainland found that the populations were moderately dense when compared with the north-east of Scotland and more numerous comparatively than those on other Scottish islands or on the west and north-west mainland. The reasons for the relatively high density in Shetland was said to be the fact that the heather moorland of Shetland is not widely burned and therefore there is more of it suitable for hares. The habitat down to sea level in Shetland is also submontane, and the short heather, due to exposure and heavy grazing, is a natural part of the blue hare's range. However, this also offers little protective cover from its usual predators, such as the fox, wildcat or golden eagle, which are absent in Shetland, although the *bonxie* (great skua) and the *swaabie* (greater black-backed gull) will take leverets. This suggests that if any of these predators were introduced to Shetland they would soon make an impact on the hare population; if the sea eagle ever colonized, which it could well do, the mountain hare could be an easy target.

The date of the introduction of the rabbit is not known, although warrens were present on West Burra, and the isles of Oxna, Hildasay and Papa Little were 'somewhat stored with Coneys' by 1654. Shetland rabbits are unusual in being polymorphic for coat colour: black, chocolate, spotted and even true albino forms occur in significant frequencies. Dominantly inherited black rabbits survive on islands and headlands in other parts of Britain in situations where food is limited, apparently because they are more stolid than normal agouti animals and continue feeding when their sibs are scared into their burrows. The extra food they get in this way presumably more than offsets the risk of being predated; of course, several of their mainland predators are absent from Shetland. The reason for the survival of the other colour forms is completely unknown and the occurrence of wild-living albinos is particularly surprising.

There are no bat colonies in Shetland, but vagrants are regularly recorded and have been seen at least since Low was informed in 1774 that they occasionally appeared. Bats feed on the wing, like the swallow, the martins and the swift, and like them do not thrive in cool, windy areas where food availability can be difficult. It is not surprising therefore that although there are a few records for several species, they occur only as a handful of records, lost or blown off course. A full list is given in Appendix 3.

There are three naturalized carnivores in Shetland and there might be a fourth; in addition there are feral cats in some areas. Each in their way demonstrates the contribution or danger that introduction or translocation of new species can have in island situations. The otter (*draatsi*) (see Chapter 7), which is abundant, has been on the islands perhaps as long as any terrestrial mammal. The stoat on the other hand, whose local name is the Scots *whitrit* for the weasel, has been present only since the seventeenth century, when a Zetland Court Statute (dated 1 August 1615) ordered that the head of a *quitred* be presented to the Court by every local minister and gentleman. It has been suggested that stoats may in fact have been introduced to control rabbits. Certainly stoats were once released on Whalsay in an attempt to control rats and rabbits, although they are now extinct there.

The third naturalized carnivore at present on the loose is the ferret-polecat (*Mustela putorius* × *M. furo*). Animals either deliberately or accidentally released in the early 1980s, apparently in Central Mainland, have become feral and spread. They have proved to be a threat to poultry and duck and possibly have local detrimental effects on wildlife, such as ground-nesting birds like the lapwing. In 1993 a control scheme was set up by Shetland Islands Council. In the 18 months up to October 1996 almost 250 were trapped. It is too early yet to be sure but it does appear that the scheme is working. A fourth carnivore, which escaped from captivity, was the mink, a native of eastern Canada. This animal was farmed in Shetland in the 1960s and 1970s and a number became feral; however it seems that it has died out. The latest predator to get loose in Shetland is the fox. Rumours of one living in North Mainland were confirmed when a dog fox was killed on the main road in 1996, but unfortunately the rumours persist. Feral cats are known to predate several seabird colonies and they have been a particular threat to the Manx shearwaters of Fetlar and could eliminate that species from the island if predation continues. All these species of carnivores could have a serious effect on Shetland's wildlife locally, particularly the waders and terns (*tirricks*) that are so successful in their absence. It is sheer folly to introduce animals, or plants, into an island environment and there are plenty of examples of disasters throughout the world due to this practice. Animals and plants should never be introduced without a great deal of thought and planning, and even then one should hesitate.

Field and house mice

The field mouse is common throughout the larger islands of Shetland in all places away from the larger townships. Indeed it is usually called the 'hill mouse', which fairly accurately describes its habitat, certainly more accurately than its European and English name of 'wood mouse'. One of the reasons for its success in Shetland is that there are no voles; it shares with the house mouse the drier areas where voles would live. Shetland field mice are among the more brightly coloured races of the species and are often referred to as 'red mice' in distinction to house or 'grey mice'. Field mice are more common in Shetland than in Orkney, where they have to compete with voles (*Microtus arvalis orcadensis*). The only small mammal in Faroe is the house mouse.

Both field and house mice in Shetland are large forms of their species (Table 7). Indeed the house mice are among the biggest recorded in the world. No one knows why this should be so, although increased size is an almost invariable characteristic of mice living on small islands. The most likely reason is that mice are usually smaller than their most efficient physiological size because of the need to escape down small holes when chased by predators that are themselves capable of squeezing into the holes. The relative absence of such predators in places like Shetland means that the larger animals are not continually eliminated, and the mean size of the mice is consequently able to increase. The main advantage of larger over smaller size is that body surface is reduced in relation to body volume, which means that the proportion of energy lost as heat is reduced. Since the main cause of death in mice is cold, even a small increase in size is likely to be important. Other effects of greater body size will be demonstrated by intraspecific fighting and intrauterine competition between embryos.

TABLE 7 *Average sizes of Shetland mice with other populations for comparison (mature animals only)*

No. in sample		Weight (g)	Length (mm)		
			Head and body	Tail	Hind foot
Apodemus sylvaticus					
60	Iceland *(A. s. grandiculus)*	—	130.0	90.8	23.2
95	Foula *(A. s. thuleo)*	26.8	101.2	92.1	24.0
5	Yell *(A. s. granti)*	—	100.9	88.2	23.6
30	Fair Isle *(A. s. fridariensis)*	32.1	112.9	98.6	23.9
76	St Kilda *(A. s. hirtensis)*	42.6	114.4	99.2	25.1
38	Rum *(A. s. hamiltoni)*	30.1	105.9	92.9	24.6
33	Perthshire	18.4	92.3	82.6	21.8
40	Surrey	20.4	87.6	86.2	21.9
Mus musculus					
55	Mykines, Faroe	25.4	96.1	87.9	19.0
49	Sandøy, Faroe	20.9	96.7	84.4	18.6
54	Foula	25.1	97.7	82.5	18.2
95	Bressay*	16.7	86.5	78.5	18.7
53	Scalloway*	15.5	83.2	72.8	18.1
91	Dunrossness*	17.4	86.5	75.1	18.4
12	Fair Isle	21.1	98.5	82.9	18.6
77	Sanday, Orkney*	17.9	87.6	73.1	17.7
64	Harray, Orkney*	14.8	84.0	69.5	17.7
104	Somerset*	13.5	86.6	74.3	16.8

* Caught when ricks threshed, and hence from a different environment to the other house mouse samples, which were trapped in fields and on the cliffs.

Shetland field mouse

Shetland field mice differ in more ways than size from other forms of the same species. A new subspecies of field mouse (*Apodemus sylvaticus fridariensis*) was described in 1906 from six adult mice caught on Fair Isle; in 1914 another subspecies (*A. s. granti*) was described from Yell; and in 1919 the subspecies *A. s. thuleo* was discovered in Foula. Both the Yell and Foula races are smaller than the Fair Isle one, the Yell form having in addition a slightly shorter tail and the Foula one particularly large hind feet. The description of the Shetland subspecies was part of a general recognition during the early years of this century that a great deal of differentiation has occurred in small mammals on the islands of the western North Atlantic (especially the Hebrides, Orkney and Shetland). As far as the field mouse is concerned, three species containing 16 subspecies were characterized, all of them on small islands. This diversity becomes significant when contrasted with the uniformity of the species on the continent of Eurasia, where its range extends from the Atlantic coast to western China.

The Shetland field mice are more closely related to Norwegian animals than to Scottish ones, which is one of the facts demonstrating the lack, or short-lived nature, of any land-bridge connecting Shetland to the Scottish mainland following the last glaciation. This has been shown by a comparison of as many gene frequencies as possible in population samples from Shetland and elsewhere. When these comparisons are carried out, Yell field mice were found to be much closer to Norwegian than Scottish animals. Comparisons within an island (or between samples collected on a single landmass, such as the Scottish Highlands) consistently show little or no divergence: the statistic is around zero. The Fair Isle and Foula populations are unlike both Scottish and Norwegian mice, but are more like the Yell mice than anything else (Fig. 16). These relationships seem to indicate that the Yell field mouse population was derived directly from Norway and that the smaller islands were colonized from Yell (or one of the other large islands; no large collections have been made from Mainland, which is the most likely source). Since each colonizing event presumably involved a few animals getting ashore, their gene frequencies will almost inevitably differ from those in the ancestral population (see Fig. 2). The founder effect is the most powerful way of changing gene frequencies (see Chapter 1). Consequently it is not surprising that the Foula and Fair Isle populations are as distinct as they are.

Now, discussion about relationships between populations leads us back to the question of how long field mice have been on the Shetland islands. Since massive genetic change can take place so easily, there is no need to assume that the distinctiveness of the Shetland forms implies they have been isolated for a very long time. The maximum antiquity for the Yell population will be a time when boats began sailing from Norway to Shetland; the Foula and Fair Isle populations could have been established at any time since. Probably field mice got ashore from one of the early Viking ships, perhaps in a cargo of seeds or in the bedding of animals being introduced for the settlers' farms, about 1200 years ago.

The research carried out on Shetland field mice has not only thrown light on *their* origins, but also on those of the people who inadvertently transported them. Since we think that the otter may also have been introduced to Shetland it would be very interesting to examine the relationships of the otter populations of the Northern Atlantic islands, Scandinavia and Scotland. Where did they come from?

The field mouse situation is also important, not only because of the confusion that has arisen through past assumptions that field mice are 'relics' rather than introductions into Shetland, but also because of the light it throws on the

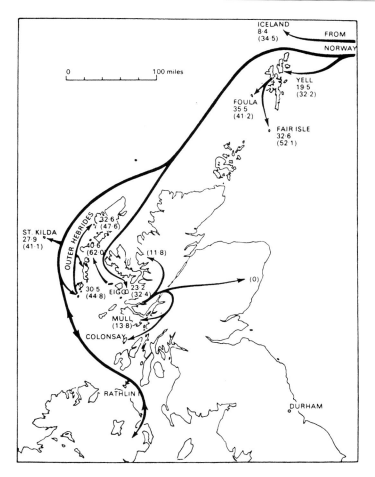

FIGURE 16 *Map to show the suggested routes by which Shetland and the Western Isles were colonized by field mice. The figures are estimates of divergence (the higher the value, the more distant the relationship), those without parentheses being the 'genetic distance' from the closest related population, and those within parentheses the distance from the Loch Sunart population (taken as typifying Scottish Highland field mice)* (from Berry, 1969a).

mechanisms of biological change in general. If subspeciation can happen suddenly, new gene combinations can be 'tried out' by natural selection, and evolution will be able to proceed much more rapidly than forecast by the classical mechanisms of genetic change.

Not surprisingly, house mice in Shetland show a parallel situation to field mice. The house mice of both St Kilda (where house mice became extinct in 1932 but had previously been separated as the only distinct British species, *Mus muralis*) and Faroe have a narrowing of the mesopterygoid fossa on the ventral surface of the skull (i.e. the place where the internal nostrils open). This is a sign of common ancestry, since Shetland mice also possess it. As would be expected from the operation of the founder effect, its frequency is different on different islands: on Fetlar it occurs at 91%, on Foula at 9%. There are two stories of the introduction of house mice to Foula: they were released there by some Walls fishermen in dispute with Foula men about fishing rights, or they came over in a packing case when a shop was first opened on the island. Both stories put the introduction about 1830.

The unravelling of the history of the house mouse and its colonization of the Northern (and Western) Isles of Scotland and Faroe is, however, far from as obvious as it appears to be for the field mouse. Narrowing of the mesopterygoid fossa has not been found in Orkney field mice, so perhaps they do not share a common ancestry with those of the other islands. The history of the house mouse on Shetland has also very recently been found to be much older than that of the field mouse. An archaeological dig at Scatness by Bradford University and the Shetland Amenity Trust has identified house mice remains in a secure Iron Age context. Having been on Shetland for around 1500–2000 years at least, the house mouse comes as close as any Shetland mammal to being indigenous.

Domestic animals

The terrestrial mammals that have the longest history in Shetland are humans and their farm animals, cattle and sheep, for which there is evidence at Sumburgh settlement, the Scord of Brouster, at 5500 BP. However it appears that these primitive domestic beasts were largely cross-bred, with the introduced Scandinavian animals brought by the Norse settlers 1200 years ago.

Almost all visitors to Shetland are aware of the Shetland pony, somewhat fewer know of the Shetland sheep, but very few are aware that there are Shetland cattle. They are small, black, fine-boned animals said to be most closely related to the rare South and Westland breed of south-west Norway and it has even been suggested that they are closely akin to a subspecies. The outstanding feature of the breed is their 'hardiness and ability to convert poor quality fodder into beef and milk'. Those who still raise Shetland cattle emphasize that hardiness, which they suggest

45. *Shetland cow: a relatively small and hardy animal, with mainly Scandinavian ancestry, well adapted to the hardships of the Shetland climate.* (Courtesy of L. Johnston.)

makes the 'native' cattle cheaper to look after than the modern non-Shetland breeds. Most important in these northern latitudes, where winter feed is often critically scarce, is that the breed is very slow growing; a Shetland calf takes 2 years to mature in contrast to the usual 1 year. A fat Shetland cow weighs 100–130 kg and gives 5–10 litres per day. The breed was in danger of dying out in the face of crossing with other mainland breeds but was safeguarded by the formation of the Shetland Cattle Herd Book Society in 1910–11 and support from Shetland Islands Council latterly. The breed received recognition from the European Economic Community in 1985.

Ponies are probably the most well-known Shetland animals outside Shetland. Basically they are the same breed as those of Norway. A skeleton of a pony of 12 hands was found in a midden at Jarlshof, and ancient stones from Bressay and Papil have a carving of a pony ridden by a hooded figure, presumably a priest or a monk. They must have been fairly numerous and valuable at that time judging by the number of Shetland place names derived from the Old Norse *hestr* (horse), such as Hestaness and Hestinsetter. The Shetland Court Books of the sixteenth century have a number of mentions of 'horsis' in connection with offences committed in the islands. These show the importance placed on the hair of the tails, which was of great economic value and was used for making cords, fishing lines, and so on. Early in the seventheeth century, an Act was passed making it an offence to 'row or cut' the hair from the tail of another man's horse.

The 'Shetland Pony Stud Book Society' was formed in 1890 and has published a register of horses and breeders most years since. The objects of the Society are to maintain the purity and promote the breeding of Shetland ponies. In 1956 a Premium Stallion Scheme was set up in collaboration with the Scottish Department of Agriculture. Under this, up to 18 registered stallions are placed on *scattalds* in the islands, and these have produced a great improvement in the present stock.

46. *Shetland ponies: here grazing on the sedge-rich serpentinite grassland of Unst where they are particularly common. One of the smallest ponies of the world, well adapted to keeping a low profile through the worst winter weather.* (Courtesy of L. Johnston.)

In the eighteenth century, the largest animals were exported and complaints were made that the breed was becoming smaller. However, the Marquis of Londonderry established stud farms on Bressay and Noss in 1870–99 to produce horses for use down coal mines with the appearance but not the prohibitive size of the Clydesdale. In fact selection for big feet seems to have led to an overall increase in body size and even today, decades after the introduction of more careful breeding, ponies in Shetland are frequently larger than 'Shetland ponies' in other places. The traditional use of ponies was as pack animals, particularly for bringing home peats from the hills; nowadays they are bred for riding and export. The first mention of the Shetland pony for road transport seems to have been made by Christian Ployen, Governor of Faroe, who visited Shetland in 1839. He tells that he was driven in Lerwick by his host in a carriage drawn by a pony, that he rode a pony for trips further afield and that he was much impressed.

Shetland sheep are world renowned for their fine, soft wool. Like Shetland cattle they are relatively small, fine-boned and hardy, with an average fleece weight of about 1 kg. They are also prolific and long-lived and the only sheep that can thrive on the exposed and poor hill land. If kept on the hill entirely they produce very tasty lamb and mutton. Only the rams have horns, and the breed has several features that suggest an affinity with primitive sheep, such as the Soay sheep of St Kilda. One of these features is the short tail, another is the tendency for the fleece to be moulted annually, and a third is the occurrence of coloured wool. Archae-ological evidence points to the presence of a primitive sheep in Shetland nearly 4000 years before the Vikings arrived with their own breed. Today's Shetland sheep are similar to the Spaelsau breed of south-west Norway and were probably crossed with the original inhabitants.

Only about 2% of Shetland sheep are coloured today, and of these the most common colour is *moorit* (brown). However there are also black, piebald and grey

47. *Shetland sheep: the small and variously coloured native sheep, introduced by the Norse but presumably crossed with those husbanded by Shetland's earlier inhabitants, produce a very fine and warm wool.* (Courtesy of R. J. Tulloch.)

48. *Lichen* Ramalina: *a common lichen that hangs like an unkempt beard from exposed rocks and stone; once used for dyeing wool.* (Courtesy of D. H. Dalby.)

sheep and some variations. One of these, known as *shaela* (greyish-black), is said to resemble hoar frost on old, rain-sodden snow. To these indigenous colours many others were added by the use of natural dyes from plants and lichens. In the past there was a 'hairy' variety of sheep, which may have been the result of Norse influence. This may survive as the 'hardback' on Foula. A similar method of inheritance of colour in Orkney and Iceland sheep suggests that they have a common origin. Shetland sheep are not very different to those of Orkney, including the well-known seaweed-eating sheep of North Ronaldsay. However precise relationships are difficult to ascertain. For example, the range of fleeces from hairy to woolly was a common feature of primitive sheep and provides the basis for selective breeding everywhere.

The tendency to shed their fleece in the spring or early summer is caused by a thinning of the wool fibre during the slow winter growth, causing a break to occur between the old and new fibres. In the past it led to the custom of *rooin* or plucking the wool, so that the fleece would not be lost. Complaints about this practice were periodically made. As long ago as 1619 the Scottish Privy Council forbade *rooin* on the ground that it was 'grievous and noisome to the puir harmless beasts'. Shetlanders protested, explaining 'that the undirgrowth of young woll cast off the auld groith of the awn accord, without pulling or clipping, and as naturallie as gif the wool wes taen off by industrie or art', and that consequently their practice was not 'grievous to the puir beastis'. The Council appointed a Commission, which confirmed the facts were as stated by the islanders, whereupon the prohibition was withdrawn.

As cattle numbers have declined in Shetland so sheep numbers have increased. In the early seventeenth century a typical family would keep nine cows and 22 sheep on average, and probably also a pig, goats and some geese. Cross-breeding with other mainland breeds began in the eighteenth century, and with the clearances of the nineteenth century sheep numbers rose dramatically. Although there are *soumings* that control the number of Shetland sheep on the *scattald*, there is no such control on the apportioned and improved land, so that the number of breeding ewes and gimmers is now around 220 000, of which only around 25% are pure-bred Shetland. Cross-breeding has resulted in continued deterioration of wool quality, associated with a decline in the woollen industry. These increasing numbers of sheep and the decline in cattle are driven by the (European) Common Agricultural Policy and wool prices are now so low that it is hardly worth the effort of shearing or *rooin*. Summer pastures, and even the hill, are becoming increasingly littered with wool and it is not uncommon to see *shalders* (oystercatchers) trailing long fibres or even with their legs entirely entangled.

The Shetland sheepdog perhaps ought to be included with the other farm animals. It probably originated from a cross of a Scottish collie with the all-purpose *toonie* dog that scavenged the crofting township. At some time crosses with the 'Yakkie' dog of the Greenland whalers must have also taken place, giving the Shetland dog a black muzzle. Since 1908 breed standards have been established and the modern selected dog probably bears little resemblance to the early crofters' scavenger.

AMPHIBIANS

There are no amphibians native to Shetland. The common toad has been introduced in small numbers by way of adults and tadpoles several times with limited success. There is only one authenticated record of spawning after the last recorded release in Lerwick in 1950 and only a handful of sightings of adults since then. It may well be that the toad has not become naturalized and these infrequent sightings may be due to continuing and very occasional unrecorded introductions that do not survive for very long.

The common frog, on the other hand, has become established through introduction. The first recorded introduction was at Brough Lodge in Fetlar in 1895 (Evans and Buckley, 1899). In the 1920s further introductions were released at Scalloway and Lerwick. It appears that these two introductions are the sources for most of the Shetland mainland population from North Roe to West Mainland and to Sandwick in South Mainland, although there could well have been other unrecorded introductions. Frogs are also present now in most of the inhabited islands, including Foula and Fair Isle.

FRESHWATER FISH

Compared with the mainland of Scotland the freshwater fish fauna of Shetland is relatively impoverished (see Appendix 3) with only seven species definitely established, all of which have a marine phase or are tolerant of high salinities. As with other groups this is mainly due to the isolation of the islands, but it is also due to the preponderance of nutrient-poor lochs (see Table 6) and burns that normally support few species. However, the islands are famed among anglers for their brown trout fishing; in all but the smallest peaty lochans and the few that have no access for fish from the sea, the brown trout is ubiquitous. Their colour and marking vary a great deal. For example, the Spiggie trout tend to be silvery and close to being sea trout; those on the serpentinite are tinged with red on the belly; while those from the peaty lochs are dark and brightly spotted. 'Sea' trout too are common, but generally restricted to the the larger burns and lochs close to the sea. Unfortunately they are nowhere as common as they were earlier in the century. It has been suggested that overfishing and particularly illegal netting by burn mouths may have been one of the original causes for their decline and that more recently sea-lice from fish farms and even seals may be exacerbating the problem. The otter takes some trout undoubtedly but it seems to eat eels more often. There appear to be enough young fish leaving fresh water for the sea, but few returning at 2 years old. The sea trout decline in Scotland is of course not limited to Shetland; there are serious problems on the west coast too.

Salmon occur only in the largest burns and lochs, such as the lochs of Strom, Tingwall and Voxterby. Presumably salmon were very much more common in at least two sites in the early Norse period or why would they have been named Laxo Voe and Laxo Firth from the Old Norse name for salmon. Rainbow trout have been introduced to several lochs, have overwintered and grown, but there is no evidence for spawning. Recently, non-indigenous brown trout have been introduced in quite large numbers to lochs that come under heavy angling pressure, such as the Loch of Tingwall. Unfortunately, there is no control or definitive record of which lochs have been stocked with fish, nor of which lochs that have never had trout and which should remain so. Breeding between different 'races' of trout may invigorate local stock; on the other hand, the characteristics of Shetland trout that have allowed them to adapt and survive for so long may be lost.

In the late 1950s Dr M. A. Swan, a retired surgeon and a keen angler, decided to investigate the 'rumours' of the presence of arctic char in the Loch of Girlsta. This species is a relict of the colder climate following the last Ice Age and is a migratory species in the arctic. It occurs in a few lochs in Scotland, where it is now virtually 'trapped', usually occupying the deeper and cooler waters than its near relative the brown trout. As Dr Swann said in the *New Shetlander* (1964): 'When I first visited Shetland in 1953, the Girlsta char was thought to be probably extinct, as none had been caught for several decades in spite of some attempts to find it'. Undeterred he set a herring-net overnight in 1955 and caught 57! It appears that Loch of Girlsta, the largest loch by volume, is the only suitable site for this species in Shetland and the population is the most northerly in the British Isles. Although it spends much time in deeper water, it appears that the littoral (shallow) zone is very important for feeding where it preys on the water flea, the water 'lice', snails and caddis fly larvae among others. As the feeder streams to Loch of Girlsta appear to be impassable it is likely that the char also spawns in the littoral zone.

Experiments are now going on with raising char in Shetland commercially. Trials of sea trout farming have very recently also proved successful. Shortly they may join salmon as part of Shetland's very successful fish farming industry. Great care will be needed to ensure that there will be no threats to the indigenous populations from these farms, the parasites they attract or the chemicals that are used.

Other common fish species are the eel, which is fairly widespread; the three-spined stickleback, found in all situations from fresh to brackish water, except the most acidic and peaty lochs; and the flounder, which is found in only those lochs with easy access to the sea and a suitable substrate. The only other fish species that may be common in Shetland is the lamprey. Finally, the ten-spined stickleback has been recorded from the Loch of Cliff in Unst, but this requires confirmation.

BUTTERFLIES AND MOTHS

Once again it is the climate and relative isolation of the islands that conspires to limit the Lepidoptera fauna, particularly the butterflies. Only the large white (*Pieris brassicae*), which was said to have colonized via NAAFI (Navy, Army and Air Force Institute) cabbages during the Second World War, is now resident, as the common blue (*Polyommatus icarus*) appears to be extinct. It is not therefore for the large colourful forms that Shetland is renowned, but for the less flamboyant moths, the Shetland ghost moth (*Hepialis (humuli) thulensis*) for example, which was first described in 1865 and exhibited in London 15 years earlier. It was not until later that century that professional collectors began to visit Shetland and also Orkney, usually to Hoy, although the Shetland forms were more spectacular (and saleable) than those found in Orkney and consequently Shetland was much more intensively collected. Not until the mid-twentieth century did research commence (see Chapter 10). In *The Natural History of Shetland* (1980) the number of species of Lepidoptera for Shetland was given as 145. Since then much work has been done by M. Pennington (see Appendix 3) and others and the Shetland total now stands at around 280.

The chief peculiarity of the Shetland moths that attracted so many outsiders was a high frequency of melanic forms. About one-third of the non-migrant species are represented in Shetland by a form much darker than the typical (e.g. *Standfussiana lucernea, Diarsia mendica, Hadena confusa, Eupithecia venosata*) or by a range of forms between melanic and typical (e.g. *Amathes xanthographa, Eulithis populata, Apamea monoglypha*). Melanics apparently identical to some of the Shetland forms occur as industrial melanics in England, for example 4% of the black form of *A. monoglypha* occurs at Bradford, 17% at nearby Guisley. However, industrial melanism is a result of changes in the daytime resting places of moths caused by pollution (eliminating, among other effects, vegetative lichens from trees and fences), whereas there is negligible air pollution in Shetland. In fact melanics are found in both Orkney and Faroe, but at a much lower frequency than in Shetland (only 2% of indigenous species in Faroe). The occurrence of melanism is high at the same latitude as Shetland in both Norway and Canada, and must be an adaptation to climatic or biological conditions at 60° N.

However, the reason for the high number of lepidopteran melanics in Shetland is still unknown. The most reasonable hypothesis is that the long twilight period in summer means that nocturnal moths are flying before darkness fully falls, thus exposing them to predation by insectivorous birds. Under these conditions, a dark moth could have a cryptic advantage. However there is no evidence for this suggestion and the correct explanation could as easily be that the coloration is a physiological response to the cool conditions of Shetland.

A determined attempt to discover the factors maintaining the melanics was made by B. Kettlewell and collaborators using the autumnal rustic (*Paradiarsia glareosa*). This species was chosen because it has a distinct melanic form (f. *edda*) that cannot be confused with the typical form (f. *typica*) except in very worn specimens. It is unusual in this respect; most of the Shetland melanics do not have a sharp distinction between the dark and light forms. This piece of research was described in Berry and Johnston (1980) and although it did not succeed in finding the answer to this apparently simple question it revealed a situation of considerable complexity. Frustrating as it must have been not to have found the answer, the facts that emerged, as so often, were probably of greater general significance and illustrated the value of Shetland, and islands generally, in investigating adaptation and its general mechanism.

In 1987 the Fair Isle Bird Observatory obtained a moth trap, while in 1992 the Shetland Entomological Group was formed and another trap was set up by Mike Pennington in Unst. In the past new records have been added only through visiting entomologists. One of the main aims of the group therefore has been to take advantage of several enthusiastic entomologists now living in Shetland. Since the formation of the group many new migrants have been added to the list. Work carried out by the group suggests that several montane species discovered last century, such as the northern dart, the broad-bordered white underwing, and the small dark yellow underwing, have either become extinct or very rare. In contrast the less choosy of the grass-feeding species, especially dark arches and the clouded-bordered brindle, have become much commoner, with the last-mentioned species not even recorded until 1959. Both of these alterations in abundance could be due to changes and pressures in agriculture, apportionment and reseeding accounting for increases in the grass-feeding species and heavy grazing and erosion of the hill land (see Chapters 4 and 12), which is also affecting certain bird species (see Chapter 6), being responsible for decline of the montane species.

FLIES AND OTHER INSECTS

The latest list of flies (Diptera), by B. R. Laurence (1997), lists over 200 species, several of which are boreo-arctic species, but most of which have a wide distribution and are found also in Orkney, the Hebrides and on the Scottish mainland. Some are migratory species, notably certain hover-flies.

Flies do not normally arouse the interest of the Shetlander or the visitor, but we should all be grateful that the female of a blackfly found only in Shetland does not, like other blackflies, feed on blood before laying her eggs. This unique species is found in Shetland in rapid, stony and peaty burns, whereas in lowland Britain its cousin is normally found in broader and slower streams and rivers. This species is another example of one of the features of island fauna mentioned in the opening chapter: adaptation in isolation. Several other fly species also demonstrate the lowering of altitudinal zones in Shetland compared with the mainland of Scotland, being found on mountains and moorlands on the Scottish mainland but down to sea level in Shetland; an example is a tiny empid fly of about 7 mm, which is regarded on the mainland as a mountain species but which occurs at sea level also in Orkney. This species has been found as a frequent pollinator of Edmondston's chickweed on the Keen of Hamar and it is possible that it, like the chickweed, is a relict of the postglacial period.

We cannot cover all the insect orders in this book and have included in the species lists in Appendix 3 only those groups which have been well covered. Like the groups mentioned above there are, as we have come to expect, relatively few species present and in some orders no representatives at all, for example there are no grasshoppers or crickets. The Odonata, the largest flying members of the insects of the British Isles, are also noticeable by their absence: there are no dragonflies resident on Shetland and only the common blue damselfly occurs in a few pools in North Mainland and the southern half of Yell. Since both dragonflies and damselflies are carnivorous insects, usually requiring reasonably productive and sheltered waters edged by tall vegetation in which to patrol and hunt, it is not surprising in exposed Shetland that they are lacking. What is surprising perhaps is that the common blue damselfly manages to survive at all. Likewise there are only four species of stonefly and three mayflies so far recorded.

A characteristic of Shetland lochs that affects all orders is that the summer water temperature is on average 3°C cooler than at similar heights on the Scottish mainland. This allows organisms normally restricted to higher altitudes to survive at much lower altitudes in Shetland. For example, the flatworm *Crenobia alpina*, which is confined to springs at high altitudes in most of Britain, replaces the normal lake-dwelling species in lochs near sea level in Shetland. The lower temperatures have also allowed colonization by arctic aquatic organisms, for example the water flea (*Eurycerus glacialis*), which occurs in the highest loch on Ronas Hill and has otherwise been recorded only once in Scotland. Has this been introduced by transport on the feet of migrating birds from Iceland or Greenland?

Surprisingly little systematic work has been done on the bees, wasps, ants and their allies (Hymenoptera), although this is by far the largest British order of insects. Apparently there is only one species of ant, *Myrmica ruginodis*. While there are six species of bumblebees (*Bombus*), of which one subspecies, the small heather bumblebee (*Bombus jonellus* subsp. *vogti*), is restricted to Shetland, the honey-bee, common on the Scottish mainland, is not native. The beetles (Coleoptera), on the other hand, have been reasonably well covered with some 350 species characterized (see Appendix 3). Among the interesting individuals are a possible Shetland endemic, *Apion ryei*, and several distinct Shetland varieties; also the click beetle (*Athous subfuscus*), otherwise unknown in Britain but quite common in woods and copses in Europe and Scandinavia – another introduction by courtesy of the Vikings perhaps!

SPIDERS

A total of 111 spider species have been recorded from Shetland (see Appendix 3), representing just over 17% of the UK fauna. Some of these are ubiquitous pioneer and disturbed-land species, but the majority are more or less characteristic of the limited range of habitats in Shetland.

All the species found are also recorded from Scotland and Scandinavia, but only half the species recorded from Iceland and two-thirds of those from Faroe are also known from Shetland. Although it is likely that a number of species in Shetland still await discovery, some are undoubtedly absent due more to a failure to colonize than an ability to survive. A number of species, several of them restricted to mountains further south, occur in Shetland at much lower altitudes. For example *Latithorax fausta*, found at the Brig of Fitch at 50 m altitude, *Walckenaeria clavicornis* at 200 m on Fair Isle and *Scotinotylus envansi* at 150 m also on Fair Isle are all recorded from their lowest known British localities; elsewhere they are regarded as montane species. Spider assemblages found on the upper slopes of even quite small hills in Shetland are characteristic of altitudes of 900 m and more on the Cairngorms. Once again this illustrates the lowering of altitudinal zones as we travel northwards.

However a number of montane species that occur in Scotland and even further south in England and Wales are absent from Shetland. Species that may be found when more extensive collecting has been carried out include *Erigone psychrophila* and *E. tirolensis*, which are both present in very small areas on the Scottish mountains. While no northern species appear to reach the limit of their distribution in Shetland, a number of southern species appear to reach their northern limit; two examples are the littoral *Xerolycosa miniata* and a grassland species *Trichopterna thorelli*.

Habitats well represented in Shetland have a higher proportion of species found in Britain than the 17% overall. For example, Shetland has half the species recorded from Moor House in the northern Pennines, but no woodland species have been recorded in the islands. That is not to say that none exist, only that spiders have yet to be collected from the relict scrub sites on holms and inaccessible crags.

LAND AND FRESHWATER MOLLUSCS

The terrestrial mollusc fauna of Shetland (see Appendix 3) is rather poor in diversity. Shetland lacks woodland and has few eutrophic lochs, both habitats that normally support a good variety of molluscs; heavy grazing pressure also has a deleterious effect on numbers. Investigations by Roger Tallack in 1994 at the lochs of Bardister and Kirkigarth illustrates the last point: 'Within the small fenced area there was a limited but quite abundant fauna, yet elsewhere around both lochs they were difficult to find'. He also pointed out a 'decimation' of the *Pisidium* (pea shell) molluscs at Hillwell following pollution (see Chapter 4). In both these cases there are strong knock-on effects on the more obviously attractive fauna of Shetland, the birds. Overgrazing and pollution reduces their food supply and undoubtedly limits their diversity and numbers. The best mollusc habitats in Shetland are on the calcareous dune systems, limestone and the few eutrophic lochs. A number of the Shetland species are at the northern limit of their distribution and therefore probably under some climatic stress already. If the majority of the existing fauna is to be conserved there is need for good management of these areas, otherwise the additional stress may be enough to topple them into extinction, as has no doubt already happened to some species.

No doubt further work will reveal further invertebrate species. However it has to be recognized that the diversity of invertebrates is extremely low in comparison with Orkney and the Scottish mainland, and many British groups and species are absent. For example there are only 65 species of non-marine molluscs recorded whereas there are well over 700 native to Britain; in the Lepidoptera there are under 300 species recorded as against more than 2500 in Britain; and in the Crustacea there is only one freshwater shrimp. Once again though, as we found with some of the plants and lichens, and as we will find later with the birds, in addition to British species many species with strong northern and/or Scandinavian links also appear.

FRESHWATER PLANKTON

In the zooplankton there are relatively few species and these recur in varying combinations in a whole range of conditions. Five cladoceran and five copepod species have been recorded, with only two of each group appearing in appreciable numbers in a sample of 56 lochs. These are the copepods *Cyclops streuus abyssorum* and *Diaptomus wierzjeski* and the cladocerans *Bosmina corgoni* var. *obtusirostris* and *Daphnia hyalina* var. *lacustris*, the first named being the most abundant species in each case. In general the majority of lochs at the time of sampling contained only one species of each group (population numbers vary according to the season), with one species representing over half the total zooplankton population. Only four species altogether are found in any one loch. Although the species composition is generally uniform, obvious distinctions are that large lochs, except the most acidic and those with a maritime influence, tend to have the greatest diversity. An improvement of trophic status of a sample is always associated with a greater abundance.

Otters

CHAPTER 6

Residents and Migrants

Golden plover and dunlin

Supraeme sits he
His fedders prinkin
Sun-bricht,
Ita da grit sun's glinkin

A lown flame
Wi' black een blinkin
Nor deevil een
Keens what he's tinkin!

Da Corbie, Jack Peterson

One of the real characters of Shetland birdlife is the raven (*rafn*), better known today under the Scots name corbie. In Shetland its history goes back a thousand years to the Viking navigator Flokki, who released ravens, caught in Shetland, *en route* to Iceland. Unfortunately while searching for young birds his daughter Gerhilda was drowned in a loch, which was named the Loch of Girlsta in her memory. It is not a bird immediately noticed by the visitor, except perhaps on the helmet of a member of the Jarl's squad at *Up-Helly-Aa*. However in the dead of winter, when the skuas and gulls are absent from moorland, the raven is often the only large bird one may meet, drifting lazily along in the wind like a great scrap of black paper. The raven is one of those birds that seems to take a delight in flying

Merlin and lark

and in the early days of the year it is a joy to see its exuberant and acrobatic display, folding its wings in steep dives, rolling and tumbling, and calling out with its deep and husky *kwaark*.

However, ask a visitor what is their most evocative memory of the birds of Shetland and you will probably get a dozen different answers: the laverock (lark) singing above colourful pastures; the primitive wail of a *raingoose* (red-throated diver) circling a loch; a *tirrick*'s (tern) dancing summer flight on transparent wings above a shingle beach; a *bonxie*'s (great skua) lumbering and threatening attack on a remote hill; the delicate and completely unafraid red-necked phalarope spinning on a pool among the reeds; the cacophony and chaos of a huge seabird colony on a dramatic headland; or perhaps the bubbling call of the whimbrel (*peerie whaap*).

There are around 70 species of birds that breed regularly in Shetland (see Appendix 3) and although the islands are probably best known for their huge and

49.   *Laverock: one of the commonest birds and one of the contributors to the joyous sounds of spring and summer over Shetland's grasslands.* (Courtesy of B. Jackson.)

spectacular seabird colonies, at Herma Ness and Noss for example, its terrestrial species, those dependent on the land for their food, are equally attractive and perhaps even more worthy of interest in terms of their peripheral and fluctuating populations. There are 13 breeding species of waders, including overlapping northern and southern species; both the British and continental subspecies (*alba*) of wagtail; the ubiquitous *steynshekker* (wheatear); and of course Shetland's own wren (*Troglodytes troglodytes* subsp. *zetlandicus*) and starling (*Sturnus vulgaris* subsp. *zetlandicus*). Then there are the wintering species that come south from beyond the Arctic Circle, such as the whooper swan, long-tailed duck and great northern diver, and the migrants driven in from Iceland, Scandinavia and Siberia that precipitate out of an empty sky on to the outlying islands of Fair Isle and Out Skerries, sometimes arriving in huge flocks, as in the autumn of 1976 and 1987 when tens of thousands of the large Scandinavian thrushes, fieldfares and redwings descended on Shetland like flocks of locusts.

This chapter is called Residents and Migrants because the terrestrial species that breed, the residents, first have to arrive on the islands in sufficient numbers or regularly enough, as migrants, to establish a stable population. When species do settle on these relatively remote and inhospitable islands, lacking as they do many of the diverse and sheltered habitats of mainland Scotland or Scandinavia, they often only survive or stay to breed for a few years. Of the 38 or so passerines that have bred in the last quarter of a century, only one-third or so are securely established and almost two-thirds have been irregular or sporadic breeders; uniquely in the British Isles, the origin of over one-third of these passerines (and almost half of the irregular or sporadic breeders; Table 8) is Scandinavia not Scotland as one might think.

To make the account of Shetland's birds more coherent I have arbitrarily pigeon-holed them in what I hope is a sensible manner. The major division will be between those commonly termed 'seabirds', dependent on the sea for their presence, and the 'landbirds', those constrained more by available terrestrial breeding and feeding habitat and the geographical location of the islands in relation to the British Isles, Scandinavia and the other islands to the north and south. This chapter deals with the landbirds, Chapter 8 with the seabirds and Chapter 9 with Fair Isle and migration. It should be noted that any conclusions drawn on the status change of species must be qualified by the limitations of earlier records and the contrasting very comprehensive cover of today.

WOODLAND, WHAT WOODLAND?

We have seen that all but the merest scraps of native scrub and woodland probably disappeared over 2000 years ago, and may well have become restricted to ravines, scree slopes and isolated patches much earlier. Thus, all the 'woodland' bird species that now breed in Shetland use broad-leaved plantations, many now over 100 years old, shelterbelts such as those at Kergord, Sullom and Gott (see Chapter 4) and the occasional mature garden especially in Lerwick or Scalloway, all established with great effort in the face of the destructive force of the Shetland elements. Twenty

TABLE 8   *Irregular and new breeding species, and species with small populations, to 1996*

New or irregular breeding species since 1970 (breeding at least once)		Regular breeding species with small populations (less than 10 pairs most years)
Mute swan‡	(established 1992)	Shelduck
Whooper swan*‡	(established 1994)	Shoveller
Greylag goose†‡	(established 1985)	Tufted duck
Common scoter§	(last bred 1993)	Moorhen
Pintail	(bred 1994)	Black-tailed godwit†
Kestrel‡	(bred 1992)	Greenshank‡
Peregrine§	(last bred 1996)	Wood pigeon
Coot§	(last bred 1989)	Swallow
Corncrake§	(last bred 1986)	Pied‡/white* wagtail
Cuckoo	(last bred ?)	Redwing*
House martin	(last bred 1996)	Goldcrest*‡
Yellow wagtail‡	(last bred 1988)	Chaffinch*
Grey wagtail	(last bred 1993)	Reed bunting
Robin*‡	(last bred 1992)	
Stonechat*‡	(last bred 1977)	
Ring ouzel‡	(last bred 1989)	
Fieldfare*‡	(last bred 1993)	
Song thrush§	(last bred 1988)	
Reed warbler*‡	(bred 1973)	
Whitethroat‡	(last bred 1996)	
Blackcap*	(last bred 1988)	
Willow warbler*	(last bred 1994)	
Red-backed shrike*‡	(bred 1990)	
Jackdaw§	(last bred ?)	
Siskin*‡	(bred 1992)	
Mealy redpoll*‡	(bred 1982)	
Lesser redpoll*‡	(bred 1992)	
Tree sparrow‡	(bred 1979)	
Corn bunting§	(last bred 1983)	

Only *confirmed* breeding dated; some species with labelled 'last bred' have possibly bred since the date given. See Appendix 3 for further details.

Of the passerines, 38 species thought to have bred in the last 25 years; of those only 30% (12 species) could be said to be securely established, three (swallow, pied and white wagtails) have only small populations, while 60% (23 species) are irregular or sporadic breeders.

*Species with Scandinavian origin.

†Species with Icelandic origin.

‡Not recorded as breeding in 1955 (by Venables and Venables). NB Collared dove (1965–), greenshank (1871, 1980–), tufted duck (1952, 1979?–), long-eared owl (1935, 1960s–75), snowy owl (1967–75).

§Lost as a regular breeding species since 1955. NB Moorhen declining still.

years ago there were under 40 ha of planted woodland throughout Shetland. Today, through renewed interest in the ameliorating benefits of shelter and in native and broad-leaved trees, that figure has possibly doubled. It is an interesting thought that the mixed plantation at Kergord, which just happens to be the largest area of woodland in Shetland, is still the most important single breeding site for woodland species, which suggests that woodland birds in Shetland would probably most benefit from relatively large plantings. The present woodland areas are too small to allow the establishment of many woodland species and accounts for the fact that there are few regularly breeding species and they only occur in small numbers, while many species only breed irregularly. However, these limited areas of woodland are very important for migrants, as was noted by Saxby (1874) when speaking of the Halligarth trees, which date from the mid-nineteenth century:

> The planting of a few trees carefully sheltered by stone walls from the sweeping gales of the Atlantic, has had a curiously marked effect in attracting birds hitherto unknown as visitors to the islands; an effect indeed altogether disproportionate to the small scale on which the experiment has been tried.

Halligarth, which is the only scrap of 'woodland' in Unst, has an impressive record of breeding woodland species, including the redwing and the only Scottish record of the reed warbler in 1973. This last record is a clear-cut example of colonization, however briefly, from Scandinavia rather than by a British migrant, since in Britain this species is confined as a breeder to England and the south of Scotland.

When discussing 'woodland' birds in Shetland one must bear in mind that few are necessarily restricted entirely to woodland. They may make use of garden shrubs or very small clumps of trees in the towns or, in the case of the blackbird, be equally at home in buildings; the long-eared owl has been recorded as breeding for several years from the mid-1960s on moorland in Tingwall. Adaptability is an important survival tool in Shetland where there are finite limits to both the variety of habitats and to their physical size. Immigrants may find their usual niche just not large enough, or they may find another overlapping race or species. A recent immigrant to Shetland, not present on the 1955 list, that has adapted its behaviour and found a new niche throughout Britain is the collared dove. This species appeared in Shetland in 1961, first nesting in 1965 and now has a small but fairly widespread population mostly confined to Lerwick and Scalloway and Central Mainland.

There is only one 'woodland' species confined to woodland that is truly successful in Shetland and that is the rook. Other woodland and shrub species that breed regularly, albeit in very small numbers, are redwing, goldcrest and chaffinch. Species that have bred sporadically are robin (Scandinavian race), fieldfare, song thrush, whitethroat, blackcap, willow warbler, tree sparrow, siskin, lesser redpoll (*Carduelis flammea* subsp. *cabaret*) and mealy redpoll (*Carduelis flammea* subsp. *flammea*). Quite a list and each with its own story! The blackbird, song thrush, wood pigeon and tree sparrow possibly have arrived in Shetland as a result of a general expansion and immigration from Britain and Orkney, whereas the others appear to have come from Scandinavia.

The song thrush is a regular spring and autumn migrant, but has gradually decreased as a breeding species from a peak in the first half of this century to the mid-1950s when it ceased to breed every year, partly due to reduction of the small population during the severe winter of 1947. It bred annually until 1978 but the last record is 1988. The song thrush first bred in Shetland at the turn of the century shortly after the blackbird became established. The latter is now fairly numerous and widespread in Shetland, adapting its lifestyle in the absence of woodland and has even become a regular breeder in the small plantation woodland in Tórshavn, Faroe.

The rook underwent a gradual expansion in the British Isles through the middle part of this century and has been a regular, if not common, migrant to Shetland for many years. At the time the Kergord plantations were maturing in 1952 rooks were abnormally abundant in Shetland; nine nests were established in that year, averaging a success rate of three young per nest. These birds then became resident and their numbers have steadily increased to 344 pairs in 1979, though this was somewhat reduced by misguided 'management' to 79 pairs in 1980. If the initial wave of immigration is numerous enough in 1 or 2 years and breeding attempts are successful, a species that is not normally a numerous migrant can become established. Crop production, excluding grass, has fallen dramatically in Shetland, by almost 80% over the last 25 years, but the rook, whose population had recovered to 166 pairs in 1996, appears to be coping well with this change.

At the close of the summer season, as the female *dunter* (eider) are flocking in the voes, as the auks move out to sea, as the terns are winging their way on their long journey south and the twite, merlin and rock pipit move *innadaeks*, the Shetland moorland seems to die with only a few straggling skuas, gulls, crows and ravens flapping over the landscape. This is when the migrant flocks of redwing, fieldfare, brambling and chaffinch can arrive in their thousands. The majority pass through on their way to the Scottish mainland, the redwing flashing its red underwing and often accompanied by the dumpier fieldfare with its almost slate-blue head and rump. In recent years the latter has been expanding its range in Europe and in 1968 it bred in Shetland for the first time. Thereafter it bred on about 10 occasions up to 1993, often in woodland but not always. It first bred in the British Isles in Orkney in 1967 and has been a sporadic breeder there and on the Scottish mainland since.

50. *Redwing: an intermittent Scandinavian immigrant that can descend on passage in tens of thousands.* (Courtesy of RSPB.)

51. *Traditional crofting, Fladdabister, 1997: in fewer and fewer places traditional crofting practices survive.*
(Courtesy of L. Johnston.)

Redwing have had a similar recent history in the islands; it bred on four occasions between 1953 and 1975, four times in the 1980s, failing twice, and bred four times again up to 1996. On the Scottish mainland it has bred in the Highlands in small numbers regularly since 1967. Saxby states, 'By merely substituting the name of Redwing for that of the Fieldfare, my remarks upon the former scarcity and present abundance of the one would apply with equal truth to the other'. Redwing are more confined to woodland than fieldfare and this is reflected in its breeding sites in Shetland.

It is impossible to know exactly how many of these species bred in the past, but it is a safe bet that woodland bird diversity has always reflected the diversity of the habitat and that the present 'impoverished' woodland bird fauna is a measure of the lack of woodland and scrub in today's environment.

INNADAEKS

One of the most attractive and, as far as wildlife is concerned, most positive contributions that Shetlanders have made to the Shetland landscape has been the development of small-scale farming or crofting, a diverse system of land use adapted to the small pockets of good land, the framework of which was established very early in Shetland's human history. This system, common to the west coast and islands of Scotland too, evolved to make maximum use of meagre natural resources and involved fairly intensive land and crop management. In the mid-1990s the pattern of hill dyke, scattered township and *rigs* (strip cultivation) is still evident, but is fast being obscured by the pressures of modern agriculture. For 100 years, since the crofter has had security of tenure and since some capital has made its way back into the croft from incomes made elsewhere, the landscape of Shetland, outwith the few large farms and lairds' gardens, has been dominated by a well-managed and intricate system of crofting that has added colour, texture and many rich habitats for flowers, invertebrates and birds. In very recent years increasing grazing pressures, 'improvements' to permanent pastures, increasing drainage, the demise of crops and the taking-in of hill land by reseeding and fertilizing has perhaps changed that irrevocably – it is as if the patchwork quilt has been thrown away for a plain blanket.

There are still corners where more traditional methods are practised, where croft and byre provide shelter for elder, rose, flowering currant, escallonia and fuschsia; where there are *rigs*, edged on the low-lying wet ground with natural hayfields. In the spring, especially on the limestones, the soft yellow and green of the primrose adorn the grassland, giving way in the summer to the harder yellow of the marsh marigolds in the ditches and the rich red of the Shetland campion around the houses and along the road edges. Although unimproved grasslands carry a diversity of plant species, by far the most luxuriant flora occurs on the wetter margins of the croft, which traditionally remained uncut until the late summer, bright with red and yellow rattles, ragged robin, iris, forget-me-not, orchids, tall grasses, sedges and horsetails. Apart from the buildings themselves, these last two habitats are the most important for the characteristic birds of croftland.

Common breeding birds around buildings are the house sparrow, blackbird, wren, the occasional swallow and, very rarely, the house martin. Probably the most numerous species associated with people in Shetland is the starling. This must be one of the most successful birds in Shetland, being found throughout the islands, across all the habitats from the croft and farm to the hill and to the shore. Elsewhere in the British Isles and in Europe the starling is on the decline, in the former after a recolonization of Scotland from England following an earlier decline in the eighteenth century. During this earlier decline the species withdrew from the north and west of Scotland and only recolonized in the nineteenth century. However the starling survived in the Outer Hebrides and in Shetland two centuries ago, so that today these (and Fair Isle) are relict populations. Tulloch and Hunter (1972) suggested that the species might be decreasing, although it seems to have increased again in recent years, possibly through taking advantage of the additional food resources provided by the large areas of reseeded grassland and maybe also from the shelter and food provided by the new large sheds erected for holding wintering animals and agricultural and fish farm food stocks. Venables and Venables (1955) noted that starlings appear often to be associated with sheep, and therefore presumably benefit from access to shorter vegetation and even bare soil and therefore food. It is perhaps not surprising then that as sheep continue to increase dramatically in Shetland so does the starling. In the winter months starlings are the most numerous birds around the crofting townships and houses, wheeling round, sometimes in large flocks, to scatter the sparrows and twittering twite (*lintie*) from any spare food available. They often roost in coastal caves and a particularly delightful memory is of returning to Snarraness from line fishing in a very early summer dawn and being welcomed home by a starling chorus issuing from beneath a dark and rocky proscenium.

The Shetland starling, as we have noted, is a recognized local and perhaps relict race (*Sturnus vulgaris* subsp. *zetlandicus*). Recognized by some perhaps, but not reliably in the field! Tulloch (1992) describes it as having a measurably wider bill

Twite

and the juveniles as being 'recognisably darker' than the nominate race. The Shetland form (like its Hebridean counterpart) is intermediate between the European and Faroe subspecies and not very distinctive in its own right. Where physical trends in island races are continuing over large areas in this way, one can reasonably say that they are adaptations to particular environments; where they are not (as with the Shetland field mouse, see Chapter 5) differentiation is more likely due to the founder effect.

In the drier meadows and grassland, meadow pipit are common as is also the little grey sentinel who pops up everywhere on the rock outcrop or the fence-post with his *chack chack*, the *steynshekker* (wheatear). The other very common bird of grassland and the hill and often the earliest harbinger of spring on a mild February day, with a song that lifts the heart weary of winter, is the laverock (lark) and occasionally on dry banks, the twite. In the wetter ground, curlew (*whaap*), oystercatcher (*shalder*) and lapwing (*tieve's nacket*) are commonly found, and less commonly snipe and redshank, which are virtually confined to this habitat; also found, but in no great number, is the reed bunting. The curlew is a fairly common species in Shetland, a rare breeder in Faroe and absent in Iceland. In Shetland it overlaps with whimbrel, which replaces it to the north. Their breeding habitats are quite different, however, the former preferring damp pastures with longer vegetation while the latter prefers drier heathery hills with short vegetation. There is nowhere else in Britain where the two can be so easily compared. The simplest way of distinguishing the whimbrel from the curlew is by its call, which is a higher and more delightful bubbling trill than the latter: once heard never forgotten. It is also a smaller bird with a shorter bill and has a distinctive striped head pattern lacking in the curlew. However practice is needed to distinguish them.

The *shalder* is one of Shetland's ubiquitous species. Its scolding cry can be heard all over the islands. In recent years it has changed its behaviour and exploited grasslands and meadows across its whole range. In Faroe the *shalder* is so numerous and popular that it has become the national emblem of those islands. Sharing the same origin, the Faroese name, *tjaldur*, is very similar to that used in Shetland. If one was to make a list of the local boat names in Shetland, *shalder* would rank alongside *tystie* (black guillemot) and *tirrick* (tern). The snipe is a shy bird, and where a disturbed grouse explodes heavily from cover like a shell, the snipe emerges like an errant missile, fizzling out and dropping back out of sight as unexpectedly as it appeared. Its fast and erratic flight has always been a challenge to the gun and the autumn migrant flocks of 100 years ago seem to have been the favourite quarry of Shetland's sporting, and not-so-sporting, gentlemen.

These wetland areas that grade into marshland in Shetland, although not quite as important as the machairs of the Hebrides, are key sites nationally and internationally for wader species, holding more than 1% of the British breeding populations of *shalder* and curlew for example. One of the rarest and most elegant waders in Shetland's marshland, with its chestnut-red head and breast, black-tipped bill and white tail also tipped with black, is the black-tailed godwit. There are only between 50 and 100 pairs breeding in Britain as a whole and most of these are in Norfolk. Whereas the birds elsewhere in Britain recolonized from the Continent, the Shetland (and Orkney) birds have colonized from Iceland and are of a different race (*Limosa limosa islandica*). They have been breeding continuously

52. *Black-tailed godwit: an elegant Icelandic immigrant with a very small population; a northern element of Shetland's fauna.* (Courtesy of B. Jackson.)

as only one or two pairs, occasionally a few more, since 1949 and similarly in Orkney since 1956.

As we have seen, many regularly breeding woodland species must have been lost from Shetland some time ago, On the other hand, several species associated with croftland have become rare and even extinct only within the last decades. How very much part of our time we are. If we listen today to the birds of the croftland we are aware of no discord, no absence of a particular sound and yet the generation that grew up on a croft from the turn of the century will remember evenings punctuated by the insistent rasping of the corncrake, winding itself up with its rusty key. In the nineteenth century it could be heard in every cultivated district throughout the islands, but then 100 years earlier Henry Cockburn spoke of listening 'to the ceaseless rural corn-craiks' from a corner of Charlotte Square in the centre of Edinburgh New Town. In 1948 Venables and Venables recorded 48 nests, in 1974 it was still a common breeding species, but the last definite breeding record was in 1986, since when only occasional birds have been heard calling. The Shetland decline is unfortunately part of an overall decline of this species in Europe. Oddly enough for a bird with a very distinctive call and habits it does not have a common Shetland, or Old Norse, name: was it an uncommon species during the Norse period? Another regularly breeding bird of the traditional hayfield, the quail, has also ceased to breed and a third species, the corn bunting (*docken sporrow*), said by Evans and Buckley to be the most conspicuous bird in Shetland, has also declined to the point where it has not even been seen on the islands for several years.

Why has all this happened? One just has to look at the changes in agriculture in Shetland (see Table 16) and across the crofting areas of Scotland generally: firstly, loss of traditional crops including the traditional croft stackyard, which used to provide important winter feeding; secondly, mechanization and the move to the

making of silage; and thirdly, increased areas of improved grassland via fertilization, reseeding, drainage and heavy grazing. In the spring there is now very much
less tall and rank cover than there used to be; in the summer there is no longer the
diversity of vegetation rich with seed, or soils rich with invertebrates; no longer the
undisturbed summer days to allow the incubation of eggs or growth of chicks, but
the harsh and early cut of the silage machine. The same unremitting process is now,
via the further conversion of marginal wetland through drainage, threatening
redshank, snipe and curlew; and, via the 'improvement' to traditional dune and
other 'natural' pastures and increased sheep grazing, impoverishing the grassland
flora and the bird populations it supports such as the laverock and the twite.

Some species, however, have benefited or taken advantage of the changes.
Peewits and *shalders* are happy to nest and breed on the improved grasslands and
even whimbrel if there is no preceding ploughing. The reed bunting too, only seen
by Saxby on three occasions, has increased to become a more widespread, if still
uncommon, breeding resident since first recorded as a breeder by Venables and
Venables in 1949. This is a species that has expanded its ecological range from a
breeding dependence on nearby fresh water to a toleration of drier habitats.
However, its hold in Shetland is very tenuous.

A spectacular addition to the Shetland bird fauna that has obviously taken
advantage of the increase in reseeded grasslands is the grass-eating greylag goose.
This species is indigenous in the North-west Highlands and Western Isles of
Scotland where it is at present making a slight recovery. However the Shetland
birds are most probably Icelandic birds, migrants and wintering birds that have
been staying on into the summer in Shetland in increasing numbers since the mid-
1970s at least. They first bred in 1981 and for a few years were confined to Unst, but
since 1991 they have begun to prospect and breed in other parts of Shetland. With
large areas of reseeded pasture throughout Shetland there is no doubt they will
continue to increase until someone decides they are eating just too much grass. This
situation has already arisen on Tiree in the Western Isles, where the local crofters,
voluntary bodies and the government's advisory body, Scottish Natural Heritage,
are trying to agree a management programme.

Shetland's somewhat intermediate geographical position with regards to bird
races is further illustrated by the wagtails, insect feeders usually associated with
open or running water. Both the yellow and grey wagtail have bred occasionally,
but the regular breeding wagtail is the white wagtail (*Motacilla alba* subsp. *alba*),
which is the continental race also breeding in Faroe and Iceland. This race is more
migratory than the pied wagtail (*M. a.* subsp. *yarelli*), which is the British race. In
appearance they are very similar and the only distinct difference is that the mature
pied has a solid black back of the same tone as the bib and the back of the head,
whereas the white has a grey back of lighter tone than head or bib. Saxby was as
confused about the two as most of us, and confessed that he might have overlooked
the white, identifying it wrongly as the pied. Venables and Venables (1955) stated
that they had never seen the pied in Shetland, although they accepted that it
probably occurred. Possibly because of this they suggested that the hearsay records
of pied breeding, given in Evans and Buckley (1899), may have referred to the
white, which they knew first hand sometimes bred. However, the pied was a not
uncommon breeder in Orkney at the turn of the century and only decreased there

from the late 1930s. It did in fact breed sporadically in Shetland early this century, although by the time of the Venables' report it had become very scarce.

As far as the white wagtail is concerned, Saxby may not have overlooked it and his first recording of the species in 1852 may have been the beginning of a more regular appearance. Evans and Buckley do not record any further occurrences until the first record of breeding in 1900. Breeding then became sporadic and in the last couple of decades probably regular. A few pairs of both races breed annually, mostly mixed and more usually the white than the pied. Single pairs of white wagtail have bred a few times in the Western Isles and on the Scottish mainland and mixed white/pied occasionally, but single whites and mixed pairs are not as common as in Shetland. Shetland is thus a boundary between the two races where fraternizing is common and racism absent!

Croftland and farmland therefore provide an important habitat in Shetland for its breeding birds and have shown, and continue to show, some substantial changes in bird fauna over the years. They are also an important winter habitat for migrants seeking shelter and food on passage, for the resident croftland species such as the house sparrow, and for resident moorland and coastal species, such as rock pipit (*banks sparrow*), hoodie crow, raven, gulls and rock dove, and even merlin and peregrine.

OOTADAEKS

The predominant vegetation of Shetland on the lower and intermediate hill and many dales is blanket bog (see Chapter 4), intermixed with drier heather moorlands and acid grasslands. Although moorland stretches from sea level to well over 300 m, most of the moorland from sea level is classified as submontane. This means that differences in moorland habitat are a reflection of local conditions, topography, underlying geology and drift, rather than altitude. Moorland breeding bird species are therefore well distributed in Shetland and only a very few are restricted to either 'lowland' or 'upland'. There is also quite an overlap between marginal land within the hill dyke and that on the hill, so that although some species, such as the redshank, snipe and black-tailed godwit, are virtually confined to the lower-lying acidic wetland, others such as the curlew and *shalder* are not uncommon on the hill.

One of the less common waders on the hill is the common sandpiper, which is restricted to loch and burnside. There seems to have been little change in its status over the last century. Although it reaches the Arctic shore in northern Europe, it does not breed in Faroe or Iceland. Relatively scattered but with a stable population is the dunlin or *plivver's page*, so called from its peculiar habit of often shadowing the *plivver* (golden plover) on its display flights. Both Saxby (1874) and Venables and Venables (1955) give the low-lying wet areas as its main breeding habitat, but this solitary bird can also be found on higher and drier areas and can breed in very high densities on small islands. Another species found on the blanket bog that has recently colonized Shetland is the greenshank. Saxby recorded a bird on eggs in 1871 and it was not until just over 100 years later in 1980 that the second confirmed breeding was recorded. From then until the present possibly between six and nine pairs have bred or attempted to breed annually, although there are signs that breeding numbers may have declined recently again. The greenshank's stronghold in Scotland is on Lewis and in the far northern mainland where there are several hundred pairs.

We will come back to other birds of Shetland moorland in a moment, but for the present we will continue our discussion of Shetland's wader species. Athough never seen as such a spectacle as its seabirds, this group of birds and their habitat is equally as important internationally (Table 9), especially as more and more of their moorland habitat throughout Britain is being lost. Shetland, with 13 breeding wader species, several of them northern species uncommon elsewhere in the British Isles and several breeding in high densities, must be one of the single most important places for this group of birds in the country.

One of the best places in Shetland where one can see almost the whole range of these waders is Unst. Many well-travelled visitors there have noted, as we have discussed in Chapter 4, the resemblance of some of the heaths and sparsely vegetated areas on the metagabbro summits of Colvadale and the Sobul and on the serpentinite of the Keen of Hamar (also the North Roe plateau and the serpentinite of Fetlar) to the subarctic tundra and fellfields of Faroe, Iceland and Scandinavia. Such sparsely vegetated areas are not common in the British Isles, being normally confined to the northern and outlying western islands, and particularly to the high tops of the central Scottish Highlands. Their attraction therefore to northern bird species, and especially waders, is not surprising, particularly as Shetland lies closer to the centres of population of many of these species than any other part of the British Isles and also lies on the migration routes of many of them. Such is the variety of breeding birds on Unst today that it is difficult to imagine how Evans and Buckley were able to describe a walk on Unst 100 years ago in the following terms: 'From Baltasound to Uyea Sound birdlife is more remarkable for its absence than its presence, and throughout the whole distance of some six miles little can be seen except a few Ringed Plover and Wheatear'.

However at that time the only place where whimbrel were seen on Unst was Herma Ness, with 'one or possibly two pairs' (Evans and Buckley, 1899) and one pair between Belmont and Uyeasound; none were found on Fetlar, which is one of their other present-day strongholds. Breeding birds were noted on the smaller

TABLE 9   *International significance of breeding population of waders on Shetland 1996* (Adapted from Bates, *et al.*, 1994)

Species	Shetland population	British population	Proportion of British population (%)	Biogeographic population	Proportion of biogeographic population (%)
Ringed plover	900	8 600	10.47	13 100	6.87
Golden plover	2 000	22 600	8.85	609 000	0.33
Dunlin	1 700	9 150	18.58	11 100	15.32
Black-tailed godwit	3	35	8.57	133 000	
Whimbrel	480	c. 530	90	203 000	0.23
Red-necked phalarope	40	40	100	150 000	0.03

islands between Unst and Yell where they are now absent (apart from Hascosay between Yell and Fetlar) and reference was made to a few pairs scattered throughout the main island. Earlier they had been a common species (Dunn, 1837) but by the time of Evans and Buckley they had decreased substantially, becoming extinct for a time on Orkney where there are small numbers today. This decline coincided with an amelioration of the climate during the first half of this century, which ended in the 1940s.

The recovery in Shetland has been very recent and fairly spectacular, gaining in momentum in the last couple of decades. Venables and Venables (1955) quote J. Peterson who failed to find a breeding pair on Unst in 1938 and they themselves only found 35 pairs there in 1949. In the 1970s there were thought to be around 70 pairs on Unst and by the early 1980s the population there had reached between 110 and 115 pairs. Whimbrel are now breeding widely over Shetland from Dunrossness in the south to Unst in the north. There are single pairs scattered over Mainland and on Yell, but the bulk of the population, now around 480 pairs, breed in about a dozen colonies. The preferred habitat is dry heather moorland with short vegetation where breeding density is greatest, but such has been the expansion that breeding now takes places quite widely on blanket bog. In fact the annual rate of increase of the whimbrel population since the 1970s is thought to be 7.5%, too great an increase to come from the local breeding population and therefore there must be a steady immigration from outwith Shetland. It has been suggested that the increase in the Shetland whimbrel population is due to the cooling of the climate in the last few decades allowing the southern expansion of the species, such a change also being linked to the increase in other cold temperate/subarctic species in Shetland such as the raingoose, the skuas and the successful breeding of the snowy owl in Shetland during the late 1960s and early 1970s (Richardson, 1990). Whether expansion (and retraction of

53. *Whimbrel: a characteristic northern wader of short moorland with its distinctive trilling call, where it replaces the curlew. Shetland is the stronghold for this species in the British Isles.* (Courtesy of B. Jackson.)

some) of these species is entirely due to climatic change is a moot point. A recent decline in the *raingoose* population in some parts of Shetland is unlikely to be related to climate. However the whimbrel does illustrate the dynamic nature of many of Shetland's bird populations, quite outwith the influence of humans. Elsewhere in the British Isles there are less than 50 pairs in Orkney, the Western Isles and the northern mainland.

It is perhaps a slight misnomer to call any area of Shetland moorland 'dry', but it does occur where more permeable rocks allow reasonably free drainage or on exposed slopes where peat has not formed and the vegetation is almost prostrate. The common wader of this habitat is the golden plover, which is also quite widespread on most heather moorland in Shetland, making up almost 9% of the British population. However it does not appear to be as common as it was 100 years ago when Saxby said that it bred 'even on the outlying holms', which it certainly does not do today and seems a rather odd breeding habitat for it. It is the southern form that breeds in Shetland, lacking the complete dark band from the head to the back of the belly that is found in the northern race of Iceland and northern Scandinavia. When disturbed, the golden plover has the most plaintive and pathetic cry of all the waders. Like the ringed plover or *sandy-loo* (the *loo* element deriving from the Old Norse *lo* from the sound of the call of both species) it will try and lead the intruder away from the nest. It also has the most beautiful and intricate gold and black plumage.

Moving on from Shetland's wader populations, but remaining on the moorland, we come to a species not well adapted to the heavily grazed heather and wet climate, the grouse. Although it may be indigenous to Orkney, it was introduced to Shetland by sporting lairds mainly in the last century. The fresh heather growth on which the bird depends requires a better summer than the Shetland one and the longer heather, in which it prefers to nest, rarely occurs due to heavy grazing and exposure to the fierce maritime winds. However, the introductions have survived and spread, but thinly, across Mainland.

The hoodie crow also breeds occasionally on flat moorland, but more often on dry inland and coastal banks, ravine sides and in bushes and trees. The hoodie, frequently seen at the decaying body of a sheep or lamb or flattened hedgehog on the road, is a very common Shetland bird and not much loved. Like so many birds that we take for granted (like the starling), it is only when we observe them at close quarters that the subtlety of the plumage can be seen. In certain lights, especially in the low winter and *simmer dim* sun, the soft grey of the body can look pale brown and almost pink in contrast with the dark head and wings.

To return briefly to our discussion of birds of the 'arctic-type' terrain in Shetland. At the turn of the last century, Evans and Buckley's description of the absence of bird life from Baltasound to Uyeasound could well have applied also to Ronas Hill and the plateau of North Roe, from Ronas Hill to Fethaland. This almost barren and relatively undisturbed wilderness area is bounded on the east by the road and on the other three sides, from Ronas Voe to Uyea Isle and then to Sand Voe, by 12 km of magnificent, crumbling, red, granite cliffs and 6 km of eroding and ancient gneiss. Bird life, especially on the higher slopes and summit of Ronas Hill is as sparse as the vegetation that clings to the lee of the boulders and the risers of the terraces (see Chapter 4).

Even today, looking north over the landscape from the summit there is little movement to catch the eye, perhaps a mountain hare loping across the lower slopes, a *raingoose* winging in to one of the ice-scoured lochs or peaty lochans, a raven or *bonxie* drifting lazily across the sky and more recently a whimbrel or two. Now there are only sheep scraping a living on the plateau, whereas not so long ago there were crofts at Uyea. Apart from the view, the arctic–alpine flora and the fascinating signs of past glacial and periglacial action, it is worth keeping an eye out for the ring ouzel, which bred here from 1970 to 1972, or for the *sna ful* (snow bunting), which one day may nest on this terrain. A bird that also might have nested here, on what would have been a familiar arctic-like environment, is the snowy owl or *catyogle* (cat-owl). An irruption of this species in the early 1960s led to the establishment of a pair on the similar terrain on Fetlar in 1967. This was the first confirmed breeding in the British Isles. Snowy owls went on to breed for 9 years and then the male disappeared during the winter of 1975–76. Since then there have been many females, gradually reducing in number over the years and latterly only immature females have appeared. It may be many years alas until we see this spectacular bird breeding again in Shetland.

The principal food of the snowy owl on the Continent is of course the lemming. On Fetlar it was the rabbit, which is confined *innadaeks* and to the moorland edge. All in all there are relatively few small mammalian prey in Shetland suitable for many of the avian predators common on the Scottish mainland or even Orkney, such as the short-eared owl, hen harrier, kestrel and buzzard. The first two, and the sparrowhawk, have been said to have bred in Shetland in the last century, but this should be treated with a modicum of caution. There is no breeding record for the buzzard. The kestrel, which is the only common migrant of this group, bred fairly regularly last century and has bred twice this century in 1905 and 1992. Presumably at the peak of Shetland's human population, when there were far more active crofts and townships, more available food and cover, and therefore greater numbers of mice and small birds, kestrels and even perhaps sparrowhawks were not short of food. Perhaps an increasing tree cover will prove more attractive again for these birds of prey. The only moorland predator today, apart from the *bonxie*, hoodie and larger gulls, is the merlin (*smirl* or *peerie hawk*). This species must have been around for a long time as there are Norse place names, such as Smirlee, to testify to its past presence.

We are particularly indebted to Saxby for information on the feeding habits of kestrel and merlin last century. He noted that the kestrel was obliged to take small birds, such as the corn bunting and blackbird, as its prey. It might therefore have come into direct competition for food with the merlin, which itself may be rather less common than in Saxby's time as he said of it 'Of all the Shetland Falconidae this is by far the most abundant', although at the close of the nineteenth century Raeburn thought the kestrel a more numerous species than the merlin in Northmavine. The latter's diet today is known to consist of the smaller grassland and moorland passerines, such as the *steynshekker* and laverock and to a lesser extent meadow pipit. The last is the common prey of the merlin elsewhere in Britain, making the Shetland population, of around 25–30 pairs, a little unusual. Like their mainland cousins, however, they breed only where heather predominates and usually on a slope, knoll or bank. It has been shown that the distance between nest sites in Shetland is usually around 4 km. This is a greater distance apart than on the mainland, suggesting a relatively poorer availability of suitable prey species, but also might be a reflection on the condition of the heather on a Shetland hill.

Between 1981 and 1983 Shetland's merlin population fell dramatically by about 50%, although it subsequently recovered again, prompting an investigation of the possible causes. Over several years from 1983 (even though the population recovered) it was found that of all the pairs examined annually, 97% of all nest failures occurred at the egg stage. Examination of the eggs showed that the levels of organochlorines and polychlorinated biphenyls (PCBs) were low in comparison with the rest of Britain, but that mercury levels from Orkney and Shetland were the highest. As the Orkney population also crashed in 1984 it seems that mercury is implicated in some way. It is known from other studies that the mercury levels in Shetland eggs are sufficient to markedly affect productivity. The only known source of this mercury in the northern isles is marine and the contamination may be through wind-blown spray.

Two other interesting facts arose out of both the recent merlin studies, the first academic perhaps, but the second salutary. Firstly, some of Shetland's merlins fall into the size range of Icelandic merlins. This may be due to increasing size with latitude or with the source of colonization; although many adults may be resident, there are also passage migrants. Secondly, during the surveys of nest sites it was found that in three sites where birds no longer bred the heather had been greatly reduced by overgrazing, while in two others burning had destroyed the heather. Mercury from the sea may be, presumably always was, a threat to the Shetland merlin population and perhaps there is nothing we can do about that, but poor management of the hill is likely to be an increasing threat and it is a factor we *can* do something about.

LOCHS AND SHUNS

Putting on our 'wellies' and moving firmly into the marshland and associated open-water habitat of mesotrophic and eutrophic lochs such as Hillwell, Spiggie and Tingwall, we find a very small but regular moorhen breeding population and occasional coot at the first site. The coot used to be more common but has declined as a breeding species since the 1960s, just as it has in Orkney and in the north of Scotland generally, and presently breeds only occasionally at Hillwell. If, and until, it recovers further south, it is unlikely to re-establish itself in Shetland.

With only a limited number of productive lochs supporting sufficient food and the cover of emergent vegetation, Shetland has a limited breeding wildfowl population. None the less it has an interesting range of species. Apart from mallard and teal, which are fairly common and widespread, all the other ducks only breed in small numbers and sometimes sporadically. The shelduck, one of the most boldly plumaged ducks, also breeds on sheltered sandy seashores as well as by eutrophic lochs. South Mainland has been its stronghold for two centuries at least. Even though this bird is breeding on the northern edge of its range there seems to have been little change in its status over the past 50 years, albeit there is a suggestion that numbers have declined slightly in recent years. There are usually pairs at Hillwell and Boddam, with several at Virkie by Sumburgh. Unfortunately developments at Sumburgh Airport in 1975, adjacent to the Virkie site, caused too much disturbance for the birds and they did not breed there for several years. Occasionally birds breed elsewhere, such as Burra Isle, Papa Stour, Yell and Unst, but the total number in any year is probably less than 10 pairs. The birds leave Shetland in the autumn to moult, possibly joining other European birds in the Heligoland Bight, and return to Shetland in midwinter.

Duck species with very small populations, often only one or two breeding pairs, include wigeon, shoveller and tufted duck, while pintail have been recorded breeding in 1994. The tufted duck is a recent breeder, probably as a result of its general expansion in the British Isles. In the last century it was an irregular visitor to Shetland, but by the 1950s was a common wintering species particularly in South Mainland.

A number of Shetland birds can be described as 'magnificent' or 'attractive', but perhaps only the red-necked phalarope can be described as 'charming' and 'intriguing': charming, because so small, colourful and unafraid of humans; intriguing, because here is a wader that swims and because the female, the handsomer of the pair, leaves the male to incubate and raise the young. This is an arctic species very rare in Britain.

The phalarope's main breeding preference is for shallow water with plenty of cover: in the margin of a reasonably productive or brackish loch or in old sedge-peat cuttings. They have little fear of people, probably because they have such little knowledge of us as they winter at sea, feeding off plankton, off the Arabian peninsula. Though they are difficult to spot, they are not difficult to identify as they

54. *Red-necked phalarope: a shy and delicate little wader yet almost unafraid of humans, with very few breeding in the British Isles outwith Shetland. The RSPB is carrying out active management on one of their reserves to improve its breeding habitat.* (Courtesy of R. J. Tulloch.)

have such distinctive plumage and are always darting with quick movements through the emergent vegetation, or spinning and bobbing on the water as they pick off disturbed insect larvae. Of all Shetland's migratory breeders it is the last to return to breed, even later than the *tirricks*, usually towards the end of May but sometimes not until the first week of June. They also depart early from their breeding grounds, usually early August but often before the end of July; birds obviously familiar with the Shetland summer!

The status of the species has fluctuated somewhat over the last century. The Unst population has dwindled from 10–20 pairs in the last century to virtually none today. Similarly, numbers fell steadily on the few sites on Mainland until they were finally abandoned. This left just a small population on Fetlar, which was estimated in the early 1980s to be less than 20 pairs, falling to a nadir of six in 1989. Since then, through the active management of the Royal Society for the Protection of Birds (RSPB) on their reserve on Fetlar in re-creating breeding habitat, the phalarope has made such a remarkable recovery that there are now thought to be 40 breeding pairs. Hopefully recolonization of old breeding sites will follow so that the Shetland population, which is almost 100% of the British population, will once more be securely established.

That would have been the end of our description of the water-fowl of the Shetland mesotrophic lochs had this book been written only 5 years ago. In the 1990s, however, we have two of the largest of Britain's breeding birds meeting each other on the edges of their range, one of which is the only non-feral pair breeding in Britain. The species are of course the mute and whooper swans.

The mute swan was first introduced to Shetland at Spiggie from Orkney early in the century. They bred for a few years and apparently numbers rose to about 10 in 1919. However locals returning from the First World War shot them all. Further unsuccessful introductions were made in the 1930s and until the 1970s the mute swan remained a rather rare migrant. Since then there have been migrants in most years with some staying on through the summer. In 1990 an immature stayed on through the winter into 1991 and then into 1992, when it was joined by an adult and they then bred on the Loch of Tingwall. Subsequently they bred successfully in 1993 and 1994. In 1995 two pairs bred, while elsewhere in Shetland 10 non-breeding immatures summered (presumably the progeny of the first pair) and in 1996 breeding pairs increased to five, three of which were successful. The nearest breeding mute swans are in Orkney and it has been assumed that this is the origin of the Shetland birds; however in 1996 one was found to have been ringed in Norway.

Whooper swans have been regular winter visitors to Shetland from Iceland for at least 300 years and probably for a lot longer. Bones of swans have also been found from Bronze Age and Viking dwellings at Sumburgh. They have also bred in Orkney in the past but became extinct in the eighteenth century. Otherwise in Scotland, as wild birds, they are very occasional breeders. The earliest recorded breeding in Shetland occurred, as with the mute, at Spiggie, in 1907. Two birds with wings damaged from being shot bred, successfully but irregularly, for several years. At the end of the First World War alas, they suffered the same fate as their cousins. We do not know why the birds were shot, but presumably it was for food rather than sport. In 1994, just 2 years after the first mute swan success, a pair of whooper bred and successfully raised two young. In 1995 and 1996 they returned and bred again. Both species may stay on and breed for a few years, but who knows for how long. In the mean time we should just enjoy the pleasure of seeing these attractive and majestic birds on the lochs of Shetland throughout the year.

If we leave the lower-lying productive lochs and move on to the hill land and the more acidic lochs we find even fewer species. Those that are dependent on the sea for food and move there with their young as quickly as they can, the *raingoose*, red-breasted merganser and *dunter* (eider duck), we discuss under seabirds. This leaves only the common scoter, of which a few have perhaps bred regularly from 1911, not long after they first bred on the Scottish mainland; however none have been recorded breeding since 1993. This is a northern species commonly breeding in Norway and the tundra and also in Iceland. In Scotland there are less than 500 pairs, mainly in the north. Neither Saxby nor Evans and Buckley record many wintering or summering birds. All these species of duck and their chicks (including the eider and merganser) suffer the depredations of the *bonxie* and the larger gulls.

THE BANKS

A number of species that breed inland, such as the *shalder*, ringed plover, starling, wren and sparrow, may also be found on the coast. The ringed plover is predominantly a low coastal breeding species and so is the wren, but the latter, quite a common bird in Shetland, in addition to being a frequent inhabitant of old dykes also occurs on high cliffs. Even where there is the fiercest updraught one can come across this tiny bird, cocking its tail nervously and whirring from one crevice to another with its amazingly loud *tit-tit-tit*. A nest has even been recorded at the top of the Kame of Foula, 370 m above the sea. Like the only other Shetland subspecies of bird (starling) and the field and house mice, the Shetland wren illustrates the tendency to increasing size in northerly latitudes. The wrens of the Scottish islands, St Kilda, Fair Isle and Shetland, all have different songs, with differences occurring even between the islands of Shetland itself. The Shetland wren also has a darker plumage than its mainland cousin, a common occurrence in local races found in mild wet climates. A common passerine of the coast is the rock pipit, which rarely moves far inland. It is one of those 'small brown jobs' that confuse the ornithological beginner. It is larger and greyer than the meadow pipit (*hill sparrow*). A less common passerine is the twite, which is most usually found on coastal banks but occasionally inland too. This used to be a more common species around the croft, especially in the winter months. The population may be less than it was and has suffered again recently in Shetland from the bad winter of 1995–96.

The last widespread breeding bird of the low coast we discuss here is the ringed plover, which nests mainly on open sandy or shingly ground. The Shetland population is thought to be around 1000 pairs, representing over 10% of the British population. When disturbed on the nest or when feeding on the shore it runs away with a clockwork precision, like a little thief with its black eye-mask. In the winter months small flocks are extremely common on the sandy beaches, flitting out in tight arcs from the shore to alight nimbly again at a safe distance. Often seen

55.   *Shetland wren: a bird that sings above its weight and that over many years of isolation has evolved into a subspecies.* (Courtesy of RSPB.)

in the company of the ringed plover in winter and occurring as often on the rocky foreshore is the turnstone or *steyn pekker*. This is one of the most northerly breeding species that occurs all round the Scandinavian coast, but has not yet been proved to breed in Scotland. Adults regularly occur in summer, in small numbers, in Orkney and Shetland, and are occasionally seen displaying or behaving in an agitated manner. Saxby described finding a nest with eggs last century, but did not see the adults. It just seems a matter of time before the first breeding record is confirmed by a sharp-eyed or lucky bird-watcher. Another northern wader species that Saxby thought had bred in the nineteenth century is the purple sandpiper or *ebb sleeper*. Saxby stated that eggs were brought to him from a suitable habitat, but alas with a degree more cynicism it could be suggested that they had been brought to him *via* a suitable habitat. There were rewards to be had in importing eggs to sell to the credulous! On the other hand, the purple sandpiper breeds in Faroe, Iceland and Norway, recently has occasionally bred in Scotland and is seen in Shetland, where there is suitable 'tundra-like' habitat, in all months; so perhaps Saxby was correct. Although it has not been seen on its breeding habitat in the summer months, it is perhaps another bird to watch out for.

The rock dove, or *blo doo*, is a common species around Shetland's cliffs and has been for a very long time: Tulloch (1992) describes caves on the Holm of Gloup with faecal deposits several feet thick. Shetland and the other remote northern areas of Scotland probably have the last 'pure' populations left in the British Isles, as feral pigeons, arising from racing and 'show' pigeons, have now interbred with most of the more 'accessible' rock dove populations. However, as the origin of these breeds was probably the rock dove in the first place, there is a question of the importance that should be attached to 'purity' anyway.

The terrestrial bird *par excellence* of the banks is the raven. Like the *bonxie* (great skua), the larger gulls and the hoodie crow, the raven has long been persecuted by humans because of its association with carrion, and nests, eggs and young are still regularly destroyed. Although ravens will attack sick or helpless sheep and lambs,

56. *Ravens: characteristic opportunists of the cliff and hill and the lords of the winter scene when the breeding seabirds are largely absent.* (Courtesy of B. Jackson.)

there is little evidence that they will harm healthy animals. An investigation into the predation of sheep by birds in Shetland suggested that the problem had become more acute recently because of the changes taking place in crofting, with less attention being given to hill lambing than in the past, rather than because of an increase in predation. The real culprit may be the *bonxie*, which will also drive sheep, dogs and people from their nesting area.

Recent studies have established that there are some 200 pairs of ravens in Shetland predominantly breeding on the coast, some 4–5% of the British population. Although they breed in Shetland at greater densities than many other places, it appears that breeding success is somewhat lower than most other places within their range. In fact, as there appears to be no lack of food (sheep carrion and rabbits) and only a limited amount of persecution, it is possible that there is a density-dependent effect operating. In other words, breeding is at capacity. The raven's close relative, the jackdaw, apparently bred first in 1943 'and has occurred regularly ever since though the numbers continue to be small' (Venables and Venables, 1955). However there have been no confirmed breeding records for a number of years and the status of this bird requires investigation.

The story of the peregrine, or *stock hawk*, in Shetland is a sad one. Bones of peregrines have been found from Viking times and there is no reason to think that the species was not present long before that. In the seventeenth century the King's Falconer used to visit Shetland to collect young peregrines. In the nineteenth century they were considered to be 'pretty numerous' (Dunn, 1837) and even Venables and Venables (1955) thought Shetland was still 'one of the strongholds in Britain for this species'. Alas today none of these statements hold up, as in 1991 Shetland held the dubious distinction of being the only county in Scotland without breeding peregrines. A pair bred in 1996, but previous to that the last successful pair was in 1993; 1994 was probably the first time in at least 1000 years that no known peregrine nests were occupied. Why has this happened?

There is little doubt that Shetland peregrines suffered, though to a lesser extent, from the same effects of organochlorines from seed-dressings in the 1950s and 1960s as did peregrines in the rest of Britain. However, following controls on the use of insecticides in the late 1960s, while mainland populations began to recover, those on the coast either showed no recovery or, in the case of Shetland, continued to decline. In fact it may well be that Shetland's (and other coastal) peregrine population was already declining prior to the use of organochlorines. When the diet of these coastal birds was examined it was, as expected, largely seabirds, waders and rock doves. However, Shetland peregrines, even compared with Orkney, rely more on seabirds and waders than any other group. When the chemical residues in the eggshells of the Shetland birds were analysed it was found that the levels of PCBs and mercury were high enough to depress breeding success. The origins of these contaminants is of course industry and the sea, and the peregrine is accumulating them through its diet. However, Orkney's peregrines seem to be holding their own, so why have Shetland's peregrines apparently almost reached extinction?

There are two exacerbating factors that may be the proverbial nails in the Shetland peregrine's coffin. The first is the huge and increasing population of the *maalie* (fulmar) breeding on the same cliffs and even taking over the nest sites of the peregrine. There have been several cases in Shetland of both adults and juveniles being found so badly coated with *maalie* oil that they could not fly. A similar event happened to one of the juvenile sea eagles introduced to Fair Isle 25 years ago. The *maalie* population is, and has been, much greater than anywhere else in Britain, which could account for the longer-term decline, a decline steepened by the effects of pollutants. Shetland's isolated position relative to the Scottish mainland (and Norway, a dead peregrine found in 1997 was found to have been ringed in Norway), which can be a critical factor in the success or lack of recolonization, may well be the reason that although Orkney's low population can be boosted by immigrants, Shetland's is less likely to be so, as peregrines are unfortunately uncommon passage migrants. The problem for Shetland's peregrines is therefore quite complex and there seems no way back for this magnificent bird in the foreseeable future.

The last pair of Shetland's most magnificent bird of prey, the *erne* or sea eagle, nested in the early part of this century. This was a much reviled bird in Shetland in the past with a price on its head, at least during the eighteenth and first part of the nineteenth centuries, due to its reputation for taking lambs. In Foula the great skua (bonxle) used to be protected because it mobbed the *erne* and presumably distracted it from taking lambs. In the late nineteenth century there were around five pairs in Shetland and previous to that they must have been reasonably common, with ample summer food supplies of seabirds and seaduck. In 1968 attempts were made to reintroduce sea eagles to Fair Isle with the release of four immature birds from Scandinavia. However, they all disappeared or died, one being found virtually helpless and covered in fulmar oil. With the recent comprehensive programme of reintroduction, initially to Rum from 1975 to 1984, sea eagles have gone from being vagrants in Shetland to becoming an occasional visitor. In the 1980s birds appeared almost annually and during 1983–84 two immature birds were resident at Fitful. As the reintroduction programme to Scotland continues once more, it may just be a matter of time, even with the low level of persecution that still persists on the mainland, until birds settle once again in Shetland. There is certainly plenty of food for sea eagles in Shetland today, from seabirds to sheep carcasses and mountain hares, but they may not be welcomed back.

WINTERING WILDFOWL AND WADERS

The winter is a harsh time for Shetland's wildlife. With little good shelter and poor feeding on the hill, in the field, on freshwater lochs or inshore, most of Shetland's breeding birds move south and even migrants, generally speaking, only pause long enough to regain strength before moving on. When the wind blows in the winter months, which it does most days, even though the air may be mild wind chill soon lowers body temperatures. The naturalist or the walker feels almost entirely exposed on the landscape at this time of year. On the beaches the wind can whip sand across the face so that one has to turn one's back, when even the ringed plover

57.   *The calloo: an attractive and relatively small winter visitor to the sounds and voes, whose long tail curls elegantly over its back in stiff sea breezes.* (Courtesy of B. Jackson.)

58.   *Whooper swans: magnificent winter visitors from the north that have recently stayed to breed in small numbers.* (Courtesy of B. Jackson.)

seems to drop its head and crouch lower. In the teeth of a gale, searching the swell and the galloping white-horses in the sound for seaduck and divers, the short chop of the waves and the driven spume on the lochs brings tears to the eyes. Then there are days when the wind has all but disappeared over the horizon, when all is still but the sea, and on its surface, bobbing on the swell, the unforgettable sight of a flock of black and white *calloos* (long-tailed duck), running up signals with their long tails over their heads and calling to each other. Or magic moments when the sun is low relatively early in the afternoon in the brief winter days, when a family of whooper swans, the wind whistling through their powerful wings, their all-white bodies tinged with pink, descend out of the sky with immense grace and with breathtaking beauty, to plough across the surface of a loch and come to rest, heads held high on their aristocratic necks.

Whereas Orkney to the south has large shallow lochs set in the rich soils of its Old Red Sandstones, Shetland, with its predominantly acidic rocks, has few productive lochs. Relatively speaking therefore Shetland supports few wintering wildfowl on freshwater lochs, although some species, such as goldeneye, mallard, wigeon, teal and whooper swans, are regularly found in brackish and marine situations, while others, such as the Slavonian grebe, great northern diver and the *calloo*, are almost exclusively found on the sea. The absence of many large cultivated fields and eel grass (*Zostera*) has traditionally meant there has been little feeding for geese. There may not be very many different wildfowl to see in winter in Shetland, but their is a special leavening of northern species and the setting is rarely less than dramatic.

With the increasing number of ornithologists and keen local amateurs now in Shetland, regular and comprehensive counts of freshwater wintering wildfowl have been taking place for some 20 years, although these counts are not always consistent and cannot cover all the outlying holms where geese and wigeon graze. Counts of the principal sites therefore are only of minimum numbers, although they cannot be far short of the totals. The principal sites are shown in Fig. 17 and the monthly counts for 13 of those sites (1991–92) are given in Table 10. To estimate change in status over the last century and a half is quite difficult as Saxby's records refer only to Unst, Evans and Buckley were not present for long periods throughout the winter and Venables and Venables could not adequately cover the whole of Shetland. Comparisons therefore should be treated with caution.

Whooper swans appear to have been wintering in Shetland since at least the seventeenth century; subsequently they were shot and by the middle of the nineteenth century the birds that did turn up showed little inclination to winter, while at the end of that century Evans and Buckley also thought they were unusual. Early this century, following the cessation of persecution, they began again to regularly winter in small numbers on Loch of Spiggie and by the late 1940s and early 1950s the November and October peaks were regularly just under 100, with a maximum of 122 in the winter of 1950–51. More recently, average peaks have been slightly higher, with that for the period 1990–91 to 1991–95 being 130. The peak number given for Easter Loch (Unst) in the winter 1948–49 is 54, which is not dissimilar to today's counts. Loch of Spiggie and Easter Loch remain the two most important wintering sites for whooper swan in Shetland, although they also occur in quite small numbers on several other lochs. There has clearly been an increase in the wintering population over the last 50 years with one of the highest monthly counts being 430 in October 1986. However, the average peak monthly count (September–March) for the whole of Shetland over the last decade is around 250, which is 4% of the UK wintering population. Whoopers arrive in October, usually peak in numbers in that month or November and decrease rapidly thereafter, the last departing around March with occasional stragglers staying on to summer.

TABLE 10   *Monthly wintering wildfowl counts 1991–92, from 13 principal freshwater/brackish sites (from Wildfowl and Wader Counts 1991–92, WeBS— WWT, BTO, RSPB, JNCC)*

Species	September	October	November	December	January	February	March	Peak monthly count
Little grebe	0	0	0	0	0	0	1	1
Cormorant	0	1	0	1	0	1	1	1
Mute swan	1	1	1	1	1	1	1	1
Whooper swan	2	141	241	198	38	42	16	241
Pink-footed goose	0	1	0	0	0	0	0	1
Greylag goose	0	59	32	93	116	136	79	136
Barnacle goose	0	42	0	0	0	0	0	42
Shelduck	0	1	0	0	0	1	2	2
Wigeon	28	278	26	6	35	24	2	278
Teal	13	18	9	18	19	57	14	57
Mallard	105	106	101	63	154	111	28	154
Shoveller	0	0	1	0	0	0	0	1
Pochard	0	37	81	80	122	161	55	161
Tufted duck	110	214	258	231	269	151	146	269
Scaup	0	8	0	0	1	0	2	8
Long-tailed duck	0	14	4	3	2	3	26	26
Goldeneye	3	50	150	194	127	123	90	194
Smew	0	0	0	0	2	2	1	2
Red-breasted merganser	4	1	0	1	0	2	2	4
Goosander	0	0	0	0	1	1	2	1
Coot	0	3	0	1	0	0	0	3
Monthly total	266	975	904	890	887	816	466	975

FIGURE 17　*Principal freshwater wintering sites of wildfowl (whooper swans, tufted duck, wigeon, teal, pochard, mallard, goldeneye)* (from Berry & Johnston, 1980).

Mallard have been a common wintering species for at least 200 years and numbers do not seem to have changed very much recently. South Mainland, with the lochs of Spiggie, Brow and Hillwell and Clickhimin at Lerwick, seems to be the most important area, with overall monthly counts varying from 100 to almost 300 over the last decade. Similarly, pochard have been wintering in Shetland for some time and again predominantly on the more productive lochs of South Mainland; peak numbers for the whole of Shetland vary between 100 and 200. The other relatively common wintering duck are tufted duck and goldeneye, with the former usually the most numerous duck counted in Shetland. The peak count in South Mainland in the 1950s was 80 birds, which is similar to numbers over the last 20 years. Today, the lochs of Clickhimin, Tingwall, Snarravoe and to a lesser extent Easter Loch can hold more than double that number between them. It seems unlikely that the birds would have been missed if they had been present in these numbers in the 1950s, so it seems that wintering tufted duck numbers must have continued to expand since then. The highest monthly peak for tufted duck for the whole of Shetland for the period 1984/85–1994/95 is 432 in November 1984 and the average peak is around 280. The situation regarding goldeneye is less clear. Previous estimates by Saxby ('common in winter'), Evans and Buckley ('large numbers, sometimes of great numbers, usually 30') and Venables and Venables

('Common in Shetland from autumn to spring, with peak numbers of just over 100 in the Dunrossness area') compare reasonably with the picture today, with peak numbers for the whole of Shetland over the last decade regularly around 100, but occasionally 200.

Wigeon and teal also winter in small numbers, the former numbering usually over 100 and the latter usually less. Other species in quite small numbers, but of some interest, are little grebe, Slavonian grebe especially from Whiteness Voe to Bixter Voe, scaup, common scoter, red-breasted merganser and goosander (all to be found on salt as well as fresh water), with a whole range of others appearing occasionally or as vagrants. Few geese winter in Shetland and usually only greylag or pink-footed geese, plus occasional white-fronted, barnacle or brent, pass through in small numbers in the autumn. Latterly, greylag wintering numbers have increased in Unst and South Mainland; increasingly, greylags have stayed on to breed, courtesy of central and local government reseeding grants.

There may be only a handful of freshwater sites in Shetland that regularly hold over 100 freshwater wintering wildfowl in total, which in terms of the British Isles wintering populations is very small beer, but there are numerous bays, sounds and voes that hold several thousand seaduck. The most common, as we shall see in the following chapter, is the *dunter* or eider duck, of which there are about 7000. Following breeding they form into moult flocks and around October move into other preferred areas to winter, particularly north and south of Bressay, between Whalsay and Mainland, and between Burra Isle and Skelda Ness. For almost 30 years now, the magnificent king eider has been seen almost annually among them, sometimes several individuals and often in the same areas.

Not far from Sumburgh Head, which is one of the regular king eider moulting spots, is Quendale Bay, perhaps one of the best sites for viewing wintering seaduck and divers. Among the eider can be seen *calloo*, great northern diver and, very occasionally, black-throated diver. Overall Shetland probably supports 250–300 or between 5 and 6% of the British wintering total of great northern divers. That birds or species can be extremely faithful to their wintering grounds is well known and illustrated in Shetland by a leucistic (white) great northern diver that has returned to Sandsound Voe each winter now for around 15 years and a white-billed diver that returned to Linga Sound (Whalsay) annually between 1979 and 1991, a characteristic which also makes this specific wintering population rather vulnerable, as we shall see in a later chapter.

Apart from the *dunter* the most common wintering seaduck in Shetland, and certainly the most attractive, is the *calloo*. Venables and Venables (1955) also described them as common in winter, but it is impossible to know if numbers have changed over recent times. Surveys around the coast over the winter of 1990–91 for the Nature Conservancy Council (NCC) and Shetland Oil Terminal Environmental Advisory Group (SOTEAG) counted around 1500 birds and the total wintering population has been estimated at nearer 3000. This latter figure would give Shetland around 15% of the British wintering population. However it must be remembered that there are several million *calloos* in north-west Europe!

Although Shetland's coastline is very long, there are relatively few sheltered shores with suitable 'estuarine' substrate for supporting wintering waders. Even where such sites occur, the catchment from which they have obtained their material and the burns that empty into them are generally acidic and bring few nutrients. Waders such as curlew, lapwing and snipe are therefore often found in fields as well as on the shore. One of the best wader sites is the Pool of Virkie in South Mainland; otherwise there are only the few sandy beaches scattered throughout the islands, the sheltered beaches at the very head of the long voes, the few *houbs* and *vadills* and the innumerable tiny areas of soft shore scattered along the length of the coast. Nevertheless, a survey by the Tay Ringing Group and the Shetland Bird Club in December 1985 counted some 12 000 waders, the most abundant of which were turnstone (5104), followed by redshank and purple sandpiper. Also found in numbers were ringed plover (612) and curlew (1400). Shetland is therefore important nationally for these wader species and internationally for curlew numbers. Other species encountered in number were golden plover (min. 1000) and lapwing (min. 1000). Very few *shalders* were seen, supporting the notion that most of Shetland's very large population go south for the winter.

The winter is not a time associated with visiting northern islands for watching wildlife. However, there is a lot to see and for those from the cities there is an incredibly stimulating contrast, both physical and spiritual, between relatively unchallenging urban streets and the raw power and beauty of an exposed and wild landscape, which can only be described by a succession of superlatives: the almost overpowering strength of gale-force winds and the reverberations of crashing waves and roaring surf pounding across sands or up against the bulwark of black unbending cliffs; when the sun shines, the enormous shadows cast across the wide-open landscape; the steely-blue northern winter light; the overwhelming intensity of a clear night sky with no city lights to diminish the myriads of stars; the sight of the ocean, clear to the horizon, bathed in unearthly moonlight; or the silent majesty of the sweeping curtains and ever-shifting bands of the aurora borealis, which makes city laser displays look like pocket-torch beams.

STATUS AND RELATIONSHIPS OF THE SHETLAND LANDBIRDS

Table 11 illustrates the decrease of species diversity with increasing latitude. This table should be taken as a guide for illustrative purposes only, as several species in all the island groups see-saw between being regular and irregular breeders. The first thing to notice is that at least half of the 37 birds that regularly breed in the north of Scotland but not in Orkney are associated with woodland (coniferous or broad-leaved), a habitat that is limited and fragmentary in Orkney. Of the 27 or so that breed regularly in Orkney but not in Shetland, 'a further half are associated with woods, shrubby heath or gardens, five with eutrophic lochs, marsh and emergent vegetation, both limited in Shetland, while four have a diet of small mammals or birds that are not sufficiently abundant in Shetland. Of the 15 or so species that breed regularly in Shetland but not in Faroe, two major factors are the much greater isolation of the latter and the even more restricted range of habitats, particularly a lack of many freshwater bodies. This is illustrated further by the fact

TABLE 11   *Bird species reaching their northern and southern limits*

Birds breeding regularly in north of Scotland mainland but not Orkney

Black-throated diver	Swift	Chiffchaff
Common scoter	Sand martin	Spotted flycatcher
Goosander	Tree pipit	Long-tailed tit
Ptarmigan	Grey wagtail	Coal tit
Partridge	Dipper	Blue tit
Woodcock	Redstart	Great tit
Greenshank	Whinchat	Treecreeper
Wood sandpiper	Ring ouzel	Magpie
Little tern	Mistle thrush	Siskin
Cuckoo	Grasshopper warbler	Redpoll
Tawny owl	Whitethroat	Goldfinch
Long-eared owl	Blackcap	Crossbill
		Bullfinch

Birds breeding regularly in Orkney but not Shetland

Little grebe	Pheasant	Song thrush
Grey heron	Water rail	Sedge warbler
Gadwall	Corncrake	Willow warbler
Pintail	Coot	Goldcrest*
Hen harrier	Sandwich tern	Jackdaw
Sparrowhawk	Short-eared owl	Chaffinch*
Buzzard	Dunnock	Greenfinch
Kestrel	Robin	Linnet
Peregrine*	Stonechat	Corn bunting

Birds breeding regularly in Shetland but not Faroe

Cormorant	Shoveller	Greenshank
Mute swan*	Tufted duck	Common sandpiper
Whooper swan*	Common scoter*	Common tern
Shelduck	Red grouse	Rook
Teal	Moorhen	Reed bunting

Birds breeding regularly in Faroe but not Iceland

Lapwing	Skylark	Hooded crow
Curlew	Swallow	Starling
Rock dove	Rock pipit	House sparrow
Collared dove	Blackbird	

Birds breeding regularly in Iceland but not Faroe

Great northern diver	Shoveller	Gyrfalcon
Slavonian grebe	Tufted duck	Ptarmigan
Cormorant	Scaup	Grey phalarope
Whooper swan	Harlequin duck	Glaucous gull
Pink-footed goose	Long-tailed duck	Brunnich's guillemot
Wigeon	Common scoter	Little auk
Gadwall	Barrow's goldeneye	Short-eared owl
Teal	Goosander	Redpoll
Pintail	White-tailed eagle	Snow bunting

Birds breeding regularly in Faroe but not Shetland

Canada goose
Purple sandpiper

Birds breeding regularly in Shetland but not Orkney
Leach's petrel* Common scoter*
Whooper swan* Red-necked phalarope
Greenshank

Birds breeding regularly in Orkney but not north of Scotland mainland

Manx shearwater	Gadwall	Whimbrel
Storm petrel	Pintail	Sandwich tern
Gannet	Black-tailed godwit	Corn bunting

Approximate number of species breeding regularly
North of Scotland mainland: *c.* 150
Orkney: *c.* 90
Shetland: *c.* 70
Faroe: *c.* 50
Iceland: *c.* 80

*Consult Table 8 and Appendix 3 for these species.

that Iceland, further north than Faroe but with a far greater landmass including many freshwater lakes and marsh, has some 27 more breeding species than the latter, half of them water-fowl.

All the species breeding in the north of Scotland but absent as regular breeders in Orkney breed further north in Europe. At the present moment there are three species breeding in Orkney that do not regularly breed further north, either in the islands or in Europe. These are the sandwich tern, the stonechat and the corn bunting. All of these have bred irregularly in Shetland and the last two have suffered a general decline and retraction of their range in the British Isles due to loss of habitat and agricultural changes. Only the mute swan reaches its northerly limit in Shetland and it only became established as a breeding species in 1992. The pied wagtail is one of Shetland's interesting anomalies in that the British race (*M. a.* subsp. *yarelli*) does not occur further north than Shetland, either in the islands or further north in Europe where it reaches south Norway. The European race, the white wagtail (*M. a.* subsp. *alba*), which does breed further north in Scandinavia, also breeds in Shetland. Two other species have bred in Shetland at about the same northerly limit as in Scandinavia, the reed warbler in 1973 (only) and the whitethroat, which has bred in just 4 years out of the last 25.

Looking at the composition of the bird fauna from the other direction, of the 27 or so species breeding regularly in Iceland but not Faroe, only Barrow's goldeneye, the grey phalarope, glaucous gull and Brunnich's guillemot do not breed further south. Of the two species (Canada goose and purple sandpiper) that regularly breed in Faroe but not Shetland, the origin of the first is probably the feral population of the British Isles, while the second has bred a few times on the Scottish mainland. There are therefore no Faroese breeding species reaching their southern limit. Of the 'northern' species breeding regularly in Shetland but not Orkney, all breed, or have bred, either in the Hebrides or the Scottish mainland, at least in small numbers. The greylag is another interesting anomaly, in that while it also breeds in Orkney in small numbers (where it was introduced), there is a large

Scottish population in the North-west Highlands and Western Isles. Are the Shetland (and Orkney) birds of Scottish or Icelandic origin? They may well be the latter, like the black-tailed godwit. The three species, all seabirds, that 'officially' breed in Orkney but not Caithness and Sutherland in fact breed on Sule Stack and Sule Skerry and could therefore equally well be considered as birds of the north of Scotland.

Thus although Shetland can claim, at least since 1992, to have one species that reaches its northerly breeding limit (the mute swan), it cannot claim to have any breeding species reaching its southern limit (although the snowy owl reached its southern limit 1967–75). However it can claim to have the bulk of the British population of several northern species, e.g. the whimbrel, red-necked phalarope, arctic skua and great skua; and it can claim breeding records of several Scandinavian or Icelandic races, some of which do not, or only rarely, breed further south in the British Isles (Table 11). Moving northwards from Britain through the islands, therefore, avifauna diversity is seen to depend on habitat diversity, relative landmass and geographical isolation, while the fact that few species reach their latitudinal limit can be accounted for by the fragmented and isolated nature of the islands in contrast to the unbroken European north–south corridor to the east.

It is in this context that the effect of Shetland's geographical position becomes apparent (see Fig. 1). To illustrate the situation, the islands can be regarded as the northern apex of a triangle drawn around the British Isles and the southern apex of another triangle drawn through Iceland and Scandinavia. The western and eastern boundaries of this second triangle are the potential migration routes that pass through Shetland, allowing the establishment in Shetland of immigrants from Iceland, Faroe and Scandinavia, in some cases winter or spring visitors staying on into the summer. At the apex of the first triangle Shetland is also in a position to benefit from the expansion of a British population or from an 'overshoot' in the spring migration. Shetland is both isolated and sufficiently closer to Scandinavia than either Orkney or Faroe to be in a position to be the landfall for a greater variety and number of migrants and therefore potentially hold them as breeding species. As we have seen, however, the position is always changing. Shetland is a stepping stone, but because of its lack of a number of habitats common to the south and the east it is a kind of 'no-man's land', where a species' hold may be very tenuous. It is likely therefore that there will always be a high proportion (60%) of irregular and sporadic breeders, even if environmental management is improved and habitats such as woodland substantially increased.

Since the end of the last Ice Age there have been many fluctuations in the climate that undoubtedly have effected the breeding bird populations of Shetland. In fact it has been suggested that a number of breeding species new to the British Isles and western Europe as a whole in the last 150 years, including many Shetland species such as the tufted duck, black-tailed godwit, whimbrel, redwing and fieldfare, are a result of recolonization from refuges further east and south following the last Ice Age. Certainly early this century an amelioration allowed the northern expansion of several species and a similar amelioration in the early 1960s probably allowed the expansion of the breeding range of the tufted duck into Shetland, while short periods of hard winters in the early and late 1940s were probably responsible for the loss of an established song thrush population. When food is abundant and breeding success and chick survival high, some species expand rapidly into new areas. It was probably a few years' abundance of lemmings in Scandinavia that allowed the snowy owl to expand into Shetland in the 1960s, and the huge increase in conifer planting in the north of Scotland and in Europe that, respectively, has drawn the siskin (1992) northwards and the lesser redpoll (1992) westwards. Such waves of advancement and retraction of populations are continuous features that ebb and flow over Shetland. Comparing Table 8 with the breeding list in Venables and Venables (1955), it can be deduced that although 16 additional species (including collared dove) have bred since 1955 (partly a reflection of better coverage in recent years), only five of these have become regular breeding species, while six have since been lost as regular breeding species, and of those that have been lost three are probably due to loss of habitat. Continuous change in the fauna and flora is the norm for islands.

CHAPTER 7

The Plankton, the Fish and the Whale

Fishing boat

O it's ane o' the bonniest sichts in the warld
To watch the herrin' come walkin' on board
In the wee sma' 'oors o' a simmer's mornin'
As if o' their ain accord

With the Herring Fishers, Hugh MacDiarmid

Both human history and natural history in Shetland are inextricably bound up with the surrounding seas. Were it not for the productivity of the neighbouring waters, the human settlers and their descendants, particularly through the periods of climatic deterioration, would have had a very different and even more chequered time than they have. In addition, the cliffs would not be adorned in the summer months with immense seabird colonies, nor would there be the *bonxie* or the *raingoose* on the hill, nor the *tirrick* on the shore, the *selkies* on the skerry, the *neesick* in the voe, nor in the sounds the big whales that are now reappearing after so many years, nor many other birds and animals that contribute so much to the rich diversity of wildlife that Shetland offers.

To appreciate the reasons for the productive wealth of Shetland seas it is first necessary to understand the oceanography of the north-eastern Atlantic. In this chapter we shall look at this first, then at the inshore algae and other marine life of Shetland that has been described through survey over 150 years. Then we will look at the demersal and pelagic fish, shellfish and fish farming, their history and position today and will conclude with a section on Shetland's marine mammals. The seabirds, which equally depend on the food resources of the North Sea, are described in the next chapter.

PRIMARY PRODUCTION

As on land, all life in the sea (with a few rare exceptions in the deep ocean) ultimately depends for its food, through photosynthesis (primary production), on the energy of the sun. Since it is dependent on sunlight, photosynthesis is restricted to the surface layer of the ocean where sunlight can penetrate. The maximum depth at which photosynthesis can take place is dependent on a number of factors, including the latitude, season, weather conditions and amount of suspended material in the water. In general, however, photosynthesis is limited to depths of less than 100 m in the open ocean, while in coastal areas the maximum depth is no more than 30–40 m, and in some areas may be reduced to only a few centimetres.

On land most primary production is carried out by large plants, such as grass, trees, etc., which grow firmly rooted in the ground. In the sea, however, the equivalent plants (the large seaweeds) are restricted to areas where the sea bed is shallow enough for sunlight to reach it. Over the vast majority of the world's oceans (>99.9%), the sea bed lies below the zone where photosynthesis can take place, so the contribution of these large seaweeds to the overall production of food in the sea is relatively insignificant. In contrast to the large plants found on the earth's land surfaces, the vast majority of primary production in the sea is carried out by untold billions of phytoplankton, microscopic plants that drift suspended in the surface layers of the ocean. The largest of these plants are no more than a millimetre in size, and their small size and light weight help keep them afloat.

Feeding on the phytoplankton are the zooplankton, countless millions of tiny animals, the largest of which are a few millimetres in size. Crustacea, tiny shrimp-like creatures that may be as large as a grain of rice, predominate, but there is a host of other types of animal as well: small worm-like animals, little jellyfish, and many other forms. The tiny plants and animals that drift freely with the ocean's currents (as opposed to actively swimming and moving at will, as animals such as fish and whales can do) are collectively known as 'plankton' from the Greek word for 'wandering'. A number of species of fish, such as herring and mackerel, feed directly on the plankton, as do basking sharks and the huge baleen whales, while others feed on smaller fish that have fed on the plankton. Many species of shellfish also feed on plankton that they filter out of the water.

Like their terrestrial counterparts, phytoplankton require an abundant supply of nutrients (such as nitrate and phosphate), as well as sunlight and carbon dioxide, in order to photosynthesize. On land, dead plants and animals generally decay in the soil, the nutrients incorporated in them being released into the soil for plants to take up again. In the sea, however, dead zooplankton and other animals tend to sink, causing a steady drain of nutrients out of the sunlit surface layers of the oceans, where photosynthesis can occur. As a result, primary production is limited over large areas of the world's oceans by a shortage of nutrients in the surface waters, while the deeper waters are rich in nutrients but too dark for photosynthesis to occur. The vast sunlit open oceans of the tropics are relative deserts, almost totally devoid of nutrients and so of life. Phytoplanktonic food production is greater in coastal areas where rivers provide a constant supply of new nutrients from the land. However, production is greatest in areas of the world's oceans where ocean currents bring deep, nutrient-rich water to the surface, allowing the phytoplankton to grow and multiply.

THE TOPOGRAPHY OF THE SHETLAND SEAS

Shetland sits on the northernmost extension of Britain's continental shelf, the platform of relatively shallow water (maximum depth about 200 m) that extends off most of the world's coastlines. Offshore the sea bed initially plunges steeply downwards, matching the topography above sea level of much of the islands' outer coast, to reach depths of 50 m within a few hundred metres of most of the coastline (and much closer in many areas). Further from the shore the sea bed gradually flattens out to join the general continental shelf at a depth of 75–100 m, generally within 10 km, and in places less than 2 km, from the coast.

To the south of Shetland the continental shelf stretches for 1000 km, gradually shallowing, to the southern coastline of the North Sea, while to the east it extends for some 200 km, gradually deepening to a depth of about 200 m before dipping into the Norwegian Trench, off the Norwegian coast. To the north and west, however, deep water is found much closer to Shetland, with the edge of the continental shelf lying between 50 and 75 km from the coast. Beyond, the sea bed drops relatively steeply into the 1500 m depths of the Faroe–Shetland Channel, a southern extension of the deep Arctic Ocean Basin. There is one further important topographic feature of the sea bed near Shetland: a relatively shallow ridge extends west of Fair Isle at a depth of about 500 m, linking Britain's continental shelf to that of the Faroe Islands and forming a physical barrier that separates the deep cold waters of the Arctic Ocean from the relatively warm waters of the Atlantic.

The sea bed itself around Shetland is generally composed of relatively coarse sediments, with sands and sandy gravels (sand, 0.6–2.0 mm; gravel, >2.0 mm) predominating. The nature of the sediments is a reflection of the relatively rapid movement of the waters around the islands, which do not allow finer sediments to accumulate. Muddy sediments are only found in a few locations, such as St Magnus Bay, where glacial scouring has left deep basins in the sea bed, or sheltered, glacially deepened voes, where water movements are slower and finer sediments have been able to accumulate.

THE HYDROGRAPHY OF THE SHETLAND SEAS

The waters of the ocean are not, as might appear, simply one homogeneous mass. Countless thousands of measurements of the salinity (saltiness) and temperature of sea water at different depths and in different areas have revealed that the oceans contain many different bodies of water, each with a characteristic salinity and temperature. Although some mixing does occur between these water masses, their boundaries are generally fairly distinct and in some places can even be seen as a sharp line on the surface.

Nor are the waters static; ocean and tidal currents are constantly moving them around over short and long distances. Ocean currents are large, relatively slow flows of water that generally move consistently in the same direction at the same speed, usually transporting large volumes of water over long distances. These currents are driven either by steady winds, such as the trade winds, or by differences between the densities of adjacent water masses. Tidal currents, by contrast, are driven by changes in water level linked to the ebb and flow of tides, so they change direction and strength during each tidal cycle.

Descriptions of Shetland's hydrography have traditionally described a great ocean current, usually referred to as the Gulf Stream or North Atlantic Drift, which sweeps across the Atlantic Ocean from the Caribbean and bathes Shetland's shores in relatively warm water. Thus Shetland's (and northern Europe's) relatively mild climate is attributed to the arrival of warm Caribbean water. In fact, the Gulf Stream and North Atlantic Drift (now more usually known as the North Atlantic Current) are both parts of the same great current that circulates endlessly round the North Atlantic, driven by the prevailing winds in the tropics and subtropics. The Gulf Stream is that part which flows north along the east coast of the USA before swinging eastwards about 40° N of the equator to flow across the Atlantic as the North Atlantic Current. It used to be believed that a branch of this current turned to the north as it approached the coast of Europe and swept northwards past Ireland, Scotland and Shetland before rounding the north of Norway.

Extensive studies over the last two decades have substantially increased our understanding of the ocean currents around Shetland and in the north-east Atlantic in general. It is now clear that although a large current does flow northwards to the west of Shetland, it is *not* part of the Gulf Stream/North Atlantic Current and that the water which reaches Shetland's shores does not originate in the Caribbean. A branch of the North Atlantic Current does turn northward as it approaches Europe, but it flows much further offshore than previously thought, passing around the Faroe Islands.

The current that flows past Shetland (Fig. 18) is known as the Slope Current or Shelf Edge Current because it occurs above the continental slope between the 200 and 800 m depth contours, just off the edge of the continental shelf. Between these contours the Slope Current extends from the surface to the sea bed and flows

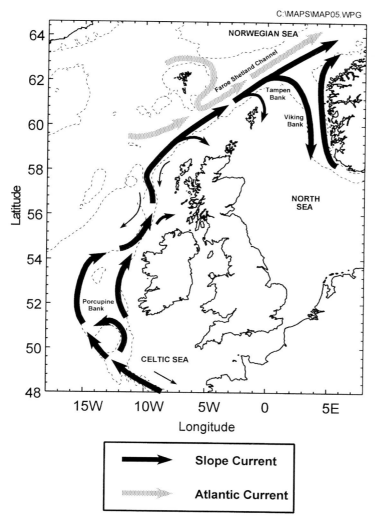

FIGURE 18   *Continental shelf, showing the main circulation patterns of the Atlantic and Slope Currents* (from Reid *et al.*, 1997, reproduced with permission of FRS Marine Laboratory.

throughout the year. It is a relatively fast-flowing ocean current, carrying some 5 million m^3 of water northwards at speeds of between 30 and 70 cm s^{-1} (0.6–1.4 knots approximately).

The Slope Current originates in the Bay of Biscay/Rockall Trough area and is driven by the difference in density between these waters and those of the Norwegian Sea where it terminates. The waters of the former area are relatively warm (thanks to the influence of the North Atlantic Current) and saline, while those of the Norwegian Sea are cooler and less saline. Salinity has a more significant effect on the density of the waters in these areas than their temperatures, and makes the waters of the Biscay/Rockall Trough area more dense. As a result they flow north into the less dense waters of the Norwegian Sea, carrying with them heat that originated in the Caribbean and which moderates Shetland's climate. So although the Gulf Stream itself does not reach Shetland its warmth does, via the Bay of Biscay and the Slope Current. (In the same way items of flotsam, such as the seed pods of Caribbean trees, occasionally reach Shetland's shores.)

Between the Slope Current and the coast, on the continental shelf itself, the currents are relatively weak and, being predominantly wind driven, their direction and strength is much more variable. There is, therefore, considerable mixing of the waters at the edge of the continental shelf, where the Slope Current flows past the relatively slow-moving waters on the continental shelf. This mixing brings nutrient-rich water up into the sunlit surface zone, boosting primary productivity along the shelf edge. Hence the attraction of this area for some of the large cetaceans, as we will see (Fig. 21).

In the area around North Rona, north-west of Cape Wrath, the Slope Current itself spills on to the continental shelf, partly as a result of sea-bed topography, particularly the shallow Wyville–Thomson Ridge which deflects the Slope Current upwards. This is an area of intense mixing as the Slope Current merges with the waters on the continental shelf, again bringing an abundant supply of nutrients up into the sunlit surface waters. This well-mixed, nutrient-rich water flows north and then generally east through the Fair Isle gap, between Orkney and Shetland, into the North Sea. The exact position of this inflow varies from year to year depending on the direction and strength of the prevailing winds, and may pass to the north or the south of Fair Isle. In occasional years it will be deflected so far north that it enters the North Sea around the north of Shetland. Once in the North Sea this flow of water turns south and roughly follows the 100-m contour south into the North Sea.

To the north of Shetland the Slope Current gradually disperses into the Norwegian Sea, some of it flowing a short distance into the North Sea via the Norwegian Trench before turning north again. During the summer, water from the Slope Current spills on to the continental shelf to the north and north-west of Shetland, again mixing with the waters on the shelf. This mixed water flows around the north of Shetland and south down the east coast, again boosting primary productivity in these waters.

SEASONS IN THE SEA

In the waters around Shetland (as throughout the North Sea and other temperate areas of the ocean), the level of primary production varies in a marked seasonal cycle throughout the year. Primary production in these areas may be limited by two main factors, sunlight and nutrient supply. In winter, nutrients are abundant in surface waters, as winter storms bring deep nutrient-rich water up to the surface, but photosynthesis is limited by low light levels. In spring the supply of sunlight increases as the days get longer until it reaches the critical level where photosynthesis can take place. The phytoplankton are now able to grow and multiply rapidly on the rich supply of nutrients stirred up during the winter, giving rise to a 'spring bloom' of phytoplankton. As the season progresses, however, improving weather means less mixing of the waters so the nutrients consumed by the phytoplankton (and lost as they or the animals that eat them die and sink) are not replenished from below. Eventually, as spring passes into summer, the supply of nutrients falls so low that photosynthesis more or less ceases and the spring bloom collapses, as phytoplankton abundance declines dramatically.

Throughout the summer, there is abundant sunlight but little phytoplanktonic growth due to the scarcity of nutrients in the absence of mixing of the waters. A second, smaller and shorter, bloom occurs in the autumn as the first equinoctial gales stir up the water bringing nutrients back to the surface while the sunlight is still strong enough to support photosynthesis. Although the winter gales continue to provide a rich supply of nutrients, phytoplanktonic production wanes as the days get shorter and light levels fall.

The spring and autumn blooms provide an abundant supply of food for the herbivorous zooplankton, which increase dramatically in abundance as a result (there is a time-lag of a few days between the phytoplankton and zooplankton blooms). When the phytoplankton bloom collapses, however, the zooplankton starve and their abundance declines equally rapidly.

Most large marine organisms, including most commercial fish and shellfish species, produce larvae that spend the first few days or weeks of their lives as members of the zooplankton. Here they drift with the ocean's currents with the other plankton, feeding on phytoplankton and other zooplankton (and themselves being fed on), until they metamorphose into juvenile adults, either settling to the sea bed and adopting sedentary lifestyles or becoming free-swimming. This planktonic phase is a difficult and dangerous time for these young animals and only a small proportion survive this phase of their lives, the majority starving, being eaten or being transported into areas where they cannot survive as adults. It has become clear in recent years that this stage of the life cycle plays a critical role in determining the abundance of many marine organisms. A small change in the survival rate of the planktonic stage, perhaps due to a variation in the availability of food or the numbers of predators, can significantly change the numbers of juveniles that join the adult stock each year.

Reproduction and spawning by many marine animals is timed to coincide with the spring phytoplankton bloom, which will provide a rich food supply for their larvae, and many species undertake annual spawning migrations to areas where conditions for the larvae will be most favourable. However, if the spring phytoplankton bloom is delayed by even a few days (by bad weather, for example) then the larvae may starve, while if the bloom is early there may be large numbers of zooplanktonic predators present, which will again cause heavy mortality. Similarly, a slight change in the pattern of currents, perhaps due to a period of strong winds, may carry the larvae into unfavourable areas, where few survive.

VARIABILITY IN THE OCEANS

Descriptions of the hydrography of the oceans, primary production or other oceanic processes, like those above, often paint a rather static picture of the oceans. By summarizing and generalizing they tend to describe the 'average' conditions in the sea, and often give the impression that the ocean is a very constant environment. It might be imagined, therefore, that currents always follow the same path at the same speed, that the temperature of the waters varies by the same amount each year, that it is always equally rough in winter and calm in summer, or that primary production always follows the same predictable annual cycle.

This picture is quite misleading, however, as we now know, from the systematic collection of biological and physical data over large areas of the oceans over long periods of time, that significant fluctuations occur in the seas from year to year and from decade to decade. These fluctuations are related to changes in atmospheric weather patterns, as there is an intimate relationship between the earth's atmosphere and oceans. Perhaps the best known of these atmosphere–ocean fluctuations are the El Niño events that periodically afflict the Pacific coast of northern South America.

The seas around Shetland, together with the whole North Atlantic, also experience large-scale fluctuations, which can have a profound effect on their natural history. These fluctuations, known as North Atlantic Oscillations (NAOs), are linked to changes in the atmospheric pressure over the Iceland/Greenland area. At some times, this area is dominated by a low pressure area over Iceland that deflects the Atlantic's prevailing westerly winds to the south, bringing warm south-westerly winds and relatively mild winters to Europe and the north-east Atlantic. This pattern may persist for anything up to a decade or more, but eventually the Icelandic low gradually fades as a high pressure area over Greenland becomes dominant. This high deflects the westerlies to the north, bringing cool north-westerly winds and colder winters to the north-east Atlantic. The Greenland high, too, may persist for many years before the system changes back again.

The NAO can have significant effects on the waters of the north-east Atlantic Ocean and North Sea, and thus on their biota. Between the 1950s and 1970s, for example, there was a substantial decline in the abundance of both phytoplankton and zooplankton in the North Sea and in the north-east Atlantic in general. This coincided with a period when the NAO was developing an increasingly strong Greenland high phase, resulting in an increased frequency and strength of cold northerly winds over Europe. Not only did northerly winds become more frequent but they were stronger; the incidence of gales in Shetland was 20% greater in the 1970s than in the 1950s, and this figure rose to 50% in some parts of the North Sea.

These winds delayed the onset of the spring phytoplankton bloom by up to 1 month, with the result that the phytoplankton had a shorter season in which to grow and multiply which, in turn, has a knock-on effect on the herbivorous zooplankton and all the organisms that feed on them. In the 1980s the Greenland high diminished in strength as the Icelandic low became established. This reduced the frequency of cold north-westerly winds and thus the delay to the onset of the spring phytoplankton bloom.

During the 1960s there was a dramatic increase in the abundance of gadoid fish (cod, haddock, saithe, etc.) in the North Sea, with their numbers increasing almost five-fold; the 1962 haddock year class was 25 times larger than the average year-class strength over the previous 50 years. This increase in the abundance of gadoid fish, known as the 'gadoid outburst', resulted from much better than average larval survival over several years due to the changed timing of the spring phytoplankton bloom described above. It appears that a later bloom suits the gadoid larvae better and that their mortality rate is lower in years when the spring phytoplankton bloom is delayed. During the 1980s, as the delay to the spring phytoplankton bloom diminished, the survival rate of gadoid larvae fell to more 'normal' levels with a resulting decrease in the abundance of gadoid fish in the North Sea.

The changes in North Sea plankton and the gadoid outburst during the 1960s dramatically illustrate the large-scale fluctuations that occur in the seas and the knock-on effects they can have on all marine organisms. Most fluctuations that occur in the sea are not of such a large scale nor do they have such dramatic effects, but they do occur all the time on various temporal and spatial scales. In order to understand the natural history of the seas around Shetland and the 'natural' fluctuations of dependent groups, such as seabirds or cetaceans, and to keep events such as the 'sandeel crisis' in perspective, it is essential to appreciate that change is the natural state of affairs in the seas. Conditions in the sea are constantly changing in response to various influences, and these strongly influence the distribution and survival of many marine organisms.

INSHORE FLORA AND FAUNA

In understanding the marine flora and fauna of Shetland we must recall again some of the factors that affect its terrestrial flora, namely that the islands are an isolated archipelago at the most northerly point of the British Isles and almost as close to Scandinavia. In addition, it has a prodigiously long and complex coastline with many islands, often with fast tides flowing between. In fact Shetland has probably one of the most exposed coasts in Britain, particularly the outer coast, with deep water, in excess of 100 m, within 1 km of the shore at many points. Here waves from the open Atlantic are almost continuously shattering their immense energy against the rocks. Its inner coast on the other hand can be very sheltered, particularly at the head of long voes where the clear oceanic water can be subject to a high organic input from peat.

Because of the length and complexity of the shore, there are a large range of marine habitats and therefore a wide range of communities. Not surprisingly much of the coast has a hard substratum of rock, boulders or gravel, otherwise it would not be there. Most of the rocky shores have fewer crevices and pools than other places and this reduces the faunal and floral diversity of exposed shore, since these form a niche for sheltered shore organisms; there are only limited areas of sediment where, in contrast, there are relatively diverse communities. The former habitat is poor as much from exposure as from the islands' northerly position and its cold waters, while the latter habitat benefits from shelter and stability. Like the terrestrial flora, the marine flora is relatively impoverished when compared with coastlines further south.

The Shetland situation was put very clearly by Howson (1988) in a report to the NCC: 'There are fewer northern species entering the [marine] flora and fauna than southern species dropping out and this trend continues between Shetland and Faeroe and beyond'. However the Shetland marine flora and fauna *are* strongly northern in character. For example, some arctic–boreal species not recorded elsewhere in shallow water in the British Isles include the sea cucumber, the sea urchins *Strongylocentrotus droebachiensis* and *S. pallidus*, a northern species of hydroid (*Halecium* sp.) that has not yet been given a specific name and there are several other northern species found 100 years ago. Similarly very few southern species have been found but include the jewel anemone, the cup coral and the blenny, which all appear to be at their northern limit. On the other hand, several northern species, such as the anemone *Protanthea simplex*, that might be expected and which occur on the west coast of Scotland are absent or at least not recorded. The situation therefore regarding Shetland's position in a boreal–arctic continuum is not entirely clear.

One of the features of Shetland's marine biology is the elevation and widening of the littoral and sublittoral zonation pattern, particularly in exposed situations. Here the combination of the regular occurrence of large waves, which surge high up the shore and subsequently drag far out, and the high humidity in these conditions has raised the normal intertidal zone by several metres while extending the subtidal zone to considerable depths. For example, kelp is present beyond its normal range to depths of at least 32 m.

One of the features in Shetland, in common with the west coast of Scotland, is the domination by the sea urchin at moderately exposed sites, where it apparently controls the species composition by creating 'urchin barrens'. Two further areas of interest in the sheltered waters of Shetland require further investigation. The first is the still and isolated waters at the heads of some voes. Shetland's voes are quite different to the sea lochs of the west coast of Scotland in that they have very little water exchange with the sea. At the head of Ronas Voe unusual rock communities have been found in deep water where anemone larvae suggested the presence of a very rare anemone (*Arachnanthus sarsii*). The second is the communities of the *houbs* and at The Vadills (West Mainland). Investigations into the ecology of a number of voes has found the occurrence of bottom-living forms to be controlled by the presence of 'organically rich reduced sediment', i.e. peat is highly important in determining the species present. The peat comes from both submerged peat beds (see Chapter 2) and erosion of blanket peat on surrounding land. The *houb* at Dales Voe, where the submerged peat is very visible on the shore, has been found to be rich in species and, like the community at The Vadills, unlike any other community so far found.

A consequence of the climate in Shetland, with its low daytime temperatures, is that it has allowed species which live entirely below the low-tide mark in England to extend into the littoral zone in both Orkney and Shetland and there are probably other unique features of Shetland shore. Certainly the growth habit of the toothed wrack and knotted wrack are different to that in similar habitats in Norwegian fiords and there are no unattached forms of the latter in Shetland, unlike both Norway and the Hebrides; sea pinks extend down to the upper spiral wrack zone of the extremely sheltered Shetland shores, whereas in the south they are confined to well above the splash zone; there are likely to be many more local and significant features if the shores were better known. Many species grow to a very large size in Shetland: the acorn barnacle is two or three times larger in Shetland than in the south. Some species, the barnacle *Elminius modestus* (incidentally an introduction to Britain from the antipodes) and the prosobranch mollusc *Littorina neritoides* reach their northern limit in Shetland. Only one species of top-shell occurs, compared with four in the south of Britain. Many more small snail species (up to about 1.25 cm long) than larger are found. An association not known outside Shetland is a commensal nemertean, *Malacobdella grossa*, in the cockle.

THE FISH IN SHETLAND'S WATERS

A total of 224 species of fish have been recorded in the North Sea, ranging in size from 5-cm gobies to the 10-m basking shark. No separate list is available for Shetland, but it is likely that a high proportion of the North Sea fish may be found there. Most of the common species are those typical of continental shelf seas, although deep-water species are found along the edge of the continental shelf to the north and west of Shetland and along the edge of the Norwegian Trough to the east.

The species recorded from the North Sea vary widely in their abundances; few can be regarded as common and even fewer are exploited commercially. It has been estimated that just 20 species (Table 12) make up over 95% of the total fish biomass

TABLE 12   *The 20 most abundant fish species in the North Sea in terms of biomass (thousands of tonnes), from analysis of survey records 1977–86* (from Daan *et al.*, 1990)

Common name	Latin name	Biomass
Demersal species		
Common dab	*Limanda limanda*	2110
Haddock	*Melanogrammus aeglefinus*	826
Cod	*Gadus morhua*	670
Whiting	*Merlangus merlangus*	643
Saithe	*Pollachius virens*	585
Plaice	*Pleuronectes platessa*	485
Starry ray	*Raja radiata*	308
Long rough dab	*Hippoglossoides platessoides*	227
Grey gurnard	*Eutrigla gurnardus*	206
Lemon sole	*Microstomus kitt*	178
Poor cod	*Trisopterus minutus*	92
Sole	*Solea solea*	54
Pelagic species		
Herring	*Clupea harengus*	1439
Sprat	*Sprattus sprattus*	474
Horse mackerel	*Trachurus trachurus*	427
Mackerel	*Scomber scombrus*	349
*Not easily classified**		
Sandeel	mainly *Ammodytes marinus*	1789
Norway pout	*Trisopterus esmarkii*	752
Spurdog	*Squalus acanthias*	175
Blue whiting	*Micromesistius poutassou*	84
Total all other species		427
Total of all species		12 300

* These species typically live close to the sea bed but feed mainly on organisms that live in the water column.

Flounder

of the North Sea (some 12.3 million tonnes). Many of these species are fished commercially around Shetland, but some which are not of commercial importance may be equally abundant.

As in other areas, most of the fish in the waters around Shetland can be broadly classified into demersal and pelagic species, as shown in Table 12. Demersal fish typically live in close association with the sea bed and tend to be relatively solitary, not forming large shoals, and generally lying on, or swimming a short distance above, the sea bed (although they do on occasion swim much higher in the water). By contrast, pelagic fish spend their lives swimming in mid-water, well above the sea bed, where they form shoals that can be both extremely large and very dense. The diet of these fish consists mainly of small planktonic animals, such as copepods, as well as juvenile fish. Pelagic fish have streamlined bodies and powerful muscles and are capable of sustained swimming over long distances, many species following regular migrations over distances of hundreds or thousands of kilometres. Their dark upper surface and silvery sides and underside help to camouflage them in the light conditions encountered in mid-water in the oceans. As shown in Table 12, a few species do not fit neatly into either group as their lifestyles exhibit characteristics typical of both demersal and pelagic fish.

In the waters around Shetland (and throughout the North Sea) different depths and sea-bed sediment types tend to have different assemblages of demersal fish species. In the waters to the north and west of Shetland the demersal fish assemblage is characterized by saithe (44%), haddock (12%), Norway pout (11%), whiting (9%), blue whiting (4%) and cod (4%), while to the east the dominant species are haddock (42%), whiting (14%), cod (9%), Norway pout (5%) and saithe (4%).

The spawning grounds of fish that spawn their eggs into the water column (as most do) are widely distributed over the continental shelf, the eggs drifting freely as part of the plankton. However, a few species, including herring and sandeels, lay eggs that adhere to the sea bed and so remain in one place during their development. These fish have much more localized spawning grounds that are determined by the availability of an appropriate sediment (gravel in the case of herring, sand for sandeels) and good water exchange to oxygenate the developing eggs.

Depending on species, young fish spend the first 1–7 months after hatching as larvae before metamorphosing into young fish. During this period the larval fish form part of the zooplankton, drifting with the sea's currents and feeding on phytoplanktonic and other zooplanktonic organisms. As has been mentioned earlier, the vast majority of young fish do not survive this phase of their lives, most either starving or being eaten. The survival rate of fish larvae, however, plays a key role in determining the abundance of adult fish; the gadoid outburst of the 1960s, for example, was a result of improved survival of gadoid larvae.

FISHING AROUND SHETLAND

It were as if the mould
was the trough of a wave
taken by the eye to the land
and by the hand filled around
with larch. First with adze
he carved out the wooden keel
to lie as heavy flotsam
against the drag of the sea,
and then with template, bowed
the strakes like swans' wings
from stem to stern, and finally
he cut the ribs – a wishbone
for their flight.

Willie's Shetland Boat, Laughton Johnston

Fish have been an important resource for Shetlanders since the islands were first settled some 5000 years ago. For much of this period fishing was carried out from small open boats, initially using hand-lines to catch species such as cod, saithe and ling. Perhaps the most significant influence on fishing in Shetland was the arrival of the Vikings between AD 800 and 900, with their technologically advanced sea-going ships. These wooden, clinker-built, double-ended craft combined stability and seaworthiness with strength and lightness, and their significance to the future development of Shetland's fisheries was immense. Fishing boats such as the *yoal*, *fourareen* and *sixern* that were to develop in Shetland, and which were the dominant craft in the islands until little more than a century ago, were their direct descendants.

Commercial fishing began in Shetland in the twelfth century with dried cod and ling being exported to Europe, initially via the Hanseatic League's merchants in Bergen and, from the fifteenth century onwards, via German merchants who came to Shetland each summer to trade directly with the islanders. The islanders caught cod and ling from small boats on inshore fishing grounds (usually within 16 km of the shore) using long-lines, lines of baited hooks laid along the sea bed, which had by this time been introduced to the islands. Their catches were sold to the German merchants, who cured the fish by drying them on clean stony beaches and were either salted or unsalted. In exchange the islanders received fishing gear, cloth, meal, alcohol, tobacco and other goods, as well as cash. This trade continued in Shetland until the early eighteenth century, when the German merchants were forced out by new laws, particularly the Salt Tax, brought in following the union of Scotland and England to obstruct foreigners trading on British soil.

Following the departure of the German merchants a locally based fishing industry developed, with the lairds (landowners) themselves exporting fish to Europe (see Chapter 3). About this time the *sixern*, a relatively large (7.5 to 9 m) open boat propelled by six oars or a sail, was introduced to the islands. Being larger and more seaworthy than the boats used hitherto they allowed fishing to extend to new grounds some 50–80 km offshore, primarily to the north and west of Shetland. The fishery that developed on these deep-sea fishing grounds, and which was to dominate Shetland life for more than 150 years, came to be known as the *haaf* or *far haaf*, *haaf* being the Old Norse word for ocean; this era is today seen as something of a heroic age.

The *sixerns* made trips of 2 or 3 days' duration during the summer months, setting long-lines some 11–13 km in length with about 1000–1200 baited hooks. The principal fish caught were cod, ling and saithe, which were cured by salting and drying on stony beaches. An average catch for a *sixern* was about 5 tonnes, and at the height of the *haaf* fishery, in the early nineteenth century, some 2500 tonnes of fish were being landed annually.

Despite their seaworthiness the *sixerns*, far out in the open ocean, were vulnerable to the gales that can spring up even in summer in Shetland. In the worst disaster a sudden gale in July 1832 resulted in the loss of 31 boats and 105 men, while in 1881 10 boats and 51 men were lost in similar circumstances. Such losses were felt particularly hard in Shetland as many of the men lost came from the same small communities and even from the same families. The 1881 disaster badly shook the long-standing confidence in the *sixern*, which in addition to appearing less safe than the decked fishing boats that were starting to appear in Shetland was increasingly unable to compete with them economically. The final blow to the *haaf* fishery came from the Truck Commission Report of 1872 and the Crofters' Act of 1886, which crushed the power of the lairds and freed the tenant fishermen from their serfdom (see Chapter 3).

In the nineteenth century Shetlanders began, for the first time, to progress beyond the small open fishing boats they had been using till then and break into two major 'new' fisheries, for cod and herring, which Dutch fishermen had been pursuing in Shetland waters for several centuries using large seaworthy sailing vessels.

The cod fishery started in Shetland with the investment in larger sailing vessels or 'smacks', fore and aft rigged vessels of up to about 35 tonnes in size. Unlike the *sixerns*, the smacks were able to stay at sea for more than a couple of days at a time and trips of a week to 10 days became the norm in 'home' waters, with a good catch being about 25–30 tonnes. By the 1860s over 1000 men, one-third of Shetland's fishermen, were regularly employed on the smacks and the cod fishery had spread beyond Shetland to Faroe, Iceland and Rockall and, eventually, as far as west Greenland and the North Cape of Norway. The fishery declined towards the end of the nineteenth century as a result of decreasing catches, increasing competition from other countries, the growth of the more attractive herring fishery and the increasing difficulty of obtaining crews; many of the ambitious young men were being attracted into the merchant navy where conditions were better and their wages guaranteed.

Herring, on the other hand, were fished with drift nets in which the shoals of herring became trapped as they tried to swim through the meshes. The fishery boomed in the early 1830s but collapsed as rapidly as it had grown, probably due to a scarcity of herring in local waters. Further damage to the fishery was caused in 1840 by a great storm that sank at least 30 boats at sea and destroyed the rest of the fleet's nets, leading to the failure of the Shetland Bank and of the main local supplier of fishing gear. Herring shoals returned to the traditional fishing grounds in the 1850s, but it was not until the 1870s that the industry picked up momentum once more, thanks to the opening of new markets and the adoption of large, fully decked, sailing drifters that could pursue the herring further afield (up to 112 km offshore) in years of apparent failure. The first steam drifters appeared in Shetland in 1900 and by the end of the decade over 500 were operating in Shetland waters. With this boom in the herring fishery, curing stations sprang up all over the islands, wherever suitable harbours existed, to process the catches; the gutted herring were packed in barrels of salt, mainly for export to Germany and Russia.

The introduction in 1894 of selling fish by auction and, later, the advent of the steam drifters, which required more sophisticated harbour facilities where coal and water were available, resulted in a steady centralization of the curing industry in a few places: Lerwick, Scalloway, Baltasound and Sandwick; later, most particularly in Lerwick. By 1905 over half the entire Scottish herring catch was landed in Shetland but the fishery declined thereafter possibly due to one of the periodic changes in the movements of the herring shoals, until the First World War brought a virtual end to the fishery.

With the decline of the long-line fishery before and after the First World War catches of large fish, such as ling and cod, decreased. At the same time the winter small-line fishery for small fish, such as haddock and whiting, was maintained, so that as total demersal catches decreased, the proportion of small fish increased. Although the demersal fishery in Shetland between the wars was merely a small-scale subsidiary to the enfeebled herring fishery, it established the basis on which the local fishing industry was to develop after the Second World War: the supply of fresh haddock and whiting to the British market.

The post-war years saw the development of what was virtually a completely new fishing industry in Shetland, with one of the most important changes being the wholesale adoption of the reliable, economical and powerful diesel engine, which, in addition to lower fuel, maintenance and repair costs, enabled fishing vessels for the first time to tow fishing gear such as the seine net across the sea bed. Another

59.   *Traditional yoals, Westing, Unst: beautiful examples of the local boats that still faithfully follow the Norse design introduced to Shetland some 1200 years ago.* (Courtesy of R. J. Tulloch.)

important change in the post-war fishing industry was the widespread adoption of the seine net, which is designed to catch demersal fish in a light sock-like net with long protruding wings. The seine net has a higher catch rate than lines, but it can only be used on clean, flat, sandy sea beds, as any obstructions will catch the warps and net as they are hauled.

In the post-war decade the converted sailing boats of the Shetland fleet were largely replaced by purpose-built, diesel-engined, dual-purpose inshore fishing vessels of up to 21 m in length designed for fishing with either drift net or seine net. Following an initial post-war upswing the herring fishery again declined. However, after the mid-1950s the herring stocks became more stable and a more profitable fishery was once again established for the next decade or so.

There was an abrupt change in the pace of fishing around Shetland with the arrival in the mid-1960s of a fleet of modern Norwegian purse-seine fishing vessels. While a drifter would consider 5 tonnes of herring to be a good night's catch, the pursers could take more than 100 tonnes with a single cast of the net. Following a slow start, Shetland fishermen gradually adopted the new technology, initially in relatively small multi-purpose vessels equipped for purse-seining, demersal seining and for trawling. Although these vessels' catches were comparatively small compared with the Norwegian pursers, they were consistently better than the drift netters. The success of the new vessels soon led to the demise of the dual-purpose fishing vessel in the early 1970s, with the local fleet splitting into seine-net boats, which fished for demersal species such as cod, haddock and whiting, and the new pursers, which fished exclusively for pelagic species.

Since the 1970s the successive generations of Shetland pursers have grown in size and sophistication. The collapse of North Sea herring stocks in the 1970s was largely offset by the development of a fishery for mackerel, which is still fished in

60.   Serene *(1995)*, *pelagic trawler: a modern Shetland fishing boat and part of the backbone of the industry that has been important to Shetlanders for hundreds of years.* (Courtesy of I. Napier.)

addition to the recovered North Sea herring and, in recent years, Atlanto-Scandian herring in the Norwegian Sea far to the north of Shetland. The mid-1990s, however, saw the replacement of all the local pursers by more flexible pelagic trawlers, which tow immense trawl nets in mid-water (i.e. well above the sea bed) down to depths of several hundred metres. Unlike the pursers, which were limited to catching dense shoals of fish near the surface, the pelagic trawlers can target shoals at greater depth as well as more scattered shoals of fish. The current vessels in the Shetland fleet are 60 m or more in length and can carry up to 1000 tonnes of fish in refrigerated sea-water tanks to keep the catch fresh.

The demersal sector too has seen large changes since the 1970s, primarily the widespread adoption of the trawl net in place of the seine. The local demersal fleet is now composed almost entirely of modern steel-hulled vessels, although a few wooden-hulled trawler/seine netters still remain.

The cod, saithe and ling, which have been the mainstay of Shetland's commercial fisheries since the twelfth century, continue to be important components of demersal fish catches today, together with the haddock and whiting which became important early this century. Since the mid-1980s, however, there has been a dramatic growth in the importance of monk fish (angler fish), a species that until then had been discarded as it had no market. However, monks now attract high prices and account for about one-third by value of all demersal fish landings in Shetland.

Despite the growth of commercial fishing in Shetland, the tradition of small-scale inshore fishing for personal consumption is still carried on in Shetland today, as it has been for 5000 years. Known locally as *da eela*, this fishery is carried out with rod or hand-line from small boats within a few kilometres of the shore. Today, though, *da eela* is a leisure pursuit, a pleasant way to spend a fine evening, rather than, as it was not so long ago, a necessity for survival.

Vaila darkenin fae aest ta wast,
wind faa'n awa;
eela nichts i da simmer dim

Gyaain Ta Da Eela, Christine De Luca

SHELLFISH

In addition to the demersal and pelagic sectors, an important fishery for shellfish has developed in Shetland since the 1960s. We know that prehistoric humans harvested intertidal shellfish such as limpets, cockles and razorshells (*spoots*), the latter still harvested on a subsistence basis. Species such as the common mussel and horse mussel were important sources of bait for the small-line fishery, and large quantities of oysters were harvested commercially at the end of the nineteenth century until overexploitation destroyed the beds.

Commercial exploitation of shellfish did not really start until after the Second World War, when improved transport links made it possible to ship lobsters alive to mainland markets. The lobster fishery boomed in the early 1960s but stocks collapsed and as they have never recovered the fishery has continued since then at a relatively low level. Fishing for edible crabs also started in the 1960s and despite a decline through the 1970s is now once more increasing in importance. Scallop fishing started in the late 1960s with queen scallops following soon after; the former continues to be an important local fishery, although the queen fishery has all but collapsed. Fisheries have started for a number of new species in recent years, including whelks for export to the Far East, scampi, periwinkles and razorshells.

Although the quantities of shellfish landed in Shetland are relatively small (about 1% of all fish landings), their relatively high value means that the shellfishery accounts for about 10% by value of local landings. Recent years have seen a steady increase in fishing effort for shellfish, with more boats joining the fleet and an increase in their size and power, and there are fears that some species may again be overexploited with possible detrimental effects. In an effort to improve the management of local shellfish stocks a local body has been set up to apply to the government for a Regulating Order, which would give them powers to manage shellfish fishing in Shetland's inshore waters. Plans are also being developed to enhance lobster stocks through the release of large quantities of post-larval juveniles raised in hatcheries.

INDUSTRIAL FISHING

Industrial fishing refers to the use of fish for purposes other than direct human consumption. Instead, the fish are usually reduced to fish-meal and oil, which are in turn used in the production of animal feeds, some human foods and, more recently, feeds for farmed fish, especially salmon. Industrial fishing has always attracted criticism from those who regard it as a 'waste' of fish that could be used for direct human consumption. Other concerns have centred around the effects of harvesting small fish near the bottom of the food chain on other commercial fish species or on other marine organisms, such as mammals and seabirds, which may depend on them to a greater or lesser extent for food.

The issue is not, however, as simple as is often portrayed. Although some of the raw material for the production of fish-meal comes from directed industrial fisheries, where fish are harvested specifically for reduction, many of the species caught are not suitable for direct human consumption or have no markets for human consumption. In addition, surplus fish from conventional food fisheries (when supply exceeds demand), and offal from fish processors, are also significant sources. The question of the possible effects of industrial fishing on other marine organisms remains, however, an open question.

Industrial fish processing began in Shetland in the 1880s, when factories were built on Unst and Bressay to produce fish manure (i.e. fertilizer), and later fish-meal and oil, from surplus and spoiled herring catches. This continued throughout the century, with surplus herring and white fish reduced regularly to fish-meal, although only the Bressay factory survives. The 1960s saw the first directed industrial fishery in Shetland waters (although there was no Shetland participation) with Norwegian fishing vessels targeting herring. In the absence of any controls on catches the Norwegians took up to 600 000 tonnes of herring per annum from Shetland waters for reduction to fish-meal, contributing to the collapse of North Sea herring stocks in the early 1970s.

During the early 1970s there was a small local fishery for sprat, a small pelagic fish, in some Shetland voes, with most of the catches being reduced to fish-meal. Sprat first appeared around Shetland in large numbers in 1965 and had largely disappeared again by 1978, but between those years there was a large spawning population centred on the Fair Isle area. Catches peaked at almost 700 tonnes per annum in 1973 but this was exceptional, catches in other years being not much more than, and often less than, 100 tonnes.

It seems likely that the appearance, and disappearance, of sprat in Shetland waters was associated with the periodical environmental changes (mentioned earlier) in the seas around Shetland, which allowed them to extend their range northwards in the mid-1960s but pushed them back to their more normal range in the central and southern North Sea in the late 1970s. There have been occasional catches of sprat since 1978 but there has never been another local fishery.

A second short-lived industrial fishery took place in Shetland waters in the 1970s for Norway pout, and by 1974 the annual catch by the local fleet had reached almost 10 000 tonnes. However, the fishery was the subject of strong criticism from the main demersal sector of the local and UK fishing fleets because of the large numbers of immature haddock and whiting that were unavoidably caught with the Norway pout. Scientific studies supported the fishermen's claims and the European Commission then introduced various legislation to reduce the *bycatch* of immature whitefish. As a result, interest in the Norway pout fishery waned rapidly in Shetland after 1975 and the fishery ceased altogether in 1980.

A third fish, the sandeel, has been the subject of industrial fishing in Shetland waters in recent years. The sandeel is one of the most abundant fish in the North Sea, making up 10–15% of the total fish biomass (see Table 12). Five species of

61.   *Sandeels: these little fish are a vital component of the marine food chain, supporting the larger fish, seabirds, cetaceans, seals and, of course, the fishermen of Shetland.* (Courtesy of R. J. Tulloch.)

sandeel are found in Shetland and UK waters: three species of lesser sandeel that grow to lengths of up to 20 cm; and two species of greater sandeel that reach around 45 cm. Of these, *Ammodytes marinus*, a lesser sandeel, is by far the most abundant and forms the basis of both the Shetland sandeel fishery and the other North Sea fisheries. The sandeel fishery is without doubt the most controversial local fishery of recent years because of the importance of sandeels in the diets of many other marine animals, including fish, seals and seabirds, and in particular because of the fishery's implication in the disastrous breeding failures of several seabird species in the mid and late 1980s (see Chapter 8). Furness (1990) has estimated the proportion and quantities consumed at Shetland by the various predators (Table 13); note that he estimates that around 30% are consumed by seabirds and only 7% by seals.

Sandeels are small eel-like fish that divide their time (both on a daily and seasonal basis) between free-swimming in dense shoals and lying buried in sandy sediments. Although sandeels are found throughout the North Sea, those around Shetland have generally been considered as a distinct stock and the Shetland

TABLE 13   *Estimated quantities of sandeels consumed by the various groups of natural predators and caught by the industrial fishery at Shetland, 1981–83* (from Furness, 1990)

Consumer	Best estimate of consumption (tonnes)	Probable min. and max. consumed (tonnes)
Industrial fishery	45 000	
Seabirds	47 000	33 000; 62 000
Predatory fish	25 000	12 000; 50 000
Seals	9 000	4 000; 15 000
Total consumed per year	126 000	
Estimated production	100 000	

sandeel fishery as separate from other North Sea fisheries. Sandeels have been fished in the North Sea since the 1960s but the Shetland fishery only started in 1974. From an initial annual catch of 8000 tonnes, and in the absence of any regulation of the fishery, catches increased rapidly to a peak in 1982 of over 52 600 tonnes with a value of around £1 million. This fishery was mainly pursued by vessels that fished for whitefish in winter and sandeels in summer.

Sandeels have patchy distributions, but in Shetland waters are commonly found over sandy substrata in depths between 20 and 70 m. The fishery is limited to areas suitable for towing the light trawls needed to catch them, and which provides economic catch rates, but constitutes only a small proportion of the area over which sandeels are found. A 10% bycatch limit further restricts the fishery to areas where bycatch species are mainly absent, although the average bycatch rate in Shetland waters is much less than this (2% other sandeel species and less than 1% other fish species on average).

In Shetland waters, sandeels spawn (Fig. 19) over sandy substrata in December– January, the demersal eggs adhering to sand grains. The larvae occur in the plankton from February to April and metamorphose into the adult form at a length of 3–4 cm during May and June. These 0-group sandeels (so called because they are less than 1 year old, i.e. '0' years old) are first taken by the fishery in June when they are 4–6 cm long, and their major entry to the fishery takes place in July. The Shetland sandeel fishery was unusual in that it depended heavily on 0-group sandeels, which predominated in catches from July onwards when the catch rates of older sandeels diminished.

After 1982 sandeel catches in Shetland waters decreased rapidly, falling to 12 000 tonnes in 1986 and only 1500 tonnes in 1989 (Fig. 20). Although there was a decrease in fishing effort during this period of decline, as decreasing sandeel prices and increasing whitefish prices encouraged boats to abandon the sandeel fishery and concentrate on whitefish all year round, there is no doubt that there was a substantial real decline in sandeel abundance in Shetland waters during this time.

As discussed more fully in the next chapter, several species of seabirds that breed in Shetland suffered increasingly severe breeding failures from about 1980 onwards. Given the coincidence of breeding failures in seabirds that rely on 0-group sandeels and a fishery that was taking large quantities of these same 0-group sandeels (and whose catches soon went into decline), it is not surprising that many people concluded that the fishery was directly responsible for the decline in sandeel abundance and, consequently, for the seabird breeding failures. In 1988, in recognition of a declining resource, Shetland fishermen introduced a voluntary restriction on the catch of 0-group sandeels. However, pressure from seabird groups and the declining catches eventually resulted in the Scottish Office officially closing the Shetland sandeel fishery part way through the 1990 season, although the fishery had by then virtually ceased anyway.

As a result of the seabird breeding crisis, a number of research programmes were initiated in the late 1980s to study the summer food supplies of the most affected seabird species, the distribution and biology of sandeels in Shetland waters, and the links between the two. The results of the investigation of sandeel biology indicated for the first time that the Shetland sandeel stock was not, as had been generally believed, a discrete self-reproducing stock. Although sandeels do reproduce in

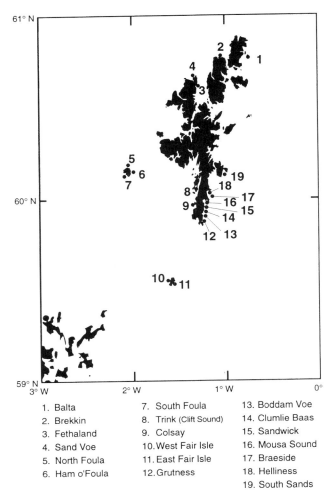

FIGURE 19   *Sandeel fishery grounds around Shetland* (from Wright & Bailey, 1993).

1. Balta	7. South Foula	13. Boddam Voe
2. Brekkin	8. Trink (Clift Sound)	14. Clumlie Baas
3. Fethaland	9. Colsay	15. Sandwick
4. Sand Voe	10. West Fair Isle	16. Mousa Sound
5. North Foula	11. East Fair Isle	17. Braeside
6. Ham o'Foula	12. Grutness	18. Helliness
		19. South Sands

Shetland waters, there is a major influx every year of juvenile sandeels spawned on grounds to the west of Orkney and which are transported northwards as planktonic larvae into Shetland waters, where they metamorphose and join, or are 'recruited' to, the local sandeel stock as 0-group sandeels. It now appears that this annual recruitment may be the most important factor determining the abundance of 0-group (and so of older) sandeels in Shetland waters.

There is good evidence that this recruitment of sandeels into the Shetland stock largely failed during the 1980s, although the reasons for this are uncertain. The most likely explanation is that for some reason the larvae spawned off Orkney did not reach Shetland waters (or if they did, they did not survive). In the absence of this annual 'top-up' local reproduction would have been unable to maintain the Shetland sandeel stock at its normal size, so the stock (and the fishery) declined, while the resulting shortage of 0-group sandeels affected the seabirds that feed on

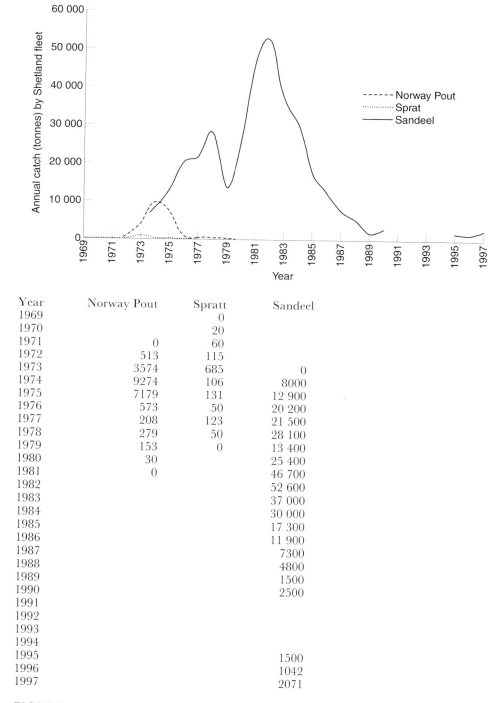

Year	Norway Pout	Spratt	Sandeel
1969		0	
1970		20	
1971	0	60	
1972	513	115	
1973	3574	685	0
1974	9274	106	8000
1975	7179	131	12 900
1976	573	50	20 200
1977	208	123	21 500
1978	279	50	28 100
1979	153	0	13 400
1980	30		25 400
1981	0		46 700
1982			52 600
1983			37 000
1984			30 000
1985			17 300
1986			11 900
1987			7300
1988			4800
1989			1500
1990			2500
1991			
1992			
1993			
1994			
1995			1500
1996			1042
1997			2071

FIGURE 20 *Annual catch off Shetland of sandeel, Norway pout and sprat 1969–97.* (Courtesy of Ian Napier, NAFC)

them. While the fishery would have hastened the decline in abundance of older sandeels, fisheries scientists do not believe that it could have significantly affected the abundance of 0-group sandeels.

There is good evidence that a number of subtle changes in physical and biological conditions have occurred throughout the north-east Atlantic and North Sea over the last 30 years or so, such as a slight increase in surface water temperature, a gradual delay in the spring phytoplankton bloom and a decrease in zooplankton abundance. It seems likely, therefore, that rather than being an isolated local phenomenon Shetland's sandeel crisis was tied into much wider-scale oceanographic fluctuations. Rather than being the villains of the piece, as has been widely supposed, it may be that the Shetland sandeel fishermen were to some extent as much victims of greater forces as the seabirds were.

The Shetland sandeel stock apparently enjoyed high levels of recruitment in the early 1990s and evidence of increased sandeel stocks soon led to calls for the fishery to be reopened. The Scottish Office eventually agreed to this in 1995 for a trial period of 3 years, but under tight restrictions. Most importantly, an annual quota of 3000 tonnes was set, the fishery was limited to vessels under 18 m in length and the fishery was closed at the end of June, before the period when seabirds need sandeels for their chicks. A locally based sandeel data collection and monitoring programme has also been initiated by the North Atlantic Fisheries College, with partial funding from the European Union and in conjunction with the Scottish Office's Marine Laboratory in Aberdeen, to continue and extend the work previously carried out by the Marine Laboratory.

Up to half a dozen local boats annually have fished for sandeels since the fishery reopened, but they have consistently failed to reach their quota, taking only between 1000 and 1500 tonnes per annum. This might reflect a shortage in the abundance of sandeels but could arise from a variety of other reasons, including the effects of poor weather on the small boats allowed to participate in the fishery, the early closure of the fishery and the attractions of other fisheries (such as scalloping) that can offer better returns than sandeel fishing. What will happen to the fishery after 1997, when the 3-year trial period ends, remains to be seen.

AQUACULTURE

Fish farming only began in earnest in Shetland in 1980, yet in less than 20 years it has expanded into a major industry that now produces a greater income than the centuries-old fish-catching industry (see Fig. 39).

Shetland's waters are too cold for many species which are farmed in other parts of the world, but are ideally suited to the growing of Atlantic salmon. Shetland's numerous voes provide sheltered sites for the floating cages in which the salmon are grown, while the long summer days enhance the growth of the salmon during their main growing season. The oceanic currents that flow around Shetland provide water of stable and relatively mild temperature and stable salinity (thanks also to limited run-off of fresh water from the land), all factors that encourage the growth of salmon. Finally, strong tidal currents, wind and wave action flush out the voes (and the detritus from the fish farms), providing a continuous source of clean water. Here

62. *Salmon cages: aquaculture is now more important economically than deep-sea fishing and there is hardly a voe or sound without its salmon farm.* (Courtesy of R. J. Tulloch.)

Shetland scores over many too-sheltered sites on the west coast of Scotland and in Norwegian fiords, where limited water exchange can result in large fluctuations in salinity and water temperature, the accumulation of fish farm waste and a general deterioration in water quality, all of which reduce salmon growth rate.

Salmon farming is an intensive farming process, with large numbers of fish being grown in very small areas, large inputs of feed and, increasingly, inputs of various chemicals and drugs to treat the diseases and infestations that afflict farmed fish. These factors have given rise to considerable concerns about the effects that salmon farming may have on the marine environment and these are discussed in Chapter 12.

CETACEANS

There are very few natural history sights as moving as the emergence of a leviathan from the deep. In Shetland, experiencing the overwhelming numbers

Whales and shearwaters

and cacophony of a large seabird colony or attempting to combat a winter gale on the Atlantic coast as it hurls huge rollers on the shore perhaps comes closest. However, neither elicit the mystery and the frisson of fear at the appearance, and almost as abrupt disappearance, of something that was not there a moment before. Something immense, alive and breathing; for if one is close enough there is a sound like a gasp for air as the back breaks the waves, in reality exhalation rather than inhalation.

In 1996, details of cetacean sightings from seismic survey vessels around the British Isles were recorded for the Joint Nature Conservation Committee, in connection with assessing the effects of seismic surveys on these animals. Although the survey did not cover the whole sea area around the British Isles, the findings showed three important areas for cetaceans, by far the most important being the edge of the continental shelf and the deep sea not far to the north-west of Shetland (Fig. 21). Four of the five most frequently sighted species are the fin, pilot and killer whales and the white-sided dolphin, all in this area and in the summer months most commonly. It is not perhaps surprising therefore that individuals of the large

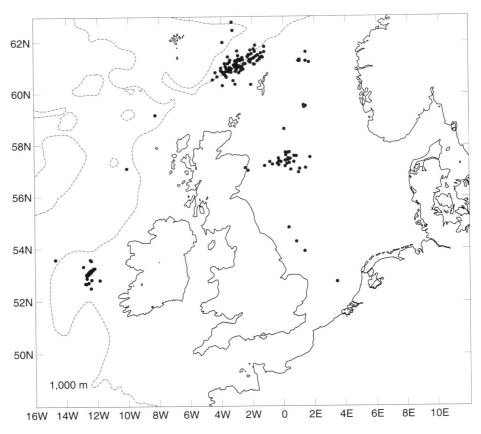

FIGURE 21   *Cetacean sightings (all species) from seismic survey vessels during 1996* (from Stone, 1997).

whales, which prefer the deep waters, are regular visitors to Shetland, while some of the smaller whales are regular, if not common, visitors closer inshore. Shetland must be one of the best places in Britain to see a whole variety of cetaceans, whose numbers by and large appear to be no less than they were prior to the whaling industries of the last few hundred years. One of the most recent concerns of marine mammal experts is the possible disturbance factor to whales from seismic soundings in oil exploration, an activity fairly common in the North Sea and western Atlantic in recent years. However there is no evidence of long-term harm at the moment and it may be that cetaceans become habituated to the noise, just as terrestrial animals have become habituated to our many activities on land.

Shetlanders have been familiar with whales for as long as they have voyaged. Particularly to the west and north of the islands, they would occasionally have come across both large baleen whales, such as the fin and the sei feeding mainly on planktonic crustacea, and large-toothed whales, such as the sperm. Nearshore the largest whale seen would probably have been one of the smaller baleen whales, the minke or *herring hog* as it is known by Shetland fishermen, which grows to about 9 m, less than half that of many of the larger species. Inshore they would undoubtedly have encountered the killer whale hunting seals and the much smaller *caain'* or log-finned pilot whale, as well as abundant *neesick* or harbour porpoise and several dolphin species.

Although whales of all sizes are occasionally stranded – whalebones have been found associated with humans even from the Bronze Age – Shetlanders would have exploited cetaceans just as soon as they had the capability. The traditional local catch was only of the *caain'*, which is the most common whale seen off the coast of north Scotland. This 'small' black whale grows to almost 8 m, feeds mainly on squid and fish and is found usually in a pod of a number of individuals. It often comes close to the Shetland shore and is particularly seen during the winter months. There are several recent records of strandings, including a large pod of 40 at Hillswick in 1983, of which several were successfully refloated. In the past when a pod ventured into the confined waters of bays or voes, boats were launched and the whales driven or *caa'd* into shallow water, where they were stranded and killed. Only the blubber was utilized, being boiled and turned into oil, while the carcasses were left to rot, attracting the local carrion-eating birds in large numbers. In Faroe this practice still continues, but there the meat is eaten as well, being considered a delicacy.

The largest known *caa* was at Quendale in South Mainland in 1845 when some 1540 animals were killed, while the last known *caa* was of 83 animals at Weisdale in 1903. Many *caas* were of well over 100 animals, so the whale must have been present in large numbers in the nineteenth century. Between 1969 and 1973, Captain Alan Whitfield, the local Loganair pilot, recorded over 2000 individuals with pods numbering seven to over 100 individuals. In recent years pods seen have been generally smaller, but one of 100 individuals was seen some way off Foula in 1994.

In the late eighteenth and early nineteenth centuries many Shetlanders were engaged at the Greenland whaling (see Chapter 3), despite the protestations and threats from the lairds who wanted the men for their fishing industry. At that time hunting was confined to open boats and the pursuit of the slower whales. These were harpooned and then killed with lances. In the late nineteenth century modern whaling was founded with steam-powered catchers, using an explosive harpoon fired from a cannon mounted on the bow. This technique allowed the exploitation of the previously little-hunted faster species such as the fin and sei, and those such as the blue whale which sinks on death. Whaling stations then sprang up all round the North Atlantic from Newfoundland to Spitsbergen.

The Greenland whaling collapsed before the turn of the twentieth century, by which time there were whaling stations in Iceland and Faroe. In north Norway whaling was banned as a result of a bitter dispute with cod fishermen and the Norwegian companies involved with the whaling had to look elsewhere for new bases, such as Shetland. However even in Shetland there was a dispute at this time between the herring fishery, the most important industry in Shetland at that time, and the whalers. The herring fishermen suffered damaged nets from whales, believed that they consumed large amounts of herring, which proved to be unfounded and also believed that the pollution of blood and offal from the shore stations drove off the herring. In 1903 two whaling stations were set up in Shetland, firstly at Ronas Voe, followed in 1904 by two more, at Olnafirth and Collafirth, but because of the complaints from the herring fishermen they were forced to hunt farther offshore. At the same time, whaling stations were set up in Ireland and in the Hebrides; however the Shetland stations were always the most important.

Of the 4893 whales recorded in the 12 operating seasons before the First World War, 67% were fin and 30% sei. Between the end of the war and the termination of whaling from Shetland in 1929, some 1500 whales were caught in nine seasons, the species ratio being similar, although all species except the blue whale showed a net decrease (Table 14). Before the First World War there was no evidence for overexploitation, but afterwards it became obvious that the stocks of whales passing through Shetland waters, particularly blue, humpback and right whales, were not large enough to sustain the hunting pressure. Of the west North Atlantic species, neither the blue whale nor the right whale have been seen in Shetland waters since; however the humpback is now a regular visitor again and has been recorded in successive years since 1992. These sightings and others elsewhere off the west coast of Britain suggest this species has recovered to pre-exploitation levels. The sperm whale population was never hunted to the same degree and is presumably relatively stable. Although a deep-water species, it has regularly been recorded in Shetland waters in recent years. All the individuals are males as the females remain in warmer waters.

The whaling season in Shetland lasted from April to September, not because of the restrictions of winter weather but because this is the season that the larger

TABLE 14   *Species of whale landed at Shetland during the whaling 1903–14 and 1920–29* (from Berry & Johnston, 1980)

	Blue	Fin	Humpback	Sei	Right	Sperm	Bottle-nosed
1903–14	25	3287	49	1492	6	11	23
1920–29	60	1069	2	347	0	8	2

63. *Killer whales and grey seals: these large predators have become almost a common spectacle around Shetland, striking fear and confusion into the seal population when they appear.* (Courtesy of B. Jackson.)

whales generally make their appearance in northern waters. As the spring sunshine warms the surface waters of the sea, a relatively dense phytoplankton 'soup' develops on which growing numbers of zooplankton graze, and on which the herring, mackerel, sprat and whales come to feed. Towards the end of the summer, the baleen whales at least depart to warmer waters. It is clear from the catches of the British whaling stations that most of the large whales, such as the right whale and the largest of them all, the blue whale, were caught to the west of Britain and few were to be found in the north around Shetland.

These larger whales perform an annual migration from warmer waters, where they have their young, to colder waters in the North Atlantic, where they come to feed. The migration routes of the blue, the right and the humpback lie to the west of Britain and Faroe. The fin and the sei, on the other hand, appear to migrate through the Shetland–Faroe Channel, although both appear to prefer to remain far offshore beyond the 180-m contour. The smallest of the baleen whales, the minke, which occurs in Scottish waters throughout the year, is one of the commonest whales to be seen from the Shetland shore. In the last few years there have been many more sightings of this species in Shetland, particularly from June to September, off the south-east coast, possibly filling the niche vacated by the larger whales after their overexploitation. International protection has been given to the humpback since 1955 and to the blue since 1960. The Norwegians have stepped up their kill of minke whales in the North Sea from 23 in 1996 to 57 in 1997 and it has been suggested that this may have an effect on the numbers around Shetland. However, the Norwegians reassuringly point out that the north-east Atlantic population is estimated to be around 12 000.

Undoubtedly, the other common whale in Shetland waters is the spectacular killer whale. Captain Whitfield, the local Loganair pilot, recorded 127 sightings of over 600 individuals in the 4 years between 1969 and 1973, generally between April and October and usually in fast tidal streams around headlands and between large islands. In the last few years the number of sightings has increased all around Shetland, the animals often in pods of 3–12 individuals and one record of a pod of 100 animals seen by fishermen off Muckle Flugga in late May 1995. This large (the male can grow in excess of 9 m) fast predator hunts large fish, seals and all the smaller whales, porpoises and dolphins. They are very distinctive and menacing, with their white markings underneath and behind a very large dorsal fin (the saddle patch) on an otherwise black background. In many parts of the world where killer whales are studied individuals are recognized by the pattern of their saddle patch or the nicks or notches in the dorsal fin. This latter approach is just being investigated in Shetland and it will be fascinating to find out a little more about the Shetland killer whale society and the movements and territories of the animals. Although usually in small pods, they can join to form large pods of up to 30 animals to hunt larger prey. Sometimes they herd dolphins to attack them, producing spectacular sights as their prey leap clear of the water in their attempts to escape. Recently it appears that the Shetland population of seals has become a target of killer whales, which have normally hunted further offshore. Pods of killer whales are now more regularly seen inshore around areas frequented by seals, for example around Sumburgh Head. In Shetland, where seals, although much loved, are seen to be a threat to salmon farms and other commercial fish species, this particular element of the killer diet is welcomed and the killer whale has been dubbed the *culler* whale. Killer it may be, but it is itself vulnerable: a stranded bull at Catfirth in 1994 was found to have died from an internal septic wound caused by a small fish-hook in its stomach. Like seabirds (see Chapter 8) killer whales are now being seen around whitefish boats and apparently benefiting from fish discard largesse. This is probably the source of the fish-hook in the Catfirth bull.

It used to be that when out on the sea on a summer's evening in Shetland fishing for a few days' supply of whitefish or mackerel, for the home and for the neighbour, invariably a few *neesicks* (harbour porpoise) would roll around a headland or an island and across the bay, often passing within yards of the boat. In the 1980s there was a decline in their presence, during the same period that several seabird species suffered declines in their breeding success. The *neesick* has declined more widely in north-west Europe as a whole, particularly in the southern part of the North Sea. However in Shetland they can still be seen in large groups, of up to 50, particularly off the east coast and in the summer months, and the Shetland population remains probably the largest in Britain.

The apparent decline in the population was picked up by Evans and Gilbert (1991) and others following surveys and repeated transects from 1977. Although the *neesick* is seen all round Shetland, it is most common in certain areas such as east of Yell Sound, Whalsay, Out Skerries, Bressay and from Mousa south to Sumburgh Head (Fig. 22). Although seen all year round, adults with newborn calves appear from after midsummer to late autumn; when they are observed foraging, the fish they appear to be most frequently associated with is the sandeel. It is undoubtedly no coincidence that the area of Shetland most frequented by the *neesick* is the south-east coast from Noss to Sumburgh, which is also one of the most important areas for sandeel fishing. One of the sandeel sites in that area, much frequented by seabirds in the summer months also, is Mousa Sound. Here the study found that almost all of *neesick* behaviour was related to foraging. The breeding failure of certain seabird species during the 1980s (see Chapter 8) was closely associated with the lack of young sandeels. The apparent decline in the *neesick* population, and signs of recovery in the late 1980s and early 1990s, mirrored the trends in these seabird species. Perhaps the decline was in the presence of *neesicks* reflecting a decline in sandeels-prey known to be important to these predators, rather than a decline in the actual neesick population. Does the *neesick* depend on an abundance of sandeels during the critical stage in July and August when it is raising its young, just like the guillemot, the shag and the *tirrick*? It appears so. An additional reason for the presence of adults and calves at this period of the year may be related to social behaviour and the need for the young to learn to forage for themselves in reasonably safe and food-rich waters.

Other small cetaceans that are regular visitors to Shetland waters include the Atlantic white-sided dolphin and the white-beaked dolphin. Both are North Atlantic species, but the latter is usually seen inshore more frequently than the former. Evans (1992) suggests that the white-beaked dolphin has been under-recorded in Shetland in the past because of its similarity to the white-sided dolphin and that the former is in fact the commonest dolphin in Shetland waters. These species are the most exuberant of the smaller cetaceans, leaping clear of the water

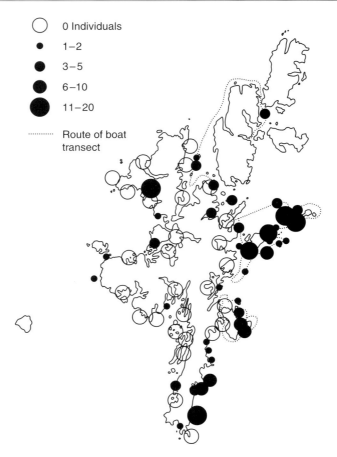

FIGURE 22   *Distribution of harbour porpoises in Shetland from land-based watches and boat transects (for timed watches, expressed as numbers of individuals per 100-minute observations) in 1992* (from Evans, 1992).

and bow-riding boats and ships; in Shetland tradition they have not been distinguished and are known as the *looper dog*. Both can be seen in the summer months in fairly large pods around headlands and off islands. The white-beaked is also seen regularly from the *Good Shepherd* plying between Shetland and Fair Isle. Other members of the dolphin family that are regularly seen in small numbers are the common dolphin, a creature normally of warmer waters but not seen annually, and Risso's dolphin, small pods of which are seen annually.

A complete list of the 21 (22 if doubtful records of the bottle-nosed are included) cetacean species occurring or recorded can be found in Appendix 3, but we cannot leave this section without mentioning two arctic species that have occurred. The first is a narwhal, apparently driven ashore in Weisdale in 1808; the second is the rare white whale or beluga, first seen by Whitfield in the early 1970s offshore, and on a second occasion seen very close, within 15 m, at Hoswick on South-east Mainland in 1996.

Today it appears that there are increasing sightings of a number of cetacean species around Shetland and not just because there are many more observers. One just has to look at the local paper through the summer months to see photographs and articles, with headlines such as 'Dolphins create a stir', 'Killer whales feast off Shetland', 'Whale of a tale', almost every week. Even a Shetland primary school nature outing was able to watch whales in 1996.

SEALS

In the month of June, at the height of the *simmer dim* when the long summer days stretch into and almost through the night and when the breeding birds are sitting on eggs or feeding young, the *selkie* or harbour seal hauls out in one of the small colonies under the protection of cliffs or on a skerry or uninhabited island and gives birth to her pup. Although one can come across harbour seals almost anywhere on the coast of Shetland, Mousa, where numbers can reach 500 in August, is one of the best places to see them (Fig. 23).

The other seal that breeds in Shetland, the grey seal, pups in the late autumn in October–November, when the weather may be at its most variable and often at its worst. When migratory breeding birds are far away to the south, when even the tenacious fulmar has vacated the cliffs and the boats are snug in their winter *noosts*, the grey seal female hauls out in small colonies, sometimes up to 100 individuals. She can be found on exposed cliff-foot beaches, in narrow *geos*, in caves, on skerries such as Ve Skerries and, very occasionally, on grassy islands such as Gruney in North Mainland and holms around Sumburgh (Fig. 24). There she gives birth to her young as far as possible above the reaches of the long winter swells that pound the shore.

These two seals are the only species normally found on the coasts bordering the temperate seas of the North Atlantic, although other vagrant species appear from time to time. To the non-expert, indeed sometimes to the expert, they can be hard to distinguish. However the grey seal is much the larger, with bulls around 2.3 m and cows 1.8 m, while the harbour seal bull is slightly smaller than the female grey and the harbour seal female a few centimetres smaller again. The difference between the sexes is therefore much greater in the grey than the harbour seal. The old Shetland name for the grey seal is the *haaf fish*, or deep-sea fish, and for the harbour seal, the *tang fish* or seaweed fish, indicating the former's preference for open sea conditions and the latter's preference for more sheltered shores. One of the most obvious distinguishing features is the shape of the head: the grey seal has a high muzzle and a 'roman nose'; in contrast the harbour seal has a low dog-like muzzle, with a relatively rounded head and distinct forehead, giving it a more expressive and appealing appearance.

In world conservation terms, the grey seal is the more important as it is largely confined to the eastern side of the North Atlantic, whereas there are five recognized subspecies of the harbour seal in the North Atlantic and North Pacific oceans. In the British Isles the population of the European subspecies of the harbour seal is around 28 000, of which, following the large-scale mortality of harbour seals in

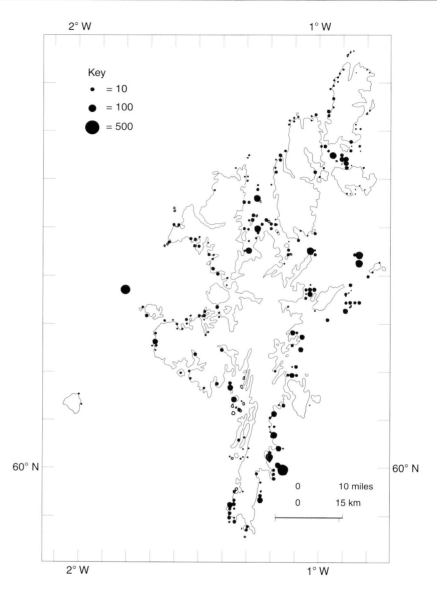

FIGURE 23   *Harbour seals in Shetland in August 1993.* (Courtesy of Sea Mammal Research Unit)

Europe from phocine distemper virus in 1988, the British population is 40%. The Shetland population is estimated to be 6200, i.e. 22% of the British population or 9% of the total population of the subspecies. The British population of grey seals, about 36% of the world population, is estimated to be around 115 000, by far the majority of which are in Scotland. The Shetland population, which has not been surveyed for several years, is estimated at 3500, just 3% of the British population. The Shetland harbour seal population is of interest in a British context as it occurs

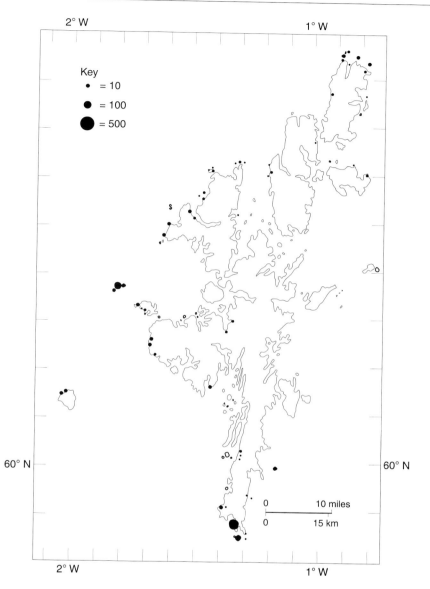

FIGURE 24 *Breeding sites and distribution of grey seals in August 1993.* (Courtesy of Sea Mammal Research Unit)

in much more exposed situations in the islands than it does on the mainland of Britain.

Seal history in Shetland is long and the bones of both grey and harbour seal have been found from Iron Age levels at Jarlshof, while the prefix *seli* (seal) in the names of many localities attest to their former abundance. In the past Shetlanders have hunted seals with nets in the sea, with clubs in the caves and latterly with rifles, but they have always had an ambiguous attitude towards them. Folklore of the northern and western isles has it that *selkies* possess magical powers and are able to cast off their skins and come ashore to bewitch the people.

> I am a man upo' the land
> I am a selchie in the sea
> And when I'm far frae every strand
> My home is on Sule Skerry

Traditionally this only occurred in Shetland at Johnsmas (midsummer) and folklore has it that many an islander has fallen in love with a *selchie* in their human guise and followed it back to the sea! Recently it has been suggested that the myth of the seal people may have stemmed from sightings of the Finns (from modern Lapland), whose culture was once very closely linked with the sea, some of whom may have been blown across the North Sea in their low-lying kayaks and mistaken for half-man, half-sea creature or seal.

Notwithstanding a certain fondness for seal, they were hunted in Shetland and their blubber used for oil, their skins for garments and *rivlins* (footwear) and their meat occasionally eaten. Most recently the main purpose of hunting was for skins for the fur trade and local knick-knacks. Although only the skin was utilized, the purpose of hunting remained as it had always been: a means of income and survival when times were hard.

The most valuable skins were those of the pup, particularly the harbour seal pup, followed by adult skins just after moult. As the harbour seal has her pups in fairly accessible places in the quiet month of June, they were the main target for shooting.

64.   *Harbour seals, Sandwick pier: the smaller and more sociable of the two seal species that occur and the one that generally prefers more sheltered waters.* (Courtesy of E. Brown.)

It was also the case that, whereas hunting the grey seal required a permit (since 1914), the harbour seal was unprotected until relatively recently. Protection for the harbour seal was in fact sought specifically because of their high rate of exploitation in Shetland.

Following the Second World War, the demand for sealskins increased and their value rose sufficiently to encourage the hard-pressed Shetlanders to take part in the sealskin trade. In the 1950s and 1960s the price continued to rise and many individuals took to hunting part-time at the weekends in addition to the existing hunting groups. Between 1960 and 1970 over 700 harbour seal pups were culled annually; it has been estimated that of the 1000 or so pups born in 1968, 900 were culled. What this meant was that there was very little recruitment to the population, which was slowly ageing. If hunting had not been controlled then eventually the existing adult population, which itself was being hunted at a much lower level, would have died out. In the late-1960s it was obvious that the Shetland population was decreasing. For example, at Fitful Head harbour seal numbers declined four-fold, from around 400 in the 1950s to around 100 in the early 1970s, and this pattern was repeated throughout the islands. Another indication of the pressure on the population was a delay in the date of breeding similar to that which occurred with heavily exploited elephant seal in South Georgia.

With the experience of Faroe in mind, where harbour seals were hunted to extinction this century, a Seals Conservation Bill was passed in 1970 to protect the harbour seal, requiring permits for hunting. A further survey of the population in 1971 revealed that it had slumped to 1800 animals, excluding the young of the year. In 1973, therefore, a total ban on hunting in Shetland was introduced on an annual basis. Happily a survey carried out in 1978 showed a marked improvement in the population to 3800 seals, with many more young animals. Although numbers rose to an estimated 4784 in 1991, this suggested a quite slow increase in the population, which may have been partly due to illegal control. Salmon farmers and other fishermen can obtain licences to cull 'rogue' seals, but it is well known that many more are culled regularly. As a result of the concern for the population, an order came into force in 1991 prohibiting the taking of harbour seals (except under licence) for an indefinite period. A further survey was carried out in 1993, which estimated that there were 6200 harbour seals; however pup recruitment still remains low. Notwithstanding, the Secretary of State for Scotland lifted the ban on killing harbour seals in Shetland in 1998.

The exploitation of grey seal pups in Shetland has never been so intense as that of the very much larger population in Orkney, nor even as intense as that on the Shetland harbour seal. This is probably because of the inaccessibility of many of the pupping sites and the unfavourable late-autumn weather for hunting from a boat. The highest recorded number of grey seal pups killed in any one year was 365 in 1964, although during the 1970s not more than 75 were killed in any one season and often many fewer. However natural mortality of the grey seal pup is high in Shetland. For example, in one cliff-foot colony on the west side of Ronas Hill, in the early 1970s, 100 pups were counted at an early stage of moult just prior to a severe gale. Following the gale a few days later only half a dozen pups could be found scattered over a wide area. Similar occurrences are known for Fetlar colonies. Although specific localities are favoured for pupping, the actual site chosen may sometimes depend on the strength and direction of the wind at the time. The size of the Shetland grey seal population in fact seems little changed over the past 20 years; however there is an indication that pup production has been increasing very recently and that new and more sheltered breeding sites are being explored. It may be that low recruitment due to continuing high pup mortality at the more exposed sites has been the cause of population stability. In contrast the Scottish population, estimated at 30 000 in 1963 and 60 000 in 1978, was last estimated at 105 000 in 1995. There is no doubt that there are many suitable uninhabited grassy holm sites in Shetland, similar to Orkney, which would be available to an expanding grey seal population.

First-year grey seals are known to disperse widely and apparently randomly outwith Shetland, east to Scandinavia and south down the west and east coasts of the British Isles, while individuals from the Farne Islands, Orkney and the Western Isles have been tracked by satellite to haul-outs off Sumburgh Head and the Ve Skerries. However, there does not seem to be recruitment of adults of any number into the Shetland population. Harbour seals, on the other hand, have a much greater tie to their place of birth, although they may move in September from the immediate neighbourhood of their breeding sites.

It has been suggested that harbour seals remain hauled out for particularly long periods in Shetland because food resources are so ample. When ashore they can be seen loafing on the rocks in a very characteristic manner, balanced on their sides with heads and tails up forming a long 'U'. It looks extremely uncomfortable but it seems to work for the seal. They frequently sleep in the water also, hanging in a vertical position and rising periodically, their heads emerging every so often like fat black bottles.

In their first few months the young of both species seem to favour invertebrates such as crabs and squids, but as they get older they turn to whatever fish is available. Identifying what seals eat, particularly offshore, is obviously very difficult. The grey seal, which is probably the most abundant marine mammal in the North Sea, apparently feeds mainly on sandeel, although 30% of its diet by weight consists of the larger fish species such as saithe, skate, haddock and cod. On the west coast of Scotland they take less sandeels and more of the larger predatory fish. In Shetland annual fish consumption is estimated to be of the order of 8400 tonnes.

Until very recently no detailed work had been done on the food of the seals around Shetland. However, in a study of harbour seals through 1995–96 that tried to establish the fish species taken and its possible impact on commercial fisheries, it was estimated that Shetland's population of harbour seals consume around 10 000 tonnes of fish annually. Of that, 40% consists of sandeels and it is not surprising therefore that one of the largest breeding colonies and haul-outs is on Mousa, where there is a large sandeel spawning and fishing ground. The bulk of the remainder of fish taken, a further 46%, is a wide variety of gadoids, e.g. saithe, haddock, ling, whiting and cod. Pelagic fish such as mackerel and herring are also taken, but as the harbour seal feeds mainly within 10 km of the coast they make up only 9% of their diet.

At 1996 prices the total fish taken was reckoned to be worth about £1.5 million of commercial fish. However this has to be put in perspective by comparing the uptake of fish by the other top natural predators around Shetland. In fact the overall figure for seals, porpoises and seabirds is 77 400 tonnes, with seals therefore taking only 12.9%. When available, both seal species will take sea-trout and salmon. Fish farming and overfishing of fish stocks have exacerbated the conflict between people and seals. If seal culling is seriously considered again, proponents will have to be prepared to argue why seabirds and cetaceans should not therefore be culled also: compare the figure of 10 000 tonnes of fish consumed by seals with the figure of 600 000 tonnes estimated to be consumed by seabirds in the North Sea. Fishermen will also have to defend some very wasteful fishing methods.

OTTER

It may be surprising to some readers to find *draatsi*, or the otter, included in the marine section of this book; however in Shetland the otter is mainly a coastal animal, just as on the west and north coasts of Ireland and Scotland and on the Western Isles and Orkney. Otters were once widespread in Europe and Britain but were persecuted for sport and fishery protection, particularly in the eighteenth and

65. *Otters: a relatively large and predominantly marine animal in Scotland, occurring all around the coast and, with a little patience, easily seen.* (Courtesy of B. Jackson.)

nineteenth centuries. From the late 1950s, as with some bird of prey species, otters suffered a steep decline on the mainland of Britain due to the effects of the organochlorine pesticides brought into use in agriculture. There has been a slight recovery from this setback, but nowhere possibly are otters so relatively numerous in Britain as they are in Shetland. On the other hand, the habitat and lifestyle of the coastal otter is quite different from its terrestrial cousin and in the cool coastal waters of Shetland they have a harder and shorter life.

It is estimated that the Shetland population of otters numbers between 700 and 800 and they inhabit the more sheltered shores. They are particularly fond of small uninhabited islands but also occur inland by loch and burnside. As they feed almost entirely in the daytime they are almost a common sight on the coast. The most frequently taken prey is the eelpout, which makes up one-third of their diet; they also take many butterfish, but in terms of weight the rockling is the most important. However, otters have a catholic diet, as the density of fish varies considerably through the year, and they will take several other fish species and crustaceans. These bottom-living fish are caught fairly close to the shore, in depths up to 15 m and are most common where there are rocks and small boulders on relatively sheltered coasts with a thick growth of seaweeds, such as *Laminaria* species. These conditions are found in the west and north of the British Isles, hence the distribution of the coastal otter in this country. Fish biomass is most abundant in late autumn and it is interesting that Shetland otters, by and large, have their litters between May and August just before food availability peaks. However it may be just as important, for an animal that can lose its insulation fairly rapidly in the sea, that the sea temperature (at 12°C) is at its warmest then. Not surprisingly, in the early spring, when food abundance is least and sea temperature at its coldest (6°C), mortality is highest. The majority of otters that die from natural causes are found to have empty stomachs. Although a large number of otters are killed on the roads in Shetland, it is thought, with the present health of the population, that this is not a threat to their numbers.

What is of interest in the Shetland situation and something that will require monitoring is the fact that the rate of mortality in adult otters increases gradually with age, in contrast to what is found in other mammals. It appears that Shetland otters have high levels of mercury, which occurs naturally in Shetland waters in high concentrations They also have relatively high levels of PCBs, industrial derivatives known to affect reproduction. In times of stress, when food is in short supply, it may be that these pollutants have an additional minor effect. In Shetland today, of course, otters face another pollutant that can have a fairly direct effect on an individual's chance of survival and that is oil. A small quantity of oil can have a serious effect on the insulating quality of the coat and therefore can cause death from hypothermia; at least 10 otters died from oil pollution from the *Esso Bernicia* in 1978.

Otters use areas of food availability quite intensively; however food availability is not the only factor that determines the distribution of the coastal otter in Shetland. Essentially the coastal otter is an 'ordinary' otter that has taken to feeding, and therefore spending a lot of time, in the sea. However, unlike the true sea-otter (*Enhydra lutra*), its coat is adapted for fresh water; if it spends too long in salt water, the coat loses its insulating properties and the animal rapidly chills. Coastal otters therefore need to wash and preen in fresh water fairly frequently and in Shetland it has been found that otter holts almost invariably have fresh water within or very close by. This fact suggests that it is very unlikely that otters arrived in Shetland on their own initiative, as any otter trying to swim between Orkney and Fair Isle or the latter and Shetland would have become 'waterlogged' and probably died of hypothermia long before it reached a shore. The question is: who introduced otters, when and why? We do not know.

Although otters in captivity can live for up to 25 years, the stresses required to find enough food to keep a relatively small mammal, adapted to fresh water, warm and alive in the harsh maritime climate of Shetland are such that the average life expectancy is only just over 3 years, although individual wild otters can live much longer. Such is the struggle – just as the *tirrick* has to cope with an unpredictable food supply – that a female will abandon her litter, usually only two, if she cannot find enough time or strength to keep herself alive. All being well, however, the cubs will stay with their mother through their first winter and will part company either during the more difficult time for food in the early spring or not long after.

Shetlanders have a soft spot for the otter, even if they exploited them in the past for their pelt. Otters were caught in 'otter-houses', a stone box-trap built on a known run, with a trip-wire releasing a trap-door from above once the otter was inside. The Shetland equivalent of the phrase 'live and let live' is 'lat be for lat be, as Robbie Glen said to the otter'. The story is that the unfortunate Robbie Glen once stunned an otter and, thinking it dead, slung it over his shoulder and set off home, holding the creature by its tail. Unfortunately for Robbie, the otter recovered consciousness and gripped Robbie's own tail from behind, and this forced him to make the bargain!

CHAPTER 8

The Seabird Saga

Herma Ness and gannets

You can sing me a sang o da black-kyeppit maa
At follow da furr efter stoaries.
Da grace o da solan, da grey-happit craa,
An dunters an swaabies an nories;
Da bunxie an leeries, da skarfs, brungawheedies,
Or da tirricks aye flytin an tirn;
Bit me bird abön aa is da blue-backit maa
At follows da boats ta da herrin.

Löd A Langer – Song of Homesickness, Rhoda Bulter

Shetland, with well over a million breeding seabirds, is one of the key seabird stations in the north-east Atlantic. These seabirds have exploited the same rich marine resources, described in the last chapter, as generations of fishermen from the adjacent continental seaboard and offshore islands. In the not too distant past, we had little impact on this shared resource but probably controlled the population of

201

some seabird species through harvesting. However, as we have seen, our more recent relentless exploitation of the marine biological resource, including oil, has the capacity to more seriously affect seabird numbers, upsetting the dynamic balance between seabirds and their food resources and between seabird species themselves. The apparently remote, and often physically inaccessible, seabird colonies of the north-east Atlantic Ocean are now increasingly under our influence.

The British Isles are in the ideal geographical situation, relative to the North Atlantic Current, the Shelf Currents and the freshwater debouch from the Continent, to take advantage of the resulting rich planktonic resources and thus supports large seabird colonies all down its west, north and north-east coasts. The largest colonies, however, occur in the areas nearest to that resource, in the north and north-west, and the largest of these are the seabird colonies of St Kilda, Orkney and Shetland. These colonies comprise a high proportion of the temperate North Atlantic seabirds and hold internationally important numbers of several species. The other comparable and very large seabird colonies of the north-east Atlantic occur even further to the north, on Faroe, Iceland and in north-west Scandinavia.

The rich variety and abundance of the marine food resource and its annual cycle of appearance is reflected in the great variety of seabirds, their many feeding adaptations and the annual patterns of breeding and migration. For example, the petrels skim the sea and with their small bills delicately graze on the zooplankton. The kittiwake picks plankton from the surface and also plunges briefly into the sea to catch the smaller fish, such as sandeels, just below the surface. Larger pelagic fish, such as herring and mackerel, are taken by the gannet, which with its specially strengthened head and dagger-like bill plunges spectacularly from up to 30 m above the sea to depths of several metres. Sandeels are similarly caught inshore by the terns, though from less heady heights; they annually migrate across the globe and back, from the fringes of the Antarctic to the fringes of the Arctic. Terns share the inshore feeding grounds with the surface-diving auks, shag, cormorant, *tystie* (black guillemot), *dunter* (eider duck) and *raingoose* (red-throated diver). The larger gulls and the skuas are ubiquitous, often harrying the others birds as pirates or even predators.

The pelagic seabirds are so highly adapted to marine life, with long narrow wings for effortless gliding over large distances (gannet, fulmar and shearwater) or small narrow wings and strong legs placed well to the rear for powerful and extended diving (auks), that they are ill-suited for manoeuvring on dry land. They therefore seek nesting sites inaccessible to ground predators, such as cliff faces and stacks, crevices and burrows. Even the inshore seabirds prefer isolated and protected breeding sites, such as stacks and small sea or freshwater holms. However, the skuas, which can look after themselves, breed on open moorland. Such preferred sites are abundant in Shetland (Fig. 25), and where the rocks provide tiers of ledges on high cliffs, as at Noss, Herma Ness, Foula, Sumburgh and Fair Isle, they can support immense colonies of seabirds.

In the summer months seabirds take over the Shetland coast, many moorland areas and the inshore waters. Even though they are no longer exploited for food and feathers, and no longer traditional cues for a variety of seasonal activities, the beginning and the end of the season is still defined for many Shetlanders by their appearances and their departures.

66. *Noup of Noss: one of the most spectacular and accessible, by land or sea, of Shetland's several very large seabird colonies and a National Nature Reserve.* (Courtesy of SNH.)

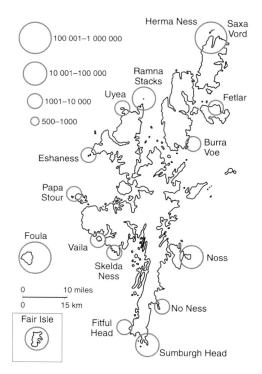

FIGURE 25   *Main seabird breeding colonies* (from Berry & Johnston, 1980).

In the British Isles there are 24 regularly breeding seabird species, in addition to divers, seaduck and phalarope. Of these 24 species, the greatest diversity (21 species) is in Shetland. Two of these 21 species, the great skua and arctic skua, have the bulk of their British populations in Shetland as does the red-throated diver. Several other species, e.g. fulmar, shag, arctic tern, guillemot, black guillemot and puffin, also have a very significant proportion of their British populations in Shetland (Table 15). Their significance is not only on a national scale. For 13 of these species Shetland holds between 25 and 100% of the total breeding population of the North Sea coast, while for one subspecies, the great skua, Shetland holds 45% of the whole Northern Hemisphere and world population.

Two of the best places for getting a sense of the vast numbers of breeding seabirds in Shetland are the National Nature Reserves of Herma Ness and Noss. For slightly smaller but still spectacular colonies, the site with the easiest access is the RSPB Reserve at Sumburgh Head. For the more intrepid, who will be rewarded for their efforts with magnificent scenery, there is also Fair Isle and Foula. In addition, there are many places round the coast, including Mousa and Papa Stour, where a great variety of seabirds can easily be seen.

In Chapter 11 we look at the oil industry and its impact on seabirds, but it is important to acknowledge that much of the information presented here on Shetland's seabirds comes from the 20 years of seabird monitoring sponsored by the Shetland Oil Terminal Environmental Advisory Group (SOTEAG). Other

TABLE 15   *Approximate numbers and percentages of Great Britain and Ireland populations (where known), of Shetland's seabirds (pairs unless otherwise stated)* (from various sources including SNH, RSPB, SOTEAG and JNCC)

Species	Number	Percentage of Great Britain and Ireland population
Red-throated diver	430	50–70
Fulmar	300 000	52
Manx shearwater	10	
Storm petrel	4 000	
Leach's petrel	20	
Gannet	21 000	9
Cormorant	212	2
Shag	6 000	13
Eider duck	7 000	10
Arctic skua	1 900	60
Great skua	6 200	70
Black-headed gull	250	0.1
Common gull	2 300	3
Lesser black-backed gull	450	0.5
Herring gull	4 000	2
Greater black-backed gull	2 500	10
Kittiwake	36 000	6.5
Common tern	500	3
Arctic tern	10 000	22
Guillemot (individuals)	180 000	15
Razorbill (individuals)	13 000	7
Black guillemot (individuals)	15 000	40–60
Puffin	100 000	20

information comes from Scottish Natural Heritage (SNH) and its predecessor bodies, the RSPB, the Shetland Bird Club and the Shetland Ringing Group and various ornithological survey and research projects, particularly work on Foula, initiated by the Brathay Trust but then developed into a long-term and intensive monitoring and research study by R. W. Furness of Glasgow University.

HISTORY OF SHETLAND'S SEABIRDS

The history of seabirds in Shetland undoubtedly goes back to the end of the Ice Age long before the Neolithic people arrived on the scene, bringing with them other terrestrial predators. The population of several species may well have been much larger and more widespread, particularly those vulnerable to exploitation, such as the gulls and eider. With the arrival of people, eggs would have been harvested from the most accessible and numerous species, while the young of many species, and even the adults of some, would have been caught, as they still are today in Faroe and by the men of Lewis. In fact accessible nests have been harvested regularly until relatively recently.

Periods of climatic change throughout the Holocene would have affected sea temperatures and there may have been associated fluctuations in the strength and direction of the Atlantic and Shelf Currents. This would have had knock-on effects on plankton and fish populations and therefore also caused periodic fluctuations in seabird numbers and diversity. Human immigrants, although they may have controlled numbers, did not threaten their existence, with the exception of one species, the great auk, which could well once have bred in Shetland, as it certainly did in Orkney and St Kilda. There is no conclusive evidence of its presence, but bones of this species have been found at the Jarlshof excavations

During certain periods of human expansion – on initial colonization, during the Iron Age, after the Norse colonization and in the nineteenth century – many outlying islands and remote corners of the mainland were inhabited that have since been abandoned. The disturbance caused by the presence of people and the increased *fowling* (harvesting of young birds for food) would have had the effect of reducing certain seabird populations locally. Several species, such as the raven and sea eagle, also had a price on their head and the latter was of course exterminated. With the introduction of the gun, the taking of birds became relatively easy and shooting reigned uncontrolled during the eighteenth and nineteenth centuries. Shooting birds, sometimes to obtain samples of rare birds, was the 'sport' of the gentry and of visitors and dealers who sold the skins to collectors for good prices. They, of course, regarded any shooting by the crofter as unproductive labour and attempted to discourage it. An extract from Saxby well illustrates the establishment's ambivalent view of fowling in Shetland in the middle of the nineteenth century:

> Fowling is now very little practised except by some of the old hands, [although] considerable quantities of eggs are taken annually, either for home consumption or for local dealers. The cause of this decline has not been any failure in the supply, but the steady manner in which the proprietors have endeavoured to persuade the men to turn their time to better account. A somewhat ludicrous occurrence took place some years ago when a well-known landowner who was shooting from a boat was suddenly interrupted in his aim at a row of guillemots by one of the crew, who explained that there was a man up there; and so there was – one of his tenants, lying flat upon the ledge, perhaps not in a very tranquil state of mind, but for all that more willing to risk the receipt of a charge of shot than to incur the inevitable anger of the Laird.

Such was the extent of fowling and egg-collecting that a new seabird colonizer that arrived in the eighteenth century, the great skua, was almost exterminated before it got a foothold. With the introduction of the Gun Tax and the first bird protection Acts in the 1880s shooting became much less common. About that time, too, the fulmar first settled in Foula, beginning an incredible period of expansion. As a prescient James Hay (RSPB Watcher in the early part of this century) said of it 'getting a firm hold along the coast and promises to become the most numerous of any bird'. It kept its promise!

During the harder years of this century seabird eggs were undoubtedly taken for food. After the First World War, as we saw in the previous chapter, swans were shot; even after the Second World War, shags were shot in some numbers and exported to the restaurants of London as 'Highland Duck'. Today, a few eggs are still harvested from seabirds, but this has no serious effect on seabird numbers. However, the history of many seabird species in Shetland in the first two-thirds of this century, following the cessation of fowling and shooting as elsewhere in the British Isles, has been one of expansion and population growth (e.g. the gannet, *dunter*, *bonxie*, the auks and the kittiwake). It has also been suggested that the new food opportunities resulting from the wasteful methods of the North Sea fishing industry has aided the growth of some seabird populations in the latter half of the century. However, apart from a few species able to take large fish or to adapt their feeding behaviour, several seabird species that depend on smaller fish have shown serious declines in the last 10 or 15 years.

We begin our account of Shetland's seabirds, therefore, by looking at those species that were the first to indicate recent serious problems with the availability of some marine food resources.

TIRRICKS, KITTIWAKES AND SANDEELS

Terns on a fence

The arctic tern, or *tirrick* (onomatopoeic), must see more sunlight than almost any other of earth's creatures, for it enjoys the long summer days in the high latitudes of both the Northern and Southern hemispheres by commuting annually between Shetland and the fringes of the Antarctic, a distance of 16 000 km. In fact the Shetland (and British Isles) population is only at the southern edge of its breeding range, which extends also into the high Arctic. The *tirrick* is probably the best-loved

67.   Tirrick: *the lightsome harbinger of summer that crosses the globe twice annually, and the seabird that suffered most during the 'sandeel crisis'.* (Courtesy of P. Ellis.)

bird in Shetland, partly because of its dancing flight and lightsome nature but also because its return, with the first birds appearing usually around the first week of May, heralds the end of the somewhat rumbustious spring and the arrival of the more peaceful and warmer summer. However, Shetland winters sometimes seem to go straight into summer in June without a spring! Indeed there are some years when summer itself never seems to arrive; there is an old Shetland saying for this: 'as da day lentens da cowld strentens'.

Generally the *tirrick* prefers to nest on short vegetation or shingle, the former habitat often found on moorland never far from the sea. For a small bird, it defends its nest with vigour and the unwary visitor will find that it 'punches' well above its weight. A few common terns can be found with the arctics and there are occasional small colonies, mostly on low holms, almost purely of the common tern. Like the *maalie* (fulmar) and the *bonxie* (great skua), the common tern is a relative newcomer to Shetland with the first proven breeding record in 1901. Its present population is around 250 pairs. The only other terns that have bred in Shetland are the sandwich tern, a few pairs of which bred on Whalsay between 1955 and 1960, and the roseate tern, one of which unsuccessfully attempted to breed with an arctic tern in 1984.

The Shetland population of the (arctic) *tirrick* is probably of the order of 11 000–15 000 pairs, which is only one-third of what it was in 1980, and comprises a few large colonies of over 1000 pairs and numerous smaller colonies of over 100 pairs. Any figure, however, must be tentative as *tirricks* are notoriously capricious in their attachment to breeding sites and overall numbers may rise or fall by several thousand in one year. The figures for Foula well illustrate these fluctuations (Fig. 26).

Numbers rose substantially from the 1960s until the mid-1970s and then fell back somewhat over the next few years. In 1979, in Shetland as a whole there was a poor breeding season for *tirricks*, mainly due to the weather. A second bad year followed in 1980, when there were large-scale desertions and a noticeable change in food items from sandeels to other small translucent fry. This raised some concerns about

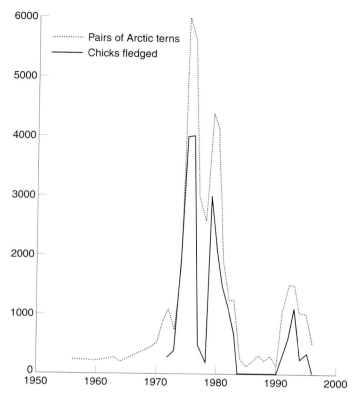

FIGURE 26   *Number of pairs of arctic terns and chicks fledged Foula 1956–96* (data courtesy of R. W. Furness).

the inshore sandeel fishery in Shetland that had commenced in 1974 (see Chapter 7). In 1981, there was a substantial decline in the number of pairs at Foula and a continuing drop in breeding success. In 1982, there was a further drop in the number of adults present and many desertions of nests, which was reflected in many parts of Shetland. This downward trend continued in 1983 and in 1984, when there was the lowest number of adults recorded on Foula in 20 years of monitoring and for the first time there was complete abandonment of breeding with no young fledged at all.

Other signs suggested feeding problems among other species at this time. For example, in both 1980 and 1982 *raingeese*, where monitored, raised only single chicks on average. Further, *bonxies* on Herma Ness appeared to be turning from sandeels to Norway pout, haddock and whiting and it was noted that the kittiwake, the arctic skua and the guillemot also had poor breeding success in 1984. In 1985 most *tirrick* colonies failed to rear any young and many kittiwake nests were abandoned. Alarm bells rang as a third disastrous breeding season for *tirricks* followed in 1986, accompanied by falling numbers of kittiwakes attending monitored colonies. At the same time *Tammy Nories* (puffins) were seen to be feeding their young with unusually small sandeels at Herma Ness, where a study

68.   *Kittiwakes: seemingly the noisiest seabird on the cliff and unfortunately another species that suffered breeding failure during the 'sandeel crisis'; now facing increasing predation by the bonxie.* (Courtesy of L. Johnston.)

also indicated that gannets had changed their diet from sandeels to predominantly larger fish, such as mackerel and herring. Several seabird species were therefore showing various signs of changes in their normal diet. However, the only species that appeared to be suffering as badly as the *tirrick* during this period was the kittiwake.

There are indications that the kittiwake was quite numerous in the past and might have suffered, like many seabirds, from exploitation for food and from shooting. When these practices ceased at the end of the last century the kittiwake population began to increase in the British Isles and possibly Shetland. In the first three-quarters of this century several new colonies were founded, for example on Bressay, Yell, Out Skerries and Wats Ness, but there also appears to have been some declines at other existing colonies. During the 1970s, however, there began a decline in Shetland and also in Orkney.

This decline continued and steepened at many Shetland colonies in the latter half of the 1980s with a run of very poor breeding years at most colonies, including five seasons of almost complete breeding failure. This coincided with the poor breeding performances of the *tirrick*, which failed completely on Foula (Fig. 26) and elsewhere in Shetland for the 7 years from 1984 to 1990. Overall the population of kittiwakes in Shetland dropped from a high of around 42 700 in 1969–70 (Operation Seafarer) and 50 000 in 1985–87 (Lloyd *et al.*, 1991) to around 36 000 in 1996 (SNH). The decline in Shetland in the 1980s was severe (40% on Herma Ness and 61% on Noss between 1980 and 1985), with desertion of nests and chicks and abandonment of colonies, not all entirely due to food shortages as we will see.

This was a catastrophic time for Shetland's breeding seabirds, when 'tens of thousands of tern, kittiwake and puffin chicks starved to death' (Heubeck, 1989a) on a scale not seen before among British seabirds. The *raingoose*, *bonxie*, arctic skua, *Tammy Norie* and *skarf* (shag) also exhibited poor breeding performances or changes in feeding behaviour, and even the *maalie*, whose population had been expanding steadily on Shetland for 100 years, showed signs of poor breeding success. At the same time it was realized that little was known of the underlying causes, except that all these species had a common dependence on sandeels, which for some reason were in poor supply (see previous chapter).

Under pressure particularly from concerned local ornithologists, research programmes into the relationship between the most affected seabird species and their summer food supply were initiated in 1987 by SOTEAG, SNH, RSPB and Glasgow University. The following year, 1988, the Shetland Bird Club came of age when it called a conference in Lerwick that brought all the interested parties – fishermen, fisheries scientists, seabird biologists, statutory and voluntary conservation bodies and the public – to the table. This resulted in the collaborative research effort to address the issues of the relationship of sandeels to Shetland's seabirds and the possible effects of the fishery.

Sandeel and sprat are favoured fish for seabirds because of their high calorific (energy) value and they are particularly important in the breeding season for the rapid growth and development of chicks. Off the Shetland coast, as there are relatively few sprats or small herring, the lesser sandeel is the major food for the *tirrick*, kittiwake, the auks (apart from the *tystie*) and, indirectly through kleptoparasitism, for the arctic skua. They are also important for the *raingoose* and the *skarf*, and for gannets and *bonxies*. But what did we know of sandeel biology around Shetland, particularly the relationship between its abundance and its availability to seabirds and other predators? We knew very little, no more than we knew anywhere else in the North Sea, even though we were taking some 800 000 tonnes from there in the mid-1980s.

We have seen (in Chapter 7) just how important is the fishing industry to Shetland, but perhaps we do not quite appreciate just how much we exploit the North Sea. To quote Monaghan (1992):

> Each year, over 2 million tonnes of fish and 200 000 tonnes of molluscs and crustaceans are caught, some 25 million tonnes of sand and gravel are extracted and more than 10 million tonnes of sewage and industrial waste are dumped. To date over 1100 oil exploration wells have been drilled. While there are considerable pollution and fisheries management problems, we lack much of the fundamental knowledge of the North Sea ecosystems necessary for their resolution, particularly in relation to the ecological impact of marine fisheries.

It is the smaller 1-year-old sandeels and the 0-group sandeels hatched that year that are the essential food used by seabirds with small chicks, such as the *tirrick*, kittiwake and *Tammy Norie*, to feed themselves and their young. These 0-group sandeels become available from June and July, coinciding with seabird breeding. A successful breeding season for many Shetland seabirds thus depends on a reasonable abundance of sandeels in the summer months. Species with smaller chicks require a reasonable recruitment of 0-group sandeels that year and, critically for surface feeders such as the *tirrick* and the kittiwake, availability of this 0-group at, or within about 0.5 m of, the sea surface. During the mid and late 1980s for one reason or another, possibly simply because a small numbers of sandeels were evenly distributed through the whole water column and therefore there were few proportionally at the surface, there were very few suitable sandeels available at the surface layer for these two species and that is why they suffered such poor breeding seasons. Other seabirds, such as the *raingoose*, guillemot and *skarf*, were able to dive through the water column to feed where there were relatively higher numbers of sandeels available, or switched, as did the gannet and the *bonxie*, to other food sources and therefore did not suffer such dramatic breeding failures.

On the evidence so far there does seem to have been poor recruitment to the sandeel population in Shetland during the mid–late 1980s and the shortage of available sandeels of the year (0-group) may have been exacerbated by fishing. There was probably also poor levels of immigration. However, as suggested in the previous chapter, there are probably deeper underlying factors affecting sandeel availability, only we do not know exactly where these begin. Casual observation by experienced observers has suggested that sandeels are not so numerous as they were prior to the 1980s. For example, it has been said that the large masses of sandeels, which used to appear regularly at the surface as 'balls' of fish, no longer occur nearly so frequently. Also, there were indications on Foula that breeding success for some seabird species was declining well before there were breeding failures due to lack of 0-group sandeels.

On a wider front, during this period of seabird breeding failure in Shetland in the 1980s it was noticeable that kittiwake breeding failure extended far down the east coast of the British Isles. It was also apparent that the further north the kittiwake colony the more severe was the breeding failure and the earlier in the season it occurred and significantly, there was poor breeding success at some colonies where there was no sandeel fishing. The oceanographical changes that could well have affected both Shetland's sandeel spawning and the levels of their immigration from Orkney could be perfectly natural long-term cyclical events, part of the NAOs mentioned in the previous chapter, which presently may, or may not, be exacerbated by fishing. More seriously, these changes could be caused by global warming. The reason for the 'sandeel crisis' of the 1980s is clearly therefore very complex and we cannot simply blame only one of the factors.

To return to the lightsome *tirrick*, which has struggled so hard to survive in Shetland in the 1980s. It used to be thought that the *tirrick* was a 'fickle' bird, nesting one year here and the next there, as if by whim. The *tirrick* is a relatively small seabird and like all small birds and mammals must keep up a relatively high food intake compared with larger species. Its foraging range is relatively short and it has to spend much time on this activity with little margin for error. It is also a long-lived bird that can afford to miss out breeding for a few years. When food is scarce during the breeding season it is therefore in its own interests to delay, desert or abandon breeding attempts in order to ensure its own survival and the option to breed again in better years. The *tirrick* has, of course, evolved to cope with the shifting fortunes of sandeel recruitment, leaving its decision on where, or if, to nest until the last possible moment, to ensure it is as close as possible to the best food resource for its young. The 'fickle' behaviour is in fact part of its survival strategy. The loss of recruitment to the Shetland *tirrick* population through the latter half of the 1980s, and the possibility that many may have moved their breeding site to areas with more secure food supplies, means that Shetland may need a run of good breeding seasons before we see again white bickering clouds of *tirricks* on Foula and Papa Stour. In the last few years *tirricks* have had mixed breeding success, partly due to poor weather at critical times, but there are signs of a gradual recovery.

For the kittiwake, following 4 years of complete breeding failure, from 1987 to 1991, there has since been a run of several better breeding years (apart from 1993) and there are now signs of a reduction in the rate of its decline at some colonies. However, unlike the *tirrick*, another factor is involved in the kittiwake decline and is a further obstacle to its recovery. Breeding success is very varied across Shetland and one colony at least, at Kettlaness, which has fledged virtually no chicks since 1986, has dropped from a population of 260 nests in 1987 to 42 in 1993, mainly due to *bonxie* predation; while at Eshaness from 1994 to 1996, at a colony of more than 670 pairs, there was total breeding failure due to *bonxie* predation. At other sites it is the raven that is the main predator. Where there is no predation, breeding success has been relatively good.

Predation of kittiwake adults, chicks and eggs by *bonxies* is nothing new. Reductions of the kittiwake colonies on Foula due to *bonxie* predation were observed in the 1950s. However, *bonxie* numbers have increased very greatly since the 1950s, possibly partly due to the increase in discards available from fishing boats and to healthy sandeel stocks (prior to the 1980s). This expanded population of *bonxies* then found itself short of food during the 1980s and a significant proportion (see Skuas and piracy) turned for their main source of food to predating adult kittiwakes and chicks as well as other species. The threat to several kittiwake colonies from *bonxie* predation is now severe. So much so that breeding success at some colonies occurs only where there is natural physical protection from *bonxies*, such as caves or overhangs, while a few colonies have been abandoned and new subcolonies, safe from predation, established. Part of the reason for the vulnerability of kittiwake chicks to the attacks of the *bonxie* has probably been the fact that during the sandeel crisis both kittiwake parents were forced to go on longer foraging trips, with some evidence of journeys of greater than 50 km, to gain whitefish offal from fishing boats, leaving chicks alone and unprotected. What is causing most concern among seabird biologists, however, is that the present rate of predation of adult kittiwakes by *bonxies* is not sustainable and unless there is a reduction in predation Shetland's kittiwake colonies face a bleak future.

Dramatic and tragic as the story is, we need to keep a perspective on the events of the 1980s as far as the majority of Shetland seabirds are concerned. Firstly, sandeel shortage appears to be a problem for only certain species. Secondly, from 1991 most seabirds have shown signs of improved breeding success with a halt to the decline, apart from the kittiwake. Thirdly, as far as the *tirrick* is concerned, the numbers breeding in the mid-1990s are still greater than that estimated for Shetland in the seabird survey of 1969–70. Fourthly, seabirds are generally long-lived and are therefore adapted to withstand a run of a few years of poor breeding success. Fifthly, we have seen already that the populations of many have increased dramatically this century. It was suggested that this was partly due to the end of exploitation and persecution in the nineteenth century. It has also been suggested that the overfishing this century of herring and mackerel, the predators of the small fish species such as sandeels and sprats, has allowed these latter populations to grow and this is also responsible for fueling the seabird population expansion. Whatever the reasons, and one must include the increased provision of discards and offal from the fishing industry, it could be argued that some of the present seabird populations are 'unnaturally' high and that therefore what is happening is simply an adjustment of overall numbers and that no species is under real threat. If we look at other similar events in the world, we see that what has happened in Shetland is not unique and perhaps we may learn some lessons.

The North Sea is one of the most productive marine areas in the world. Another is off the coast of Peru where the strong Peru Current is partly responsible for a similar mixing of water to produce abundant food for the Peruvian anchovy, upon which feed large seabird populations. Natural events (El Niño) regularly disrupt this regime and fish stocks and seabird populations plummet. Until recently, with the resumption of normal currents and productivity, the seabird populations rapidly recovered. However overfishing of the anchovy has now withdrawn that resource upon which recovering seabird populations depended and has seriously depressed seabird numbers. Ironically, in the world fish-meal market, a poor catch of Peruvian anchovies means better prices and more pressure on the North Sea sandeel. Nearer home, guillemot populations in northern Norway crashed after 1985, apparently due to similar food shortages. In this case capelin was identified as the probable food source and although overfishing by a new industrial fishery, as in Shetland, was probably not the initiator of the problem, at a time of low stocks it could well have been a critical factor.

DIVERS AND SEADUCK

Divers in courtship display

Singing to an infant
of the raingoose
riding the hypotenuse to the sea

Gudrun, Laughton Johnston

69. *Raingeese: a primitive-looking bird of the hill and sea, which in the summer is the haunting voice of Shetland's moorlands and lochans.* (Courtesy of R. J. Tulloch.)

There are many bird calls evocative of Shetland, but few as primitive as the melancholy wail of the *raingoose* (red-throated diver) on a remote lochan, or its high and rapid *we're a' weet, we're a' weet . . . waur wadder, waur wadder* as it passes overhead to descend in a long glide to the sea or a loch. With its weird call and distinctive 'hump' shape in flight it seems such an ancient creature. Like so many of the features of Shetland that one could take for granted it deserves close inspection, revealing the precise definition of the red throat patch, delicate grey head, beady eye and the white velvet-cord striping of the nape of the neck. It has been called the *lum* (Old Norse *lomr*) and hence the many Shetland lochans called *loomieshun* (Old Norse *tjorn*, tarn) in Foula, on Saxa Vord and at Girlsta and Swinnister to name a few; the similarly named 'loon' in North America has the same derivation. It is more commonly in Shetland called the *raingoose* (Old Norse *regn gas*) as it was supposed to foretell the coming rain, not a hard task in Shetland! Signs such as these were important in Shetland folklore, providing assurance or guidance when decisions might lead to life or death.

> If the rain goose flees ta da hill,
> du can gane to da haf whin du will;
> Bot whin sho gangs to da sea,
> du maun draw up du'r boats an flee

> Anonymous

The *raingoose* is one of several northern 'seabird' species reaching its southern limits in Scotland, Shetland being its stronghold in the British Isles with around 50–70% of that population. However, the species has a holarctic distribution across northern North America, Scandinavia and Russia. The status of the *raingoose* in Shetland is that of a common and widespread species. In the nineteenth century and even early in the twentieth century it was not a common species. Venables and Venables (1955), who recorded over 100 nests in the 1950s, suggested that this was partly due to egg collecting. By the late 1970s estimates of several areas suggested an overall population in the order of 500 pairs. The first complete survey, carried out by the RSPB in 1983, found just over 600 pairs and estimated the total population at 700 pairs. Since then sample areas have been monitored annually, demonstrating a substantial annual variation in breeding succcess and several years of poor breeding success in the late 1980s. A second complete survey carried out in 1993 (RSPB/SNH) recorded approximately 430 pairs, indicating a 40% decline since the early 1980s. Breeding numbers and success is however very variable over Shetland.

Another diver seen regularly in Shetland is the *immer gos* or great northern diver. It has been claimed that it bred in Shetland in the nineteenth century and as Venables and Venables (1955) have stated 'the data presented are extremely suggestive'. Today the *immer gos* is still seen regularly as a migrant in breeding plumage in the summer months, though very rarely on fresh water. In Scotland it has been proved to have bred only once, in 1972 in Wester Ross.

The aura of legend that clouds the history of the great northern diver in Shetland also obscures the record of the long-tailed duck or *calloo* (onomatopoeic), and there is not a Shetland ornithologist who would not throw away a pair of binoculars to be the first this century to record the *calloo* as a breeding bird. Evans and Buckley noted two records of fresh eggs purchased in Lerwick, which must have been a thriving market for eggs in the late nineteenth century. Of these Venables and Venables have said 'that if subsequent investigations prove that the bird breeds in Shetland, they may fairly be taken as genuine'. But how subsequent is 'subsequent', for there has been no proof of breeding for 95 years. Certainly the species is more common in recent years as a summer visitor and it has bred in Orkney this century. One therefore feels compelled to admit that the *calloo* could well have bred in Shetland in the past and may yet do so again.

The other common but not numerous 'seaduck', actually a 'sawbill', breeding in fresh water in Shetland is the red-breasted merganser, though it prefers the clear oligotrophic lochs and stream sides to the peaty loch. Unlike the *raingoose* it takes its family of chicks down to the sea as soon as they are hatched. By far the most numerous 'seaduck' breeding in Shetland, however, is the eider or *dunter*, which breeds ubiquitously on the moorland and low-lying offshore holms. The local name sounds rather descriptive of its stocky appearance, but according to *Jamieson's Scottish Dictionary*, the name comes from *dun* (down) and *taer* (gnaw), from the female's habit of plucking down from her breast to line her nest. Unfortunately *dunters* do not nest in sufficient density to allow easy harvest for the making of eiderdown quilts. At first glance the male is a simple contrast of black and white during the breeding season; however if one looks closely it will be seen that his breast has a tinge of pink and that the nape of his neck is an extremely soft and pale green. In eclipse, in the autumn, he wears a shabbier coat and looks completely different. On a still day in the spring the relatively soft *woo-woo* call of the 'wooing' males carries surprisingly far across the water as the winter flocks disperse. The female's uniformly dark-brown, cryptic colouring allows her to sit secure and tight for long periods where there is little cover, so she is difficult to find when she is incubating.

As with so many of the vulnerable and edible birds of Shetland, the *dunter* may have been more numerous before the nineteenth century. Saxby deplored the efforts of many who took birds for the table, although his apology for this habit illuminates the scarcity of food and the social conditions of the time:

> should ... ornithologists ... meditate passing a winter in the north isles, I would advise them to withold their criticism until ... they can conscientiously aver that failing health has not driven them to a like extremity; unless, indeed, their sojourn has been with the laird, the minister, or still better with the factor.

However the introduction of the Gun Tax reduced the persecution so that by the end of the century, like the *raingoose*, the *dunter* population was probably recovering.

Recent work on *dunters* in Shetland, arising from the general need to know more about the numbers and movements of seabirds in relation to oil developments, has shed some light on their distribution and population size. After mating the males gather in tight flocks in very specific areas, where there is shelter, good and reliable food supplies and a relatively undisturbed shore on which to roost. By August, when they are completely flightless due to their wing moult, they are joined by the females and young of the year and by September–October they all move to wintering areas, mainly off Sumburgh, north-west Bressay and Ronas Voe, where they may remain until the spring. Flock sizes range from only a few birds to up to several thousand and are a spectacular sight on a winter's day bird-watching, when it is also worth keeping an eye out for the occasional and handsome king eider from arctic Norway and Russia.

The first estimate of the Shetland *dunter* population, including Fair Isle and Foula, was made in 1977 when total numbers were thought to be 15 500. This was subsequently revised upwards by 1000 to 16 500 (Heubeck, 1989a). In 1984 the total population was estimated at 11 000, in 1989 at 10 000 and in late summer 1992 at 7000, less than half the population of 20 years ago. Two separate events are known to have had some effects on the population, but an apparent long-term decline, not detected elsewhere in the British Isles, remains largely unexplained.

The decline between 1977 and 1984 was partly caused by the *Esso Bernicia* oil spill in 1979 in Sullom Voe; another, an apparently unrelated, large mortality of birds in the Bluemull and Colgave Sounds occurred in the winter of 1979–80 when possibly 2000 birds died. The cause of this latter event is not known, but it has been suggested that it might have been a disease, which could have spread rapidly through the flock. However these two events and small-scale chronic oil pollution incidents do not explain the long-term and continuing decline. An increased predation of adults and chicks by expanding great skua populations, by gulls and by feral ferrets may well be having an effect, but there is little documented

70.   Dunters: *a common but declining seaduck. The female is so well camouflaged and sits so tight on her eggs that one may almost tread on her.* (Courtesy of R. J. Tulloch.)

evidence. In addition, otters have also been seen to take adult *dunters*, although it is unlikely that the number taken are significant. On the one hand, we should keep these changes in perspective, as this species was not at all common 150 years ago; on the other, a decline that appears to be long term suggests a deep-rooted cause requiring further investigation.

THE *MAALIE*, OTHER PETRELS, OFFAL AND DISCARDS

One of the most graceful of Shetland's seabirds is surely the *maalie* (fulmar). The effortlessness and ease with which the *maalie* continually swings through the updraughts of cliff faces, or rides the uplift from the wave-trough and crest, following the constantly shifting surface in a pattern of perfection, is as hypnotizing as following the apparently effortless movements of a ballet dancer. Its stiff and narrow wings allow it to sail far over the oceans with little effort. Ironic that such a handsome bird, with its large soft eye, should have such a devastating spit!

The *maalie* is a very widespread species, occurring in both the Pacific and Atlantic. It varies in colour in the eastern North Atlantic, from mainly light birds in the southern part of its range to a high proportion of dark grey or 'blue' in the northern part. In Shetland the blue phase is rarely seen in the breeding season, but regularly seen on passage in the autumn.

Saxby, in the mid-nineteenth century, said of the *maalie* that 'it never breeds in Shetland' and that to make its acquaintance one had to go offshore with the *haaf* fishermen. The fact that few adult bones of the *maalie* have been recovered from the tenth-century deposits at Jarlshof and that the Shetland common name *maalie* is not related to the Scandinavian or Faroese name for that species (although could it be related to Old Norse *mar*, a gull and *aol*, to squirt out, as in *aalamootie*, the storm petrel?) suggests that it was never common in Shetland in the past. Although the

71.   Maalie *and* Tammy Norrie: *the former, almost unknown in Shetland just over 100 years ago, is now the commonest seabird, scattered right around the coastline and even inland. The latter, with its clownish costume, nests in burrows in large colonies on sloping grassy cliffs.* (Courtesy of B. Jackson.)

maalie bred on St Kilda from at least the seventeenth century, the first confirmed breeding in Shetland, and the first in the British Isles outwith St Kilda, was on Foula in 1878. Thereafter the *maalie* spread rapidly around Shetland, nesting on Herma Ness in 1897. The rate of expansion there, as elsewhere in Shetland, is illustrated in Fig. 27. This expansion continues at around 3.3% per annum, not as rapidly as in the first half of the century. It is interesting that there was reduced breeding success in both the mid and late 1980s, similar to other Shetland seabirds, during the sandeel scarcity and indications of a switch in the *maalie* diet to whitefish offal.

It is incredible that a bird known only offshore in Shetland just over 100 years ago should now be by far the most numerous seabird in Shetland, numbering around 300 000 pairs, breeding from high cliffs to low shore, from peat banks to dykes and derelict buildings, especially as it lays only one egg, does not re-lay if that is lost and does not breed until it is 8 years old. The reason for the sudden southward expansion of the *maalie* has never been fully explained, although a number of explanations have been put forward: from Fisher's theory that there has been an increase of available food from human activity beginning in the early Greenland whaling and fishing days; through behavioural changes associated with genetic changes, proposed by Wynne-Edwards; to the recent warming of the eastern North Atlantic, put forward by Salomonsen. The natural food of the *maalie* is zooplankton; however it is known that the *maalie* fed on the offal from the whaling industry at the turn of the century and that it also fed, and continues to do so very successfully today, on the offal from fishing boats.

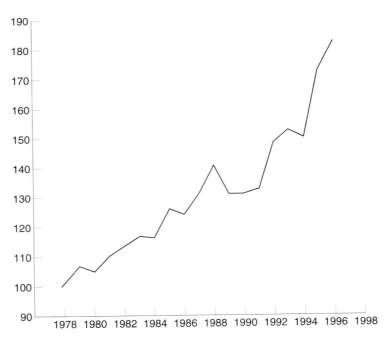

FIGURE 27   *Indices (1978 = 100) of mean annual counts of fulmar (apparently occupied nests) of four colonies, 1978–96* (data courtesy of M. Heubeck, SOTEAG).

There is surely something very wrong when the principal commercial fish stocks everywhere have fallen through overfishing, when in the 1990s the fishing industry in the North Sea is annually discarding 320 000 tonnes of (mostly undersized) fish, 70 000 tonnes of offal and 180 000 tonnes of benthic invertebrates. Much of this is consumed by seabirds and it has been calculated that in total this weight of food could support an additional 200 000 seabirds. It might seem little wonder then that many seabird populations have expanded so dramatically this century and it can be no surprise that on Foula, for example, it has been found that fish offal and whole fish discards are a major source of potential food. The most abundant of the scavenging seabirds are the kittiwake and the *maalie*. The former is probably the least successful scavenger of offal, when challenged by the other larger birds, and the latter the most successful. A recent survey estimated that in the autumn months almost 2 million *maalies* are in the area west of Norway (including Orkney and Shetland) and north of Buchan Ness. However when it comes to the discards of undersized and unwanted species of fish, it is the larger birds, the *solan* (gannet), *bonxie* and great black-backed gull, which are the most successful feeders, the *bonxie* often robbing the others and its own species.

However, the simple deduction that more food means more seabirds does not necessarily stand up. Recent research of fish discard consumption by birds in the North Sea demonstrates that there is no direct correlation between the presence of fishing boats, and therefore discards and offal, and seabird numbers. The results suggest that the *maalie* (and most other seabirds) are opportunistic feeders at fishing boats. However it may well be that the additional food made available from the fishing industry is enough either to ensure breeding success when it might not otherwise have happened through shortage of the normal food supply, especially for birds like the *maalie* that can travel long distances with ease, or to improve winter survival when otherwise there would have been higher levels of mortality. This would be sufficient to increase the populations of several seabird species that now may be dependent on these additional food sources to sustain the present level of their populations. The situation is very complex and there are too many unknowns at the moment to be able to measure the effect. The only species that appear to be positively influenced by the presence of fishing boats are the large gulls and it must be assumed that in their case the additional food supply is a direct influence on population size.

If the availability of discards and offal from fishery practices is partly responsible for the increased population of certain seabird species, it is a potential North Sea seabird time-bomb. Because of the poor state of fish populations in the North Sea, sooner or later there will have to be severe reductions in fishing quotas and other conservation measures, such as the introduction of larger net sizes (to allow small fish to escape) and other regulations, to reduce or cease the dumping of discards (as has happened in Norwegian waters) and offal. When this happens seabirds are going to struggle to find food to fill this gap. Those capable of kleptoparasitism (stealing from others) or predation will have an increasing effect on the populations of their prey, who may already be under stress themselves. The future is very unsure for these species, although reductions may only return the populations of some species to previous levels.

To return to the *maalie*. With such a vast increase in the population of one bird species, fears naturally arise that other birds may be affected directly or indirectly. The *maalie* produces an oily secretion that can be projected and clog up the feathers of other birds, even to the extent of impairing flight. At least one young sea eagle introduced to Fair Isle in the early 1970s died as a result of such an attack and there have been similar attacks on many migrant raptors on Fair Isle and on peregrines in Shetland itself. The *maalie* may be the reason why the peregrine has failed to recover in Shetland from the impact of DDT. In addition, the *maalie* seems to have little hesitation in taking over the nests of other birds, for example the raven and the peregrine, and the author has seen *maalies* take over both *shalder* and herring gull nests, complete with the eggs of the former occupant. Moreover the *maalie* will happily nest in dense vegetation and this is threatening some of the few 'shrubby' sites still surviving on sheltered Shetland coasts, both by direct physical damage and by overenrichment from the nitrogenous guano.

The other petrel with long, narrow wings designed for gliding that breeds in Shetland is the manx shearwater or *lyrie*, derived from the Old Norse for fat, which undoubtedly refers to the chick at the point where the parents desert it. Alas this species seems to be gradually declining towards extinction in Shetland. From comments made last century and from the existence of place names such as Lyra Stack and Lyra Skerry, the species must have been more common, perhaps consisting of only relatively small colonies, in the past. Two, at Foula and Yell, of the three known extant colonies may no longer be occupied (although they can be difficult to find on cliff faces such as those on Foula), which leaves only a tiny colony of nine pairs (1996) on Fetlar that itself has seen a diminishing number of young being fledged. It is known that the latter colony is predated by cats and it may well be that the others have suffered in the same way. On the positive side the RSPB on Fetlar have initiated a management programme aimed at protecting this last colony in Shetland.

As with the *lyrie* the *ala-mootie* or storm petrel and Leach's petrel are pelagic outwith the breeding season and only return to their breeding sites at night and so are not easy to census. The storm petrel is the smallest of our seabirds and is very much like a house martin in flight, moving in bursts of fluttering and gliding. The tarsii are very long compared with the body and when feeding on surface plankton and fish the birds patter along the surface. On land both small petrels are very awkward and can only shuffle short distances to their nests in burrows or crevices. The distribution of storm petrels in Shetland, to quote Bobby Tulloch, is on 'the scree cliffs of Fetlar, Foula and Fair Isle and the famous broch on the island of Mousa ... Most of the small offshore islands have nesting "Stormies"'. He reckoned that there were probably several thousands on the scree sites and there is also thought to be a total of 4000–5000 on Mousa, including the broch. Mousa is probably the most beautiful and romantic place, as well as the easiest, to see these birds, and if there is not time to stay the night just put an ear to the walls of the broch or the nearby dykes and listen to the chatterings and purrings. In the *haaf* fishing days last century, storm petrels were familiar birds to Shetlanders in their boats well away from the land and no doubt a lamp at night attracted them, but for most of us today they are merely fluttering ghosts in the night at their breeding grounds.

The storm petrel's near relative, Leach's petrel, has only recently been proved to breed in Shetland, in very small numbers, on Foula in 1973 then on Ramna Stacks in 1981. The latter, where breeding had been suspected for a number of years, is one of only six sites in the British Isles. In 1996 it held between 17 and 20 pairs. Whereas the storm petrel's breeding range stretches south to the Mediterranean, Leach's petrel is a seabird of the eastern North Atlantic, breeding only on oceanic islands from the Westmanns (Iceland) to Faroe, St Kilda, the Flannans, Sula Sgeir, North Rona and of course Shetland.

Before leaving the order Procellariiformes, or the 'tubenoses', we must salute Albert, one of Shetland's most curious and regular visitors over the last 30 years. Albert is a black-browed albatross who strayed over the equator some time ago, arriving in Shetland in 1970. From 1974 Albert has regularly made his summer home among the gannets at Saito on Herma Ness, although 'he' did not appear in 1996 or 1997. A bird of the same species was also seen with the gannets at the Bass Rock in the 1960s and Albert could well be this same bird. What a fascinating situation there would be if a mate ever turned up for Albert!

THE *SOLAN*

With its brilliant white plumage, black wing-tips, 2-m wing-span, yellow head and piercing eyes, the gannet is a most conspicuous bird, and raucous too in its huge colonies. In Shetland it can be seen around the coasts throughout the year,

72.   *Gannet: Shetland's largest seabird that plunges so spectacularly into the sea to seize fish with its dagger-like bill.* (Courtesy of R. J. Tulloch.)

although most adults and the mottled-brown first-year birds tend to migrate south in the winter months. Anywhere shoals of mackerel or herring occur, gannets can be seen plummeting with half-closed wings into the sea. Except in high winds they require a run to gain enough momentum to take off and at this point they are especially vulnerable to the *bonxie*, which will repeatedly knock a gannet back into the sea until it gives up its catch. It will also commonly tip the gannet up in flight by grabbing a wing-tip.

The gannet or *solan*, from Old Norse *sula* (of Sule Stack and Sule Skerry), is our largest seabird and hence Albert's attachment to it. It has been present in Shetland waters for a great many years; bones have been found in ninth and tenth century dwellings, and as far back as the Bronze Age its bones were fairly numerous in the Jarlshof middens. That it bred at that time cannot be assumed, since the *solan* was taken for food as late as the mid-nineteenth century when they were certainly not breeding. Saxby noted that in windless conditions with a flat sea 'these birds may not unfrequently be knocked down with an oar'. At that time they were seen throughout the year and in the breeding season on the North Stack of Muckle Flugga and the Outstack; however, even today they have never been known to breed on either, although they now breed in large numbers in adjacent areas. If the *solan* was not breeding in Shetland before the twentieth century it must have been a summer visitor in fairly large numbers.

Around the end of the nineteenth century the species began to settle and expand, first at Noss in 1914 and then at Herma Ness in 1917. Expansion at these sites (Fig. 28) and other British sites probably led to the founding of the Norwegian colonies as recently as 1946. In more local waters the *solan* began roosting at several new sites recently, for example Foula, Fair Isle and Sumburgh Head (and Copinsay in Orkney). In 1975 they bred on Fair Isle for the first time, where there are now over 1000 pairs, in 1980 on Foula, and they may soon be breeding at Sumburgh Head where many have been regularly roosting for several years. The rate of expansion varies at the different colonies with the new ones being the most rapid, for example 17% (1994–95) at Fair Isle. At Herma Ness the rate of increase over the last decade has been 2% and at Noss 4%. The Shetland population is around 8.5% of the total population of the British Isles, which itself is around 60% of the world population. Coincidentally this continuing expansion in Shetland is also happening at nearly all the other British colonies (at around 2–3%) and at the only colonies on the western side of the North Atlantic in Newfoundland and the Gulf of St Lawrence.

The expansion of the gannet population has taken place at the same time as the failures of the herring and mackerel fishery and has continued through the sandeel

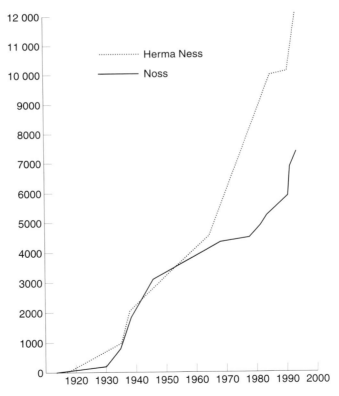

FIGURE 28   *Increase in gannet numbers at Herma Ness and Noss 1914–1994* (from various sources including SNH).

crisis of the 1980s. It seems that the *solan* can relatively easily switch from one prey to the other, depending on availability. One study in Shetland showed that whereas the sandeel had been 90% of its diet in 1981, by 1986 it was only 15%. The *solan* also scavenges at fishing boats in the North Sea, but will ignore fishing vessels relatively close to the colony to forage naturally at greater distances. Thus the waste from the fishing industry has probably only played a small part in the *solan*'s continued expansion.

SKUAS AND PIRACY

> I'll be the Bonxie, that noble scua.
> That infects a' ither birds wi' its qualms.
> In its presence even the eagle
> Forbears to pounce on the lambs.
>
> *The Bonxie*, Hugh MacDiarmid

Most probably the least-loved seabird but the most important on a global scale that breeds in Shetland is the great skua or *bonxie*, the name possibly deriving from the Old Norse *bunksi* used to describe a thickset person. It is estimated that 8500 pairs, which is around 60% of the Northern Hemisphere population of this very restricted species, breed in Scotland (there is an ongoing discussion as to whether or not it is a full species or a subspecies), of which 6200 or approximately 70% breed in Shetland; this means that Shetland probably holds around 45% of the total population of this species in the Northern Hemisphere (Fig. 29). The history of the evolution of the skua group and the *bonxie* specifically is only slowly becoming unravelled. The story is complicated and not yet resolved, but one theory has it that the skuas, related to the gulls which evolved in the Northern Hemisphere, maybe originated here too. Their ancestors then colonized the Southern Hemisphere and evolved into three closely related species, including the southern great skua, which is very similar to the Northern Hemisphere great skua (*bonxie*). It appears that some tens of thousands of years ago the ancestors of the *bonxie* recolonized the Northern Hemisphere, becoming a seperate subspecies from the Southern Hemisphere great skua.

The history of the species in the Northern Hemisphere is confused. For example, how long has it been here? Prior to becoming established in Scotland some time before the mid-eighteenth century, its main stronghold was Iceland and Faroe, the former continuing to hold the greatest part of the present Northern Hemisphere population. There have been no bones found in Viking or earlier times at Jarlshof and the first record in Shetland is from Low in 1774 when he refers to a few pairs in Unst and on Foula. Amusingly, considering today's lack of love of the *bonxie*, there was a very different attitude to the bird on Foula described by Low 200 years ago:

> In Foula this is a priviliged bird, no man will dare to shoot it under the penalty of 16s 8d. Ster., nor destroy its eggs; when they meet it at sea, whatever fish they have in the boat Skua always gets a share, and all this out of gratitude for beating off the eagle, who does not venture to prey on the island [lambs] during whole breeding season.

73. **Bonxie:** *may be the villain of the piece, but with the majority of the Northern Hemisphere population, by far Shetland's most important bird in international conservation terms.* (Courtesy of R. J. Tulloch.)

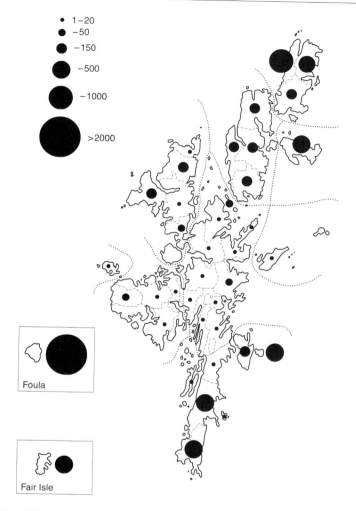

1–20
–50
–150
–500
–1000
>2000

Foula

Fair Isle

FIGURE 29   *The number of great skuas (apparently occupied territories) in different areas* (from Sears *et al.*, 1995).

For the next 100 years the *bonxie* struggled to establish itself on Shetland in the face of persecution, first by collectors such as Dunn (1837) who ruthlessly shot the birds for taxidermy and then later by the Victorian egg collectors. *Bonxies* were also harvested in Shetland for food at that time, as they were on Skuvoy (named after the Old Norse word for skua) in Faroe. It was only through the active protection of Dr L. Edmonston (1793–1879) (of Buness) at Herma Ness and John Scott of Foula, and the *bonxie*'s inclusion later in the Wild Birds' Protection Act of 1880, that it recovered. Since then there has been a steady increase in the Shetland population, which may now be slowing and has certainly peaked at the original Shetland strongholds and even fallen at Foula in recent years (Fig. 30). However, apart from poor breeding years during the late 1980s, breeding success has allowed a continued expansion elsewhere. For example, on Hoy in Orkney there are now

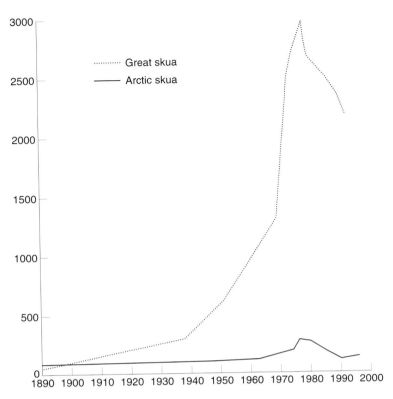

FIGURE 30   *Great skua and arctic skua numbers (pairs and apparently occupied nests) Foula 1890–1996* (data from Cramp *et al.*, 1974 and R. W. Furness).

just over 2000 pairs; in Iceland around 7000 pairs; while Bear Island and Spitsbergen were colonized in 1970 and north Norway in 1975. However in Faroe the population has declined to around 450 pairs. Shetland therefore is in the unique position of supporting a very high proportion of this Northern Hemisphere species and the only terrestrial vertebrate species that breeds in both polar regions of the globe.

Why is the *bonxie* such a disliked creature? In Shetland it is predominantly an opportunistic feeder, catching sandeels on the sea surface when they are available, taking discards from fishing boats and generally scavenging. However, it is also a kleptoparasite, a mugger, of most seabird species and can also predate almost any bird species from the smallest bird upwards. In Iceland, Faroe and St Kilda it is more of a predator, while in the Southern Hemisphere its near-relative is almost entirely predatory. In Shetland the *bonxie* has also been blamed for falls in the population of *dunters*, the smaller arctic skua and the kittiwake, and it will threaten and often attack any intruder, human, sheep or sheepdog, on its breeding territory in the nesting season. Having said that, it is thrilling to watch a *bonxie* from the cliff-top or from a boat, putting on the power like a well-muscled sprinter and harrying a *solan* or a gull, and rather exciting, if one is a visitor, to dodge its diving attacks on the moorland where it breeds. It is not so pleasant watching a *bonxie* dine off a *Tammy Norie* or, acting in consort with another, unmercifully distracting a *dunter* female while picking off her chicks and swallowing them whole. It is also very difficult to work your sheep when the dog will not leave the shelter of your legs. Notwithstanding, there has been little evidence, until very recently and in relation only to the kittiwake, that the *bonxie* actually has a detrimental effect on the populations on which it preys. Nor is there any evidence to suggest that loss of lambs to *bonxies* comes anywhere near the loss caused by other factors. The normal kleptoparasite (or predator) – prey relationship depends on the availability of the prey and as the prey decreases so does the predator. In the case of the *bonxie* and the kittiwake in Shetland this balance may have become upset lately. How is this?

To take the example of Foula. In the 1970s, sandeels were abundant and the *bonxie*'s principal source of food. However during the 1980s when the sandeel was in short supply, both for the *bonxie* and the kittiwake from which it stole, it turned more to discards from the fishing industry and to killing and even cannibalism to feed its own young. For reasons we cannot yet fully explain, although it may be related to the need to hold individual territories in high-density populations, *bonxies* continue to try and breed during times of food shortage, when other seabird species may abandon the effort if their own survival is threatened by starvation. When other species have ceased to breed through lack of food, the *bonxie* will persevere and some will have to turn to killing to support themselves and their chicks. The other side of this coin is that in times of food shortage, ironically just like the kittiwake they predate, they are forced to leave their own chicks unguarded more often in pursuit of food, leaving them to their hungry neighbours.

This has resulted in an apparent permanent change in the behaviour of an expanded *bonxie* population at a number of colonies, Fair Isle and Foula for example, where it has been estimated that 5–15% of the breeding *bonxies* have become 'specialists', turning from scavenging and kleptoparasitism to predation. By 1995, with some recovery in the sandeel stock, *bonxies* were once again feeding sandeels to their young; however the specialists have continued to predate on seabirds, particularly the kittiwake. This level of predation requires a large prey population if it is to be sustainable. Such a population of kittiwakes does not exist in Shetland, and as we have already mentioned in the section on *tirricks*, kittiwakes and sandeels, if this level of predation, particularly on adults, continues it will have a severe effect on an already declining kittiwake population. Sadly and ironically, the problem may be compounded by future fishing conservation measures.

Much of our present information on the breeding biology and feeding behaviour of the *bonxie* we owe to R. W. Furness and co-workers, including some of the inhabitants of Foula over the past 25 years. Furness has calculated that if there was a 50% reduction in discards Foula *bonxies* would eat over half a million birds a year, which is approximately the size of the present seabird population of Foula; not surprisingly, this is not sustainable. Even taking birds at the present proportion of less than 2% of their diet, *bonxies* are having a noticeable effect on the local Foula populations of a number of species. However, at present the largest *bonxie* colonies seem to have reached their peak. On Foula, in fact, *bonxie* numbers have been falling, from 3000 pairs in the mid-1970s, to 2495 in the mid-1980s, to around 2000 in the mid-1990s. Numbers of non-breeders have also fallen, suggesting a reduced recruitment into a falling breeding population and increased adult mortality. Elsewhere, away from the large colonies and also in Orkney, numbers continue to expand.

Bonxies and arctic skuas both establish a much larger territory around their nest sites than the kleptoparasitic gulls. When the off-duty bird is present, it uses a particular vantage point, very often a slight hummock that becomes a conspicuous green from constant guano enrichment, contrasting with the otherwise drab or brown heather in which it makes a scrape for its nest. Similarly green are the 'clubs' where immature and non-breeding birds gather. Outwith the breeding season the *bonxie* is a pelagic bird travelling as far south as Brazil, though most winter recoveries of ringed birds are from off France and Spain.

Where the *bonxie* makes more use of weight and strength, and reputation, in obtaining food, the arctic skua relies more on speed, manoeuvrability and sharper aggression in tackling its lighter weight prey: an Artful Dodger to the *bonxie*'s Bill Sykes! Although they take young birds and may even occasionally take adults, the arctic skua is mainly a kleptoparasite on *tirricks*, *Tammy Nories*, guillemots, razor-bills and kittiwakes, from which it takes sandeels. In pursuit of these birds, particularly *tirricks*, it demonstrates magnificent aerobatic skills and tenacity, pursuer and pursued drawing increasingly tighter circles around one another until the latter drops its load of food. Furness (1987) has said that the 'Arctic Skua is probably the only species of bird in which individuals may exist solely by kleptoparasitism at all times of the year'.

The Shetland names for the arctic skua are the *scooty aalin* or the *sjui*. The first is apparently derived from the Shetland word for excrement, *skoot*, as it was thought that it was the *tirrick*'s dropping that were eaten. The second is derived from the Old Norse *tju*, a thief. The arctic skua, unlike the *bonxie*, is a fairly common bird in the Northern Hemisphere with a holarctic breeding distribution extending in the British Isles as far south as the islands of Argyll. It also has a much longer history in

74.   *Arctic skua: the swift and aggressive harrier of* tirricks *and other small seabirds and, like the* bonxie, *not afraid to tackle humans on its territory.* (Courtesy of B. Jackson.)

Shetland than the *bonxie*, perhaps longer than that of humans. The present Shetland population is estimated to be around 1900 pairs, with just over 1000 pairs in Orkney and perhaps 200 in the rest of Scotland, which means that Shetland has some 60% of the British population (Fig. 31). However to put this in perspective there are probably over half a million across Canada, Alaska and Russia.

In Shetland, as in Orkney, arctic skua numbers have decreased at the main *bonxie* colonies, where they have been pushed out mainly by new *bonxie* breeders on the periphery of the *bonxie* colony who arrive back on the breeding grounds 2 weeks ahead of the arctic skuas. On Foula, predation of the chicks by *bonxies* has also had an effect in some cases. Elsewhere numbers are either relatively stable or falling slowly. Although breeding success was poor and many chicks starved to death during the sandeel crisis in the late 1980s and there were signs that some pairs did not breed at all in some years, food does not seem to be a limiting factor and so there

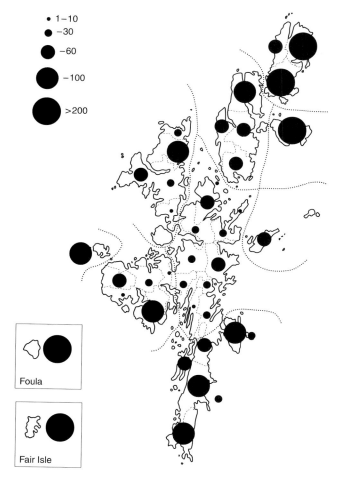

FIGURE 31   *The numbers of arctic skuas (apparently occupied territories) in different areas* (from Sears *et al.*, 1995).

is no reason to think that there will be much change in the population. That is, of course, as long as the kittiwake, auk and *tirrick* populations are sustained. Unlike the *bonxie*, the arctic skua will abandon breeding when there are food shortages; this may be because its adult survival rate is relatively low and it cannot therefore risk its own health in hopelessly trying to sustain a chick.

Although there is a lot of variation in the plumage of the *bonxie*, it does not have the polymorphism of the arctic skua, which can vary from almost completely dark chocolate, with the only light feathers in the wing-flash, to very light almost creamy underparts, usually with a dark breast-band and a more intermediate form with a dark back and dark head cap separated by a buff collar. The arctic skua is in fact the most strikingly dimorphic breeding bird in the British Isles. Due to the labours of successive wardens of the Fair Isle Bird Observatory and researchers there and on Foula, including Berry, Hudson and Furness, considerable knowledge of the biology of the species has been amassed. Over a long period details have been kept of times of arrival on the island in the spring, laying, hatching, fledging, survival and, most important, colour phase. As a result it has been possible to show that the colour phases are determined not simply by two alleles at a single locus, one dominant and one recessive, but also by the sex of the bird. The frequency of pales increases as a clinal variation in a northerly direction and northernmost colonies have few or no darks, for example Spitsbergen has 99% pale and Shetland around 25%. In Shetland there is also a higher than expected frequency of the dark phase among the males than the females.

What is the reason for the pale–dark dimorphism? There has been a great deal of debate and research on this, but the genes that produce the colour phases also appear to affect the age of recruitment to the breeding population and the timing of breeding. The dark allele appears to bring advantages to the birds breeding at low latitudes and in fact the dark-phase arctic skua does appear to be increasing in Shetland. It seems that the colour phases are simply secondary consequences, rather like guillemot bridling, of a genetic mechanism that has to allow for slightly different behaviour across the arctic skua's wide latitudinal range to ensure survival.

Outside the breeding season the arctic skua follows the migrating *tirricks* down the coasts of Africa and South America, wintering in the region of 40° S. The return is usually about the middle of April, between the 14th and 17th at Fair Isle.

AUKS AND WRECKS

The other seabirds in Shetland, predominantly pelagic outwith the breeding season but dependent particularly on sandeels in the summer months, are the guillemot, razorbill and *Tammy Norie*. All three feed also on sprat and herring, although there are not many of the former species around Shetland. These fish occur in shoals and the auks very often prey on them in well distributed flocks, travelling to and from the fishing grounds in long strings just a metre or so above the sea often with all three species flying together. Where they must pass around headlands or through sounds there is often a massive stream of traffic, which includes also the other pelagic colonial species such as the *solan* and the kittiwake. Two of the best known of these maritime highways are through Bluemull Sound between Yell and Unst, and at Sumburgh Head. The *Tammy Norie* appears to feed the furthest offshore, perhaps right out to the continental shelf, while the razorbill feeds nearest the shore. Whereas the *Tammy Norie* disperses well offshore at the close of the breeding season before it begins its moult, the guillemot and razorbill moult shortly after joining their flightless young on the water into which they have plunged from the cliffs in June and July.

The puffin, which is the most numerous auk in Shetland, is known as *Tammy Norie*, a nickname, or *lundi*, from the Old Norse to walk heavily with a stoop. The former name is used in Orkney and the Scottish mainland and is an affectionate name for this 'Pierrot' of the great cliff circus, this dumpy little bird with its disproportionately large red, blue and yellow bill and its shuffling gait.

The Shetland population of the *Tammy Norie*, which is a difficult bird to survey, is thought to be around 100 000 pairs, or about 20% of the British Isles population. The main colonies are on Foula (50 000) and Fair Isle (20 000) and at Herma Ness (20 000) and Saxa Vord in Unst, with smaller colonies scattered around the steeply sloping grassland and scree cliffs on Fetlar, Noss, Sumburgh and Mainland. Elsewhere this is a widespread species from northern Scandinavia to Brittany. In Shetland it was thought that the population was expanding until the 1980s. The *Tammy Norie* did not appear to suffer quite so seriously from the sandeel shortage in the 1980s as other Shetland seabirds, although there were breeding failures at several colonies, notably Herma Ness, Foula and Sumburgh Head, but not Fair Isle, in the late 1980s. The overall picture is uncertain at the moment, but it does appear that the Herma Ness colony may be lower in 1995 than it was in 1987. Feral cats are thought to be part of the problem at Foula, while ferret-polecats are known to have been a problem at Sumburgh and also may be elsewhere. Like the kittiwake, the *Tammy Norie* can provide a substantial share of the *bonxie* diet and it is regularly waylaid on its return from long fishing trips when it is carrying its mouthful of sandeels. Its return from the open sea after winter is later than the other pelagic auks, not until early April, when it can gather offshore in huge rafts for a few days before tentatively setting foot on dry land.

The guillemot, or *longvie* from the Old Norse description of its slightly elongated shape, is the third most common seabird in Shetland. It breeds in dense and usually large colonies, shoulder to shoulder on ledges or shelves on the cliff or within caves. The largest colonies are at Foula, Fair Isle, Herma Ness, Noss and Sumburgh, with colonies of several thousand also at Eshaness, Papa Stour and Ramna Stacks. Neither the guillemot nor the razorbill make nests and their eggs are held on the crowded ledges by the birds' body and feet.

Like the kittiwake, Saxby (1874) suggested that the guillemot had become less numerous in the nineteenth century due to exploitation for food and there is no doubt that there has been a substantial increase in its population this century. Prior to the last quarter of this century little attempt was made to census the numbers. In the mid-1950s the only place they were definitely declining was on Noss, where they were losing breeding space to the advancing gannets. The Seafarer Count of 1969–70 put the Shetland population at 77 400. Thereafter several counts, at Fair Isle (1969–70, 10 000; 1975, 19 200), Herma Ness (1969–70, 15 990; 1978, 22 760),

75 Guillemots: breed on bare rocky ledges in large cliff colonies, perhaps the seabird species most vulnerable to oil pollution. (Courtesy of R. J. Tulloch.)

Foula and Noss for example, indicated a strong increase up to the late 1970s and then a steady fall through the 1980s. In the late 1980s this fall was spectacular at some colonies, at around 50%. However, two points need to be made about this 'apparent' fall. Firstly, this may simply be a reduction in attendance due to poor food availability, particularly of non-breeding birds, e.g. at Noss counts in 1991 were spectacularly up on 1990 and attendance by breeders increased by several orders of magnitude. Secondly, on Noss, it was noted that 'good numbers' (Shetland Bird Report, 1990) fledged from the cliffs most years. Therefore, if it is not merely a reduction in attendance then adult winter mortality may be responsible for low numbers. In the early to mid 1990s there are signs of a stabilization and recovery. To put the 1980s decreases in perspective, however, we should note that at least in some colonies the 1990s populations are still higher than those almost 30 years ago, e.g. individuals on Noss in 1969–70 totalled 14 155, in 1991 38 967 and in 1996 45 696. Overall they appear to be recovering (Fig. 32).

The variant 'bridled' guillemot has a white ring and tail around the eyes that is inherited as a recessive trait. It is more common in northern populations, with about 20% in Shetland compared with 10% in Orkney and less than 1% in the

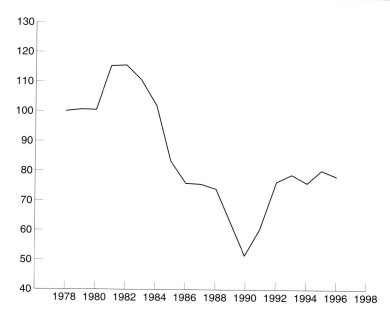

FIGURE 32 *Indices (1978 = 100) of mean annual counts of guillemots at four sites (five from 1988) 1978–96* (data courtesy of M. Heubeck, SOTEAG).

south of England. As with the colour phases of the arctic skua, bridling frequency occurs as a consistent latitudinal cline and the definitive explanation for its occurrence is as yet still not fully explained.

The razorbill, also called *sea craa* (its head does have a profile like the *craa*) or *wolkie* (from the Old Norse for an auk), usually breeds in association with the guillemot, although it prefers crannies and corners to open ledges. Its nesting preference makes it a difficult bird to census, but it is certainly much less numerous in Shetland than the guillemot, with a population of around 13 000 individuals. The history of population numbers this century – expansion to the 1980s then breeding failures and finally signs of a recovery in the 1990s (e.g. Noss: 1981, 1432; 1986, 1219; 1988, 709; 1991, 1180; 1996, 1793) – is similar to that of its cousin the guillemot. However there are still signs of a decline in the mid-1990s at some sites (e.g. Herma Ness: 1974, 1100; 1978, 1844; 1986, 942; 1990, 471; 1992, 569). This variation in breeding success of the same species but at different sites throughout Shetland, which is mirrored by other species such as the red-throated diver, guillemot, *Tammy Norie* and kittiwake, is an indication that food availability, i.e. the recruitment of sandeels at the various spawning grounds, also varies.

All three species of auk are vulnerable to oil pollution, severe winter weather offshore and probably winter food shortages, acting separately or in combination; these events undoubtedly add to the problems of populations trying to recover from summer food shortages. Numerically affected the most is the guillemot, which has suffered increased mortality in the North Sea in the 1980s, but of course the razorbill population is very much smaller than the other two and it could be the most seriously affected. We deal with oil spill-related events in more detail in

Chapter 11, but now is an appropriate time to look at the beached-bird surveys and the interesting, but sad, data that they cast up on the Shetland shore.

Beached-bird surveys have been carried out since 1979, in order to provide some baseline for mortality at sea. Up to 1992, 34 320 corpses of seabirds and seaduck have been found (SOTEAG, 1995); of these, 9% were oiled prior to death, but 92% or 27 456 were unoiled. This latter figure may seem very high, but we must remember that mortality, both winter and summer, is a very natural event in the biological world and very often a population-controlling factor.

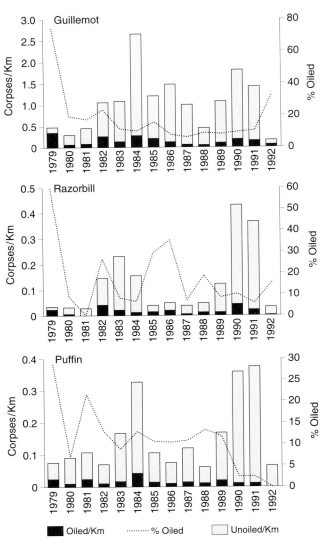

FIGURE 33   *The number of guillemot, razorbill and puffin corpses recorded on the Shetland Beached Bird Survey 1979–92* (from Heubeck, 1995).

There has been quite a variation in the number and size of 'wrecks' of guillemots over the last decade (Fig. 33), culminating in the massive wreck of emaciated birds in February 1994 from Shetland southwards. The number picked up in Shetland was around 1500, but it is estimated that the number dying could have been 10 times that, while the RSPB estimated that anywhere between 20 000 and 50 000 were wrecked nationally. In the 1994 wreck most of the birds were from colonies outwith Shetland. The number dying in this one event is within the range of natural winter mortality for the guillemot population of the North Sea; in fact, monitoring of breeding guillemots in the 1994 summer season in Shetland showed no statistically significant changes from 1993. However, it is the immatures that are particularly affected by starvation, probably from a number of colonies and over an age spread of several years, so that their additional loss from wrecks over a prolonged period will not be easy to detect. On the other hand, auk wrecks are not recent phenomena, *pace* Saxby: 'large numbers are often found dead along the shore, thus giving rise to the idea of epidemics, owing to the miserable condition of the birds and the absence of food from the stomachs'.

The razorbill was also affected to an unknown degree by wrecks, particularly in 1983 and 1990, following which there was a drop in numbers at colonies; however, as with the guillemot, another factor (sandeel shortage) was acting on the population and it is not possible to separate the two or to say just how much the winter mortality exacerbated the summer recruitment problems. A common part of the winter diet of the auks is the sprat, favoured because of its high calorific value, and there appears to be a connection between increasing industrial fishing for sprat and Norway pout and a decrease in their populations in the 1980s and the former's present distribution. The sprat population also seems to have diminished and moved away from Shetland, possibly due to other oceanographic reasons referred to earlier. Although links are very difficult to establish, there is much concern as to the possible effects of the industrial exploitation of these fish on the auk populations and a need therefore to continue the beached-bird surveys over the long term. A further threat to seabirds generally and to the guillemot in particular are gill-net fisheries. Research in the Kattegat has shown that between 1982 and 1987 probably 20 000 seabirds became caught and drowned, and of these 90–95% were guillemots. Modern monofilament nets are an even more deadly trap for seabirds in that they are not easily seen.

TYSTIES AND SKARFS

The black guillemot is known locally as the *tystie*, from the Old Norse *teisti*, after its thin, high whistle of a call. This is almost identical to the name for the bird in Orkney, Faroe, Iceland and Norway today. Like the *Tammy Norie* and the razorbill it nests out of sight and is a difficult bird to census. Counts are therefore carried out of pre-breeding birds at communal gatherings on the sea. Shetland is thought to hold around 12 000–15 000 pre-breeding birds, or approximately 60% of the British Isles population of this circumpolar species. Its other main stronghold is

Orkney with around 2250 pairs, while there are very much smaller numbers as far south as the Scottish west coast and islands, Ireland and Cumbria.

In Shetland it is thinly scattered all around the rocky and outer coasts mostly, but in the autumn congregates in very specific localities, where the tide race is not strong and which provide good feeding and some shelter, as it becomes flightless for several weeks. There are normally a few localities with several hundred and a number of others with around 50–100; however, over 1000 were recorded off Hascosay in 1974. Being an inshore species that flocks outwith the breeding season it is particularly at risk from oil spills and suffered badly from major pollution events, in 1978, 1991 and 1993 (see Chapter 12). Notwithstanding these setbacks, the population appears to have recovered and stabilized.

Several times in this book birds or their calls have been singled out as being quintessentially Shetland, the *raingoose*, the *bonxie* and the *shalder* for example. Well the *tystie* is another and appropriately, the emblem of the Shetland Bird Club, for it has well-defined, sharp and contrasting colours, with its white wing flashes against a uniformly black body and brilliant red gape, legs and feet. At one time it was persecuted, but is now a local favourite.

> I look at this running scene
> Of islands in the eye
> Water slaps water and a cormorant glides by
> Such zero in its eye.

> *Cormorant,* James Rankin

Both the cormorant and the shag are known locally as *skarf*, an onomatopoeic name imitating the croaking sound, as if issuing from a rubber tube, made by both birds. Sometimes the cormorant is known as the *muckle skarf*, or *lorin* from the white patch on the thigh (Old Norse *laer*, thigh). The cormorant's diet in Shetland is thought to be quite catholic, taking what is available near the colony; 13 species of fish have been recorded from young at the St Ninian's colony. The cormorant has been present in Shetland from at least the Bronze Age, through the Viking period and was recorded on the Heads of Grocken and Brae Wick in the eighteenth century. At present they breed almost exclusively on rocky stacks and cliffs on the west side of Shetland apart from one holm in Yell Sound. There used to be more than twice as many colonies as there are now (five) with several on the east coast and undoubtedly overall numbers were higher in the nineteenth century than they are today. Venables and Venables also noted the decline, especially on the east coast colonies. The 1969–70 Seafarer Count recorded *c.* 500 pairs; this became 444 pairs by 1975, 369 by 1985, 215 in 1995 and 212 in 1996. However there is a suggestion that over the last 4 years numbers are now stabilizing. Elsewhere in the British isles the population is increasing, apart from north-west Scotland where there is also a decline but, as with Shetland, there is no information as to the cause. Coincidentally, the Faroese colonies have declined to the point where the cormorant is now a rare bird there. It has been suggested that what the north-west coast of Scotland and Shetland have in common is fish farming and therein may lie a cause of the decline, but there is no evidence to support this. In the 1950s it was noted that there were far fewer colonies than there had been last century, but nothing was said of a decline at that time. Therefore, it is difficult to know whether or not the most recent Shetland decline is in reality part of a historic decline.

Feeding dispersal during the breeding season appears to be quite widespread: there is a regular flight line over the lochs of Spiggie and Brow to Boddam Voe, presumably from the St Ninian's Isle colony, and another across Mavis Grind to Sullom Voe from the Muckle Roe colony. Outwith the breeding season the cormorant disperses in small numbers within the sheltered voes and sounds, particularly in the Nesting area and in Yell Sound and also around the Scalloway islands, but also on the freshwater lochs. Recently, ringing returns have indicated that a small number of birds disperse as far south as Wales; however most returns suggest Grampian, Tayside and Lothian to be the more regular wintering areas for first-year birds particularly. As there appears to be no breeding problem in Shetland, it could be that part of the reason for the decline may lie in winter mortality in Scotland.

The smaller *skarf* likewise is a long-time resident of Shetland going back at least to the Bronze Age. Numbers appear to have fallen over 30% since the Seafarer Count of 8600 in 1969–70; elsewhere in the British Isles it has increased. Latterly, however, there are signs of stabilization and an increase of the Shetland population, which now stands at 6000; this still represents 13% of the British Isles population. The *skarf* feeds mainly on sandeels and may have been affected by the sandeel crisis. The local *skarf* population was of course badly hit in the southern end of Shetland by the *Braer* incident in 1993 (see Chapter 11).

*M*AAS

The Old Norse name for a gull is *mar*, and *maa* is the name given to gulls generally and to the herring gull in Shetland (*white maa* in Orkney), with variations on the name for several of the other gulls. All young gulls are called *scories* from the Old Norse *skari*, a young gull. The kittiwake, which we have dealt with already, is of course a gull, lighter in build, though similar in size, to the common gull and with a very different way of life. It also has a very distinctively buoyant flight, somewhat between that of a gull and a *tirrick*. If one imagines the regular and rhythmic wing stroke of the common gull, for every three strokes it makes the kittiwake makes only two and the *tirrick* only one.

Shetland gulls, the larger especially, have had changing fortunes over the years. In the last century a degree of control was exercised over all the gull species by the harvesting of eggs. The most famous example is that of the great black-backed, or *swaabie*, colony on the Holm of Noss (*swaabie* shortened from the Old Norse *svartbakr* for black back). In the eighteenth century there was a large colony there, but a rope cradle was erected between the Holm and Noss itself for ease of access and by the early nineteenth century the *swaabie* had all but abandoned the Holm. With the cessation, or almost, of persecution and harvesting and increase in food supplies from fishing boats and from rubbish dumps earlier this century, the *swaabie* population and those of all the large gull species expanded. The *swaabie* is in fact one of the most successful feeders at fishing boats. In Shetland they have taken to nesting on the moorland in some situations, not mentioned by Venables and Venables. More recently this expansion in the coastal colonies has come to an end and in Shetland there has been a gradual fall in the population over the last 20 years or so, perhaps stabilizing again. For example, on Noss there were an estimated 200–250 pairs in the early 1970s that fell to 80–90 in the mid-1980s, since when the population has hovered between approximately 60 and 80 pairs. The Shetland *swaabie* population today at around 2500 pairs is around 10% of that of the British Isles.

The lesser black-backed gull is known locally as the *peerie swaabie* or *sed ful*; *peerie* means 'small', *sed* comes from the Old Norse for the saithe (the saithe is the mature and larger version of the *piltock*, which was for a very long time an important part of the diet of Shetlanders) and *ful* comes from the Old Norse *fugl* for bird (NB, Foula, 'bird island'). Whereas more generally in the British Isles this species has expanded in numbers and range this century, in Shetland there has apparently been a huge reduction in numbers. In the nineteenth century Saxby (1874) described the *peerie swaabie* as nesting in 'countless numbers' in Unst; Evans and Buckley (1899) found them 'nearly, if not quite as numerous as the Herring Gull'; while Venables and Venables (1955) suggested 'this is very far from the case now'. Similarly Raeburn (1891) considered the *peerie swaabie* the most numerous gull on Papa Stour in 1890, including about 300 pairs on Lyra Stack, but Venables and Venables found only 'a few pairs' there. Curiously in 1969 there were 180 pairs. That numbers continued to decrease is well recorded, for example on Noss in 1946 there were 100 pairs (Perry, 1948) but by 1984 the bird had ceased to breed. The overall population in Shetland in 1969–70 was 541 pairs, while in 1985–87 it was estimated at around 464 pairs; this suggests that the population is stabilizing or at least that the decline has slowed. Although we know that the *peerie swaabie* is much less a scavenger than the other large gulls and that it is less successful than the other large seabirds in obtaining food from fishing boats, we do not know if this, or the fact that it is the only migratory large gull in Shetland, has anything to do with its demise over more than a century. Nor do we know if there is any link with the large increase in the population in Iceland that began in the 1920s.

The last of the large gulls breeding in Shetland, the herring gull or *maa*, is the most numerous. Like the *swaabie*, its population in the British Isles expanded substantially earlier this century, but over the last 30 years there has been a dramatic general decline of around 50%. In Shetland this decline has reduced numbers from around 9273 pairs in 1969–70 to around 4392 pairs in 1985–87 and around 4000 pairs today. There are a number of possible reasons for this decline in Britain generally, including death from botulism picked up from refuse tips, which visiting immature birds from Shetland could also contract. In Shetland itself, the very large population earlier this century was no doubt supported by the local herring fishing boom, which provided plenty 'pickings' during the summer breeding season. Latterly fish waste has been less available locally, both on land and probably in inshore waters, and we know from research (Camphuysen *et al.*, 1995) that the larger gulls are scavenging at fishing boats offshore. It is therefore likely that food has been the limiting factor and that the fall in the population, and possible stabilization over the last decade, is a reflection of fishery changes. Though the decline may have halted generally in Shetland, herring gull numbers are increasing in Lerwick, where they are nesting on rooftops. At the last count in 1993 there were over 60 pairs, which is a sharp rise in the last couple of decades, perhaps because they find the thin plastic, domestic rubbish bags easy to open!

The much smaller common gull is known in Shetland as the *peerie, pikka* or *tinna maa*, the terms *pikka* and *tinna* from the Old Norse to pick. It is equally at home 'picking' small fish from the sea or invertebrates from fields and meadows. In Shetland it has become an almost ubiquitous breeder, found on sloping banks above the sea to freshwater and marine holms and even dry moorland sites, but mainly inland. Similarly, the black-headed gull, known as *hoodie maa* or *heedie craa* from its dark head, also breeds mainly inland but is virtually confined to holms in freshwater lochs or in marshes or salt marshes. Both gulls were probably subject to egg harvesting in the past, although unlikely on the scale of exploitation of the herring gull and *peerie swaabie*. Since they both nest inland it is likely that the Seafarer survey in 1969–70, which was mostly coastal, probably underestimated both populations. Nevertheless, it seems that there has been a genuine expansion of numbers of the common gull in the last 30 years and a fall in the relatively small numbers of the black-headed gull. The 1969–70 numbers of the black-headed gull seem to be similar to those suggested by Venables and Venables (1955), but the 1985–87 numbers are 50% less at 258 pairs. Because of its inland or estuarine feeding preference, is is unlikely that the black-headed gull will ever be very numerous in Shetland. In Orkney, where numbers of both species are higher, they appear to have decreased in numbers recently.

CHAPTER 9

The Fair Isle

Sheep Craig

'As I said, this is Fridarey,' Ingrid pointed across the fields. 'The Orkneyjar, a day's sail, maybe.' She pointed back through the house. 'Hjaltland, the same again. If it's weather, that is. You can see Hjaltland from the island on a clear day. It's harder to see the Orkneyjar because there are fewer hills there, though we see them sometimes.'

Islanders, Margaret Elphinstone

There are a number of isolated islands on the fringes of Shetland, each with its own character, culture and attraction for visitors, for example Foula, with its huge cliffs and *bonxies*; Papa Stour, with its fretted coastline of stacks, arches and caves; Out Skerries, with its low fragments of limestone and flowers; and Fair Isle, an almost cliff-bound, green stepping stone, halfway between Shetland and its nearest neighbour Orkney.

Fair Isle is divided in two by a hill dyke that separates mainly fertile agricultural land to the south, where the crofts are situated, from moorland rising to a height of 217 m at Ward Hill to the north. This moorland is the common grazing of the crofters, a mixture of heather, maritime grassland and blanket bog and the home for *bonxies* and a much-studied arctic skua colony. There are around 60 people resident on Fair Isle and despite being one of the most isolated communities in Britain, the future seems assured with a steady number of children at the school. There is only one safe landing on Fair Isle at North Haven, where the island's sea

243

link, the *Good Shepherd*, unloads supplies and visitors arriving from Grutness, by Sumburgh. Fair Isle also has an airstrip and air-link with Shetland.

Although this chapter concentrates on bird migration, Fair Isle has an internationally important breeding seabird population of which there are 14 species. The island is also renowned for its coastal scenery and, not least, for the management of its crofting township: in 1996 the community won the Crofting Township of the Year award. This combination of the aesthetic grandeur of its coast, its seabirds, migration studies and its cultural heritage won the island the European Diploma from the Council of Europe in 1985, which it has held ever since.

Since 1954 Fair Isle has been owned by the National Trust for Scotland. Today the island is one of those few examples of a community and landlord working in harmony and this appears to be as much a result of a supportive Trust as of a vibrant and confident community. The economy of the island now depends to a great extent on visitors, who are warmly welcomed and who come predominantly to sample remote island life and to see the seabirds in their element. In turn those seabird colonies, as in the rest of Shetland, depend on the rich and unpolluted marine resource on their doorstep. This resource, mainly sandeels, is under pressure from fishing and under threat from nearby oil exploration, oil extraction and tanker traffic passing close to the island. A partnership led by the community and supported by the Trust, the RSPB and the Fair Isle Bird Observatory Trust has therefore sprung up to establish a Marine Nature Reserve that will protect the resource for the seabirds and for the people of Fair Isle.

The cliff coast of Fair Isle that supports the seabird colonies is heavily indented with deep and narrow *geos*, especially on the west coast. On the east side the coast is dominated by Sheep Craig, a block of steeply pitched sandstone rising to 132 m and joined to the main island by a knife-edge of crumbling stone. Until relatively recently sheep were kept on its roof of 4.5 ha of rabbit-free grassland, but now only seabirds live there. There are two endemic races on Fair Isle: the Fair Isle wren (*Troglodytes troglodytes fridariensis*) and the Fair Isle field mouse (*Apodemus sylvaticus fridariensis*). Besides the latter, the only other mammals are house mice, rabbits, feral cats and grey seals, although harbour seals and many cetaceans are seen regularly.

Why is it that this particular, tiny, exposed island of rock that is Fair Isle, with its bleak outlook and, for most of the year, rather barren surface, should rate as a Mecca for bird migration enthusiasts from around the world? What makes it so different and important? Firstly, its geographical location. Fair Isle is almost 40 km from both Orkney and mainland Shetland, well to the north of mainland Britain where the Atlantic and the North Sea merge. Secondly, weather systems with winds from the easterly quarter coincide with the annual migrations of birds on the European continent and sweep them westerly across the open sea. Therefore, Shetland and Fair Isle, and to a lesser extent the islands of Orkney, provide the first landfall for tired migrants in need of respite from the rigours of their migratory journey and an opportunity to rest and refuel before continuing (Fig. 34). Other islands, including mainland Orkney and Shetland, and more isolated outposts such as North Ronaldsay to the north of the former and the Out Skerries to the east of the latter, also attract migrants. On the large islands the migrants are widely scattered and less observable; however, with dedicated staff, absent elsewhere, observer effort per unit area is most intense on Fair Isle. This simply means that although migrants may occur quite widely in the Northern Isles, they are many times more likely to be recorded on Fair Isle. Finally, the island is small with little natural shelter or cover and so few migrants alight and depart without being seen. It is all these factors combined that has given Fair Isle the coveted status as one of the best all-round migration watch-points in the British Isles and many years of regular observation and documentation there has given us our present under-standing of bird migration patterns. In this chapter we look at the history of migrant observation on Fair Isle and at many of the species that regularly, and rarely, descend exhausted off an easterly wind on to terra firma.

The early writers on Shetland's birds, such as Low and Dunn, described the massive seabird colonies and discussed the breeding species, but the importance of Shetland as a bird migration focus was not appreciated. It was the Edmondstons and Saxbys of Unst who were the first to record migrant passage in detail. These records naturally concentrate on the birds of Unst but the posthumous publication in 1874 of *The Birds of Shetland* by Henry Saxby, edited by his brother, does give us an accurate insight into Shetland's visiting species that had been sighted or taken.

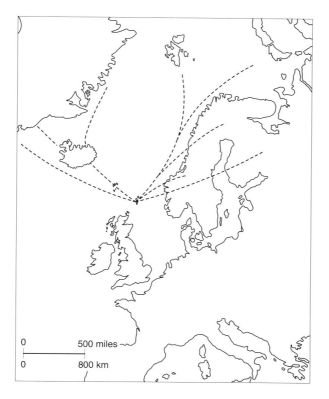

FIGURE 34 *Approximate routes followed by migrating birds that use Fair Isle and Shetland as 'stepping stones'* (from Berry & Johnston, 1980).

76.   *Sheep shearing, Fair Isle: crofters still cooperate to bring in the sheep from the hill and to dip and shear.*
(Courtesy of P. Harvey.)

HISTORY OF MIGRATION OBSERVATION

At the turn of the last century a growing interest nationally in the phenomenon of bird migration led to the appointment, by the British Association, of Dr William Eagle Clarke, then a Keeper of Natural History at the Royal Scottish Museum, to investigate the migration of birds in the British Isles. Eagle Clarke collected observations from lighthouses and coastal areas and, in 1903, produced five reports to the British Association Committee on the *Migration of Birds as Observed on the British and Irish Coasts*. In completing these digests he realized that much information was missing, so he decided to undertake a series of investigations himself and visited lighthouses, lightships and remote islands all round the British coast. These investigations resulted in the publication, in 1912, of the two-volume work *Studies in Bird Migration*. In the second volume he covered his research on Fair Isle in three chapters, describing the island as 'the British Heligoland'. Between 1905 and 1911 he visited Fair Isle eight times to cover both the spring and autumn migration seasons and during these visits recorded 207 species, half the number on the then British list.

Others then became interested in the island. Mary, Duchess of Bedford made several long visits between 1910 and 1914 in her yacht *Sapphire*, staying at Pund. After an interruption due to the First World War, Eagle Clarke again visited the island in 1921, this time accompanied by Surgeon Rear-Admiral John H. Stenhouse. The latter was to visit the island annually until 1928. The islanders themselves also contributed (and still do) greatly to the recording of migrants. For example, George Stout of Busta, his brother Stewart and their cousin Jerome Wilson of Springfield all assisted Eagle Clarke with his enquiries, collecting and recording in his absence. Since the Second World War, Jerome Wilson, George Stout of Field (known widely as *Fieldy*) and J. A. Stout of Midway have all contributed to Fair Isle's records.

These islanders had considerable ornithological ability. Without the advantage of modern field guides, detailed information was obviously not available. Field glasses were of poor quality, but of course in those days many of the more unusual migrants were shot and preserved for later identification. This in itself must have required considerable skill and patience, as powder and shot were in short supply and there is no evidence of large numbers of birds being taken simply on the chance of finding a rarity. It was obvious that these men were excellent at field recognition and only collected the unusual birds to confirm the record. This tradition of ornithological skills has continued down the years and through generations of Fair Islanders.

Meanwhile, in 1933, almost at the other end of Britain, R. M. Lockley established a bird observatory, as a private venture, on the island of Skokholm off the Welsh coast. The following year the Midlothian Ornithological Club set up the first Scottish Bird Observatory on the Isle of May in the Firth of Forth. An enthusiastic young member of this club was George Waterston. As a schoolboy he met John Stenhouse at the Royal Scottish Museum and was also influenced by the Misses Baxter and Rintoul. Following visits to the Isle of May he made his first trip to Fair Isle in 1935. After this visit George Waterston returned annually until the start of the Second World War in 1939. He often stayed with Fieldy on his croft and it was then that he began to form a plan to start a bird observatory on Fair Isle. These ideas, together with the possibilities of building a Heligoland trap, were discussed with a range of other interested visitors including Pat Venables, H. F. Witherby, P. A. D. Hollom, C. A. Norris and Theo Kay of Lerwick. The Heligoland trap, named after the famous German island, was developed to catch migrants so that they could be examined, ringed and released without harm. It became the main method of securing in-hand migrants for many years and still is today.

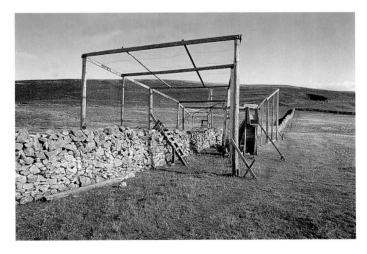

77. *Double-dyke trap, Fair Isle: migrant birds, tired and hungry from a long flight over the sea, follow the meagre shelter of the dyke and are caught in the narrows of the trap, identified, recorded, ringed and released.* (Courtesy of R. Riddington.)

Just as with Eagle Clarke before him, a war interrupted George Waterston's visits to Fair Isle. In 1941, while on service on Crete, he was taken prisoner and subsequently transferred to a prisoner-of-war camp in Germany. While incarcerated there he made further plans for the bird observatory with a fellow prisoner, Ian Pitman, who also became a supporter of the project. In 1943, due to ill-health, George Waterston was repatriated and incredibly, whilst aboard the home-coming liner, his first sight of the British coast was Sheep Craig on Fair Isle. The following year he was back on the island determined to press forward the plans for the establishment of a bird observatory with research facilities and accommodation for visitors. After a series of setbacks he bought the island from Sumburgh Estates in early 1948. Coincidentally, the war-time naval huts at North Haven became vacant and these were refurbished to form the long-planned observatory.

The original observatory committee included Sir Arthur Duncan as chairman, Ian Pitman as treasurer and George Waterston himself as secretary. The Fair Isle Bird Observatory Trust (FIBOT) was then formed to oversee the running of the operation. Later, in 1954, George Waterston made the island over to the National Trust for Scotland, leaving the observatory to be run independently by FIBOT. In the mid-1960s it became obvious that the ageing naval huts were coming to the end of their useful life and, after an appeal through the Friends of Fair Isle, a new observatory overlooking North Haven and Sheep Craig was opened in 1969. These building were extended and modernized in 1988–89 and the observatory continues its work today as a tribute to the foresight and perseverance of George Waterston who died in 1980. During this time more Heligoland traps were designed and constructed and those such as the gully, the double dyke and the single dyke have become classics in trap design. It is the opportunity these traps gave to observatory staff to handle and ring large numbers of migrants that has provided the basic data from which we have developed an insight into the origin and destination of Fair Isle migrants.

However, to follow the development on Fair Isle of our understanding of bird migration we must return to 1948, to the appointment of the observatory's first director, Kenneth Williamson, and the start of systematic migrant records. Eagle Clarke had thought that Fair Isle was on a major migration route for north European migrants; however, through regular observation it became apparent that the large arrivals of birds on Fair Isle coincided mainly with some well-established weather conditions and wind directions. Information that rapidly accumulated from trapping enabled Williamson to develop new ideas on *drift migration*, which he extensively described in *Fair Isle and Its Birds* (1965). His theories on migration largely hold good today and have been further refined by data from the bird observatory network around the British coast and radar studies.

MIGRATION THEORY

To understand migrant falls on Fair Isle we need to see the process of bird migration on the wider stage. A common life strategy is for birds to breed in high latitudes, where abundant summer resources confer greater chances of successful reproduction, and then undergo a potentially hazardous migration to southern climes where less-pronounced seasonality offers a richer environment in the winter (or non-breeding season). Vast numbers of birds breed in north-western and northern parts of Europe, across into Siberia and Asia, and most of these move south in winter. Populations of some species traditionally move south-west to winter in the British Isles, for example plovers such as golden plover and lapwing, and thrushes, such as blackbird, fieldfare and redwing. In the autumn these species cross the North Sea to eastern Britain before continuing their journey overland. For species such as these, especially the smaller birds, Fair Isle may provide a vital stepping stone. Other species, including many chats, such as whinchat and redstart, and warblers, such as garden warbler, willow warbler and chiffchaff, travel further south, some to the Mediterranean region, some continuing into Africa, crossing the Sahara to rich equatorial zones. The normal route of these species is overland and south across the Continent, but sometimes weather conditions may force them away from their normal route. For example, good weather conditions of clear skies and light winds in northern Europe may encourage birds to begin their journey south. Once underway, developing easterly winds may *drift* them off course and out over the North Sea. Following the line of least resistance, they continue on a south-west flight path until cloud and poor weather bring them lower and lower and eventually on to the northern isles. The flashing light from lighthouses probably pull birds in from a considerable distance and night migrants, in poor visibility, probably hear the fog-horns or even waves crashing on the shores. Williamson showed that the typical weather system that produced these landfalls was high pressure over Scandinavia with low pressure across southern Britain, Ireland or southern Europe (Fig. 35).

Other birds in the autumn come from the north-west (Fig. 34), from Faroe, Iceland and Greenland. They migrate south-east to winter either in the British Isles or, further south, in the Iberian peninsula or Africa. Many wildfowl, for example whooper swans and barnacle geese, and some passerines, such as meadow pipits and wheatears, are involved. These species are regular and intentional migrants through Fair Isle.

The situation in the spring is the reverse of the autumn, but numbers tend to be lower for a number of reasons. Firstly, autumn birds include the young of the year, many of whom will succumb, either on the wintering grounds or during migration. Secondly, there is a greater sense of urgency in the spring, as the drive to get back to the breeding grounds is strong. In most cases, the first individuals to arrive at the breeding grounds can claim the best territory and mate. Stops to feed and regain strength therefore tend to be fewer and shorter. The strong desire to get back to the breeding grounds also produces the phenomenon of *spring overshooting*, when north-bound migrants in their eagerness overshoot their normal destination and end up further north or west than they should. This process enhances the variety of species that arrive on Fair Isle in spring with the, almost regular, appearance of south-eastern species such as short-toed lark and subalpine warbler. Some birds also take a more eastern migration route in spring and are therefore less likely to appear than in the autumn. However, the basic principles of drift migration still apply and can explain the appearance of many species on Fair Isle in spring on easterly winds.

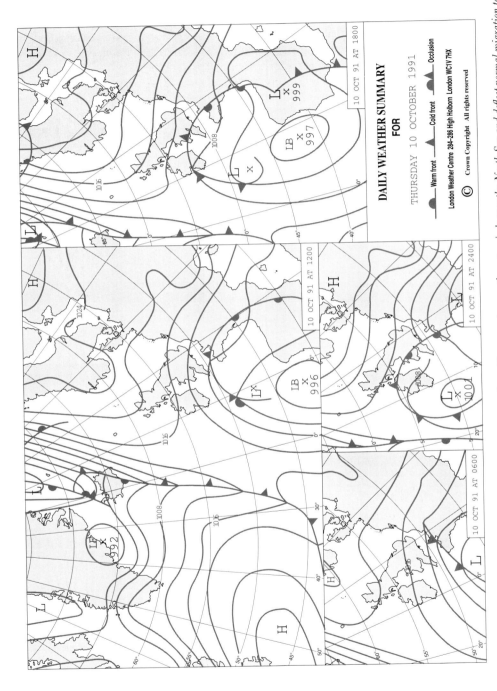

FIGURE 35   *High pressure over Scandinavia and a low to the south combine to produce south-easts winds over the North Sea and deflect normal migration to bring birds to Fair Isle and Shetland* (courtesy of the London Weather Centre).

As well as a large number of regular migrants, Fair Isle is justifiably famous for its long list of species that are vagrants or accidental visitors to Britain. Fair Isle in fact has more records of such species than any other single site in Britain. Typically, these are Far Eastern, Siberian or Asian breeding species that winter in southern parts of Asia. Essentially the same processes that bring the regular migrants are responsible for the appearance of such waifs and strays; however, in this case, more extreme weather patterns are required, for example if a large blocking anticyclone sits over the Eurasian landmass, birds travelling with the wind from the Far East are swept west along its southern flank. Another mechanism that brings rarities to Britain and Fair Isle is that of *reverse migration*, where the orientation, usually of young birds, is impaired. Individuals may then migrate in the wrong direction, often in completely the opposite direction to that which they should be travelling. For example, a paddyfield warbler, caught on migration in Lithuania on 8 September 1996, was trapped on Fair Isle 11 days later. A straight line from the western part of this species' breeding grounds, through Lithuania to Fair Isle, is a mirror image of the direct route to its wintering grounds. Fair Isle has recorded several species that are virtually annual visitors, yet which are virtually unknown outside the Northern Isles, species such as lanceolated warbler (from Siberia) and yellow-breasted bunting (from north-east Europe to eastern Siberia).

Migration through Fair Isle and the other Northern Isles, including Shetland, is not only a reflection of the geographical position and physical characteristics of the islands, but also of the migration characteristics of the species themselves and often the prevailing meteorological conditions. It is these complex interrelationships that help to explain both regular and occasional breeding occurrences in Shetland of species from the north, south and east, discussed in Chapter 6. Having described the processes and some general patterns of migration, the rest of the chapter gives a brief chronological account of spring and autumn migration on the island; for a systematic list see Appendix 1.

SPRING

As early as the end of February, the first signs of spring migration materialize. The first *shalders* (oystercatchers) announce their return in shrill tones, and small numbers of other waders appear for the first time since winter: a few ringed plovers and small parties of golden plovers and lapwings. Weatherwise, the winter is far from over, but the days are already lengthening and on warmer, less windy days fragments of courtship and display are seen. The numbers of waders increases steadily through March, with flocks of *shalders* being the most visible sign of the approaching breeding season. In the latter half of March particularly, the early passerines begin to appear. The few hardy laverocks that have endured the winter on the island are swelled by increasing numbers of migrants, which are more restless than the locals and form tight, jittery flocks. Towards the end of the month more passerines appear, typically a mix of those heading north and north-west, such as the meadow pipit and pied wagtail, and those making for the Continent, such as dunnocks, robins, thrushes and finches. Although numbers are usually small compared with autumn, in some years the end of March and the beginning of April produces large concentrations of thrushes and finches, e.g. day counts of 3000 blackbirds in 1958 and 1984, and 1000 chaffinches, also in 1958. Commonly by the end of March the first long-distance spring migrants, *steynshakker* (wheatear) and chiffchaff, appear. Seabirds, too, provide evidence of the new breeding season, with guillemot and razorbill once again crowding inshore waters, gannets on their nest sites, the first *bonxies* patrolling the hill and, around the first few days of April, the first *Tammy Nories* returning to land.

Arctic skua and tern

April, the main month for spring migration further south in Britain, can still be a cool and very variable month in the Northern Isles as we have seen in earlier chapters. Wintry weather is still common, and many species flooding into Britain from the south are dissuaded from pushing further north by the weather. In years when the month is warmer, with favourable southerly winds, there can be a wonderful variety of migrants, but essentially the pattern established in late March is reinforced. Passage of many species of waders peaks in April, especially of those that wintered in Europe, for example the plovers, curlew, woodcock and turnstone. Species from further afield, such as whimbrel, green and common sandpiper, make their first showing. Passerines are often still dominated numerically by the robin, thrushes, starling, finches and buntings, but more of the African-wintering species appear as the month progresses: the first hirundines, chats and warblers appear at this time. The early spring is a good time also for several species that are scarce, though annual, visitors to Fair Isle, such as stonechat (in March), grey wagtail, mistle thrush (late March/early April) and great grey shrike and bullfinch (April). Woodlark, dipper and hawfinch peak in April, but these visitors are more elusive and less than annual. A few memorable vagrants have been recorded during April, among them pallid harrier, sandhill crane, calandra lark and three song sparrows (including Britain's first, on 27 April 1959), but for the most part the early spring is not noted for extreme rarities.

May is typically *the* month for spring migration in Shetland, although some of the most unexpected and extreme rarities occur in June. As always, the weather patterns are crucial, for example the whole of May 1991 was dominated by westerly winds and just one single *Sylvia* warbler was logged by despondent observers during the entire month! However, May has produced some outstanding *falls* down the years too. As April merges into May, so the emphasis turns from thrushes and finches to chats, warblers and flycatchers. One of the most memorable falls occurred on 8–9 May 1970, when 700 redstarts, 350 whinchat, 1000 willow warblers and 120 pied flycatchers all descended on Fair Isle. More recently, a similar fall occurred on 18–21 May 1996, when the main species involved peaked at 700 *steynshekkers*, 220 redstarts, 75 whitethroats, 750 willow warblers, 125 pied flycatchers and 80 reed buntings. In most years the number of these species are smaller, but seeing them on a sunny May day on Fair Isle, decked in their fresh spring finery, is a memorable experience.

Associated with common species, many scarce migrants to Britain are seen regularly in May on Fair Isle, sometimes in surprising numbers. Bluethroat perhaps typifies spring on Fair Isle more than any other species. Males of the red-spotted race appear in dazzling plumage, so different from the drab autumn birds. The record count for Fair Isle is 70 on 13 May 1985, and since 1970 they have been regular visitors during the middle 2 weeks of that month. Other scarce species, such as wryneck, short-toed lark, red-backed shrike and ortolan bunting, are recorded most springs. So too are species that are 'officially' rare in Britain, for example red-throated pipit, thrush nightingale, subalpine warbler and rustic bunting. The list of extreme vagrants in May is long and impressive, including five species that have been added to the British list from Fair Isle: American kestrel (25 May 1976), western sandpiper (27 May 1956) and white-crowned sparrow (15 May 1977), all from America, in addition to pallid harrier (8 May 1931) and thrush nightingale (15 May 1911).

From the end of May the number of migrants passing through declines markedly and through June migrant activity gradually dwindles. Notwithstanding, there are some species for which numbers are often highest in early June rather than late May, such as quail, turtle dove, icterine warbler, red-breasted flycatcher, golden oriole and common rosefinch. Arctic-breeding waders, such as knot and sanderling, often put in an appearance in early June, whilst hirundines (particularly swallows and house martins) typically peak during the last few days of May and the first week of June. As mentioned above, many weird and wonderful vagrants are the province of June: red-rumped swallow from southern Europe (2 June 1905), hermit thrush from North America (2 June 1975) and Cretzschmar's bunting from south-east Europe (10 June 1967) were all new to the British list from Fair Isle in June, whilst in the past 10 years both lesser kestrel and olivaceous warbler were new to Shetland during this month.

Even the extreme tail-end of spring can hold major surprises. In 1992 Britain's first brown flycatcher was trapped on 1 July, followed next day by Fair Isle's first Pacific golden plover. In mid-July 1997, a black-eared wheatear of the eastern race (*Oenanthe hispanica melanoleuca*) spent 9 days on the island in full primary moult; although truly a midsummer record, it is probably more sensible to talk about this in ecological terms as a late spring record. Crossbills are typically recorded during the summer and these are very definitely post-breeding movements. The species is essentially an *irruptive* visitor to the Northen Isles, arriving in large numbers in some years when a combination of good breeding success and food shortages in northern breeding grounds stimulates these movements. The largest and most prolonged irruption during the last 50 years was in 1990, with a peak count of 225 common crossbills on 23 August; associated with these came a total of six two-barred crossbills.

AUTUMN

Autumn begins early in the Northern Isles, with waders returning from the far north at the end of July. Species such as knot, sanderling, dunlin, purple sandpiper and bar-tailed godwit are frequently recorded, although all these species reach peak numbers a little later, in August or early September. Movements of common and black-headed gulls are apparent at this time, too, both species reaching a peak in early August. Sifting through these concentrations of common species can often yield surprises, such as Fair Isle's first ring-billed gull in August 1992. During August, the magic easterly winds are viewed with increasing optimisim and expectation by watchers on Fair Isle. Barred warbler is a regular autumn visitor (up to 14 have been recorded in a day) and the first usually arrive early in the month. Red-backed shrike and common rosefinch are other early migrants that frequently entertain the visitor in early August. Common warblers, particularly willow warbler and flycatchers, begin to appear in early August given the right conditions. In a good year it is clear that autumn has begun by the middle of the month. More unusual visitors that appear in mid-August may typically involve species from eastern Europe, such as aquatic warbler or rose-coloured starling, or species from further east, such as an early citrine wagtail. However, the end of August signals the onset of more realistic vagrant potential. At this time, a number of migrant species reach their peak autumn passage, among them wood and common sandpipers, wryneck, pied wagtail, whinchat, wood warbler and red-backed shrike. Eastern species, such as citrine warbler, greenish warbler and yellow-breasted bunting, are the more typical rarities of late August, but exceptional vagrants do occur, such as the first recorded juvenile red-necked stint in Europe (from east/north-east Asia) found newly dead in South Harbour on 31 August 1994.

Early September marks the peak passage for several common southbound species, meadow pipit, redstart, garden warbler, willow warbler and pied flycatcher among them. At this stage in the season, the volume of migrants flowing through the Isle is high, and discovering a vagrant requires patient sifting through the abundant and commoner congenors. But the effort can be very rewarding, such as Britain's first booted warbler (3 September 1936) and the first Tennessee warbler (6 September 1975).

As mid-month approaches, the volume of southbound species declines, but the variety remains unaffected or even increases. Mid-September is traditionally the time when observers seeking Fair Isle's 'big four' tend to book in at the observatory.

The four species, pechora pipit, lanceolated warbler, Pallas' grasshopper warbler and yellow-breasted bunting, are all closely associated with Fair Isle. Although today there is vastly increased observer coverage in Britain with records from many other areas (especially mainland Shetland), Fair Isle remains the most reliable site in western Europe to see this quartet. Yellow-breasted bunting (breeding from Finland through to east Asia) and lanceolated warbler (central and southern Siberia, with its first British record on Fair Isle on 9 September 1908) are annual visitors, or nearly so. Pechora pipit (from Asia, with the first British record on Fair Isle on 23 September 1925) has been recorded in most recent years, while Pallas' grasshopper warbler, another Asian breeder, is recorded more sporadically. Great snipe, another Fair Isle speciality, is most frequently recorded during September. As well as these special vagrants, other more regular species reach peak numbers in mid-September, among them blackcap and common rosefinch, whilst arctic warbler is most frequently recorded at this time too. Numbers of skylarks start to build up around the crofts, favouring the harvested oat crops, though the largest flocks are recorded at the end of the month and into October.

Late September, however, is Fair Isle's zenith. For the enthusiast the list of vagrants is long and mouth-watering. Additions to the British list at this time include Pallas' reed bunting (29 September 1975), citrine wagtail (20 September 1954), river warbler (24 September 1961), Blyth's reed warbler (29 September 1910) and paddyfield warbler (26 September 1925), all from the east and the last four of which have all been recorded more than once in the last decade. Other momentous finds at this time include northern oriole, bobolink and savannah sparrow (from America), and rufous turtle dove and red-flanked bluetail from the East. Late September is the peak time for several more regular visitors from the East, notably Richard's pipit and yellow-browed warbler.

Early October holds almost as much promise as the latter part of September. The roll-call of notable finds includes three firsts for Britain: grey-cheeked thrush from America (5 October 1953) and from Asia, thick-billed warbler (6 October 1955) and Siberian rubythroat (9 October 1975). Buff-bellied pipit (1953), yellow-browed bunting (1980) and Blackburnian warbler (1988) were all second records for Britain. This is also the best time for other, more regular eastern species such as short-toed lark, little bunting and rustic bunting. October also brings much more in the way of wildfowl passing through Shetland on their way south for the winter, with peak counts of whooper swans amd pink-footed geese (from Iceland) and barnacle geese (from Spitsbergen) in the first half of the month. By the end of September robins, thrushes and finches begin to out-number warblers and chats, and this becomes more pronounced through October. Robins, redwings and song thrushes move through in their largest numbers in mid-October, whilst fieldfares and blackbirds reach their highest numbers later in the month. The spectacle of vast numbers of geese and thrushes is one of the most dramatic sights of October bird-watching on Fair Isle. On 14 October 1979 an estimated 65 000 redwings literally carpeted Fair Isle. Such mass arrivals of common species invariably includes scarcer species; the fall of 25 000 redwings on 11 October 1991 brought olive-backed pipit, lanceolated warbler and Radde's warbler, one of the great days of autumn migration on Fair Isle.

As October nears its end, wildfowl and thrushes become larger components of the daily log totals, but there are still many diversions. Northern bullfinches peak at this time, the huge invasion of 1994 peaking at 77 individuals on 1 November. Rarities still trickle through at this late stage, at least in those years when the weather conditions remain favourable into November. Britain's first pine bunting arrived on Fair Isle on 30 October 1911 and the first week in November has produced little bustard, little swift, Blyth's pipit and pine bunting in recent years. Other scarce migrants at this time might typically include woodlark, shorelark and waxwing, whilst this is the best time to see species such as woodcock, little auk and long-eared owl. Even the darkest days of the winter months on Fair Isle can provide excitement – an ivory gull in December, a great bustard and harlequin duck in January – and keep the migration enthusiasts on their toes.

Although migrant recording, established by Eagle Clarke all those years ago, is still the principal activity of the observatory, over the last 50 years its work has expanded considerably to include recording of all aspects of wildlife on the island. Fair Isle is now one of the four National Seabird Monitoring Programme sites in Britain (the others being Canna, Isle of May and Skomer) and much of the summer work of the observatory staff is devoted to recording seabird breeding numbers, productivity and survival as well as supporting research. Most recently the observatory has taken part in the Europe-wide study organized by the European Science Foundation called the European–African Songbird Migration Project, which aims to study patterns of migration and different habitat use by migrant birds: a collaborative project covering many migration centres across Europe and Africa, using standardized recording and measurement techniques and computers to analyse the mass of field data. It has also joined in a partnership with SNH to provide a ranger service to interpret the wildlife of the island for visitors. What a great distance, metaphorically, the observatory has travelled since those early days and, it must be recognized, what a positive contribution it has also made to the life of the islanders.

CHAPTER 10

Shetland Naturalists

Whooper swans on Spiggie Loch

Mr. Thos. Edmondston has been long known to me personally and by correspondence. From his earliest years he evinced the most uncommon zeal in the cause of Natural History, and has never ceased to improve himself in the various branches of it, especially in Botany. With this knowledge is combined a liberal education and an ardent desire to devote his whole life to the cause of science. I consider him well qualified to lecture upon Natural History in general, and to fulfil the duties of a Professor in any Academy or University.

Sir William Hooker's testimonial for Thomas Edmondston in support of
his application for Professor of Botany at Glasgow University, 1844

Early naturalists in Shetland were visiting a foreign land, and their comments are important but have to be read critically. The earliest accounts are those of ministers who, generally speaking, were more interested in antiquities than natural history. Around 1800 medically trained men began to write about the islands and they have left us more information about natural history. Then in Victorian times, rarity seekers braved the journey north and laid the basis for our modern understanding of the islands' fauna and flora. Since 1945, natural historians in the modern sense have flocked to the islands, recording the species present and more recently interpreting the interactions and adaptations of local forms. However, apart from visitors from the south, many Shetlanders have become expert naturalists by any standards: Bruce, Kay, Henderson and particularly Edmondston, Saxby, Tullock and Scott have recorded the Shetland scene and provided the base upon which 'scientific' natural history can build.

EARLY TRAVELLERS AND NATURALISTS

In 1700 the General Assembly of the Church of Scotland sent seven ministers and one ruling elder 'to settle the ecclesiastical affairs of the islands on a presbyterian basis'. One of the ministers was John Brand, who published *A Brief Description of Orkney, Zetland, Pightland Firth and Caithness* in 1701. He was a wondermonger whose comments are always interesting even when gloriously wrong. For example, he recorded at length how shellfish in Shetland are often found buried alive in the ground a mile or more from the sea without realizing that this was a fishermen's habit so that bait was ready to hand. But he is worth reading; his account of arctic skua (*Scooty-aalin* in Shetland) habits is far more entertaining than some modern ornithological pomposity:

> There is a fowl called the Scutiallan, of a black colour and as big as a Wild Duck, which doth live upon the vomit and Excrements of other Fowls whom they pursue and having apprehended them, they cause them to Vomit up what they have lately taken and not yet digested: The Lord's Work both of Nature and Grace are wonderful, all speaking forth His Glorious Goodness, Wisdom and Power.

However the first real naturalist to leave a record of Shetland was George Low, minister of Birsay in Orkney, who made tours of the northern group in 1774 and 1778 on the instigation of Pennant, who published some of the results in his *Arctic Zoology* of 1784. Low's own account was not published in Kirkwall until 1879 as *A Tour through the Islands of Orkney and Schetland*.

At much the same time Sir John Sinclair of Ulbster, Caithness was collecting answers to 166 questions that he sent to every parish in Scotland, and which were published as *The Statistical Account of Scotland* between 1791 and 1799. (This is known as the 'Old Account' in distinction to the 'New Account' which appeared in 1845.) Answers to the natural history questions varied enormously. The minister of Northmavine deals with migratory birds simply: 'The Kettywakes and Thomas Norie birds nestle in great numbers, and come herein May and return in August'. Other ministers are more informative, but in general they were more interested in archaeology than natural history.

However the most important Shetland naturalists also emerged at this time. The first was Dr Arthur Edmondston of Hascosay (1776–1841), a family that had come into Shetland perhaps 100 years previously. His two-volume work *A View of the Ancient and Present State of the Zetland Isles* (1809) was the most comprehensive account of Shetland so far, and included a complete list of the Shetland fauna as

78. *Laurence Edmondston: the father of Thomas Edmondston and a naturalist and polyglot who planted the sycamores at Halligarth.* (Courtesy of J. Coutts.)

known at that time. His younger brother Laurence (1795–1879) became doctor in Unst, first living at Buness and then moving to Halligarth where he planted a small plantation, still the northernmost wood in the British Isles. He too was interested in natural history, writing papers on the subject and adding the glaucous, Icelandic and ivory gulls and the snowy owl to the British list. He was also a linguist and a musician. Authorship was not confined to the male side of the family: his wife Eliza wrote *Sketches and Tales of Shetland* and his daughter Jessie (with Biot her brother) wrote *The Home of a Naturalist*. Jessie, Laurence Edmondston's youngest daughter, married Henry Saxby in 1859, who later took over from his father-in-law as Unst doctor. His book *The Birds of Shetland* was published posthumously in 1874. Their son, Thomas Edmondston Saxby, continued the ornithological interests of his father and went on to publish regular articles on Unst's birds. Laurence's eldest son, Tom (brother of Jessie), carried on the family tradition in pursuing natural history from an early age. He became a professional botanist and produced the first *Flora of Shetland* (1845). But for a tragic accident he would have outshone them all. We return to him later in the chapter.

GEOLOGISTS

The first account of the geology of Shetland was published in 1798 by Robert Jameson. Before this only a few mineralogical notes in travellers' accounts of Shetland had been published.

Robert Jameson, who descended from a Shetland family, was interested in natural history from childhood. His interests led his father to apprentice him to an Edinburgh surgeon. Among the lectures he attended at the university were those of the first active Professor of Natural History, John Walker, a noted geologist. Soon he was a favourite student, was given charge of the museum and taken on field excursions. His chief interest became geology and in 1794, at the age of 20, he gave up his medical career before graduation and spent 3 months in Shetland during the summer studying geology and natural history. In 1797 he visited Arran and his *Outline of the Mineralogy of the Shetland Islands and of the Island of Arran* appeared in the next year. In 1799 he made a 6-week survey of Orkney and declared it the most uninteresting journey he ever made. In 1800 an account appeared in his book *An Outline of the Mineralogy of Scottish Isles*. In modern terms both are geology books.

In 1804 he became Professor of Natural History at Edinburgh and remained in this post until his death 50 years later. Jameson was extraordinarily successful in producing geologists and for many years most of the geologists working in Shetland were his students. He was a poor lecturer, but students were attracted by his subject matter, his field excursions, his genial nature and his ability to befriend them. Charles Darwin, his most famous student, declared that Jameson's lectures were so dull that they made him determined never to read a book on geology. However, Darwin found virtually all lecture courses dull.

One of Jameson's earliest students was an Orcadian, T. S. Traill, who went on to have an eminent career in medicine but whose lifelong interest was chemistry, mineralogy and mineral collecting. He also made an important collection of fossil fish from Orkney. He qualified in 1803 and immediately visited Shetland. His account of the geology was published in 1806 in Patrick Neill's *A Tour Through the Islands of Orkney and Shetland*. Some of the minerals he collected may be seen in Lerwick Museum. Later in life he became Professor of Medical Jurisprudence at Edinburgh and on a number of occasions gave Jameson's course of lectures.

In 1805 John Fleming graduated at Edinburgh. He was an ordinand but in 1802 had attended chemistry classes as well as his theological ones and gained a love for chemical analysis, which he concluded was the only true basis for mineralogy. This sentiment is so close to Jameson's views that it is almost certain that he was also a student of Jameson. In 1807 he embarked on a tour of Orkney and Shetland and, finding the Bressay ministry vacant, became minister there. He immediately began to publish geological and zoological papers. He was engaged to carry out an economic mineralogical survey in Shetland in 1809 for the sum of £20. The report was published in Shirreff's book *A General View of the Agriculture of the Shetland Islands* (1814). Soon afterwards he moved to mainland Scotland and by 1815 was regarded as Scotland's foremost zoologist. Eventually he became Professor of Natural History at Edinburgh and at the end of a long life was still publishing both zoological and geological papers. As a minister, a geologist and a zoologist he was active in the controversies over the Book of Genesis and evolution. After his death he was remembered as a tall, rather grim figure, full of personal kindness and gifted with a keen critical power. He seemed never happier than when he had an opportunity of exercising that power in sarcastically demolishing the arguments of those to whom he was opposed.

In 1817 two of Jameson's medical students qualified and became geologists. One was Ami Boué who returned to the Continent and wrote the book *Essai Geologique sur l'Écosse* (1820), which contained the first geological map of Scotland and the first attempt at correlation between the rocks of Scotland and Shetland. He became one of France's more eminent geologists.

The knowledge of Shetland Boué exhibited in his book and map was largely from Samuel Hibbert, who graduated the same year. On qualifying at the age of 35, 'sick of grinding', Hibbert departed for Shetland. He spent 3 months in 1817 and 6 months in 1818 surveying the islands. He had long been keen on 'pedestrian tours' and now scoured the hills and coasts of Shetland, a tall slightly stooped figure in a battered hat, a disreputable coat with capacious leather pockets stuffed with specimens, wearing leather gaiters and followed by his dog Silly. He spent his nights wherever was most convenient, sometimes on the straw-covered floor of a smoke-filled crofter's cottage, at others in a laird's house. His vagabond appearance seems to have been no disadvantage to him in Shetland but in England it once got him imprisoned on suspicion of poisoning a racehorse! His wife wrote to him urging him to return home from Shetland but not to bring his 'mineralogical dress ... for fear of lively company'. In 6 months he collected 4000 specimens, a prodigious number to collect in that length of time even today. His greatest difficulty lay in the lack of a good base map on which to record his observations. This involved him in much laborious topographical survey work. By 1820 he had published a detailed interpretation of the geology of Shetland, far more advanced than any previous account and, more important, the first geological map of Shetland, which was one of the earliest geological maps of any part of Scotland. His account was considerably expanded to include the antiquities of Shetland and published as *A Description of the Shetland Islands* (1822).

Hibbert discovered chromite in Unst in 1817 and this enabled Thomas Edmondston of Buness (elder brother of Arthur and Laurence Edmondston and uncle to the botanist) to start a chromite mining industry there. He endeavoured to start a kaolin mining industry by sending samples of kaolin from Fetlar via his friend W. Henry (discoverer of Henry's law) to Josiah Wedgwood in England. In the same year Thomas Edmondston was visited by another scientist, the great French astronomer and physicist J. B. Biot, who stayed with him for 2 months while determining the gravitational field with a pendulum, part of a project to determine the shape of the earth. In 1818 H. Kater, the English surveyor arrived to repeat the experiment. This was the first geophysical work done in Shetland. More than 100 years were to elapse before any further geophysical work was done there.

These two visitors were followed in 1820 by John MacCulloch, who had been a student with Jameson and who was then employed as a geologist by the Ordnance Survey of the time. He was sent to Shetland to determine what allowances should be made in the gravity determinations for local gravitational anomalies, and to add the geology of Shetland to the geological map of Scotland that he was making. He is a much-neglected and undervalued geologist. He was probably the world's first government-employed geological surveyor and for a time constituted a national (Scottish) geological survey; his map published in 1836 is the first official geological map of a country.

R. J. H. Cunningham attended chemistry classes at Edinburgh in 1833–36 including almost certainly Jameson's classes; even within that time he was already reading papers on his own geological survey work. In 1838 he read a paper on the geology of southern Mainland of Shetland, based on a survey made in 1837, which was unfortunately never published. Five years later he died having already surveyed six Scottish counties and six islands and published five papers.

Another of Jameson's students was W. F. Heddle, an Orcadian. He was a medical student qualifying in 1851. As a child he was already a fanatical collector.

A prize-winning herbarium of his was dropped into a stream by a fellow pupil and destroyed. Heddle immediately resolved to collect only indestructible objects and became a mineral collector. He spent some of his undergraduate years in Germany studying mineralogy and chemistry and his graduation thesis was entirely mineralogical. Nevertheless, on graduation he became a doctor in Edinburgh, but gave up after 5 years and departed to Faroe to collect minerals. He spent the next 20 years teaching in St Andrews University. He was one of the most dedicated, ruthless and successful mineral collectors who ever lived. He attacked the rocks with 13-kg hammers, wedges and explosives and, when possible, travelled in yachts to save time. His detailed mineralogical survey of the cliffs of Shetland was carried out in company with Patrick Dudgeon of Cargen in the latter's yacht and his geological map contains the navigational instructions needed to repeat the operation. His description of Shetland minerals published first in 1878 in *The County Geognosy and Mineralogy of Scotland, Orkney and Shetland* remained unimproved for about 80 years. His collection of Scottish minerals grew to be the greatest collection of any single country made by one man. However, he was much more than a collector, analysing his minerals both chemically and crystallographically, describing them in detail, and publishing the results.

The next major contribution to Shetland geology was made by very different men. B. N. Peach and J. Horne were career Geological Survey officers trained in London and Glasgow. Peach's father, C. W. Peach, a customs officer, was a very talented amateur geologist. In 1858 he visited Orkney and Shetland on the annual cruise of the ship belonging to the Commissioners of Northern Lights in company with Stevenson, the lighthouse engineer who constructed the Bound Skerry (Out Skerries) and Muckle Flugga lighthouses. Later, in 1865, he published the first paper to attribute the effects of glaciation visible in Shetland to ice action.

In 1876 B. N. Peach, as part of his duties, accompanied his chief A. Geikie, another great geologist later to become the first Professor of Geology at Edinburgh University and still later Director General of the Geological Survey, on a tour of Shetland. Disillusioned by having the results of his researches published by his superiors, Peach proposed to Horne in 1878 that they spend their summer holidays together carrying out work they could publish in their own names. Glaciation by major ice sheets was then just becoming accepted, and in 1870 Croll had proposed that the Scottish and Norwegian ice sheets had filled the North Sea and flowed to the west across Orkney and Shetland. They resolved to test this hypothesis by field work and to start work that summer in Shetland.

In 1879 they published an improved geological map of Shetland, an updated account of the geology and at the same time confirmed that Shetland had been glaciated by an ice sheet from Norway. In the following years they went on to survey Orkney and Caithness in the same way and completely vindicated Croll's hypotheses. They worked together for the rest of their lives. Their names became inseparable and famous in the geological world as they solved major problems in the Highlands of Scotland. Nevertheless, their work in Shetland was partly wrong: much of the evidence they cited for the glaciation of the central and northern parts of Shetland by Scandinavian ice was in fact produced by ice moving eastwards towards Scandinavia, as indeed C. W. Peach had originally suggested. The Dalsetter erratic, which confirms the presence of Scandinavian ice in the southern part of Shetland in an earlier glaciation, was discovered in the 1900s by a Bressay schoolmaster, T. Mainland.

In the 1930s the Geological Survey of Scotland returned to survey Shetland officially. A team of geologists devoted several summers to the project. Unfortunately, a backlog of work in the economically more important coal-field areas of Scotland interfered with the publication of the results. Consequently the first official geological map of Shetland did not appear until 1963; this map was on the scale of $\frac{1}{4}$ inch to 1 mile, about the same as Hibbert's map. The Survey returned again to Shetland in the 1960s to update the work. One inch to the mile maps appeared in 1968 and 1971 and the first memoir, *The Geology of Western Shetland*, by W. Mykura and J. Phemister was published in 1976.

It is interesting to compare Hibbert's map of 1822, Peach and Horne's somewhat smaller map of 1879 and the survey map of 1963. If Hibbert's boundaries are transferred to a modern base map and his archaic nomenclature is translated into modern terms, his map is seen to be very similar to the more recent maps. It is obvious that Peach and Horne based their work on his map, copying some of his boundaries and correcting others. The survey map differs from Peach and Horne's chiefly in the addition of more details. Taking into account the inaccuracy of the base map Hibbert had to use, the rudimentary state of geology in his time and the complexity of Shetland geology, his map is extraordinarily accurate. There can have been few maps made at that time that were as good.

Several members of the original Geological Survey team, in particular J. Phemister and H. H. Read, produced very accurate maps of parts of Shetland, which were published at the time of the survey or soon after. H. H. Read became a professor and in 1934 published the first paper on the geology of Shetland, which interpreted the rocks in terms of their history of development rather than merely describing and identifying them. This interpretative work inspired one of his students, Derek Flinn, to start a survey of Shetland that has lasted 30 years and which has contributed to and extended our knowledge and understanding of both the geology and geomorphology of Shetland; a glance at the Bibliography illustrates the scale of that contribution. Professor Flinn contributed Chapter 2 of this book and much to this chapter.

Wren

BOTANISTS

The most detailed account of botanical exploration in Shetland is by Walter Scott and Richard Palmer, to whom we will return, in *The Flowering Plants and Ferns of the Shetland Islands* (1987). A James Robertson is credited with some of the first identifications and descriptions of the Shetland flora around 1769, particularly with the first record of the northern plant, curved sedge. Close on his heels came the minister and naturalist George Low (1774) who added more records. Reports from Shetland ministers in *The Statistical Account of Scotland* at the end of that century and observations from further visitors to Shetland, naturalists, mineralogists and ornithologists in the early part of the nineteenth century continued to add interesting specimens to the growing botanical list. However, by far the most important development in the early history of our knowledge of the Shetland flora came from a Shetlander already mentioned, Thomas Edmondston of Unst (1825–1846).

Thomas Edmondston was born at Buness, Baltasound, but the family soon moved to Halligarth nearby where Thomas' father planted the trees that still grow there. Coming from such a gifted family it is perhaps not surprising that Thomas was a bright and precocious child, apparently teaching himself to read, from the Bible, at age 4 while at the age of 8 he took up the study of botany. In 1837 Dr W. D. Hooker (the son of Sir W. J. Hooker) called at Baltasound on his way back from an expedition to North Cape and, naturally, Thomas' father, a keen amateur naturalist, met him and introduced his son aged 11 to him. Thomas showed Dr Hooker his list of plants and the latter was so impressed that he included it in his book, *Notes on Norway* (1839). This was the first published list of Shetland's plants. In that same year, on the serpentinite soils of Unst, Thomas discovered a plant that he could not identify. In the following year he was credited in the *British Flora* (1838) with the first record in Shetland of the Norwegian sandwort, an arctic–alpine plant rare in Britain. He also discovered another unusual flowering plant on the serpentinite, but it was to take until 1843 before he was able to publish an account of it in *The Phytologist*. The paper was entitled 'Notice of a new British *Cerastium*' and began

> Having for some years entertained the opinion that the plant (above figured), although generally referred to *Cerastium latifolium*, was distinct from the plant called by that name in Britain, I have paid considerable attention to our Cerastia, and am disposed to conclude that my plant is truly distinct from the *C. latifolium* of Smith and Hooker.

Through this paper Thomas Edmondston was able to gain the recognition that *Cerastium nigrescens* subsp. *nigrescens*, the Shetland mouse-ear chickweed (or Edmondston's chickweed as it is informally known) was a new British *Cerastium*.

Meanwhile in 1841, at the age of 16, he had gone to Edinburgh University to study medicine. Things did not go well for him there and eventually he went on to

Aberdeen University in 1843. The following year he worked on his botanical records for Shetland and in 1845 his career must have seemed to have reached a peak when he published *A Flora of Shetland*, one of the earliest local floras of Britain, and at the same time was elected, at the age of 19, Professor of Natural History at the Andersonian University of Glasgow. The testimonial written in December 1844 by Sir William Hooker (then Director of the Royal Botanic Garden, Kew) in support of his application to the Glasgow professorship (see beginning of the chapter) demonstrates the impression Thomas had made on those at the pinnacle of the British botanical establishment.

An illustrious academic future seemed assured for Thomas, but it was not to be. Before he had given any lectures to the university he accepted what must have seemed a thrilling prospect: an offer to sail on HMS *Herald* as a naturalist on a government expedition to California to follow in the wake of Charles Darwin and the *Beagle* only 10 years earlier. In fact Darwin, among other eminent scientists, overwhelmed him with advice and requests. A year later and many thousands of miles under the keel and having passed around Cape Horn, Thomas arrived on the Galapagos islands where, like Darwin before him, he made a collection of as many new plants and animals as he could. After Galapagos the *Herald* returned to the South American coast and on the evening of 23 January 1846 anchored in Sua Bay (Peru). From the ship they were taken to the shore by boat and as Thomas was being carried from the boat to the beach, someone accidentally caught the hammer of a loaded gun in his trousers and discharged it. The ball passed through the arm of another sailor and struck Thomas on the temple killing him instantly.

It is impossible to know what Thomas might have gone on to achieve, but one could imagine that he might have returned with his natural history collection to meet up with Darwin among others and then? As it is, he is one of Shetland's prodigies and undoubtedly would have gone on to rank in achievement with the likes of Arthur Anderson (the founder of the P & O Shipping Co.). Thomas Edmondston was not without his faults, however, and his Shetland flora came in for some criticism from the next person, Ralph Tate in 1865, to study Shetland's plants.

Further visitors continued to add to the list, but it was not until 20 years later with the arrival of William H. Beeby in 1886, 'the most discerning botanical explorer Shetland has had' (Scott and Palmer, 1987), that a really extensive survey was made of most of Shetland. Beeby made a number of contributions to the Shetland flora, which he published in *The Scottish Naturalist* over several years, including the recognition of the relict scrub sites on the holms of islands in the freshwater lochs of west Mainland. The first person to study Shetland's plant communities, rather than simply identifying species and adding to the list of their localities, appears to have been William West in 1912 and it was to be almost half a century until another botanist picked up this particular torch.

The second flora of Shetland, the Flora Zetlandica of George Druce, was published in 1922, following his visit a year earlier. However this did not add much to Beeby's work and there were a number of errors. It was not until his second

79.   *Thomas Edmondston: the promising young genius who wrote the first flora of Shetland and who was the first to discover several rare plants including the unique Shetland mouse-ear chickweed, but who died so tragically after visiting the Galapagos Islands.*

visit to Shetland in 1924 that he really contributed to the records. Another visitor in the 1920s was a retired army doctor, Colonel Henry Halcro Johnston, who over a period of several years made the definitive collection for Fetlar.

After Thomas Edmondston himself and W. H. Beeby perhaps, the next most significant contributions to our knowledge of the Shetland flora came from three botanists working from the 1950s onwards. The first was David H. N. Spence (1925–1985). His was an old Shetland family, originally Scottish (Spens), who for a time owned and lived on the island of Uyea at the south end of Unst and who, coincidentally, married into the Edmondston family in the nineteenth century. David Spence spent many boyhood holidays on Unst where he developed his keen interest in natural history and in the serpentinite flora, which he returned to study in his adult life. After graduating from Edinburgh University he lectured there, then at Glasgow and finally St Andrews University, where he became Professor of Botany in 1977.

David Spence's particular contribution to our knowledge of the flora of Shetland was through his pioneering ecological studies on the vegetation. Three specific areas of Shetland's flora drew his attention. One was the aquatic freshwater vegetation of the lochs. Another was the relict scrub vegetation, on which he wrote several papers describing the community and which he tried to promote as a precious reminder of Shetland's past environment and as a resource for future use. The third was the most unusual vegetation community on Unst, the serpentinite debris flora he saw as a boy on the Keen of Hamar and on which he wrote a series of papers exploring its origins and dynamics, comparing it with other serpentinite flora in Britain. His papers on the scrub vegetation encouraged this author to explore for further relicts and also members of the Shetland Amenity Trust to carry out conservation protection work on the most vulnerable sites. Papers on the serpentinite flora stimulated others, notably John Proctor and David Slingsby, to carry out further research that still continues. However, David Spence was not just an academic, eminent as he was. In 1979 he wrote *Shetland's Living Landscape*, a fascinating account of Shetland's plant ecology, and in 1980 he contributed the chapter on vegetation to *The Natural History of Shetland* (Berry and Johnston). In the former David Spence drew attention to the damage being done to Shetland's unique landscape through developments such as sand extraction and particularly to the impoverishing effects of overgrazing. Chapter 4 of this book is based substantially on these two works.

The two other significant botanists, who like many of their illustrious amateur predecessors have added so much to our knowledge, are Walter Scott and Richard Palmer. The former is a Shetlander from the Scalloway area who, like other Shetland naturalists such as Thomas Edmondston, David Spence and Bobby Tulloch, developed a childhood interest into an adult vocation. He makes his living with a shipping agency, but his life is Shetland's botany. The latter makes his living in Oxford with the University Press compiling dictionaries, but has been visiting Shetland and pursuing its botany along with Walter Scott since the mid-1950s. In 1969 they published the first check-list of Shetland's flowering plants and ferns since Druce's day, and in 1987 *The Flowering Plants and Ferns of the Shetland Islands*, the most comprehensive flora of Shetland to date. It is this flora that Walter Scott has updated in Appendix 3 of this book. For over 40 years Scott and Palmer have patiently combed all of Shetland's habitats, from its hills to its holms and skerries, lochs, hayfields, sand dunes, shingle beaches and cliffs. In that time they have identified several new species to Shetland and endemic microspecies, and alas also recorded the demise of several others.

Apart from the flowering plants and ferns, our knowledge of the lichen flora has been built up by the successive visits of U. Duncan and D. L. Hawksworth in the 1960s, with a check-list published in *The Natural History of Shetland* (Berry and Johnston, 1980) and updated in this volume by D. H. Dalby who has worked on Shetland lichens, and both the limestone and salt-marsh communities, since the 1980s. The first list of bryophytes was compiled for the Nature Conservancy Council (now SNH) by M. O. Hill and J. A. Paton, also published as a check-list in *The Natural History of Shetland* (1980) and updated in this volume by M. E. Newton. The first list of the fungi of Shetland was published by R. W. G. Dennis and E. G. Gray (1954) and the first fungus flora was published by R. Watling in 1992 (reproduced in this book).

Since the 1960s many other academics and students have contributed to our knowledge through their studies, for example Goode's (1974) phytogeographical study; Britton's (1974) freshwater ecology of Shetland; the phytosociological studies of Lewis (1977), Hilliam (1977) and Roper-Lindsay and Say (1986); and Hulme's (1985) work on peat erosion, to name but a few.

Otter and eider

BIOLOGISTS

Steamship transport between Shetland and the Scottish mainland was introduced in the 1830s, and a weekly service was instituted in 1838. This was a spur for many naturalists to visit the islands. One of these was John R. Tudor, who wrote a series of 'Rambling and Angling Notes from Shetland' for the *Field* between 1878 and 1880. In 1883 he produced his *Orkneys and Shetland: their Past and Present State*, a book of considerable achievement. It contains many observations on birds and mammals as well as chapters on botany and geology (the last by Peach and Horne).

The closing decades of the nineteenth century were dominated by record and specimen collectors. For example, Harold Raeburn, an Edinburgh ornithologist, trudged vast distances on four visits between 1885 and 1895, recording his exploits in a journal now in the Royal Scottish Museum. The Duchess of Bedford cruised the northern seas in her yacht, making many useful observations. Rich entomologists from the south sent professional collectors to the islands where the unique local varieties were being discovered and proving highly marketable in London.

The first lepidopterist to visit Shetland was the collector MacArthur, sent by E. G. Meek. He visited Mainland in 1880 and 1881, and Unst in 1883. Following publicity about some of the distinct forms caught, Shetland aquired a fame that attracted a flutter of lepidopterists: C. A. Briggs, Meek himself, P. M. Bright, J. F. X. King, W. Reid, W. Salvage and E. Roper-Curzon. The last perhaps was the most notable as he stayed later than most of the others and so recorded several species not seen again until recently. The first list of Shetland Lepidoptera was compiled by South in 1888 and visitors continued to make the trek north to Shetland in the early part of this century, although they tended to visit the established sites to collect the known forms and varieties, with Unst being the favoured destination. Relatively little new information was published, although a new list of Lepidoptera, bringing together all the new information, was compiled by B. Beirne in 1945. In the 1950s Bernard Kettlewell and his collaborators, particularly Cadbury and Sam Berry, contributed much to our understanding of Shetland's melanic moths through an extended study in the Tingwall valley. Since then much valuable work has been done by Mike Pennington and the Shetland Entomological Group that was set up in 1992, which has virtually doubled the existing Lepidoptera species and has added many more to other insect groups. Others who have added to our knowledge of invertebrates have included, among others, Philip Ashmole and John Godfrey in 1974 and, notably, those who have contributed species lists for this book, including Brian Laurence (flies), Edward Milner (spiders) and Roger Tallack (non-marine molluscs). As far as the vertebrates are concerned, recognition must be given to Sam Berry's whole range of work in Shetland including that on the genetics of Shetland's mice and polymorphism of the arctic skua, Pete Evan's work on Shetland's cetaceans and the very recent work by Ed Brown on seals.

ORNITHOLOGISTS

Arthur Edmondston and his brother Laurence became the first of a long and distinguished line of Shetland's many ornithologists in the early eighteenth century by making detailed and scientific records of their observations. The latter's son-in-law, Henry Saxby, then went on to complete the first comprehensive account of Shetland's birds before his death in 1871. Later in the eighteenth century J. A. Harvie-Brown and his colleagues from mainland Scotland made a gallant attempt to cover the whole of Scotland in a series of vertebrate faunas. Harvie-Brown himself circumnavigated Shetland in his yacht in 1890 with Eagle Clarke of the Royal Scottish Museum, who, as we have seen, was more or less to found modern bird migration studies with his work on Fair Isle around the turn of the century (despite having been originally trained as a civil engineer). At Uyeasound they met and were joined by two ornithologists, A. H. Evans and T. E. Buckley, and together visited many of the outlying stacks and holms. From this partnership came Evans and Buckley's *A Vertebrate Fauna of the Shetland Islands* (1899), which was the standard work of Shetland natural history (albeit with limited coverage) for over 50 years. They covered the islands very thoroughly and arranged for local naturalists to send them further observations and the result was one of the best volumes of the vertebrate fauna series.

In 1900, 1902 and 1913 a poor Suffolk barrister, Edmund Selous, visited Shetland and the modern biological era can be said to have dawned. He did not add greatly to our knowledge of Shetland birds in themselves, but he observed carefully and accurately, and laid a much firmer basis for future ornithological studies than is apparent from reading his rambling descriptions. For this reason, Lack has argued that he has had a more profound influence on ornithology than any other British pioneer.

Since then, regular flocks of bird-watchers have invaded Shetland, many of them producing much sought-after books: Frances Pitt with *Shetland Pirates* (1923) of the earlier generation; Niall Rankin *Haunts of British Divers* (1947), G. K. Yeats *Bird Haunts in Northern Britain* (1948) and Richard Perry *Shetland Sanctuary* (1948), books of the immediate post-war period; and Pat and Ursula Venables who had lived in Shetland since 1947 produced their book *The Birds and Mammals of Shetland* (1955), which magisterially reviewed and summarized much information. It replaced *A Vertebrate Fauna of the Shetland Islands* as the standard work for another 35 years, until the publication of *The Natural History of Shetland* by R. J. Berry and J. L. Johnston (1980).

Another ornithological development of the twentieth century in Shetland was of course the establishment of the Fair Isle Bird Observatory by Eagle Clarke, George Waterston and others, covered in detail in Chapter 9. Jerome Wilson and George Stout, who assisted with the development of FIBOT, can be regarded as part of an indigenous Shetland naturalist tradition. To them must be added G. T. Kay and G. W. Russell of Lerwick, J. A. Stout of Fair Isle, S. Bruce and J. Simpson of Whalsay, Tom Henderson of Dunrossness, Fred Hunter and Dennis Coutts (the photographer) of Lerwick and many, many others.

However, the man who above all put Shetland's wildlife on the world map in recent times was R. J. Tulloch (1929–96). Bobby Tulloch was a Yell man with no formal academic qualifications who, from a childhood interest in birds, became Shetland's foremost naturalist with a wide knowledge and love of not only its birds, but its mammals and plants as well. In addition to this Bobby Tulloch had the gift of communication and his infectious interest and enthusiasm stimulated and encouraged both native Shetlanders and many, many amateur ornithologists and professional scientists. Because of his ability to popularize – along with Fred Hunter he produced the first guide to Shetland birds in 1970 and many more publications illustrated with his beautiful wildlife photographs – many did not realize the true depth of his knowledge and understanding of Shetland's ecology that came from a lifetime of acute and patient observation. Anybody studying Shetland's natural history had something to learn from him. Outwith Shetland he will probably be remembered most for his bird photography and famous discovery of the breeding snowy owl on Fetlar in 1967. Within Shetland he will be remembered as someone to whom scientists and naturalists annually beat a path, a great entertainer and a man without pretension.

An increasing number of naturalists and researchers have visited Shetland in recent years and contributed to our further understanding of the ecology of the islands: a glance at the bibliography and the preface to this book reveals just the tip of the iceberg. However a handful have stayed or made annual pilgrimages to continue studies over a period of years. However interesting these short-term studies and surveys, it is the long-term continuous pieces of work that give us the really valuable information and that often explain the underlying 'natural' and 'artificial' pressures that are behind 'unexpected' events, for example the apparent changes in seabird breeding success and behaviour resulting from changes to the food supply (see Chapter 8). Recognition should therefore be given to people like Bob Furness, who has carried out many years of research on the seabirds of Foula and whose studies on the skuas and on the 'conflict' between seabirds and the commercial North Sea fishery have been major contributions to a more holistic understanding of the ecology of Shetland's seabirds. Martin Heubeck also, particularly through his patient and intensive monitoring of seabirds for SOTEAG (and SVEAG), has provided the enormous amount of background detail throughout the rest of Shetland without which we could only guess at what was happening to Shetland's seabirds, both as a result of food changes and oil pollution. To these should be added Mike Richardson, David Okill and Pete Ellis for their work on a number of Shetland's bird species.

OTHER FIELDS

However it is not just geologists and naturalists who have built up our knowledge of Shetland's environment, past and present, but geographers, historians, archaeologists and Shetland's own writers of its past society and way of life: geographers such as Alexander Fenton, whose comprehensive book on the Northern Isles (1978) has given us valuable insights into the way of life in the nineteenth and twentieth centuries especially; historians such as F. T. Wainwright, Gordon Donaldson, Shetland's own Dr Mortimer Manson and the present archivist Brian Smith; archaeologists such as Alan Small and Noel Fojut of Historic Scotland, with his perceptive overview of thousands of years of Shetland history; also those whose recent digs and careful analysis, such as K. D. Bennett, G. F. Bigelow, J. Birnie, S. B. Butler, B. Crawford, J. Johansen, M. Keith-Lucas, G. Whittington and A. Whittle among others, supported by Val Turner of Shetland Amenity Trust, have added an almost overwhelming amount of information on Shetland's past environment.

Undoubtedly a major step forward for Shetland's natural history was the formation of the Shetland Bird Club (SBR) by Pete Kinnear and Ian Robertson in 1973. This organization has come a long way since then and perhaps one of its greatest achievements was the conference it held in Lerwick in 1988 on the 'sandeel crisis', which attracted the attendance of many experts from the world of seabirds and fisheries in Scotland. A year after the formation of the Bird Club, in 1974, the Sullom Voe Environmental Advisory Group was established by Shetland Islands Council and the oil industry. This organization (and its successor SOTEAG), through monitoring of the environment, has contributed enormously to our knowledge of Shetland's ecology, particularly its seabirds, and has additionally pressed for the most effective contingency plans in dealing with oil spills. For 20 years it was led by its indefatigable chairman George Dunnet and to him, more than any other individual, Shetland should be grateful for the fact that the Shetland oil industry has had so little impact on its wildlife.

In 1993, with the rising interest in the occurrence of whales, a Shetland Cetacean Group was formed and like the SBR it too produces an annual report. There is also a Shetland Ringing Group, a Shetland Entomological Group and a Field Studies Group, the last of which produces *The Shetland Naturalist* with excellent articles on all aspects of Shetland's natural history. Finally there is the Field Trust, an environmental education trust set up by Shetland Islands Council, and a local natural history computer network. Little happens therefore on the natural history front in Shetland today without anyone who is interested, within or outwith Shetland, needing to miss it. Shetland must be one of the best-served places in Britain for its contemporary natural history. Little did the pioneers of our knowledge of Shetland realize what interest there would be among the inhabitants one day!

CHAPTER 11

Black Gold or Black Death

Sullom Terminal

The SVEAG will advise on environmental aspects of the developments associated with the oil terminal at Sullom Voe Shetland, including the onshore sealine (out to the SIC limit), landfalls, terrestrial pipeline corridors, storage and other related installations and the tanker jetties and ship handling facilities. The aim is to ensure that environmental considerations are taken into account in the planning, development and operation stages of the project.

Terms of reference for the Sullom Voe Environmental Advisory Group
1974

Shetland has seen a number of 'booms' come and go, such as the herring industry, but none has posed such potentially major environmental threats in its relatively short life as North Sea oil. Commencing with the Shetland Oil Terminal at Sullom in 1978, connected to the North Sea oil fields by pipeline, the oil industry is now gearing up to take advantage of the new oil fields to the west, from which it is intended to transport oil to the terminal by shuttle tanker. In this chapter we look at the impacts to date of the oil industry on Shetland's environment generally and its seabirds in particular, an industry that by 1996 had exported 10 000 cargoes of North Sea oil and gas from Sullom across the globe and whose peak flow of oil in the 1980s was 1.5 million barrels per day, falling to around 0.75 million barrels in 1996.

SHETLAND OIL TERMINAL

With the discovery in the North Sea of the large Brent oil field in 1971, and later finds including the Ninian field, it became clear that the best way to transport oil to land would be to pipe it to the nearest landmass, Shetland. The following year Zetland County Council (ZCC, now the Shetland Islands Council, SIC), realizing that Shetland was the inevitable landfall for oil, appointed consultants to identify sites that would be suitable for a major oil terminal. This led to the selection of Calback Ness, a small headland within Sullom Voe, as the site for the development of the oil terminal. At the same time the far-sighted ZCC quickly realized that the scale of the coming oil industry would be enormous and that there would be huge commercial pressures for development in Shetland that would overshadow anything that had gone before and that, most importantly, the decisions concerning these developments would be unlikely to be made in Shetland by Shetland people. The Council, in an extraordinary move, therefore promoted a bill through Parliament, the Zetland County Council Act 1974, which gave the Council very considerable powers over the oil development. Using these powers the Council purchased the land around Sullom Voe and leased it to the oil companies as the

80.   *Shetland Oil Terminal, Sullom: the source of Shetland's recent prosperity, potential threat to its seabirds and marine habitat, and subsidizer of most of Shetland's seabird monitoring over the last 20 years.* (Courtesy of RSPB.)

only site to be developed into Shetland's oil terminal, in the process setting up the Sullom Voe Association Limited (SVA), a partnership with the oil companies to run the port. The Act also made the Council the harbour authority for all Shetland waters (outwith Lerwick harbour) up to one mile offshore, allowing the Council to influence and control both sea traffic and pollution management within Sullom Voe and Yell Sound.

Because of Shetland's unique natural environment, with its huge seabird colonies, concerns were immediately expressed regarding the dangers of pollution posed by such an immense oil development. ZCC and the oil industry therefore jointly established the Sullom Voe Environmental Advisory Group (SVEAG). Membership of SVEAG was made up of both ZCC and the oil industry, plus representatives of the Nature Conservancy Council and the Countryside Commission for Scotland (now amalgamated as Scottish Natural Heritage), the Natural Environment Research Council and two professors from Scottish universities both with special interests in Shetland.

SVEAG was totally funded from the SVA and one of its main aims was to assess the environmental impact of the terminal development, not on a once-and-for-all basis before construction began but while it was in progress. While the impact assessment was being drawn up, SVEAG was fulfilling another of its roles, that of giving advice to the Council and the oil-terminal constructors. It was also making a description and inventory of all the important features of the natural environment of Shetland that could be adversely affected by the development using

81.   Braer, *Garths Ness, January 1993: the origin of one of the largest oil spills in the British Isles and an awful reminder of the potential damage the oil industry could cause to Shetland's environment and people.* (Courtesy of RSPB.)

numerous biological and chemical surveys. The formation of SVEAG (and its successor Shetland Oil Terminal Environmental Advisory Group, SOTEAG), the way it operated and the baseline information it produced for the purpose of monitoring the oil industry in Shetland therefore represented a unique 'joint' step in the conservation and environmental considerations for such a major development, following in the ground-breaking footsteps of the Zetland County Council Act.

SOTEAG was not involved formally with oil pollution contingency planning, but examined the ecological advice that went into the SVA contingency plan and upon which the oil spill clean-up strategy was based. The whole of Sullom Voe, Yell Sound and associated waters form a natural geographical area on which the contingency plan was based. Outwith the SIC limits of one mile offshore, the responsibility for oil clearance lies with the Department of Trade and Industry (DTI). At the oil fields themselves, the oil companies retained responsibility for drawing up their own contingency plans, which required the approval of the DTI. In 1991 a Wildlife Response Coordinating Committee (WRCC) was established. This is the committee that made the plans to deal with birds and mammals killed or injured by oil spills. The WRCC has a Shetland-wide remit and is part of the SIC Anti Oil Spill Plan. With SVA funds a bird rehabilitation centre and a wildlife centre were established. It was the WRCC and the operation it set up that so effectively dealt with the *Braer* spill in 1993.

Thus, half a millenium after the Hanseatic traders had made Shetland a centre for the fishing industry, northern shipping routes (this time for oil tankers) once again led to Shetland, bringing unprecedented income to Shetlanders and their families. After exceptional environmental deliberation and with well-prepared contingency plans the Shetland Oil Terminal (SOT) opened for business in the late autumn of 1978.

Prior to the opening of the SOT, the only oil pollution incident of any scale recorded in Shetland was in the summer of 1971 when at least 1200 birds (and perhaps five times that number), predominantly guillemots, died of oil pollution from unknown sources off the east coast of Mainland. When the SOT opened therefore in late 1978 all were aware of the potential for disaster to Shetland's seabirds and what were thought to be the best possible care and precautions taken to prevent spills. These plans were made with the knowledge that Sullom Voe itself and Yell Sound are important wintering and, in the case of the latter, breeding areas for seabirds and seaduck.

ESSO BERNICIA AND AFTER

It had been estimated that the terminal might average 15–22 crude oil spillages annually, most of a minor size, so it was a great shock when within only 1 month of the new port being opened there was a spill of 1200 tonnes of fuel oil (still the largest spill to date at the SOT), which escaped from the *Esso Bernicia* following a collision with the mooring dolphins at the loading jetty. Partly because of the nature of the heavy fuel oil and through a series of equipment failures, 700 tonnes of this oil eventually escaped from Sullom Voe into Yell Sound. Once there, strong tidal streams quickly spread the oil northwards to the west coast of Yell and Unst and east as far as Out Skerries, polluting large sections of the shore and resulting in almost 4000 seabird and seaduck deaths. The bulk of the deaths were great northern diver (146), at least 40% of Shetland's wintering population, shag (683), *calloo* (306), *dunter* (570) and *tystie* (633); other deaths included at least 13 otters and around 50 sheep (with a further 2000 contaminated). At the time, 95% of all diving seabirds were estimated to have been killed within Sullom Voe and 75% in southern Yell Sound. Subsequently it was estimated that probably double the number of seabirds and seaduck died.

The result of the *Esso Bernicia* spill was therefore very serious for the local wintering and breeding birds. For example, in the summer of 1980 a survey in Yell Sound found only one-third of the *tysties* that were present in 1978. However, recovery of the population to pre-spill levels, around 500–600 pairs, appears to have taken only around 10–15 years. Although shags and cormorants from a wide area were affected, their numbers recovered quite quickly. *Dunter* numbers did not however, with part of the reason being the additional unexplained mortality of the winter of 1979–80 (see Chapter 8). Most worrying since then has been the almost total lack of great northern divers and long-tailed duck in Sullom Voe. Even in Yell Sound today the number of great northern divers are still less than one-third of what they were. It seems that the local breeding populations were fairly quickly replaced by immigration from healthy adjacent populations. A possible explanation for the lack of replacement of wintering great northern divers and long-tailed duck is that these particular birds were attuned to wintering in Sullom Voe and Yell Sound and that the populations to which they belonged have now lost most, if not all, of the birds with the knowledge of that traditional wintering area.

Some light on the origin of the wintering great northern divers in Shetland and additional information on other threats to the species was shed by the examination of the corpses at the Royal Scottish Museum. In total just over 100 corpses were examined, 82% of which were from Shetland. It was suggested that the origin of approximately 45% was Iceland, another 45% Greenland and Baffin Island and the remainder from mainland Canada. The examination also found that one-third had gunshot wounds!

Following the *Esso Bernicia* incident and the adverse publicity it generated, the SVA authorities readdressed their oil pollution contingency plan. The original emphasis on clearing up spills by dispersant was radically changed to one of containment and recovery and £7 million was invested in spur and mobile booms, skimmers, staff, boats and specialist equipment. The SOT became the first oil installation in Europe to establish and maintain a dedicated workforce to tackle oil pollution.

In Chapter 8 we discussed the Shetland Beached Bird Surveys (BBS) in relation to wrecks of auks. Since 1980, these surveys have also served to monitor seabird mortality in relation to oil spills at Sullom Voe or from tankers leaving or arriving. The SOT had in fact opened, under some public protest, before its ballast treatment plant was operational and the temptation for unscrupulous tanker captains to empty oil tanks of ballast before entering the port proved to be too much. Analyses of the BBS results showed an increase in oiled birds during 1977–79 coincident with the opening of the terminal. In fact only 10 days after the SOT opened unusual numbers of oiled birds began coming ashore in Orkney and over the next 6 months there was a series of incidents stretching from the east coast of Caithness to Shetland involving over 4000 oiled birds, probably a mere fraction of the numbers that died. This included 1700, mostly guillemots, found in Shetland in early March 1979. One of the sources of the oil was undoubtedly from tanker washings, in addition, a tanker was spotted on its way to Sullom allegedly trailing oil, possibly ballast from oil tanks.

Further public concern, following the pollution and oiling of seabirds, led to the SOT Port Authority making the carrying of 35% ballast a condition of charter for tankers visiting Sullom, in order to stop this dumping. Other far-sighted controls of tankers entering Sullom were also initiated. For example, through their surveillance aircraft, the harbour authority was aware that several tankers were passing far too close to the Shetland shore, so another clause was entered into the conditions of contract for doing business with Sullom: all vessels were required to stay at least 16 km offshore until making their final approach. Furthermore, tankers were required to contact the SOT Port Authority approximately 320 km out and to give their passage plan to Sullom so that each approach could be monitored. The SOT authorities were also becoming very concerned about the deteriorating quality of the tankers arriving at Sullom. In the first quarter of 1991 there had been six main engine failures in tankers using the SOT, while the huge oil company Shell had found that 20% of the vessels it inspected for charter were below their minimum standard. Pressure was therefore put on the oil companies to ensure a higher standard of tankers entering Sullom.

These actions all had an effect on reducing spills and damage to the environment, including the oiling of seabirds. When the Shetland figures are compared with results from the rest of the British Isles and indeed with the European North Sea coast they are generally lower. In fact 'since 1980, there have been no instances of significant mortality of seabirds arising from oil spillages at the Sullom Voe Terminal' (Royal Society of Edinburgh, 1995). This is a very encouraging reflection on the measures taken to control oil spill in Sullom Voe itself and from trading tankers. However there are still oil pollution incidents around Shetland's coasts, such as April–August 1995 when 192 oiled birds were found and December 1995–April 1996 when 443 were found, mostly on the east coast. Analysis showed that a variety of fuel and crude oils were involved, but that a high proportion probably came from illegal discharges from tankers.

However we also have to remember that there are internationally agreed legal discharges of oil at sea, including oily water from the slop tanks of oil tankers, which actually make up one-third of all the oil entering the marine environment; these are obviously very difficult to monitor. In other words, until there are much more stringent controls on legal discharges, there will always be a background level of oil in the sea affecting seabirds and shores. Since the north of Scotland is a major sea route from the Continent to North America, deliberate oil spills will continue. Unfortunately it only needs one relatively small incident to have a serious effect, such as that in March 1991 when oil pollution was thought to have killed some 100–150 *tysties* between Sumburgh and Levenwick, approximately 25% of the local breeding population.

BRAER

It is reckoned that annually hundreds of oil tankers by-pass Shetland to the north and south. Thus it was a rather sad irony that the origin of the largest oil spill in Shetland (and Scotland), 87 000 tonnes of Norwegian crude oil and 1600 tonnes of heavy bunker fuel, was from a vessel *en route* from Norway to Canada, with no connection with the Shetland oil industry. It was also a mercy that the incident occurred in the middle of winter, when most of Shetland's seabirds were far away; during appalling weather (which was partly responsible for the incident), so that the oil was quickly mixed on the surface by ferocious winds; on the very tip of the Shetland archipelago, where the oil was further dispersed in strong tidal waters and by powerful seas smashing and rebounding against a rocky coastline; and finally that the oil involved was 'light' and therefore could break up and evaporate relatively quickly. Even then, it was bad enough.

Dunrossness, 'ness of the roaring tideway', was not so named by the Norse for nothing. The *Braer* went ashore at Garth's Ness on 5 January 1993 in winds of 20 m s^{-1} (45 m.p.h.) gusting to 40 m s^{-1} (90 m.p.h.), in other words 'strong gale' to 'hurricane'. Immediately she began spilling oil. For the following 8 days she was buffeted by almost continuous gale-force winds and high seas as she gradually broke into pieces. During that time, when weather permitted, some effort to spray the oil on the sea by six low-flying DC3 aircraft of the government's Marine Pollution Control Unit (MPCU) was carried out, but it was fairly ineffective and not continued for long. The weather around the south end of Shetland did not abate but continued for 25 of the 31 January days, blowing at or near gale force. As the crude oil the *Braer* was carrying was a 'light' oil, the action of the wind, the high seas and the tidal currents rapidly diluted it through the water column or speeded its evaporation into the atmosphere. The direction of the wind caused much of thisoil-laden atmosphere to sweep across Dunrossness, polluting winter crops, damaging roofs and causing discomfort to the locals. The tidal currents took the oil-laden waters up the coasts, both west and east, but predominantly the former, polluting valuable salmon in the fish farms. During January, while 87 000 tonnes of oil gradually dispersed and disappeared, 1538 seabirds were found oiled and dead, a number of grey seals and two otters.

The count of seabirds killed by the *Braer* was, as always, only a fraction of the actual mortality. By far the majority of those found dead were shags (857); among others were *tysties* (203), kittiwake (133), long-tailed duck (96), *dunter* (70) and, importantly, great northern diver (13). Relatively few *maalie* (31) or guillemot (17) were found as they apparently remained well offshore in the poor weather. No waders were found, although many were observed oiled while feeding on the shores.

The operation developed by the WRCC to cope with all the complexities of this incident, the scale of whose eventual outcome could not initially be predicted, turned out to be very successful and a tribute to all the local and national organizations and the volunteers who took part. Efforts were made to save as many of the birds and seals as humanly possible and all the bird corpses were collected and frozen for later examination The most serious implications of the oil spill were for the great northern diver, which had lost 40% of its wintering population in the 1978 (*Esso Bernicia*) oil spill and which probably lost a further

10% this time, and for the long-tailed duck, which may have lost up to 7%. Approximately 4% of the British Isles wintering population of both species occurs in Shetland. Examination of breeding success of the southern Shetland seabird colonies in 1993 indicated that there had been no effect of the *Braer* oil on the normal food sources. Numbers of shags were significantly down at Sumburgh and of *tysties* along the south-west coast. However, counts during 1994–96 indicated the beginnings of a recovery in both populations.

The non-ornithological environmental effects of the largest oil spill in Shetland have been found to be surprisingly little. The conclusions of the report of the Environmental Steering Group on the Oil Spill in Shetland (ESGOSS, 1994) stated:

> It would appear that the shallow coastal sediments around south-west Shetland harbour very little hydrocarbon contamination arising from the *Braer*.... It is likely that, following an initial toxic impact to sedentary marine animals, much of the coastal pollution was dispersed, redistributed or deeply buried within 3–4 months.

It was concluded therefore that there was limited and local contamination of shellfish; however a residue of oil still appears to remain in the seabed, so that a ban on prawn and scallop fishing in the area is still in force (1997). There appeared to be no long-lasting effects on wild fish, but the immediate damage was done by oil pollution driven up the west coast to several salmon farms, which were forced to close. Seals in the area at the time were seen to be suffering from respiratory problems, but there were no signs of significant mortality of the local population. It is incredible that the eleventh greatest amount of oil ever spilled in one incident, twice as much as spilled from the *Exxon Valdez*, should have resulted in such little environmental damage.

Shetlanders are thankful for that and more aware than ever just what might be the result of a similar incident if a tanker passing Shetland too close got into difficulties but in the summer months, when the islands and the surrounding seas teem with over a million seabirds. In order to address this the SIC has been pressing Parliament to get international legislation to control the routes of tanker traffic, shore stations to monitor them, a salvage vessel stationed in Shetland to deal with any future breakdowns and a whole range of measures regarding tanker classification and construction. Much of this was looked into in the public inquiry carried out by Lord Donaldson (Safer Ships, Cleaner Seas, 1994) set up by the government following the *Braer* incident. This pointed out that Shetland waters had exceptional protection against shipping accidents, being surrounded by Areas to be Avoided (ATBA) or Precautionary Areas. Lord Donaldson proposed a range of measures to tackle the dangers of oil pollution from tankers around the British coast, but nearly all voluntary. The inquiry also pointed out that on average only one tanker a day passed through the Fair Isle Channel and that therefore the threats of oil pollution were greater elsewhere. So far, pressure from the SIC has only resulted in a voluntary agreement with oil companies on routeing and the positioning by the government of a salvage vessel on the Western Isles of Scotland. It has been argued by the government that the existing harbour tugs in Shetland and Orkney could be used in an initial response to a tanker incident like the *Braer*; however SIC has always pointed out that these tugs are not adequate to deal with tankers in the kind of conditions that the *Braer* went ashore in 1993. The requests and the arguments are continuing.

As if threats of oiling from tanker discharge or spills were not enough, Shetland's seabirds and seaduck, especially *dunter*, have been under threat for a number of years from east Europeans. That is, from the 40–50 regular *klondykers*, the fish factory and processing ships that used to gather off Lerwick in the autumn and winter to fill up with mackerel and herring before returning home. These ships have never been obliged to meet western standards of care and maintenance and have regularly got into trouble in the poor weather of a Shetland winter. Oil and sewage discharge from these ships in a limited and sensitive area have been a constant worry to the local environmental authorities and conservationists. Sensitive because of the local human population, but also because the Lerwick and Bressay area holds Shetland's largest flock of moulting eiders. In 1993 the largest fleet of klondykers ever recorded in Shetland, 90 vessels, anchored off Lerwick. It was estimated that the total number of crew on board was over 7000, greater than the population of Lerwick itself. Almost inevitably in that winter two of the klondykers were wrecked, but mercifully no one was lost and few seabirds were affected. The following autumn, in October 1994, a third vessel, the *Pionersk*, was wrecked at Gulberwick. On this occasion it is thought that at least 45 *dunter* were oiled and died. With the fall in fish prices and the collapse of the east European economies, klondykers no longer visit Lerwick in such numbers, so for the moment that threat has gone.

Dead puffin

ATLANTIC OIL

New oil developments in the Atlantic, to the west and north-west of Shetland, may now bring new potential threats to Shetland's shores, seabirds and fish farms. How real are the dangers and what will be the environmental cost to Shetland from Foinaven, Schiehallion and the giant Clair oil fields and what precautions are being taken by the oil companies? The Clair field, only 70 km north-west of Shetland (Fig. 36) and the largest yet discovered in the British sector of the North Sea and Atlantic, is a year or two away from production and BP say it plans to pipe that oil to Shetland, although there is still some doubt about the whole project. Therefore we concentrate on the others here.

The oil fields to the west of Shetland were actually discovered 20 years ago, but only now has full exploration of the reserves, the technology and the price of oil combined to make to its extraction viable. The oil companies have argued that the limited reserves in Foinaven and Schiehallion and the immense depth of water in which they are situated (the former at depths of 400–600 m) precludes transport of oil by pipeline and that there is little increased risk of spillage by using other transport methods. Although the industry's assessment of the effect it might have on the environment was generally accepted in an appraisal by the Institute of Offshore Engineering (IOE), the analysis of risk of spills was heavily criticized as

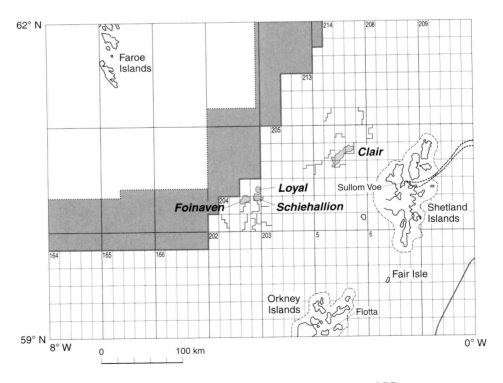

FIGURE 36   *BP/Shell Atlantic Oilfields* (courtesy of BP).

inadequate comparisons had been made between pipeline and offshore loading systems. The IOE went as far as to say that the risks of spills would be higher than that suggested. Nevertheless, the industry's proposals have been accepted by the Board of Trade. The oil industry has therefore developed the offshore loading and shuttle tanker system, first used in the North Sea at the Argyll field in 1975. The system that will be in use at these fields from 1997 will be the Floating Production, Storage and Offloading Facility (FPSO) (Fig. 37). This is basically a large ship that will be at permanent anchor above the oil field and which will collect the oil via risers from the sea bed, then process, store and finally supply it to dedicated shuttle tankers. The tankers will ply back and forth between the field and an oil terminal, one every 3 days approximately, from where the oil will be transhipped across the world. In the case of Foinaven, which will be the first field to come on stream, the FPSO will be the *Petrojarl Foinaven*, which will be capable of processing 95 000 barrels of oil a day and storing up to 300 000 barrels. The oil will then be pumped aboard shuttle tankers to be taken to the Flotta Oil Terminal in Orkney. In the case of Schiehallion, the oil will be shuttled to the Shetland Oil Terminal at Sullom Voe. That is the plan, but technical problems in establishing the sea-bed well-head and securing the FPSO have continually delayed the project with transport of oil to Shetland now due to commence in the late summer of 1998. These delays have been an indication of the enormous difficulties in extracting oil from the harsh and unpredictable environment of the North Atlantic.

From the environmental point of view the problems with extracting oil from the Atlantic fields are, firstly, that the fields lie in some of the most exposed waters in

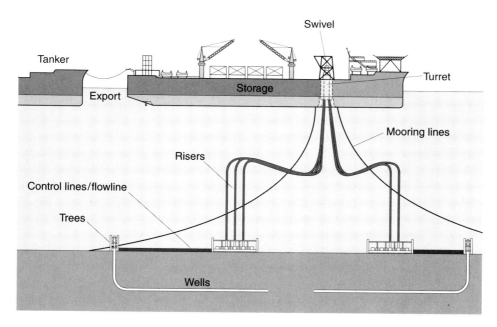

FIGURE 37 *Foinaven Phase 1 Development, Floating Production Storage and Offloading Facility (FPSO)* (courtesy of BP).

the world, with oceanic swells much greater than those experienced in the North Sea, and also at considerably greater depth. Secondly, the fields are in the path of migrating whales and also close to the edge of the continental shelf, where there are recently discovered deep-water corals and very important plankton communities that are the basic food source for a large fishery, particularly mackerel, for cetaceans and for some of the huge breeding seabird populations of Orkney and Shetland. In addition, the fields are only some 110 km west of Foula and 190 km north-west of Orkney, in that quarter of the compass from which come over 30% of Shetland's winds. It has been calculated that with a westerly wind of some 15 m s^{-1} (35 m.p.h.), which is only twice Shetland's mean annual wind speed, oil spilled from the Atlantic fields could be ashore on Shetland in 48 hours. It may be some comfort to know that 'design analysis' by the oil industry calculates that spills of over 100 tonnes from offshore operations are unlikely but if such a spill occurs, with winds of 15 m s^{-1} natural dispersion should result in removal of much of the surface oil before it reaches Shetland's shores. However, the reality is that it is not the Shetland shore – perhaps the safest place for oil to be, if it *has* to be anywhere outwith a tanker or a pipeline, as far as the natural environment in Shetland is concerned – that is most at risk, it is the marine environment itself and the seabirds, seaduck, mammals and fish therein. Prior to oil extraction, during the exploration phase, concerns have been raised as to the auditory effect of seismic explosions on cetaceans and on their communications, but so far there has been little evidence of more than local disturbance.

It is almost certainly inevitable that there will be regular 'small' spills from FPSO systems (if that system is used) to the west of Shetland, that some will be so small as to have undetectable effects and that some will be dealt with immediately and efficiently from the support vessel and helicopters. And it is inevitable that some will occur in weather conditions and in the short winter days that will limit some, if not all planned remedial action. Therefore there will be regular seabird casualties in relatively small numbers annually that should not affect seabird populations unless, that is, fate decrees that the incident significantly affects Shetland's smallest seabird populations, such as Leach's petrel or Manx shearwater. What is also feared is that if spills are chronic, oil may affect plankton, sensitive larvae or taint fish, although with the huge dilution rate that will occur in the Atlantic this should only be a remote possibility.

So what contingencies are being taken by the oil industry, the government and SIC to avoid accidents at the offshore fields and to deal with them should they occur? At the scene of operations offshore the systems are designed to reduce the maximum size of any spill compatible with reasonable flow of production. On the FPSO and support vessel there will be stocks of dispersant for immediate use and pods that can be quickly fitted to helicopters to deal with spill under 200 tonnes. Above that amount, additional stocks of dispersants or equipment would have to be obtained from Shetland or the mainland; for a large spill the MPCU would take charge, coordinating with other arms of national and local government. Response time to deal with a large spill, with the importation of equipment and aircraft, is said to be within 24 hours, half the time it could take the oil to reach the Shetland shore. By that time, presumably, the oil would be widely dispersed and although it is feasible in good weather to spray oil with dispersant from the air, it is highly unlikely that corralling and recovery of oil would be successful. Under the present contingency plan it is likely that a large number of seabirds (depending on the season) could be affected by a major spill at the oil field. It is also hard to imagine that temporary booms could protect fish farms, inshore seabirds and seaduck, or soft shores against widely dispersed oil over a large part of Shetland's western shore, even under very calm conditions. Unfortunately, in the case of fish farms, if booms have to be deployed to protect them physically from surface oil, then oil in the water column itself will probably have contaminated the fish anyway.

Shetland (Orkney and Faroe) cannot therefore be fully protected against spills from the offshore production operations and we have to put our trust in oil industry care and the government's controls in limiting the number of spills in the first place. As far as tanker accidents from transportation are concerned, however, there is more that could be done and the presence of a salvage tug on station in Shetland, requested by SIC since 1981, is more than ever required. In an effort to reassure the public and to measure any environmental impact, a monitoring group, the Atlantic Frontier Environmental Forum (AFEF) modelled on the lines of the very successful SOTEAG, was set up in 1996, consisting of officials from both SIC and Orkney Island Council, the wild fish and fish farm industries, the oil industry, and representatives of government and non-governmental environmental organizations. This body, with an independent chairman, will allow direct involvement of all interested parties in the monitoring of the environmental effects of the Atlantic oil developments and in advising the industry. If it is half as successful as SOTEAG it will have a very positive effect on the oil industry and its operating procedures. However this body was only set up, with the encouragement of the industry, *after* it had carried out its environmental assessment and established its contingency plans.

Accepting that we all want fuel for our cars, central heating and the many other 'benefits' to which oil is put, we must also accept that there will be consequences, and since the government has sanctioned its exploitation by offshore loading rather than by pipeline, we must be prepared for the worst scenario. However to put these threats in perspective, a recent study suggested that only 458 tonnes of oil were known to have been accidentally or deliberatedly discharged into the sea surrounding the British Isles in 1995, that only 20% or so originated from the oil industry and that a similar amount originated from fishing boats lost at sea. Even if the figures from the oil industry are questionable, they should be seen in the context of the huge extractive industry which is North Sea oil. However, when considering oil extraction and all its economic benefits, particularly to Shetland, we should also bear in mind the contribution fossil fuels are making to the 'greenhouse effect' and to global warming. If there is a direct relation between this phenomenon and the posited fundamental oceanographic changes occurring in the north-west Atlantic (see Chapter 7) and therefore a relationship also with the availability and timing of appearance of plankton, the basic energy resource for both Shetland's fish and seabirds, it would be a sad irony for Shetland and a high price to pay.

To date, though, the oil industry has had mercifully little proven impact on the environment and indeed the establishment and operation of SOTEAG and SOT itself has gained Shetland an international reputation as a model of good practice. However, as the *Braer* demonstrated, some events *are* outwith the control of Shetland's watchdogs. We can only hope, for the sake of Shetland's rich marine environment, that any future failure of machinery or human judgement within the North Sea or Atlantic oil industry similarly chooses the right time and place to happen! However the most important decision that could have been taken to reduce the threat of Atlantic oil to Shetland, its wildlife, its tourism and its aquaculture would have been to have waited until the technology was secure and then pipe all the oil direct to the land from the Atlantic fields.

Skuas

CHAPTER 12

Sustainability and Survival

Kittiwakes

Conservation of biodiversity requires the care and involvement of individuals and communities.

To help reverse this trend [progressive loss of biodiversity] local communities need to build pride in the distinctiveness of their own localities.

Local Authorities provide the main framework within which environmental care is organised at local level and public attitude to the environment cultivated.

UK Biodiversity Action Plan, 1994

In the preceding chapters we have discussed the special geological and geomorphological features of Shetland, identified the special plants and animals, both terrestrial and marine, and their habitats. We have identified Shetland's important birds species, of which many are of national and international importance. We have also looked at the history of Shetlanders themselves and their contribution to the shaping of Shetland's habitats and communities. The British government and

287

the Shetland people have a special responsibility to safeguard all these, not only for ourselves but for the rest of mankind, just as we expect others to do in their own countries. The sum total of these features is what makes Shetland such a unique group of islands and such a special place to live and to visit.

Identifying and safeguarding these features in Shetland was originally purely an amateur pursuit. The history of environmental conservation in Shetland could be said to have begun with the efforts of Dr L. Edmondston and John Scott in the nineteenth century to protect the great skua and with Thomas Edmondston, the son of the former, when he published the first *Flora of Shetland* (1845). Another key figure was Eagle Clarke, through his appointment of a 'bird-watcher' on Fair Isle in the early twentieth century. At that time, too, Shetland had its RSPB 'watchers'. However it was not until the 1960s that the RSPB appointed its first part-time warden and the (then) Nature Conservancy its first full-time resident officer. Since then RSPB staff have become full-time, there are several SNH staff resident and dedicated to Shetland and, in addition, there are environmental staff contracted to SOTEAG and advisory staff appointed to Shetland's Crofting Farming and Wildlife Advisory Group (SCFWAG), as well as SIC's own Amenity Trust and Field Studies Trust.

DESIGNATION AND PROTECTION

The first of a now rather complicated plethora of designations, designed to provide legal protection to the whole range of Shetland's locally and nationally valuable natural heritage features, arose following the passing of the National Parks and Access to the Countryside Act 1949. In 1955 the then Nature Conservancy* (NC) designated the island of Noss and the headland of Herma Ness as National Nature Reserves (NNR), to protect and promote the study of the great seabird colonies. Since then a third NNR has been declared at the Keen of Hamar, in Unst, and over 70 SSSIs, of which 10 have been designated as Special Protection Areas (SPA) under the European Community (EC) Directive on the Conservation of Wild Birds (1979). Additionally, a further seven are candidate Special Areas for Conservation (SAC) under another EC Directive, the Habitats and Species Directive (1992). Under its powers in the 1970s, the Countryside Commission for Scotland (CCS) identified a large National Scenic Area (NSA) subdivided into seven parts. In 1990 the Nature Conservancy Council (NCC) identified four (non-statutory) Marine Consultation Areas (MCA), while in 1994 the whole of Shetland became an Environmentally Sensitive Area (ESA) designated by the Secretary of State for Scotland. There is also one Area of Special Protection (ASP) and one Council of Europe Diploma Site. Figure 38 shows the areas covered by the designations mentioned above.

The total area covered by statutory conservation legislation as SSSIs in Shetland amounts to some 16 000 ha or approximately 10% of the islands. Some of the SSSIs

---

* In 1973, the Nature Conservancy became the Nature Conservancy Council; in 1992 the Nature Conservancy Council amalgamated with the Countryside Commission for Scotland to become Scottish Natural Heritage.

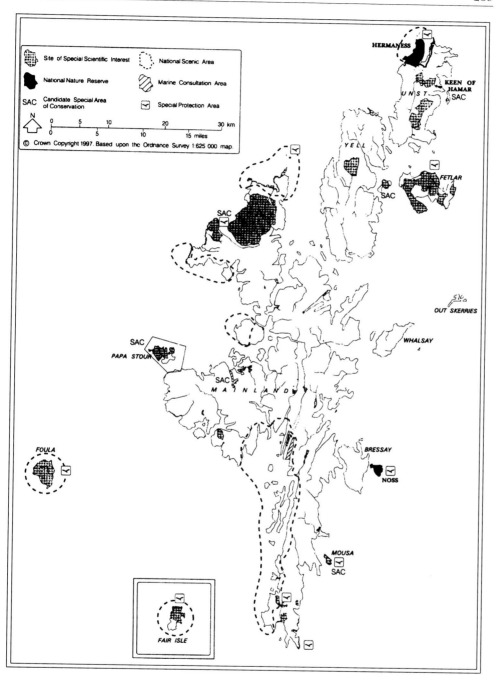

FIGURE 38 *Protected Areas in Shetland* (courtesy of SNH).

are also RSPB Reserves, for example Loch of Spiggie and part of north Fetlar, while Fair Isle, with its internationally famous bird observatory, is owned by the National Trust for Scotland (NTS). Many of Shetland's sites of course have more than one designation, but such a comprehensive award of 'gongs', confusing as they are, is only a just recognition of Shetland's standing in the field of international conservation. A full list of designated sites can be found in Appendix 2.

There is only room here to discuss the designations briefly, but I hope what follows will shed a little light on the implications and the differences of the various types. Let us begin with the SSSIs (which include the NNRs), which are so designated by the government's advisory body, SNH. These require the owner or tenant to consult with SNH before management changes are made that may be damaging to the natural heritage features. Management agreements can be made with SNH and financial support given to environmentally positive actions. Generally there are few conflicts between the needs of protection and management and some of the most fragile of Shetland's SSSIs are those which have been created and sustained by generations of traditional management, for example the limestone herb-rich grasslands of Whiteness, the machair grasslands of Quendale, the hay meadows of Aith or Norwick and the serpentinite and greenstone fellfield and heathlands of Unst. NNRs are special SSSIs where the owner has made a management agreement with SNH. Usually they are places of more general interest, often spectacular and where there is pressure for public access.

The EC Directives (on wild birds and on habitats and species) are laws of the European Union applying across all the member states. SPAs, according to the Directive, should be 'sufficient in number and area to ensure the favourable conservation status of 175 particularly vulnerable bird species and subspecies' and 'other migratory species with special reference to wetland', while the SACs should 'maintain or restore natural habitats and species of European interest' with 'special priority to be given to over 200 habitat types and the sites of 193 animal species and over 300 plant species' (IUCN, 1994). Together the sites will form an ecological network called Natura 2000 and when completed there will be thousands of such sites right across Europe. Examples of SPAs are the seabird colonies of Herma Ness, Fair Isle, Foula and Fetlar; the Loch of Spiggie, which regularly holds more than 3% of the wintering whooper swans in the British Isles; North Roe and Tingon, which together hold 5% of both the British and EC populations of *raingeese* and whimbrel, 1% of British merlins, 3% of arctic skuas and 2% of *bonxies*; as well as 16 breeding species of waders and wildfowl and 12 species of seabirds. To date 10 SPAs have been designated and 10 candidate SACs identified for designation by 2004 under the EC Directive. Protection under the EC Directives requires more than maintenance of the status quo under SSSI legislation and forbids development that might damage the integrity of the site unless for reasons 'of overriding public interest, including those of a social or economic nature'.

Statutory protection of the NSAs in Shetland requires planning authorities to notify SNH where they intend to grant planning permission for specified categories of development proposals likely to have a significant effect on the scenic interest within the NSA. An interesting omission from the Scottish Office Circular 9/1987, particularly in Shetland's case, was fish farm development. However Whiteness Voe, within the NSA, was one of the few voes not given planning permission for fish farms.

MCA are non-statutory sites that were developed to protect coastal areas in the face of the rapid development of fish farms in the mid-1980s (although some in Shetland already contained fish farms), as SSSIs do not extend beyond the low-water mark. They were identified by the NCC (now SNH) as 'deserving particular distinction in respect of the quality and sensitivity of their marine environment and where the scientific information available fully substantiates their nature conservation importance', to assist and guide the Crown Estate Commissioners (CEC) in their role as the approving body for developments onshore and just offshore. In Shetland, however, the Zetland County Council Act 1974 gave SIC special coastal powers up to 4.8 km offshore. Strong feelings of their more recent cultural and historical associations with *udal* law encouraged Shetland to challenge CEC's jurisprudence and it was not until 1991 that the latter regained control in Shetland. By then, of course, by far the majority of fish farms were established. To be fair to the Shetland Salmon Farmers Association they did follow the environmental and planning guidelines developed by the CEC, although they did not encourage use of CEC's environmental impact assessment until 1991. There are four MCAs in Shetland, covering the unique tidal *houbs* and *vadills* at Swinister, Fugla Ness and Brindister, whose marine communities are found nowhere else in Britain (see Chapter 7), and Whiteness Voe, with its relatively rich sublittoral flora and fauna.

ESAs were first established under the Agriculture Act 1986 in order to protect areas where traditional farming practices supported distinctive landscapes and maintained valuable wildlife habitats, historic and cultural features. The whole of Shetland became an ESA in 1994 in recognition of its crofting and farming landscape and the diverse and unique range of wild flowers and birds that its traditional agricultural practices supported. In Shetland's case these are particularly the heather moorlands, hay meadows, herb-rich grasslands and unimproved pastures, and the nationally important populations of waders that inhabit them in the summer months. Under the ESA scheme, which is voluntary, grants are available to carry out agreed forms of management compatible with conserving the 'natural' habitats and to enhance or extend them under a farm conservation plan. In 1996 a second environment advisor was appointed by SCFWAG to assist Shetlanders in taking advantage of the ESA grants. In the long term these appointments may be seen as just as important as those of the first RSPB warden or government conservation officers.

The above is a very impressive list of designations and Shetlanders are rightly proud of them, many owing their existence to years of sensitive management. Alas, however, experience has shown that the statutory designation of a site in Shetland, or anywhere, does not necessarily give it full protection. Indeed SSSI designation of specific areas may give the false impression that the remaining 90% of Shetland is an environment without value, a supposition manifestly not true. An example of mistreatment and damage to SSSIs, sites recognized as being of national and sometimes international importance, was the sand extraction from St Ninian's Isle and the Quendale dunes. At St Ninian's Isle, extraction has forever removed the natural form of the dunes on both sides of perhaps the most symmetrical and beautiful sand tombolo in Europe and threatened the very existence of the structure itself. At Quendale, the largest and the only complete dune system in Shetland, where history has tried to tell us that interference with the stability of the system can result in serious erosion problems, the structure is still being exploited. The only machair lochs in Shetland within the sand system at Quendale have also suffered the indignity of a sewage outfall, which has caused eutrophication and the loss of several plant species. Further damage to the diverse flora of the 'machair' of Quendale and other non-SSSI sand systems, such as that at Scousburgh, has been caused by overgrazing. Prior to the Wildlife and Countryside Act 1981, there was no requirement for owners or tenants on SSSIs to consult the government's conservation arm on agricultural (or forestry) development. It was the destruction of many important semi-natural habitats throughout Britain by these developments that provided the impetus for new statutory controls. Events in Shetland played their part too, such as the reseeding of half of the Keen of Hamar, the relict fellfield from the retreat of the ice from Shetland. Happily the remainder of the Keen of Hamar is now an NNR with a management agreement.

GREEN INITIATIVES IN SHETLAND

We return to Shetland's conservation problems and opportunities later in the chapter when we look at the impact of the main industries on the environment. Here we look at international, national and local initiatives that are providing some hope for a more enlightened approach in Shetland to what used to be seen as a conflict between development and conservation, for today there is a quiet environmental revolution starting in Shetland's primary schools.

At the Earth Summit in Rio de Janeiro in June 1992, among many great and noble declarations, world leaders, including those of Europe and of course Great Britain, endorsed the principle that the protected area system, although central to sustaining biological diversity (itself the key to a healthy and economically productive environment) was not enough, and that to support humanity without destroying the environment in the process there must be a global partnership to achieve sustainable development and that each country must 'develop national strategies, plans or programmes for the conservation and sustainable use of biological diversity' (this was an endorsement of earlier proposals taken at UNCED under Chapter 15 in Agenda 21). In part fulfilment of the Earth Summit's declarations the UK published its Biodiversity Action Plan in 1994. All the worthy goals, principles and objectives of the UK Action Plan can be found in this document, but the underlying thrust is for the wise and sustainable use of our natural resources, guided by the precautionary principle, and the principle that action requires 'the care and involvement of individuals and communities'. In Shetland, perhaps more than many places, where there is a strong sense of identity and community in a distinctive and well-defined geographical area, there must be a real opportunity to take this forward.

Has Shetland adopted local Agenda 21 initiatives adopted by the Earth Summit? There is no formal Agenda 21 programme for Shetland, but an environmental coordinator to draw one up has been appointed by SIC. There are also several ambitious and far-sighted initiatives that have been promoted or encouraged by the SIC, as well as the adoption of a whole range of green policies and procedures within council departments. In addition SIC has made use of its additional oil funds to set up two 'environmental' trusts.

On the world stage of environmental concerns, Shetlanders have never allowed the physical limits of their relatively small group of islands to inhibit their vision: from the earliest days they have always looked beyond their shores to the seemingly unlimited horizons of the sea. The history of their control of the development of the oil industry well illustrates this. It is also evident in SIC being a founder member, and the secretariat, of Kommunenes Internasionale Miljøorganisasjon or KIMO. KIMO is a pressure group of local governments on the North Sea coasts, set up to lobby for the protection and improvement of the environment of the North Sea and includes all the Scandinavian countries, Faroe and Germany. KIMO has agreed a number of green resolutions, such as the establishment of marine nature reserves, controls on many aspects of shipping relating to oil transport and dumping, pollution control, and is seeking to form a consensus on fishing. Shetland has also launched KIMO's programme of research into the social and economic impacts of marine debris in the North Sea, i.e. the flotsam and jetsam that gets entangled in nets, lies unsightly on beaches and sometimes gets ingested by farm stock. The results of this research will be delivered to the environmental ministers of the North Sea states at the fifth North Sea Conference in the year 2000.

A second major initiative, over and above programmes for recycling glass, paper, CFCs, metals, compost, solvents and plastics throughout the islands, is to replace the ageing council incinerator and do away with the landfill sites, which will shortly become illegal under European regulations. It is intended to build a waste-to-energy plant close to Lerwick, which may take in additional combustible waste from the oil industry and from Orkney also, and use the energy generated to provide a district heating system for the town.

With the advent of the oil industry revenue from the Sullom Oil Terminal, SIC established the Shetland Amenity Trust in 1983. Since its inception the Amenity Trust has annually dispensed around £1 million in amenity and environmental improvements throughout Shetland. On the environmental side, there have been numerous positive projects over the years, such as the anti-litter campaign under the slogan *Dinna chuck bruck* and an annual *Voar redd up* (spring clean-up). There are coastal protection schemes, access improvements, repair of old buildings with historical or cultural associations to form low-key holiday accommodation or *camping bods*, and recently very imaginative efforts to protect the last scraps of native Shetland scrub and to establish a nursery of these plants through cuttings and seed collection. The Trust has also been experimenting with other hardy non-native trees and shrubs, all of which can be used to create new 'native' woodland or shelterbelts. In addition to amenity and environmental work, the Amenity Trust has an archaeologist on its staff whose direct involvement and stimulus to other archaeologists is steadily increasing our knowledge of the past flora and fauna of the islands, how the environment has been managed and how it has changed over time. In association with SNH and the Shetland Tourist Board, the Amenity Trust is also producing interpretative material for visitors and the local schools.

82. *Camping bod, Walls: another of the many Amenity Trust projects has been the renovation of buildings of local historical importance and their transformation into basic and cheap accommodation for backpackers, walkers and cyclists.* (Courtesy of Shetland Amenity Trust.)

In the UK's Biodiversity Action Plan it was stated that 'formal education has a crucial role to play' and it is perhaps in this field that Shetland is making its most exciting and important environmental investment. An investment that has been taken up so enthusiastically by its primary schools, supported by SIC's Field Studies Trust, that they are cornering the market in the annual national environmental awards for schools. For example, Shetland primary schools won the first two ECO Schools accreditations (Tidy Britain Group) to be won in Scotland, in 1995 a junior high school won a World Wide Fund for Nature prize for a multi-habitat nature trail and another received a community award during the BT Environment Week for designing gull-proof litter receptacles. There is little doubt that the support of the Field Studies Trust and Shetland's exciting environment has helped to stimulate the local childrens' interest. For example, a nature field trip to the shore, led by Trust staff, for a primary 3 class in the summer of 1996 was entertained by a wildlife spectacular, perhaps equivalent to a city group being taken to see a *Jaws* movie, except this was live and the Shetland children saw a pod of eight killer whales trying to make lunch out of a group of seals!

The Education Department of SIC is also developing the 5–14 Environmental Education Programme for Shetland's children, which will ensure that some projects can be locally based and that therefore the stimulus from the local environment can be used to develop environmental awareness where it matters most. In addition the principal secondary school is rewriting the social and moral education programme, which will encourage older pupils to examine the social and moral implications of their current lifestyle and its effect on their local environment. Finally, the local link with the tertiary element of environmental education is now almost in place, with the development of modules on Shetland's natural environment by Aberdeen University's Centre for Continuing Education through the North Atlantic Fisheries College in Scalloway.

Environmental education is obviously making great strides in Shetland and will eventually, maybe shortly, ensure that those who make the decisions locally – as, increasingly, democratic responsibilities and decisions are being devolved – will have an even better understanding of their environment. Shetland is thus doing a great many things to promote green issues.

AGRICULTURE

The arable

Arable farming combined with pastoralism is the oldest traditional Shetland industry, stretching back 5000 years to the first-known settlers, and it has been this industry, combined with long-term climatic fluctuations, that has transformed the face of Shetland and continues to do so.

Paradoxically, where management has been most intensive *innadaeks* (as opposed to the hill), the most diverse wildlife habitats, agriculturally productive and attractive landscapes have been created, but only where and when this management has been carried out at a sustainable level, compatible with the productivity of the soil and the prevailing climate. We have seen evidence from the distant past that suggests soils became exhausted at different periods, via climatic deterioration accompanied by poor land management, causing the abandonment of arable land. More recently, this trend has continued for other reasons, for example resulting from the clearances of last century and changes in the agricultural markets and support systems through the latter half of this century. In his long and perceptive perspective Fojut (1993) has suggested that 'The whole history of Shetland seems to show a decline in arable farming from the earliest days onwards'. Today one just has to cast an eye over the crofting scene to see that this trend has accelerated in the last decade or so. It is only on the farms in the most fertile areas, Dunrossness and Tingwall for example, that there are still mixed arable systems.

83. *Ireland: the original long* rigs *are still in evidence, but are now predominantly down to silage or permanent grassland.* (Courtesy of L. Johnston.)

84.   Grazing effects, Stromfirth: a prolonged period of differential grazing on either side of the dividing fence demonstrates how the 'natural' dwarf-shrub heath can be transformed by increased grazing into grassland. The remains of old arable rigs *can also be seen in the grassland.* (Courtesy of L. Johnston.)

85.   Spiggie, Dunrossness: on the best Shetland land are the relatively few farms. (Courtesy of SNH, Lerwick.)

In Shetland today there are around 2000 crofts and 20 farms, with 12% of the rural population involved in agriculture and by far the majority of crofts run on a part-time basis. The total income from agriculture (Fig. 39) is around £13 million, about one-third of the income from fish farming or wild fishing; almost 50% of that income is from subsidies. In financial terms, crofting is not therefore the most important industry in Shetland, but it is part of the very fabric of the island way of life. SIC has always recognized this and in its 1981 10 Year Agricultural Plan it stated that 'every solution for agriculture must also conform to the sociological requirements. The long term aim should be to maintain the rural community as well as to improve agricultural production'. SIC has therefore invested substantially, almost £1 million a year, over the last decades to improve agricultural production.

The driving forces behind the loss of arable and wetland to permanent pasture and the loss of heather moorland in Shetland (as elsewhere) are the subsidies under

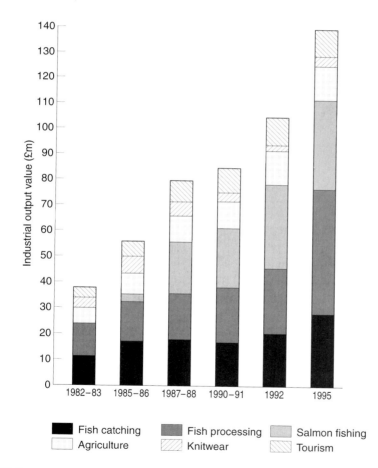

FIGURE 39 *Industrial output and growth of traditional industries 1982–95* (note that the figures for output are absolute and not relative) (courtesy of Development Department SIC).

the Hill Livestock Compensatory Allowance (HLCA) and the Sheep Annual Premium (SAP) under the Common Agricultural Policy (CAP) of the European Union. These are paid on 'headage', i.e. simply on the number of cattle and sheep, and not on their quality. The area of permanent grassland has been slowly rising through the 1970s and 1980s, while the area under crops (cereals, turnip, kale and potatoes) has halved in the same period (Table 16). This dramatic change in the area of arable land is well illustrated by the fact that in 1966 there were some 1000 ha of oats and barley, while in 1996 there were only around 100 ha. In acknowledging that it is the subsidy system that is the major driving force in agricultural change in Britain generally, we must also recognize that recent climatic trends in Shetland have mitigated against growing grain crops and made a haymaking tradition less easy. Some changes we are powerless against and must adapt to.

In the middle of the nineteenth century there were around 50 000 sheep in Shetland, mostly the small Shetland breed, in the 1960s around 264 000 and today around 400 000, eight times as many. More than ever before, as in the Scottish Highlands and islands generally but most seriously in Shetland, there is an overwhelming dependency on sheep and on the subsidy they bring. Approximately 95% of Shetland's agricultural subsidy comes from sheep and at around £6 million

TABLE 16   *Agricultural statistics 1971–96 Shetland* (reproduced with permission of SIC)

Main and minor holdings	1971	1981	1991	1995	1996
Land use (figures to nearest hectare)					
Tillage	1 410	1 062	749	493	411
Grassland and crops	8 407	8 400	15 232	18 954	19 311
Rough grazing (incl. common grazing)	129 019	133 160	130 516	126 388	126 466
Total area rented	38 130	36 046	36 738	39 568	40 041
Total area owned	28 161	30 368	34 400	33 663	34 541
No. of holdings	2 439	2 240	2 433	2 333	2 193
No. of common grazings	93	93	100	100	100
Area under crops (figures to nearest hectare)					
Grass (excl. rough grazings)	6 998	7 338	14 482	18 461	18 900
Barley and oats	857	511	214	107	78
Turnips and swedes	134	103	110	62	59
Kale and cabbage	73	34	35	19	15
Potatoes	256	232	147	99	91
All other crops	17	25	144	145	120
Livestock					
Beef cows and heifers	2 492	1 896	2 139	2 316	2 361
Dairy cows and heifers	791	593	648	636	731
Total cattle	6 945	5 103	5 750	5 907	6 276
Breeding ewes and gimmers	—	—	214 881	220 210	219 350
Total sheep	264 779	297 558	394 193	401 710	400 466

Source: Scottish Office Agriculture, Environment and Fisheries Department.
Note: 1995 minor holdings results not available. Some figures are estimates.

this is actually double their sales income. This is not a healthy situation for Shetland's agriculture, nor for the environment trying to support them.

Through the combination of increasing grazing pressure and agricultural 'improvement' the quality of the semi-natural permanent grassland is actually being reversed. The replacement of once lightly grazed permanent grassland with commercial varieties of grasses and those few native species of tough grasses and rushes that can stand up to heavy grazing or fertilizer use is gradually depleting the diversity of lower plants, grasses, sedges and flowering plants that used to support livestock *and* soil invertebrates, insects *and* the birds that fed on them. The number of cattle in Shetland is almost what it was in 1966, but they are now concentrated on the large farms and by and large absent from the crofts, which means the crops and hayfields are no longer required and cattle dung is no longer returned to the field, nor is there the ploughing of that land to help retain its fertility. Also lost, or declining, are those species of birds that depended on the crops and the micro-habitats they created, the corn bunting and the corncrake for example.

On the other hand, where diversity is lost there may be an increase in other populations that can take advantage; species like the *shalder*, lapwing and starling have probably benefited and expanded. However, the recent move towards silage will exacerbate the loss of semi-natural grassland and thus the availability of food and habitat to insects and birds. This imbalance between sheep and cattle has been recognized by SIC. In 1981 it stated 'much land in Shetland would be greatly improved if cattle numbers were increased along with the associated production of arable crops' (10 Year Agricultural Plan). We have to move forwards of course with our agricultural techniques and become more efficient, but it is too easy to dismiss the loss of just one 'insignificant' animal or plant when measured against the increase of income and employment. We need to recognize that the loss of each individual species, caused by our management, is another warning light on the health of the natural environment and another step down a series of events leading to monocultures and the loss of what is also a *cultural* environment.

While *innadaeks* traditional Shetland croftland is dramatically changing in its agricultural and landscape quality and wildlife diversity, the old defining border between it and the hill, the hill dyke, has almost disappeared. Hill reclamation, the creation of grassland by the application of fertilizer and commercial grass seed (reseeding), first received government assistance in the mid-1950s and this continued up until the mid-1980s. Between 1976 and 1989 approximately 11 242 ha of hill land was improved in Shetland, about 7% of the *scattald*. Since this central government support ceased, SIC has continued to support the maintenance of these reclaimed areas by the annual addition of fertilizer. In fact between 1983 and 1991 SIC has put over £1 million into promoting 6220 ha of land improvement schemes, including inbye land and 1 million m of drains and ditches. These schemes, by and large, support additional sheep to gain the Sheep Annual Premium (SAP) and HLCA grants. In the long term, without a continuous input of fertilizer and public funds in the shape of grants, most of these 'improvements' are unsustainable. Even only a few years after reclamation many of the less suitable areas that should not have been improved are reverting not to the original heather, which has been killed off, but to unpalatable rushes and grasses, which like their 'improved' counterparts in the inbye are of less value to Shetland's livestock and to its traditional breeding birds. What was once a landscape of patchwork *rigs* and fields around crofts, bordered by semi-natural grassland and wetlands, giving way beyond the hill dyke to the wild brown heather of the hill, is fast becoming an artificial green, stretching out from the crofthouse and rising like a tide up the hill.

There are, of course, many areas of Shetland where management *innadaeks* remains sympathetic to the colourful and diverse crofting heritage and can still give a livelihood. However, the sort of management required is becoming increasingly uneconomical in the face of present subsidies, and if we want to retain this inheritance we need to look very carefully as to how we can support this.

Sheep, waders, starlings and gulls

The hill

And what of the hill itself? While the 'reclaimed' areas were created first by *apportioning* parts of the *scattald* to individual crofters with grazing rights, 80 000 ha of the remaining rough grazings remains a shared resource. The individual grazing shares (number of sheep), or *soumings*, on the *scattald* were set over 100 years ago after a period of heavy exploitation by a variety of grazing stock, including cattle, pigs and many more Shetland ponies, and by a long period of exploitation for peat, peat mould, heather, etc. The *soumings* were probably set as much for pertinent political as agricultural reasons and are unlikely to have borne much relation to the sustainable stocking rates at that time, nor of course can they be related to carrying capacity today.

In fact several factors have probably increased the original *soumings* and grazing pressures. For example, there were *c.* 20 000 cattle on the hill in the summer last century, which have since been replaced by an 'equivalent' number of sheep; these of course remain on the hill to graze through the winter months, are more selective grazers and recycle less nutrients. Although most hill sheep are the traditional small and hardy Shetland breed, not all are and therefore more pressure has been put on the grazing resource. Finally, in some areas, numbers are kept higher than the land can otherwise support by the provision of winter supplements, which in itself creates additional grazing pressure.

It was pointed out in the first chapter of this book that the climate at sea level in Shetland is submontane, equivalent to that at 350 m in Scotland. It is not surprising therefore that heather, the dominant plant on Shetland's blanket bog and an important food supply for sheep especially in winter, is reaching its geographical limits. A recent study has shown that the rate of heather growth in Shetland is equivalent only to the lower end of the range for mainland Britain. If heather shoots are eaten back faster than they can grow, the plant will not grow and may even die.

There is plenty evidence to show the results of overgrazing of the hill in Shetland (see Chapter 4). For example, a striking feature of the Shetland blanket peat is the widespread occurrence of mat grass and ling communities on areas that once would have supported bell heather and bog moss communities; in effect a vegetation change has been caused by heavy and prolonged grazing, which has removed the active bog ingredient (*Sphagnum* moss). Many parts of the hill, like the Muness phylittes, also bear thin peat on waterlogged soil, which is the remains of former deep peat removed for fuel. There, the natural drainage structure has been

86.   *Peat erosion, Ward of Culswick: alas a feature of the unsustainable management of many parts of the Shetland hill where exposure, exacerbated by overgrazing, has resulted in the removal of the protective living vegetation and the initiation of active peat erosion, which now may be very difficult to stop.* (Courtesy of P. Harvey.)

damaged and the substitute plant cover is dominated by mat grass or heath rush, which in itself is a further loss of grazing value. This is still happening today where some mechanical peat cutting, which extracts the peat from below the surface, is also destroying the drainage structure. Where peat cutting is carried out in the traditional manner by the *tushkar* and divots replaced carefully in the *greff* (previous year's cut) such damage should not occur.

There is also a serious erosion problem, possibly partly due to climate but very much exacerbated by overgrazing. Hulme and Birnie (1990) has pointed out that in Dunrossness and Sandwick districts 17% of peatland is unvegetated. It has also been estimated that almost 90% of Shetland's blanket bog, which makes up half of the Shetland moorland, is suffering from erosion; in a recent study the rate of erosion of peat in Shetland was put at 1–4 cm per year. Although the initial causes of peat erosion are probably climatic, there is evidence that reduction of stocking levels could allow recolonization of peat by vegetation. The situation is unfortunately on a downward spiral, because the less heather there is to graze through its loss by erosion or conversion to poor grassland, or overstocking through supplements, the more pressure falls on the remainder.

The problems for hill do not end there. We have seen that recent studies of the effects of a changing climate have also indicated that 'woody' plants, like heather, are coming under increasing climatic pressure due to milder winters. Also recently, it has been found that some areas of heather are suffering from invertebrate and fungal attack. It is difficult to know at present whether this event is a case of invertebrates and fungi taking advantage of an already weakened system or if they are responsible for causing weakness.

Why should we worry about this? Heather moorland and blanket bog is a resource that has sustained the traditional Shetland sheep and pony, and people, over many generations and is the habitat for many of Shetland's characteristic and internationally valued birds and plants. Neither sheep nor wildlife can live on peat or bedrock and if the erosion continues there will not be any feeding for sheep, or any other grazer eventually. And maybe sooner than later, as the indications are that the problems will get worse and because of climatic change will become increasingly difficult to remedy. What action can we take?

Calculations, using the tried and tested Macaulay Land Use Research Institute grazing model (given temperature and altitude and information on the composition of the plant community), can calculate the production of a heather shoot for each month of the year. Knowing the grazing impact of a sheep, a conclusion can be drawn as to the optimum number of sheep per type of vegetation community and area of moorland to ensure the survival of heather; this gives the hill's carrying capacity. This has been done for some areas in Shetland and could be completed in a relatively short time, then the results applied. That is the management answer to the question, but of course there will also be difficult financial and political problems to overcome.

Subsidies, grants and traditions

Today there are a number of large and successful farms on Shetland, but there are fewer and fewer 'agricultural' units one could call a traditional croft any longer.

This is partly due to an almost irreversible loss of people from the crofts attracted by well-paid and secure jobs. A new generation has grown up, where both partners may work and who no longer want to work the land. Neither is it easy in the modern workplace to get away at short notice to carry out the seasonal work required on a croft. It is an odd fact that three-quarters of a century ago, an enlightened government gave the fathers of some of today's older generation new crofts, from the break-up of larger landholdings, when they returned from fighting in the First World War. These same crofts are now being reunited under one tenant to become sheep 'ranches', with abandoned and derelict crofthouses. The irony is that the original idea was to give more people land to help them and their families survive and prosper in a healthy rural environment, while today, again with public subsidy, the government and ourselves support a system (sheep subsidies) that is doing exactly the opposite. We seem to have forgotten that it was sheep, or rather the greed for money from the raising of them, that also caused the abandonment of many crofts and the exodus of people from the land last century. If ever there was a subsidy that was bad for the rural population and the countryside, including its wildlife, it is the present CAP with its heavy emphasis on sheep numbers. The system for assigning crofts, designed to keep them in use and provide subsistence support for as many people as possible, seems also to have fallen into abuse.

The establishment of the ESA in Shetland, the appointment of advisors to support the many crofters who have indicated that they wish to manage their land in a more environmentally friendly way, retaining unimproved grasslands and wetlands and reducing grazing pressures on the hill, is heartening for the future. However, it must be recognized that the overall amount of money available for such management is almost infinitesimal when compared with the finance available from the EC or SOAFED to develop production unrelated to sustainability, never mind similarly targeted local SIC agricultural grants. In addition, the level of grant available for individual management elements of the ESA may not be attractive enough, except for the already converted and they may not be properly targeted. If we are to sustain the fertility and diversity *innadaeks* there needs to be a *cropping* grant to encourage the growing of crops and the traditional ploughing of land.

If the soils and remaining wildlife diversity are going to be sustained on the crofts and on the hills of Shetland, so that they are a resource for the use of future generations of Shetlanders once oil has gone, there is going to have to be some major rethinking at all levels of government. We need to persuade the EC to rethink the balance of the CAP, stop wasting public money in supporting the very successful lowland farms and direct it to the margins, to the less favoured areas, ensuring 'cross-compliance', i.e. environmental gain for public subsidy. We need to encourage the British government to recognize that agricultural subsidies for marginal farming areas such as Shetland are in reality 'rural population support' subsidies and therefore they should ensure that grants and subsidies support diversity and extensification, that *headage* payments become *area* payments. Local government, SIC, needs to adopt an agricultural 'strategy' that pays regard to carrying capacity and the natural environment and that integrates with the ESA and other legitimate land uses. The public and voluntary conservation bodies need to keep pressing central government for 'positive' incentives for crofters, farmers and wildlife. We need to look more radically at the crofting regulations regarding croft-holding. This list of needs is an illustration of the number of public agencies and bodies involved and perhaps the essential need is to get them all together to act in unison. We must recognize that *people* are the landscape: good management is vital for both soil and wildlife conservation.

Some evidence of the historical overexploitation of the land has been recounted in this book. There is now a desperate need to get an agreement on grazing levels, between those who define overgrazing in terms of 'ecology' and those who define it in terms of 'agriculture'. It is a strange anomaly that Shetland gives such strong support to its rich cultural and historical heritage and tradition, and recently to environmental education, but yet so little to its diverse crofting traditions. SIC today could not do better than emulate their colleagues of 1974 who took control of an enormous oil industry in order to mitigate its impact on the landscape and wildlife and to ensure benefits for all the Shetland people. Shetland needs a vision of what it wants from its land and needs a SLUAG, a Shetland Land Users Advisory Group, to bring together all interested parties to integrate the grant and subsidy systems and to agree a strategy for a sustainable agricultural future that also supports its unique landscape and wildlife. In a few years there will be substantial reform of the CAP and now is the opportunity for Shetland to get its act together before it finds itself fitted up with a new agricultural straitjacket.

AQUACULTURE

It is not surprising that an island with limited 'terrestrial' natural resources, but surrounded by productive seas, should earn the bulk of its wealth from fishing. What is remarkable today is that the fish farming element, virtually all salmon, and less than 20 years old, now produces a greater income than fish catching (Fig. 39). It should not be forgotten of course that the genesis of aquaculture arose partly from the loss of traditional wild fish stocks as a result of overexploitation. Neither should it be forgotten that a great deal of the food pellets fed to caged salmon are manufactured from the produce of industrial fishing, i.e. from sandeels and sprat.

Standing on a fish farm set in the sparkling waters of a Shetland voe and looking down into the sea of silvery and elegant salmon, it all looks as clean as a health farm. In fact a fish farm works on the same basis as any other intensive rearing operation: it is just like a packed chicken-shed with all the waste and surplus food dropping out of the bottom (a recent study suggested that for every 10 tonnes of feed put into a salmon cage, 1 tonne of solid waste sinks to the sea bed). The only difference, and here Shetland scores over many of the fish farms developed in fresh waters and those in too-sheltered situations on the west coast of Scotland or deep in the fiords of Norway, is that powerful tidal currents and swells around Shetland flush the cages and water column beneath them. To conclude the chicken-shed analogy, it is as if the chicken-shed in Shetland were suspended in the air and subjected to continuous gales that blow the waste away before it hits the ground!

The danger in Shetland's sheltered voes and freshwater lochs is that the additional nutrients in the feed dropping on to the sea bed from a fish farm or hatchery cause a sharp rise in tiny organisms, which in turn increasingly use up all the oxygen until finally they deoxygenate the water, making it and the sediment uninhabitable to many of the other larger marine organisms, shellfish etc. that would normally live there. In some situations in Shetland, where much organic matter in the form of peat already washes into the voe, deoxygenation already happens in the summer months. So far, studies suggest that by far the bulk of Shetland's fish farms are well located in areas of reasonable water movement and that any change to the macrofauna on the sea bed is confined to up to 15 m from the cages, even after several years. The Scottish Environmental Protection Agency (SEPA), continuing from where SIC left off, requires fish farmers to carry out continuous self-monitoring of the biological impact below the fish farms and itself carries out occasional audits. If this is to be a long-term industry, it is vital that with so many farms a close watch is kept on any low-level chronic impact. SEPA are also responsible for licensing substances used to control diseases or infestations in the tightly packed cages. In this regard, recent approval to use the neurotoxin ivermectin against sea-lice has raised some environmental concerns, although SEPA has given assurances that any effects on the natural environment will be closely monitored; if the agent is found to be damaging, licences will be withdrawn. However, the widespread use of chemicals could have very subtle and damaging effects, for example, interfering with the traces of 'messenger' chemicals used by shellfish in their reproductive cycle

Even with so many fish farms scattered around Shetland there is no evidence to suggest that the industry has any direct effect on Shetland's seabirds and seaduck. However, indirect forms of biological impact, such as 'management' to protect the fish from predators, are difficult to assess. Undoubtedly there will have been some shooting of individual seals or cormorants persisting in attack, but with today's anti-predator nets this should not be necessary. In fact, though there may be *ad hoc* culling of birds, there is little evidence to suggest that the killing of predators is at all regular or having an effect on the local populations. Another suggested impact is disturbance to seaduck by the semi-continuous movement of boats, for example to *dunter* creches, with *bonxies* and gulls taking advantage of distracted adults to take chicks. Once again there is little evidence this is having a serious impact.

An environmental problem that has gained a lot of attention, particularly in Norway, in Ireland and on the west coast of Scotland, is the impact of escaped salmon on local populations through transmission of disease, competition for food and breeding sites, and the danger of interbreeding with the native stock and destroying the unique genetic imprint associated with each individual river. That there are many escaped salmon in the wild is undisputed: a recent study in Norway showed that 20% of salmon caught by the commercial fishery were from fish farms. In Shetland, as there are very few 'native' salmon (although several Norse place names, e.g. Laxo, suggest that there were more in the past) it could be that escaping salmon could virtually replace the native stock. There is also the problem of large concentrations of sea-lice in fish farming and their effect on local sea-trout populations. There is no indication that fish farming in Shetland has affected already depleted local sea-trout populations, but the great concentration of fish farms could well mitigate against their recovery.

The industry is now diversifying into sea trout and other commercial species, such as char and halibut, and may well also develop into cod and haddock. Future threats to the environment from fish farming lie in the danger of over-intensification of the industry, particularly now that some of the industry is passing into Norwegian hands, who will use the Shetland base as a means of entry to the EC. Shellfish too will no doubt be farmed, especially mussels, whose success or failure should be a good indication of the 'health' of the sea. Since mussels are an important food for *dunters*, precautions will have to be taken to ensure that these ducks, presently declining, do not become entangled in any anti-predator nets.

Although it is possible to minimize the impact to the sea bed from fish farms, it is almost impossible to limit the visual impact. There are now around 50 fish farms in Shetland and hardly a voe or sound is not now adorned by the floating rectangles and circles of fish cages. In areas of existing activity, with piers, slipways and moored boats, fish cages can merge with the background activity. In entirely new sites there is no way of hiding them. By and large, however, fish farms sit well in Shetland waters, continuing the tradition of the Shetlander's involvement with the sea. Where there should be restriction from further development should be in the areas of highest scenic value, Weisdale Voe for example, and in the areas of highest wildlife value, for example MCAs and in any designated SPAs.

FISH CATCHING

Fishing has many effects on the marine environment, some of which attract considerable attention, others largely hidden. The nature of the fishing operations around Shetland means that some of the highest profile problems, such as catches of dolphin or seabirds, are fortunately rare. With the exception of scallop and suction dredges, which have severe but localized effects, the type of fishing gear used means that disturbance to the sea bed and the animals which live on it is much less serious around Shetland than in other areas, such as the southern North Sea. This does not mean that Shetland has not been guilty of overexploiting some of its marine resources locally, e.g. lobsters, queens and oysters. However, the most significant effect that fishing around Shetland has on the marine environment and fish predators is simply that of catching, and discarding, fish.

The last century or so, and the last few decades in particular, have seen an immense increase in total fishing effort as fishing vessels have become larger, more powerful and more sophisticated. Fish are a finite resource, however, and this increase in fishing effort has left today's fishing industry, not just in Shetland but throughout Europe and the world, facing a simple fact: there is too much catching power (i.e. too many big boats) chasing too few fish. The result is overfishing, which has two main effects. Firstly, many fish are caught at a small size so that the fishermen's total catch (in terms of weight) is less than it would have been if the fish had been allowed to grow larger. Secondly, overfishing may reduce the size of a fish stock until it no longer produces enough eggs to replace the fish that are caught or die. The latter is more serious, since it can result in (or contribute to) the total collapse of stocks, as occurred with North Sea herring in the past and more recently in the Canadian cod fishery.

If fishing effort could be significantly reduced for a period of several years, fish stocks would have a chance to recover so that they would be able to provide greater yields than they do today and would be at less risk of collapse. The facts are simple, but the solutions are less so. Reducing fishing effort essentially means forcing fishermen to either stop fishing or accept substantial cuts in earnings; such measures invariably meet with considerable opposition from the fishing industry if they are proposed, and to date the political will to impose such measures has been lacking.

One of the most significant problems in fisheries management is the gulf that exists between fishermen and the fisheries scientists who advise the politicians, which results in misunderstanding and a generally confrontational approach to fisheries management. A secondary problem is the unwillingness of politicians to heed the warnings of their fisheries scientists, and so take effective management measures, until problems are so severe and obvious that they can no longer be ignored.

In the absence of reductions in fishing effort, endeavours have been made to conserve young fish by allowing more of them to escape from fishing nets. Attempts to achieve this by increasing mesh sizes have largely failed, and minimum landing sizes simply result in large quantities of small fish being *discarded*, or dumped back in the sea, usually dead. A major problem is that allowing more young fish to escape inevitably also means the escape of some commercially sized fish, and so less earnings for the fishermen. Attention has focused in recent years on so-called Technical Conservation Measures, i.e. modifications to fishing gear that make them more selective, reducing the numbers of juvenile fish and non-target species which they catch, while retaining the maximum number of commercially sized fish. Research results on measures such as square-mesh panels in trawl nets have shown some promise, but it remains to be seen how effective they can be in practice.

A related problem is that of catches of *over-quota* species. Fish stocks in European waters have traditionally been managed by single-species quotas, i.e. limits on how much of each species a fisherman can catch. However, this ignores the fact that most fisheries in these waters are multi-species: several different species are taken simultaneously. Thus the situation can and does arise where a fisherman has used up his quota for cod (and so cannot legally land any) but is still able to catch haddock, for which he still has a quota. But because cod and haddock occur together, it is impossible to catch one without the other and the fisherman is forced to discard the cod that he inevitably catches. This results in considerable wastage of perfectly good, legally sized fish as very few survive the trauma of being caught and discarded. Hence the resentment among fishermen.

Politically Shetland is not an island, and the management of the fisheries in the surrounding waters (just as with agriculture on the land) is largely regulated at a national and, through the EU, international level. As a result the management is often seen as remote and uncaring of fishermen's problems.

What effect does the state of fish stocks and fishing methods have on the natural predators in the North Sea, such as Shetland's seabirds? Of the larger pelagic fish, either herring or mackerel, or both, must be present in reasonable numbers to support the continuing expansion of the gannet. The smaller and relatively short-lived species, sandeels, sprats and Norway pout for example, are perhaps not as abundant or as available as they were when they helped support the population growth of several seabird species up until the 1980s. Catch levels will also have to be directly related to recruitment to ensure no overfishing and further studies are needed on these species. Indeed the current methods of assessing most fish stocks, by 'catch per unit effort' or by 'virtual population analysis', need now to investigate all interspecific dynamics: other predatory fish, seabirds and marine mammals. These studies need to be integrated with studies of the predators themselves to ensure that we are clear about their links and dependencies, so that we can pinpoint the necessary monitoring areas that can tell us quickly when and what things are going wrong.

One of the effects of the drop in the presence or availability of sandeels, linked with a previous abundance, has been the change in feeding behaviour of the *bonxie* at many colonies (see Chapter 8). If these *bonxies*, which have switched to predating on kittiwake chicks, do not revert to feeding on sandeels as the latter's abundance recovers, there are very real problems for Shetland's kittiwakes or at least for some colonies. Only long-term research, such as that on Foula and monitoring of seabird colonies by SOTEAG, will tell us what is happening, although there is not much we can do about it.

Inshore small, non-commercial, fish (and crustacea) appear to be abundant enough to continue to support several seabird species, such as the shag and the *tystie*, and the otter. However, the falls in the populations of cormorants and *dunters* suggest some problems, perhaps with shellfish in the case of the latter; in the case of the former, problems may lie outwith Shetland. It has been noticeable also for a number of years now that the catch of local traditional hand-line recreational fishing from open boats does not include so many haddock, whiting, ling or tusk as in the past.

Bonxie chasing gannet

The scale of fish offal and discard being dumped by the fishing industry in the North Sea and north-eastern Atlantic has been pointed out earlier in this book, along with the fact that this has probably supported the expansion of several seabird species and possibly continues to support higher numbers of seabirds than otherwise might be the case. There is a very real danger that much-needed changes to fishery regulations that reduce wastage will have a marked effect on some seabird populations. In the case of the *maalie* some would say this would be no bad thing; however it might force the large gulls to seek other food sources from the land. This may only have a 'nuisance' effect around coastal towns, but it may also impact directly on other seabirds, seaduck and coastal species through the taking of chicks or even adults, as has happened with some *bonxies*. Whatever the specific effect on each species now making use of the surplus food, there could well be an observable and increased mortality of seabirds, depending on how effective were new regulations and how rapidly they were applied.

The fishing industry, by overfishing, may have contributed to seabird declines through the exacerbation of both summer and winter food shortages, themselves possibly caused by natural fundamental oceanographic changes. On the other hand, discards and offal from fishing boats have provided additional food resources for seabirds that may well have contributed to the expansion of populations. Finally, the other potentially serious area of the marine fishery that directly impacts on Shetland's seabirds, divers and seaduck is some of the fish-catching techniques, especially the non-biodegradable monofilament nets that have been proved to have killed numerous auks off Norway and elsewhere. With new 'exotic' target species being sought by the fishing industry, pressure will need to be kept up to ensure seabirds are not endangered by new fishing techniques. Perhaps there is a role for KIMO here and an opportunity for Shetland to show the lead in its environmental concern as it has in so many other areas. All the indications are that we have now created a situation where the coming inevitable changes in fishing practice to conserve North Sea stocks may lead to wilder swings in some Shetland seabird populations than we have yet seen, and possibly calls for the 'management' of some seabird species whose behaviour has changed to predation.

The history of the shellfish industry in Shetland is not a happy one; however, two things are happening now in Shetland that give hope that these days are over. Firstly, a project to rear lobsters, funded by SIC and carried out by the North Atlantic Fisheries College in Scalloway, has been very successful and has now reached the point of 'reseeding' Shetland's coastline with young lobsters. A similar project with Shetland oysters is also under way. Such projects could be a waste of time and investment, of course, if fishermen continue their uncontrolled exploitation. Secondly, the establishment of a Regulating Order gives the Shetland Fishermens Association (SFA) powers to manage all shellfish in Shetland's inshore waters, including crustacea such as crabs and lobsters. However, control will not lie solely with the SFA, and in an imaginative step a 'regulating committee' is to be formed that will comprise members from the North Atlantic Fisheries College, SIC, the fish-processing industry and SNH, as well as the SFA. How the management of the major deep-sea fish stocks will be carried out in the future remains to be seen. It is possible that there will be a shift towards more regional management, but whatever direction it takes politically, for the future of Shetland's fishermen and the other natural predators of fish a move towards a sustainable fishery is becoming increasingly urgent.

There is an old Shetland saying: 'Da laand cries "Hadd dee hand!" but the sea says "come again!"'. This might have been relevant 100 years ago, but alas no more.

AGGREGATES AND MINERALS

As far as extraction of sand for building or agricultural use is concerned, Shetland has a poor record environmentally. On an island with very limited sand resources it has always been the temptation to use what is there rather than import from more extensive sources at extra cost. Despite fairly unequivocal historical precedents warning against disturbance to sand-dune systems, Quendale and Sandwick (Unst) for example, considerable damage by insensitive exploitation has been caused in the past to coastal sites. With today's relatively healthy economy and demand for much larger scale supplies this local practice has now stopped at most sites, but still continues at one at least to the detriment of its structure.

Equally, the local resources of stone for road-building and other industrial and agricultural purposes present problems for Shetland. The smooth and rounded contours of the Shetland landscape, resembling an upturned saucer, mean that any development, i.e. building or extraction, is rarely hidden from view. The nature of the climate and the soils also mean that any disturbance to the vegetation and topsoil takes a long time to recover and that any remedial effort to hide development usually results in 'unnatural' landscape forms and vegetation, which only draw attention to what is intended to be hidden. Operating quarries cannot be disguised in Shetland so efforts have to be made to choose the locality and outlook with great care, very often not successfully in the past, or to ensure sensitive reinstatement after use, as recently at Dales Voe and Voe. Super quarries, although not on the scale of the proposed Harris quarry, have been mooted from time to time in Shetland and there appears to be suitable rock material for export for road-building in the Sullom area, where there is also shelter and deep water; however no proposals have actually gone ahead.

Peat should be considered in this section, as to all intents and purposes when extracted by commercial techniques it is a finite resource. Problems of erosion of peat due to heavy grazing have been discussed in the section on agriculture, and some reference made to the effects on the vegetation by 'mechanical' extraction rather than traditional methods. Such is the effect of extracting peat from beneath the surface layer, even on a small scale, that planning controls should be applied. If not, there will be a continuing loss of grazing plants and their replacement by unpalatable species. In some cases damage to the surface vegetation may also lead to erosion. Where the surface vegetation is first removed in commercial extraction, a layer of peat should be left above the bedrock and there must be an acceptable form of replacing the vegetation when extraction is completed.

Rarer minerals dictate the site of exploitation and difficult decisions must be made as to whether or not to exploit the resource at all, particularly when the damage done to the landscape and vegetation may be irreparable and the returns short-lived. Too often SIC has allowed short-term development to go ahead and all future generations of Shetlanders are going to have to live with the results. The extension to the talc industry at Haroldswick and the speculative preparations for extraction at Hoo Field in Cunningsburgh, a site that once exported steatite utensils all over the Viking world, have left ugly scars in otherwise undeveloped landscapes. Shetland's geology contains a great range of rocks and some, for example those in Unst contain small amounts of precious minerals such as gold.

Attractive as the income and employment might be from a gold mine there is no doubt that the environmental impact would be extensive, partly through the process of rendering by-products such as arsenic and cyanide harmless and partly in purifying the water from the extractive process itself.

TOURISM

Although it does not bring a return as great as any element of the fishing industry, at about £10.9 million per annum it is similar in economic importance to agriculture (if one takes into account that 50% of the latter income is subsidy and that over one-third of visitors to Shetland are either there for business reasons or to see relatives and friends) and makes up almost 10% of Shetland's total ouput. Relative to tourism in other areas of Scotland, numbers are low at 20000, while half of the visitors are from abroad, particularly Scandinavia. In Shetland a large number of visitors arrive only for very short visits on board cruise liners, of which there were between 30 and 40 in 1997.

A recent study for SIC stated that

> The features that attract visitors to Shetland are essentially 'natural' – the unique scenery and landscape, the feeling of remoteness and difference, the opportunities for natural activities (particularly bird watching) and the enjoyment of the ancient history which the islands have inherited through archaeological remains.

In fact approximately half of all visitors to Shetland come for the birdlife, the scenery and to walk. The natural heritage of Shetland is therefore its primary resource for tourism. In the long term this could be a secure and important industry for Shetland with the potential to increase without any harm to the resource on which it depends. Particularly appropriate in Shetland are the low-key developments, such as the *bods* and the local museums, and visitor centres and guided wildlife tours, which are becoming increasingly popular.

As we have seen, the unique wildlife and flora of Shetland that attracts the visitor is intimately bound up with traditional management of the land and its fisheries. Any substantial break with those traditions and/or damage to the natural environment will have a knock-on effect on tourism. The wreck of the *Braer* in 1993 is a good example: it had a serious effect on tourism with the numbers of all visitors dropping in 1994. Shetland's moorlands and wetlands are of national and international importance for birdlife, but these habitats are coming under increasing pressure. Also, present agricultural subsidies are pushing Shetland's traditional croftland into permanent improved grassland. If Shetland loses its unique landscape and wildlife, tourists are not going to be prepared to meet the additional cost and effort to come to the islands and that potential income is going to become increasingly important as the oil industry runs down. Once the natural resource has gone, it cannot be replaced. But it is not just for the visitor and the income they bring that Shetland should seek to sensitively manage its natural resources.

87.   *Mill repair, Huxter, Sandness: the Shetland Amenity Trust has initiated repairs to many traditional buildings, bringing them back into working order for both tourists and local education.* (Courtesy of Shetland Amenity Trust.)

88.   Dunter *under the Noup of Noss: taking a boat from Lerwick and getting close to the immense cliffs and seabird colonies of Noss is one of the 'natural' thrills for visitors.* (Courtesy of SNH, Battleby.)

PLANNING AND THE FUTURE

The Shetland Structure Plan was approved in 1980 and at present is under review for completion in the late 1990s. The plan recognized all the statutory designations and the sites they cover; however, important as these designations are, all the natural heritage wealth of the islands cannot be contained within

89. *Housing, Hellister, Weisdale: council housing in the middle ground, and beyond large and bright — sometimes garish in the landscape — new private homes, built on the strength of recent prosperity.* (Courtesy of S. Johnston.)

them. Many of the unique Shetland habitats and species are widely and thinly spread, particularly the very limited populations of some of Shetland's endemic species, where each unit by itself may appear unimportant and yet is essential in supporting the viability of the others. Every time an important habitat is destroyed, an option closes for a number of species; if the habitat is unique, like a tiny island site for relict scrub, it may mean extinction for some of Shetland's species.

The same could be said for Shetland's built heritage. The attractive and traditional groupings of crofts, outbuildings and walls, and the natural materials used to build them, that lie so naturally within the landscape are disappearing. In the last two decades housing conditions for Shetlanders have improved immeasurably, but in the rush to build, particularly new housing for the expanded employment opportunities in Lerwick, there seems to have been no time to develop the Shetland vernacular building. Many unsuitable and off-the-shelf buildings, appropriate to the urban mainland but inappropriate in scale, colour and shape to the Shetland landscape, have transformed some rural areas, such as Quarff and Gulberwick, into sprawling commuter suburbias. Only time, by wearing off the sharp edges and harsh colours, and the camouflage of shrub, tree and flower will eventually soften the impact.

FINAL COMMENTS

Shetland is an isolated group of islands where species diversity is naturally low and where many species have very small populations with no adjacent reservoir for easy replacement of losses. The islands also have generally poor soils with a short growing season and 'suffer' a relatively harsh, though mild climate, with ever-present erosion pressures from strong, salt-laden winds. These same factors that are responsible for the uniqueness of its natural features also make the islands a fragile ecosystem.

We have looked at the immigrations of people and their effect on the natural environment of Shetland over a period of 4000–5000 years, particularly at the transformation of habitats, at the continuing retraction of arable agriculture and the increased pressure on the *scattald*. We have also looked at the impact of a marine fishing policy that now needs to take into account other natural and legitimate users of the same resource. However, we have to remember that to survive in this northern and isolated group of islands Shetlanders have often had to exploit the local resources, even sometimes to the point of exhaustion. On the other hand, we have seen that where people's actions have been at a level sympathetic to the nature of the resource, the meadows and herb-rich grasslands for example, there has been harmony and often an environmental gain. And where, after careful appraisal of exploitation, it has been predicted that there might be damage to the environment, precautions and monitoring have proved valuable in ensuring sustainable management.

Shetland's geographical context to a great extent dictates the presence or absence of species. We know that diversity and quantity is limited and therefore we must ensure that we do not allow species to become extinct or unnecessarily allow the loss of individual native plants, animals or communities. Conversely we must be very careful with our choice of introductions. They may be benign or even enhance our wildlife, like the monkey flower that fills so many ditches with colour; but they could be very destructive and difficult to eliminate, like the polecat. The same applies to Shetland's physical resources: whereas we can 'harvest' biological resources, the exploitation of physical resources is inevitably unsustainable and therefore demands the greatest justification and care. Shetland's climate is the other major influence on its soils and vegetation, whose effects we exacerbate at our peril. We must learn from the lessons of history.

Since the arrival of people on Shetland, two of the greatest changes brought about by management have probably been, firstly, the loss of the woodland and scrub communities and the brown soils that were an integral part of them and, secondly, the creation of diverse and attractive communities such as the herb-rich grasslands, both changes effected by the Neolithic settlers and their descendants. The greatest change triggered by natural forces, and possibly exacerbated by management, has undoubtedly been the formation of blanket bog over much of the islands. In combination these events have created potential resources for Shet-landers *and* habitats of outstanding international importance for waders and seabirds.

The scale of today's changes to the Shetland landscape cannot be compared to these events, but their impacts may have a bearing on many generations to come. Unless steps are taken to balance the pressures on the hill, erosion and loss of heather will continue to transform parts of the hill to an environment both unsuitable as a grazing resource and impoverished in terms of its wildlife. In a sense, the management changes required to sustain the hill are fairly straight-forward; however, those required to sustain the rich diversity of communities *innadaeks*, which have only been established by centuries of input, are much more complex. The loss of arable fields and herb-rich 'natural' grasslands from the crofts and the creation of permanent 'improved' grasslands and establishment of silage crops are creating new patterns of landscape that are undoubtedly more economic under today's agricultural support system but which are, equally undoubtedly, 'poorer' landscapes in terms of their attractiveness and wildlife.

In the perspective of the several thousand years that have elapsed since the first immigrants, we may consider that our modern impacts are of small significance, but we must reflect that the natural capital on which we draw today is now substantially diminished and through lack of reinvestment is still declining. In the absence of an amenable climate, and possibly in the presence of a deteriorating one, this capital is not easily recoverable once damaged or lost.

Because of its island geography, Shetland demonstrates in a relatively clear and simple manner the inter-connectedness of the whole environment. Adjust the balance here and something else will be unbalanced there. The natural heritage of Shetland is not something apart from its culture but is on the contrary very much an integral part of it. Just as the loss of other elements – language, art, poetry or music – are an impoverishment of Shetland's spiritual roots, threaten its present health and its future creative and economic potential, so the loss of its natural heritage is also an impoverishment. At this stage in Shetland's history we probably have the greatest opportunity we will ever have, because of the islands' present financial wealth, to reinvest in the croft, the hill and the sea in a sustainable manner. If this opportunity is taken, the unique natural heritage of Shetland, so much a part of the lives of its inhabitants and also fascinating and attractive to visitors, may be handed on in a healthy state that will take it through the next millennium.

The islands of Shetland may not support the range of endemic species that Charles Darwin and Thomas Edmondston found on the Galapagos; however, because of their isolation, the Galapagos cannot boast the fascinating range of overlapping species found in Shetland (an area of study that has not yet been fully explored by naturalists). The islands may have been the *ultima thule* for the Romans and not thought worth a visit, but in reality they are a stepping stone, across which, from almost all points of the compass, sweep tides of life: one day bringing an exotic creature from here, the next day one from somewhere else and the next, washing them away.

Despite and because of all that has happened to it, Shetland is a place of special magic that I have not found easy to translate into language. Hopefully, Shetland will always remain this way. Its apparent timelessness belies its fragility, the shingle beach is as vulnerable as the bird, and Shetland, like MacDiarmid's bird, is 'open' like very few other places.

Deep conviction or preference can seldom
Find direct terms in which to express itself.
Today on this shingle shelf
I understand . . . ,
. . . These stones with their resolve that Creation shall not be
Injured by iconoclasts and quacks. Nothing has stirred
Since I lay down this morning an eternity ago
But one bird. The widest open door is the least liable to intrusion,
Ubiquitous as the sunlight, unfrequented as the sun.
The inward gates of a bird are always open.
It does not know how to shut them.
That is the secret of its song, . . .

On a Raised Beach, Hugh MacDiarmid
(written on the island of Whalsay)

Bibliography

Otter

Adams, C.E. (1995) *The Arctic char* Salvelinus alpinus *population of Loch Girlsta, Shetland*. Fish Behaviour and Ecology Group, Glasgow University. Unpublished report for SNH, Edinburgh.

Allot, G. (1971) A report on the lowland vegetation of Foula. *Brathay Exploration Group Field Studies Report*, no. 11: 48–57.

Anderson, S.S. (1974) Seals in Shetland. *In* Goodier, R. (ed.), *The Natural Environment of Shetland*: 114–118. NCC, Edinburgh.

Anderson, S. (1981) Seals in Shetland waters. *Proceedings of the Royal Society of Edinburgh*, **80B**: 181–188.

Angus, J.T. (1910) *An Etymological Glossary of some Place-names in Shetland*. Manson, Lerwick.

Armstrong, E.A. (1952) The behaviour and breeding biology of the Shetland wren. *Ibis*, **94**: 220–242.

Armstrong, E.A. (1953) Island wrens: conditions influencing subspeciation and survival. *British Birds*, **46**: 418–420.

Ashmole, N.P. (1979) The spider fauna of Shetland and its zoogeographic context. *Proceedings of the Royal Society of Edinburgh*, **78B**: 63–122.

Aston University Sub-Aqua Club (1974) *The Wreck of the Kennemerland*. Aston University, Birmingham.

Avery, M.I., Burgess, D., Dymond, N.J., Mellor, M. & Ellis, P.M. (1993) The status of Arctic Terns *Sterna paradisaea* in Orkney and Shetland in 1989. *Seabird*, **15**: 17–23.

Bailey, P. (1971) *Orkney*. David & Charles, Newton Abbot.

Bailey, R.S., Furness, R.W., Gauld, J.A. & Kunlik, P.A. (1991) Recent changes in the population of the sandeel (*Ammodytes marinus* Raitt) at Shetland in relation to estimates of seabird predation. *ICES Marine Science Symposia*, **193**: 209–216.

Baker, J. (1971) The ecological effects of successive oil spillages. *In* Cowell, E.B. (ed.), *The Ecological Effects of Pollution on Littoral Communities*: 21–32. Elsevier, London.

Baldwin, J.R. (ed.) (1978) *Scandinavian Shetland*. Scottish Society for Northern Studies, Edinburgh.

Baldwin, J.R. (1978) Norse influences in sheep husbandry on Foula, Shetland. *In*: Baldwin,

J.R. (ed.), *Scandinavian Shetland*: 97–127. Scottish Society for Northern Studies, Edinburgh.

Balfour, E. (1968) Breeding birds of Orkney. *Scottish Birds*, **5**: 89–104.

Balfour, E. (1972) *Orkney Birds. Status and Guide*. Senior, Stromness.

Ball, D. F. & Goodier, R. (1974) Ronas Hill, Shetland: a preliminary account of its ground pattern features resulting from the action of wind and frost. *In*: Goodier, R. (ed.), *The Natural Environment of Shetland*: 89–106. NCC, Edinburgh.

Balneaves, E. (1977) *The Windswept Isles. Shetland and its People*. Gifford, London.

Barclay, R.S. (1965) *The Population of Orkney 1755–1961*. Kirkwall Press, Kirkwall.

Barkham, J.P. (1971) A report on the upland vegetation of Foula. *Brathay Exploration Group Field Studies Report*, no. 11: 25–47.

Barnes, R.S.K. & Hughes, R.N. (1988) *An Introduction to Marine Ecology*. Blackwell Science, Oxford.

Barret, C.G. (1895–1904) *The Lepidoptera of the British Isles*. Reeve & Co., London.

Barrett-Hamilton, G.E.H. (1900) On geographical and individual variation in *Mus sylvaticus* and its allies. *Proceedings of the Zoological Society of London*, 397–428.

Barrett-Hamilton, G.E.H. & Hinton, M.A.C. (1910–21) *A History of British Mammals*. Gurney & Jackson, London.

Bates, M.A., Shepherd, K.B., Whitfield, P. & Arnott, D.A. (1994) *Breeding waders and upland birds*. Unpublished report of SNH, Edinburgh.

Baxter, E. V. & Rintoul, L.J. (1928) *The Geographical Distribution and Status of Birds in Scotland*. Oliver & Boyd, Edinburgh.

Bedford, Mary Duchess of (1937) *A Bird-watcher's Diary*. London (privately printed).

Beenhakker, A.J. (1973) *Hollanders in Shetland*. J.F. Clausen, Lerwick.

Beirne, B.P. (1943) The relationships and origins of the Lepidoptera of the Outer Hebrides, Shetland, Faroes, and Iceland. *Proceedings of the Royal Irish Academy*, **49B**: 91–101.

Beirne, B.P. (1945) The Lepidoptera of Shetland. *Entomologists' Record and Journal of Variation*, **57**: 37–40.

Beirne, B.P. (1947) The origin and history of the British Macro-Lepidoptera. *Transactions of the Royal Entomological Society of London*, **98**: 273–372.

Beirne, B.P. (1952) *The Origin and History of the British Fauna*. Methuen, London.

Benediktsson, G. & Bjarnason, O. (1959) Lepra i Island. *Nordisk Medicia*, **62**: 1225–1227.

Bennet, K.D., Boreham, S., Sharp, M.J. & Swiur, V.R. (1992) Holocene history of environment, vegetation and human settlement on Catta Ness, Lunnasting, Shetland. *Journal of Ecology*, **80**: 241–273.

Bennett, K.D., Bunting, M.J. & Fossit, J.A. (1987) Long-term vegetation changes in Western and Northern Isles, Scotland. *Botanical Journal of Scotland*, **49**: 127–140.

Berry, A.C. (1974) The use of non-metrical variations of the cranium in the study of Scandinavian population movements. *American Journal of Physical Anthropology*, **40**: 345–358.

Berry, R.J. (1967) Genetical changes in mice and men. *Eugenics Review*, **59**: 78–96.

Berry, R.J. (1968) The biology of non-metrical variation in mice and men. *In*: Brothwell, D.R. (ed.), *Skeletal Biology of Earlier Human Populations*: 103–133. Pergamon, London.

Berry, R.J. (1969a) History in the evolution of *Apodemus sylvaticus* (Mammalia) at one edge of its range. *Journal of Zoology, London*, **59**: 311–328.

Berry, R.J. (1969b) Non-metrical variation in two Scottish colonies of the Grey Seal. *Journal of Zoology, London*, **157**: 11–18.

Berry, R.J. (1970) Viking mice. *Listener*, **84**: 147–148.

Berry, R.J. (1972a) Genetical approaches to taxonomy. *Proceedings of the Royal Society of Medicine*, **65**: 853–854.

Berry, R.J. (1972b) *Ecology and Ethics*. Inter-Varsity, London.

Berry, R.J. (1973) Chance and change in British Long-tailed field mice. *Journal of Zoology, London*, **170**: 351–366.

Berry, R.J. (1974) The Shetland fauna, its significance or lack thereof. *In*: Goodier, R. (ed.), *The Natural Environment of Shetland*: 151–163. NCC, Edinburgh.

Berry, R.J. (1975) On the nature of genetical distance and island races of *Apodemus sylvaticus*. *Journal of Zoology, London*, **176**: 293–296.

Berry, R.J. (1977) *Inheritance and Natural History*. Collins New Naturalist, London.

Berry, R.J. (1979) The Outer Hebrides: where genes and geography meet. *Proceedings of the Royal Society of Edinburgh*, **77B**: 21–43.

Berry, R.J. (1985) *The Natural History of Orkney*. Collins, London.

Berry, R.J. & Crothers, J.H. (1974) Visible variation in the Dog-whelk, *Nucella lapillus*. *Journal of Zoology, London*, **174**: 123–148.

Berry, R.J. & Davis, P.E. (1970) Polymorphism and behaviour in the Arctic Skua (*Stercorarius parasiticus* (L.)). *Proceedings of the Royal Society of London B*, **175**: 255–267.

Berry, R.J. & Johnston, J.L. (1980) *The Natural History of Shetland*. Collins, London.

Berry, R.J. & Muir, V.M.L. (1975) The natural history of man in Shetland. *Journal of Biosocial Science*, **7**: 319–344.

Berry, R.J. & Rose, F.E.N. (1975) Islands and the evolution of *Microtus arvalis* (Microtinae). *Journal of Zoology, London*, **177**: 359–409.

Berry, R.J. & Tricker, B.J.K. (1969) Competition and extinction: the mice of Foula, with notes on those of Fair Isle and St. Kilda. *Journal of Zoology, London*, **158**: 247–265.

Berry, R.J., Evans, I.M. & Sennitt, B.F.C. (1967) The relationships and ecology of *Apodemus sylvaticus* from the Small Isles of the Inner Hebrides, Scotland. *Journal of Zoology, London*, **152**: 333–346.

Berry, R.J., Jakobson, M.E. & Peters, J. (1978) The house mice of the Faroe Islands: a study in microdifferentiation. *Journal of Zoology, London*, **185**: 73–92.

Bevan, J. (1987) *A survey of Hieracia (Hawkweeds) in Shetland 1987*. Unpublished report of NCC, Edinburgh.

Birks, H.J.B. (1973) *Past and Present Vegetation of the Island of Skye*. Cambridge University Press, Cambridge.

Birks, H.J.B. & Ransom, M.E. (1969) An interglacial peat at Fugla Ness, Shetland. *New Phytologist*, **68**: 777–796.

Birnie, J. (1984) Trees and shrubs in the Shetland islands: evidence for a post-glacial optimum. *In*: Mörner, N. & Karlen, A. (eds), *Climatic Changes on a Yearly to Millenial Basis*: 155–161. D. Reidel.

Birnie, J.F., Gordon, J.E., Bennet, K.J. & Hall, A.M. (eds) (1993) *The Quaternary of Shetland: Field Guide*. Quaternary Research Association, Cambridge.

Birnie, R.V. (1993) Erosion rates on bare peat surfaces in Shetland. *Scottish Geographical Magazine*, **109**: 12–17.

Birnie, R.V. & Hulme, P.D. (1990) Overgrazing of peatland vegetation in Shetland. *Scottish Geographical Magazine*, **106**: 28–36.

Birse, E.L. (1971) *Assessment of climatic conditions in Scotland. 3. The bioclimatic subregions*. Macaulay Institute for Soil Research, Aberdeen.

Birse, E.L. (1974) Bioclimatic characteristics of Shetland. *In*: Goodier, R. (ed.), *The Natural Environment of Shetland*: 24–32. NCC, Edinburgh.

Bjarnason, O., Bjarnason, V., Edwards, J.H., Fridriksson, S., Magnusson, M., Mourant, A.E. & Tills, D. (1973) The blood groups of Icelanders. *Annals of Human Genetics*, **36**: 425–458.

Black, G.P. (1976) *Shetland. Localities of Geological and Geomorphological Importance*. NCC, Newbury.

Blackburn, T. (1874a) Notes on beetles occurring in the Shetland Isles. *Entomologist's Monthly Magazine*, **11**: 112.

Blackburn, T. (1874b) Description of a new species of *Apion* from the Shetland Isles. *Entomologist's Monthly Magazine*, **11**: 128.

Blackburn, T. & Lilley, C.E. (1874) Notes on the entomology of Shetland. *Scottish Naturalist*, **2**: 346–349.

Bloch, D., Jensen, J.K. & Olsen, B. (1996) *List of Birds seen in the Faroe Islands*. Foroya Fuglafrooifelag, Tórshavn.

Bloomfield, E.N. (1904) Diptera from the Shetlands and Orkneys. *Entomologist's Monthly Magazine*, **15**: 88.

Bogan, J.A. & Bourne, W.R.P. (1972) Polychlorinated biphenyls in North Atlantic seabirds. *Marine Pollution Bulletin*, **3**: 171–175.

Bonner, W.N. (1971) An aged Grey seal (*Halichoerus grypus*). *Journal of Zoology, London*, **164**: 261–262.

Bonner, W.N. (1976) *Stocks of Grey Seals and Common Seals in Great Britain*. NERC Publications Series C, no. 16. NERC, London.

Bonner, W.N. (1978) Man's impact on seals. *Mammal Review*, **8**: 3–13.

Bonner, W.N., Vaughan, R.W. & Johnston, J.L. (1973) The status of common seals in Shetland. *Biological Conservation*, **5**: 185–190.

Borgesen, F. (1903) The marine algae of the Shetland. *Journal of Botany, London*, **41**: 300–306.

Bott, M.H.P. & Browitt, C.W.A. (1975) Interpretation of geophysical observations between the Orkney and Shetland Islands. *Journal of the Geological Society of London*, **131**: 353–371.

Bott, M.H.P. & Watts, A.B. (1970) Deep sedimentary basins proved in the Shetland–Hebridean continental shelf and margin. *Nature*, **225**: 265–268.

Boué, A. (1980) *Essai Geologique sur l'Écosse*. Paris.

Bourne, W.R.P. (1974) Geographical variation in Shetland birds. *In* Goodier, R. (ed.), *The Natural Environment of Shetland*: 145–146. NCC, Edinburgh.

Bourne, W.R.P. & Johnston, J.L. (1971) The threat of oil pollution to north Scottish seabird colonies. *Marine Pollution Bulletin*, **2**: 117–120.

Bowie, S. (1994) *Shetland Sheep*. Shetland Publishing Company, Lerwick.

Bowie, S.H.U. (1995) *Shetland Cattle. History and Breeding Characteristics*. Abbey Typesetting, Crewkerne.

Boyce, A.J., Holdsworth, V.M.L. & Brothwell, D.R. (1973) Demographic and genetic studies in the Orkney Islands. *In*: Sunderland, E. & Roberts, D.F. (eds), *Genetic Variation in Britain*: 109–128. Taylor and Francis, London.

Boycott, A.E. (1936) The habitats of freshwater Mollusca in Britain. *Journal of Animal Ecology*, **5**: 116–186.

Boyd, J.M. (1963) The grey seal (*Halichoerus grypus* Fab.) in the Outer Hebrides in October 1961. *Proceedings of the Zoological Society of London*, **141**: 635–662.

Bradley, J.D., Tremewan, W.G. & Smith, A. (1973, 1979) *British Torticoid Moths*, Vols 1 & 2. Curwen Press, London.

Brand, J. (1701) *A Brief Description of Orkney, Zetland, Pightland Firth and Caithness*. Brown, Edinburgh.

Brathay Exploration Group (1969–76) *Field Studies on Foula*. Brathay, Ambleside.

Briggs, C.A. (1884) A week's collecting on Unst. *Entomologist*, **17**: 197–201.

Brindley, E., Mudge, G., Ellis, P., Meek, E., Dymond, N., Lodge, C., Ribbands, B., Steele, D. & Suddaby, D. (1994) *A survey of Arctic Terns in Shetland and Orkney in 1994*. NCC, Edinburgh.

Bristowe, W.S. (1931) The spiders of the Orkney and Shetland Islands. *Proceedings of the Zoological Society of London*, 951–956.

British Petroleum (1996) *Foinaven Phase 1 Development. Environmental Assessment*. Halcon, Stonehaven.

Britton, R.H. (1974) The freshwater ecology of Shetland. *In*: Goodier, R. (ed.), *Natural Environment of Shetland*: 119–129. NCC, Edinburgh.

Brøgger, A.W. (1929) *Ancient Immigrants*. Oxford University Press, Oxford.

Brown, E.G. (1995) *Survey and review of data on grey seal population in Shetland*. Unpublished report of SNH, Edinburgh.

Brown, E.G. & Pierce, G.J. (1994) Diet of Harbour seals at Mousa, Shetland, during the third quarter of 1994. *Journal of the Marine Biological Association*, **77**: 539–555.

Brown, E.G. & Pierce, G.J. (1997) *The diets of common seals* (Phoca vitulina) *around the Shetland Islands*. Unpublished report of Shetland Wildlife Fund, SNH, Hunter & Morrison Trust and the Shetland Fishermens Association.

Brown, E.S. (1965) Distribution of the ABO and Rhesus (D) blood groups in the north of Scotland. *Heredity*, **20**: 289–303.

Brown, S.G. (1976) Modern whaling in Britain and the north-east Atlantic Ocean. *Mammal Review*, **6**: 25–36.

Brown, S.G. (1978) Twenty-ninth annual meeting of the International Whaling Commission, 1977. *Polar Record*, **19**: 59–61.

Bullard, E.R. (1972) *Orkney. A Checklist of Vascular Plants, Flowering Plants and Ferns*. Rendall, Stromness.

Bullock, I.D. (1980) The breeding population of terns in Orkney and Shetland 1980. *In*: *Shetland Bird Report 1980*: 45–52. University of Strathclyde Press, Glasgow.

Bulter, R. (1986) *Snyivveries: Shetland Poems*. Shetland Times, Lerwick.

Bundy, G. (1978) Breeding red-throated divers on Shetland. *British Birds*, **71**: 199–208.

Burrows, E.M. (1963) A list of the marine algae in Fair Isle. *British Phycological Bulletin*, **2**: 245–246.

Burrows, E.M., Conway, E., Lodge, S.M. & Powell, H.T. (1954) The raising of intertidal zones on Fair Isle. *Journal of Ecology*, **42**: 283–288.

Butler, S. (1992) *Archaeopalynology of ancient settlement at Kebister, Shetland Islands*. PhD thesis, University of Sheffield.

Button, J. (ed.) (1976) *The Shetland Way of Oil*. Thuleprint, Lerwick.

Cadbury, J. (1975) A note on ancient melanism in the Lepidoptera of North Scotland. *In*: Goodier, R. (ed.), *The Natural Environment of Orkney*: 80. NCC, Edinburgh.

Calder, C.S.T. (1958) Report on the discovery of numerous Stone Age sites in Shetland. *Proceedings of the Society of Antiquaries of Scotland*, **89**: 340–397.

Campbell, L.H. (1987) The importance of breeding waders on croft and farmland in Shetland. *RSPB Conservation Review*, **3**: 5–78.

Camphuysen, C.J. (1990) Fish stocks, fisheries and seabirds in the North Sea. *Technical Rapport Vogelbescherming*, **5**: 84–93.

Camphuysen, C.J., Calvo, B., Durinck, J., Ensor, K., Follestad, A., Furness, R.W., Garthe, S., Leaper, G., Skov, H., Tasker, M. L. & Winter, C.J.N. (1995) Consumption of discards by seabirds in the North Sea. *Final report EC DG XIV Research Contract BIOECO/93/10. NIOZ Rapport 1995*, vol. 5. Netherlands Institute for Sea Research, Texel.

Carlquist, S. (1974) *Island Biology*. Columbia University Press, New York.

Carpenter, R.M. (1962) On the invertebrate fauna of Fair Isle. *Scottish Naturalist*, **70**: 91–95.

Carter, J.R. & Bailey-Watts, A.E. (1981) A taxanomic study of diatoms from standing freshwaters in Shetland. *Nova Hedwigia*, vol. XXXIII: 513–628. J. Cramer, Braunschweig.

Carter, S.P., Proctor, J. & Slingsby, D.R. (1987) Soil and vegetation of the Keen of Hamar serpentine. Shetland. *Journal of Ecology*, **75**: 21–42.

Central Unit on Environmental Pollution (1976) Pollution of the sea. Pollution Paper no. 8. HMSO, London.

Chaloner, W.G. (1972) Devonian plants from Fair Isle, Scotland. *Review of Palaeobotany and Palynology*, **14**: 49–61.

Chapelhow, R. (1965) On glaciation in North Roe, Shetland. *Geographical Journal*, **131**: 60–70.

Cherrett, J.M. (1964) The distribution of spiders on the Moor House National Nature Reserve, Westmorland. *Journal of Animal Ecology*, **33**: 27–48.

Childe, V.G. (1946) *Scotland Before the Scots*. Methuen, London.

Christensen, I. (1977) Observations of whales in the North Atlantic. *Report of the International Whaling Commission*, **27**: 388–399.

Clapham, A.R., Tutin, T.G. & Warburg, E.G. (1962) *Flora of the British Isles*. Cambridge, London.

Clarke, W.E. (1912) *Studies in Bird Migration*, vols 1 & 2. Oliver & Boyd, Edinburgh.

Cloudsley-Thompson, J.L. (1956) On the arachnid fauna of Fair Isle. *Annals and Magazine of Natural History*, **9**: 830–832.

Cluness, A.T. (1951) *The Shetland Isles*. Hale, London.

Cluness, A.T. (1955) *Told Round the Peat Fire*. Hale, London.

Cluness, A.T. (ed.) (1967) *The Shetland Book*. Zetland Education Committee, Lerwick.

Cohen, B.L., Baker, A.J., Blechschmidt, K. *et al.* (1997) Enigmatic phylogeny of skuas (Aves: Stercorariidae). *Proceedings of the Royal Society of London B*, **264**: 181–190.

Conchological Society (1976) *Atlas of the Non-marine Molluscs of the British Isles*. Institute for Terrestrial Ecology, Cambridge.

Conroy, J.W.H. & Jenkins, D. (1986) Ecology of otters in northern Scotland. VI. Diving times and hunting success of otters (*Lutra lutra*) at Dinnet Lochs, Aberdeenshire and in Yell Sound, Shetland. *Journal of Zoology, London*, **209**: 341–346.

Consultative Committee (1963) *Grey Seals and Fisheries*. HMSO, London.

Coope, G.R. (1969) The contribution that the Coleoptera of glacial Britain could have made to the subsequent colonization of Scandinavia. *Opusc. Ent. Land.*, **34**: 95–108.

Corbet, G.B. (1961) Origin of the British insular races of small mammals and of the 'Lusitanian' fauna. *Nature*, **191**: 1037–1040.

Corbet, G.B. (1970) Vagrant bats in Shetland and the North Sea. *Journal of Zoology, London*, **161**: 281–282.

Corbet, G.B. & Southern, H. (1977) *The Handbook of British Mammals*, 2nd edn. Blackwell, Oxford.

Costin, A.B. & Moore, D.M. (1960) The effects of rabbit grazing on the grassland of Macquarie Island. *Journal of Ecology*, **48**: 729–732.

Coull, J.R. (1967) A comparison of demographic trends in the Faroe and Shetland Islands. *Transactions of the Institute of British Geographers*, **41**: 159–166.

Coull, J.R. (1996a) *The Sea Fisheries of Scotland*. John Donald, Edinburgh.

Coull, J.R. (1996b) Towards a sustainable economy for the Shetland Islands: development and management issues in fishing and fish farming. *GeoJournal*, **39**: 185–194.

Cowie, J.R. (1871) *Shetland and Its Inhabitants*. Lewis, Smith, Aberdeen.

Cox, M.C. (1965) *The Shetland Pony*. Adam & Charles, London.

Cox, M.C. (1976) *The Ponies of Shetland*. Shetland Times, Lerwick.

Cramp, S., Bourne, W.R.P. & Saunders, D. (1974) *The Seabirds of Britain and Ireland*. Collins, London.

Crampton, C.B. (1911) *The vegetation of Caithness considered in relation to the geology*. Committee for the Survey and Study of British Vegetation, Cambridge.

Crawford, B.E. (1984) *Scandinavian Scotland: Scotland in the Early Middle Ages*, 2. University Press, Leicester.

Crawford, B.E. (1985) The Biggings, Papa Stour: a multi-disciplinary investigation. *In*: Smith, B. (ed.), *Shetland Archaeology*: 125–128. Shetland Times, Lerwick.

Crawford, R.M.M. (1997) Oceanity, the ecological disadvantage of warm winters. *Botanical Journal of Scotland*, **49**: 205–221.

Curtis, C.D. & Brown, P.E. (1969) The metasomatic development of zoned ultrabasic bodies in Unst, Shetland. *Contributions to Mineralogy and Petrology*, **24**: 275–292.

Daan, N., Bromley, P.J., Hislop, J.R.G. & Nielsen, N.A. (1990) Ecology of North Sea fish. *Netherlands Journal of Sea Research*, **26**: 343–368.

Dalby, D.H. (1985) Salt-marsh vegetation in the Shetland Islands. *Vegetatio*, **61**: 45–54.

Dalby, D.H. (1989) *The limestone grasslands of Shetland*. Unpublished report of NCC, Edinburgh.

Dalby, D.H. (1991) An introduction to Shetland lichens. *The Shetland Naturalist*, **1**: 13–21.

Dalby, D.H., Cowell, E.B., Syratt, W.J. & Crothers, J.H. (1978) An exposure scale for marine shores in western Norway. *Journal of the Marine Biological Association*, **58**: 975–996.

Daniel, G.E. (1941) The dual nature of the megalithic colonization of prehistoric Europe. *Proceedings of the Prehistoric Society*, **7**: 1–49.

Darling, F.F. & Boyd, J.M. (1964) *The Highlands and Islands*. Collins, London.

Davidson, D.A. & Simpson, I.A. (1994) Soils and landscape history: case studies from the Northern Isles of Scotland. *In*: Foster, S. & Smout, T.C. (eds), *The History of Soils and Field Systems*. Scottish Cultural Press, Beith.

Davie, L. & Laurence, B.R. (1992) The distribution of *Calliphora* species in Britain and Ireland (Diptera, Calliphoridae). *Entomologist's Monthly Magazine*, **128**: 207–213.

Davies, L. (1966) The taxonomy of British blackflies (Diptera: Simuliidae). *Transcripts of the Royal Entomological Society, London*, **118**: 413–511.

Davies, L. & Laurence, B.R. (1992) The distribution of *Calliphora* species in Britain and Ireland (Dipt., Calliphoridae). *Entomologist's Monthly Magazine*, **128**: 207–213.

Davis, J.E. & Anderson, S.S. (1976) Effects of oil pollution on breeding grey seals. *Marine Pollution Bulletin*, **7**: 118.

Davis, P. (1965) A list of the birds of Fair Isle. *In*: Williamson, K. (ed.), *Fair Isle and Its Birds*: 251–296. Oliver & Boyd, Edinburgh.

Davis, P.E. & Dennis, R.H. (1959) Song-sparrow at Fair Isle: a bird new to Europe. *British Birds*, **52**: 419–421.

Degerbøl, M. (1939) The field mouse of Iceland, its systematic position (*Apodemus sylvaticus grandiculus* sub sp. nov.) and biology. *Zoology Iceland* Pt. 76. Appendix.

Degerbøl, M. (1942) Mammalia. *Zoology Faroes* Pt. 65, 1–133.

Delany, M.J. (1963) A collection of *Apodemus* from the Island of Foula, Shetland. *Proceedings of the Zoological Society of London*, **140**: 319–320.

Delany, M.J. (1964) Variation in the Long-tailed field mouse (*Apodemus sylvaticus* (L.)) in north-west Scotland. I. Comparison of individual characters. *Proceedings of the Royal Society of London B*, **161**: 191–199.

Delany, M.J. & Davis, P.E. (1961) Observations on the ecology and life history of the Fair Isle field mouse *Apodemus sylvaticus fridariensis* (Kinnear). *Proceedings of the Zoological Society of London*, **136**: 439–452.

De Luca, C. (1995) *Voes and Sounds*. The Shetland Library, Lerwick.

Demoulin, V. & Marriot, J.V.R. (1981) Key to the Gastromycetes of Great Britain. *Bulletin of the British Mycological Society*, **15**: 37–56.

Dennis, R.W.G. (1972) Fungi of the Northern Isles. *Kew Bulletin*, **26**: 427–432.

Dennis, R.W.G. & Gray, E.G. (1954) A first list of the fungi of Zetland (Shetland). *Transactions of the Botanical Society of Edinburgh*, **36**: 215–223.

Dennis, R.W.G., Orton, P.J. & Hora, F.B. (1981) New check list of British Agarics and Boleti. *Transactions of the British Mycological Society*, **43** (Suppl.): 1–225.

Denny, P. (1963) Vegetation of Ronas Hill, analysed by a new technique. BSc thesis, University of St Andrews.

Department of the Environment (1994) *Biodiversity: The UK Action Plan*. HMSO, London.

Deyell, A. (1975) *My Shetland*. Thuleprint, Lerwick.

Dickson, J.H. (1992) North American Driftwood, especially *Pices* (spruce) from Archaeological sites in the Hebrides and Northern isles of Scotland. *Review of Palaeobotany*, **73**: 45–96.

Dif, G. (1989) *Shetland Terre Du Vent*. Fournie, Milan.

Dixon, I. (1987) *Fish farms in Shetland, August 1986*. Unpublished report to NCC, SIC and Shetland Salmon Farmers Association.

Dixon, P.S. (1963) Marine algae of Shetland collected during the meeting of British Phycological Society, August 1962. *British Phycological Bulletin*, **2**: 236–243.

Donaldson, G. (1958) *Shetland Life under Earl Patrick*. Oliver & Boyd, Edinburgh.

Donaldson, G. (1966) *Northwards by Sea*. Grant, Edinburgh.

Donaldson, G. (1969) The Scottish settlement. Inaugural address at Quincentenary Historical Congress, Lerwick. *Shetland Times*, 22 August 1969.

Donaldson, Lord (1994) *Safer Ships, Cleaner Seas. Report of the inquiry into the prevention of pollution from merchant shipping*. HMSO, London.

Donk, M.A. (1966) Check list of European hymenomycetous Heterobasidae. *Persoonia*, **4**, 145–335.

Dore, C.P., Ellis, P.M. & Stuart, E.M. (1996) Numbers of Whimbrel breeding in Shetland in 1989–1994 and previously. *Scottish Birds*, **18**: 193–196.

Dott, H.E.M. (1967) Numbers of Great Skuas and other seabirds of Hermaness, Unst. *Scottish Birds*, **4**: 340–350.

Drosier, R. (1830–31) Account of an ornithological visit to the island of Shetland and Orkney in the summer of 1828. *Magazine of Natural History* for 1830: 321–326; 1831: 193–199.

Druce, G.C. (1922) Flora Zetlandica. *Report of the Botanic Exchange Club for 1921*: 457–546.

Druce, G.C. (1925) Additions to Flora Zetlandica (1924). *Report of the Botanic Exchange Club*, **7**: 628–657.

Dudman, A.A. & Richards, A.J. (1997) *Dandelions of Great Britain and Ireland*. Botanical Society of the British Isles, London.

Duidan, C.A. (1991) The re-discovery of the Cladoceran *Eurycerus glacialis* (Lilljeborg 1889) in Scotland. *Freshwater Forum*, **1**: 184–194.

Duncan, U.K. (1961) A visit to the Shetland Isles. *Lichenologist*, **1**: 267–268.

Duncan, U.K. (1963) A list of Fair Isle lichens. *Lichenologist*, **2**: 171–178.

Dungal, N. (1961) The special problem of stomach cancer in Iceland. *Journal of the American Medical Association*, **178**: 789–798.

Dunn, R. (1837) *The Ornithologist's Guide to the Islands of Orkney and Shetland*. Hull.

Dunn, R. (1848) Some notes on the birds of Shetland. *Zoologist*: 2187–2188.

Dunnet, G.M. (1974) Impact of the oil industry on Scotland's coasts and birds. *Scottish Birds*, **8**: 3–16.

Dunnet, G.M. & Heubeck, M. (1995) The monitoring of breeding seabirds and eiders. *Proceedings of the Royal Society of Edinburgh*, **103B**: 137–164.

Dunnet, G.M. & MacIntyre, A.D. (1995) Monitoring at an oil terminal: the Shetland experience. *Proceedings of the Royal Society of Edinburgh*, **103B**: 1–258.

Dymond, J.N. (1991) *The Birds of Fair Isle*. Privately published.

Earll, R. (1975) An extensive survey of the shallow sublittoral fauna of Shetland. *In*: Adolson, J. (ed.), *Proceedings of the 4th World Congress of Underwater Activities. Vol. I Archaeology and Biology*: 193–200. Vorderwater, Stockholm.

Edmondston, A. (1809) *A View of the Ancient and Present State of the Zetland Islands*. Ballantyne, Edinburgh.

Edmondston, B. & Saxby, J.M.E. (1889) *The Home of a Naturalist*. Nisbet, London.

Edmondston, T. (1843) Notice of a new British *Cerastium*. *Phytologist*, **XXII**: 497–500.

Edmondston, T. (1845) *A Flora of Shetland*. Oliphant, Anderson & Ferrier, Aberdeen.

Eggeling, W.J. (1964) A nature reserve management plan for the Island of Rhum, Inner Hebrides. *Journal of Applied Ecology*, **1**: 405–419.

Ellis, P.M. & Okill, J.D. (1990) Breeding ecology of the Merlin *Falco columbarius* in Shetland. *Bird Study*, **37**: 101–110.

Ellis, P.M. & Okill, J.D. (1992) The breeding population of the Peregrine in Shetland. *Shetland Bird Report 1991*: 91–93.

Ellis, P.M. & Okill, J.D. (1993) Breeding numbers and breeding success of the Peregrine in Shetland, 1961–1991. *Scottish Birds*, **17**: 40–49.

Ellis, P.M., Ewins, P.J., Bird, D.R. & Prior, A. (1987) Shetland Skua Survey. *Shetland Bird Report 1986*: 91–93.

Ellis, P.M., Okill, J.D., Petrie, G.W. & Suddaby, D. (1994) The breeding performance of Ravens from a sample of nesting territories in Shetland during 1984–1993. *Scottish Birds*, **17**: 212–234.

Elphinstone, M. (1994) *Islanders*. Polygon, Edinburgh.

Erdtman, G. (1924) Studies in micropalaeontology of post-glacial deposits in North Scotland and the Scotch Isles with especial reference to the history of the woodlands. *Journal of the Linnean Society of Botany*, **46**: 449–504.

Evans, A.H. & Buckley, T.E. (1899) *A Vertebrate Fauna of the Shetland Islands*. Douglas, Edinburgh.

Evans, F.C. & Vevers, H.G. (1938) Notes on the biology of the Faeroes mouse (*Mus musculus faeroensis*). *Journal of Animal Ecology*, **7**: 290–297.

Evans, P.G.H. (1976a) An analysis of sightings of Cetacea in British waters. *Mammal Review*, **6**: 5–14.

Evans, P.G.H. (1976b) *Guide to Identification of Cetaceans in British Waters*. Mammal Society, Reading.

Evans, P.G.H. (1992) Whales and dolphins in Shetland waters. *Shetland Bird Report 1991*: 80–86.

Evans, P.G.H. & Borges, L. (1996) Ecological studies of harbour porpoises in Shetland. *In*:

Evans, P.G.H. & Nice, H. (eds), *European Research on Cetaceans 9*: 173–178. European Cetacean Society, Kiel, Germany.

Evans, P.G.H. & Gilbert, L. (1991) The distribution ecology of harbour porpoises in the Shetland Islands, North Scotland. *In*: Evans, P.G.H. (ed.), *Proceedings of 5th Annual Conference of the European Cetacean Society*: 47–53. European Cetacean Society, Cambridge.

Evans, P.G.H., Fisher, P., Rees, I. & Wainwright, J. (1993) *Ecological studies of the Harbour porpoise in Shetland, North Scotland*. Report for WWFN. Seawatch Foundation Conference, Oxford.

Evans, P.G.H., Nice, H.E. & Weir, C.R. (1997a) Sighting frequency and distribution of cetaceans in Shetland waters. *In*: Evans, P.G.H. (ed.), *European Research on Cetaceans 10*: 143–147. European Cetacean Society, Kiel, Germany.

Evans, P.G.H., Weir, C.R. & Nice, H.E. (1997b) Temporal and spatial distribution of harbour porpoises in Shetland waters, 1990–95. *In*: Evans, P.G.H. (ed.), *European Research on Cetaceans 10*: 233–237. European Cetacean Society, Kiel, Germany.

Ewins, P.J. (1983) Arctic Terns: the 1982 breeding season. *Shetland Bird Report 1982*: 47–53.

Ewins, P.J. (1986) The status, distribution and breeding of shelducks in Shetland. *Shetland Bird Report 1986*: 54–61.

Ewins, P.J., Bird, D.R., Ellis, P.M. & Prior, A. (1987) *The distribution amd status of Arctic and Great Skuas in Shetland, 1985–86*. Unpublished report for NCC, RSPB, Seabird Group and Shell UK.

Fenton, A. (1973) *The Various Names of Shetland*. Privately printed.

Fenton, A. (1978) *The Northern Isles: Orkney and Shetland*. Donald, Edinburgh.

Fenton, E.W. (1937) The influence of sheep on the vegetation of hill-grazings in Scotland. *Journal of Ecology*, **25**: 424–430.

Ferguson, T. (1960) Mortality in Shetland a hundred years ago. *Scottish Medical Journal*, **5**: 107–112.

Ferreira, R.E.C. (1959) Scottish mountain vegetation in relation to the geology. *Transactions of the Botanical Society of Edinburgh*, **37**: 229–250.

Finlay, T.M. (1926a) A tongsbergite boulder from the boulder-clay of Shetland. *Transactions of the Edinburgh Geological Society*, **12**: 180.

Finlay, T.M. (1926b) The Old Red Sandstone of Shetland. Part I: South-eastern area. *Transactions of the Royal Society of Edinburgh*, **53**: 553–572.

Finlay, T.M. (1930) The Old Red Sandstone of Shetland. Part II: North-western area. *Transactions of the Royal Society of Edinburgh*, **56**: 671–694.

Fisher, J. (1952) *The Fulmar*. Collins, London.

Fisher, J. & Lockley, R.M. (1954) *Sea Birds*. Collins New Naturalist, London.

Fisher, J. & Venables, L.S.V. (1938) Gannets (*Sula bassana*) on Noss Shetland with an analysis of the rate of increase in this species. *Journal of Animal Ecology*, **7**: 305–313.

Fisher, J., Stewart, T.M. & Venables, L.S.V. (1938) Gannet colonies of Shetland. *British Birds*, **32**: 162–169.

Fisher, P. & Richardson, M.G. (1983) *Whimbrel and Wader Distribution. Shetland 1983*. Unpublished report for NCC, Edinburgh.

Fisher, R.A. & Taylor, G.L. (1940) Scandinavian influence in Scottish ethnology. *Nature*, **145**: 590.

Flinn, D. (1958) On the nappe structure of North-east Shetland. *Quarterly Journal of the Geological Society of London*, **114**: 107–136.

Flinn, D. (1959) Extension of the Great Glen Fault beyond the Moray Firth. *Nature*, **191**: 589–591.

Flinn, D. (1964) Coastal and submarine features around the Shetland Islands. *Proceedings of the Geologists Association*, **75**: 321–339.

Flinn, D. (1967) The metamorphic rocks of the southern part of the mainland of Shetland. *Geological Journal*, **5**: 251–290.

Flinn, D. (1969a) On the development of coastal profiles in the north of Scotland, Orkney and Shetland. *Scottish Journal of Geology*, **5**: 393–399.

Flinn, D. (1969b) A geological interpretation of the aeromagnetic maps of the continental shelf around Orkney and Shetland. *Geology*, **6**: 279–292.

Flinn, D. (1970a) The glacial till of Fair Isle, Shetland. *Geological Magazine*, **107**: 273–276.

Flinn, D. (1970b) Some aspects of the geochemistry of the metamorphic rocks of Unst and Fetlar, Shetland. *Proceedings of the Geologists Association*, **81**: 509–527.

Flinn, D. (1973) The topography of the sea floor around Orkney and Shetland in the northern North Sea. *Quarterly Journal of the Geological Society of London*, **129**: 39–59.

Flinn, D. (1974) The coastline of Shetland. *In*: Goodier, R. (ed.), *The Natural Environment of Shetland*: 13–23. NCC, Edinburgh.

Flinn, D. (1977) The erosion history of Shetland: a review. *Proceedings of the Geologists Association*, **88**: 129–146.

Flinn, D. (1978) The most recent glaciation of the Orkney–Shetland Channel and adjacent areas. *Scottish Journal of Geology*, **13**: 109–123.

Flinn, D. (1983) Glacial meltwater channels in the northern islands of Shetland. *Scottish Journal of Geology*, **19**: 311–320.

Flinn, D. (1985) The Caledonides of Shetland. *In*: Gee, D.G. & Stuart, B.A. (eds), *The Caledonian Orogen: Scandinavia and Related Areas*: 1159–1172. Wiley, Chichester.

Flinn, D. (1989) *Travellers in a Bygone Shetland*. Scottish Academic Press, Edinburgh.

Flinn, D. (1990) Richard Trevithick, Arthur Woolf and the Shetland Mining Company. *Journal of the Trevithick Society*, **17**: 23–30.

Flinn, D. (1992) The Milldale glacial lake, Herma Ness, Unst. *The Shetland Naturalist*, **1**: 29–36.

Flinn, D. (1994a) *Geology of Yell and Some Neighbouring Islands in Shetland*. Memoir of the British Geological Survey, Sheet 130 (Scotland). HMSO, London.

Flinn, D. (1994b) Ice flow in Unst during the last glaciation. *The Shetland Naturalist*, **1**: 73–80.

Flinn, D. (1995) The melt-down of the Shetland ice cap in Unst. *The Shetland Naturalist*, **1**: 109–115.

Flinn, D. (1996) The Shetland Ophiolite Complex: field evidence for the intrusive emplacement of the 'cumulate' layers. *Scottish Journal of Geology*, **32**: 151–158.

Flinn, D., May, F., Roberts, J.L.V. & Treagus, J.E. (1972) A revision of the stratigraphic succession of the east mainland of Shetland. *Scottish Journal of Geology*, **8**: 335–343.

Flinn, D., Frank, P.L., Brook, M. & Pringle, I.R. (1979) Basement-cover relations in Shetland. *In*: Harris, A., Holland, C.H. & Leake, B.E. (eds), *The Caledonides of the British Isles*: 109–115. Geological Society, London.

Fog, M. & Hyllested, K. (1966) Prevalence of disseminated sclerosis in the Faeroes, the Orkneys and Shetland. *Acta Neurologica Scandinavica*, **42** (Suppl. 19): 9–11.

Fojut, N. (1993) *A Guide to Prehistoric and Viking Shetland*. Shetland Times, Lerwick.

Fojut, N. (1996) Not seeing the wood: an armchair archaeology of Shetland. *In*: Waugh, D.J. (ed.), *Shetland's Northern Links*: 103–116. Scottish Society for Northern Studies, Edinburgh.

Ford, E.B. (1945) *Butterflies*. Collins New Naturalist, London.

Ford, E.B. (1955a) *Moths*. Collins New Naturalist, London.

Ford, E.B. (1955b) Polymorphism and taxonomy. *Heredity*, **9**: 255–264.

Fowler, J.A. (1977) *Preliminary studies on the fauna and flora of Yell, Shetland*. Leicester Polytechnic, School of Life Sciences, Leicester.

Fowler, J.A. (1982) Leach's petrels present on Ramna Stacks, Shetland. *Seabird Report*, **6**: 93.

Fowler, S.L. (1989) *Nature conservation implications of damage to the seabed by commercial fishing operations*. Unpublished report for NCC, Edinburgh.

Fraser, F.C. (1934, etc.) *Reports on Cetacea Stranded on the British Coasts*. British Museum (Natural History), London.

Fraser, F.C. (1966) *Guide for the Identification and Reporting of Stranded Whales, Dolphins and Porpoises on the British Coasts*. British Museum (Natural History), London.

Fresson, E.E. (1967) *Air Road to the Isles*. Rendel, London.

Furness, R.W. (1977) The effect of Great Skuas on Arctic Skuas in Shetland. *British Birds*, **70**: 96–107.

Furness, R.W. (1978) Energy requirements of seabird communities: a bioenergetics model. *Journal of Animal Ecology*, **47**: 39–53.

Furness, R.W. (1987) *The Skuas*. T. & A.D. Poyser, London.

Furness, R.W. (1989) Declining seabird populations. *Journal of Zoology, London*, **219**: 177–180.

Furness, R.W. (1990) A preliminary assessment of the quantities of Shetland sandeels taken by seabirds, seals, predatory fish and the industrial fishery in 1981–83. *Ibis*, **32**: 205–217.

Furness, R.W. (1997) *Impact of predation by Great Skuas on other seabird species, with particular reference to SPAs in Shetland*. Unpublished report for SNH, Edinburgh.

George, R.S. (1970) Fleas, and a few other animals, from the island of Foula in Shetlands. *Entomologists' Gazette*, **21**: 30–32.

Gibson, G.A. (1877) *The Old Red Sandstone of Shetland*. Williams & Norgate, Edinburgh.

Gifford, T. (1786) *An Historical Description of the Zetland Islands*. J. Nichols, London.

Gill, J.P., Williams, H.A., O'Brien, M. & Ellis, P.M. (1994) *Numbers of breeding waders on lowland areas of Shetland 1993*. RSPB Birdlife, Sandy.

Gillham, M.E. (1967) *Sub-antarctic Sanctuary*. Gollancz, London.

Gimingham, C.H. (1964a) Dwarf shrub heaths. *In*: Burnett, J.H. (ed.), *The Vegetation of Scotland*: 232–287. Oliver & Boyd, Edinburgh.

Gimingham, C.H. (1964b) Maritime and sub-maritime communities. *In*: Burnett, J.H. (ed.), *The Vegetation of Scotland*: 67–129. Oliver & Boyd, Edinburgh.

Gimingham, C.H. (1972) *Ecology of Heathlands*. Chapman & Hall, London.

Goater, B. (1969) Entomological excursions to the Shetlands, 1966 and 1968. *Entomologists' Gazette*, **20**: 73–82.

Goater, B. (1973) Some further observations on Shetland Lepidoptera, 1972. *Entomologists' Gazette*, **24**: 7–12.

Goldsmith, F.B. (1975) The sea-cliff vegetation of Shetland. *Journal of Biogeography*, **2**: 297–308.

Gomersal, C.H., Morton, J.S. & Wynde, R.M. (1984) Status of breeding red-throated diver in Shetland 1983. *Bird Study*, **31**: 223–229.

Goode, D.A. (1974) The flora and vegetation of Shetland. *In*: Goodier, R. (ed.), *The Natural Environment of Shetland*: 50–72. NCC, Edinburgh.

Goodier, R. (ed.) (1974) *The Natural Environment of Shetland*. NCC, Edinburgh.

Goodier, R. (ed.) (1975) *The Natural Environment of Orkney*. NCC, Edinburgh.

Goodlad, C.A. (1971) *Shetland Fishing Saga*. Shetland Times, Lerwick.

Goodlad, J. (1989) Industrial fishing in Shetland waters. *In*: Heubeck, M. (ed.), *Seabirds and Sandeels*: 50–59. Shetland Bird Group, Lerwick.

Goodlad, J. (1993) Sea fisheries management: the Shetland position. *Marine Policy. The Journal of Oceanic Affairs*, **17**: 350–361.

Goodlad, J. & Napier, I. (1997) Assessment of the Shetland sandeel fishery: 1996. Fisheries Development Note No. 6. North Atlantic Fisheries College, Scalloway.

Gore, A.J.P. (1975) An experimental modification of upland peat vegetation. *Journal of Applied Ecology*, **12**: 349–366.

Gorham, E. (1958) The physical limnology of northern Britain: an epitome of the Bathymetrical Survey of the Scottish Freshwater Lochs, 1897–1909. *Limnology and Oceanography*, **3**: 40–50.

Goudie, G. (1904) *The Celtic and Scandinavian Antiquities of Shetland*. Blackwood, Edinburgh.

Graham, J.J. (1993) *The Shetland Dictionary*. The Shetland Times, Lerwick.

Graham, J.J. & Smith, B. (1995) *Shetland Folk Book*. **IX**, Shetland Folk Society, Lerwick.

Graham, L. & Smith, B. (1992) *MacDiarmid in Shetland*. Shetland Times, Lerwick.

Grant, M.C. (1988) Use of re-seeds and established pastures during the pre-laying period by whimbrel (*Numenius phaeopus*). *Shetland Bird Report 1987*: 55–62.

Grant, M.C. (1991) Nesting densities, productivity and survival of breeding whimbrel *Numenius phaeopus* in Shetland. *Bird Study*, **38**: 160–169.

Grant, M.C. (1992) The effects of re-seeding heathland on breeding whimbrel *Numenius phaeopus* in Shetland. 1. Nest distribution. *Journal of Applied Ecology*, **29**: 501–508.

Greenstreet, S. & Tasker, M. (1995) *Aquatic Predators and their Prey*. Blackwell Scientific, Oxford.

Grewal, M.S. (1962) The rate of genetic divergence of sublines in the C57BL strain of mice. *Genetic Research*, **3**: 375–391.

Grime, P. & Hunt, R. (1975) Relative growth rate: its range and adaptive significance in a local flora. *Journal of Ecology*, **63**: 393–422.

Grimshaw, P.H. (1905) Diptera Scotica. IV. Orkney and Shetland. *Annals of Scottish Natural History for 1905*: 22–35.

Groundwater, W. (1974) *Birds and Mammals of Orkney*. Kirkwall Press, Kirkwall.

Haldane, J.B.S. (1948) The theory of a cline. *Journal of Genetics*, **48**: 277–284.

Haldane, R.C. (1904) Whaling in Shetland. *Annals of Scottish Natural History for 1904*: 74–77.

Haldane, R.C. (1905) Notes on whaling in Shetland in 1904. *Annals of Scottish Natural History for 1905*: 65–72.

Hale, M.E. (1974) *The Biology of Lichens*, 2nd edn. Arnold, London.

Hall, A.J., Watkins, J. & Hiby, L. (1996) The impact of the 1993 *Braer* oil spill on grey seals in Shetland. *Science of the Total Environment*, **186**: 119–125.

Hall, M.R. (1993) Problems of pollution and litter in the seas around the Scottish Isles: the Shetland perspective. *Marine Policy. The Journal of Oceanic Affairs*, **17**: 418–421.

Hall, R.E. (1954) Some Chironomidae from the Shetland Isles. *Journal of the Society for British Entomology*, **4**: 66–69.

Hamer, K.C. & Furness, R.W. (1991) Age specific breeding performance and reproductive effort in Great Skuas *Catharctica skua*. *Journal of Animal Ecology*, **60**: 693–704.

Hamer, K.C., Furness, R.W. & Caldow, R.W.G. (1991) The effects of changes in food availability on the breeding ecology of Great Skuas *Catharctica skua* in Shetland. *Journal of Zoology, London*, **223**: 175–188.

Hamer, K.C., Monaghan, P., Uttley, J.D., Walton, P. & Burns, M.D. (1993) The influence of food supply on the breeding ecology of Kittiwakes *Rissa tridactyla* in Shetland. *Ibis*, **135**: 255–263.

Hamilton, F. (1974) The importance of Shetland birds in a United Kingdom context. *In*: Goodier, R. (ed.), *The Natural Environment of Shetland*: 147–150. NCC, Edinburgh.

Hamilton, J.R.C. (1956) *Excavations at Jarlshof, Shetland*. HMSO, Edinburgh.

Hamilton, J.R.C. (1962) Brochs and broch-builders. *In*: Wainwright, F.T. (ed.), *The Northern Isles*: 53–90. Nelson, Edinburgh.

Hamilton, J.R.C. (1968) *Excavations at Clickhimin, Shetland*. HMSO, Edinburgh.

Hammond, P.S., Hall, A.J. & Prime, J.H. (1994) The diet of Grey seals on the Inner and Outer Hebrides. *Journal of Applied Ecology*, **31**: 737–746.

Hardy, A.C. (1956) *The Open Sea: its Natural History. Part I: The World of Plankton*. Collins New Naturalist, London.

Hardy, A.C. (1959) *The Open Sea: its Natural History. Part II: The World of Plankton*. Collins New Naturalist, London.

Hare, E.J. (1963) Shetland macro-lepidoptera. *Entomologists' Record*, **75**: 238.

Harmer, S.F. (1914, etc.) *Reports on Cetacea Stranded on the British Coasts*. British Museum (Natural History), London.

Harris, D. & Goto, H.E. (1982) Collembola from Shetland. *Entomologists' Gazette*, **33**: 143.

Harris, M.P. (1976) The seabirds of Shetland in 1974. *Scottish Birds*, **9**: 37–68.

Harris, M.P. (1984) *The Puffin*. T. & A.D. Poyser, Calton.

Harris, M.P. & Wanless, S. (1990) Breeding success of British kittiwakes (*Rissa tridactyla*) in 1986–88: evidence for changing conditions in the northern North Sea. *Journal of Applied Ecology*, **27**: 172–187.

Harrop, H.R. (1994) *Where to Watch Birds in Shetland*. Harrop, Shetland.

Harvie-Brown, J.A. (1892) Hedgehog (*Erinaceus europaeus* L.) in Shetland. *Annals of Scottish Natural History for 1892*: 132.

Harvie-Brown, J.A. (1893) Contributions to a fauna of the Shetland Islands. *Annals of Scottish Natural History for 1893*: 9–25.

Harvie-Brown, J.A. (1895) The starling in Scotland, its increase and distribution. *Annals of Scottish Natural History for 1895*: 2–22.

Harwood, J. (1978) The effect of management policies on the stability and resilience of British grey seal populations. *Journal of Applied Ecology*, **15**: 413–421.

Harwood, J. (1991) The 1988 seal epizootic. *Journal of Zoology, London*, **222**: 349–351.

Harwood, J. (1992) Assessing the competitive effects of marine mammal predation on commercial fisheries. *South African Journal of Marine Science*, **12**: 689–693.

Harwood, J. & Prime, J.H. (1978) Some factors affecting the size of British grey seal populations. *Journal of Applied Ecology*, **15**: 401–411.

Hawksworth, D.L. (1966) The lichen flora of Foula (Shetland). *Lichenologist*, **3**: 218–223.

Hawksworth, D.L. (1969a) Notes on the flora and vegetation of Foula, Shetland (V.C. 112). *Proceedings of the Botanical Society of the British Isles*, **7**: 537–547.

Hawksworth, D.L. (1969b) The bryophyte flora of Foula (Shetland). *Review of Bryology and Lichenology*, **36**: 213–218.

Hawksworth, D.L. (1970a) Studies on the peat deposits of the Island of Foula, Shetland. *Transactions of the Botanical Society of Edinburgh*, **40**: 576–591.

Hawksworth, D.L. (1970b) Notes on Shetland lichens 1. *Transactions of the Botanical Society of Edinburgh*, **40**: 283–287.

Hawksworth, D.L. (1980) Lichens. *In*: Berry, R.J. & Johnston, J.L. (eds), *The Natural History of Shetland*: 276–281. Collins, London.

Hawksworth, D.L. & Rose, F. (1976) *Lichens as Pollution Monitors*. Arnold, London.

Hawksworth, D.L. & Seaward, M.R.D. (1977) *Lichenology in the British Isles 1568–1975*. Richmond Publishing, Richmond.

Heddle, M.F. (1878) *The County Geognosy and Mineralogy of Scotland, Orkney and Shetland*. Truro.

Heineberg, H. (1972) *Die Shetland-Inseln ein Agrarisches Problem gebiet Schott lands*. Bochumer Geographische Arb. vol. 5.

Henderson, T. (1978) Shetland boats and their origins. *In*: Baldwin, J.R. (ed.), *Scandinavian Shetland*: 49–55. Scottish Society for Northern Studies, Edinburgh.

Heubeck, M. (1985) Tystie distribution in Shetland. *Shetland Bird Report 1984*: 48–55.

Heubeck, M. (1986) The recent decline of the Kittiwake in Shetland. *Shetland Bird Report 1985*: 40–48.

Heubeck, M. (1987). Changes in the status of the common eider (*Somateria mollissima*) in Shetland, 1977–1984. *Scottish Birds*, **14**: 146–152.

Heubeck, M. (ed.) (1989a) *Seabirds and Sandeels: Proceedings of a Seminar held in Lerwick, Shetland, 5–16 October 1988*. Shetland Bird Club, Lerwick.

Heubeck, M. (1989b). *A survey of moulting Eiders in Shetland, August–September 1989*. Unpublished report for SOTEAG, Aberdeen.

Heubeck, M. (1989c) *Changes in wintering numbers of seabirds and waterfowl in Sullom Voe and Yell Sound following the 'Esso Bernicia' oilspill*. Unpublished report for SOTEAG, Aberdeen.

Heubeck, M. (1989d) *The status of seabirds and seaduck in Bluemull and Colgrave Sounds during winter 1976–1988*. Unpublished report for SOTEAG, Aberdeen.

Heubeck, M. (1990) *The Shetland Beached Bird Survey, March 1987–February 1990*. Unpublished report for SOTEAG, Aberdeen.

Heubeck, M. (1992) The occurrence of dead auks on Shetland beaches, March 1979 to February 1992. *Shetland Bird Report 1991*: 94–103.

Heubeck, M. (1993a) Moult flock surveys indicate a continued decline in the Shetland Eider population, 1984–92. *Scottish Birds*, **17**: 77–84.

Heubeck, M. (1993b) Eider mortality in Shetland in early 1980. *Shetland Bird Report 1992*: 95–101.

Heubeck, M. (1995) Shetland beached bird surveys: national and European context. *Proceedings of the Royal Society of Edinburgh*, **103B**: 165–179.

Heubeck, M. (1997) *Ornithological Monitoring Programme. 1996 Summary Report*. Unpublished report for SOTEAG, Aberdeen.

Heubeck, M. & Ellis, P.M. (1986) Shetland seabirds 1985. *BTO News*, **143**: 10.

Heubeck, M. & Robertson, I.S. (1987) Chick production of kittiwake (*Rissa tridactyla*) colonies in Shetland, 1986. *Seabird*, **10**: 34–42.

Heubeck, M., Richardson, M.G. & Dore, C.P. (1986) Monitoring numbers of Kittiwake (*Rissa tridactyla*) in Shetland. *Seabird*, **9**: 32–42.

Heubeck, M., Meek, E. & Suddaby, D. (1992) The occurrence of dead auks *Alcidae* on beaches in Orkney and Shetland, 1976–1991. *Sula*, **6**: 1–18.

Heubeck, M. Harvey, P. & Uttley, J. (1995) *Dealing with the wildlife casualties of the* Braer *oil spill, Shetland, January 1993*. SOTEAG, Aberdeen.

Hewer, H.R. (1964) The determination of age, sexual maturity, longevity and a life-table in the grey seal (*Halichoerus grypus*). *Proceedings of the Zoological Society of London*, **142**: 593–624.

Hewer, H.R. (1974) *British Seals*. Collins New Naturalist, London.

Hewson, R. (1988) Spacing and habitat preference of mountain hares in Shetland. *Journal of Applied Ecology*, **25**: 397–407.

Hibbert, S. (1822) *Description of the Shetland Islands*. Constable, Edinburgh.

Hilliam, J. (1977) *Phytosociological studies in the southern isles of Shetland*. PhD thesis, University of Durham.

Hinton, M.A.C. (1919) The field mouse of Foula, Shetland. *Scottish Naturalist for 1919*: 177–181.

Hiscock, K. (1986) *Marine biological surveys in Shetland*. Unpublished report for NCC, Edinburgh.

Hiscock, K. & Johnston, C. (1989) *Review of marine biological information for Shetland*. Unpublished report for NCC, Edinburgh.

Holbourn, I.B.S. (1938) *The Isle of Foula*. Manson, Lerwick.

Holdgate, M.W. (1960) The fauna of the mid-Atlantic islands. *Proceedings of the Royal Society of London*, **152**: 550–567.

Holdgate, M.W. & Wace, N.M. (1961) The influence of man on the floras and faunas of southern islands. *Polar Record*, **10**: 475–493.

Hoppe, G. (1965) Submarine peat in the Shetland islands. *Geografiska Annaler*, **47A**: 195–203.

Hoppe, G. (1974) The glacial history of the Shetland Islands. *Transactions of the Institute of British Geographers*, Special Publication no. 7: 197–210.

Howarth, D. (1951) *The Shetland Bus*. Nelson, London.

Howe, G.M (1963) *National Atlas of Disease Mortality in the United Kingdom*. Nelson, London.

Howson, C. (1988) *Marine Nature Conservation Review: Survey of Shetland, Foula and Fair Isle 1987*, Vol. 1. OPRU/Field Studies Council, Orielton.

Hulme, P.D. (1985) The peatland vegetation of the Isle of Lewis and Harris and the Shetland Islands, Scotland. *Aquilo Series Botanica*, **21**: 81–88.

Hulme, P.D. & Birnie, R.V. (1990) Cause for concern. *Discover Scotland*, issue 39.

Hulme, P.D. & Blyth, A.W. (1985) Observations on the erosion of blanket peat in Yell, Shetland. *Geografiska Annaler*, **67A**: 119–122.

Hulme, P.D. & Durno, S.E. (1980) A contribution to the phytogeography of Shetland. *New Phytologist*, **84**: 165–169.

Huxley, T. (1974) Wilderness. *In*: Warren, A. & Goldsmith, F.B. (eds), *Conservation in Practice*: 361–374. Wiley, New York.

Ing, B. (1968) *Census Catalogue of British Myxomycetes*. British Mycological Society, London.

Irvine, D.E.G. (1962) The marine algae of Shetland: a phyto-geographical account. *British Phycological Bulletin*, **2**: 181–182.

Irvine, D. (1974) The marine vegetation of the Shetland Isles. *In*: Goodier, R. (ed.), *The Natural Environment of Shetland*: 107–113. NCC, Edinburgh.

Irvine, S.G. (1968) An outline of the climate of Shetland. *Weather*, **23**: 392–403.

IUCN Commission on National Parks and Protected Areas (1994) *Parks for Life: Action for Protected Areas in Europe*. IUCN, Gland, Switzerland and Cambridge, UK.

Jackson, E.E. (1966) The birds of Foula. *Scottish Birds*, **4** (suppl.).

Jakobsen, J. (1928) *An Etymological Dictionary of the Norn Language in Shetland*. Vilhelm Prior, Copenhagen and Nutt, London.

Jakobsen, J. (1936) *The Place-names of Shetland*. Vilhelm Prior, Copenhagen and Nutt, London.

Jameson, R. (1798) *Outline of Mineralogy of the Shetland Islands and of Arran*. Creech, Cadell & Davies, Edinburgh.

Jamieson, R.A. (1986) *Shoormal*. Polygon, Edinburgh.

Jamieson, R.A. (1992) Ootadæks. *In*: MacDonald, M. (ed.), *The Edinburgh Review*, vol. 88. University Press, Edinburgh.

Jay, S.C. (1993) *Relict trees of Shetland. Their status and survival*. Unpublished report of Shetland Amenity Trust, Lerwick.

Jefferies, D.J. (1989) The changing otter population of Britain 1700–1989. *Biological Journal of the Linnean Society*, **38**: 61–69.

Jefferies, D.J. & Parslow, J.L.F. (1976) The genetics of bridling in guillemots from a study of hand-reared birds. *Journal of Zoology, London*, **179**: 411–420.

Jeffreys, J.G. (1869) Last report on dredging among the Shetland Isles. *Report of the 38th Meeting of the British Association*: 232–247.

Jensen, A.D. (ed.) (1928–72) *The Zoology of the Faroes*. Høst, Copenhagen.

Jewell, P.A., Milner, C. & Boyd, J.M. (1974) *Island Survivors: the Ecology of the Soay Sheep of St. Kilda*. Athlone, London.

Joensen, A.H. (1966) *The Birds of Faroe*. Rhodos, Copenhagen.

Johansen, J. (1975) Pollen diagrams from the Shetland and Faroe Islands. *New Phytologist*, **75**: 369–387.

Johansen, J. (1978) The age of the introduction of *Plantago lanceolata* to the Shetland Islands. *Geological Survey of Denmark Yearbook for 1976*: 45–78.

Johnston, J.L. (1968) *Meetings*. Outpost Publications, London.

Johnston, J.L. (1974) Shetland habitats, an outline ecological framework. *In*: Goodier, R. (ed.), *The Natural Environment of Shetland*: 33–49. NCC, Edinburgh.

Johnston, J.L. (1975a) *Parkland Poets*, vol. 13. Akros Publications, Preston.

Johnston, J.L. (1975b) *Native woodland in Shetland*. Unpublished report of NCC, Edinburgh.

Johnston, J.L. (1976) The environmental impact. *In*: Button, J. (ed.), *The Shetland Way of Oil*: 58–71. Thuleprint, Lerwick.

Johnstone, J. (1846) *Jamieson's Scottish Dictionary (Abridged)*. Simpkin, Marshall & Co., London.

Jones, A.M. (1975) The marine environment of Orkney. *In*: Goodier, R. (ed.), *The Natural Environment of Orkney*: 85–94. NCC, Edinburgh.

Jones, A.M., Jones, Y.M. & James, J.L. (1979) The incidence of the nemertine *Malacobdella grossa* in the bivalve *Cerastoderma edule* in Shetland. *Journal of the Marine Biological Association*, **59**: 373–375.

Jones, N.V. & Mortimer, M.A.E. (1974) Stream invertebrates on Foula. *Glasgow Naturalist*, **19**: 91–100.

Jonsson, J. (1965) Whales and whaling in Icelandic waters. *Norwegian Whaling Gazette*, **54**: 245–253.

Kay, G.T. (1947) The young Guillemot's flight to the sea. *British Birds*, **40**: 156–157.

Kay, G.T. (1948) The gannet in Shetland in winter. *British Birds*, **41**: 268–270.

Kennedy, K. (1996) Caddis flies (Trichoptera) from Fetlar. *Glasgow Naturalist*, **23**: 44–47.

Kent, D.H. (1992) *List of Vascular Plants of the British Isles*. Botanical Society of the British Isles, London.

Kettlewell, H.B.D. (1961a) Geographical melanism in the Lepidoptera of Shetland. *Heredity*, **16**: 393–402.

Kettlewell, H.B.D. (1961b) Selection experiments on melanism in *Amathes glareosa* Esp. (Lepidoptera). *Heredity*, **16**: 415–434.

Kettlewell, H.B.D. (1965) Insect survival and selection for pattern. *Science*, **148**: 1290–1296.

Kettlewell, H.B.D. (1973) *The Evolution of Melanism*. Clarendon Press, Oxford.

Kettlewell, H.B.D. & Berry, R.J. (1961) The study of a cline. *Heredity*, **16**: 403–414.

Kettlewell, H.B.D. & Berry, R.J. (1969) Gene flow in a cline. *Heredity*, **24**: 1–14.

Kettlewell, H.B.D. & Cadbury, C.J. (1963) Investigations on the origins of non-industrial melanism. *Entomologists' Record*, **75**: 149–160.

Kettlewell, H.B.D., Berry, R.J., Cadbury, C.J. & Phillips, G.C. (1969) Differences in behaviour, dominance and survival within a cline. *Heredity*, **24**: 15–25.

Kikkawa, J. (1959) Habitats of the field mouse on Fair Isle in spring, 1956. *Glasgow Naturalist*, **18**: 65–77.

King, H.G.R. (1969) *The Antarctic*. Blandford, London.

King, J.J.F.X. (1890) Tipulidae from the Island of Unst. *Entomologist's Monthly Magazine*, **26**: 176–180.

King, J.J.F.X. (1896) Notes on Trichoptera (including *Agrypnia picta* Kol.) taken in Unst, Shetland. *Entomologist's Monthly Magazine*, **32**: 151–152.

King, J.F.F.X., Bright, P.M. & Reid, W. (1896) Ten weeks collecting Lepidoptera in Unst (Shetland). *Entomologist's Monthly Magazine*, **32**: 5–9.

Kinnear, N.B. (1906) On the mammals of Fair Isle with a description of a new subspecies of *Mus sylvaticus*. *Annals of Scottish Natural History for 1906*: 65–68.

Kinnear, P. (1976) Birds and oil. *In*: Button, J. (ed.), *The Shetland Way of Oil*: 92–99. Thuleprint, Lerwick.

Kirby, J.S., Ferns, J.R., Waters, R.J. & Prys-Jones, R.P. (1991) *Wildfowl and Wader Counts 1990/91*. Wildfowl and Wetland Trust, Slimbridge.

Kirpatrick, A.H. & Simpson, I.A. (1996) *The moorlands of Shetland and their natural heritage interest*. Unpublished report of SNH, Edinburgh.

Kloet, G.S. & Hincks, W.D. (1972) *A Check List of British Insects. Part 1: Lepidoptera*, 2nd edn, revised. Royal Entomological Society, London.

Klomp, N.I. & Furness, R.W. (1992a) Non-breeders as a buffer against environmental stress: declines in numbers of great skuas on Foula, Shetland, and prediction of future recruitment. *Journal of Applied Ecology*, **29**: 341–348.

Klomp, N.I. & Furness, R.W. (1992b) The dispersal and philopatry of Great Skuas from Foula, Shetland. *Ringing and Migration*, **13**: 73–82.

Kruuk, H. & Balharry, D. (1990) Effects of sea water on thermal insulation of the otter, *Lutra lutra*. *Journal of Zoology, London*, **220**: 405–415.

Kruuk, H. & Hewson, R. (1978) Spacing and foraging of otters (*Lutra lutra* L.) in a marine habitat. *Journal of Zoology, London*, **185**: 205–212.

Kruuk, H. & Moorhouse, A. (1990) Seasonal and spatial differences in food selection by otters (*Lutra lutra*) in Shetland. *Journal of Zoology, London*, **221**: 621–637.

Kruuk, H., Conroy, J.W.H. & Moorhouse, A. (1987) Seasonal reproduction, mortality and food of otters (*Lutra lutra*) in Shetland. *Symposia of the Zoological Society of London*, No. 58: 263–278.

Kruuk, H., Wansink, D. & Moorhouse, A. (1990) Feeding patches and diving success of otters, *Lutra lutra*, in Shetland. *Oikos*, **57**: 68–72.

Kruuk, H., Conroy, J.W.H. & Moorhouse, A. (1991) Recruitment to a population of otters (*Lutra lutra*) in Shetland in relation to fish abundance. *Journal of Applied Ecology*, **28**: 95–101.

Kunzlik, P.A. (1989) Small fish around Shetland. *In*: Heubeck, M. (ed.), *Seabirds and Sandeels*: 38–49. Shetland Bird Group, Lerwick.

Kurtén, B. (1959) Rates of evolution in fossil mammals. *Cold Spring Harbor Symposia in Quantitative Biology*, **24**: 205–215.

Lacaille, A.C. (1954) *The Stone Age in Scotland*. Oxford University Press, London.

Lack, D. (1942) Ecological features of the bird faunas of British small islands. *Journal of Animal Ecology*, **11**: 9–36.

Lack, D. (1959) British pioneers in ornithological research 1859–1939. *Ibis*, **101**: 71–81.

Lack, D. (1960) A comparison of 'drift migration' at Fair Isle, the Isle of May, and Spurn Point. *Scottish Birds*, **1**: 295–327.

Lack, D. (1969) The numbers of bird species on islands. *Bird Study*, **16**: 193–209.

Lack, D. (1976) *Island Biology*. Blackwell, Oxford.

Laing, L. (1974) *Orkney and Shetland. An Archaeological Guide*. David & Charles, Newton Abbot.

Laurence, B.R. (1992) A relict fly from a glacial past. *The Shetland Naturalist*, **1**: 57–58.

Laurence, B.R. (1997) Diptera in the Northern Isles of Britain. *Entomologist's Monthly Magazine*, **133**: 225–232.

Laws, R.M. (1977) Seals and whales of the Southern Ocean. *Proceedings of the Royal Society of London B*, **279**: 81–96.

Lea, D. & Bourne, W.R.P. (1975) Birds of Orkney. *In*: Goodier, R. (ed.), *The Natural Environment of Orkney*: 98–128. NCC, Edinburgh.

Lewis, A. (1977) *Phytosociological studies in the northern isle of Shetland*. PhD thesis, University of Durham.

Lewis, F.J. (1907) The plant remains in the Scottish peat mosses. III. The Scottish Highlands and the Shetland Islands. *Transactions of the Royal Society of Edinburgh*, **46**: 33–70.

Lewis, F.J. (1911) The plant remains in the Scottish peat mosses. IV. The Scottish Highlands and the Shetland Islands. *Transactions of the Royal Society of Edinburgh*, **47**: 793–833.

Lindroth, C.H. (1955) Insects and spiders from Fair Isle. *Entomologist's Monthly Magazine*, **91**: 216.

Lindroth, C.H. (1970) Survival of animals and plants on ice-free refugia during the Pleistocene glaciations. *Endeavour*, **29**: 129–134.

Linklater, E. (1965) *Orkney and Shetland. A Historical, Geographical, Social and Scenic Survey*. Hale, London.

Livesey & Henderson (1973) Sullom Voe and Swarbacks Minn area. Master Development Plan related to oil industry requirements: report to Zetland County.

Livingstone, W.P. (1947) *Shetland and the Shetlanders*. Nelson, Edinburgh.

Lloyd, C. (1975) Timing and frequency of census counts of cliff-nesting auks. *British Birds*, **68**: 507–513.

Lloyd, C., Tasker, M.L. & Partridge, K. (1991) *The Status of Seabirds in Britain and Ireland*. T. & A.D. Poyser, London.

Lockie, J.D. (1952) The food of the Great Skua on Hermaness, Unst. *Scottish Naturalist*, **64**: 158–162.

Lockley, R.M. (1966) *Grey Seal, Common Seal*. Deutsch, London.

Lorimer, R.I. (1975) Lepidoptera in Orkney. *In*: Goodier, R. (ed.), *The Natural Environment of Orkney*: 57–79. NCC, Edinburgh.

Low, G. (1774) *A Tour through the Islands of Orkney and Shetland* (1978 reprint). Melven, Inverness.

Lyle, A.A. & Britton, R.H. (1985) The freshwaters of Shetland: II. Resources and distribution. *Scottish Geographical Magazine*, **101**: 157–164.

Macan, T.T. & Worthington, E.B. (1951) *Life in Lakes and Rivers*. Collins New Naturalist, London.

MacArthur, R.H. & Wilson, E.O. (1967) *The Theory of Island Biogeography*. University Press, Princeton.

McBride, J.H. & England, R.W. (1994) Deep seismic reflection structure of the Caledonian orogenic front west of Shetland. *Journal of the Geological Society of London*, **151**: 9–16.

MacDiarmid, H. (1934) *Stony Limits and other Poems*. Victor Gollanz, London.

McGillivray, J.W. (1920) Agriculture in Shetland. *Scottish Journal of Agriculture*, **3**: 414–429.

MacIntosh, J. (1984) *Shetland Meadows Survey*. Unpublished report of NCC, Edinburgh.

McIntyre, A.D. (1961) Quantitative differences in the fauna of boreal mud associations. *Journal of the Marine Biological Association*, **41**: 599–616.

McIntyre, A.D. (1970) The range of biomass in intertidal sand, with special reference to the bivalve *Tellina tenuis*. *Journal of the Marine Biological Association*, **50**: 561–575.

McIntyre, A.D. (1993) Control of pollution of the sea. *Marine Policy. The Journal of Oceanic Affairs*, **17**: 394–398.

McKay, A.G. (1974) A sub-bottom profiling survey of the St. Magnus Bay deep, Shetland. *Scottish Journal of Geology*, **10**: 31–34.

McKee, J. (1986) The Caribidae (Col.) of Unst, Shetland. *Entomologist's Monthly Magazine*, **122**: 243–248.

MacKenzie, J. (1993) *Arboriculture in the Faroe Islands and the implications for Shetland.* Unpublished report of Shetland Amenity Trust, Lerwick.

McLachlan, R. (1884) Trichoptera from Unst, North Shetland. *Entomologist's Monthly Magazine*, **21**: 91; 153–155.

McVean, D.N. & Ratcliffe, D.A. (1962) *The Plant Communities of the Scottish Highlands.* HMSO, London.

Maitland, P.S. (1972) A key to the freshwater fishes of the British Isles. *Scientific Publications of the Freshwater Biological Association*, **27**: 1–139.

Maitland, P.S. (1995) *The Fresh Waters of Shetland.* Unpublished report of SNH, Edinburgh.

Maitland, P.S. & Britton, R.H. (1985) The freshwaters of Shetland: I. The strategy of a synoptic resource analysis. *Scottish Geographical Magazine*, **101**: 150–156.

Maitland, P.S. & East, K. (1976) The freshwater fish and fauna of Shetland. *Glasgow Naturalist*, **19**: 321–324.

Manly, B.F.J. (1975) A second look at some data on a cline. *Heredity*, **34**: 423–426.

Marchmont, J.H., Hudson, R., Carter, S.P. & Whittington, P. (1990) *Population Trends in British Breeding Birds.* BTO, Tring.

Marwick, E. (1975) *The Folklore of Orkney and Shetland.* Batsford, London.

Mather, A.S. & Smith, J.S. (1974) *Beaches of Shetland.* University Department of Geography, Aberdeen.

Matthews, J.R. (1955) *Origin and Distribution of the British Flora.* Hutchinson, London.

Matthews, L.H. (1952) *British Mammals.* Collins New Naturalist, London.

May, F. (1970) Movement, metamorphism and migmatization in the Scalloway region of Shetland. *Bulletin of the Geological Survey of Great Britain*, no. 31: 205–226.

Mayr, E. (1954) Change of genetic environment and evolution. *In*: Huxley, J., Hardy, A.C. & Ford, E.B. (eds), *Evolution as a Process*: 157–180. Allen & Unwin, London.

Mayr, E. (1963) *Ancient Species and Evolution.* Oxford, London.

Mayr, E. (1967) The challenge of island faunas. *Australian Natural History*, **15**: 369–374.

Meek, E.R. (1988) The breeding ecology and decline of the merlin (*Falco columbarius*) in Orkney. *Bird Study*, **35**: 209–218.

Meek, E.R. (1995) *Islands of Birds. A Guide to Orkney Birds.* Shetland Times, Lerwick.

Mercado, G.I. (1967) *Notes on Shetland Freshwater Life and Arthropods.* Manson, Lerwick.

Metcalfe, G. (1950) The ecology of the Cairngorms. II. The mountain Callunetum. *Journal of Ecology*, **38**: 46–74.

Meyrick, E. (1928) *A Revised Handbook of British Lepidoptera.*. London.

Miller, J.A. & Flinn, D. (1966) A survey of the age relations of Shetland rocks. *Geological Journal*, **5**: 95–116.

Milner, C. (1978) Shetland ecology surveyed. *Geographical Magazine*, **50**: 730–753.

Milner, J.E.D. (1987) The spiders of Fair Isle. *Glasgow Naturalist*, **21**: 331–334.

Milner, J.E.D. (1988) New and rare spider records from the Orkney and Shetland Islands. *Newsletter of the British Arachnology Society*, **54**: 2.

Milner, J.E.D. & Riddiford, N. (1997) *Spider Studies on Fair Isle (Shetland).* (In press.)

Moffat, W. (1934) *Shetland: the Isles of Nightless Summer.* Cranton, London.

Monaghan, P. (1992) Seabirds and sandeels: the conflict between exploitation and conservation in the northern North Sea. *Biodiversity and Conservation*, **1**: 98–111.

Monaghan, P., Walton, P., Wanless, S., Uttley, J.D. & Burns, M.D. (1993) Effects of prey abundance on the foraging behaviour, diving efficiency and time allocation of breeding Guillemots *Uria aalge*. *Ibis*, **136**: 214–222.

Moore, D.M. (1968). *The vascular flora of the Falkland Islands.* British Antarctic Survey Scientific Report no. 60.

Moore, P.D. (1975) Origin of blanket mires. *Nature*, **256**: 267–269.

Mordue, J.E. & Ainsworth, G.C. (1984) Ustilaginales of the British Isles. *Mycological Paper*, **154**: 1–96.

Morris, K.H. (1987) The freshwaters of Shetland: chemical characteristics of running waters. *Hydrobiologia*, **144**: 211–221.

Morrison, I. (1973) *The North Sea Earls. The Shetland/Viking Archaeological Expedition.* Gentry, London.

Morrison, I.A. (1978) Aspects of Viking small craft in the light of Shetland practice. *In*: Baldwin, J.R. (ed.), *Scandinavian Shetland*: 57–75. Scottish Society for Northern Studies, Edinburgh.

Moss, D. & Ackers, G. (1987) *A sub-littoral survey of Shetland, 1987*. Unpublished report of NCC, Shetland Amenity Trust and Sullom Oil Terminal, Edinburgh.

Murray, J. & Pullar, L. (1910) *Bathymetric Survey of the Scottish Freshwater Lochs*. Challenger, Edinburgh

Murray, R.A. (1979) Colonization of Scotland by northern birds, 1820–1977. *Scottish Birds*, **10**: 158–174.

Murray, S. & Wanless, S. (1992) *A count of the Noss Gannetry in 1992 and analysis of Gannet monitoring plots on Noss NNR 1975–92*. JNCC, Peterborough.

Mykura, W. (1972a) Tuffisitic breccias, tuffisites and associated carbonate-sulphide mineralization in south-east Shetland. *Bulletin of the Geological Survey of Great Britain*, no. 40: 51–82.

Mykura, W. (1972b) The Old Red Sandstone sediments of Fair Isle, Shetland Islands. *Bulletin of the Geological Survey of Great Britain*, no. 41: 1–31.

Mykura, W. (1972c) Igneous intrusions and mineralization in Fair Isle, Shetland Islands. *Bulletin of the Geological Survey of Great Britain*, no. 41: 33–53.

Mykura, W. (1974) The geological basis of the Shetland environment. *In*: Goodier, R. (ed.), *The Natural Environment of Shetland*: 1–12. NCC, Edinburgh.

Mykura, W. (1975) The geological basis of the Orkney environment. *In*: Goodier, R. (ed.), *The Natural Environment of Orkney*: 1–9. NCC, Edinburgh.

Mykura, W. (1976) *Orkney and Shetland (British Regional Geology)*. HMSO, Edinburgh.

Mkykura W. & Phemister, J. (1976) *The Geology of Western Shetland*. Memoirs of the Geological Survey of Great Britain no. 125.

Nelson, G. (1977) *Reminiscences of the Shetland Fireside*. Thuleprint, Lerwick.

Nelson, J.G. & Butler, R.W. (1993) Assessing, planning, and management of North Sea oil development effects in the Shetland islands. *Environmental Impact Assessment Review*, **13**: 201–269.

Neustein, S.A. (1964) A review of pilot and trial plantations established by the Forestry Commission in Shetland. *Scottish Forestry*, **18**: 199–211.

Newton, I. & Haas, M.B. (1988) Pollutants in merlin eggs and their effects on breeding. *British Birds*, **81**: 258–269.

Nicholson, J.R. (1978) The slaughter of the herring. *Shetland Times*, 21 July.

Nicolson, J.R. (1972) *Shetland*. David & Charles, Newton Abbot.

Nicolson, J.R. (1975) *Shetland and Oil*. Luscombe, London.

Nicolson, J.R. (1978) *Traditional Life in Shetland*. Hale, London.

Norman, A.M. (1869) Shetland final dredging report. II. On the Crustacea, Tunicata, Polyzoa, Echinodermata, Actinozoa, Hydrozoa, and Porifera. *Report of the 38th Meeting of the British Association*, 247–340.

North Sea Task Force (1993) *North Sea Quality Status Report 1993*. Olsen & Olsen, Fredensborg.

Oddie, B.C.V. (1959) The composition of precipitation at Lerwick, Shetland. *Quarterly Journal of the Royal Meteorological Society*, **85**: 163–165.

O'Dell, A.C. (1939) *The Historical Geography of the Shetland Isles*. Manson, Lerwick.

O'Dell, A.C. (1940) *Zetland. Report of the Land Utilisation Survey of Britain*. Geographical, London.

O'Donald, P. (1983) *The Arctic Skua. A Study of the Ecology of a Seabird*. Cambridge University Press, Cambridge.

Okill, J.D. (1992) Natal dispersal and breding site fidelity of Red-throated Divers *Gavia stellata* in Shetland. *Ringing and Migration*, **13**: 57–58.

Okill, J.D. (1993a) Environmental impacts on wildlife, land, food and soil. *Marine Policy. The Journal of Oceanic Affairs*, **17**: 449–452.

Okill, J.D. (1993b) *Report to ESGOSS. The recoveries of ringed birds during the 'Braer' oil spill, Shetland, 1993*. Shetland Ringing Group, Lerwick.

Okill, J.D. (1994) Ringing recoveries of Red-throated Divers *Gavia stellata* in Britain and Ireland. *Ringing and Migration*, **15**: 107–118.

Okill, J.D. (1995) *Report to SOTEAG on red-throated divers in Shetland in 1995*. Unpublished report of Shetland Ringing Group, Lerwick.

Okill, J.D. & Osborn, K. (1993) *A report to ESGOSS. A review of the seabird breeding season in Shetland 1993 in the aftermath of the 'Braer' oil spill*. Unpublished report of Shetland Ringing Group, Lerwick.

Okill, J.D. & Wanless, S. (1990) Breeding success and chick growth of Red-throated Divers *Gavia stellata* in Shetland in 1979–88. *Ringing and Migration*, **11**: 65–72.

Okill, J.D., Ginnever, J.A. & Jones, A. (1980) Shetland's Merlins. *Shetland Bird Report 1979*: 51–54.

Okill, J.D., Fowler, J.A., Ellis, P.M. & Petrie, G.W. (1990) The diet of Cormorant (*Phalacrocorax carbo*) chicks in Shetland in 1989. *Seabird*, **14**: 21–26.

Okill, J.D., Fowler, J.A., Ellis, P.M. & Petrie, G.W. (1993) *A report to ESGOSS. The effect of the 'Braer' on the diet of the cormorant in Shetland*. Unpublished report of Shetland Ringing Group, Lerwick.

Oldham, C. (1930) Notes on the land and freshwater Mollusca of Foula. *Scottish Naturalist for 1930*: 37–38.

Oldham, C. (1932) Notes on some Scottish and Shetland Pisidia. *Journal of Conchology*, **19**: 271–278.

Ostenfeld, C.H. (1908) The land vegetation of the Faeroes. *Botany of the Faeroes*, **3**: 867–1026.

Ostenfeld, C.H. & Grontved, J. (1934) *The Flora of Iceland and the Faeroes*. Williams & Norgate, London.

Palmer, R.C. & Scott, W. (1969) *A Check-list of the Flowering Plants and Ferns of the Shetland Isles*. Buncle, Arbroath.

Palsson, H. & Edwards, P. (1978) *The History of the Earls of Orkney*. Hogarth Press, London.

Parke, M. & Dixon, P.S. (1976) Check-list of British marine algae: third revision. *Journal of the Marine Biological Association*, **56**: 527–594.

Parslow, J.L. (1973) *Breeding Birds of Britain and Ireland*. Poyser, Berkhamstead.

Paton, J.A. (1965) *Census Catalogue of British Hepatics*, 4th edn. British Bryological Society.

Paton, J.A. (1973) Hepatic flora of the Shetland Islands. *Transactions of the Botanical Society of Edinburgh*, **42**: 17–29.

Peach, B.N. & Horne, J. (1879) The glaciation of the Shetland Isles. *Quarterly Journal of the Royal Society of London*, **35**: 778–811.

Peach, B.N. & Horne, J. (1884) The old red volcanic rocks of Shetland. *Transactions of the Royal Society of Edinburgh*, **32**: 359–388.

Peach, C.W. (1865) On traces of glacial drift in the Shetland Islands. *Report of the British Association for the Advancement of Science Meeting Bath 1864*: 59–61.

Pearson, T.H. & Stanley, S.O. (1977) The benthic ecology of some Shetland voes. *In*: Keegan, B.F., Creidigh, P.O. & Boaden, P.J.S. (eds), *Biology of Benthic Organisms*: 503–512. Pergamon, Oxford.

Pennant, J. (1784–85) *Arctic Zoology*. London.

Pennington, M.G. (1992) Moths and butterflies in Shetland (excluding Fair Isle) in 1991. *Shetland Naturalist*, **1**: 37–47.

Pennington, M.G. (1993) Recent Lepidoptera records from Shetland. *Entomologists' Record and Journal of Variation*, **105**: 173–174.

Pennington, M.G. (1995) The Common Blue Damselfly *Enallagma cyathigerum* and other Odonata records in Shetland. *Entomologists' Record and Journal of Variation*, **107**: 165–170.

Pennington, M.G. & Rogers, T. (1994) Notes on Lepidoptera in Shetland in 1993. *Entomologists' Record and Journal of Variation*, **106**: 186–187.

Pennington, M.G., Rogers, T.D. & Bland, K.P. (1997) Lepidoptera new to Shetland. *Entomologists' Record and Journal of Variation*, **109**: 265–281.

Perring, F.H. & Walters. S.M. (1962) *Atlas of the British Flora*. Nelson, London.

Perry, R. (1948) *Shetland Sanctuary*. Faber, London.

Persson, I. (1969) The fate of the Icelandic Vikings in Greenland. *Man*, **4**: 620–628.

Peterson, G.B.S. Da Wren. *In: Draw de up, du's welcome*. Smith, Mossbank.

Peterson, J. (1964a) Da Corbie. *In*: Graham, J. & Robertson T.A. (eds), *Northern Limits: An Anthology of Shetland Verse and Poetry*. T. & J. Manson, Lerwick.

Peterson, J. (1964b) Shetland Sea Trout I. *New Shetlander*, **68**: 27–30.

Peterson, J. (1964c) Shetland Sea Trout II. *New Shetlander*, **69**: 20–22.

Phemister, J. (1978) *The Old Red Sandstone intrusive complex of northern Northmaven, Shetland*. Report of the Institute of Geological Sciences no. 78/2.

Phillips, R.A., Furness, R.W. & Caldow, R.W.G. (1995) Behavioural responses of Arctic Skuas *Stercorarius parasiticus* to changes in Sandeel availability. *In*: Greenstreet, S. & Tasker, M. (eds), *Aquatic Predators*: 17–25. Blackwell Scientific, Oxford.

Phillips, R A., Caldow, R.W.G. & Furness, R.W. (1996) The influence of food availability on the breeding effort and reproductive success of Arctic Skuas *Stercorarius parasiticus*. *Ibis*, **138**: 410–419.

Pitt, F. (1923) *Shetland Pirates*. Allen & Unwin, London.

Ployen, C. (1840, English translation 1896) *Reminiscences of a Voyage to Shetland, Orkney and Scotland*. Manson, Lerwick.

Poore, M.E.D. & McVean, D.N. (1957) A new approach to Scottish mountain vegetation. *Journal of Ecology*, **45**: 401–439.

Powell, H.T. (1957) Studies in the genus *Fucus* L. II. Distribution and ecology of forms of *Fucus distichus* L. emend. Powell in Britain and Ireland. *Journal of the Marine Biological Association*, **36**: 663–693.

Powell, H.T. (1963) New records of *Fucus distichus* subspecies for the Shetland and Orkney Islands. *British Phycological Bulletin*, **2**: 247–254.

Powell, M. (1938) *200,000 Feet on Foula*. Faber, London.

Price, W.R. (1929) Notes on the vegetation of Zetland. *Report of the Botanic Exchange Club*, **8**: 770–781.

Pringle, J.R. (1970) The structural geology of the North Roe area of Shetland. *Geological Journal*, **7**: 147–170.

Pritchard, D.E., Housden, S.D., Mudge, G.P., Galbraith, A. & Pienkowski, M.W. (eds.) (1992) *Important Bird Areas in the United Kingdom*. RSPB/JNCC, Bedford.

Proctor, J. (1971) The plant ecology of serpentine. II. Plant responses to serpentine soils. *Journal of Ecology*, **59**: 397–410; 827–842.

Proctor, J. (1991) *A corporate environmental strategy*. Shetland Salmon Farmers Association, Lerwick.

Proctor, J. & Woodell, S.R.J. (1975) The ecology of serpentine soils. *Advances in Ecological Research*, **9**: 255–366.

Raeburn, H. (1888) The summer birds of Shetland. *Proceedings of the Royal Society of Edinburgh*, **9**: 542–562.

Raeburn, H. (1891) The birds of Papa Stour, with an account of the Lyra Skerry. *Zoologist*, 3rd series, **15**: 126–135.

Rankin, J. (1969) *Parkland Poets No. 4*. Akros Publications, Preston.

Rankin, N. (1947) *Haunts of British Divers*. Collins, London.

Rasmussen, R. (1952) *Føroya Flora*. Thomsen, Tórshavn.

Ratcliffe, D.A. (1968) An ecological account of the Atlantic bryophytes in the British Isles. *New Phytologist*, **67**: 365–439.

Ratcliffe, N., Towl, H. & Suddaby, D. (1996) *The Breeding Performance of Arctic Terns, Arctic Skuas and Great Skuas in Orkney and Shetland (1990–1995)*. RSPB, Edinburgh.

Rawes, M. (1983) Changes in two high altitude blanket bogs after the cessation of sheep grazing. *Journal of Ecology*, **71**: 219–235.

Read, H.H. (1934) The metamorphic geology of Unst in the Shetland Islands. *Quarterly Journal of the Geological Society of London*, **90**: 637–688.

Read, H.H. (1937) Metamorphic correlation in the polymetamorphic rocks of the Valla Field Block, Unst, Shetland Islands. *Transaction of the Royal Society of Edinburgh*, **59**: 195–221.

Reed, T. (1981) The number of breeding landbird species on British islands. *Journal of Animal Ecology*, **50**: 613–624.

Reid, D.G., Turrel, W.R., Walsh, M. & Corten, A. (1997) Cross-shelf processes north of Scotland in relation to the southerly migration of Western mackeral. *ICES Journal of Marine Science*, **54**: 168–178.

Reinert, A. (1971) Højere dyr på land. *Danmarks Natur*, **10**: 537–538.

Reinikainen, A. (1937) The irregular migration of the crossbills and their relation to the cone-crop of the conifers. *Ornis Fennica*, **14**: 55–64.

Rendall, R. (1946) *Country Sonnets and Other Poems*. The Orcadian, Kirkwall.

Rendall, R. (1960) *Orkney Shore*. Kirkwall Press, Kirkwall.

Richardson, M.G. (1982) *Amphibians in Shetland*. Unpublished report of NCC, Edinburgh.

Richardson, M.G. (1986) Recent decline of the Kittiwake in Shetland. *Shetland Bird Report 1985*: 40–48.

Richardson, M.G. (1990) The distribution and status of Whimbrel *Numenius p. phaeopus* in Shetland and Britain. *Bird Study*, **37**: 61–68.

Richardson, M.G. (1995) Status and distribution of the Kittiwake in Shetland in 1981. *Bird Study*, **32**: 11–18.

Richardson, M.G., Heubeck, M., Lyster, I. & McGowan, R. (1979) *Great Northern Divers in Shetland*. Joint report of NCC, SOTEAG, Royal Scottish Museum, Edinburgh.

Riddiford, N.J. & Harvey, P. (1992) New moth records, and a wasp, from Fair Isle. *Entomologists' Record and Journal of Variation*, **104**: 263–264.

Riddiford, N.J. & Thompson, G. (1997) *Managing the Sea for Birds: Fair Isle and Adjacent Waters*. Fair Isle Bird Observatory Trust, National Trust for Scotland and RSPB, Edinburgh.

Ritchie, W. (ed.) (1994) *The Environmental Impact of the Braer*. Report of the Ecological Steering Group on the Oil Spill in Shetland (ESGOSS). Scottish Office Environment Department, Edinburgh.

Robertson, M.S. (1991) *Sons and Daughters of Shetland, 1800–1900*. Shetland Publishing Company, Lerwick.

Robertson, T.A. (1975) *Collected Poems of Vagaland*. Shetland Times, Lerwick.

Roper-Lindsay, J. & Say, A.M. (1986) Plant communities of the Shetland Islands. *Journal of Ecology*, **74**: 1013–1030.

Rothschild, M. (1958) The bird-fleas of Fair Isle. *Parasitology*, **48**: 382–412.

Royal Commission on Environmental Pollution (1974) *Pollution control, progress and problems*. Cmnd. 5780. HMSO, London.

Royal Society for the Protection of Birds & Scottish Crofters Union (1992) *Crofting and the environment: a new approach*. RSPB, Edinburgh.

Ryder, M.L. (1968) The evolution of Scottish breeds of sheep. *Scottish Studies*, **12**: 127–167.

Ryder, M.L. (1971). Cycles of wool follicle activity in some Shetland sheep. *Animal Production*, **13**: 511–520.

Ryder, M.L., Land, R.B. & Ditchburn, R. (1974) Coat colour inheritance in Soay, Orkney and Shetland sheep. *Journal of Zoology, London*, **173**: 477–485.

Salomonsen, F. (1935) Aves. *Zoology Faroes*, **3**, part 64: 1–269.

Sandison, S. (1968) *Unst, My Island Home and its Story*. Shetland Times, Lerwick.

Saxby, C.F.A. (1903) *Edmondston's Flora of Shetland*. Oliphant, Anderson & Ferrier, Edinburgh.

Saxby, H.L. (1874) *The Birds of Shetland*. MacLaren & Stewart, Edinburgh.

Saxby, J.M.E. (1932) *Shetland Traditional Lore*. Grant & Murray, Edinburgh.

Scanlon, G.M. & Harvey, P. (1988) *The breeding success of Arctic Skuas in Shetland in 1988 and proposals for monitoring both species of Skuas breeding in Shetland*. Unpublished report of NCC, Edinburgh.

Schei, L.K. & Moberg, G. (1988) *The Shetland Story*. Batsford, London.

Scott, D. & Duthie, R. (1894) The inland waters of the Shetland Islands. *Thirteenth Report of the Fish Board Scotland*, **3**: 174–191.

Scott, W. (1822) *The Pirate*. Constable, Edinburgh.

Scott, W. (1962) Profile from the past: Thomas Edmondston. *New Shetlander*, **62**: 7–9.

Scott, W. & Palmer, R. (1987) *The Flowering Plants and Ferns of the Shetland Islands*. Shetland Times, Lerwick.

Scott, W.K. & Palmer, R.C. (1995) A new Shetland *Hicracium* of the Section Alpestria [Fries] F.N. Williams. *Watsonia*, **20**: 282–284.

Scottish Office Agriculture and Fisheries Department (1994a) *Crofting Counties Agricultural Grants Scheme: guidance notes*. HMSO, Edinburgh.

Scottish Office Agriculture and Fisheries Department (1994b) *Shetland Isles: Environmentally Sensitive Area: explanatory leaflet for farmers and crofters*. HMSO, Edinburgh.

Scottish Office Environment Department (1995) *An interim report on survey and monitoring*. ESGOSS, Edinburgh.

Sears, J., Ellis, P.M., Suddaby, D. & Harrop, H.R. (1995) The status of breeding Arctic Skuas *Stercorarius parasiticus* and Great Skua *S. skua* in Shetland in 1992. *Seabird*, **17**: 21–31.

Seaward, M.R.D. (ed.) (1977) *Lichen Ecology*. Academic Press, London.

Select Committee on Science and Technology (1978) *Fourth Report: House of Commons*, **684**.

Selous, S. (1905) *The Bird Watcher in the Shetlands*. Dent, London.

Sheldrick, M.C. (1976) Trends in the strandings of Cetacea on the British coasts. *Mammal Review*, **6**: 15–23.

Shepherd, S. (1971) *Like a Mantle, the Sea*. Bell, London.

Shetelig, H. (1940) *Viking Antiquities in Great Britain and Ireland*. Aschehoug, Oslo.

Shetland Amenity Trust (1983–96) *Annual Reports*. Shetland Amenity Trust, Lerwick.

Shetland Bird Reports (1969–96) *Annual Reports*. Shetland Bird Club, Lerwick.

Shetland Cetacean Group (1993–96) *Annual Reports*. Shetland Cetacean Group, Lerwick.

Shetland Islands Council (1977) *Shetland's Oil Era*. SIC Res. & Dev. Dept, Lerwick.

Shetland Islands Council (1981) *Ten Year Plan for Shetland Agriculture*. SIC Res. & Dev. Dept, Lerwick.

Shetland Islands Council (1993) *Shetland Economic Review*. SIC Res. & Dev. Dept, Lerwick.

Shetland Islands Council (1995a) *Economic Strategy*. SIC Res. & Dev. Dept, Lerwick.

Shetland Islands Council (1995b) *Environmental Statement: Waste to Energy Facility: Non-technical Summary*. SIC Env. Services Dept, Lerwick.

Shewry, P.R. & Peterson, P.J. (1976) Distribution of chromium and nickel in plants from serpentine and other sites. *Journal of Ecology*, **64**: 195–212.

Shirreef, J. (1814) *General View of the Agriculture of the Orkney and Shetland Isles, with Report on Mineralogy by Rev. John Fleming*. Board of Agriculture, Edinburgh.

Sibbald, R. (1711) *Description of the Islands of Orkney and Zetland*. Stevenson, Edinburgh.

Silcocks, A. (1991) Population changes and breeding success of seabirds on the isle of Noss, 1981–90. *Shetland Bird Report 1990*: 74–77.

Sinclair, C. (1840) *Shetland and the Shetlanders or The Northern Circuit*. Whyte, Edinburgh.

Sinclair, J. (1795) *General View of the Agriculture of the Northern Counties and Islands of Scotland*. Board of Agriculture, London.

Sissons, J.B. (1974) The Quaternary in Scotland: a review. *Scottish Journal of Geology*, **10**: 311–337.

Slaitkin, N. (1973) Gene flow and selection in a cline. *Genetics*, **75**: 733–756.

Slingsby, D.R. (1980) The Keen of Hamar, Shetland: a general survey and census of some of the rarer plant taxa. *Transactions of the Botanical Society of Edinburgh*, **43**: 297–306.

Slingsby, D.R. (1981) Britain's most northerly desert. *Shetland Life*, October: 30–31.

Small, A. (1968a) Distribution of settlement in Shetland and Faroes in Viking times. *Saga – Book of the Viking Club*, **17**: 145–155.

Small, A. (1968b) The historical geography of the Norse Viking colonization of the Scottish Highlands. *Norsk geogr. Tidsskr.*, **22**: 1–16.

Small, A. (1969) Shetland: location the key to historical geography. *Scottish Geographical Magazine*, **85**: 155–161.

Small, A., Thomas, C. & Wilson, D.M. (1973) *St Ninian's Isle and its Treasure*. Oxford University Press, Oxford.

Smit, F.G.A.M. (1955) The recorded distribution and hosts of Siphonaptera in Britain. *Entomologists' Gazette*, **8**: 75.

Smit, F.G.A.M. (1957) *Handbook for the Identification of British Insects: Siphonaptera*. Royal Entomological Society, London.

Smith, B. (ed.) (1985) *Shetland Archaeology: New Work in Shetland in the 1970s*. Shetland Times, Lerwick.

Smith, E.A. (1966) A review of the world's grey seal population. *Journal of Zoology, London*, **150**: 463–489.

Smith, H.D. (1977) *The Making of Modern Shetland*. Shetland Times, Lerwick.

Smith, J. (1661) *The Trade and Fishing of Great Britain Displayed, with a description of Orkney and Shetland* (reprinted 1971). Toucan, Edinburgh.

Smith, R. (1992) Shetland and the Greenland Whaling Industry: 1780–1872. *Northern Studies*, **12**: 67–83.

South, R. (1888) Distribution of Lepidoptera in the Outer Hebrides, Orkney and Shetland. *Entomologist*, **21**: 28–30; 98–99.

South, R. (1961) *The Moths of the British Isles*, 3rd edn. Warne, London.

Southern, H.N. (1943) The two phases of *Stercorarius parasiticus* (Linnaeus). *Ibis*, **85**: 443–485.

Southern, H.N. (1962) Survey of bridled guillemots, 1959–60. *Proceedings of the Zoological Society of London*, **138**: 455–472.

Speakman, R., Racey, P.A., McLean, J. & Entwhistle, A.C. (1993) Six new records of Nathusius' Pipistrelle (*Pipistrellus nathusii*) for Scotland. *Scottish Bats*, **2**: 14–16.

Speed, J.G. & Speed, M.G. (1977) *The Exmoor Pony*. Countrywide Livestock, Chippenham.

Spence, D.H.N. (1957) Studies on the vegetation of Shetland. I. The serpentine debris vegetation in Unst. *Journal of Ecology*, **45**: 917–945.

Spence, D.H.N. (1958) The flora of Unst, Shetland, in relation to the geology. *Transactions of the Botanical Society of Edinburgh*, **37**: 163–173.

Spence, D.H.N. (1959) Studies on the vegetation of Shetland. II. Reasons for the restriction of the exclusive pioneers to serpentine debris. *Journal of Ecology*, **47**: 641–649.

Spence, D.H.N. (1960) Studies on the vegetation of Shetland. III. Scrub in Shetland and in South Uist, Outer Hebrides. *Journal of Ecology*, **48**: 73–95.

Spence, D.H.N. (1964) The macrophytic vegetation of lochs, swamps and associated fens. *In*: Burnett, J.H. (ed.), *The Vegetation of Scotland*: 306–415. Oliver & Boyd, Edinburgh.

Spence, D.H.N. (1970) Scottish serpentine vegetation. *Oikos*, **21**: 22–31.

Spence, D.H.N. (1974) Subarctic debris and scrub vegetation in Shetland. *In*: Goodier, R. (ed.), *The Natural Environment of Shetland*: 73–88. NCC, Edinburgh.

Spence, D.H.N. (1979) *Shetland's Living Landscape: a Study in Island Plant Ecology*. Thuleprint, Lerwick.

Spence, D.H.N. & Millar, E.A. (1963) An experimental study of the infertility of a Shetland serpentine soil. *Journal of Ecology*, **51**: 333–343.

Spence, J. (1899) *Shetland Folklore*. Johnson & Greig, Lerwick.

Stace, C. (1997) *New Flora of the British Isles*, 2nd edn. Cambridge University Press, Cambridge.

Stephen, A.C. (1929–30) Studies on the Scottish marine fauna: the fauna of the sandy and muddy areas of the tidal zone. *Transactions of the Royal Society of Edinburgh*, **56**: 219–306; 521–535.

Stewart, G.C. (1962) Kergord Plantations, Shetland. *Forestry*, **35**: 35–36.

Stewart, I. (1965) Shetland farm names. *In*: Small, A. (ed.), *Fourth Viking Congress*: 247–266. Oliver & Boyd, Edinburgh.

Stewart, J. (1954) Udal law and government in Shetland. *In*: Simpson, W.D. (ed.), *Viking Congress, Lerwick, July 1950*: 83–111. Oliver & Boyd, Edinburgh.

Stewart, J. (1987) *Shetland Place Names*. Shetland Times, Lerwick.

Stone, C.J. (1997) *Cetacean observations during seismic surveys in 1996*. JNCC Report No. 228. JNCC, Aberdeen.

Stone, C.J., Webb, A., Barton, C., Ratcliffe, N., Reed, T.C., Tasker, M.L., Camphuysen, C.J. & Pienkowski, M.W. (1995) *An Atlas of Seabird Distribution in north-west European waters*. JNCC, Peterborough.

Strange, I. (1972) *Falkland Islands*. David & Charles, Newton Abbot.

Suddaby, D. (1991) *Winter Seabird Monitoring Project Shetland, February/March 1991*. Unpublished report of NCC, Edinburgh.

Suddaby, D. & Ellis, P.M. (1994) *Winter Seabird Monitoring post MV* Braer *oil spill, Shetland: November 1993 to March 1994*. Unpublished report to RSPB, Bedford.

Sullom Voe Environmental Advisory Group (1976) *Oil Terminal at Sullom Voe: Environmental Impact Assessment*. Thuleprint, Lerwick.

Summers, C.F. (1978) Trends in the size of British grey seal populations. *Journal of Applied Ecology*, **15**: 395–400.

Summers, C.F., Bonner, W.N. & Van Haaften, J. (1978) Changes in the seal populations of the North Sea. *Rapp. P.-v. Reun. Couns. Int. Explor. Mer.*, **172**: 278–285.

Summers, R.W., Ellis, P.M. & Johnston, J.P. (1988) Waders on the coast of Shetland in winter: numbers and habitat preferences. *Scottish Birds*, **15**: 71–79.

Sutherland, G. (1933) Management and control of shipping around Shetland. *Marine Policy. The Journal of Oceanic Affairs*, **17**: 371–379.

Svardson, G. (1957) The 'invasion' type of bird migration. *British Birds*, **50**: 314–343.

Svensson, R. (1954) *Lonely Isles*. Faber, London.

Swan, M.A. (1957) Specimens of char from Shetland and the Faroes. *Scottish Naturalist*, **69**: 67–70.

Swan, M.A. (1964) The Girlsta Char. *New Shetlander*, **69**, 21–26.

Swan, W.B. & Senior, W.H. (1972) *Survey of Agriculture in Caithness, Orkney and Shetland*. HIDB Special Report No. 8. Highlands and Islands Development Board, Inverness.

Tait, E.S.R. (ed.) (1925) *The Statistical Account of Shetland 1791–1799*. Manson, Lerwick.

Tait, W. (1980) *Collected Poems*. P. Harris, Edinburgh.

Tallack, R.M. (1994) *The Non-marine Molluscs of Selected SSSIs in Shetland*. Unpublished report to SNH, Edinburgh.

Tallack, R.M. (1995) A list of the non-marine Mollusca of Shetland. *The Shetland Naturalist*, **4**: 93–100.

Tasker, M.L. & Pienkowski, M.W. (1986) *Vulnerable concentrations of birds in the North Sea*. NCC, Edinburgh.

Tasker, M.L., Webb, A., Hall, A.J., Pienkowski, M.W. & Langslow, D.R. (1986) *Seabirds in the North Sea*. NCC, Edinburgh.

Taylor, A.B. (1955) British and Irish place-names in Old Norse Literature. *In*: Falk, K. (ed.), *Annen Viking Kongress*: 113–122. University Press, Bergen.

Thom, V. (1986) *Birds in Scotland*. T. & A.D. Poyser, Calton.

Thompson, D.R., Hamer, K.C. & Furness, R.W. (1991) Mercury accumulation in Great Skuas *Cathartica skua* of known breeding age and sex, and its effect upon breeding and survival. *Journal of Applied Ecology*, **28**: 672–684.

Thompson, K.R., Brindley, E. & Heubeck, M. (1996) *Seabird numbers and breeding success in Britain and Ireland, 1995*. JNCC, RSPB & SOTEAG, Peterborough.

Thompson, K.R., Brindley, E. & Heubeck, M. (1997) *Seabird numbers and breeding success in Britain and Ireland, 1996*. JNCC, RSPB & SOTEAG, Peterborough.

Thomson, W.P.L. (1970) Funzie, Fetlar: a Shetland run-rig township in the nineteenth century. *Scottish Geographical Magazine*, **86**: 170–185.

Thorne, R. (1977) *Fetlar: Some Facts and Stories*. Bluebell, Cambridge.

Tickell, W.L.N. (1970) The exploitation and conservation of the Common Seal (*Phoca vitulina*) in Shetland. *Biological Conservation*, **2**: 179–184.

Time Management Consultancy (1995) *Shetland Visitor Survey*. Unpublished report of Shetland Islands Tourism, SIC and Shetland Enterprise, Lerwick.

Tonessen, J.N. & Johnsen, A.D. (1982) *The History of Modern Whaling*. Hurst, London.

Toyne, S.M. (1948) *The Scandinavians in History*. Arnold, London.

Traill, J.W.H. (1889–90) Revision of the Scotch Discomycetes. *Scottish Naturalist*, **10**: 125–142; 171–190; 220–223.

Traill, T.S. (1806) Observations chiefly mineralogical on the Shetland Islands made in the course of a tour through these islands in 1803. *Nicholson's Journal*, **15**: 353–367.

Tudor, J.R. (1883) *The Orkneys and Shetland: Their Past and Present State*. Stanford, London.

Tulinus, S. (1965) Personal communication cited by Mourant, A.E., Kopec, A.C. & Domaniewska-Sobozak, K. (1974) *The Distribution of the Human Blood Groups*, 2nd edn. Oxford University Press, Oxford.

Tulloch, R.J. (1967) Birds on Out Skerries, Shetland 1966. *Scottish Birds*, **4**: 467–480.

Tulloch, R.J. (1968) Snowy owls breeding in Shetland in 1967. *British Birds*, **61**: 119–132.

Tulloch, R.J. (1978) *A Guide to Shetland Mammals*. Shetland Times, Lerwick.

Tulloch, R.J. (1988) *Bobby Tulloch's Shetland*. Macmillan, London.

Tulloch, R.J. (1992) *A Guide to Shetland's Breeding Birds*. Shetland Times, Lerwick.

Tulloch, R.J. & Hunter, F. (1972) *A Guide to Shetland Birds*. Shetland Times, Lerwick.

Turner, V. (1993) *How to be a Detective. An Introduction to Shetland's Archaeology for Bairns of All Ages*. Shetland Amenity Trust, Lerwick.

Tyldesley, J.B. (1973) Long-range transmission of tree-pollen to Shetland. *New Phytologist*, **72**: 175–181; 183–190; 691–698.

Uttley, J.D., Walton, P., Monaghan, P. & Austin, G. (1993) The effects of food abundance on breeding performance and adult time budgets of Guillemots *Uria aalge*. *Ibis*, **136**: 205–211.

Vaughan, H. (1880) The micro-lepidoptera of the Shetland Isles. *Entomologist*, **12**: 291–292.

Vaughan, R.W. (1975) Seals in Orkney. *In*: Goodier, R. (ed.), *The Natural Environment of Orkney*: 95–97. NCC, Edinburgh.

Vaughan, R.W. (1977) A review of the status of the Common Seal *Phoca vitulina* in Scotland. *ICES Marine Mammals Committee*, **18**: 1–5.

Venables, L.S.V. & Venables, U.M. (1948) A Shetland bird population: Kergord Plantations. *Journal of Animal Ecology*, **17**: 66–74.

Venables, L.S.V. & Venables, U.M. (1950a) The corncrake on Shetland. *British Birds*, **43**: 137–141.

Venables. L.S.V. & Venables, U.M. (1950b) The whooper swans of Loch Spiggie, Shetland. *Scottish Naturalist*, **62**: 142–152.

Venables, L.S.V. & Venables, U.M. (1952) The Blackbird in Shetland. *Ibis*, **94**: 636–653.

Venables, L.S.V. & Venables, U.M. (1955) *The Birds and Mammals of Shetland*. Oliver & Boyd, Edinburgh.

Venables, U.M. (1952) *Tempestuous Eden*. Museum, London.

Venables, U.M. (1956) *Life in Shetland. A World Apart*. Oliver & Boyd, Edinburgh.

Venables, U.M. & Venables, L.S.V. (1955) Observations on a breeding colony of the seal *Phoca vitulina* in Shetland. *Proceedings of the Zoological Society of London*, **125**: 521–532.

Venables, U.M. & Venables, L.S.V. (1957) Mating behaviour of the seal *Phoca vitulina* in Shetland. *Proceedings of the Zoological Society of London*, **128**: 387–396.

Venables, U.M. & Venables, L.S.V. (1959) Vernal coition of the seal *Phoca vitulina* in Shetland. *Proceedings of the Zoological Society of London*, **132**: 665–669.

Verspoor, E., Wright, P.J. & Mitchell, A. (1994) Part III. Population structure in the lesser sandeel, *Ammodytes marinus*, in Scottish waters. *In*: *The Impact of the* Braer *Oil Spill on Sandeel Availability to Seabirds around Shetland*. SOAFED, Marine Laboratory, Aberdeen.

Wace, N. (1960) The botany of the southern oceanic islands. *Proceedings of the Royal Society of London B*, **152**: 575–590.

Wainwright, F.T. (1962a) Picts and Scots. *In*: Wainwright, F.T. (ed.), *The Northern Isles*: 91–116. Nelson, Edinburgh.

Wainwright, F.T. (1962b) The Scandinavian settlement. *In*: Wainwright, F.T. (ed.), *The Northern Isles*: 117–162. Nelson, Edinburgh.

Walsh, P.M., Avery, M. & Heubeck, M. (1990) *Seabird numbers and breeding success in 1989*. CSD report. NCC, Edinburgh.

Walsh, P.M., Sears, J. & Heubeck, M. (1991) *Seabird numbers and breeding success in 1990*. CSD report. NCC, Edinburgh.

Walsh, P.M., Sim, I. & Heubeck, M. (1992) *Seabird numbers and breeding success in Britain and Ireland, 1991*. JNCC, RSPB & SOTEAG, Peterborough.

Walsh, P.M., Sim, I. & Heubeck, M. (1993) *Seabird numbers and breeding success in Britain and Ireland, 1992*. JNCC, RSPB & SOTEAG, Peterborough.

Walsh, P.M., Brindley, E. & Heubeck, M. (1994) *Seabird numbers and breeding successs in Britain and Ireland, 1993.* JNCC & RSPB & SOTEAG, Peterborough.

Walsh, P.M., Brindley, E. & Heubeck, M. (1995) *Seabird numbers and breeding success in Britain and Ireland, 1994.* JNCC, RSPB & SOTEAG, Peterborough.

Wanless, S. (1987) *A survey of the numbers and breeding distribution of the North Atlantic gannet* (Sula bassana) *and an assessment of the changes which have occurred since Operation Seafarer 1969/71.* Research and Survey in Nature Conservation 4. NCC, Edinburgh.

Warren, A. & Harrison, C.M. (1974) *A proposed nature conservation plan for Shetland.* Discussion Paper in Conservation No. 7. University College, London.

Waterston, G. (1937) Scottish Naturalist, 25–31.

Waterston, G. (1946) Fair Isle. *Scottish Geographical Magazine,* **62**: 111–116.

Watling, R. (1992) *The Fungus Flora of Shetland.* Royal Botanic Gardens, Edinburgh.

Watling, R. (1994) Larger fungi of Shetland and their habitats. *The Shetland Naturalist,* **1**: 6–11.

Watson, H. (1978) *Coastal Otters in Shetland.* Privately printed.

Watt, A.S. & Jones, E.W. (1948) The ecology of the Cairngorms. I. The environment and the altitudinal zonation of the vegetation. *Journal of Ecology,* **36**: 283–304.

Waugh, D. (ed.) (1996) *Shetland's Northern Links, Language and History.* Scottish Society for Northern Studies, Lerwick.

Weir, D.N., McGowan, R.Y., Kitchener, A.C., McOrist, S. & Heubeck, M. (1996) Effects of oil spills and shooting on Great Northern Divers which winter in Scotland. *Dansk Ornitologisk Forenings Tiddskrift,* **90**: 29–33.

Weir, J.J. (1880) The macrolepidoptera of the Shetland Isles. *Entomologist,* **13**: 249–251; 289–291.

Welch, S.G. & Mears, G.W. (1972) Genetic variants of human indophenol oxidase in the Westray Island of the Orkneys. *Human Heredity,* **22**: 38–41.

Welch, S.G., Barry, J.V., Dodd, B.E., Griffiths, P.D., Huntsman, R.G., Jenkins, C.G., Lincoln, P.J., McCathie, M., Mears, G.W. & Parr, C.W. (1973) A survey of blood groups, serum protein and red cell enzyme polymorphisms in the Orkney Islands. *Human Heredity,* **23**: 230–240.

West, J.F. (1972) *Faroe, the Emergence of a Nation.* Hurst, London.

West, W. (1912) Notes on the flora of Shetland with some ecological observations. *Journal of Botany, London,* **1**: 265–275; 297–306.

West, W. & West, T.G.S. (1904) Freshwater algae from the Orkneys and Shetlands. *Transactions of the Botanical Society of Edinburgh,* **23**: 3–41.

Westoll, T.S. (1937) Old red sandstone fishes of the north of Scotland, particular by Orkney and Shetland. *Proceedings of the Geologists Association,* **48**: 13–45.

White, F.B. (1882) The Lepidoptera of Orkney, Shetland and the Outer Hebrides. *Scottish Naturalist,* **6**: 289–291; 337–344.

Whittington, G. (1980) A sub-peat dyke on Shurton Hill, Mainland, Shetland. *Proceedings of the Society of Antiquaries of Scotland,* **109**: 30–35.

Whittington, G. & Edwards, K.G. (1993) Vegetation changes on Papa Stour, Shetland, Scotland: a response to coastal evolution and human interference. *The Holocene,* **3**: 54–62.

Whittle, A. (ed.) (1986) *Scord of Brouster. An Early Agricultural Settlement on Shetland.* Oxford University Press, Oxford.

Wickham-Jones, C.R. (1994) *Scotland's First Settlers.* Batsford/Historic Scotland, London.

Williamson, K. (1948) *Atlantic Islands.* Collins, London.

Williamson, K. (1951a) The wrens of Fair Isle. *Ibis,* **93**: 599–601.

Williamson, K. (1951b) The moorland birds of Unst, Shetland. *Scottish Naturalist,* **63**: 37–43.

Williamson, K. (1958a) Population and breeding environment of the St Kilda and Fair Isle wrens. *British Birds,* **51**: 369–393.

Williamson, K. (1958b) Bergmann's rule and obligatory overseas migration. *British Birds,* **51**: 209–232.

Williamson, K. (1965) *Fair Isle and its Birds.* Oliver & Boyd, Edinburgh.

Williamson, K. & Spencer, R. (1960) Ringing recoveries and the interpretation of bird movements. *Bird Migration,* **1**: 176–181.

Wills, J. (1978) *The Lands of Garth. A Short History of Calback Ness.* Shetland Times, Lerwick.

Wills, J. (1991) *A Place in the Sun: Shetland and Oil, Myths and Realities.* Mainstream, Edinburgh.

Wills, J. & Warner, K. (1993) *Innocent Passage. The Wreck of the Tanker Braer.* Mainstream, Edinburgh.

Wilson, G.V. & Knox, J. (1936) The geology of the Orkney and Shetland Isles. *Proceedings of the Geologists Association,* **47**: 270–282.

Wilson, M. & Henderson, D.M. (1966) *British Rust Fungi.* Cambridge University Press, Cambridge.

Wolff, N.L. (1971) Lepidoptera. *Zoology Iceland,* **3**(45): 1–193.

Wright, P.J. (1995) Is there a conflict between sandeel fisheries and seabirds? A case study at Shetland. *In*: Greenstreet, S. & Tasker, M. (eds), *Aquatic Predators and their Prey.* Blackwell, Oxford.

Wright, P.J. & Bailey, M.C. (1993) *Biology of sandeels in the vicinity of seabird colonies in Shetland.* Fisheries Research Report 15/93. SOAFED, Aberdeen.

Yeats, G.K. (1948) *Bird Haunts in Northern Britain.* Faber, London.

Zetland County Council (1974) *Sullom Voe District Plan.* ZCC Planning Dept, Lerwick.

Ziegler, P.A. (1978) North-western Europe: tectonics and basin development. *Geologie en Mejnbouw,* **57**: 589–626.

APPENDIX 1

Places to Visit

Otter

Approximately 100 sites and walks have been listed, aiming at the best examples of as many of the features, ecosystems and habitats as possible. They are arranged roughly from north to south, although the smaller islands are left out of this regular sequence (see Fig. 40). It is advisable, particularly on the longer and more rugged walks, to wear proper clothing and footwear, to take a map and compass, and to inform someone at the place of residence of one's intended route and time of return. Be extra cautious on the cliffs, especially on windy days. Walkers should follow the normal countryside code with respect to gates, fences and dykes and should familiarize themselves with the laws concerning the disturbance of nesting birds, including those regulating photography of certain protected species. In this respect, the local officers of SNH or RSPB will be able to help. They can be contacted through the Information Centre in Lerwick (see below). Because so much grazing is unfenced and because many birds nest on open moorland, pets must be kept under particularly strict control.

There is a wonderful tradition of freedom of access in Shetland, almost unique in the British Isles, but it is both good manners and good practice to seek advice and permission before entering agricultural land. NNRs are open to the public, but it should be remembered that other designations do not give automatic public access rights.

Shetlanders are proud of their environment and many are very knowledgeable about their wildlife; a great deal can be learned from a few minutes' conversation.

Maps

Shetland is covered by Sheets 1–4 of the Ordnance Survey 1:50 000 series: Yell and Unst; Whalsay; North Mainland; South Mainland (including Foula and Fair Isle). Shetland is contained within a single sheet, at 1:128 000, produced by Shetland Islands Tourism.

There are also the following geological (solid and drift) maps available from the Geological Survey: Yell, Scotland Sheet 130; Central Shetland, Scotland Sheet 128; Northern Shetland, Scotland Sheets 130 and 131; Western Shetland, Scotland Sheet 127; and Southern Shetland, Scotland Sheet 126.

Getting about in Shetland

Bus services in Shetland are infrequent, with the exception of those running between the two main towns of Lerwick and Scalloway. An 'overland' bus runs on most days from Lerwick via the inter-island ferries to Yell and Unst.

Regular vehicle ferries run between the larger islands of Mainland, Bressay, Yell, Whalsay, Unst and Fetlar. Other boat services run from Mainland to Fair Isle, Foula, Papa Stour, Mousa, and Out Skerries.

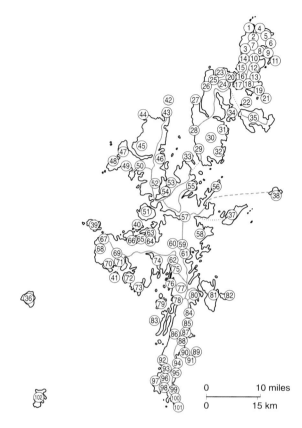

FIGURE 40   *Places to visit.*

Unless experienced, it is hazardous to navigate oneself in Shetland waters due to dangers from rapid changes of weather and strong tides.

Scheduled air services operate between the main airport of Sumburgh and Tingwall, Whalsay, Unst and Fair Isle; it is possible to charter a plane to Foula, Papa Stour or Out Skerries.

Information about travel and accommodation within the islands, and on boat-trips and wildlife tours, can be obtained from Shetland Islands Tourism, Market Cross, Lerwick, Shetland ZE1 OLU (tel. Lerwick 693434) . Information on NNRs and on open days can be obtained from SNH (tel. Lerwick 693345) and on the RSPB Reserves from their office at Sumburgh Lighthouse (tel. Sumburgh 460800).

UNST

1 *Herma Ness (NNR)* (HP 600160)

A peninsula approximately 4.8 km by 1.6 km, with cliffs rising from 60–150 m with stacks and skerries, overlooking Muckle Flugga and North Stack. The latter is the most northerly part of the British Isles. With the cliffs of Saxavord it has one of the largest seabird colonies in Britain, including gannet, guillemot, razorbill, kittiwake, an immense number of puffins, and both *bonxie* and arctic skuas. Grey and harbour seals breed around the coast in small numbers. Glacial meltwater overflow channel at the car park. Part of Shetland's National Scenic Area (NSA) with spectacular cliffs. A rugged walk. There is a small SNH visitor centre at the old lighthouse base and there is a leaflet available.

2. *Burrafirth* (HP 615140)

Beach and machair system of muscovite sands with garnet–magnetite sands at the east end of the beach, physiographically unique to Shetland. Gradation from beach to machair grassland without the presence of dunes, controlled by a complex interrelationship of past and present fluvial, marine and aeolian processes.

3. *Loch of Cliff* (HP 600120)

Formed by the barrier of sand. A mesotrophic loch and minor wintering wildfowl site. Washing area for Hermaness seabirds. At the southern end, the effect of a crystalline limestone band on the vegetation can be recognized.

4. *Saxa Vord* (HP 630165)

Fourth highest hill in Shetland. The coastline on the west and north (part of the NSA) of this large block of chloritoid schist is heavily eroded and has a continuation of the puffin, guillemot and kittiwake colonies of Herma Ness, with *bonxies* and arctic skuas on the moorland. Fine view on a good day.

5. *Nor Wick* (HP 650148)

Excellent exposure of the fault between the Saxa Vord schists and the Clibberswick serpentinites at the Taing of Nor Wick. Sand dunes support the only Shetland site for the sea pea. To the south of the dunes and the road, and extending almost as far as Haroldswick, the Norwick Meadows are one of the best and most extensive examples of a species-rich Shetland marsh. The 1-km square at Norwick has one of the greatest variety of breeding birds in the county.

6. *Cross Geo* (HP 652122)

Mylonite–steatite seperating the Clibberswick serpentinite from the underlying Lower Nappe. Serpentinite well exposed on beach at back of *geo* and adjacent steatite quarry.

7. *Crussa Field and The Heogs* (HP 625105)

Herb-rich sedge-grassland of serpentinite heath supporting a wide range of attractive and restricted plants and supporting 17 bird species, including almost one-tenth of Britain's whimbrel population and important numbers of arctic skuas. The quarry at Quoys has the largest exposure of talc in Britain. These serpentinites, which weather to form the distinctive ochrous rocks, are slices of the earth's mantle upthrust 500 million years ago when two parts of the old continental plate collided.

8. *Nikkavord* (HP 627104) *and Hagdale* (HP 640103)

Disused chromite quarries. Best sites for studying these ore deposits in Britain.

9. *Keen of Hamar* (*NNR*) (HP 643099)

The finest example of serpentinite debris vegetation in Europe, supporting Edmondston's chickweed among a number of other attractive and rare arctic–alpine plants, and exhibiting active periglacial stone stripes on fellfield at its lowest altitude in the British Isles. There is a leaflet available.

10. *Baltasound* (HP 630085)

Minor seaduck, diver and grebe site. Good salt marsh at the head of the sound. Halligarth plantation adjacent at HP 625093.

11. *Balta Island* (HP 660080)

A highly eroding beach–machair continuum covering most of the island.

12. *Hill of Colvadale* (HP 620060) *and Sobul* (HP 605040)

Metagabbro rocks supporting both a herb-rich sedge-grass heath and species-poor dwarf-shrub heath, giving way on the higher slopes to a woolly-moss heath. Supports an outstanding diversity of wader species, including almost one-tenth of Britain's whimbrel population, as well as important numbers of arctic skuas.

There are also several of Shetland's restricted plant species. A good place to see Shetland ponies and greylag geese. The gabbro rocks of this area were the oceanic crust that overlay the mantle rocks (serpentinite) upthrust 500 million years ago.

13. *Sand Wick (Eastings)* (HP 620020)

Severely deflated dune and machair area representing a late stage in the evolution of this type of system. The erosion, which is relatively recent, has uncovered a Viking site. Muness Castle nearby at HP 630010.

14. *Valla Field* (HP 585050)

High and rugged walk from the Westing to Herma Ness over acidic dwarf-shrub heaths. Excellent view of the effects of the various rocks of Unst on the vegetation. Rocks rich in garnet, kyanite and staurolite along crest of ridge.

15. *The Westing* (HP 575060)

Example of effect of limestone band. Compare flora with that of the acid gneisses to the west and on Valla Field, and of the serpentinites towards the main road (A968) to the east. Adjacent to site of archaeological interest at Underhoull (HP 576041).

16. *Lunda Wick* (HP 570040)

Limited sand-blow site. Coastal cliffs with exposures through metasomatically zoned ultrabasic bodies; classical locality for their study.

17. *Loch of Snarravoe* (HP 570015)

Wintering wildfowl site for tufted and goldeneye among others. Coarse chloritoid–garnet schists with best roche moutonnées in Shetland.

18. *Easter Loch* (HP 598013)

A small brackish loch cut off from the sea by a shingle barrier bar. Important wintering wildfowl site for whooper swan, tufted duck and goldeneye.

19. *Mu Ness* (HP 638006)

Serpentinite Upper Nappe thrust over metagabbro with sheeted dykes.

20. *Bluemull Sound* (HP 555000)

Very large passage of seabirds from Hermaness through to the east and back, particularly in winter and early spring. Both *dunter* and *tystie* flocks can be seen in the winter months, occasionally very large. A site where killer whales can sometimes be seen.

21. *Haaf Gruney* (HU 635983)

A small uninhabited but fertile grassy holm with a flora resembling that of other areas of serpentinite rock on Unst. Breeding ground of *dunter*, *tystie*, storm petrel and larger gulls. Favourite haul-out site for grey and harbour seals in summer months.

22. *Islands between Unst and Fetlar*

Small attractive grassy holms similar to Haaf Gruney.

YELL

23. *Breckon* (HP 529052)

The largest area of blown shell sand in the islands, important for the unusual assemblage of accreting dunes and severely deflated hill machair. Supports several plants otherwise rare in Shetland and is the only Shetland station for bog orchid. Includes the tiny eutrophic Kirk Loch, which is Yell's most important wintering wildfowl site.

24. *Cullivoe* (HP 540030)

Beautiful example of traditional crofting area with herb-rich meadows.

25. *Gloup* (HP 505050)

Isolated and attractive deep Shetland voe, with several mid-bay bars – a partly drowned glacial meltwater channel cut through watershed.

26. *Gloup* (HP 505050) *to Whalefirth* (HU 480930)

A 13–16 km walk along attractive cliff. From Bratta (HU 475990) to Ramna Geo (HU 470967) is a 3.2-km stretch of cliffs where the coarse garnet-rich gneiss is cut by spectacular pegmatite veins with mica crystals. Few seabirds other than the *maalie*.

27. *Nev of Stuis* (HU 460970)

Rugged walk to the site of one of the last sea eagle eyries in Shetland at Erne Stack.

28. *West Sandwick* (HU 446890)

Small and attractive dune and machair complex, although unfortunately the machair area has been worked for sand and much disturbed. Red streaks of garnet visible in the sand. To landward are hay meadows.

29. *Ness of Sound* (HU 450825)

Excellent example of large, undisturbed, shingle double tombolo.

30. *Alin Knowes* (HU 509813) *(Lumbister SSSI)*

Deep, eroded blanket peat with innumerable lochs and lochans; *raingeese*, skuas and waders, including whimbrel.

31. *White Hill* (HU 547890)

Two small and easily accessible kittiwake colonies.

32. *Horse of Burravoe* (HU 535813)

Kittiwake, guillemot and puffin colonies.

33. *Yell Sound Islands*

Puffin and possibly storm petrel colonies, harbour seals and roosting for wintering wildfowl. The area is important for wintering eider, long-tailed duck, great northern divers and *tysties*.

34. *Hascosay* (HU 555925)

Attractive little island between Yell and Fetlar with cross-section of Shetland breeding birds, including *raingeese*, *bonxies* and arctic skuas and one of the highest densities of dunlin in the islands. It also has a very large harbour seal haul-out. However its main interest is its fine undisturbed peatland, which is the best example of Shetland's blanket bog, making it the 'type-site' in the national series of mires.

FETLAR, FOULA AND OTHER ISLANDS OUTWITH MAINLAND

35. *Fetlar* (HU 600900)

Part RSPB Reserve. An extremely diverse island. The greater part of the geology is serpentinite, supporting many breeding waders on herb-rich sedge-grasslands and heath composed of a great diversity of flowering plants. There are also sedge-mires, maritime heaths and lichen heaths. Breeding birds include one-fifth of Britain's population of whimbrel. There are also skuas, *tirricks* and *raingeese*. Perhaps the most important species is the red-necked phalarope, whose small population represents at least three-quarters of Britain's breeding population. A band of gneiss forms Lamb Hoga on the south-east headland with heather moorland and blanket bog. The latter supports several wader species, notably a high density of dunlin, *raingeese* and skuas. On the cliffs of Lamb Hoga are kittiwake, guillemot, puffin and storm petrel colonies. At the foot of the north-eastern cliffs are small grey seal colonies and on the surrounding skerries and holms many sites for the harbour seal. Papil Water, impounded by a barrier bar, is a minor wintering wildfowl site. The east end of Fetlar is formed of deformed quartzite conglomerate best seen between Staves Geo and The Snap (HU 655885). At Tressa Ness (HU 618948) are veins of rodingite, a very rare garnet-rich rock. A wonderful island on which to walk.

36. *Foula* (HT 960400)

The most spectacular island in Shetland (part of the NSA), both for its topography and immense number of seabirds, including one of Britain's largest colony of *bonxies*. Another notable seabird is Leach's petrel, whose breeding was confirmed only a few years ago. In all, Foula supports some 18 breeding seabird species. The Old Red Sandstone cliffs rise on the western coast to 370 m at The Kame of Foula, and dip to the south with an unconformity at Smallie. The Kame cliffs are precipitous and can justly be regarded as second in the British Isles only to those of St Kilda. Access from Walls.

37. *Whalsay* (HU 560640)

Important island for migrant birds with many lochs, marshes and a wader *houb* at Kirk Ness (HU 553655) formed from three tombolos. Small kittiwake and puffin colony at the southern extremity. Harbour seals breed on the surrounding holms.

38. *Out Skerries*

Extremely attractive group of little islands with a band of crystalline limestone; probably has as many migrants as Fair Isle. Small colonies of eider, *tystie*, gulls and *tirricks*.

39. *Papa Stour* (HU 167609)

An island of basaltic lavas and tuffs of Old Red Sandstone, the disparity in hardness of which has been eroded by the sea to produce the most impressive series of caves, stacks and arches in Britain. The caves themselves are formed from volcanic rhyolite and basalt. There are also small seabird colonies and breeding harbour seals. The 'scalped' lichen-rich heathland usually supports large *tirrick* colonies. The flat nature of the island makes for easy walking. The Ve Skerries to the west support one of Shetland's largest grey seal colonies. Access from West Burrafirth.

40. *Vementry* (HU 300600)

Rugged and extremely attractive little island of deep heather; few seabirds except *maalies*, *tysties* and gulls. Several lochs with divers and on the coast harbour seals.

41. *Vaila* (HU 230460)

A compact island with a good cross-section of Shetland seabirds. Granite and Old Red Sandstone contact in cliffs; thermal metamorphism, caves and stacks.

42. *Ramna Stacks* (HU 380970)

A forbidding and impressive group of stacks with guillemots, kittiwakes and a small colony of Leach's petrel. The associated island of Gruney has a grey seal colony

MAINLAND

43. *Fethaland* (HU 375945)

A beautiful peninsula of gneiss and schists with a band of serpentinite giving rise to a herb-rich grassland, partly maritime. One of the few sites for the early flowering purple saxifrage. Seabirds passing from the south-west to and from the colonies of Unst can be seen from here. An added interest is the presence of picturesque ruins of a *haaf* fishing station. Easy walking.

44. *Uyea Isle* (HU 310930)

A small undisturbed sand tombolo, under water at high tide, connects the island to the mainland. Small colonies of guillemots, puffins and kittiwakes among others. Grey seals breed here in late autumn. The coast from Uyea to Fethaland has important exposures of Lewisian, Moine and Dalradian rocks. A long walk. To the south at Fugla Ness is an exposure of mid and late Pleistocene (interglacial) peat, which has provided evidence of the vegetation of that period.

45. *Ronas Hill and North Roe* (HU 315845)

This is a remote mountain area of red granite of great interest on account of its virtually undisturbed periglacial features, including active and relict wind- and frost-patterned ground, turf-banked terraces, wind stripes, hill dunes and blockfields. Of the 25 arctic–alpine plants that occur in Shetland 15 can be found on the Ronas Hill fellfield. On the southern coast, which drops dramatically to Ronas Voe, and on some of the loch holms to the north of the hill are some of the best examples of relict scrub. At Heylor (HU 290810) and on the opposite northern shore of Ronas Voe are fine examples of looped bars, and the voe itself is well known for its April population of great northern divers and occasional king eider. The voe is an extremely scenic fiord in red granite.

On the western coast, steeply eroding cliffs, backed by crevasses parallel to the coast, due to land sliding from Stonga Banks to Valla Kames have given rise to two remote and utterly unspoilt granite shingle beaches, each almost 1.6 km long. This has also produced an impressive series of arches and stacks. At Hevdadale (HU 310890) is a grey seal colony, but both seal species may be seen on this coast. The topography just to the north of Ronas Hill consists of incipient corries with ice-moulded, oligotrophic lochs (e.g. Roer Water HU 340860) and roche moutonnées that give way to the North Roe plateau dominated by *Racomitrium* moss, with interesting features such as peat cones. The numerous peaty lochans and pools of North Roe support the second highest breeding density of *raingeese* in Britain and there are also skuas and waders. On the holms of some of the lochs and on inaccessible crag ledges are good examples of Shetland's relict trees and scrub. This is the largest wilderness area in Shetland with extremely rugged, but highly rewarding, walking.

46. *Ollaberry* (HU 370810)

An attractive crofting area on a small area of limestone. At the Back of Ollaberry is the best example of a major tear fault in the British Isles, the Walls Boundary Fault, which itself is a continuation of the Great Glen Fault in Scotland. At Gluss (HU 370775) is a fine shingle tombolo.

47. *Villians of Hamnavoe* (HU 240824) *and Tingon* (HU 255840)

This section of coastline, exposed to the full force of the North Atlantic, shows some of the best examples of the power of storm waves in Britain. A 'shelved' storm beach has been formed along the junction between andesite tuffs and lavas of Middle Old Red Sandstone: at one point at over 18 m above sea level. The rocks are well jointed so that sections are removed in blocks and cubes, giving deep rectangular shafts. At the northern end, there is a stairway inlet and waterfall and an immature blow-hole. Inland from the coast is another excellent example of undisturbed blanket bog (Tingon) with innumerable pools that support a high density of *raingeese* and waders including whimbrel. Magnificent views from the northern coast to Ronas Hill.

48. *Eshaness* (HU 209790)

Cliffs of Old Red Sandstone with fine exposures of volcanic rocks including basaltic and andesite tuffs, lavas and ignumbrites. At the Villians of Ure (HU 213800) is the spectacular stairway inlet and storm beach of the Grind of Navir and just to the south the Holes of Scraada, a collapsed blow-hole. At Eshaness, Stenness (HU 214772) and Dore Holm (HU 220762) there are guillemot and kittiwake colonies. At the Loch of Houlland (HU 215790) there is the remains of a broch and *tirrick* colonies. At Stenness there are the ruins of the *haaf* fishing station and a shingle beach. Overall, low cliff with beautiful maritime grassland and easy walking.

49. *Heads of Grocken* (HU 265775) *and The Neap* (HU 255775)

Eroded red granite cliffs with series of stacks and arches, and a cliff-foot sand beach. Cormorant colony at The Runk. The spectacular stacks called The Drongs (HU 260755) at Hillswick can be seen from here.

50. *Urafirth* (HU 300788)

Fine example of a shingle barrier, with the beautiful oyster plant.

51. *Muckle Roe* (HU 320650)

Extremely rugged cliffed coast of granite, with isolated and abandoned settlement at South Ham and cormorant colonies at Grusterwick (HU 296648) and Erne Stack (HU 304672). Inland the heather moorland makes for tough but dry walking, with occasional juniper, bearberry and honeysuckle.

52. *Sullom* (HU 350728)

One of the best examples of the 1950s forestry plots. At Haggrister (HU 349701) fine salt marsh and looped bar. Magnetite scarn deposit.

53. *Sullom Voe* (HU 380740)

Good wintering populations of eider, long-tailed duck, great northern diver, velvet scoters and grebes. At the Houb of Scatsta (HU 395730), opposite the oil terminal, fine wader feeding area.

54. *Burn of Valayre* (HU 369693)

Accessible ravine with ungrazed relict scrub vegetation high on the sides, rowan, honeysuckle, dog-rose and willows.

55. *The Houb* (HU 449723)

Composite sand and shingle tombolo connects the island of Fora Ness to the mainland and forms a voe to the north with a mid-bay bar and a bay-head bar. Provides an interesting variant to the sand tombolos and shingle bars in the rest of Shetland. Fine example of drowned peat on the shores, while the tombolo usually has a *tirrick* colony.

56. *Lunna Ness* (HU 500700)

Fine example of ice-moulded topography with tombolos and bay-mouth bar at West Lunna Voe (HU 480690), plus tombolo at Hamna Voe (HU 495714). The former was the site of the Shetland Bus in the Second World War (Howarth, 1951). Harbour seal colony at Lunna Holm (HU 528750). Fine walking on the Ness with many lochs and lochans supporting *raingeese*. Further interest in the old chapel at Lunna (HU 485691) and Stanes of Stofast, the largest erratic in Shetland. Many exposures of the spectacular Val Ayre microcline–porphyroblast gneiss.

57. *Voe* (HU 410630)

Scenically attractive with limestone band and associated flora on the south approach from Aith.

58. *Dury Voe* (HU 455630) *to Dales Voe* (HU 450450)

Large coastal strip with wide variety of depositional features typical of Shetland, including tombolos at

Skellister, Eswick Holm, Little Holm (HU 475548, HU 483530, HU 448530); a double tombolo at Railsborough (HU 456523); barrier bars at Lingness, Aswick and Wadbister (HU 490550, HU 474529, HU 430500); mid-bay bars at Dury (HU 460605); bay-head bars at Laxo, Dury, Wadbister and Dales Voe (HU 450634, HU 460605, HU 430500, HU 438438); looped bar at Stavaness (HU 510600). The last site has a fine large and rounded boulder beach. Lingness may be the only pure shell sand beach in Shetland. The South Nesting area is a particularly attractive example of crofting townships on a crystalline limestone band. The Loch of Benston (HU 460535) is a wintering wildfowl site. At Catfirth (HU 439538) is a good example of an ungrazed limestone flora in the ravine and one of only two sites for native hazel. The bay of Catfirth is a wintering seaduck, diver and grebe site.

59. *Sandwater* (HU 415547)

Relatively shallow loch, surrounded by acidic dwarf-shrub heath, strongly influenced by underlying band of crystalline limestone; breeding and wintering wildfowl. Also noted for large bed of common bulrush, unusual in Shetland.

60. *Kergord* (HU 395540)

Series of mixed coniferous and broad-leaved shelterbelts, first established early in the century and added to since; makes up the largest and longest established woodland in Shetland and provides a habitat for woodland flora and breeding birds including rook and woodpigeon and occasionally tree sparrow, goldcrest and fieldfare, among other woodland species. Excellent site for migrant and wintering woodland and shrub birds. The Burn of Weisdale is one of the few Shetland salmon rivers. There are fluvio-glacial mounds, and a large landslide scar (HU 385524) is visible on the east side of Weisdale Hill overlooking the voe.

61. *Girlsta* (HU 433522)

Deepest Shetland loch (25 m) lying on a band of crystalline limestone and the only Shetland site for the arctic char. Also noted for its large brown trout.

62. *Weisdale Voe* (HU 380490)

Wintering site for goldeneye, tufted duck, divers and grebes and also local mergansers. Last site of a pilot whale *caa*.

63. *Loch of Clousta* (HU 315582)

Islands in the loch provide an interesting comparison of grazed and ungrazed vegetation; several islands support relict Shetland scrub.

64. *Clousta* (HU 310575) *to Vementry* (HU 310600)

Attractive and relatively easy area for walking on the coast and inland. Compare vegetation of Vementry gneiss and schists with that of the sandstones of the Walls peninsula.

65. *Brindister* (HU 287570) *and The Vadills* (HU 290550)

Salt-water and brackish wintering wildfowl site with exceptional marine flora and fauna. Tombolos at The Vadills.

66. *West Burrafirth* (HU 260575) *to Brindister* (HU 287570)

Attractive and relatively easy walk from the limestone band at Burrafirth, past the deserted crofts at Whalwick (HU 258584), to the Neeans (HU 273596). Varied coastal scenery with maritime and acid grasslands.

67. *Sandness* (HU 200570)

The crofting area of Sandness lies on schists and gneiss (compare with surrounding hills of sandstone). At Melby (HU 195576) and Norby (HU 200577), barrier bars of sand block off the wintering wildfowl lochs. To the east are other wintering wildfowl sites at the Loch of Collaster (HU 210574) and the Ness Lochs (HU 217578). The latter lie on gneiss and crystalline limestone whose rugged topography is quite distinct from the rest of Sandness and the surrounding hills. The last group of lochs have breeding tufted duck. On the road above Collaster and further east to Bousta are small but excellent examples of unimproved herb-rich dwarf-shrub heaths.

68. *Sandness* (HU 200570) *to Dale* (HU 180530)

Rugged coastal walk with high cliffs and deep valleys. Sandness Hill (250 m) has relict periglacial features. Interglacial till at Sel Ayre.

69. *Walls Peninsula*

Almost 52 km^2 of relatively easy hill walking on the Old Red Sandstone hills. Innumerable lochs with *raingeese* and occasional common scoter, and very occasionally with exotic water-lilies, the last notably at Lunga Water (HU 235525) and Stanevatstoe (HU 217545).

70. *Wats Ness* (HU 170510) *to Walls* (HU 240490)

Undemanding walk along an extremely varied and attractive coast with views of Foula. Waders on the coastal heath and *tirricks* at Footabrough.

71. *Kirkigarth* (HU 238497) *and Bardister* (HU 238502)

Two mesotrophic lochs with a wide range of aquatic flora; important wintering wildfowl sites.

72. *Culswick Marsh* (HU 273445) *and Ward of Culswick* (HU 268463)

The largest undisturbed mesotrophic marsh in Shetland, evolved from a partially drained loch in a deep valley bottom and cut off from the sea by a barrier bar. An uncommon habitat in Shetland. It is noted for its yellow iris–water horsetail community. The short heath of the Ward of Culswick supports whimbrel and arctic skuas.

73. *Culswick* (HU 274448) *to Reawick* (HU 330450)

Spectacular and relatively easy cliff walk on maritime grasslands on red granite. Cormorants at Clett Stack (HU 293414) and small kittiwake colonies at Westerwick (HU 280420) and Skelda Ness (HU 303405). Beaches at Westerwick, Skeld and Reawick of red granite shingle and sand.

74. *Bixter Voe* (HU 330520) *and Tresta Voe* (HU 350510)

Good wintering and migrant site for seaduck, divers and grebes. Kaolinite at Sandsound and in Burn of Tactigill.

75. *Loch of Strom* (HU 400490)

Largest brackish loch in the county, grading into fresh water at Stromfirth. Wintering wildfowl.

76. *South White Ness* (HU 385445)

The largest continuous area of crystalline limestone outcrop in Shetland, supporting a fine limestone flora and containing the only marl loch in the county. There is a fine salt marsh at The Hoove (HU 393461) with breeding common and black-headed gulls. The vegetation of the peninsula makes a striking comparison with that of the adjacent Strom Ness, which is composed mainly of acidic metamorphic rocks. The head of Whiteness Voe is also noted for its rich marine flora and fauna.

77. *Lochs of Tingwall* (HU 415425) *and Asta* (HU 413415)

Two easily accessible mesotrophic lochs lying in one of the main crystalline limestone valleys. The lochs are noted for their diverse aquatic flora and wintering wildfowl, including whooper swans and pochard. There are breeding tufted duck and in very recent years the lochs have also, uniquely, supported breeding mute and whooper swans.

78. *East Voe of Scalloway* (HU 395385)

Seaduck site where occasional king eider recorded.

79. *Scalloway Islands* (HU 360400)

Extremely attractive, varied and peaceful little islands with a good variety of breeding birds and harbour seals.

80. *Clickkimin* (HU 465410)

Nearest wintering wildfowl site to Lerwick. The barrier bar blocking this loch from the sea is now disguised by the road. Added interest provided by the Broch of Clickhimin.

81. *Bressay* (HU 500400)

Relatively easy walking on heather moorland with waders and skuas. Old Red Sandstone cliffs, with magnificent caves, rising to 150 m on the southern coast.

82. *Noss (NNR)* (HU 542405)

The most accessible spectacular seabird cliffs in Shetland with the ledges formed from almost horizontally bedded sandstones. Colonies include gannets, kittiwakes and guillemots. Both skuas breed on the moorland and, on the Holm of Ness, is one of the largest greater black-backed gull colonies in Shetland.

83. *West and East Burra* (HU 370330)

At the south end of East Burra are three tombolos and relatively easy walking on Houss Ness. On West Burra at Banna Minn (HU 365306) is a beautiful curving sandy tombolo, connecting West Burra with Kettla Ness, on which there is easy walking on short heath and grassland, sometimes with *tirrick* colonies. At Meil (HU 374354) there is an attractive and sheltered shell sand beach.

84. *East Voe of Quarff* (HU 435353)

Exposure of coarse Old Red breccia conglomerates on the shoreline with oyster plants on the beach. The deep U-shaped valley through to Wester Quarff (HU 410350) is a relict of an older landscape.

85. *Fladdabister* (HU 435325)

One of the most attractive old crofting townships in Shetland, near a limestone band with herb-rich meadows and heath. On the coast are the ruins of a lime kiln.

86. *Royl Field* (HU 396285)

Second highest hill on Mainland, interesting in comparison with Ronas Hill and Sandness Hill. At 300 m shows no periglacial features and is peat-covered to the summit. Fairly rugged walk over blanket peat and acid moor and grassland.

87. *Aith* (HU 430300)

Fine example of the complex crofting township habitats with some of the best examples of hay meadows in Shetland. Floristically, the meadows are very diverse with a wide variety of botanical communities, ranging from dry meadow to wet fen.

88. *Hoo Field* (HU 425271)

Chloritoid phyllite with variably steatitized serpentinite to the east. The marks made in the burn during the carving of steatite bowls can easily be seen and a further area of turf has been removed to demonstrate only a small extent of what must have been an extensive exploitation. A bowl is in the museum at Lerwick. These steatite working are of Viking age. On the coast and to the east is an area of basic volcanic rocks: lavas, tuffs and pillow lavas. Attractive flora.

89. *Mousa* (HU 461242)

One of the most attractive and interesting of the small Shetland islands with a good cross-section of Shetland's flora and fauna, including *dunter*, skuas, *tirricks*, *tysties* and storm petrels, the last breeding within field boundary walls and the very walls of the Broch of Mousa. There is a large colony and haul-out of harbour seals. The area around Mousa is an important sandeel spawning ground and therefore feeding area for seabirds, seals and harbour porpoises.

90. *Sandwick* (HU 435237)

One of the most accessible sites to see harbour seals, often hauled out on the pier. Old peat deposits can still be seen on the beach. Site of copper mines worked in the past. Access to Mousa.

91. *No Ness* (HU 442220)

Extremely accessible small colonies of guillemot and kittiwake; easy walking on dwarf-shrub heath and maritime grassland.

92. *St Ninian's Isle* (HU 365210)

The largest example of a shell sand tombolo (HU 372208) in the British Isles, over 900 m of sandy causeway connecting the island with Mainland. Small cormorant colony on the island. Fascinating also for its chapel ruins where a Pictish silver hoard was discovered in 1958.

93. *Bigton* (HU 380210) *to Scousburgh* (HU 377177)

The road takes one past the tiny and attractive township of Rerwick (HU 375196) with its traditional *rig* (field) system. Also as one approaches Scousburgh on the coast, the roadside vegetation provides a fine example of ungrazed meadow flowers and grasses. At Scousburgh there is a section through a remarkable aureole of thermally metamorphized Dunrossness phyllites, containing andalusite, kyanite, sillimanite, staurolite, chloritoid and garnet.

94. *Levenwick* (HU 414214) *to Boddam* (HU 400153)

Undemanding walk along low cliffed and varied coastline with small kittiwake and guillemot colonies. At Levenwick small beach backed by dunes and blown sand. At Boddam wintering seaduck, divers and grebes, also breeding shelduck.

95. *Dalsetter* (HU 405163)

The largest intact remnant of short dry heathland, especially rich in lichens, in south Mainland. The heathland also supports whimbrel, arctic skuas and *tirricks*. In the dyke by the roadside at Dalsetter (HU 403160) is an erratic boulder from Norway, which must have been deposited in Shetland during a previous Ice Age. The Loch of Clumlie nearby (HU 405175) is an acidic and dystrophic minor wintering wildfowl site, interesting also for the abandoned township and water mill.

96. *Spiggie* (HU 370170) *and Brow* (HU 385157)

The Loch of Spiggie, which is an RSPB Reserve, and Loch of Brow are the largest eutrophic lochs in Shetland. Loch of Spiggie is blocked off from Scousburgh Bay by a sandy bay-mouth bar with a dune and machair system supporting a diverse flora. The sand extends on the loch floor for about 0.8 km, providing rich feeding for wildfowl. This is the most important site for wintering whooper swans in Shetland, supporting 1% of the British wintering population, and usually contains a great variety of wildfowl in the winter months, including all the usual wintering duck and occasionally grebes. The southern extremity of the loch is more acidic but has been a breeding site for red-necked phalarope. The loch is noted for its silvery trout, which come in from the sea at Spiggie Voe. Between Spiggie and Brow is an interesting mesotrophic marsh. Loch of Brow is a more minor wintering wildfowl site but has a special attraction for pochard, as does the Loch of Tingwall.

97. *Noss* (HU 360165) *to Fitful* (HU 345130) *to Quendale* (HU 370130)

Commences as a pleasant walk over maritime grassland but rapidly becomes rugged towards the top of Fitful Head. The cliffs at Fitful are formed of chloritoid phyllites and are the highest cliffs (270 m) on Mainland.

There are associated stacks and skerries. There are several seabird colonies but most are not easily observed, except at Noss. At Noss, harbour seals breed, as do grey seals under the Fitful cliffs. At Garthsness (HU 365112) is a pyrrhotite ore body on the shore in hornblende schists. Mine shafts and adits still preserved in the cliffs. Now under improved grassland are the remnants of a village cleared to Quendale in the 1870s. This is also the site of the end of the *Braer* in January 1993.

98. *Quendale* (HU 380134)

The largest sand-dune system in Shetland, containing the best examples of dune, dune slack and machair vegetation; has had considerable sand-blow in the historical past. Towards the northern limit of the sand is the only machair loch in Shetland, the Loch of Hillwell (HU 376140), which for its size is also the most productive loch, with a remarkable flora. This loch attracts a great variety of wintering wildfowl and has been the only breeding site for several aquatic bird species. The machair area is also the only Shetland breeding site for butterflies (except the cabbage white). To the north of the site in Quendale is some of the best farming land in the islands. Quendale Bay is one of the most important sites for wintering seaduck and divers.

99. *Pool of Virkie* (HU 398112)

The largest intertidal sand and mud flat in Shetland. With its rich population of *Arenicola*, it is one of the most important wader feeding sites, where a variety of interesting and rare wintering and migrant waders can be seen. It is one of several sites for breeding shelduck in South Mainland.

100. *Grutness* (HU 408102) *and Sumburgh* (HU 400100)

The north–south airport runway crosses a large sand tombolo with dune and machair on either side. At Grutness is a fine, though rather disturbed, storm boulder beach with a *tirrick* colony. The shrub gardens of Sumburgh Hotel and the borrow-pit on the road to the lighthouse are excellent sites for migrants. Interest is added by the presence of the remarkable archaeological site at Jarlshof, named by Sir Walter Scott in his Shetland novel, *The Pirate*. Access to Fair Isle.

101. *Sumburgh Head* (HU 410080)

Fine and easily observable seabird colony run by the RSPB as a viewpoint. In the autumn moulting *dunter* can be seen and in summer there is a spectacular traffic of seabirds between Noss and the Sumburgh roost, just to the south of the head. Grey seals can also be seen around the coast and on the holms and skerries. In recent years Sumburgh Head has become one of the best points to view a number of Shetland's visiting whales, including minke, killer and occasionally humpback. On a fine day Fair Isle can be seen.

FAIR ISLE (HZ 210720) (site 102)

Famous island for spectacular scenery and migrants. It is owned by the National Trust for Scotland and its bird observatory has been carrying out observations on migrants and seabirds for over 50 years. It also has a large cliff seabird colony, a large arctic skua colony and a very new gannet colony.

Most of the places described above can only be reached on foot, but most people will travel to the starting points by car. A little ingenuity in route planning can combine some of the more exciting sites in a single outing, and this may be necessary for those on whom time presses. Possible half-day excursions from Lerwick are listed below.

To the south: Gulber Wick Beach, Quarff, Fladdabister (with a spectacular view of Noss to the north), Aithsetter, Boddam, Quendale, Spiggie, Bigton and St Ninian's Isle, and back.
To the west: Scalloway, Hamnavoe and the Burra Isles (with walks to Kettla Ness or Houss Ness) and back via Tingwall.
To the north: out on the Walls Road to Whiteness and Weisdale (with a diversion to Kergord), Bixter, Aith, Voe, and then either straight back or via Nesting through Laxo and Brettabister to Girlsta and thence Lerwick.

Any of these may easily take a whole day, or can be extended, for example to the Walls Peninsula and Sandness to the west; to Lunna in the north-east; to Firth and Sullom Voe in the north, going on to Ronas Voe and Hillswick or to North Roe. It is possible to drive from one end of Shetland to the other in a day, but anyone venturing to any of the main islands would be much better advised to stay for a night or two if they wish to appreciate their flavour at all.

Most people who come to Shetland have a purpose: to watch birds, botanize, study geology, visit the numerous archaeological sites, or perhaps to 'get away from it all'. All are likely to discover that Shetland really is the group of 'friendly isles' as the tourist authorities claim, and they will almost certainly find what they are looking for. I hope that this guide will help those who want to know more about natural history. Those whose interests are more antiquarian or archaeological will find help in books such as Noel Fojut's *A Guide to Prehistoric and Viking Shetland* and many more are available in Lerwick's bookshop and the Shetland Public Library. I recommend even the most restless naturalist to take time to visit at least the Shetland Museum and Library in Lerwick and the multi-layered archaeological site at Jarlshof, near Sumburgh Airport. After that it is well worth going to Clickhimin Broch on the south edge of Lerwick, to the virtually complete broch on Mousa, to the crofthouse museum at Boddam, the Croft Trail on Trondra, Weisdale and Quendale Mills, Bressay Lighthouse, Lunna Kirk, Stanydale and Brouster Neolithic sites, the Boat Museum on Unst, the many local 'musuems', and much, much more. But all that is beyond my scope.

APPENDIX 2

Protected Areas in Shetland

Otter

The list below describes the protected areas in Shetland as depicted in Fig. 38. The various designations (with the number in parentheses) are:

ED, European Diploma (1)
ESA, Environmentally Sensitive Area (1)
FIBOT, Fair Isle Bird Observatory Trust (1)
MCA, Marine Consultation Area (4)
NNR, National Nature Reserve (3)
NSA, National Scenic Area (1)
NTS, National Trust for Scotland (1)
RSPB, Royal Society for the Protection of Birds (4)
can. SAC, Candidate Special Area of Conservation (7)
SPA, Special Protection Area (10)
SSSI, Site of Special Scientific Interest (78)

In addition, the whole of Shetland is an ESA. None of the designations mentioned below give public right of access to the sites.

Site	Grid reference	Designation	Brief description
Aith Meadows	HU 440293	SSSI	Damp hay meadows
Balta	HP 660077	SSSI	Deflated dune/machair complex
Breckon	HP 529052	SSSI	Sand dune/machair/pasture
Burn of Aith	HU 442295	SSSI	Quaternary sediment/pollen
Burn of Lunklet	HU 370573	SSSI	*Hieracium zetlandicum*
Burn of Valayre	HU 369693	SSSI	Relict tree
Catfirth	HU 437538	SSSI	Relict tree
Cletts (The), Exnaboe	HU 407130	SSSI	Fossil fish
Clothister Hill	HU 342728	SSSI	Skarn quarry mineralization and magnetite
Crussa Field and The Heogs	HP 625105	SSSI	Breeding moorland birds, serpentinite heath and debris flora, talc quarry and chromite mineralization
Culswick Marsh	HU 273445	SSSI	Mesotrophic marsh
Dales Voe	HU 408687	SSSI	Salt marsh

Site	Grid reference	Designation	Brief description
Dalsetter	HU 405163	SSSI	Lowland heath
East Mires and Lumbister	HU 495955	SSSI	Blanket bog
Easter Loch	HP 598013	SSSI	Wintering whooper swans
Easter Rova Head	HU 474453	SSSI	Devonian conglomerate
Eshaness Coast	HU 210790	SSSI	Devonian extrusive volcanics
Fair Isle	HZ 213720	SSSI, ED, SPA, NTS, FIBOT	Fossil plant, breeding seabirds, Fair Isle wren and field mouse
Fidlar Geo, Watsness	HU 190493	SSSI	Old Red Sandstone sedimentary structures
Foula	HT 960390	SSSI, SPA	Breeding seabirds
Foula Coast	HT 961391	SSSI	Coastal geomorphology
Fugla Ness	HU 312913	SSSI	Interglacial peat deposit
Funzie	HU 656884	SSSI	Deformed conglomerate
Gutcher	HU 551997	SSSI	Moine exposures
Ham Ness	HP 636017	SSSI	Ophiolite dyke complex
Hascosay	HU 553923	SSSI, can. SAC	Blanket bog and Moine structural
Herma Ness	HP 605160	SSSI, NNR, SPA (part of)	Breeding seabirds
Hill of Colvadale	HP 610052	SSSI	Breeding seabirds and waders, serpentinite heath and debris flora
Houb (The) of Fugla Ness	HU 366776	MCA	Intertidal
Keen of Hamar	HP 645097	SSSI, NNR, can. SAC	Serpentinite flora and chromite mineralization
Kergord Plantations	HU 395541	SSSI	Tree plantations
Lamb Hoga	HP 602897	SSSI, SPA (part of)	Breeding waders and seabirds
Laxo Burn	HU 445634	SSSI	*Hieracium attenuatifolium*
Loch of Clousta	HU 315582	SSSI	Relict tree flora
Loch of Girlsta	HU 433522	SSSI	Arctic char
Lochs of Kirkigarth and Bardister	HU 238497	SSSI	Mesotrophic lochs and *Potamogeton rutilus*
Lochs of Spiggie and Brow	HU 374160	SSSI, SPA, RSPB Reserve (Spiggie)	Eutrophic loch (flora and fauna), wintering whooper swans
Lochs of Tingwall and Asta	HU 417429	SSSI	Mesotrophic lochs with *P. rutilus*
Lunda Wick	HP 566044	SSSI	Zoned ultramafic bodies
Melby	HU 168565	SSSI	Fossil fish and sedimentology
Mousa	HU 461242	SSSI, SPA, can. SAC	Breeding seabirds and seals
Muckle Roe Meadows	HU 338659 and 341659	SSSI	*Hieracium* flora
Ness of Clousta, The Brigs	HU 304582	SSSI	Extrusive volcanics and sedimentology
Ness of Cullivoe	HP 550025	SSSI	Moine geology, breeding seabirds and waders
North Fetlar	HU 625930	SSSI, SPA (part of)	Serpentinite heath flora
North Roe Meadow	HU 371897	SSSI	*Hieracium northroense* and *H. zetlandicum*
North Sandwick	HU 550965	SSSI	Moine geology
Norwick	HP 650148	SSSI	Caledonian structures
Norwick Meadows	HP 461138	SSSI	Valley fen/mire complex
Noss	HU 545404	SSSI, NNR, SPA	Breeding seabirds
Papa Stour	HU 165610	SSSI, can. SAC	Breeding moorland birds and seabirds, maritime heath
Papa Stour Coast	HU 147615	SSSI	Coastal geomorphology
Papa Stour Fish Bed	HU 186605	SSSI	Fossil fish
Pool of Virkie	HU 398112	SSSI	Intertidal mudflats
Punds to Wick of Hagdale	HU 645107	SSSI	Ophiolite structures

Site	Grid reference	Designation	Brief description
Quendale	HU 380134	SSSI	Sand dune and machair complex
Qui Ness to Punds Stack	HU 400000	SSSI	Ophiolite structures
Quoys of Garth	HU 408741	SSSI	Quarternary history
Ramna Stacks	HU 380970	SSSI, SPA	Breeding seabirds
Ronas Hill, North Roe	HU 323855	SSSI, SPA (part of), can. SAC	Subalpine flora, blanket bog, breeding moorland birds, invertebrates, periglacial geomorphology
Sandwater	HU 415547	SSSI	*Schoenoplectus lacustris*
Saxa Vord	HP 628173	SSSI, SPA (part of)	Breeding seabirds
Sel Ayre	HU 177540	SSSI	Interglacial peat deposit
Skelda Ness	HU 302405	SSSI	Scapolite mineralization
Skeo Taing, Clugan	HU 647075	SSSI	Ophiolite structures
South White Ness	HU 388458	SSSI	Limestone flora
St Ninian's Tombolo	HU 372208	SSSI	Coastal geomorphology
Sumburgh Head	HU 408091	SSSI, SPA, RSPB Reserve	Breeding seabirds and fossil fish
Swinister, Ayres of	HU 449723	SSSI, MCA	Coastal geomorphology
Tingon	HU 255840	SSSI, SPA (part of), can. SAC	Blanket bog and breeding moorland birds
Tonga Greff	HP 585140	SSSI	Metamorphic mineralization
Tressa Ness, Colbinstoft	HU 615944	SSSI	Ophiolite structures
Uyea, North Roe Coast	HU 344916	SSSI	Structural geology
Trona Mires	HU 670915	SSSI, RSPB Reserve, SPA (part of)	Basin mires/coastal lichen heath
Vadills (The)	HU 290555	SSSI, can. SAC, MCA	Intertidal area, *Ascophyllum nodosum* f. *mackaii*
Villians of Hamnavoe	HU 240824	SSSI	Coastal geomorphology
Virva	HU 645920	SSSI	Ophiolite structures
Voxter Voe and Valayre Quarry	HU 365697	SSSI	Moine structures
Ward of Culswick	HU 268463	SSSI	Breeding moorland birds
White Ness Voe	HU 390440	MCA	Intertidal, eel grass beds

APPENDIX 3

Lists of Species

Otter

This appendix contains all the known species (and in some cases intraspecific categories) recorded in Shetland from a number of groups. The plant tables are almost comprehensive, with detailed information included on distribution and status of flowering plants and ferns; only the marine algae are not included. The invertebrate lists are much more comprehensive than they were only 10 years ago, with detail lacking now only in a few groups. Although there are only a few terrestrial vertebrates, details have been included. The best-known animals are the birds and comprehensive details have been included reflecting the great interest in this group, including migrant and vagrant information.

Most of the lists have been compiled by specialists in the different groups and one has been adapted from a published list. The authors are acknowledged at the head of each list.

FUNGI
by L. Johnston

The recently published fungus flora of Shetland by Roy Watling (1996) lists almost 1000 species, 3.6% of which are new records for the British Isles. However, Shetland's fungi, like so many other groups, is only a small part of the British fungus flora with even Orkney having one-third more species. Watling has noted that both 'Atlantic' and 'arctic–alpine' elements can be recognized and that, again as with some other groups, some familiar species take up slightly different roles in the Shetland plant community. For example, some mainland woodland species are found often in association with the dwarf willows such as creeping willow (*Salix repens*). This community also includes several species new to the British Isles. There are also other 'unique' communities not found elsewhere in the British Isles, such as the combination of fungi found on the small shrub bearberry (*Arctostaphylos uva-ursi*) and the community found on the herb-rich sedge-grass heath on the serpentinite of Fetlar. The last have affinities with some grasslands in Faroe and Norway. The damp oceanic climate also encourages the larger fungi and several of the favourite edible species can be found on grasslands from early summer.

Rich habitats for fungi include the herb-rich grasslands, where they have not been overgrazed or agriculturally improved, and the woodland plantations, particularly Kergord. There is no doubt that an expansion of woodland would increase the diversity of the fungus flora of Shetland. On the other hand, the traditional hay-meadow habitat is not renowned for being rich in fungi.

The following list is a distillation of that published by the Royal Botanic Garden Edinburgh in *The Fungus Flora of Shetland* by Professor Roy Watling in 1992.

Eumycota
Basidiomycotina
Authorities follow texts listed under separate sections,
unless otherwise indicated

Hymenomycetes

Boletales

Boletaceae
Boletus edulis L.: Fr
Suillus bovinus (L.: Fr.) Kuntze
S. flavidus (Fr.) Singer

S. grevillei (Klotzsch) Singer
S. luteus (L.: Fr.) S.F. Gray
S. variegatus (Sow.: Fr.) Kuntze

Agaricales (authorities follow Denis *et al.*, 1960 unless otherwise indicated)

Hygrophoraceae
Hygrocybe acutopunicea Haller & Moeller
H. aurantiolutescens P. Orton
H. aurantiosplendens Haller
H. berkeleyi (P. Orton) P. Orton & Watl.
H. calyptraeformis (Berk. & Br.) Fayod.
H. ceracea (Wulfen.: Fr.) Karsten
H. chlorophana (Fr.: Fr.) Wünsche
H. clivalis (Fr.) P. Orton & Watl.
H. coccineocrenata (P. Orton) Moser
H. coccinea (Schaeff.: (Fr.) Kummer
H. colemannianus (Blox.: Fr.) P. Orton & Watl.
H. conica (Scop.: Fr.) Kummer
H. conicoides (P. Orton) P. Orton & Watl.
H. flavescens (Kauffman) Singer
H. fornicata (Fr.) Singer
H. glutinipes (Lange) Haller
H. insipida (Lange ex Lundell) Moser
H. lacma (Fr.) P. Orton & Watl.
H. laeta (Pers.: Fr.) Karsten
H. lepida Arnolds
H. marchii Bres.
H. miniata (Fr.) Kummer
H. mollis (Berk. & Br.) Moser
H. nigrescens (Quélet) Kühner
H. nitrata (Pers.: Pers) Wünsche
H. nivea (Fr.) Murrill
H. obrussea (Fr.) Wünsche s. Kühner
H. ?ochraceopallida P. Orton
H. phaeococcinea (Arnolds) Arnolds
H. persistens (Britz.) Britz.
H. pratensis (Pers.: Fr.) Murrill
H. psittacina (Schaeff.: Fr.) Wünsche
H. punicea (Fr.) Kummer
H. quieta (Kühner) Singer
H. reai R. Maire
H. reidii Kühner
H. russocoriacea (Berk. & Miller) P. Orton & Watl.
H. splendidissima (P. Orton) Moser
H. strangulata (P. Orton) Svrcek
H. subminutula Murrill
H. subradiata (Schum.: Fr.) Orton & Watl.
H. substrangulata (P. Orton) Moser
H. subviolacea (Peck) P. Orton & Watl.

H. tristis (Pers.) Moeller
H. turunda (Fr.: Fr.) Karsten
H. unguinosa (Fr.) Karsten
H. virginea (Wulfen: Fr.) P. Orton & Watl.
H. vitellina (Fr.) Karsten

Pleurotaceae
Lentinus lepideus (Fr.: Fr.) Fr.

Tricholomataceae
Armillaria sp. possibly *A. gallica* Marxmüll.
Arrhenia acerosa (Fr.) Kühner
Calocybe carnea (Bull.: Fr.) Donk
C. ?juncicola (Heim) Singer
C. gambosa (Fr.) Donk
Clitocybe agrestis Harmaja
C. ditopus
C. aff. lituus (Fr.) Métrod
C. pseudoclusilis
C. rivulosa
C. striatula
C. vibecina
Collybia alpina Vigylas
C. dryophila
C. luteifolia
Cystoderma amianthinum
C. longisporum (Kühner) Heinem. & Thoen
Dermoloma cuneifolium
D. phaeopodium P. Orton
D. pseudocuneifolium Herink
Gerronema marchantiae Singer & Clémençon
Hohenbuehelia myxotricha
Hygrophoropsis aurantiaca
H. pallida (Peck) Kriesel
Laccaria tortilis
L. bicolor
L. laccata
L. proxima
L. proximella Singer
L. tetraspora Singer
Lepista irina
L. luscina
L. multiforme (Romell) Gulden
L. nuda

L. ovisporum (J. Lange) Gulden
L. pseudoectypa (M. Lange) Gulden
L. rickenii Singer
L. saeva
L. sordida
Lyophyllum connatum
Marasmius androsaceus
Melanoleuca schumacheri (Fr.) Singer
Merismodes fasciculatus (Schwein.) Donk
Mycena abramsii (Murrill) Murrill
M. acicula
M. aetites
M. alcalina
M. amicta
M. bulbosa
M. epipterygia
M. cinerella
M. fibula
M. filopes
M. flavoalba
M. galopus
M. leptocephala
M. lineata
M. leucogala
M. metata
M. olivaceomarginata
M. oortiana
M. pura
M. rosella
M. sanguinolenta
M. swartzii
M. tenerrima
M. vitilis
M. uracea
Omphalina cupulatoides P. Orton
O. ericetorum
O. favrei Watl.
O. fusconigra
O. hepatica
O. hudsoniana (Jenn.) Bigelow
O. luteovitellina
O. mutila
O. obscurata
O. oniscus
O. cf. *paravelutina* Irlet & Clémençon
O. pseudoandrosacea (Bull.) Fr. s. Moeller
O. pyxidata
O. rickenii
O. sphagnicola
O. velutina
Resupinatus rhacodium
Tephrocybe palustris (Peck) Donk
T. tesquorum (Fr.) Moser
Tricholoma flavovirens
T. psammopus
Tricholomopsis rutilans

Entolomataceae
Alboleptonia robellotincta Larg. & Walt.
Clitopilus cretatus
'Eccilia' carneo-alba (With.: Fr.) Quélet
Entoloma ameides

E. costatum
E. fuscomarginatum
E. helodes
E. jubatum
E. occultopigmentatum Arnolds & Noordel.
E. porphyrophaeum
E. prunuloides
Leptonia anatina
'Leptonia' asprellus s. J. Lange.
L. atromarginata
L. caesiocincta
L. catalaunica
L. caerulea
L. chalybea
L. corvina
L. cyaneoviridescens
L. fulva
L. griseocyanea
L. inocybeoides
L. intermedia
L. lampropus
L. lampropus s. Kühner & Romagnesi
L. lazulina
L. nigroviolacea
L. pyrospila
L. sericella
L. serrulata
L. spurceifolia
L. turci
Leptonia sp.
Nolanea cetrata
N. clandestina
N. cucullata
N. conferenda (Britz.) Sacc.
N. cuneata
N. farinolens
N. fernandae
N. infula
N. juncina
N. lucida
N. mammosa s. Moeller
N. minuta
N. nitens
N. papillata
N. radiata
N. sericea
Nolanea solstitialis
N. tenella
N. versatilis
Nolanea sp.

Amanitaceae
Amanita fulva

Pluteaceae
Pluteus cervinus
P. nanus
Volvariella speciosa

Bolbitiaceae
Agrocybe erebia
A. paludosa

A. pediades (Fr.) Fayod
A. praecox
A. semiorbicularis
A. sphalermorpha (Bull.: Fr.) Fayod
A. subpediades (Murrill) Watl.
Bolbitius vitellinus
Conocybe aporos van Wav.
C. dentatomarginata Watl.
C. dumetorum (Vel.) Svrcek
C. dunensis
C. filaris
C. kuehneriana Singer
C. macrocephala
C. mesospora
C. neoantipus (Atk.) Singer
C. piloselloides Watl.
C. pseudopilosella
C. rickeniana
C. siliginea
C. subovalis
C. subpubescens
C. tenera
C. tenera agg.

Coprinaceae
Coprinus atramentarius
C. comatus
C. cordisporus
C. ephemeroides
C. ephemerus
C. heptemerus
C. heterosetulosus Locq.
C. latisporus P. Orton
C. micaceus
C. miser
C. niveus
C. patouillardii
C. pellucidus
C. plicatilis
C. radiatus
C. stercoreus
C. tigrinellus
C. velox
C. xantholepis P. Orton
Lacrymaria velutina
Panaelous ater
P. acuminatus
P. campanulatus
P. castaneifolius (Murrill) Smith
P. fimicola
P. foenisecii
P. olivaceus
P. retirugis
P. rickenii
P. semiovatus
P. speciosus P. Orton
P. sphinctrinus
Psathyrella ammophila
P. atomata
P. clivensis
P. coprobia
P. ?dunensis van Wav.

P. fibrillosa
P. flexispora
P. cf. *panaeloides* Maire
P. sphagnicola
P. trepida

Agaricaceae
Agaricus arvensis
A. bernardii
A. bisporus
A. campestris
A. cupreobrunneus
A. depauperatus (Moeller) Pilát
A. fissuratus (Moeller) Moeller
A. fuscofibrillosus
A. hortensis (Cooke) Pilát
A. langei agg.
A. macrosporus
A. nivescens
A. porphyrocephalus
A. stramineus (Moeller & Schaeffer) Moeller
A. variegans Moeller

Strophariaceae
Hypholoma elongatum
H. ericaeum
H. ericaeoides
H. fasciculare
H. myosotis (Fr.:Fr.) M. Lange.
H. polytrichi
H. subericaeum
H. udum
Psilocybe apelliculosa P. Orton
P. coprophila
P. graminicola (P. Orton) P. Orton
P. merdaria
P. montana
P. muscorum
P. physaloides
P. semilanceata
P. subcoprophila (Britz.) Sacc.
Stropharia caerulea Kreisel
S. pseudocyanea (Desm.) Morgan
S. semiglobata

Cortinariaceae
Cortinarius acutostriatus Henry
C. anomalus
C. cinnamomeobadius
C. cinnamomeolutescens
C. cinnamomeus agg.
C. favrei
C. hinnuleus
C. lepidopus
C. aff. *mucosus*
C. pratensis (Bon & Gaugue) Høiland
C. pseudosalor
C. pseudostriatulus Henry
C. maxistriatulus Henry
C. striatuloides Henry
C. ?tabularis
C. trivialis

C. uliginosus
Crepidotus cesati
Flammulaster granulosa
Galerina ampullaceocystis
G. atkinsoniana A.H. Smith
G. autumnalis (Peck) Smith & Singer
G. calyptrata
G. cedretorum R. Maire
G. cerina var. *longicystis* Smith & Singer
G. clavata
G. hiemansii W. Reijnd.
G. aff. *helvoliceps* (Berk. & Curt.) Singer
G. hypnorum
G. laevis (Pers.) Singer
G. marginata
G. mniophila
G. muricellospora Atk.
G. paludosa
G. praticola
G. pseudomniophila Kühner
G. pseudopumila
G. pseudotundrae Kühner
G. pumila
G. sphagnorum
G. stordalii Smith & Singer
G. stylifera (Atk.) Smith & Singer
G. subcerina Smith & Singer
G. terrestris Wells & Kempton

Russulales

Russulaceae
Lactarius deterrimus Gröger
L. hysginus
L. lacunarum
L. lanceolatus Miller & Laursen
L. rufus
Russula alpina
R. chamiteae Kühner

Aphyllophorales

Cantharellaceae
Cantharellus cibarius Fr.

Clavariaceae
Clavaria argillacea Pers.: Fr.
C. fumosa Fr.
C. vermicularis Sow.: Fr.
Clavulinopsis corniculata (Fr.) Corner
C. fusiformis (Fr.) Corner
C. helvola (Fr.) Corner
C. luteoalba (Rea) Corner
Multiclavula vernalis (Schwein.) Petersen
Typhula placorhiza Fr.

Clavulinaceae
Clavulina cinerea (Fr.) Schroeter
C. cristata (Fr.) Schroeter

G. tibiicystis
G. ?unicolor s. Gulden
G. vittaeformis
Gymnopilus junonius
G. fulgens
Hebeloma alpinum Bruchet
H. crustuliniforme
H. fragilipes Romagn.
H. leucosarx
H. mesophaeum
H. populinum Romagn.
Inocybe acuta
I. asterospora
I. concinnula Favre
I. dulcamara
I. eugenula Favre
I. fastigiata
I. fulvella
I. geophylla
I. lacera
I. lanuginella
I. leptocystis Atk.
I. ovatocystis Boursier & Kühner
I. salicis
Phaeogalera stagnina (Fr.) Pegler & Young
P. stagninoides (P. Orton) Pegler & Young
P. zetlandica (P. Orton) Kühner
Pholiota squarrosa

R. fragilis
R. medullata Romagn.
R. nigricans
R. norvegica Reid
R. pascua (Moeller & Schaeffer) Kühner
R. persicina (Krombh.) Melzer & Zvara
R. cf. *saliceticola* (Singer) Kühner
R. xerampelina agg.

Coniophoraceae
Coniophora arida (Fr.) Karsten
Serpula lacrimans (Wulfen: Fr.) Schroeter

Corticiaceae
Athelia epiphylla Pers.
Botryobasidium subcoronatum (Höhnel & Litsch.) Donk
Brevicellicum olivascens (Bres.) Larson & Hjortst.
Cerocorticium confluens (Fr.:Fr.) Jülich & Stalpers
Galzinia incrustans (Höhnel & Litsch.) Parm.
Gloeocystidiellum cf. *ochraceum* (Fr.: Fr.) Donk
G. porosum (Berk. & Curtis) Donk
Grandinia barba-jovis (Fr.) Jülich
G. crustacea (Pers.: Fr.) Fr.
G. subalutacea (Karsten) Jülich
Grandulobasidium geogenium (Ell. & Crag.) Jülich
Hyphoderma argillacea (Bres.) Donk
H. pallidum (Bres.) Donk
H. praetermissum (Karsten) J. Erikss. & Strid
H. sambuci (Pers.: Fr.) Jülich.

Hyphodermella corrugata (Fr.) J. Erikss. & Ryv.
Hyphodontia nesopori (Bres.) J. Erikss. & Hjortst.
Hypochnicium detriticium (Bourd. & Galz.) J. Erikss. & Ryv.
Meruliopsis corium (Fr.) Ginns
Peniophora incarnata (Pers.: Pers.) Karsten
P. lycii (Pers.) Höhnel & Litsch.
Phlebia radiata Fr.
P. rufa (Fr.) Christ.
Scopuloides rimosa (Cooke) Jülich
Sistotrema subtrigonospermum Rogers
Subulicystidium longisporum (Pat.) Parm.
Trechispora farinacea (Pers.: Fr.) Liberta
T. cohaerens (Schwein.) Jülich & Stalpers
T. mutabilis (Pers.) Liberta
Tubulicrinus subulata (Bourd. & Galz.) Donk

Polyporaceae
Fomes fomentarius (L.:Fr.) Fr.
Oxyporus populinus (Schum.: Fr.) Donk

Physisporinus sanguinolentus (Alb. & Schein.: ex Fr.) Pilát
Polyporus badius (Pers.: S.F. Gray) Schwein.
P. melanopus (Pers.) ex Fr.
P. varius (Pers.) ex Fr.

Stereaceae
Stereum rugosum (Pers.: Fr.) Fr.

Thelephoraceae
Thelephora terrestris Pers.: Fr.
Tomentella cf. *galzinii* Boud.

Hymenochaetaceae
Inonotus radiatus (Sow.: Fr.) Karsten

Hydnaceae
Hydnum repandum L.: Fr.
H. rufescens Fr.

Gasteromycetes (authorities of taxa follow Demoulin & Mariott, 1981)

Lycoperdales

Lycoperdaceae
Bovista nigrescens
B. plumbea
Langermannia gigantea

Lycoperdon foetidum
L. molle
L. lividum
Vascellum pratense

Sclerodermatales

Sphaerobolaceae
Sphaerobolus stellatus

'Hymenomycetous Heterobasidiae' (authorities of taxa follow Donk, 1966)

Dacrymycetales

Dacrymycetaceae
Calocera viscosa

Dacrymyces stillatus
D. minor

Tulasnellales

Tulasnellaceae
Tulasnella araneosa Bourd. & Galz.

Ceratobasidiaceae
Thanatephorus cucumeris (Frank) Donk

Tremellales

Tremellaceae
Exidia albida
Myxarium nucleatum
Sebacina calcea
S. effusa

Auriculariaceae
Platygloea ?(Achroomyces) sebaceus

Teliomycetes (Hemi-Basidiomycetes) (rusts follow Wilson & Henderson, 1966. Smuts follow Mordue & Ainsworth, 1984)

Tilletiales

Tilletiaceae
Entyloma dactylidis
E. ficariae

Tilletia sphaerococca
Urocystis anemones

Ustilaginales

Ustilaginaceae
Anthracoidea caricis
A. pratensis (H. Sydow) Boidol & Poel
Ustilago longissima
U. segetum var. *avenae*

U. segetum var. *segetum*
U. segetum var. *tritici*
U. vaillantii
U. striiformis
U. violacea

Uredinales (abbreviations: I, Aecidia; II, Uredosori; III, Teleutosori)

Coleosporiaceae
Coleosporium tussilaginis
Melampsorella caryophyllacearum

Melampsoraceae
Chrysomyxa empetri
Melampsora epitea
M. lini
Pucciniastrum guttatum
P. vaccinii

Pucciniaceae
Puccinia acetosae
P. arenariae
P. calcitrapae
P. calthae
P. calthicola
P. caricina
P. cnici

P. coronata
P. festucae
P. galii-verni
P. glomerata
P. hieracii
P. obscura
P. poae-nemoralis
P. punctata
P. punctiformis
P. recondita
P. violae
P. virgae-aureae
Uromyces acetosae
U. dactylidis
U. fallens
U. muscari
U. nerviphilus
U. rumicis
U. viciae-fabae

Ascomycotina (note: lichenized species are not included), authorities follow Cannon, Hawksworth & Sherwood-Pike 1985, unless otherwise stated.

Hemiascomycetes

Taphrinales

Protomycetaceae
Protomyces macrosporus

Taphridium umbelliferarum

Euascomycetes

Pezizales

Ascobolaceae
Ascobolus albidus
A. furfuraceus
A. immersus
A. stictoideus
Saccobolus glaber
S. obscurus
S. versicolor

C. granuliformis
C. lacteus
C. sexdecimsporus
Iodophanus carneus
Neottiella vivida
Scutellinia scutellata
S. trechispora
Tricharina gilva

Humariaceae
Aleuria aurantia
A. bicucculata (Boud.) Grelet
Cheilymenia cf. *fimicola*
C. raripila
C. stercorea
Coprobia granulata
Coprotus aurorus
C. glaucellus

Pezizaceae
Peziza ammophila
P. cerea
P. repanda

Thelebolaceae
Lasiobolus papillatus
Thelebolus caninus
T. nanus

Helotiales

Dermateaceae
Hysteropezizella lyngei
H. prahliana
H. pusilla
Leptotrochila cerastiorum
L. ranunculi
L. verrucosa
Mollisia cinerea
M. clavata
M. discolor var. *longispora*
M. fallax
M. ligni
M. melaleuca
M. ventosa
Mollisia sp.
Pseudopeziza calthae
P. trifolii
Pyrenopeziza ?adenostylidis
P. arenivaga
P. carduorum
P. laricina f. *microsperma* le Gal.
P. petiolaris
P. pulveracea
P. revincta
P. rhinanthi
P. urticicola
Tapesia fusca

Gelatinodiscaceae
Sarcotrochila alpina

Geoglossaceae
Geoglossum cookeianum
G. fallax
G. glutinosum
G. nigritum
Mitrula paludosa

Helotiaceae
Ascocoryne cylichnium
A. sarcoides
Crocicreas cyathoidea
Claussenomyces atrovirens
Cudoniella acicularis
C. clavus
C. clavus var. *grandis*
Heterosphaeria patella
Hymenoscyphus ?conscriptus (Karsten) Korf & Kobaysi

H. repandus
H. rhodoleucus
H. robustior
H. subferrugineus
Ombrophila sp.
Pezizella eburnea
Phaeangellina empetri

Hyaloscyphaceae
Dasyscyphus acuum
D. apalus
D. carneolus var. *longisporus*
D. controversus
D. imbecillis
D. mollissimus
D. palearum
Dasyscyphus palearum var. *niger* Dennis
D. virgineus
Hyaloscypha stevensonii
Lachnellula hahniana
L. occidentalis
L. subtilissima
Psilachnum inquilinum
Unguicularia millepunctata
U. ulmariae

Orbiliaceae
Orbilia delicatula Karsten
O. sarraziniana
O. xanthostigma

Phacidiaceae
Phacidium cf. *vaccinii*

Sclerotiniaceae
Botrytinina calthae
Ciboria spp.
Ciborina ciborium (Vahlitr.) Schumacher & Kohn
Gloeotinia granigena
Myriosclerotinia curreyana
M. dennisii
M. scirpicola
Myriosclerotinia sp.
Rutstroemia henningsiana
R. plana
Sclerotinia eleocharidis
S. gregoriana
S. sclerotiorum

Ostropales

Ostropaceae
Apostemidium?

Rhytismatales

Rhytismataceae
Cyclaneusma minus
Lophodermium cf. *alpinum*
L. arundinaceum
L. conigenum
L. culmigenum
L. gramineum

L. juniperinum
L. pinastri
L. seditiosum
Propolis phacidioides
Propolomyces farinosus
Rhytisma salicinum

Lecanorales

Agyriaceae
Agyrium rufum

Dacytylospora stygia

Clavicipitales

Clavicipitaceae
Claviceps ?junci
Claviceps purpurea

Cordyceps gracilis
C. militaris
Epichloe typhina

Hypocreales

Hypocreaceae
Giberella avenacea
G. baccata
Nectria cinnabarina

N. coccinea
N. episphaeria
N. lugdunensis

Polystigmatales

Phyllachoraceae
Phyllachora dactylidis
P. graminis

P. junci
P. sylvatica

Sordariales

Chaetomiaceae
Chaetomium globosum
C. cf. *virescens* (v. Arx) Udagawa
C. warcupii

Nitschkiaceae
Coronophora annexa

Lasiosphaeriaceae
Podospora curvicolla
Schizothecium conicum
S. vesticola

Sordariaceae
Sordaria fimicola
S. humana
S. macrospora
S. minima

Sphaeriales

Amphisphaeriaceae
Monographella nivalis
Phomatospora coprophila
P. dinemasporium
Physalospora empetri

Chaetosphaeria myriocarpa

Xylariaceae
Anthostomella lugubris
A. phaeosticta
Coniochaeta discospora
Hypoxylon rubiginosum
Podosordaria ?pedunculata
Rosellinia mammiformis
Ustulina deusta
Xylaria hypoxylon

Halosphaeriaceae
Corollospora comata
Lindra inflata

Trichosphaeriaceae
Calosphaeria cf. *minima*

Sphaeriales (uncertain position)

Crinigera maritima Schmidt
Diapleella clivensis

Endoxyla sp.

Diatrypales

Diatrypaceae
Diatrype stigma
Diatrypella favacea

Eutypa acharii
E. lata

Diaporthales

Gnomoniaceae
Gaeumannomyces graminis var. *avenae*
Gnomonia cerastris

Melanconidaceae
Cryptosporella hypodermia
Prosthecium auctum

Pseudovalsaceae
Ditopella ditopa

Valsaceae
Cryptodiaporthe hystrix
C. salicella
Diaporthe arctii
D. eres
D. pustulata
Melanconis thelbola
Ophiovalsa suffusa
Plagiostoma devexum
Valsa ambiens

Erysiphales

Erysiphaceae
Erysiphe graminis
E. knautiae
E. polygoni

E. ranunculi
E. sordida
Sphaerotheca alchemillae

Elaphomycetales

Elaphomycetaceae
Elaphomyces aff. *asperulus*

Gymnoascales

Gymnoascaceae
Anixiopsis stercoraria (Hansen) Hansen

Arachniotus ?citrinus

Laboulbeniales

Laboulbeniaceae
Laboulbenia nebriae

L. vulgaris
Peyritschiella protea

Loculoascomycetes

Dothideales

Arthropyreniaceae
Arthropyrenia punctiformis

Asterinaceae
Asterina veronicae

Didymosphaeriaceae
Didymosphaeria oblitescens
D. rubicola
Didymosphaeria sp.

Dothideaceae
Didymella applanata
D. trifolii (Fuckel) Sacc.
Sphaerulina oraemaris

Dothioraceae
Dothiora ribesia

Hysteriaceae
Farlowiella carmichaeliana
Gloniopsis praelonga

Melanommataceae
M. pulvis-pyrius

Micropeltidaceae
Stomiopeltis betulae
S. pinastri

Microthyriaceae
Microthyrium pinophyllum

Mytilinidiaceae
Lophium mytilinum
Mytilidion gemmigenum

Phaeosphaeriaceae
Eudarluca caricis
Leptosphaeria acuta
L. avenaria
L. doliolum
L eustoma
L. macrospora
L. nardi
Ophiobolus acuminatus
O. cirsii

Phaeotrichaceae
Sporomiella intermedia
S. minima
Trichodelitschia bisporula

Pleosporaceae
Keissleriella culmifida
Leptospora rubella
Lidophia graminis
Mycosphaerella ascophylii
M. iridis
M. macrospora

M. recutita
M. rhododendri
M. tassiana
Pleospora herbarum
P. vagans
Pyrenophora avenae
Rhopographis filicinus

Venturiaceae
Gibbera myrtilli
Venturia inaequalis
V. rumicis

Dothideales (uncertain position)

Chitinospora ammophilae

Thyridaria rubronotata

Verrucariales

Verrucariaceae
Muellerella polyspora

Deuteromycotina

Hyphales

'Hyphomycetes'
Actinocladium rhodosporum Ehrenb.
Aegerita candida Fr.
Alatospora acuminata Ingold
A. pulchella Marvanová
Anguillospora longissima (Sacc. & Sydow) Ingold
Arthrinum phaeospermum (Corda) M.B. Ellis
Arthrobotrys cladodes Dreschler
A. oligospora Fresen.
Articulospora tetracladia Ingold
Aspergillus niger v. Tieghem
Aureobasidium pullulans (de Bary) Arnaud
Botrytis cinerea Pers.
B. globosa Buchwa.
Cercospora radiata Fuckel
Cercosporella pantoleuca (Sacc.) Sacc.
Cheiromycella microscopia (Karsten) S. Hughes
Chrysosporium pannosum (Link) S. Hughes
Cladosporium carpophilum Thüm.
C. cladosporioides (Fresen.) de Vries
C. elatum (Harz) Nannf.
C. herbarum (Pers.) Link
C. macrosporum Preuss
Clavatospora longibracheata (Ingold) Nilsson ex Marvanová & Nilsson
C. stellata (Ingold & Cox) Nilsson
Coryne dubia (Pers.) Gray
Cylindrocarpon sp.
Dendrodochium citrinum Grove
Dendrospora erecta Ingold
Didymaria kriegeriana Bres.
Drechslera avenae (Eidam) Scharif
D. poae (Baudys) Shoemaker
Enantioptera tetra-alata Descals
Endoconospora cerastii Gjaerum
Endophragmiella pinicola (M.B. Ellis) S. Hughes
Endophragmium sp.

Epicoccum purpurascens Ehrenb.
Flagellospora curvula Ingold
Fulvia fulva (Cooke) Cif.
Fontanospora eccentrica (Petersen) Dyko
Fusarium aquaeductuum Lagerh.
F. avenaceum (Fr.) Sacc.
F. culmorum (W.G. Sm.) Sacc.
F. graminacearum Schwäbe
F. lateritium Nees: Fr.
F. nivale (Fr.) Ces.
F. oxysporum Schlecht.
F. cf. solani (Martius) Sacc.
F. solani var. *caeruleum* (Lib.) C. Booth
F. sporotrichioides Sherb.
Fusarium sp.
Geotrichum candidum Link
Gliomastrix sp.
Gjoerffyella rotula (Höhnel) Marvanová
Hadrotrichum virescens Sacc. & Roum.
Heliscus lugdunensis Sacc. & Therry
Helminthosporium solani Durieu & Mont.
H. velutinum Link
Hymenostilbe verrucosa Mains
Lateriramulosa uni-inflata Matsushima
Lemonniera aquatica de Wild.
L. centrosphaera Marvanová
Malbranchea sp.
Mastigosporium rubricosum (Dearn. & Barth.) Nannf.
Microdochia bolleyi (Sprague) de Hoog
Myrothecium cf. *roridum* Tode: Fr.
Oidium sp.
Oospora pustulans Owen & Wakef.
Ovularia obliqua (Cooke) Oudem.
Penicillium cf. *funiculosum* Thom
P. oxalicum Currie & Thom
P. aff. stoloniferum Thom
Periconia cookei Mason & M.B. Ellis

P. hispidula (Pers.) Mason & M.B. Ellis
Pseudocercosporella herpotrichoides (Fron.) Deighton
Ramularia didyma Unger
R. pratensis Sacc.
R. rubella (Bonorden) Nannf.
R. taraxaci Karsten
Rhizoctonia cerealis Boerema & v. Hoeven
R. solani Kühn
Rhynchosporium secalis (Oudem.) J.J. Davis
Rhynchosporium sp.
Sarcopodium circinatum Ehrenb.
Sclerotium durum Tode
Spondylocladiella botrytioides Linder
Spiloclaea pomi Fr.
Sporodesmium folliculatum (Corda) Mason & S. Hughes
S. vagum Nees & T. Nees
Stachybotrys atra Corda
Stilbella erythrocephala (Ditmar) Lindau
Taeniolina scripta (Karsten) P.M. Kirk
Taeniospora descalsii Marvanová & Stalpers

Tetrachaetum elegans Ingold
Tetracladium marchalianum de Wild
T. setigerum (Grove) Ingold
Thysanophora penicillioides (Roum.) Kendrick
Trichoderma harzianum Rifai
T. viride Pers.
Tricladium angulatum Ingold
T. eccentricum Petersen
T. patulum Marvanová & Marven
T. splendens Ingold
Trichothecium roseum Link
Trimmatostroma betulinum (Corda) S. Hughes
T. salicis Corda
T. scutellare (Berk. & Br.) M.B. Ellis
Triposporina sp.
Tubercularia vulgaris Tode: Fr.
Ulocladium consortiale (Thüm.) Simmons
Verticillium fungicola (Preuss) Hassebr.
Valucrispora graminea Ingold
Xylohypha nigrescens (Pers.: Fr) Mason

Sphaeropsidales

Actinothyrium graminis Kunze
Aposphaeria agminalis Sacc.
Ascochyta chenopodii Fres.
A. ducisapruti Mattir
A. vulgaris Kab. & Rab.
Camarosporium ambiens (Cooke) Grove
Cheilaria agrostis Lib.
Coleophoma empetri (Rostrup) Petrak
Colletotrichum graminicolum (Cestati) G.W. Wilson
Coniothyrium wernsdorffiae Laub.
Cryptocline paradoxa (de Not.) v. Arx
Cyclothyrium juglandis (Schum. ex Rabenh.) Sutton
Cytospora ambiens Sacc.
C. salicis Rabenh.
Cytosporina lata Höhnel
Dilophospora alopecuri (Fr.) Fr.
Dinemasporium strigosum (Fr.) Sacc.
Diplodina acerina (Pass.) Sutton
D. cf. *eurhodendri* Grove
D. microsperma (Johnston) B. Sutton
Diplosporonema delastrei (Delacr.) Petrak
Disculina vulgaris (Fr.) B. Sutton
Dothiorella sp. cf. '*D. pyrenophora* var. *salicis* Karsten'
Hendersonia sambuci E. Müller
Hendersoniopsis thelebola (Sacc.) Höhnel
Lichenoconium erodens M.P. Christ. & D. Hawksw.
L. usneae (Anzi) D. Hawksw.
Microsphaeropsis olivacea (Bonorden) Höhnel
Rhodesia subtecta (Roberge) Grove
Neophoma graminella (Sacc.) Petrak & Sydow
Patellina caesia Bayliss-Elliott & Stansfield
Phoma acuta Fuckel
P. complanata (Tode) Desm.
P. cirsii Sydow
P. deusta Fuckel
P. epitricha Sacc.
P. fimeti Brun.
P. exigua var. *foveata* (Foister) Boerema

P. herbarum Westend.
P. hedericola (Dur. & Mont.) Boerema
P. aff. *leguminum* Westend.
P. oleracea Sacc.
P. pomorum Thümen
P. rhodophila Sacc.
P. stagonosporoides Trail
Phoma sp.
Phomopsis cirsii Sydow
P. controversa (Sacc.) Traverso
P. linearis Traverso
P. oblonga (Desm.) Traverso
P. ?*platanoidis* (Cooke) Died.
P. salicina Died.
Phomopis sp.
Phyllosticta grossulariae Sacc.
P. cf. *fuschicola* Speg.
Placosphaeria junci Bubák
Pleurophoma pleurospora (Sacc.) Höhnel
Pseudoseptoria donacis (Pass.) B. Sutton
Rhizosphaera kalkoffii Bubák
Sclerophoma pythiophila (Corda) Höhnel
Septoria acetosae Oudem
S. avenae Frank
S. cerastii Roberge & Desm.
S. lychnidis Desm.
S. jasiones Died.
S. paeoniae Westend.
S. ribis Desm.
S. stellariae Roberge ex Desm.
Sphaerellopsis filum (Biv.-Bern.) B. Sutton
Stagonospora compta (Sacc.) Died.
S. luzulae (Westend.) Sacc.
S. subceriata (Desm.) Sacc.
Staninwardia sp.
Steganosporium pyriforme (Hoffm.) Corda
Thyriostoma spiraeae (Fr.) Died.

Melanconiales

Melanconium sp.
Melanconium apiocarpum Link
Myxosporium bellulum (Preuss.) Sacc.

Naemospora microspora Desm.
N. strobi Allescher

Phycomycotera

Phycomycotina

Mucorales

Choanephoraceae
Cunninghamella elegans Lendner

Mortierellaceae
Mortierella bainerii Costantin

Mucoraceae
Mucor plumbeus Bonorden

Pilaira anomala Schroet.
Phycomyces nitens (C.Ag.) Kunze
Spinellus fusiger (Link) v. Tieghem

Pilobolaceae
Pilobolus crystallinus (Wigg.) Tode
P. kleinii v. Tieghem

Entomophthorales

Ichthyophonus hoferi Plehn & Muslow

Endogonales

Acaulosporaceae
Acaulospora ?laevis Gerdemann & Trappe
A. nicolsonii Walker, Reed & Saunders
A. scrobiculata Trappe
Acaulospora sp.

Glomaceae
Glomus constrictum Trappe
G. geosporum Nicol. & Gerd.
G. macrocarpum Tul. & C. Tul.

G. occultum Walker
G. scintillans Rose & Trappe
Glomus spp. 1–3

Gigasporaceae
Scutellospora calospora (Nicol. & Gerd.) Koske & Walker
Scutellospora sp. 1
Scutellospora sp. 2

Chytridales

Synchytriaceae
Synchytrium erieum Karling

Mastigomycotina

Peronosporales

Pythiaceae
Phytophthora cryptogaea Pethybr. & Laff.
P. infestans (Mont.) de Bary
Pythium sp.

Peronosporaceae
Albugo lepigoni (de Bary) Kuntze
A. tragopogonis (Pers.) Schroeter
Peronospora alsinearum Casp.
P. ficariae (Nees) Tul.

P. honkenyae H. Sydow
P. minor (Carp.) Gaum.
P. polygoni (Thüm.) A. Fischer
P. radii de Bary
P. ranunculi Gaum.
P. rumicis Corda
P. violacea Berk. in Cooke
Plasmopora densa (Rabenh.) Schroeter
P. nivea (Unger) Schroeter

Plasmodiophorales

Plasmodiophora brassicae Woronin

Spongospora subterranea (Wallr.) Lagerh.

Myxomycotina (authorities of taxa following Ing 1968)

Myxomycota

Trichiales

Trichiaceae
Arcyria denudata
A. incarnata
Trichia botrytis
T. contorta

Dianemaceae
Prototrichia metallica

Physarales

Physaraceae
Badhamia lilacina
B. panicea

B. utricularis
Physarum nutans

Liceales

Liceaceae
Licea belmontiana Nann.-Brem.
L. inconspicua
L. operculata
L. parasitica
L. testudinacea Nann.-Brem.

Reticulariaceae
Lycogala epidendrum
Reticularia lycoperdon

Echinosteliales

Echinosteliaceae
Echinostelium fragile

E. minutum

Stemonitales

Stemonitaceae
Paradiacheopsis solitaria
Comatricha nigra

C. tenerrima
C. typhina

BRYOPHYTES

by M. E. Newton, University of Manchester

This group of plants is well represented in Shetland, partly because of the islands' northern situation, strongly influenced by an oceanic climate, but also because of their immense geological diversity and the position of Britain as a whole in relation to the Continent. Some 38% of the British species of bryophytes have been found on Shetland. They include good examples of ones that have a circumboreal (e.g. *Dicranella subulata*, *Blasia pusilla*), arctic–alpine (e.g. *Encalypta rhaptocarpa*, *Catoscopium nigritum*) or bi-polar (e.g. *Andreaea alpina*, *Anthelia juratzkana*) distribution. Indeed, one arctic moss, *Sanionia orthothecioides*, is known in Britain only on Shetland. Overlapping phytogeographical elements, however, are a pronounced feature of the Shetland bryophyte flora, to such an extent that *Pottia crinita* and *Porella obtusata* represent a Mediterranean–Atlantic group of species. Those species, the Atlantics and sub-Atlantics, that are dependent on sustained high humidity are particularly evident. Over 25% of the northern and widespread Atlantic species found in Britain (Ratcliffe, 1968) occur on Shetland, and more than 50% of the sub-Atlantics and Western British species are also found here. Together, these Atlantic and sub-Atlantic species make up a very important group of species for which Britain has a special duty of responsibility in terms of worldwide conservation. As well as these ecologically restricted species, however, cosmopolitan species inevitably occur on Shetland, but so too does *Anoectangium warburgii*, which is believed to be a British endemic.

Habitat variation within Shetland is closely correlated with bryophyte distribution. There are numerous calcifuges as well as calcicoles, and both groups are characteristic of a wide range of inland habitats. Despite the fact that none of those habitats includes woodland, many bryophytes that are commonly epiphytic in Britain do occur on Shetland. Some, such as *Ulota phyllantha* and *Zygodon viridissimus*, grow instead on rock, whereas others such as the thalloid liverwort, *Metzgeria fruticulosa*, have been found on elders in gardens. Many mosses, as well as liverworts, occur in coastal situations, but only four mosses on Shetland, *Desmatodon heimii*, *Schistidium maritimum*, *Tortella flavovirens* and *Trichostomum brachydontium*, are strong halophytes, tolerant of sea spray. However, many others, including *Sanionia orthothecioides*, clearly have some level of tolerance.

In the list below, asterisks identify old records made prior to 1950.

Mosses

Amblyodon dealbatus (Hedw.) B. & S.
Amblystegium riparium (Hedw.) B., S. & G.
A. serpens (Hedw.) B., S. & G. var. *salinum* Carringt.
A. serpens (Hedw.) B., S. & G. var. *serpens*
Amphidium mougeotii (B. & S.) Schimp.
Andreaea alpina Hedw.
A. rothii Web. & Mohr var. *falcata* (Schimp.) Lindb.
A. rupestris Hedw. var. *rupestris*
Anoectangium warburgii Crundw. & M. Hill
Anomobryum julaceum (Gaertn., Meyer & Scherb.) Schimp.
Antitrichia curtipendula (Hedw.) Brid.
Archidium alternifolium (Hedw.) Schimp.
Atrichum undulatum (Hedw.) P. Beauv. var. *undulatum*
Aulacomnium palustre (Hedw.) Schwaegr. var. *palustre*
Barbula convoluta Hedw.
B. unguiculata Hedw.
Bartramia ithyphylla Brid.
Blindia acuta (Hedw.) B., S. & G.
Brachythecium albicans (Hedw.) B., S. & G.
B. mildeanum (Schimp.) Schimp. ex Milde
B. plumosum (Hedw.) B., S. & G.
B. populeum (Hedw.) B., S. & G.
B. rivulare B., S. & G.
B. rutabulum (Hedw.) B., S. & G.
B. velutinum (Hedw.) B., S. & G.
Breutelia chrysocoma (Hedw.) Lindb.
Bryoerythrophyllum recurvirostrum (Hedw.) Chen
Bryum algovicum Sendtn. ex C. Müll. var. *rutheanum* (Warnst.) Crundw.
B. alpinum With.
B. argenteum Hedw. var. *argenteum*
B. argenteum Hedw. var. *lanatum* (P. Beauv.) Hampe
B. bicolor Dicks.
B. bornholmense Winkelm. & Ruthe
B. capillare Hedw. var. *capillare*
B. dunense A. J. E. Sm. & H. Whiteh.
B. inclinatum (Brid.) Bland.
B. klinggraeffii Schimp.
B. pallens Sw. var. *pallens*
B. pseudotriquetrum (Hedw.) Gaertn. var. *pseudotriquetrum*
B. rubens Mitt.
B. ruderale Crundw. & Nyh.
B. sauteri B., S. & G.
B. subapiculatum Hampe
Calliergon cordifolium (Hedw.) Kindb.
C. giganteum (Schimp.) Kindb.
C. sarmentosum (Wahlenb.) Kindb.
C. stramineum (Brid.) Kindb.
Calliergonella cuspidata (Hedw.) Loeske
Campylium chrysophyllum (Brid.) J. Lange
C. elodes (Lindb.) Kindb.

C. polygamum (B., S. & G.) J. Lange & C. Jens.
C. stellatum (Hedw.) J. Lange & C. Jens. var *stellatum*
Campylopus atrovirens De Not. var. *atrovirens*
C. atrovirens De Not. var. *falcatus* Braithw.
C. brevipilus B., S. & G.
C. flexuosus (Hedw.) Brid.
C. fragilis (Brid.) B., S. & G.
C. introflexus (Hedw.) Brid.
C. pyriformis (K. F. Schultz) Brid. var. *pyriformis*
C. schimperi Milde
Catoscopium nigritum (Hedw.) Brid.
Ceratodon purpureus (Hedw.) Brid. ssp. *purpureus*
Cinclidium stygium Sw.
Cinclidotus fontinaloides (Hedw.) P. Beauv.
Cirriphyllum crassinervium (Tayl.) Loeske & Fleisch.
Climacium dendroides (Hedw.) Web. & Mohr
Conostomum tetragonum (Hedw.) Lindb.
Cratoneuron commutatum (Hedw.) G. Roth var. *commutatum*
C. commutatum (Hedw.) G. Roth var. *falcatum* (Brid.) Moenk.
C. filicinum (Hedw.) Spruce var. *filicinum*
Ctenidium molluscum (Hedw.) Mitt. var. *condensatum* (Schimp.) Britt.
C. molluscum (Hedw.) Mitt. var. *molluscum*
Desmatodon heimii (Hedw.) Mitt.
Dichodontium pellucidum (Hedw.) Schimp.
Dicranella cerviculata (Hedw.) Schimp.
D. heteromalla (Hedw.) Schimp.
D. palustris (Dicks.) Crundw. ex E. Warb.
D. rufescens (With.) Schimp.
D. schreberana (Hedw.) Dix.
D. staphylina H. Whiteh.
D. subulata (Hedw.) Schimp.
D. varia (Hedw.) Schimp.
Dicranodontium denudatum (Brid.) Britt. var. *denudatum*
Dicranoweisia cirrata (Hedw.) Lindb. ex Milde
Dicranum bonjeanii De Not.
D. elongatum Schleich. ex Schwaegr.
D. fuscescens Sm. var. *fuscescens*
D. majus Sm.
D. montanum Hedw.
D. scoparium Hedw.
Didymodon fallax (Hedw.) Zander
D. insulanus (De Not.) M. Hill
D. luridus Hornsch. ex Spreng.
D. rigidulus Hedw.
D. sinuosus (Mitt.) Delogne
D. spadiceus (Mitt.) Limpr.
D. tophaceus (Brid.) Lisa
D. vinealis (Brid.) Zander
Diphyscium foliosum (Hedw.) Mohr
Distichium capillaceum (Hedw.) B., S. & G.

D. inclinatum (Hedw.) B,. S. & G.

Ditrichum crispatissimum (C. Müll.) Par.

D. cylindricum (Hedw.) Grout

D. heteromallum (Hedw.) Britt.

Drepanocladus aduncus (Hedw.) Warnst.

D. exannulatus (B., S. & G.) Warnst. var. *exannulatus*

D. exannulatus (B., S. & G.) Warnst. var. *rotae* (De Not.) Loeske

D. fluitans (Hedw.) Warnst. var. *falcatus* (Sanio ex C. Jens.) Roth

D. fluitans (Hedw.) Warnst. var. *fluitans*

D. revolvens (Sw.) Warnst.

Dryptodon patens (Hedw.) Brid.

Encalypta rhaptocarpa Schwaegr.

Entosthodon attenuatus (Dicks.) Bryhn

E. obtusus (Hedw.) Lindb.

Ephemerum serratum (Hedw.) Hampe var. *minutissimum* (Lindb.) Grout

E. serratum (Hedw.) Hampe var. *serratum*

Eucladium verticillatum (Brid.) B., S. & G.

Eurhynchium hians (Hedw.) Sande Lac.

E. praelongum (Hedw.) B., S. & G. var. *praelongum*

E. striatum (Hedw.) Schimp.

Fissidens adianthoides Hedw.

F. bryoides Hedw.

F. cristatus Wils. ex Mitt.

F. curnovii Mitt.

F. osmundoides Hedw.

F. taxifolius Hedw. ssp. *pallidicaulis* (Mitt.) Moenk.

F. taxifolius Hedw. ssp. *taxifolius*

Fontinalis antipyretica Hedw. var. *antipyretica*

F. antipyretica Hedw. var. *gigantea* (Sull.) Sull.

F. antipyretica Hedw. var. *gracilis* (Hedw.) Schimp.

Funaria hygrometrica Hedw.

Grimmia donniana Sm. var. *donniana*

G. pulvinata (Hedw.) Sm. var. *pulvinata*

G. trichophylla Grev. var. *stirtonii* (Schimp.) Muell.

G. trichophylla Grev. var. *trichophylla*

Gymnostomum aeruginosum Sm.

Gyroweisia tenuis (Hedw.) Schimp.

Hedwigia stellata Hedenäs

Heterocladium heteropterum B., S. & G. var. *heteropterum*

Homalia trichomanoides (Hedw.) Brid.

Homalothecium lutescens (Hedw.) Robins.

H. sericeum (Hedw.) B., S. & G.

Hookeria lucens (Hedw.) Sm.

Hygrohypnum duriusculum (De Not.) Jamieson

H. eugyrium (Schimp.) Broth.

H. luridum (Hedw.) Jenn. var. *luridum*

H. ochraceum (Turn. ex Wils.) Loeske

Hylocomium splendens (Hedw.) B., S. & G.

Hymenostylium recurvirostrum (Hedw.) Dix.

Hyocomium armoricum (Brid.) Wijk & Marg.

Hypnum cupressiforme Hedw. var. *cupressiforme*

H. cupressiforme Hedw. var. *lacunosum* Brid.

H. cupressiforme Hedw. var. *resupinatum* (Tayl.) Schimp.

H. jutlandicum Holmen & Warncke

Isopterygium elegans (Brid.) Lindb.

Isothecium alopecuroides (Dubois) Isov.

I. myosuroides Brid. var. *brachythecioides* (Dix.) Braithw.

I. myosuroides Brid. var. *myosuroides*

Leucobryum glaucum (Hedw.) Angstr.

Mnium hornum Hedw.

M. marginatum (With.) P. Beauv.

M. stellare Hedw.

Neckera complanata (Hedw.) Hüb.

Oligotrichum hercynicum (Hedw.) Lam. & DC.

*Orthothecium intricatum (Hartm.) B., S. & G.

Orthotrichum anomalum Hedw.

O. cupulatum Brid. var. *cupulatum*

O. diaphanum Brid.

O. pulchellum Brunt.

O. rupestre Schleich. ex Schwaegr.

Philonotis caespitosa Jur.

P. calcarea (B. & S.) Schimp.

P. fontana (Hedw.) Brid.

P. tomentella Mol.

Physcomitrium pyriforme (Hedw.) Brid.

Plagiomnium cuspidatum (Hedw.) T. Kop.

P. elatum (B. & S.) T. Kop.

P. ellipticum (Brid.) T. Kop.

P. rostratum (Schrad.) T. Kop.

P. undulatum (Hedw.) T. Kop.

Plagiothecium denticulatum (Hedw.) B., S. & G. var. *denticulatum*

P. nemorale (Mitt.) Jaeg.

P. succulentum (Wils.) Lindb.

P. undulatum (Hedw.) B., S. & G.

Pleuridium acuminatum Lindb.

Pleurozium schreberi (Brid.) Mitt.

Pogonatum aloides (Hedw.) P. Beauv. var. *aloides*

P. nanum (Hedw.) P. Beauv.

P. urnigerum (Hedw.) P. Beauv.

Pohlia annotina (Hedw.) Lindb.

P. camptotrachela (Ren. & Card.) Broth.

P. carnea (Schimp.) Lindb.

P. cruda (Hedw.) Lindb.

P. drummondii (C. Mull.) Andr.

P. filum (Schimp.) Mårt.

P. nutans (Hedw.) Lindb.

P. wahlenbergii (Web. & Mohr) Andr. var. *wahlenbergii*

Polytrichum alpinum Hedw. var. *alpinium*

P. commune Hedw. var. *commune*

P. formosum Hedw.

P. juniperinum Hedw.

P. longisetum Sw. ex Brid.

P. piliferum Hedw.

P. strictum Brid.

Pottia crinita Wils. ex B., S. & G.

P. truncata (Hedw.) B. & S.

Pseudephemerum nitidum (Hedw.) Reim.

Pseudobryum cinclidioides (Hüb.) T. Kop.

Pseudocrossidium hornschuchianum (K. F. Schultz) Zander

*Pterigynandrum filiforme Hedw. var. *filiforme*

Ptychomitrium polyphyllum (Sw.) B. & S.

Racomitrium aciculare (Hedw.) Brid.

R. aquaticum (Schrad.) Brid.

R. ellipticum (Turn.) B. & S.

R. ericoides (Brid.) Brid.

R. fasciculare (Hedw.) Brid.

R. heterostichum (Hedw.) Brid.
R. lanuginosum (Hedw.) Brid.
Rhabdoweisia crispata (With.) Lindb.
R. fugax (Hedw.) B., S. & G.
Rhizomnium pseudopunctatum (B. & S.) T. Kop.
R. punctatum (Hedw.) T. Kop.
Rhodobryum roseum (Hedw.) Limpr.
Rhynchostegium confertum (Dicks.) B., S. & G.
R. murale (Hedw.) B., S. & G.
R. riparioides (Hedw.) Card.
Rhytidiadelphus loreus (Hedw.) Warnst.
R. squarrosus (Hedw.) Warnst.
R. triquetrus (Hedw.) Warnst.
Sanionia orthothecioides (Lindb.) Loeske
S. uncinata (Hedw.) Loeske
Schistidium apocarpum (Hedw.) B. & S. var. *apocarpum*
S. maritimum (Turn.) B. & S.
S. rivulare (Brid.) Podp. ssp. *latifolium* (Zett.) B. Bremer
S. rivulare (Brid.) Podp. ssp. *rivulare*
Scleropodium purum (Hedw.) Limpr.
Scorpidium scorpioides (Hedw.) Limpr.
Sphagnum auriculatum Schimp.
S. capillifolium (Ehrh.) Hedw.
S. compactum Lam. & DC.
S. contortum K. F. Schultz
S. cuspidatum Ehrh. ex Hoffm.
S. fimbriatum Wils.
S. girgensohnii Russ.
S. imbricatum Hornsch. ex Russ. ssp. *austinii* (Sull.) Flatberg
*S. lindbergii Schimp. ex Lindb.
S. magellanicum Brid.
S. palustre L.

S. papillosum Lindb.
S. recurvum P. Beauv. var. *mucronatum* (Russ.) Warnst.
S. riparium Angstr.
S. russowii Warnst.
S. squarrosum Crome
S. subnitens Russ. & Warnst.
S. subsecundum Nees. ssp. *inundatum* (Russ.) A. Eddy
S. tenellum (Brid.) Bory
S. teres (Schimp.) Angstr.
Splachnum sphaericum Hedw.
Thamnobryum alopecurum (Hedw.) Nieuwl.
Thuidium erectum Duby
T. tamariscinum (Hedw.) B., S. & G.
Tortella flavovirens (Bruch) Broth. var. *flavovirens*
T. tortuosa (Hedw.) Limpr.
Tortula intermedia (Brid.) De Not.
T. muralis Hedw. var. *muralis*
T. ruraliformis (Besch.) Grout
T. subulata Hedw. var. *angustata* (Schimp.) Limpr.
T. subulata Hedw. var. *graeffii* Warnst.
T. subulata Hedw. var. *subulata*
Trichostomum brachydontium Bruch
T. crispulum Bruch
Ulota calvescens Wils.
U. crispa (Hedw.) Brid. var. *crispa*
U. hutchinsiae (Sm.) Hammar
U. phyllantha Brid.
Weissia brachycarpa (Nees & Hornsch.) Jur. var. *obliqua* (Nees & Hornsch.) M. Hill
W. controversa Hedw. var. *controversa*
W. perssonii Kindb.
Zygodon viridissimus (Dicks.) Brid. var. *stirtonii* (Schimp. ex Stirt.) Hagen
Z. viridissimus (Dicks.) Brid. var. *viridissimus*

Liverworts

Anastrepta orcadensis (Hook.) Schiffn.
*Anastrophyllum minutum (Schreb.) Schust.
Aneura pinguis (L.) Dum.
Anthelia julacea (L.) Dum.
*A. juratzkana (Limpr.) Trev.
Barbilophozia atlantica (Kaal.) K. Müll.
B. floerkei (Web. & Mohr) Loeske
Bazzania tricrenata (Wahlenb.) Lindb.
B. trilobata (L.) S. Gray
Blasia pusilla L.
Blepharostoma trichophyllum (L.) Dum.
Calypogeia arguta Nees & Mont.
C. azurea Stotler & Crotz
C. fissa (L.) Raddi
C. muelleriana (Schiffn.) K. Müll.
C. neesiana (Mass. & Carest.) K. Müll.
C. sphagnicola (H. Arn. & J. Perss.) Warnst. & Loeske
Cephalozia bicuspidata (L.) Dum. ssp. *bicuspidata*
C. bicuspidata (L.) Dum. ssp. *lammersiana* (Hub.) Schust.
C. catenulata (Hub.) Lindb.
C. connivens (Dicks.) Lindb.
C. leucantha Spruce
C. loitlesbergeri Schiffn.
C. lunulifolia (Dum.) Dum.

C. pleniceps (Aust.) Lindb.
Cephaloziella divaricata (Sm.) Schiffn.
C. hampeana (Nees) Schiffn.
C. spinigera (Lindb.) Warnst.
Chiloscyphus pallescens (Ehrh. ex Hoffm.) Dum.
C. polyanthos (L.) Corda
Cladopodiella fluitans (Nees) Buch
Conocephalum conicum (L.) Underw.
Diplophyllum albicans (L.) Dum.
*D. obtusifolium (Hook.) Dum.
Douinia ovata (Dicks.) Buch
Fossombronia foveolata Lindb.
F. incurva Lindb.
F. wondraczekii (Corda) Lindb.
Frullania dilatata (L.) Dum.
F. fragilifolia (Tayl.) Gott. *et al.*
F. tamarisci (L.) Dum.
F. teneriffae (F. Web.) Nees
Gymnocolea inflata (Huds.) Dum. var. *inflata*
*Gymnomitrion concinnatum (Lightf.) Corda
G. crenulatum Gott. ex Carring.
Haplomitrium hookeri (Sm.) Nees
*Harpanthus flotovianus (Nees) Nees
H. scutatus (Web. et Mohr) Spruce
Herbertus stramineus (Dum.) Trev.

Hygrobiella laxifolia (Hook.) Spruce
Jungermannia atrovirens Dum.
J. exsertifolia Steph. ssp. *cordifolia* (Dum.) Vana
J. gracillima Sm.
J. obovata Nees
J. paroica (Schiffn.) Grolle
J. pumila With.
J. sphaerocarpa Hook.
J. subelliptica (Lindb. ex Kall.) Levier
Kurzia pauciflora (Dicks.) Grolle
K. sylvatica (Evans) Grolle
K. trichoclados (K. Müll.) Grolle
Leiocolea alpestris (Schleich. ex Web.) Isov.
L. gillmanii (Aust.) Schust.
Lejeunea cavifolia (Ehrh.) Lindb.
L. patens Lindb.
Lepidozia cupressina (Sw.) Lindenb.
L. pearsonii Spruce
L. reptans (L.) Dum.
Lophocolea bidentata (L.) Dum.
*Lophozia bicrenata (Schmid. ex Hoffm.) Dum.
L. incisa (Schrad.) Dum.
L. sudetica (Nees ex Hüb.) Grolle
L. ventricosa (Dicks.) Dum. var. *ventricosa*
Lunularia cruciata (L.) Lindb.
Marchantia polymorpha L. ssp. *montivagans* Bischl. et Boisselier
M. polymorpha L. ssp. *polymorpha*
Marsupella emarginata (Ehrh.) Dum. var. *aquatica* (Lindenb.) Dum.
M. emarginata (Ehrh.) Dum. var. *emarginata*
M. emarginata (Ehrh.) Dum. var. *pearsonii* (Schiffn.) Corley
*M. sphacelata (Gieseke ex Lindenb.) Dum.
Mastigophora woodsii (Hook.) Nees
Metzgeria fruticulosa (Dicks.) Evans
M. furcata (L.) Dum.
Moerckia hibernica (Hook.) Gott.
Mylia anomala (Hook.) S. Gray
M. taylorii (Hook.) S. Gray
Nardia compressa (Hook.) S. Gray
N. geoscyphus (De Not.) Lindb.

N. scalaris S. Gray
Nowellia curvifolia (Dicks.) Mitt.
Odontoschisma denudatum (Mart.) Dum.
O. elongatum (Lindb.) Evans
O. sphagni (Dicks.) Dum.
Pellia endiviifolia (Dicks.) Dum.
P. epiphylla (L.) Corda
P. neesiana (Gott.) Limpr.
Plagiochila carringtonii (Balfour) Grolle
P. porelloides (Torrey ex Nees) Lindenb.
P. punctata Tayl.
P. spinulosa (Dicks.) Dum.
Pleurozia purpurea Lindb.
Porella arboris-vitae (With.) Grolle var. *arboris-vitae*
P. cordeana (Hüb.) Moore var. *cordeana*
P. cordeana (Hüb.) Moore var. *faeroensis* (C. Jens.) E.W. Jones
P. obtusata (Tayl.) Trev.
P. platyphylla (L.) Pfeiff.
Preissia quadrata (Scop.) Nees
Ptilidium ciliare (L.) Hampe
Radula aquilegia (Hook. f. et Tayl.) Gott. *et al.*
R. complanata (L.) Dum.
Riccardia chamedryfolia (With.) Grolle
R. incurvata Lindb.
R. latifrons (Lindb.) Lindb.
R. multifida (L.) S. Gray
R. palmata (Hedw.) Carruth.
Saccogyna viticulosa (L.) Dum.
Scapania compacta (A. Roth) Dum.
S. degenii Schiffn. ex K. Müll.
S. gracilis Lindb.
S. irrigua (Nees) Nees
S. nemorea (L.) Grolle
S. ornithopodioides (With.) Waddel
S. scandica (H. Arn. & Buch) Macv.
S. subalpina (Nees ex Lindenb.) Dum.
S. uliginosa (Sw. ex Lindenb.) Dum.
S. umbrosa (Schrad.) Dum.
S. undulata (L.) Dum.
Tritomaria exsectiformis (Breidl.) Loeske
T. quinquedentata (Huds.) Buch

LICHENS

by D. H. Dalby

Lichen thrive in the clean and unpolluted Shetland atmosphere. Shetland has been fortunate, in spite of its northern and oceanic isolation, to have been visited by some specialist lichenologists, mostly in relation to environmental studies linked with oil industry developments at Sullom Voe. Even so, many parts of Shetland (and especially some remote sites and islands) remain unvisited by lichenologists, so there is still much scope for further fieldwork. At present, lichens new to Shetland are being discovered at the rate of one or two per year. A fuller introduction to the lichens of Shetland has been given by Dalby (1991), and a wholly updated and annotated check-list is in preparation. These publications, together with Hawksworth (1970b, 1980), refer to virtually all published work on the Shetland lichen flora.

The Shetland lichen flora is essentially northern oceanic in the European context, but within the British Isles its more obvious relationships are with the uplands of Scotland and northern England (though some species extend down to very low altitudes in Shetland). Only about 25% of the total British lichen list occur in Shetland. Those of strictly southern affinities are absent, including many calcicoles of soft sedimentary limestones and most tree epiphytes, though a few of the latter grow instead on fence posts or even on rock (particularly a few characteristic of open oceanic woodlands elsewhere in Britain, which may now be relicts in Shetland). Loch and river margin lichen floras are also poorly represented. Although these species that are common in northern Britain certainly grow in much of Shetland, those from the fringes of the Arctic are quite scarce. In contrast, rocky sea shore communities (and those of a generally coastal nature) are perhaps not unsurprisingly very widespread in Shetland, though lacking many species characteristic of more southerly affinities.

In fact lichens dominate the rocky sea shores and cliffs of Shetland, where they form coloured zones at different heights above the sea. The lowest of these, generally dark or blackish, is dominated by *Verrucaria maura*, with other less conspicuous species (*V. striatula* and *V. amphibia*) at or near the uppermost limits of the barnacles. Headlands and rock outcrops at higher levels, coloured grey or orange-yellow, are dominated by a rich mix of species, including *Caloplaca marina*, *Ochrolechia parella*, *Tephromela atra* and *Xanthoria parietina*. Other coastal *Caloplaca* species have quite specialized habitats, such as *C. microthallina* on *Verrucaria maura* on north and north-east facing shaded cliffs, and *C. obliterans* on rock overhangs, whilst bird-perch sites are often characterized by *C. verruculifera* (with *Lecania aipospila*). Rocks above normal wave level (but wetted by salt spray) are frequently dominated by spiky growths of *Ramalina cuspidata*.

Extensive outcrops of very hard crystalline limestone at White Ness, and a few other sites through to Unst, have a most characteristic and diverse lichen flora, exemplified by *Aspicilia calcarea*, *Caloplaca holocarpa*, *C. cirrochroa*, *Diplotomma alboatrum*, *Lecanora albescens*, *Placynthium nigrum*, *Protoblastenia immersa*, *Verrucaria nigrescens* and *V. glaucina*. Even very small limestone exposures, perhaps surrounded by acidic moor and marsh, can still carry this distinctive lichen flora. The remains of derelict crofthouses also support calcicolous species, such as *Diplotomma alboatrum*, *Lecanora albescens* and *Toninia aromatica* on decayed mortar.

Lichens are generally abundant on siliceous rock surfaces and boulders not enveloped in blanket peat, but the number of species varies considerably with rock type. Thus the flora of the hard micro-granites is much poorer than that of the chemically 'richer' basic igneous rocks. The majority of these saxicolous species (e.g. *Fuscidea cyathoides* and *Porpidia tuberculosa*) form low-growing crusts which may be relatively difficult to identify, with the result that the Shetland communities are not yet properly studied. In contrast, however, some fruticose species are very much more conspicuous, such as the shaggy mats of *Ramalina siliquosa* on wind-exposed rock faces, on standing stones and on the masonry of brochs. This species (one of the lichens used in the past by Shetlanders for dyeing wool) is particularly impressive on the walls of St Olaf's kirk at Lund on Unst. The field walls around sheep pastures in Dunrossness are clothed in *R. subfarinacea* together with *Physcia tenella*. The rust-brown stony ground of the Keen of Hamar and the other Unst and Fetlar serpentinites look at first sight to be quite sterile (apart from the white caps of *Ochrolechia parella* and *Porpidia crustulata* on scattered boulder tops) but closer study shows a more varied lichen flora developed on and even within the weathered rock surfaces.

Although trees and shrubs are now generally scarce in Shetland it is still possible to find traces of what may once have been a *Lobarion* community from earlier oceanic scrub woodland, but these relicts are no longer associated with any trees or shrubs. The willows beside burns and the introduced sycamores are often well covered by epiphytes, even if there are few lichen species present. The richest localities are the sycamores, wych elm and other trees in old gardens and plantations associated with *haa* houses. Those in the grounds of Kergord House in Weisdale provide one of the few Shetland localities for *Normandina pulchella* and *Physconia grisea*, together with extensive rosettes of *Parmelia perlata*, but the nearby conifer plantations are much less interesting for lichens. The smooth bark of ash trees carry rosettes of *Lecanora confusa* and *L. subfusca*, together with various species of *Opegrapha* and other less-conspicuous lichens, but rougher bark on elms tends to be dominated by epiphytic mosses such as *Ulota phyllantha*.

Field fences with softwood posts extend throughout the crofting lands, and if they have stood for long enough they develop a lichen cover with affinities to those of trees elsewhere in northern Britain. Oval patches of *Lecanora expallens* and *L. symmicta* are abundant, with other typical species such as *Bryoria fuscescens*, *Hypogymnia physodes*, *Pseudevernia furfuracens*, *Parmelia saxatilis*, *Usnea hirta* and *U. subflorida*, most of which contributes to conspicuous furry caps on the tops of the fence posts.

Most lichens cannot compete with more vigorous vascular plants and so are less often found growing directly on soil. Terrestrial lichens are commonest in open sites where mineral soils overlying buried rock outcrops are too shallow to support vascular plants. In these localities one finds fragmentary lichen heaths developed, typically with species such as *Coelocaulon aculeatum*, *Hypogymnia tubulosa*, *Ochrolechia frigida*, *Pannaria pezizoides* and *Parmelia omphalodes*. Detached thalli of *Cetraria ericetorum* characteristically lie loose and are dispersed by the wind. Near the summits of Ronas Hill and Mid Field *Ochrolechia androgyna* forms crusts polished by wind-blown particles, and small chalk-white thalli of *Thamnolia vermicularis* occur sparsely in very low vegetation (but are missing from taller and denser stands of grasses and rushes). Disturbed peat (particularly if previously cut for fuel) can be rich in *Cladonia* species such as *C. crispata*, *C. portentosa* and *C. uncialis*, together with *Omphalina* species and *Pycnothelia papillaria*.

Grasslands are particularly poor for lichens (especially the agriculturally improved pastures on recently enclosed moorlands), but *Peltigera membranacea* is common in older grasslands in disturbed places where shallow soils dry in summer, with *P. lactucifolia* preferring rather more moist conditions.

A few species may be included in error, but their true identity cannot be established in the absence of supporting voucher specimens.

Acarospora fuscata (Schrader) Th. Fr.
A. sinopica (Wahlenb.) Körber
A. smaragdula (Wahlenb.) Massal.
A. veronensis Massal.
A. sp. (near *A. verruciformis* Magnusson)
Acrocordia gemmata (Ach.) Massal.
A. macrospora Massal.
A. salweyi (Leighton ex Nyl.) A.L. Smith
Agonimia tristicula (Nyl.) Zahlbr.
Agyrium rufum (Pers.) Fr.
Alectoria nigricans (Ach.) Nyl.
A. sarmentosa subsp. *vexillifera* (Nyl.) D. Hawksw.
Amygdalaria pelobotryon (Wahlenb.) Norman
Anaptychia ciliaris subsp. *mamillata* (Taylor) D. Hawksw. & P. James
A. runcinata (With.) Laundon
Anisomeridium biforme (Borrer) R.C. Harris
A. nyssaegenum (Ellis & Everh.) R.C. Harris
Arthonia intexta Almq.
A. lapidicola (Taylor) Branth & Rostrup
A. phaeobaea (Norman) Norman
A. punctiformis Ach.
A. radiata (Pers.) Ach.
Arthopyrenia punctiformis Massal.
A. salicis Massal.
Aspicilia caesiocinerea (Nyl. ex Malbr.) Arnold
A. calcarea (L.) Mudd
A. contorta (Hoffm.) Krempelh.
A. grisea Arnold
A. leprosescens (Sandst.) Havaas
Bacidia arceutina (Ach.) Arnold
B. bagliettoana (Massal. & de Not.) Jatta
B. egenula (Nyl.) Arnold
B. inundata (Fr.) Körber
B. naegelii (Hepp) Zahlbr.
B. sabuletorum (Schreber) Lettau
B. scopulicola (Nyl.) A.L. Smith
Baeomyces placophyllus Ach.
B. roseus Pers.
B. rufus (Huds.) Rebent.
Belonia nidarosiensis (Kindt) P.M. Jørg. & Vězda
Brigantiaea fuscolutea (Dickson) R. Sant.
Bryophagus gloeocapsa Nitschke ex Arnold
Bryoria bicolor (Ehrh.) Brodo & D. Hawksw.
B. chalybeiformis (L.) Brodo & D. Hawksw.
B. fuscescens var. *fuscescens* (Gyelnik) Brodo & D. Hawksw.
B. subcana (Nyl. ex Stitzenb.) Brodo & D. Hawksw.
Buellia aethalea (Ach.) Th. Fr.
B. coniops (Wahlenb.ex Ach.) Th. Fr.
B. disciformis (Fr.) Mudd
B. ocellata (Flotow) Körber
B. punctata (Hoffm.) Massal.
B. stellulata (Taylor) Mudd
B. subdisciformis (Leighton) Vainio
Caloplaca arnoldii (Wedd.) Zahlbr. ex Ginzb.
C. aurantia (Pers.) Steiner
C. britannica R. Sant.
C. ceracea Laundon
C. cerina (Ehrh. ex Hedwig) Th. Fr.
C. cerinella (Nyl.) Flagey
C. cirrochroa (Ach.) Th. Fr.

C. citrina (Hoffm.) Th. Fr.
C. crenularia (With.) Laundon
C. decipiens (Arnold) Blomb. & Forss.
C. ferruginea (Huds.) Th. Fr.
C. flavescens (Huds.) Laundon
C. flavovirescens (Wulfen) Dalla Torre & Sarnth.
C. holocarpa sensu lato
C. irrubescens (Arnold) Zahlbr.
C. marina (Wedd.) Zahlbr. ex Du Rietz
C. microthallina (Wedd.) Zahlbr.
C. obliterans (Nyl.) Blomb. & Forss.
C. ochracea (Schaerer) Flagey
C. saxicola (Hoffm.) Nordin
C. scopularis (Nyl.) Lettau
C. thallincola (Wedd.) Du Rietz
C. variabilis (Pers.) Müll. Arg.
C. verruculifera (Vainio) Zahlbr.
Candelariella aurella (Hoffm.) Zahlbr.
C. coralliza (Nyl.) Magnusson
C. medians (Nyl.) A.L. Sm.
C. vitellina (Hoffm.) Müll. Arg.
Carbonea vorticosa (Flörke) Hertel
Catapyrenium cinereum (Pers.) Körber
C. lachneum (Ach.) R. Sant.
Catillaria chalybeia (Borrer) Massal.
C. lenticularis (Ach.) Th. Fr.
Cetraria chlorophylla (Willd.) Vainio
C. ericetorum Opiz
C. islandica (L.) Ach.
Chromatochlamys muscorum (Fr.) Mayrh. & Poelt
Cladonia arbuscula (Wallr.) Flotow
C. bellidiflora (Ach.) Schaerer
C. caespiticia (Pers.) Flörke
C. cervicornis subsp. *cervicornis* (Ach.) Flotow
C. cervicornis subsp. *verticillata* (Hoffm.) Ahti
C. chlorophaea (Flörke ex Sommerf.) Sprengel
C. ciliata var. *ciliata* Stirton
C. ciliata var. *tenuis* (Flörke) Ahti
C. coccifera (L.) Willd.
C. coniocraea (Flörke) Sprengel
C. cornuta (L.) Hoffm.
C. crispata var. *cetrariiformis* (Delise) Vainio
C. digitata (L.) Hoffm.
C. diversa Asperges
C. fimbriata (L.) Fr.
C. firma (Nyl.) Nyl.
C. floerkeana (Fr.) Flörke
C. foliacea (Huds.) Willd.
C. fragilissima Osth. & P. James
C. furcata (Huds.) Schrader
C. glauca Flörke
C. gracilis (L.) Willd.
C. humilis (With.) Laundon
C. luteoalba Wheldon & A. Wilson
C. macilenta Hoffm.
C. merochlorophaea Asah.
C. ochrochlora Flörke
C. pocillum (Ach.) O.J. Rich.
C. polydactyla (Flörke) Sprengel
C. portentosa (Dufour) Coem.
C. pyxidata (L.) Hoffm.
C. ramulosa (With.) Laundon

C. rangiferina (L.) Weber ex Wigg.
C. rangiformis Hoffm.
C. scabriuscula (Delise) Nyl.
C. squamosa var. *squamosa* (Scop.) Hoffm.
C. squamosa var. *subsquamosa* (Nyl. & Leighton) Vainio
C. strepsilis (Ach.) Vainio
C. subcervicornis (Vainio) Kernst.
C. subulata (L.) Weber ex Wigg.
C. sulphurina (Michaux) Fr.
C. symphycarpa (Ach.) Fr.
C. uncialis subsp. *biuncialis* (L.) Weber ex Wigg.
C. zopfii Vainio
Clauzadea immersa (Hoffm.) Hafellner & Bellem.
C. monticola (Ach.) Hafellner & Bellem.
Cliostomum griffithii (Sm.) Coppins
Coccotrema citrinescens P. James & Coppins
Coelocaulon aculeatum (Schreber) Link
C. muricatum (Ach.) Laundon
Collema auriforme (With.) Coppins & Laundon
C. crispum (Huds.) Weber ex Wigg.
C. cristatum (L.) Weber ex Wigg.
C. flaccidum (Ach.) Ach.
C. furfuraceum (Arnold) Du Rietz
C. fuscovirens (With.) Laundon
C. multipartitum Sm.
C. nigrescens (Huds.) DC.
C. polycarpon Hoffm.
C. tenax var. *ceranoides* (Borrer) Degel.
C. tenax var. *tenax* (Swartz) Ach.
C. tenax var. *vulgare* (Schreber) Degel.
Cornicularia normoerica (Gunn.) Du Rietz
Cystocoleus ebeneus (Dillwyn) Thwaites
Degelia plumbea (Lightf.) P. Jørg. & P. James
Dermatocarpon luridum (With.) Laundon
D. miniatum var. *complicatum* (Lightf.) Hellbom
D. miniatum var. *miniatum* (L.) Mann
Dimerella pineti (Ach.) Vězda
Diploicia canescens (Dickson) Massal.
Diploschistes muscorum (Scop.) R. Sant.
D. scruposus (Schreber) Norman
Diplotomma alboatrum (Hoffm.) Flotow
D. chlorophaeum (Hepp ex Leighton) Szat.
D. epipolium (Ach.) Arnold
Dirina massiliensis Durieu & Mont.
Enterographa zonata (Körber) Källsten
Ephebe lanata (L.) Vainio
Evernia prunastri (L.) Ach.
Fuscidea cyathoides var. *cyathoides* (Ach.) V. Wirth & Vězda
F. cyathoides var. *sorediata* (Magnusson) Poelt
F. kochiana (Hepp) V. Wirth & Vězda
F. lightfootii (Sm.) Coppins & P. James
F. lygaea (Ach.) V. Wirth & Vězda
F. mollis (Wahlenb.) V. Wirth & Vězda
F. praeruptorum (Du Rietz & Magnusson) V. Wirth & Vězda
Gyalecta foveolaris (Ach.) Schaerer
G. jenensis (Batsch) Zahlbr.
Gyalidea fritzei (Stein) Vězda
Haematomma ochroleucum var. *ochroleucum* (Necker) Laundon
H. ochroleucum var. *porphyrium* (Pers.) Laundon

Herteliana taylorii (Salwey) P. James
Hymenelia lacustris (With.) M. Choisy
H. prevostii (Duby) Krempelh.
Hyperphyscia adglutinata (Flörke) Mayrh. & Poelt
Hypogymnia physodes (L.) Nyl.
H. tubulosa (Schaerer) Havaas
Icmadophila ericetorum (L.) Zahlbr.
Ionaspis odora (Ach.) B. Stein
Lasallia pustulata (L.) Mérat
Lecania aipospila (Wahlenb.) Th. Fr.
L. baeomma (Nyl.) P. James & Laundon
L. cuprea (Massal.) v.d. Boom & Coppins
L. cyrtella (Ach.) Th. Fr.
L. erysibe (Ach.) Mudd
L. hutchinsiae (Nyl.) A.L. Smith
L. rabenhorstii (Hepp.) Arnold
L. suavis (Müll.Arg.) Mig.
Lecanora actophila Wedd.
L. albescens (Hoffm.) Branth & Rostrup
L. argentata (Ach.) Malme
L. campestris (Schaerer) Hue
L. carpinea (L.) Vainio
L. chlarotera Nyl.
L. confusa Almb.
L. conizaeoides Nyl. ex Crombie
L. crenulata Hook.
L. dispersa (L.) Sommerfelt.
L. expallens Ach.
L. farinaria Borrer
L. fugiens Nyl.
L. gangaleoides Nyl.
L. helicopis (Wahlenb.) Ach.
L. intricata (Ach.) Ach.
L. intumescens (Rebent.) Rabenh.
L. jamesii Laundon
L. muralis (Schreber) Rabenh.
L. orosthea (Ach.) Ach.
L. poliophaea (Wahlenb.) Ach.
L. polytropa (Hoffm.) Rabenh.
L. pulicaris (Pers.) Ach.
L. rugosella Zahlbr.
L. rupicola (L.) Zahlbr.
L. soralifera (Suza) Räsänen
L. straminea Wahlenb. ex Ach.
L. sulphurea (Hoffm.) Ach.
L. symmicta (Ach.) Ach.
L. tenera (Nyl.) Crombie
L. varia (Hoffm.) Ach.
Lecidea auriculata Th. Fr.
L. berengeriana (Massal.) Nyl.
L. brachyspora (Th. Fr.) Nyl.
L. cinnabarina Sommerf.
L. confluens (Web.) Ach.
L. diducens Nyl.
L. fuscoatra (L.) Ach.
L. hypnorum Lib.
L. lactea Flörke ex Schaerer
L. lapicida (Ach.) Ach.
L. lithophila (Ach.) Ach.
L. phaeops Nyl.
L. plana (Lahm) Nyl.
L. turgidula Fr.

Lecidella anomaloides (Massal.) Hertel & Kilias
L. asema (Nyl.) Knoph & Hertel
L. elaeochroma (Ach.) M. Choisy
L. meiococca (Nyl.) Leuckert & Hertel
L. pulveracea (Schaerer) H. Sydow
L. scabra (Taylor) Hertel & Leuckert
L. stigmatea (Ach.) Hertel & Leuckert
Lepraria caesioalba (B. de Lesd.) Laundon
L. incana (L.) Ach.
L. lesdainii (Hue) R. Harris
L. lobificans Nyl.
L. neglecta (Nyl.) Lettau
Leproloma membranaceum (Dickson) Vainio
Leptogium britannicum P. Jørg. & P. James
L. gelatinosum (With.) Laundon
L. lichenoides (L.) Zahlbr.
L. plicatile (Ach.) Leighton
L. tenuissimum (Dickson) Körber
L. teretiusculum (Wallr.) Arnold
Lichina confinis (Muller) Agardh
L. pygmaea (Lightf.) Agardh
Lithographa tesserata (DC.) Nyl.
Lobaria pulmonaria (L.) Hoffm.
L. virens (With.) Laundon
Megalaria grossa (Pers. ex Nyl.) Hafellner
Micarea bauschiana (Körber) V. Wirth & Vĕzda
M. denigrata (Fr.) Hedl.
M. leprosula (Th. Fr.) Coppins & A. Fletcher
M. lignaria var. *lignaria* (Ach.) Hedl.
M. lutulata (Nyl.) Coppins
M. melaena (Nyl.) Hedl.
M. peliocarpa (Anzi) Coppins & R. Sant.
M. prasina (Nyl.) Hedl.
M. sylvicola (Flotow) Vĕzda & V. Wirth
M. ternaria (Nyl.) Vĕzda
Miriquidica leucophaea (Rabenh.) Hertel & Rambold
Moelleropsis nebulosa (Hoffm.) Gyelnik
Multiclavula vernalis (Schw.) Petersen
Mycoblastus fucatus (Stirton) Zahlbr.
M. sanguinarius (L.) Norman
Nephroma laevigatum Ach.
Normandina pulchella (Borrer) Nyl.
Ochrolechia androgyna (Hoffm.) Arnold
O. frigida (Swartz) Lynge
O. parella (L.) Massal.
O. tartarea (L.) Massal.
O. turneri (Sm.) Hasselrot
Omphalina cupulatoides P.D. Orton
O. ericetorum (Fr.) M. Lange ex H. Bigelow
O. hudsoniana (Jenn.) Bigelow
O. luteovitellina (Pilát & Nannf.) M. Lange
Opegrapha atra Pers.
O. cesareensis Nyl.
O. gyrocarpa Flotow
O. herbarum Mont.
O. multipuncta Coppins & P. James
O. niveoatra (Borrer) Laundon
O. parasitica (Massal.) H. Olivier
O. saxatilis DC.
O. saxicola Ach.
O. sorediifera P. James
O. varia Pers.

O. vulgata (Ach.) Ach.
Ophioparma ventosum (L.) Norman
Pannaria leucophaea (Vahl) P. Jørg.
P. pezizoides (Weber) Trevisan
Parmelia conspersa (Ehrh. ex Ach.) Ach.
P. crinita Ach.
P. elegantula (Zahlbr.) Szat.
P. exasperata de Not.
P. exasperatula Nyl.
P. glabratula subsp. *fuliginosa* (Fr. ex Duby) Laundon
P. glabratula subsp. *glabratula* (Lamy) Nyl.
P. omphalodes (L.) Ach.
P. perlata (Huds.) Ach.
P. pulla Ach.
P. saxatilis (L.) Ach.
P. subaurifera Nyl.
P. sulcata Taylor
Peltigera canina (L.) Willd.
P. didactyla (With.) Laundon
P. lactucifolia (With.) Laundon
P. membranacea (Ach.) Nyl.
P. polydactyla (Necker) Hoffm.
P. praetextata (Flörke ex Sommerf.) Zopf
P. rufescens (Weis) Humb.
P. scabrosa Th. Fr.
Pertusaria albescens (Huds.) M. Choisy & Werner
P. amara (Ach.) Nyl.
P. aspergilla (Ach.) Laundon
P. chiodectonoides Begl. ex Massal.
P. corallina (L.) Arnold
P. excludens Nyl.
P. flavicans Lamy
P. hymenea (Ach.) Schaerer
P. lactea (L.) Arnold
P. leioplaca DC.
P. pertusa (Weigel) Tuck.
P. pseudocorallina (Liljeblad) Arnold
P. pupillaris (Nyl.) Th. Fr.
P. xanthostoma (Sommerf.) Fr.
Phaeophyscia nigricans (Flörke) Moberg
P. orbicularis (Necker) Moberg
Phlyctis argena (Sprengel) Flotow
Physcia adscendens (Fr.) H. Olivier
P. aipolia (Ehr. ex Humb.) Fürnrohr
P. caesia (Hoffm.) Fürnrohr
P. dubia (Hoffm.) Lettau
P. tenella subsp. *marina* (A.E. Nyl.) D. Hawksw.
P. tenella subsp. *tenella* (Scop.) DC.
Physconia grisea (Lam.) Poelt
Placidiopsis cartilaginea (Nyl.) Vainio
Placopsis gelida (L.) Lindsay
Placynthiella icmalea (Ach.) Coppins & P. James
P. uliginosa (Schrader) Coppins & P. James
Placynthium nigrum (Huds.) Gray
P. subradiatum (Nyl.) Arnold
Platismatia glauca (L.) Culb. & C. Culb.
Polyblastia cruenta (Körber) P. James & Swinscow
P. cupularis Massal.
P. dermatodes Massal.
P. gelatinosa (Ach.) Th. Fr.
P. inumbrata (Nyl.) Arnold
P. theleodes (Sommerf.) Th. Fr.

Polysporina simplex (Davies) Vězda
Porina aenea (Wallr.) Zahlbr.
P. borreri (Trevisan) D. Hawksw. & P. James
P. chlorotica (Ach.) Müll. Arg.
P. guentheri (Flotow) Zahlbr.
P. lectissima (Fr.) Zahlbr.
P. linearis (Leighton) Zahlbr.
Porpidia cinereoatra (Ach.) Hertel & Knoph
P. crustulata (Ach.) Hertel & Knoph
P. hydrophila (Fr.) Hertel & Schwab
P. macrocarpa (DC.) Hertel & Schwab
P. platycarpoides (Bagl.) Hertel
P. speirea (Ach.) Krempelh.
P. tuberculosa (Sm.) Hertel & Knoph
Protoblastenia calva (Dickson) Zahlbr.
P. incrustans (DC.) Steiner
P. rupestris (Scop.) Steiner
Protoparmelia badia (Hoffm.) Hafellner
P. ochrococca (Nyl.) P.M. Jørg., Rambold & Hertel
Pseudephebe pubescens (L.) M. Choisy
Pseudevernia furfuracea var. *ceratea* (Ach.) D. Hawksw.
P. furfuracea var. *furfuracea* (L.) Zopf
Psoroma hypnorum (Vahl) Gray
Psorotichia schaereri (Massal.) Arnold
Pycnothelia papillaria Dufour
Pyrenocollema elegans R. Sant.
P. halodytes (Nyl.) R.C. Harris
P. sublitorale (Leighton) R.C. Harris
Racodium rupestre Pers.
Ramalina canariensis Steiner
R. cuspidata (Ach.) Nyl.
R. farinacea (L.) Ach.
R. fastigiata (Pers.) Ach.
R. fraxinea (L.) Ach.
R. siliquosa (Hudson) A.L. Smith
R. subfarinacea (Nyl. ex Crombie) Nyl.
Rhizocarpon concentricum (Davies) Beltr.
R. geographicum (L.) DC.
R. hochstetteri (Körber) Vainio
R. lavatum (Fr.) Hazslin
R. obscuratum (Ach.) Massal.
R. oederi (Weber) Körber
R. polycarpum (Hepp) Th. Fr.
R. richardii (Nyl.) Zahlbr.
R. umbilicatum (Ramond) Flagey
Rinodina atrocinerea (Hook.) Körber
R. confragosa (Ach.) Körber
R. exigua Gray
R. gennarii Bagl.
R. luridescens (Anzi) Arnold
R. sophodes (Ach.) Massal.
Sarcogyne privigna (Ach.) Massal.
S. regularis Körber
Schaereria cinereorufa (Schaerer) Th. Fr.
S. fuscocinerea (Nyl.) Clauz. & Roux
Sclerophyton circumscriptum (Taylor) Zahlbr.
Scoliciosporum chlorococcum (Graew ex Stenhammar) Vězda
S. umbrinum (Ach.) Arnold
Solenopsora vulturiensis Massal.
Sphaerophorus fragilis (L.) Pers.
S. globosus (Huds.) Vainio

S. melanocarpus (Swartz) DC.
Staurothele fissa (Taylor) Zwackh
S. succedens (Rehm ex Arnold) Arnold
Stereocaulon evolutum Graewe
S. vesuvianum Pers.
Tephromela atra (Huds.) Hafellner ex Kalb
T. grumosa (Pers.) Hafellner & Roux
Thamnolia vermicularis var. *subuliformis* (Swartz) Schaerer
Thelidium decipiens (Nyl.) Krempelh.
T. incavatum Mudd
T. papulare (Fr.) Arnold
T. pyrenophorum (Ach.) Mudd
Toninia aromatica (Sm.) Massal.
T. caeruleonigricans (Lightf.) Th. Fr.
Trapelia coarctata (Sm.) M. Choisy
T. involuta (Taylor) Hertel
Trapeliopsis flexuosa (Fr.) Coppins & P. James
T. gelatinosa (Flörke) Coppins & P. James
T. granulosa (Hoffm.) Lumbsch
T. pseudogranulosa Coppins & P. James
T. wallrothii (Flörke ex Sprengel) Hertel & G. Schneider
Tremolecia atrata (Ach.) Hertel
Tylothallia biformigera (Leighton) P. James & Kilias
Umbilicaria cylindrica (L.) Delise ex Duby
U. deusta (L.) Baumg.
U. polyphylla (L.) Baumg.
U. polyrrhiza (L.) Fr.
U. proboscidea (L.) Schrader
U. torrefacta (Lightf.) Schrader
Usnea cornuta Körber
U. flammea Stirton
U. fragilescens Havaas ex Lynge
U. hirta (L.) Wigg.
U. subfloridana Stirton
Verrucaria aethiobola Wahlenb.
V. amphibia R. Clem.
V. aquatilis Mudd
V. baldensis Massal.
V. caerulea DC.
V. degelii R. Sant.
V. ditmarsica Erichsen
V. fusconigrescens Nyl.
V. glaucina auct. brit. non Ach.
V. halizoa Leighton
V. hochstetteri Fr.
V. internigrescens (Nyl.) Erichsen
V. margacea (Wahlenb.) Wahlenb.
V. maura Wahlenb.
V. mucosa Wahlenb.
V. muralis Ach.
V. nigrescens Pers.
V. striatula Wahlenb.
V. viridula (Schrader) Ach.
Xanthoria calcicola Oxner
X. candelaria (L.) Th. Fr.
X. ectaneoides (Nyl.) Zahlbr.
X. elegans (Link.) Th. Fr.
X. parietina (L.) Th. Fr.
X. polycarpa (Hoffm.) Th. Fr. ex Rieber
Xylographa vitiligo (Ach.) Laundon

FLOWERING PLANTS AND FERNS   by W. Scott & R. C. Palmer

This list updates Scott and Palmer (1987) by the addition of new records, the inclusion of corrections and amendments to previously published information, and the results of recent work on *Taraxacum* and *Hieracium*. Sequence, nomenclature and English names usually follow Stace (1997), except in the case of *Taraxacum* which conforms to Dudman and Richards (1997). Under *Hieracium* the sequence of species within the sections closely follows Kent (1992). The list enumerates 850 taxa (including subspecies) divided into the following status categories:

1. Native taxa (including seven believed extinct) (392).
2. Colonists (accidentally introduced, usually in the wake of cultivation, often widespread and permanent) (129).
3. Spontaneous hybrids involving at least one native or colonist parent (47).
4. Naturalized taxa, mostly of garden origin (20).
5. Casuals (accidentally introduced, mostly annual, usually impermanent and of unpredictable occurrence) (99).
6. Taxa of garden or agricultural origin which have not become naturalized (163).

In the list all taxa in categories 4–6 are marked by an asterisk. Categories 1–3 are not marked but all colonists are indicated by a note of their status in the text. Species believed to be extinct appear in square brackets.

Huperzia selago (L.) Bernh. ex Schrank & Mart. subsp. *selago*. **Fir clubmoss**. Heaths and moors, etc., often on bare peat. Frequent, but often as scattered plants; rarely conspicuous over a small area. Occasionally attaining 15 cm in height, but usually much shorter.

Lycopodium clavatum L. **Stag's-horn clubmoss**. Formerly rather local but now very rarely seen. Perhaps in the process of becoming extinct.

Diphasiastrum alpinum (L.) Holub. **Alpine clubmoss**. Chiefly in North Mainland, especially as a feature of the Ronas Hill area and the North Roe plateau; rare elsewhere. Needing recent confirmation in Unst and Fetlar.

Selaginella selaginoides (L.) P. Beauv. **Lesser clubmoss**. Common throughout the islands, especially on the serpentinite grass-heath of Unst.

Isoetes lacustris L. **Quillwort**. Occasional to frequent. Stony or gravelly loch bottoms.

I. echinospora Durieu. **Spring quillwort**. Less often seen than the preceding, but frequent in West Mainland. Loch bottoms, especially on fine silt.

Equisetum fluviatile L. **Water horsetail**. Frequent in watery places, often forming large stands by loch margins.

E. × litorale Kühlew. ex Rupr. (*E. fluviatile* L. × *E. arvense* L.). **Shore horsetail**. Occasional or locally frequent, probably often overlooked.

E. arvense L. **Field horsetail**. Roadsides, grassy undercliffs, cultivated fields, etc. Frequent, often a feature of sandy areas.

E. sylvaticum L. **Wood horsetail**. Occasional. Particularly attractive by ferny stream banks.

E. palustre L. **Marsh horsetail**. Common in marshy places throughout Shetland.

Ophioglossum azoricum C. Presl. **Small adder's-tongue**. Locally by the coast, often on small islands; easily overlooked.

Botrychium lunaria (L.) Sw. **Moonwort**. Short, well-drained grassland, especially on serpentinite, limestone, or sandy soils. Probably decreasing and certainly not seen so regularly nowadays. However, it is still frequent about Burravoe (Yell) and in parts of North Yell.

Osmunda regalis L. **Royal fern**. On five islands in lochs, all in West Mainland. Sporelings and young plants have been very rarely found in the same general area but are unable to form permanent colonies due to grazing.

Hymenophyllum wilsonii Hook. **Wilson's filmy-fern**. Frequent in the higher and wetter areas; usually dwarfed and browned.

Polypodium vulgare L. **Polypody**. Frequent. Rocks, steep banks, etc. Often much dwarfed.

P. vulgare L. × *P. interjectum* Shivas (*P. × mantoniae* Rothm. & U. Schneid.). Once collected at Mavis Grind.

Pteridium aquilinum (L.) Kuhn. **Bracken**. Local and chiefly near the coast, but relatively frequent in West Mainland.

Phegopteris connectilis (Michx.) Watt. **Beech fern**. Among rocks. Local in North Mainland, very rare elsewhere.

Oreopteris limbosperma (Bellardi ex All.) Holub. **Lemon-scented fern**. Rocky heaths, burnsides, etc. Local in North Mainland, rare elsewhere.

Phyllitis scolopendrium (L.) Newman. **Hart's-tongue**. Extremely rare. Long considered extinct until one small clump was found by a West Mainland loch in 1989 by W. Scott.

Asplenium adiantum-nigrum L. **Black spleenwort**. Local to frequent. A serpentinite variant with broad fan-shaped segments occurs near Cunningsburgh, and in Fetlar and Unst; it has recently been referred to subsp. *corrunense* Christ.

A. marinum L. **Sea spleenwort**. Local to occasional. The recent intensive survey of the coastline has revealed a number of previously unrecorded sites.

A. trichomanes L. subsp. *quadrivalens* D. E. Mey. **Maidenhair spleenwort**. Local and found mainly in crevices of limestone or sandstone outcrops.

A. viride Huds. **Green spleenwort**. Very rare. Crevices of serpentinite rocks, Muckle Heog, Unst, only.

A. ruta-muraria L. **Wall-rue**. On rocks in a handful of stations in West Mainland, and on a wall by Gibblestone House, Scalloway, where it was found in unusual quantity in 1993 by W. Scott (though noted earlier, but not reported, by R. Steppan in 1989).

Athyrium filix-femina (L.) Roth. **Lady-fern**. Sheltered burnsides, rocky places, etc. Frequent. The plumose form found near Boddam in 1978 still grows in a Scalloway garden.

Gymnocarpium dryopteris (L.) Newman. **Oak fern**. Among rocks or scree, etc. Local in north Mainland, rare elsewhere.

Cystopteris fragilis (L.) Bernh. **Brittle bladder-fern**. Rare and found mainly on limestone or sandstone.

Dryopteris filix-mas (L.) Schott. **Male fern**. Among rocks, by burns, on sheltered sea banks, etc. Occasional to frequent, rarely in quantity.

D. affinis (Lowe) Fraser-Jenk. **Scaly male-fern**. Rare. Rocky places, sea banks, etc. We prefer, at this stage, to give a main heading only until there is a better understanding of the delimitation and distribution of the morphotypes of this very variable fern.

D. dilatata (Hoffm.) A. Gray. **Broad buckler-fern**. The commonest fern in the county. Burnsides, rock crevices, holms in lochs, peaty hollows, old stone walls, etc.

D. expansa (C. Presl) Fraser-Jenk. & Jermy. **Northern buckler-fern**. Recently found in a few rocky places in the Ronas Hill area; very rare and at lower levels elsewhere.

Blechnum spicant (L.) Roth. **Hard-fern**. A common species of damp heathery places.

*Picea sitchensis (Bong.) Carrière. **Sitka spruce**. Very rarely outside enclosures.

*Larix decidua Mill. **European larch**. Very rarely outside enclosures.

*L. kaempferi (Lindl.) Carrière. **Japanese larch**. Very rarely outside enclosures.

Juniperus communis L. subsp. *nana* (Hook.) Syme. **Common juniper**. Generally a decreasing species in Shetland, but still frequent in the north of Fair Isle, rare or local elsewhere. Probably the best site is by the Burn of Swabiewater, North Roe. A form intermediate between subsp. *nana* and subsp. *communis* occurs as single plants (one near Levenwick, South Mainland, and one at Lamb Hoga, Fetlar).

Nymphaea alba L. subsp. *occidentalis* (Ostenf.) Hyl. **White water-lily**. Native in a few lochs and pools in West Mainland; also occasionally planted both within and outside its native area (using West Mainland stock in all cases).

Caltha palustris L. **Marsh-marigold**. Common in watery places, often covering large areas. A welcome sight in spring.

* Trollius europaeus L. **Globeflower**. Widely grown in gardens but very rarely seen outside them.

*Aconitum napellus L. **Monk's-hood**. Another popular garden plant rarely seen outside enclosures.

*Anemone nemorosa L. **Wood anemone**. Introduced at Kergord Plantations but now very scarce.

*A. coronaria L., cultivar. **Garden anemone**. Very rarely seen outside gardens.

Ranunculus acris L. **Meadow buttercup**. A common and very variable species of meadows and other grassy places, stream sides, roadsides, coastal turf, etc.

R. repens L. **Creeping buttercup**. A common colonist of arable land and gardens, in disturbed muddy places, about ruined crofts, etc.

R. bulbosus L. **Bulbous buttercup**. Rare. Dry pastures (often near the sea on sandy ground); perhaps sometimes overlooked when growing with *R. acris*. Particularly abundant in the Biggings district of Papa Stour.

R. flammula L. subsp. *flammula*. **Lesser spearwort**. A very common and variable species of watery or damp places. Subsp. *minimus* (A. Benn.) Padmore is on record from southernmost Mainland but we have not seen it ourselves and feel that it requires further study.

*R. aconitifolius L. **Aconite-leaved buttercup**. The double-flowered form is commonly grown in gardens but is rarely seen outside enclosures.

R. ficaria L. subsp. *ficaria*. **Lesser celandine**. Damp grassland, burnsides, etc. Frequent, and like marsh-marigold, a sign of approaching spring if not summer.

R. hederaceus L. **Ivy-leaved crowfoot**. Occasionally seen in burns and ditches, etc., in the south part of Mainland from Lerwick southwards, and in the Isle of Noss and Fair Isle.

R. baudotii Godr. **Brackish water-crowfoot**. A rare plant of lochs and pools. Extreme south of South Mainland, and in Maa Loch, Vementry.

R. trichophyllus Chaix. **Thread-leaved water-crowfoot**. Extreme south of South Mainland; near Walls, west Mainland, and on Haaf Gruney, near Unst.

Aquilegia cultivar or hybrid. **Columbine**. Commonly grown in gardens and thus an occasional escape or outcast. Perhaps more than one taxon is present.

Thalictrum alpinum L. **Alpine meadow-rue**. Wet burnsides, flushes, damp stony ground. Generally frequent except in southernmost South Mainland where it is absent or very rare. Descending to sea level in Shetland.

Papaver pseudoorientale (Fedde) Medw. **Oriental poppy**. Rarely seen as an escape or outcast from gardens.

P. somniferum L. subsp. *somniferum*. **Opium poppy**. An occasional garden escape; once recorded as an apparent casual among oats (at Cunningsburgh).

P. rhoeas L. **Common poppy**. Long ago almost certainly a casual of oats; nowadays a very rare casual of recently reseeded roadside verges.

P. dubium L. subsp. *dubium*. **Long-headed poppy**. A colonist of sandy soil in southernmost South Mainland, and in the north of both Yell and Unst; otherwise a very rare casual.

Meconopsis cambrica (L.) Vig. **Welsh poppy**. Garden escape or outcast, occasionally becoming well established.

[*Glaucium flavum* Crantz. **Yellow horned-poppy**. Recorded from Sullom Voe before 1845, perhaps as a casual.]

Fumaria muralis Sond. ex W. D. J. Koch subsp. *boraei* (Jord.) Pugsley. **Common ramping-fumitory**. Casual, found on one occasion (in 1968) in Trondra.

F. officinalis L. subsp. *officinalis*. **Common fumitory**. A frequent colonist on the sandy soil of southernmost South Mainland, local elsewhere.

Ulmus glabra Huds. **Wych elm**. Hardly ever seen outside enclosures.

Humulus lupulus L. **Hop**. A very rare garden straggler.

Urtica dioica L. **Common nettle**. A common colonist about past and present habitations, disturbed ground, etc.

U. urens L. **Small nettle**. A frequent colonist in parts of southernmost South Mainland, local elsewhere; prefers sandy soils.

Soleirolia soleirolii (Req.) Dandy. **Mind-your-own-business**. Remains of garden, Leagarth House, Fetlar.

Betula pubescens Ehrh. subsp. *tortuosa* (Ledeb.) Nyman. **Downy birch**. Now very rare and confined to five sites in Northmavine.

Corylus avellana L. **Hazel**. Now known only from a streamside at Catfirth, South Nesting, and an island in Punds Water, North Mainland.

Chenopodium album L. **Fat hen**. Mainly as a colonist of arable ground in the sandy south.

Atriplex prostrata Boucher ex DC. **Spear-leaved orache**. A very rare colonist known only from two sites in Fair Isle.

A. × *gustafssoniana* Tasch. (*A. prostrata* Boucher ex DC. × *A. longipes* Drejer). **Kattegat orache**. Collected in a few sites in Shetland but probably under-recorded.

A. glabriuscula Edmondston. **Babington's orache**. Distribution imperfectly known; certainly much over-recorded in the past, but perhaps less local than its handful of stations would suggest.

A. glabriuscula Edmondston × *A. praecox* Hülph. Collected once (in 1977) at Basta Voe, Yell.

A. × *taschereaui* Stace (*A. glabriuscula* Edmondston × *A. longipes* Drejer). **Taschereau's orache**. Collected once (in 1978) at Channer Wick, South Mainland.

A. praecox Hülph. **Early orache**. Frequent by sheltered voes, *vadills* and *houbs*.

A. littoralis L. **Grass-leaved orache**. Known only from around the head of the voe at Boddam.

A. patula L. **Common orache**. An occasional colonist of cultivated ground (especially in the sandy areas of South Mainland), rubbish-dumps, etc.

[*A. laciniata* L. **Frosted orache**. Native, presumed extinct. Collected at the turn of the century on the beach below Clavel, South Mainland. No later record.]

Salicornia europaea L. agg. **Glasswort**. Both sides of Balta Sound, Unst.

Suaeda maritima (L.) Dumort. **Annual sea-blite**. Both sides of Balta Sound, Unst, and at The Houb, below Swinister, Dales Voe, Delting.

Claytonia perfoliata Donn ex Willd. **Springbeauty**. A very rare garden casual.

C. sibirica L. **Pink purslane**. Commonly grown in gardens and thus locally seen as an outcast or straggler.

Montia fontana L. **Blinks**. Common in flushes and damp pastures, on wet rocks and bare soil, etc. Subsp. *fontana* is probably the dominant subspecies; subsp. *variabilis* Walters has been collected once on Fair Isle.

Arenaria serpyllifolia L. subsp. *serpyllifolia*. **Thyme-leaved sandwort**. Rare in sandy places in southernmost South Mainland, very rare on basic rocks elsewhere.

A. norvegica Gunnerus subsp. *norvegica*. **Arctic sandwort**. A national rarity. In Shetland found only on the bare serpentinite tracts in Unst where it can be locally frequent.

Honckenya peploides (L.) Ehrh. **Sea sandwort**. Frequent on sandy or shingly seashores.

[*Minuartia rubella* (Wahlenb.) Hiern. **Mountain sandwort**. Native, presumed extinct. Specimens were collected on the serpentinite near Baltasound in 1840 and 1886. Not reliably recorded since.]

Stellaria media (L.) Vill. **Common chickweed**. A common colonist in cultivated ground, waste places, on seabird cliffs, etc.

*S. holostea L. **Greater stitchwort**. Introduced in Kergord Plantations.

*S. graminea L. **Lesser stitchwort**. A rare but apparently increasing introduction of roadsides, reseeded pastures, etc., occasionally long-persistent.

S. uliginosa Murray. **Bog stitchwort**. Common in watery places.

*Cerastium tomentosum L. **Snow-in-summer**. A popular garden plant sometimes seen among rocks, etc., near houses.

C. nigrescens (H. C. Watson) Edmondston ex H. C. Watson. **Shetland mouse-ear.** Shetland's most celebrated endemic. Confined to two areas of serpentinite in Unst (Keen of Hamar and Muckle Heog).

C. fontanum Baumg. subsp. *vulgare* (Hartm.) Greuber & Burdet. **Common mouse-ear**. Common and very variable.

C. glomeratum Thuill. **Sticky mouse-ear**. A common colonist around crofting areas, etc.

C. diffusum Pers. **Sea mouse-ear**. Common by the coast.

Sagina nodosa (L.) Fenzl. **Knotted pearlwort**. Occasional on mainly basic soils (stony sides of lochs, flushes, serpentinite debris, etc.).

S. subulata (Sw.) C. Presl. **Heath pearlwort**. Frequent in dry rocky places, especially on acid soils. Mainly as the glabrous form.

S. procumbens L. **Procumbent pearlwort**. Common in a variety of habitats (wet or dry). Also a persistent garden weed.

S. maritima Don. **Sea pearlwort**. Frequent by the coast on rocks and in turf.

Spergula arvensis L. **Corn spurrey**. A common colonist in and near arable ground, about crofts, etc.

Spergularia media (L.) C. Presl. **Greater sea-spurrey**. Not uncommon by the coast in muddy turf.

S. marina (L.) Griseb. **Lesser sea-spurrey**. Coastal rocks, old piers, etc. Local and preferring drier habitats than the preceding.

Lychnis flos-cuculi L. **Ragged-robin**. Widespread in damp meadows and pastures.

[*Agrostemma githago* L. **Corncockle**. Recorded once or twice in the middle part of last century, perhaps as a scarce colonist. No later record.]

Silene uniflora Roth. **Sea campion**. A frequent coastal species; rarely inland as on the Unst and Fetlar serpentinite.

S. acaulis (L.) Jacq. **Moss campion**. Locally frequent on gravelly slopes near the sea; occasionally inland in rocky places, on serpentinite debris, etc.

*S. latifolia Poir. **White campion**. An extremely rare casual. Sandy arable ground, etc., in South Mainland, and on waste ground in Lerwick.

S. × hampeana Meusel & K. Werner (*S. latifolia* Poir. × *S. dioica* (L.) Clairv.). Twice collected, at Exnaboe (South Mainland), and at Lerwick.

S. dioica (L.) Clairv. **Red campion**. Frequent on sea banks, cliffs and beaches, less commonly inland, perhaps sometimes as a probable escape from cultivation. Usually as a handsome variety with stout hairy stems and with flowers (often deep pink) in dense clusters.

*S. gallica L. **Small-flowered catchfly**. Casual. Once collected (in 1991) at the head of the East Voe of Scalloway by W. Scott.

*Persicaria campanulata (Hook. f.) Ronse Decr. **Lesser knotweed**. Very rarely seen outside gardens.

*P. bistorta (L.) Samp. **Common bistort**. Rarely seen outside gardens.

P. vivipara (L.) Ronse Decr. **Alpine bistort**. High rocky places (Foula, Fair Isle, and on the granite debris of Ronas Hill, etc.); more often on dry, stony or heathy coastal pasture, chiefly on the west side of Mainland.

P. amphibia (L.) Gray. **Amphibious bistort**. Rare to occasional, both as the aquatic form of lochs, etc., and as the terrestrial state of low-lying places.

P. maculosa Gray. **Redshank**. A frequent colonist of arable ground.

[*Polygonum oxyspermum* C. A. Mey. & Bunge ex Ledeb. **Ray's knotgrass**. Native, presumed extinct. Only once certainly collected (in 1868, at Burrafirth, Unst).]

P. arenastrum Boreau. **Equal-leaved knotgrass**. A common colonist of farmyards, tracks, and other trampled places, rarer as an arable weed (mainly) on sandy soil.

P. aviculare L. **Knotgrass**. Known with certainty only from Fair Isle.

P. boreale (Lange) Small. **Northern knotgrass**. A frequent colonist of cultivated ground.

*Fallopia japonica (Houtt.) Ronse Decr. **Japanese knotweed**. Commonly grown in gardens and frequently seen outside them as a straggler or outcast. The var. *compacta* (Hook. f.) J. P. Bailey occurs about Reafirth, Mid Yell.

*F. sachalinensis (F. Schmidt ex Maxim.) Ronse Decr. **Giant knotweed**. Long known at Houbie, Fetlar, but now in lesser quantity than formerly.

*F. baldschuanica (Regel) Holub. **Russian-vine**. Garden relic, Leagarth, Fetlar.

*F. convolvulus (L.) Á. Löve. **Black-bindweed**. A scarce casual of arable ground, rubbishy places and gardens. Probably a colonist in the Loch of Hillwell area, South Mainland.

*Rheum × hybridum Murray. **Rhubarb**. Widely grown and frequently seen as an outcast or relic of cultivation.

Rumex acetosella L. subsp. *acetosella*. **Sheep's sorrel**. Common on poor, shallow ground, often in peaty areas.

R. acetosa L. subsp. *acetosa*. **Common sorrel**. Common in damp grassy places, stream banks, sea cliffs, etc. Subsp. *hibernicus* (Rech. f.) Akeroyd occurs on bare serpentinite gravel near Baltasound, Unst.

R. longifolius DC. **Northern dock**. Common in inhabited areas, on seashores, cliffs, etc.

R. × propinquus Aresch. (*R. longifolius* DC. × *R. crispus* L.). Collected on a few occasions but probably widely overlooked.

R. × hybridus Kindb. (*R. longifolius* DC. × *R. obtusifolius* L.). Collected here and there but probably under-recorded.

R. crispus L. subsp. *crispus*. **Curled dock**. Frequent about waste and cultivated places; also commonly by the coast where it is largely, if not always, represented by subsp. *littoreus* (J. Hardy) Akeroyd.

R. obtusifolius L. **Broad-leaved dock**. A frequent colonist about crofting areas and on waste ground, etc.

Oxyria digyna (L.) Hill. **Mountain sorrel**. Confined to a few mainly coastal sites in Northmavine (on wet stream banks and cliffy places) from Lang Clodie Wick to Heylor (including Ronas Voe).

Armeria maritima Willd. subsp. *maritima*. **Thrift**. One of Shetland's most abundant and popular coastal species.

Elatine hexandra (Lapierre) DC. **Six-stamened waterwort**. Known only from the Lochs of Spiggie and Brow (South Mainland) and the lochs of Kirkigarth and Bardister (West Mainland).

Hypericum pulchrum L. **Slender St. John's-wort**. Widely but sparingly distributed in dry, rocky or heathery places, and on serpentinite grass-heath in Unst.

*Sidalcea cultivar or hybrid. **Greek mallow**. Popular in gardens but rarely seen (and even more rarely surviving) outside enclosures. Perhaps more than one taxon is present.

Drosera rotundifolia L. **Round-leaved sundew**. Frequent in boggy, mossy moorland. Fully-opened flowers are very rarely seen.

D. anglica Huds. **Great sundew**. Known only from Roer Water and the Burn of Roerwater, North Roe, very scarce in either place. Fetlar and Yell records from last century remain unconfirmed.

Viola riviniana Rchb. **Common dog-violet**. Common in dry heathy places and among rocks, etc.

V. canina L. subsp. *canina*. **Heath dog-violet**. Rare. Short, heathy, coastal pasture (rarely a little way inland), and on the Unst and Fetlar serpentinite.

V. palustris L. subsp. *palustris*. **Marsh violet**. Common in damp or wet heathy turf, bogs and marshes.

*V. cornuta L. **Horned pansy**. Formerly outside a garden, Asta, near Scalloway.

V. tricolor L. subsp. *tricolor*. **Wild pansy**. A local colonist of cultivated ground (especially in the sandy parts of South Mainland), and in dune pastures.

V. × contempta Jord. (*V. tricolor* L. × *V. arvensis* Murray). Twice collected in South Mainland.

V. arvensis Murray. **Field pansy**. A rare colonist of cultivated or sandy soil, as in southernmost South Mainland and in the north of both Yell and Unst.

Populus tremula L. **Aspen**. Barely accessible sea banks and crags. Six stations (most in North Mainland).

*Salix pentandra L. **Bay willow**. Very rarely outside enclosures.

*S. fragilis L. var. *russelliana* (Sm.) W.D.J. Koch. **Bedford willow**. Planted at Swining, near Vidlin.

[**S. × mollissima* Hoffm. ex Elwert (*S. triandra* L. × *S. viminalis* L.). **Sharp-stipuled willow**. A willow thought to be this was once collected in Burns Lane, Lerwick.]

*S. purpurea L. **Purple willow**. Very rarely seen outside gardens.

[**S. daphnoides* Vill. Formerly occurred outside enclosures at Veensgarth (north of Scalloway), and in Foula.]

*S. viminalis L. **Osier**. Rarely planted by streams, etc.

*S. × sericans Tausch ex A. Kern. (*S. viminalis* L. × *S. caprea* L.). **Broad-leaved osier**. Planted by the Burn of Quoys (South Nesting) and at Houbans (near Sullom); probably elsewhere.

*S. × calodendron Wimm. (*S. viminalis* L. × *S. caprea* L. × *S. cinerea* L.). **Holme willow**. Planted at Northdale, Fetlar.

*S. × stipularis Sm. (*S. viminalis* L. × *S. caprea* L. × *S. aurita* L.). **Eared osier**. Very rarely outside gardens (as by the Burn of Geosetter, South Mainland), but probably under-recorded.

*S. × smithiana Willd. (*S. viminalis* L. × *S. cinerea* L.). **Silky-leaved osier**. A popular willow found in many gardens and consequently seen around crofts, by burns, etc.

*S. caprea L. **Goat willow**. Hardly, if ever, seen outside enclosures.

S. cinerea L. subsp. *cinerea*. **Grey willow**. Only on the holms in Mousavord Loch, West Mainland. Subsp. *oleifolia* Macreight. Rare. Holms in lochs and on sea cliffs, mostly in Northmavine.

S. × multinervis Doell (*S. cinerea* L. × *S. aurita* L.). Very rare. Known only from a handful of stations (mostly holms in lochs) in North Roe.

*S. × laurina Sm. (*S. cinerea* L. × *S. phylicifolia* L.). **Laurel-leaved willow**. Frequently planted outside enclosures in West Mainland (as by the Loch of Elvister, near Walls), rare elsewhere.

S. aurita L. **Eared willow**. Not uncommon, especially in the west and north, by streams, roadsides, on holms in lochs, etc.

S. × ambigua Ehrh. (*S. aurita* L. × *S. repens* L.). Local in West and North Mainland, very rare elsewhere.

S. repens L. **Creeping willow**. Shetland's most widespread and frequent willow. Heathy pastures, crags, coastal banks, etc.

S. lapponum L. **Downy willow**. Known only from a holm in Moosa Water, North Roe.

S. herbacea L. **Dwarf willow**. Frequent on high stony or rocky ground, and on cliff-tops at much lower levels in parts of North Roe.

*Sisymbrium orientale L. **Eastern rocket**. Formerly a rare casual at Lerwick.

*S. officinale (L.) Scop. **Hedge mustard**. A very rare casual with records from Lerwick and (more recently) from Scalloway.

*Descurainia sophia (L.) Webb ex Prantl. **Flixweed**. Casual. A single plant was found near the Loch of Hillwell, South Mainland, in 1982.

*Alliaria petiolata (M. Bieb.) Cavara & Grande. **Garlic mustard**. Casual. A single plant in a Lerwick garden in 1971.

*Arabidopsis thaliana (L.) Heynh. **Thale cress**. A very rare casual of gardens, etc.

*Erysimum cheiranthoides L. **Treacle-mustard**. Casual. One plant in the garden of Busta, Fair Isle, 1990 (N. Riddiford).

*Hesperis matronalis L. **Dame's-violet**. A popular garden plant (better known locally as sweet rocket) often seen as an escape or outcast.

*Malcolmia maritima (L.) W. T. Aiton. **Virginia stock**. Merely a rare garden throw-out.

*Matthiola longipetala (Vent.) DC. **Night-scented stock**. Once in Lerwick, probably from a seedsman's sweepings.

*Barbarea vulgaris W. T. Aiton. **Winter-cress**. A rare garden weed or casual.

*B. verna (Mill.) Asch. **American winter-cress**. Once found in a garden at Hoswick, South Mainland, apparently casual.

*Rorippa nasturtium-aquaticum (L.) Hayek. **Water-cress**. Naturalized in several places in South Mainland, from Sandwick southwards. Very rare elsewhere.

*R. × sterilis Airy Shaw (*R. nasturtium-aquaticum* (L.) Hayek × *R. microphylla* (Boenn.) Hyl. ex Á. &. D. Löve). **Hybrid water-cress**. Planted on low sea bank near Burrastow House, West Mainland. Found in 1993 by W. Scott.

*R. microphylla (Boenn.) Hyl. ex Á. & D. Löve. **Narrow-fruited water-cress**. Known only from Walls, West Mainland, as a probable introduction.

*R. palustris (L.) Besser. **Marsh yellow-cress**. A very rare casual, its only two recent records both from Lerwick.

*Armoracia rusticana P. Gaertn., B. Mey. & Scherb. **Horse-radish**. Merely an escape or outcast from cultivation.

Cardamine pratensis L. **Cuckooflower**. Common in damp grassland and by burns and lochs, etc.

*C.flexuosa With. **Wavy bitter-cress**. An outcast or escape from gardens where it not infrequently occurs as a weed.

C. hirsuta L. **Hairy bitter-cress**. A rare native of rocky places; otherwise a very persistent weed of gardens, waste ground, etc.

Arabis petraea (L.) Lam. **Northern rock-cress**. Only known on the serpentinite of Unst and Fetlar (on debris, rock outcrops and sea cliffs).

*A. hirsuta (L.) Scop. **Hairy rock-cress**. Casual. Found on one occasion (in 1928) in Fetlar.

*Lunaria annua L. **Honesty**. A mere garden outcast.

*Lobularia maritima (L.) Desv. **Sweet alison**. A mere garden outcast.

Draba incana L. **Hoary whitlowgrass**. Local and probably decreasing. Rocky places (especially on limestone and serpentinite).

Cochlearia officinalis L. **Common scurvygrass**. Frequent on sea cliffs and beaches (often large and luxuriant), and common as a dwarf, prostrate form (usually called *C. scotica* Druce) in fine coastal turf on mud, sand or peat. Also inland as a dwarf form on the serpentinite of Unst and Fetlar where it is accompanied by a long-podded taxon closely approaching *C. pyrenaica* DC. on morphological grounds. More research is needed into these serpentinite plants and into the status of *C. scotica*.

C. officinalis L. × *C. danica* L. Once collected in Lerwick. Perhaps elsewhere in areas where the two species are present.

C. danica L. **Danish scurvygrass**. Not infrequently found in South Mainland (often on brochs and old walls by the coast), rare or very rare elsewhere.

*Camelina sativa (L.) Crantz. **Gold-of-pleasure**. Casual. Once occurred in two consecutive years on a Lerwick rubbish-dump.

Capsella bursa-pastoris (L.) Medik. **Shepherd's-purse**. A common colonist of waste, rubbly places, gardens, etc., and as an arable weed.

*Thlaspi arvense L. **Field penny-cress**. A rare casual of gardens, waste ground, etc.

*Iberis umbellata L. **Garden candytuft**. A mere garden outcast.

*Lepidium sativum L. **Garden cress**. A very rarely recorded casual.

Subularia aquatica L. **Awlwort**. Very rare. Found in a few lochs in West Mainland.

*Diplotaxis tenuifolia (L.) DC. **Perennial wall-rocket**. Once found in a Lerwick garden, status uncertain.

*Brassica oleracea L. var *viridis* L. **Kale**. Often by burns in crofting areas as an outcast of cultivation.

B. napus L. subsp. *rapifera* (L.) Metzg. **Swede**. Merely an outcast or relic of cultivation.

B. rapa L. subsp. *campestris* (L.) A. R. Clapham. **Wild turnip**. Casual. Newly-sown road verges, rubbish-dumps, etc. *Subsp. *rapa* (**Turnip**) occurs as an outcast or relic of cultivation.

B. nigra (L.) W. D. J. Koch. **Black mustard**. Casual, twice collected in Lerwick.

Sinapis arvensis L. **Charlock**. A frequent colonist of arable ground, especially in intensively managed areas.

S. alba L. subsp. *alba*. **White mustard**. A very rare casual.

Cakile maritima Scop. **Sea rocket**. Frequent on sandy or shingly beaches.

Rapistrum rugosum (L.) J. P. Bergeret. **Bastard cabbage**. Casual, once collected in Scalloway.

Crambe maritima L. **Sea-kale**. First certainly recorded (and photographed) for Shetland by T. Angus, *c.* 1991, a single flowering plant on the boulder beach, east side of the Taing of Helliness, Cunningsburgh. Not seen again in the area.

Raphanus raphanistrum L. subsp. *raphanistrum*. **Wild radish**. A common colonist of cultivated ground.

Empetrum nigrum L. **Crowberry**. Subsp. *nigrum* is common, often abundant, on heaths and moors. Subsp. *hermaphroditum* (Hagerup) Böcher has recently been detected high up on the north side of Ronas Hill.

Loiseleuria procumbens (L.) Desv. **Trailing azalea**. Found only on bare granite debris and associated dry mossy heath above 240 m on the Ronas Hill mass.

Gaultheria mucronata (L.f.) Hook. & Arn. **Prickly heath**. Very rarely planted in semi-enclosed places.

Arctostaphylos uva-ursi (L.) Spreng. **Bearberry**. Locally frequent on dry stony heaths in Northmavine, notably on the North Roe plateau. Also in parts of Muckle Roe.

Arctous alpinus (L.) Spreng. **Arctic bearberry**. Confined to Ronas Hill northwards, on stony heaths and (rarely) on moist peat.

Calluna vulgaris (L.) Hull. **Heather**. Abundant over much of upland Shetland.

Erica tetralix L. **Cross-leaved heath**. Common on wet moors and heaths.

E. cinerea L. **Bell heather**. Common on dry (sometimes wet) moors and heaths and on rocks and crags.

Vaccinium oxycoccos L., *sensu lato*. **Cranberry**. Reported from the island of Hascosay in 1985; repeated attempts to locate it have failed.

V. vitis-idaea L. **Cowberry**. Found on or near the summits of many of the higher hills, and at lower levels on the North Roe plateau.

V. uliginosum L. **Bog bilberry**. Local. Occurs on several of the higher summits (Foula, Ronas Hill, etc.), and at a low altitude on the North Roe plateau.

V. myrtillus L. **Bilberry**. A familiar species over much of the higher moorland.

[*Pyrola* sp. **Wintergreen**. Native, presumed extinct. One or other species of this was apparently found by Edmondston (1845) near Walls (recorded by him as *P. media* Sw., but perhaps really *P. rotundifolia* L., the species known from Orkney). A report of *P. rotundifolia* from Ronas Hill by a visiting naturalist in 1806 has recently come to light but was perhaps due to a trick of memory; we know he had seen the plant in Orkney during the same year.]

Primula vulgaris Huds. **Primrose**. Frequent in grassy pastures (especially near the sea), stream banks, etc.

Lysimachia punctata L. **Dotted loosestrife**. Commonly grown in gardens and thus sometimes seen as an outcast or deliberate introduction.

Trientalis europaea L. **Chickweed-wintergreen**. A local plant of short heathy pastures, easily overlooked when not in flower.

Anagallis tenella (L.) L. **Bog pimpernel**. Local. Boggy or marshy (often mossy) ground and by damp turfy margins of lochs and streams.

A. arvensis L. subsp. *arvensis*. **Scarlet pimpernel**. A rare casual weed of gardens.

Glaux maritima L. **Sea-milkwort**. Common by the coast in muddy turf, in coastal sward and among rocks.

Ribes rubrum L. **Red currant**. Very seldom seen outside enclosures.

R. nigrum L. **Black currant**. Sometimes seen by streams where it has been planted or thrown out from cultivation.

R. sanguineum Pursh. **Flowering currant**. A popular garden shrub occasionally seen outside enclosures.

R. uva-crispa L. **Gooseberry**. Rarely seen outside enclosures.

Sedum rosea (L.) Scop. **Roseroot**. Frequent on sea cliffs.

S. telephium L. **Orpine**. Merely of garden origin when seen outside enclosures.

S. spurium M. Bieb. **Caucasian-stonecrop**. Commonly grown in gardens but rarely seen outside them.

S. acre L. **Biting stonecrop**. Recorded from two rocky sites where it was originally planted.

S. anglicum Huds. **English stonecrop**. Known only from Out Skerries and Ling Ness, South Nesting. What appears to be a small-flowered and very shy-flowering form of this occurs widely on levelled gravelly ground near the Sella Ness port administration complex. First seen by W. Scott in 1993, its origin is unknown though it must have arrived during the building of the Sullom Voe Oil Terminal infrastructure in the 1970s.

Darmera peltata (Torr. ex Benth.) Voss ex Post & Kuntze. **Indian-rhubarb**. Garden relic, Leagarth House, Fetlar.

Saxifraga × *urbium* D. Webb (*S. umbrosa* L. × *S. spathularis* Brot.). **Londonpride**. Very popular in gardens and
often seen as an outcast or where it has ben planted.
S. oppositifolia L. **Purple saxifrage**. Only in Northmavine where there are many stations (chiefly coastal)
from Colla Firth to near Fethaland, and at Snarra Ness (West Mainland).
Parnassia palustris L. **Grass-of-Parnassus**. Frequent in West Mainland and parts of central Mainland, rare
elsewhere.
*Spiraea cultivar or hybrid. **Bridewort**. Occasionally seen as a garden straggler or planted by streams. More
than one taxon may occur but it seems unlikely that any Shetland material belongs to true *S. salicifolia* L.,
to which all previous Shetland records have been referred.
Filipendula ulmaria (L.) Maxim. **Meadowsweet**. Frequent by burns and lochs, and in marshy meadows,
especially on the better soils.
Rubus saxatilis L. **Stone bramble**. A local plant of rocky places, sea banks, etc.; also on serpentinite debris in
Unst and granite debris on Ronas Hill.
*R. idaeus L. **Raspberry**. A garden outcast or straggler, sometimes planted.
*R. spectabilis Pursh. **Salmonberry**. Planted or garden outcast. Locally seen near houses and by streams,
often forming large thickets.
*R. lindebergii P. J. Müll. **Bramble**. Burn of Laxdale, Cunningsburgh, probably from a garden.
[**R. echinatoides* (Rogers) Dallman. **Bramble**. This, or a related species, formerly occurred in Kergord
Plantations.]
*R. latifolius Bab. **Bramble**. Near Moors, Sandwick, planted or garden escape. A bramble close to this occurs
in Kergord Plantations.
Potentilla palustris (L.) Scop. **Marsh cinquefoil**. Widespread, and often common, in marshes, swamps, etc.
P. anserina L. **Silverweed**. A familiar species of beaches and coastal grasslands, locally well inland in pastures,
etc.
P. erecta (L.) Raeusch. subsp. *erecta*. **Tormentil**. Abundant on peaty soils from dry heaths to bogs.
*Fragaria × *ananassa* (Duchesne) Duchesne. **Garden strawberry**. Merely of garden origin or bird-sown.
*Geum cultivar or hybrid, probably of *G. quellyon* Sweet. **Avens**. Rarely seen outside gardens.
G. rivale L. **Water avens**. Local. Burnsides and loch margins, rarely in rocky turf; prefers limestone or other
basic soils.
*Acaena anserinifolia (J. R. & G. Forst.) Druce. **Bronze pirri-pirri-bur**. Garden outcast or planted.
Currently known only from outside the Old School Centre, near Mossbank. Once found as a casual near
Scalloway in 1958.
Alchemilla alpina L. **Alpine lady's-mantle**. Known only from the Ronas Hill area.
*A. conjuncta Bab. **Silver lady's-mantle**. Garden relic, Leagarth House, Fetlar.
A. filicaulis Buser subsp. *filicaulis*. **Lady's-mantle**. Frequent on the Central Mainland limestone, rare or
absent elsewhere.
*A. glabra Neygenf. **Lady's-mantle**. Naturalized in many places throughout Shetland.
*A. mollis (Buser) Rothm. **Lady's-mantle**. Occasionally seen outside gardens as an escape or outcast, or
where planted.
Aphanes australis Rydb. **Slender parsley-piert**. Formerly a local colonist of arable ground, etc., but less
frequently seen nowadays and possibly decreasing.
*Rosa rugosa Thunb. ex Murray. **Japanese rose**. One of Shetland's most popular shrubs and frequently seen
outside enclosures, sometimes well away from houses.
*R. 'Hollandica'. **Dutch rose**. Rare in gardens and rarer still outside enclosures. A hybrid of *R. rugosa*.
R. caesia Sm. subsp. *glauca* (Nyman) G.G. Graham & Primavesi. **Glaucous dog-rose**. Many occurrences on
sea cliffs, ravines, holms in lochs, etc., particularly in parts of West and North Mainland.
*R. sherardii Davies. **Sherard's downy-rose**. Outside wall of South Nesting Primary School, probably
planted.
[**R. rubiginosa* L. **Sweet-briar**. Formerly planted by Ham Burn, Foula.]
Malus sylvestris (L.) Mill. **Crab apple**. The native apple, first found in 1991 at the Neap of Foraness, Dales
Voe, Delting, by L. A. Inkster and W. Scott, and again (the following year by the same recorders) at Quey
Firth, near Ollaberry.
*M. domestica Borkh. **Apple**. Tiny saplings are occasionally seen (from discarded pips) in quite unpredictable
situations, but very rarely become established.
Sorbus aucuparia L. **Rowan**. Almost confined to the northern parts of both West and North Mainland. At its
best by the north side of Ronas Voe.
[**S. aria* agg. **Common whitebeam**. Formerly at Veensgarth, Tingwall (planted) and at Lerwick
(probably bird-sown).]
[**S. latifolia* agg. **Broad-leaved whitebeam**. Once in Lerwick on a ruined house, probably bird-sown.]
*Crataegus monogyna Jacq. **Hawthorn**. Very rarely planted outside enclosures.
Anthyllis vulneraria L. **Kidney vetch**. Frequent. Dry grassy places by the coast, and on bare serpentinite in
Unst and Fetlar. Mostly subsp. *lapponica* (Hyl.) Jalas.

Lotus corniculatus L. **Common bird's-foot-trefoil**. Common in dry, grassy places (particularly by the coast), on stony heaths, among rocks, etc.

L. pedunculatus* Cav. **Greater bird's-foot-trefoil. Naturalized in abundance between Sand Wick and Hillswick, and similarly about the head of East Burra Firth. Both stations discovered by D. H. Dalby *c.* 1984 and in 1992 respectively. Also more recently by an overgrown burn running into Hos Wick, South Mainland, 1997 (L. A. Inkster & W. Scott). Formerly at Lerwick.

Vicia cracca L. **Tufted vetch**. Frequent in cultivated areas, sea banks, sand dunes, etc.

V. benghalensis* L. **Purple vetch. Frequent in garden of 9, Knab Road, Lerwick, as a bird-seed casual, 1994 (I. Clark).

V. hirsuta* (L.) Gray. **Hairy tare. A very rare casual with no recent records.

V. sepium L. **Bush vetch**. Rough grassy places, arable ground, etc. Not uncommon and likely to be a colonist.

V. sativa* L. **Common vetch. A very rare casual of arable ground, waste places, etc. All adequate herbarium material is referable to subsp. *sativa*.

V. faba* L. **Broad bean. Two casual occurrences in Lerwick.

Lathyrus japonicus Willd. subsp. *maritimus* (L.) P. W. Ball. **Sea pea**. Very rare. Only at Nor Wick, Unst, and in very poor condition there in 1997.

L. pratensis L. **Meadow vetchling**. Frequent in rough grassy places.

*Pisum sativum L. **Garden pea**. A very rare casual or garden throw-out.

*Melilotus indica (L.) All. **Small melilot**. A very rare casual, once collected in Lerwick and once in Scalloway.

*Medicago sativa L. subsp. *sativa*. **Lucerne**. A very rare casual, twice collected in southernmost South Mainland.

M. polymorpha* L. **Toothed medick. A very rare casual, once collected in Scalloway.

Trifolium repens L. **White clover**. A common and characteristic species of dry (often sandy) grassland, but often in marshes, etc. A vital component of reseeding mixtures.

* *T. hybridum* L. subsp. *hybridum*. **Alsike clover**. Sometimes in seed mixtures and thus occasionally recorded as a relic of cultivation.

T. dubium Sibth. **Lesser trefoil**. Colonist on sandy ground in southernmost South Mainland, but only an occasional casual elsewhere in Shetland, especially in reseeded pastures.

T. pratense L. **Red clover**. Frequent in dry grassy places.

Thermopsis montana* Nutt. ex Torr. & A. Gray. **False lupin. A large and increasing patch on site of former garden, Leagarth House, Fetlar.

Lupinus nootkatensis* Donn ex Sims. **Nootka lupin. Frequently grown in gardens and occasionally seen outside them as an outcast or straggler, or where planted.

Laburnum anagyroides* Medik. **Laburnum. Very rarely seen outside enclosures.

[**Cytisus scoparius* (L.) Link subsp. *scoparius*. **Broom**. Formerly planted at Kergord Plantations, and at Baltasound.]

*Ulex europaeus L. **Gorse**. Now rarely seen outside enclosures as at 'Wullver's Hool', Baltasound, and near Maryfield, Bressay, planted in both cases.

U. gallii* Planch. **Western gorse. Planted by a stream in Fair Isle.

Myriophyllum spicatum L. **Spiked water-milfoil**. Found in the Loch of Hillwell in 1962 but not seen again.

M. alterniflorum DC. **Alternate water-milfoil**. Common in many lochs and burns.

Epilobium hirsutum* L. **Great willowherb. Of garden origin or planted; very rare.

E. montanum L. **Broad-leaved willowherb**. Frequent as a colonist of gardens and waste ground, perhaps native in gullies and by lush stream sides in one or two places.

E. × *aggregatum* Čelak. (*E. montanum* L. × *E. obscurum* Schreb.). Once collected at Fort Charlotte, Lerwick.

E. × *mutabile* Boiss. & Reut. (*E. montanum* L. × *E. roseum* Schreb.). Once collected near the Lerwick waterfront.

E. obscurum Schreb. **Short-fruited willowherb**. Probably a colonist. Village streams and ditches, gardens, etc., local.

E. × *schmidtianum* Rostk. (*E. obscurum* Schreb. × *E. palustre* L.). Once collected near Sandsound.

E. roseum Schreb. **Pale willowherb**. A very rare colonist or casual known from Lerwick only, now almost if not quite extinct.

E. ciliatum* Raf. **American willowherb. A rare but probably increasing casual, with most records from the Lerwick area.

E. palustre L. **Marsh willowherb**. A common and widespread plant of watery places.

E. brunnescens (Cockayne) P. H. Raven & Engelhorn. **New Zealand willowherb**. A local but well established and probably increasing colonist first recorded by W. Scott in 1989 by gravelly roadsides between Voe and Laxo and subsequently found by him (and others) in several similar situations from Yell and West Mainland to the Ward of Scousburgh area.

Chamerion angustifolium (L.) Holub. **Rosebay willowherb**. Now very rare as a native and confined to a stream bank in South Mainland, a holm in a loch in North Roe and a sea bank on Gluss Isle, Northmavine, where it was found in 1992 by L. A. Inkster & W. Scott. Frequently seen as a garden relic or straggler.

Fuchsia magellanica* Lam. **Fuchsia. Merely a garden outcast or straggler.

Cornus suecica L. **Dwarf cornel**. Only on high ground in Foula, and at two low-lying sites in Yell, in one of which it is very rare.

Euphorbia helioscopia L. **Sun spurge**. A local and possibly decreasing colonist of arable ground.

*E. peplus L. **Petty spurge**. A rare garden weed.

*Linum usitatissimum L. **Flax**. A very rare casual with only two recent records, both in Lerwick and of bird-seed origin.

L. catharticum L. **Fairy flax**. Frequent in short, usually dry, turf and grassy heathland.

Radiola linoides Roth. **Allseed**. Damp heathy places usually near the coast. Local, and unrecorded for North Mainland and the North Isles.

Polygala vulgaris L. subsp. *vulgaris*. **Common milkwort**. Frequent in grassy or rocky places, preferring less acid conditions than the following.

P. serpyllifolia Hose. **Heath milkwort**. Common in dry or damp acid grassland, heaths and moors.

*Aesculus hippocastanum L. **Horse-chestnut**. Very rarely as a relict of cultivation.

*Acer pseudoplatanus L. **Sycamore**. Sometimes planted outside enclosures, as by burns, etc.

Oxalis acetosella L. **Wood-sorrel**. Very scarce as a native and confined to a few shady stream banks, etc., in North Mainland. Introduced in Kergord Plantations.

[**O. incarnata* L. **Pale pink-sorrel**. Once at Scalloway, planted.]

*Geranium endressii J. Gay. **French crane's-bill**. Once or twice at Lerwick, as a garden outcast or relict.

*G. pratense L. **Meadow crane's-bill**. Frequent and widespread as an escape or outcast from cultivation; especially well established at Netherton, Levenwick.

G. dissectum L. **Cut-leaved crane's-bill**. This very rare apparent colonist may still survive precariously in one of its two Scalloway stations, extinct in the other.

*G. ibericum Cav. **Caucasian crane's-bill**. Of garden origin in the Sandwick and Cunningsburgh areas, unrecorded elsewhere.

*G. × magnificum Hyl. (*G. ibericum* Cav. × *G. platypetalum* Fisch. & C. A. Mey.). **Purple crane's-bill**. Of garden origin and found in many places near houses and gardens.

G. molle L. **Dove's-foot crane's-bill**. Local as a probable native in sandy soil and on (usually basic) rock outcrops; otherwise a casual in gardens, etc.

G. robertianum L. **Herb-Robert**. This apparently native species still flourishes on the shingle beach at Boddam, though recent earthworks have substantially reduced its abundance.

[**G. phaeum* L. **Dusky crane's-bill**. A mere garden outcast or relic recorded once or twice last century.]

*Erodium cicutarium (L.) L'Hér. **Common stork's-bill**. Nowadays an extremely scarce casual most likely to be seen in sandy arable ground in southernmost South Mainland.

*Limnanthes douglasii R. Br. **Meadow-foam**. Very rarely outside gardens as an outcast or deliberate introduction; capable of persisting and spreading.

*Tropaeolum speciosum Poepp. & Endl. **Flame nasturtium**. Planted on a rocky face near Vementry (Mainland).

*Impatiens parviflora DC. **Small balsam**. A casual once collected (in 1986) at Garth, South Nesting.

*I. glandulifera Royle. **Indian balsam**. A rare garden escape, outcast or deliberate introduction. Formerly prevalent about Scalloway but less so now following tidying operations.

*Hedera helix L. subsp *helix*. **Common ivy**. Very rarely in unenclosed situations.

Hydrocotyle vulgaris L. **Marsh pennywort**. Widespread and common in wet places.

[*Eryngium maritimum* L. **Sea holly**. Native, presumed extinct. Four records last century, the last sighting in 1884.]

Anthriscus sylvestris (L.) Hoffm. **Cow parsley**. A frequent colonist in the inhabited areas.

*Scandix pecten-veneris L. **Shepherd's-needle**. Recorded once last century, presumably as a casual, and once this century, as a bird-seed casual in the garden of 9, Knab Road, Lerwick, 1997 (I. Clark).

*Myrrhis odorata (L.) Scop. **Sweet cicely**. A rare or local plant of garden origin seen about houses and yards, etc.

Conopodium majus (Gouan) Loret. **Pignut**. A frequent colonist of grassy pastures and meadows, sometimes abundant as about Cunningsburgh (South Mainland) and Burravoe (Yell).

*Pimpinella sp. A species of **Burnet-saxifrage**. Once collected (in 1977) as a casual at Eastshore, near Sumburgh. Specific identity not certainly known.

*Aegopodium podagraria L. **Ground-elder**. Naturalized. A frequent weed of rubbly places, gardens, sides of village streams, etc.

Berula erecta (Huds.) Coville. **Lesser water-parsnip**. Now confined as a native to the Burn of Strand, near Gott, downstream to Strand Loch. Reintroduced (in 1986) to the burn from the Loch of Asta.

*Conium maculatum L. **Hemlock**. Casual, perhaps still persisting about the Lerwick waterfront.

*Bupleurum subovatum Link ex Spreng. **False thorow-wax**. A very rare casual with single records from Whalsay and Scalloway.

Apium inundatum (L.) Rchb. f. **Lesser marshwort**. Rare. Fair Isle, Papa Stour and the Holm of Melby, several stations on Esha Ness, and in Uyea, Unst.

Ammi majus L. **Bullwort**. First recorded by R. C. Palmer (in 1991) as a casual in a Lerwick garden.

Carum carvi L. **Caraway**. Naturalized in dry grassy places (usually near habitation), chiefly in South Mainland and in parts of Yell and Unst.

Ligusticum scoticum L. **Scots lovage**. Frequent to common on sea cliffs and rocky coasts, occasional on beaches.

Angelica sylvestris L. **Wild angelica**. Common, especially in low-lying damp meadows and pastures, on sheltered sea cliffs, etc.

A. archangelica L. **Garden angelica**. Formerly as a relic or outcast of cultivation about yards in south Mainland. Recently only (status unclear) among sand dunes at Nor Wick, Unst (first noted by R. C. Palmer in 1989 and probably still surviving) and on the beach at the Sand of Meal, West Burra (a single plant found by L. A. Inkster in 1993 which did not survive long).

Levisticum officinale W. D. J. Koch. **Lovage**. A garden relic at Brough Lodge, Fetlar, since at least 1958. Once (1981) as a casual in a Scalloway garden.

Peucedanum ostruthium (L.) W. D. J. Koch. **Masterwort**. A relic or outcast of cultivation. Occasional in South Mainland, rare elsewhere.

Heracleum sphondylium L. subsp. *sphondylium*. **Hogweed**. A probable colonist. Common about limestone rocks, dune pastures, churchyards, etc.

H. mantegazzianum Sommier & Levier. **Giant hogweed**. Formerly, *c.* the mid-1940s and for many years afterwards, a well established garden escape by Leagarth House, Fetlar. By 1997 it had declined to one plant.

Gentianella campestris (L.) Börner. **Field gentian**. Dry, well-drained turfy pastures. Formerly frequent but less often seen nowadays.

G. amarella (L.) Börner subsp. *septentrionalis* (Druce) N. M. Pritch. **Autumn gentian**. A local plant of dry dune pastures; also on limestone grassland by the south-east side of the Loch of Cliff, Unst, where, however, it has not been seen for a long time. A small colony was found by R. C. Palmer in 1997 on the sandy embankment by the road near the Linkshouse Pier, Mid Yell, either native or introduced with coastal soil. Autumn gentian has certainly been introduced in this way in a handful of other (sometimes inland) areas, notably on levelled gravelly ground near the Sella Ness port administration complex, Sullom Voe, where there are thousands of plants (1997, L. A. Inkster & W. Scott), and within the confines of the Eela Water Water Treatment Works, near Ollaberry, many hundreds of plants on barish gravelly ground (same date, same recorders). It also occurs on levelled grassy ground, roadsides, etc., at the extreme eastern part of Sumburgh Airport (between Grutness Voe and and Wils Ness), in considerable abundance (1997, W. Scott) and close to a native station from which it almost certainly originated. These three occurrences are all directly associated with oil-related works during the 1970s.

Hyoscyamus niger L. **Henbane**. Casual, one plant near Quendale in 1980.

Lycopersicon esculentum Mill. **Tomato**. Casual, very rarely on rubbish-dumps.

Solanum nigrum L. subsp. *nigrum*. **Black nightshade**. Casual, once recorded near Scalloway in 1958.

S. tuberosum L. **Potato**. A predictably frequent throw-out or relic of cultivation.

Convolvulus arvensis L. **Field bindweed**. Still (and since at least 1924) a garden weed at Gardie House, Bressay.

Calystegia sepium (L.) R. Br. subsp. *sepium*. **Hedge bindweed**. A usually persistent garden outcast seen occasionally.

Menyanthes trifoliata L. **Bogbean**. Frequent. Soft-edged, deep peaty pools and lochs, streams and marshy meadows.

Polemonium caeruleum L. **Jacob's-ladder**. Merely a very rare garden outcast.

Phacelia tanacetifolia Benth. **Phacelia**. Once collected (in 1960) as a weed in a Scalloway garden.

Lithospermum arvense L. **Field gromwell**. Once collected (in 1963) as a weed in a Scalloway garden.

Pulmonaria officinalis L. **Lungwort**. A garden plant sometimes seen outside enclosures.

Symphytum officinale L. **Common comfrey**. A garden escape or outcast once found (in 1961) near a house, Mid Yell.

S. × uplandicum Nyman (*S. officinale* L. × *S. asperum* Lepech.). **Russian comfrey**. Often seen about houses and crofts, on waste ground, etc., as a garden escape or outcast.

S. tuberosum L. **Tuberous comfrey**. Locally, and of garden origin, near houses, on waste ground, etc.

Anchusa arvensis (L.) Bieb. **Bugloss**. A frequent colonist of arable ground, particularly on light sandy soils.

Mertensia maritima (L.) Gray. **Oysterplant**. Formerly (up to *c.* 1960) found on many beaches (notably at Easter Quarff) but now reduced to a handful of sites and in danger of extinction.

Plagiobothrys scouleri (Hook. & Arn.) I. M. Johnst. **White forget-me-not**. Casual. Once collected (in 1989) at the Baltasound Leisure Centre by R. C. Palmer.

Myosotis scorpioides L. **Water forget-me-not**. Naturalized. Frequent in ditches and wet places about crofts and houses, and particularly well established about lochs in southernmost Mainland.

M. secunda Al. Murray. **Creeping forget-me-not**. Common in watery places (ditches, burns, marshes, bogs, etc.).

M. laxa Lehm. subsp. *caespitosa*. (Schultz) Hyl. ex Nordh. **Tufted forget-me-not**. Frequent in watery places.

M. arvensis (L.) Hill. **Field forget-me-not**. A common colonist of cultivated ground and waste places.

M. discolor Pers. **Changing forget-me-not**. A probable colonist. Common in dry, grassy, often rocky places, cultivated ground, etc.

*Lappula squarrosa (Retz.) Dumort. **Bur forget-me-not**. A bird-seed casual in the garden of 9, Knab Road, Lerwick, 1997 (I. Clark).

*Stachys × ambigua Sm. (*S. sylvatica* L. × *S. palustris* L.). **Hybrid woundwort**. Naturalized. Apparently once grown for ornament, but now an occasional to frequent and persistent garden weed which has spread on to roadsides, waste ground, foreshores, etc.

S. palustris L. **Marsh woundwort**. A probable colonist. Occasional in or by cultivated ground, waste places, ditches, etc.

*Lamium maculatum (L.) L. **Spotted dead-nettle**. Merely a very rare garden outcast.

L. purpureum L. **Red dead-nettle**. A common colonist of cultivated and waste ground.

L. hybridum Vill. **Cut-leaved dead-nettle**. A colonist in Lerwick (as a garden weed, on waste ground, etc.) since at least 1865; formerly frequent in the town but now much diminished, though just surviving in 1996.

L. confertum Fr. **Northern dead-nettle**. A frequent colonist of cultivated and waste ground.

L. amplexicaule L. **Henbit dead-nettle**. A scarce colonist of sandy cultivated ground from Cunningsburgh southwards, otherwise a very rare casual.

*Galeopsis speciosa Mill. **Large-flowered hemp-nettle**. A very rare casual with only three recorded occurrences.

G. tetrahit L. **Common hemp-nettle**. A common colonist of cultivated ground, waste disturbed places, etc.

G. bifida Boenn. **Bifid hemp-nettle**. Status and habitat as for the preceding but with a preference for the poorer soils; less common though occurring just as widely.

*Glechoma hederacea L. **Ground-ivy**. A local but usually persistent garden escape or outcast in southern Mainland, rare elsewhere.

Prunella vulgaris L. **Selfheal**. Common in damp or dry meadows and pastures, often spreading on to dry gravelly roadsides, etc.

Thymus polytrichus A. Kern. ex Borbás subsp. *britannicus* (Ronniger) Kerguélen. **Wild thyme**. Common on dry, grassy, often rocky banks, bare granite and serpentinite debris, gravelly roadsides, etc.

*Mentha × gracilis Sole (*M. arvensis* L. × *M. spicata* L.). **Bushy mint**. Garden escape or outcast. Very rare. Long established by the Ham Burn, Foula.

M. aquatica L. **Water mint**. Ditches, streams, lochsides, etc. Not uncommon in southernmost south Mainland, the limestone valleys of Central Mainland, and in south-east Unst; rare elsewhere.

*M. × piperita L. (*M. aquatica* L. × *M. spicata* L.). **Peppermint**. Locally naturalized in watery places (burns, ditches, marshes, etc.).

*M. spicata L. **Spear mint**. Naturalized locally by stream sides and other wet places. Also as a garden escape or outcast about crofts, on waste ground, foreshores, etc. Only the glabrescent form has been seen in Shetland.

*M. × villosonervata Opiz (*M. spicata* L. × *M. longifolia* (L.) Huds.). **Sharp-toothed mint**. A garden outcast once collected in Lerwick in 1960.

[**M. × villosa* Huds. (*M. spicata* L. × *M. suaveolens* Ehrh.). **Apple-mint**. Formerly (in 1961) collected (as var. *alopecuroides* (Hull) Briq.) between Cott and Sound, Weisdale, planted or garden outcast. Not seen again.]

*M. × rotundifolia (L.) Huds. (*M. longifolia* (L.) Huds. × *M. suaveolens* Ehrh.). **False apple-mint**. Naturalized by roadsides and on waste ground about crofts mostly in South Mainland.

Hippuris vulgaris L. **Mare's-tail**. Local in sluggish streams, deep peaty pools, etc., in Unst, Yell and Fetlar. In Mainland only by the Loch of Hillwell, South Mainland, where it is now abundant, having increased enormously since 1977 when a few plants were seen, and by the Loch of Spiggie, recorded in 1981 and where there are now (1997) several medium-sized patches.

Callitriche hermaphroditica L. **Autumnal water-starwort**. Local. Often abundant in the clearer waters of the less peaty lochs.

C. stagnalis Scop. **Common water-starwort**. Common in usually shallow burns, ditches and pools, and on drying mud.

C. platycarpa Kütz. **Various-leaved water-starwort**. Distribution not well understood but perhaps frequent and preferring deep burns and ditches, etc.

C. hamulata Kütz. ex W. D. J. Koch. **Intermediate water-starwort**. Common in usually deep or fast-flowing burns, ditches, etc.

Plantago coronopus L. **Buck's-horn plantain**. Abundant by the coast in grassland and among rocks; much rarer in inland sites.

P. maritima L. **Sea plantain**. Another abundant coastal species (spray-soaked sward, cliffs, salt marshes, etc.), also inland in various habitats including the fellfield areas of Unst and Ronas Hill.

P. major L. **Greater plantain**. Colonist. Subsp. *major* is common on trodden ground about crofting areas and houses, waste rubbly places, by walls, etc. Subsp. *intermedia* (Gilib.) Lange. Distribution imperfectly known. Reliably recorded recently only from the Bay of Quendale (1996), but perhaps overlooked.

P. lanceolata L. **Ribwort plantain**. Abundant in grassland, especially on the more fertile soils, as in sandy ground near the sea and on limestone.

Littorella uniflora (L.) Asch. **Shoreweed**. Abundant in and by lochs and pools, avoiding the most peaty waters. Also in damp hollows where water has stood during the winter.

*Fraxinus excelsior L. **Ash**. Very rarely outside enclosures.

*Ligustrum ovalifolium Hassk. **Garden privet**. Very rarely outside enclosures.

*Mimulus guttatus DC. **Monkeyflower**. Naturalized. Frequent in watery places (burns, ditches, around lochs, etc.).

*M. × robertsii Silverside (*M. guttatus* DC. × *M. luteus* L.). L. **Hybrid monkeyflower**. Naturalized. Rare or occasional in burns, ditches, etc.

*M. × burnetii S. Arn. (*M. guttatus* DC. × *M. cupreus* Dombrain). **Coppery monkeyflower**. Naturalized. Occasional in burns, ditches, etc., mostly as a showy form with petaloid calyx.

*M. luteus L. **Blood-drop-emlets**. Naturalized at Noonsbrough, West Mainland, where it has grown for at least 40 years.

*M. × maculosus T. Moore. **Scottish monkeyflower**. Naturalized in the southern part of Cunningsburgh, and recently found, by the B.S.B.I. Field Meeting 1995, at the Burn of Dale, westernmost West Mainland.

*Cymbalaria muralis P. Gaertn., B. Mey. & Scherb. subsp. *muralis*. **Ivy-leaved toadflax**. A very rare garden outcast.

*Kickxia spuria (L.) Dumort. **Round-leaved fluellen**. Casual, once collected (in 1959) in a Scalloway garden.

*Linaria vulgaris Mill. **Common toadflax**. A rare garden straggler or casual. Also planted on a roadside bank at Sandness.

*L. repens (L.) Mill. **Pale toadflax**. Casual. One plant seen in a field, Daisy Park, Baltasound (in 1993) by M. G. Pennington, who also found several more in an adjoining garden the following year.

*L. maroccana Hook. f. **Annual toadflax**. A garden outcast once collected (in 1961) near Scalloway.

*Digitalis purpurea L. **Foxglove**. Sometimes seen as a garden escape or outcast or where planted.

Veronica serpyllifolia L. subsp. *serpyllifolia*. **Thyme-leaved speedwell**. Common in moist grassy places, arable ground, gardens, on gravelly roadsides, etc.

V. officinalis L. **Heath speedwell**. Common in dry grassland, on stony heaths, and among rocks and scree, etc.

*V. chamaedrys L. **Germander speedwell**. Looking native, but probably only naturalized, on roadside banks by the lochs of Asta and Tingwall where it has been known for many years; less well established elsewhere as a relict of cultivation, in churchyards, or as a garden escape or outcast.

V. scutellata L. **Marsh speedwell**. Marshy places, ditches, shores of lochs, etc. Frequent in west Mainland, occasional elsewhere (mainly in Central Mainland).

V. beccabunga L. **Brooklime**. Watery places (ditches, streams, etc.). Mostly in the limestone areas of Central Mainland (as between Asta and Gott, etc.), very rare elsewhere.

V. anagallis-aquatica L. **Blue water-speedwell**. Local in sluggish ditches, streams, pools, etc., in the limestone areas of Central Mainland, and in South Mainland from Cunningsburgh southwards (especially on sandy soils).

V. arvensis L. **Wall speedwell**. Not infrequent as a probable native in dry rocky turf and on old walls; also an occasional arable weed.

V. agrestis L. **Green field-speedwell**. An occasional colonist of arable ground; also a garden weed.

*V. polita Fr. **Grey field-speedwell**. A very uncommon weed of arable and garden ground, etc.

*V. persica Poir. **Common field-speedwell**. Occasionally seen as a weed in gardens, on waste ground, etc.

*V. filiformis Sm. **Slender speedwell**. Garden plant, a rampant weed in lawns, verges, etc., occasionally becoming established as in and around Tingwall churchyard where it has been naturalized for at least 40 years; also as a garden outcast.

V. hederifolia L. subsp. *hederifolia*. **Ivy-leaved speedwell**. A local colonist of arable and garden ground, in waste places, etc., mainly in South and Central Mainland, rare elsewhere.

*Hebe × franciscana (Eastw.) Souster (*H. elliptica* (G. Forst.) Pennell × *H. speciosa* (R. Cunn. ex A. Cunn.) Cockayne & Allen). **Hedge veronica**. One plant, presumably bird-introduced, seen by R. C. Palmer in 1991 among rocks at Fort Charlotte, Lerwick. In 1997 W. Scott noticed a further three or four small plants nearby.

Melampyrum pratense L. subsp. *pratense*. **Common cow-wheat**. Very rare. Black Butten, Ronas Hill. Collected on Saxa Vord, Unst, in 1921 but not seen again.

Euphrasia. **Eyebright**.

    E. arctica Lange ex Rostrup subsp. *arctica*. A common and large-flowered species of damp meadows and marshes.

    E. nemorosa (Pers.) Wallr. Frequent. Short, dry grassland (perhaps with a preference for the better soils), sand-dune pastures, roadsides, etc.

E. confusa Pugsley. Commonly in dry, closely grazed grassland, cliff-top sward, etc.

E. frigida Pugsley. Known only from high ground in Foula.

E. foulaensis F. Towns. ex Wettst. Common in coastal sward, less often in damp bare places, etc., inland.

E. ostenfeldii group. Occasional in coastal sward, especially cliff-tops, very scarce inland. Included here are *E. ostenfeldii* (Pugsley) Yeo, *E. marshallii* Pugsley and *E. rotundifolia* Pugsley. We have had little success in separating these three closely related species, a problem aggravated by their highly exposed habitat which leads to dwarfed, condensed plants.

E. micrantha Rchb. Common on well-drained heaths and moors, serpentinite gravel, etc.

E. scottica Wettst. Frequent in marshy places by lochs and burns, damp pastures, etc.

E. heslop-harrisonii Pugsley. Known only from Foula and the Holms of Uyea-sound, near Vementry.

In addition the following 15 hybrids have been collected in Shetland. Unless otherwise stated all have been recorded from fewer than five sites:

    (1) *E. arctica* subsp. *arctica* × *E. confusa* (probably frequent)
    (2) *E. arctica* subsp. *arctica* × *E. micrantha*
    (3) *E. arctica* subsp. *arctica* × *E. nemorosa*
    (4) *E. arctica* subsp. *arctica* × *E. ostenfeldii* group
    (5) *E. arctica* subsp. *arctica* × *E. scottica* (perhaps frequent)
    (6) *E. nemorosa* × *E. ostenfeldii* group
    (7) *E. confusa* × *E. foulaensis*
    (8) *E. confusa* × *E. micrantha*
    (9) *E. confusa* × *E. scottica*
    (10) *E. foulaensis* × *E. micrantha*
    (11) *E. foulaensis* × *E. ostenfeldii* group (probably widespread)
    (12) *E. foulaensis* × *E. scottica*
    (13) *E. ostenfeldii* group × *E. scottica*
    (14) *E. micrantha* × *E. nemorosa*
    (15) *E. micrantha* × *E. ostenfeldii* group.

Odontites vernus (Bellardi) Dumort. subsp. *litoralis* (Fr.) Nyman. **Red bartsia**. Sandy coastal pastures and arable ground near the sea. Rare or local in South Mainland, Fair Isle and Unst, very rare elsewhere.

[**Rhinanthus angustifolius* C. C. Gmel. **Greater yellow-rattle**. Once either a casual or local colonist. Last seen (at Baltasound) in 1921.]

R. minor L. **Yellow-rattle**. Common in meadows (both wet or dry), on roadsides and dry, stony, heathy ground. Subsp. *minor* (including subsp. *stenophyllus* (Schur) O. Schwarz) is found in meadows, etc., while subsp. *monticola* (Sterneck) O. Schwarz and subsp. *borealis* (Sterneck) P. D. Sell favour dry heathy pastures (especially on serpentinite) and other dry stony ground; the last-named is very rare.

Pedicularis palustris L. **Marsh lousewort**. Frequent in marshy and swampy places.

P. sylvatica L. subsp. *sylvatica*. **Lousewort**. Common and widespread on wet heathery ground and damp heathland.

Pinguicula vulgaris L. **Common butterwort**. Common on wet heaths and moors, dripping burnsides and coastal banks, etc.

Utricularia vulgaris L., *sensu lato*. **Greater bladderwort**. Deep pools in swampy places, sluggish streams, etc. Frequent in West Mainland, occasional elsewhere. Both *U. vulgaris* L. and *U. australis* R. Br. have been tentatively claimed for Shetland, but until more flowering material has been found (the plant was first and last recorded in bloom in 1959, at North Roe) the true position is not likely to be known.

U. intermedia Hayne, *sensu lato*. **Intermediate bladderwort**. Quiet, often peaty, mossy swamps, pools and small lochs. Mainly in West Mainland, very rare elsewhere. As flowering has never been recorded from Shetland, it is less easy to identify our plant to segregate level. However, recent examination of material by L. A. Inkster (confirmed by W. Scott) has shown, on the basis of bladder distribution, leaf and quadrifid hair characters, that some of our plants, at least, are clearly referable to *U. stygia* G. Thor. The examined material came from the tiny loch by the roadside opposite the Loch of Flatpunds, the burn from the Loch of Grunnavoe (both near Walls), a small pool south-east of Longa Water (near West Burrafirth), and marshy ground by the south-west side of the Loch of Spiggie.

U. minor L. **Lesser bladderwort**. Peaty pools and small lochs, swamps, etc. Frequent in West Mainland, occasional elsewhere. Its flowering period has not been monitored over a long period but it would appear that flowers are produced sporadically in some locations and more regularly in others.

Campanula rotundifolia L. **Harebell**. Perhaps formerly more widespread but now extremely rare and known only from the Ness of Islesburgh (near Mavis Grind) and Skeo Taing, Unst.

Jasione montana L. **Sheep's-bit**. Common in dry, often heathy or rocky grassland, on sea banks and rocky burnsides, etc.

Lobelia dortmanna L. **Water lobelia**. Occasional to frequent in relatively clear, stony-bottomed lochs and pools.

*Sherardia arvensis L. **Field madder**. A very rare casual of arable ground, gardens, etc. Last seen in 1970.

Galium odoratum (L.) Scop. **Woodruff**. Probably a mere garden escape at Baltasound around a century ago.

G. palustre L. subsp. *palustre*. **Common marsh-bedstraw**. Common in watery places (marshes, stream sides, etc.).

G. verum L. **Lady's bedstraw**. Dry, sandy or rocky pastures (often on limestone or sandstone), sea banks, etc. Not uncommon in central and southern parts of Shetland, occasional elsewhere.

G. mollugo L. subsp. *erectum* Syme. **Hedge bedstraw**. A very rare casual of arable ground, etc., with no recent records.

G. saxatile L. **Heath bedstraw**. Abundant on dry heaths, among rocks and on gravelly roadsides.

G. aparine L. **Cleavers**. Essentially a species of shingly beaches in Shetland, in which habitat it is frequent; seldom seen inland in gardens, etc.

Sambucus nigra L. **Elder**. Commonly grown in Shetland gardens and often seen around houses and crofts in more or less unenclosed situations.

Symphoricarpos albus (L.) S. F. Blake. **Snowberry**. A garden shrub rarely seen outside enclosures.

Lonicera periclymenum L. **Honeysuckle**. Steep rocky streamsides and crags, sea cliffs and holms in lochs. Frequent in western and northern areas, local elsewhere.

Valerianella locusta (L.) Laterr. **Common cornsalad**. A very rare colonist of sandy arable ground at Norwick, Unst (last seen 1962), and in southernmost South Mainland (last seen 1966).

Dipsacus sp. **Teasel**. A very rare casual. Root-leaves were collected in 1967 on the (then) Lerwick rubbish-dump; these belonged to either *D. fullonum* L. or to *D. sativus* (L.) Honck. More recently *D. fullonum* has been seen in Lerwick gardens where, however, it may have been intentionally grown.

Succisa pratensis Moench. **Devil's-bit scabious**. Common in meadows and pastures from coastal turf to marshy stream valleys, etc.

Arctium nemorosum Lej. **Wood burdock**. As a native still surviving, rather precariously, in the Grutness Voe area, Sumburgh. Once recorded as a garden casual at Quoyness, Loch of Strom.

Saussurea alpina (L.) DC. **Alpine saw-wort**. Now very rare and elusive on the Ronas Hill summit plateau where, 40 years ago, it could be found comparatively easily. First and last seen on the Hill of Colvadale, Unst, in 1962.

Carduus nutans L. **Musk thistle**. Casual, once reported over a century ago on a Shetland beach, allegedly at Baltasound.

Cirsium vulgare (Savi) Ten. **Spear thistle**. Common in dry grassy places, on roadside verges and upper parts of beaches, etc.

C. heterophyllum (L.) Hill. **Melancholy thistle**. A rare garden outcast or where planted, particularly well established by St Colman's Episcopal Church, Burravoe, Yell.

C. palustre (L.) Scop. **Marsh thistle**. Common in marshy meadows and pastures, damp turfy ground, by burnsides, etc.

C. arvense (L.) Scop. **Creeping thistle**. A probable colonist. Common in and by arable ground, in pastures (locally covering large areas on sandy soil), on waste ground, etc.

Centaurea montana L. **Perennial cornflower**. A popular garden species sometimes seen as an escape or outcast.

C. cyanus L. **Cornflower**. A very rare casual last seen in 1991.

C. solstitialis L. **Yellow star-thistle**. Casual. One plant in a garden, Okraquoy, near Cunningsburgh, 1980.

C. melitensis L. **Maltese star-thistle**. Casual on Lerwick rubbish-dump, 1956.

C. diluta Aiton. **Lesser star-thistle**. Casual. One plant on Lerwick rubbish-dump, 1961.

C. nigra L. **Common knapweed**. A local colonist usually in small patches by roadsides, etc.

Lapsana communis L. subsp. *communis*. **Nipplewort**. A rare weed of gardens and arable ground, etc.

Hypochaeris radicata L. **Cat's-ear**. Colonist; 75 years ago this was very rare but is now a common plant of dry pastures, roadside banks, etc., in most inhabited areas.

Leontodon autumnalis L. **Autumn hawkbit**. Very common and variable. Found in a variety of habitats from coastal (including salt marsh) turf, through meadows, pastures and heaths to the granite debris of the Ronas Hill summit.

Sonchus arvensis L. **Perennial sow-thistle**. A frequent colonist of arable ground, the higher parts of shingly or sandy beaches, and foreshore banks.

S. oleraceus L. **Smooth sow-thistle**. A weed of gardens, waste places, etc. Frequent about Lerwick, Scalloway, Symbister (Whalsay), uncommon elsewhere.

S. asper (L.) Hill. **Prickly sow-thistle**. An occasional colonist of arable and waste ground, by walls, etc.

Lactuca sativa L. **Garden lettuce**. Merely a throw-out from cultivation.

Cicerbita microphylla (Willd.) Wallr. subsp. *uralensis* (Rouy) P. D. Sell. **Common blue-sow-thistle**. A very rare garden outcast or escape, capable of persisting.

Mycelis muralis (L.) Dumort. **Wall lettuce**. One plant as a garden weed, Quoyness, Loch of Strom; collected (in 1996) by J. Clark.

Taraxacum. **Dandelion**. Sixty-one microspecies are currently accepted from Shetland. Only a handful of these are native (*T. geirhildae, T. serpenticola, T. hirsutissimum, T. faeroense* and *T. unguilobum*), the first three endemic to Shetland. To these may be added two probable natives, *T. brachyglossum* and *T. fulvicarpum*. The remainder are all considered to be colonists, although some may not be more than casuals. In this list, which follows Dudman and Richards (1997), only the natives and probable natives are given habitat details. The colonists are all inhabitants of a wide range of artificial sites in and near populated areas (by roadsides and walls, in old quarries, cemeteries and gardens, on foreshores and waste ground, etc.).

Section Erythrosperma (H. Lindb.) Dahlst.
> *T. brachyglossum* (Dahlst.) Raunk. Probably native. Found (in 1984) in sandy turf by the West Pool, Mousa, by W. Scott.
> *T. scanicum* Dahlst. Southernmost South Mainland; Scalloway.
> *T. oxoniense* Dahlst. Near the main pier, Mid Yell.

Section Spectabilia (Dahlst.) Dahlst.
> *T. faeroense* (Dahlst.) Dahlst. Native. Frequent and sometimes common in wet or dry rocky places (especially burnsides), and in marshy or damp pastures. Shetland's commonest and most widespread dandelion.
> *T. geirhildae* (Beeby) R.C. Palmer & W. Scott. Endemic. Rocky places. Very rare. First found by W. H. Beeby near Lang Clodie Loch, North Roe, in 1907 (where it still grows), and more recently discovered by W. Scott in several places on the north side of Ronas Voe, and near Kellister, West Mainland (both finds made in 1993).
> *T. serpenticola* A. J. Richards. Endemic. Extremely rare. Known only from rocky turf on serpentinite, Muckle Heog, Unst.

Section Naevosa M. P. Christ.
> *T. naevosum* Dahlst. Frequent about Lerwick and Scalloway, very rare elsewhere.
> *T. naevosiforme* Dahlst. Lerwick; Scalloway; Gulberwick.
> *T. euryphyllum* (Dahlst.) Hjelt. A frequent colonist about Lerwick and Scalloway, rare elsewhere though occurring in places as widely separated as Fair Isle and Unst.
> *T. hirsutissimum* C. C. Haw. Endemic. Local in dry, sandy coastal turf and by roadsides in South Mainland, from Cunningsburgh southwards.
> *T. maculosum* A. J. Richards. Cunningsburgh; Walls; Hillswick; West Sandwick, Yell.
> *T. pseudolarssonii* A. J. Richards. Wick of Sandsayre, Sandwick; Walls.
> *T. subnaevosum* A. J. Richards. Gremista, Lerwick; Uphouse, Bressay.

Section Celtica A. J. Richards.
> *T. gelertii* Raunk. Known only from Tingwall churchyard.
> *T. bracteatum* Dahlst. Known only from Fair Isle.
> *T. duplidentifrons* Dahlst. One of our most frequent colonist dandelions, widespread and in some areas common (Lerwick and Scalloway, etc.).
> *T. inane* A. J. Richards. Symbister, Whalsay; near Baltasound.
> *T. landmarkii* Dahlst. Near South Setter, north of Scalloway; West Sand Wick, Yell.
> *T. nordstedtii* Dahlst. North of Asta, near Scalloway; Fort Charlotte, Lerwick.
> *T. fulvicarpum* Dahlst. Probably native. Dune pasture, etc., southernmost South Mainland.
> *T. unguilobum* Dahlst. Native, at least in part. Grassy banks and pastures (often on sand), stream sides, road verges, etc. Frequent in South Mainland, rare elsewhere though extending as far as Yell and Unst.
> *T. luteum* C. C. Haw. & A. J. Richards. Hillswick, first found in 1980 by W. Scott.

Section Hamata H. Øllg.
> *T. hamatum* Raunk. Scattered localities throughout Shetland, apart from North Mainland.
> *T. hamatulum* Hagend., Soest & Zevenb. Fair Isle; Scalloway and district; Lerwick.
> *T. subhamatum* M. P. Christ. Near Loch of Tingwall; Lerwick.
> *T. quadrans* H. Øllg. Lerwick; Haroldswick, Unst.
> *T. pseudohamatum* Dahlst. Sandness.
> *T. atactum* Sahlin & Soest. Lerwick; Bressay; Sandness; Baltasound.
> *T. hamatiforme* Dahlst. A few very scattered localities from near Sumburgh to Unst.
> *T. lamprophyllum* M. P. Christ. Burravoe, Brae.

Section Ruderalia Kirschner, H. Øllg. & Štěpánek.
> *T. macrolobum* Dahlst. Pool of Virkie, Sumburgh.
> *T. pannucium* Dahlst. Sumburgh area; Scalloway area.
> *T. tenebricans* (Dahlst.) Dahlst. West Voe of Sumburgh; Muckle Roe.
> *T. dilaceratum* M. P. Christ. Scalloway; near Loch of Asta; Bixter.
> *T. alatum* H. Lindb. Lerwick; Walls.
> *T. insigne* Ekman ex M. P. Christ. & Wiinst. Levenwick, South Mainland; Fort Charlotte, Lerwick; Bressay.
> *T. laticordatum* Markl. Hamnavoe, West Burra; Hillswick.

T. pallescens Dahlst. Near Loch of Kirkigarth, Walls.

T. expallidiforme Dahlst. Sumburgh Airport.

T. croceiflorum Dahlst. Near Scalloway Castle.

T. cyanolepis Dahlst. Near Laxfirth, north of Veensgarth.

T. ancistrolobum Dahlst. Hamnavoe, West Burra; Scalloway; Tingwall churchyard; Haroldswick, Unst.

T. sellandii Dahlst. Bakkasetter, South Mainland; Scalloway; Gardie House, Bressay; Mid Yell.

T. altissimum H. Lindb. West Voe of Sumburgh.

T. adiantifrons Ekman ex Dahlst. Sumburgh Airport.

T. acroglossum Dahlst. Near Sandwick, Whalsay.

T. vastisectum Markl. ex Puol. West Voe of Sumburgh; Lerwick.

T. cordatum Palmgr. Scalloway; Brough, South Nesting.

T. ekmanii Dahlst. Cunningsburgh; Scalloway; Aith, West Mainland; Houbie, Fetlar; Baltasound.

T. oblongatum Dahlst. Hillswick.

T. tanyphyllum Dahlst. Levenwick, South Mainland.

T. dahlstedtii H. Lindb. Sumburgh Airport; Hoswick; Tingwall churchyard; Lerwick; Bressay; Hillswick.

T. latisectum H. Lindb. Ollaberry.

T. subundulatum Dahlst. Symbister, Whalsay.

T. pectinatiforme H. Lindb. Hoversta, Bressay.

T. polyodon Dahlst. Fair Isle; Sumburgh and Pool of Virkie areas; Scalloway; Bressay; Burravoe, Brae; Ollaberry.

T. incisum H. Øllg. St John's Church, Baltasound.

T. xanthostigma H. Lindb. Melby House, Sandness.

T. longisquameum H. Lindb. Lerwick.

T. scotiniforme Dahlst. ex G. E. Haglund. Old lanes, Lerwick.

T. fasciatum Dahlst. Levenwick, South Mainland; Scalloway; Lerwick; near Loch of Tingwall.

*Crepis tectorum L. **Narrow-leaved hawk's-beard**. A very rare casual of reseeded ground, etc.

*C. capillaris (L.) Wallr. **Smooth hawk's-beard**. A rare casual of arable and waste ground, etc.

*C. setosa Haller f. **Bristly hawk's-beard**. A very rare casual with single records from Lerwick and Baltasound.

Pilosella flagellaris (Willd.) P. D. Sell & C. West subsp. *bicapitata* P. D. Sell & C. West. **Shetland mouse-ear-hawkweed**. Endemic. Dry rocky pastures on the White Ness peninsula and at West Burrafirth, also on steep rocky sea banks on the north side of Ronas Voe.

*P. aurantiaca (L.) F. W. Schultz & Sch. Bip. **Fox-and-cubs**. An occasional garden escape or outcast.

Hieracium. **Hawkweed**. Twenty-four microspecies (or 25 if *H.* 'sparsifolium' includes two taxa) are currently known to grow in Shetland. All the named members of Section Alpestria are endemic to Shetland. Habitat details are not given for each microspecies; all our hawkweeds inhabit relatively sheep-proof, rocky places such as ravines, crags, sea banks, holms in lochs, etc., and are only rarely encountered in hay meadows or by the grassy sides of burns and roads. Several early identifications are now known to be erroneous and this has led to some hawkweeds (notably *H. attenuatifolium* and *H. dilectum*) being over-recorded by us (1987). More research is needed into the genus in Shetland.

Section Foliosa (Fr.) Dahlst.

[*H. obesifolium* Pugsley. Endemic. First and last seen by W. H. Beeby in 1902 on a holm in Burga Water, between Walls and Sandness. Following expert opinion we previously referred the Burga Water plant to *H. maritimum* (F. Hanb.) F. Hanb., but recent examination by us of Beeby's material has clearly shown the distinctness of his plant, now sadly lost.]

H. 'Taxon C'. Very rare. Brough (South Nesting); Burn of Skelladale, Brae; Muckle Roe, and two sites in Yell (North Burn, West Yell, and the Loch of Lumbister). This leafy plant (with up to 20 narrow stem leaves) was first collected (in 1958) on Muckle Roe by W. Scott, where it is abundant in its one station. It is apparently a new species of this section and was not previously recognized as distinct, being referred to either *H. vinicaule* or to *H. dilectum*. A hawkweed ('Taxon B') from Catfirth (South Nesting), first noted (in 1956) by W. Scott, and at Kels Wick (Lunna Ness), and which appears to be the same as 'Taxon C' but with slightly narrower leaves, was also similarly misplaced.

Section Tridentata (Fr.) Gremli.

H. gothicoides Pugsley. Very rare. A taxon thus named occurs in the Lunning area, near Vidlin, but appears to be nearing extinction in the nearby Swining Voe station.

H. lissolepium (Zahn) Roffey. Extremely rare. A taxon thus named grows in a *geo* near Eric's Ham, near Aywick, Yell. Formerly considered extinct owing to confusion over the exact location.

H. 'sparsifolium Lindeb'. Very rare in West Mainland and Fetlar, rare in Central and North Mainland, and Unst, and occasional in Yell where, particularly in places about the Loch of Vatsetter, it is especially abundant. Ongoing research is likely to reveal that the name covers two superficially similar taxa, of which one probably belongs to Section Alpestria.

Section Alpestria (Fr.) Gremli.

    H. vinicaule P. D. Sell & C. West. Rare in West Mainland, occasional or locally frequent in North Mainland.

    H. northroense Pugsley. Very rare. Known only from a hay meadow at Burravoe (North Roe) and steep sea banks by the Voe of Snarraness, West Mainland.

    H. subtruncatum Beeby. Very rare in South, Central and West Mainland, occasional in North Mainland where most stations are between Islesburgh and Ronas Voe.

    H. dilectum P. D. Sell & C. West. Very rare. Burn of Quoys, South Nesting; Voe of Snarraness; near West Burrafirth; Laxo Burn.

    H. pugsleyi P. D. Sell & C. West. Very rare. Burn of Laxdale, Cunningsburgh; Burn of Weisdale; Tumblin, near Bixter (nearly extinct), and two sites in Yell (Skurdie Geo, near Otterswick, and Whale Firth). Plants from the two Yell stations were formerly referred to 'Taxon D' and 'Taxon F' respectively.

    H. attenuatifolium P. D. Sell & C. West. Extremely rare. The true plant is known only from the Laxo Burn, and in cultivation. West Mainland records given by us (1987) refer to *H. spenceanum*.

    H. hethlandiae (F. Hanb.) Puglsey. Formerly at Mavis Grind (near Brae), its only certainly recorded station, till finally destroyed by rock removal operations in 1976. Before then rescued and brought into cultivation; introduced at the nearby Burn of Skelladale in 1987, following an earlier unsuccessful attempt to establish it at Hurda Field, close to its original site. Still surviving at the Burn of Skelladale, and in cultivation.

    H. praethulense Pugsley. Northmavine only. Rare between Mavis Grind and Ronas Voe, but becoming frequent on the north side of the voe, and abundant on the holms in Swabie Water, North Roe, where it was discovered by S. C. Jay in 1994.

    H. australius (Beeby) Pugsley. Rare. Loch of Cliff, Unst; Wick of Tresta, Fetlar; Ronas Voe.

    H. spenceanum W. Scott & R. C. Palmer. Very rare. Occurs in a handful of stations from Norby (Sandness) to West Burrafirth, including the Ward of Scollan. Formerly included under *H. attenuatifolium*, and more recently referred to as 'Taxon A'; see our note (1995).

    H. difficile P. D. Sell & C. West. Very rare. One station (a limestone ravine) near Okraquoy, north of Cunningsburgh.

    H. gratum P. D. Sell & C. West. Very rare. Head of Burra Firth, Unst, and nearby Loch of Cliff. Discovered by J. Bevan (in 1988) by the west side of Whale Firth, Yell, where further stations were later found by W. Scott.

    H. breve Beeby. Extremely rare. North side of Ronas Voe.

    H. zetlandicum Beeby. Occasional (mostly coastal) in North Roe and by the south side of Ronas Voe, very rare in Central and West Mainland.

    H. 'Taxon E'. Very rare. A colony of what may be an undescribed member of this section was found by W. Scott (in 1993) on low sea banks by the west side of Sandsound Voe, near Bixter. It is a noticeably pilose, large-headed plant with about five very lightly purple-marked leaves.

Section Vulgata (Griseb.) Willk. & Lange.

    H. uistense (Pugsley) P. D. Sell & C. West. Very rare. Ronas Voe, mainly on the north side.

Section Oreadea (Fr.) Dahlst.

    H. orimeles F. Hanb. ex W. R. Linton. Mostly in West and North Mainland, very rare or unrecorded elsewhere.

    H. scoticum F. Hanb. Very rare. Sandness area; Ronas Voe.

    H. caledonicum F. Hanb. Rare. From Sandness to entrance to Aith Voe; Ronas Voe.

    H. argenteum Fr. Rare. West Burrafirth area; Ronas Voe; west side of North Roe.

Antennaria dioica (L.) Gaertn. **Mountain everlasting**. Common in dry, heathy places (especially in parts of Northmavine, Fetlar and Unst), local elsewhere.

Anaphalis margaritacea* (L.) Benth. **Pearly everlasting. Merely a garden straggler or where planted.

Gnaphalium sylvaticum L. **Heath cudweed**. Formerly an occasional, or rarely locally abundant native (in some areas perhaps a colonist) of dry pastures, banks, dunes, etc., now apparently on the verge of extinction.

G. uliginosum L. **Marsh cudweed**. Colonist. Occasional on gravelly roadside verges, in open muddy places, etc., rarely as an arable weed.

Helichrysum bellidioides (G. Forst.) Willd. **New Zealand everlastingflower**. Planted or garden outcast. Naturalized since at least 1975 by a burn west of Tagon, Voe.

*Inula helenium L. **Elecampane**. Garden outcast or escape, or planted. Occasional about yards, crofts, etc. Known since at least 1958 by Ladysmith Road, Scalloway.

Solidago virgaurea L. **Goldenrod**. Frequent in dry, well-drained places (heaths, crags, rocky stream sides, low sea banks, etc.).

S. gigantea* Aiton subsp. *serotina* (O. Kuntze) McNeill. **Early goldenrod. Garden outcast by Voe of Leiraness, Bressay (1983, W. Scott).

*Aster novi-belgii L. **Confused Michaelmas-daisy**. An occasional garden outcast or straggler, sometimes becoming well established.

*A. lanceolatus Willd. **Narrow-leaved Michaelmas-daisy**. Once collected at Lerwick, as a garden escape or relic.

Aster tripolium L. **Sea aster**. Known only from steep sea banks and cliffs on Isbister Holm, and the nearby east coast of Whalsay.

Bellis perennis L. **Daisy**. Abundant in short, often moist, grassland, etc.

* Tanacetum parthenium (L.) Sch. Bip. **Feverfew**. Merely an occasional garden escape or outcast.

*T. vulgare L. **Tansy**. A frequent garden straggler or escape by crofts, roadsides, on waste ground, etc. Established near Breakon, Yell.

Artemisia vulgaris L. **Mugwort**. Colonist. Occasional to frequent in sandy soil (especially in South Mainland), scarce elsewhere.

*A. abrotanum L. **Southernwood**. Very seldom seen outside cultivation.

Achillea ptarmica L. **Sneezewort**. Frequent in damp, rough meadows, by field-borders, roadsides, etc.

A. millefolium L. **Yarrow**. Common in dry pastures (particularly coastal sward or on limestone).

*Anthemis arvensis L. **Corn chamomile**. A very rare casual with only three records.

*Chrysanthemum segetum L. **Corn marigold**. Formerly a rare colonist in or near arable ground (chiefly cornfields and perhaps sometimes casual), etc., but seldom seen nowadays owing to the decline in oat cultivation.

Leucanthemum vulgare Lam. **Oxeye daisy**. Meadows, pastures, churchyards, roadsides, etc. In Shetland a local and usually short-lived colonist (or perhaps sometimes only a casual).

*L. × superbum (Bergmans ex J. W. Ingram) D. H. Kent. **Shasta daisy**. Sometimes seen outside gardens, usually as an outcast.

*Matricaria recutita L. **Scented mayweed**. A very rare casual once collected in 1978 at Cunningsburgh.

M. discoidea DC. **Pineappleweed**. A common colonist about crofts and farms, and as an arable weed; also about harbours, etc. First observed in Shetland in 1911, at Baltasound.

Tripleurospermum maritimum (L.) W. D. J. Koch. **Sea mayweed**. Common on sea cliffs, shingly beaches, stacks, etc; what is apparently the same taxon occurs in arable ground, both by the coast and inland.

T. inodorum (L.) Sch. Bip. **Scentless mayweed**. A seemingly local colonist of perhaps mainly light or sandy arable ground, but distribution very unclear owing to confusion with the agrestal form of the preceding.

*Cotula squalida (Hook. f.) Hook. f. **Leptinella**. Naturalized on and near turfy roadsides at Voe; above Dales Voe; Graven, and near Tofts Voe (all in Delting), and near a house, Catfirth, South Nesting. Covering hundreds of square metres at Graven, the plant is not extinct there as we inadvertently stated (1987).

*Senecio fluviatilis Wallr. **Broad-leaved ragwort**. A very rare garden outcast or relic at Brettabister and Kirkabister, North Nesting.

*S. smithii DC. **Magellan ragwort**. Naturalized around crofts and houses, shores of lochs, etc. Frequent, notably in South and West Mainland, and Yell.

S. jacobaea L. **Common ragwort**. A colonist of 100 years' standing or more in and around Scalloway; very rare and probably casual elsewhere. In Shetland effectively replaced by a form of *S. aquaticus*.

S. × ostenfeldii Druce (*S. jacobaea* L. × *S. aquaticus* Hill). Still in and around Scalloway where it was first detected as a British plant in 1888.

S. aquaticus Hill. **Marsh ragwort**. Generally common in the crofting areas: rough meadows and pastures, arable land, ditches, stony shores of lochs, etc., often in quite dry places. In Shetland occurring as an unusual, typically neat and low-growing, variant with larger and showier capitula in a flat-topped inflorescence.

*S. squalidus L. **Oxford ragwort**. A very rare casual only twice collected (on both occasions at Lerwick).

S. vulgaris L. **Groundsel**. A common colonist of arable, garden and waste ground. The var. *hibernicus* Syme has been once collected in Lerwick.

*S. vernalis Waldst. & Kit. **Eastern groundsel**. Casual. Once collected (in 1989) at the Baltasound Leisure Centre by R. C. Palmer.

* Tussilago farfara L. **Colt's-foot**. An occasional to frequent colonist on roadside banks, waste rubbly places, etc.

*Petasites albus (L.) Gaertn. **White butterbur**. A garden outcast about houses, on roadsides, etc. Rare, but several long-persistent patches at Stove, Sandwick.

*P. fragrans (Vill.) C. Presl. **Winter heliotrope**. A very rare garden outcast or relic. Still a large patch behind the 'Aald Haa', Scalloway.

*Calendula officinalis L. **Pot marigold**. This popular garden plant is occasionally seen on rubbish-tips, etc.

*Helianthus annuus L. **Sunflower**. Casual or garden outcast. One plant on the beach at Sand of Meal, West Burra, 1995 (L. A. Inkster), and a large flowering specimen on the beach at Tarland, Sound, Lerwick, 1995 (J. McKee).

*Galinsoga parviflora Cav. **Gallant soldier**. Casual. Once collected (in 1971) at Eastshore, near Sumburgh.

Triglochin palustris L. **Marsh arrowgrass**. Frequent in wet meadows, marshes, muddy ditches, etc.

T. maritima L. **Sea arrowgrass**. Frequent by the coast in brackish turf, salt marshes, etc.; very occasionally inland in bogs or marshes.

Potamogeton natans L. **Broad-leaved pondweed**. Common in lochs and pools but avoiding strongly peaty waters where *P. polygonifolius* takes its place.

P. × gessnacencis G. Fisch. (*P. natans* L. × *P. polygonifolius* L.). Collected in 1996 in the Loch of Gards, Scat Ness, near Sumburgh, by P. M. Hollingsworth and C. D. Preston. An extremely rare hybrid known from only two other sites in this country.

[? *P. × sparganiifolius* Laest. ex Fr. (*P. natans* L. × *P. gramineus* L.). An unusual pondweed, believed to be a form of this hybrid, occurred in the Loch of Cliff, Unst, from 1974 (when it was first seen) to 1978 but appears to be now extinct. It was previously recorded by us (1987) as possibly *P. polygonifolius* × *P. gramineus* (*P. × lanceolatifolius* (Tiselius) C. D. Preston).]

P. polygonifolius Pourr. **Bog pondweed**. Very common in peaty pools and runnels, burns, and in boggy or marshy areas.

P. × zizii W. D. J. Koch ex Roth. (*P. lucens* L. × *P. gramineus* L.). **Long-leaved pondweed**. Known only from the Loch of Hillwell, South Mainland (where it still occurs), in the apparent absence of *P. lucens*.

P. gramineus L. **Various-leaved pondweed**. Frequent in lochs and streams, chiefly in the less peaty waters.

P. × nitens Weber. (*P. gramineus* L. × *P. perfoliatus* L.). **Bright-leaved pondweed**. Scattered localities from the Loch of Brow, South Mainland, to the Loch of Cliff, Unst.

P. alpinus Balb. **Red pondweed**. Known only from the Loch of Voe and its outflowing stream.

P. praelongus Wulfen. **Long-stalked pondweed**. Local. Mainly in the deeper, less peaty waters; perhaps sometimes overlooked.

P. perfoliatus L. **Perfoliate pondweed**. Common. Mainly in the less peaty lochs; occasionally in the larger, deeper streams.

P. friesii Rupr. **Flat-stalked pondweed**. Known only from the Loch of Hillwell (South Mainland), first recorded in 1977 and now plentiful, and the Loch of Clickhimin (recorded once, in 1975).

P. rutilus Wolfg. **Shetland pondweed**. Known only from the lochs of Asta and Tingwall, and the lochs of Kirkigarth and Bardister (West Mainland).

P. pusillus L. **Lesser pondweed**. Local. Lochs and pools, especially near the sea in eutrophic or brackish water.

P. berchtoldii Fieber. **Small pondweed**. In similar habitats to the preceding but scarcer.

P. filiformis Pers. **Slender-leaved pondweed**. Occasional. In more or less eutrophic lochs and pools on a sandy–muddy bottom, rarely in brackish water.

P. × suecicus K. Richt. (*P. filiformis* Pers. × *P. pectinatus* L.). **Swedish pondweed**. First collected (in 1980) in the Loch of Clickhimin by R. C. Palmer but not recognized as the hybrid until 1996.

P. pectinatus L. **Fennel pondweed**. Rare. In similar habitats to *P. filiformis*.

Ruppia maritima L. **Beaked tasselweed**. A local species of brackish water in pools, small lochs, salt marshes, etc.

R. cirrhosa (Petagna) Grande. **Spiral tasselweed**. Rarer than the preceding and preferring more saline conditions; in some sites growing with seaweed.

Zannichellia palustris L. **Horned pondweed**. Very local. Chiefly in eutrophic lochs, very rarely in brackish situations.

Zostera marina L. **Eelgrass**. Very rare. Formerly more widespread but now known only from South Voe (West Burra); Whiteness Voe; Weisdale Voe; Effirth (Bixter), and Marlee Loch (near Clousta).

Lemna minor L. **Common duckweed**. Status uncertain. Abundant in a pool near Gardie House, Bressay; still in very small quantity in the Loch of Clickhimin where for a time it appeared to have vanished.

Juncus squarrosus L. **Heath rush**. Abundant in damp, heathy ground and boggy moorland.

J. gerardii Loisel. **Saltmarsh rush**. Frequent in coastal, often muddy, turf, salt marshes, and among rocks affected by spray.

J. trifidus L. **Three-leaved rush**. Frequent on bare granite debris above 240 m on the Ronas Hill mass.

J. bufonius L. **Toad rush**. Frequent in damp, open, disturbed ground (ditches, arable land, etc.), in salt marshes and on muddy–shingly seashores.

J. ambiguus Guss. **Frog rush**. Known so far from only a handful of salt marsh locations, but details of both habitat and distribution remain to be elucidated.

J. articulatus L. **Jointed rush**. Abundant in boggy places, and by pools, burns, ditches, etc.

J. acutiflorus Ehrh. ex Hoffm. **Sharp-flowered rush**. A local colonist of damp peaty ground, turfy pastures and wet meadows; seldom far from a roadside.

J. bulbosus L. **Bulbous rush**. Abundant on wet or boggy heaths and moors, etc., and in many soft-edged peaty lochs and pools where it occurs as a submerged form bearing no resemblance whatsoever to the typical plant of wet heaths.

J. triglumis L. **Three-flowered rush**. Very rare and elusive on wet stony heath, Hill of Colvadale, Unst. Only twice collected (in 1887 and 1962); recent attempts to locate it have failed.

J. effusus L. **Soft rush**. Abundant (often in large stands) on damp heaths and moors, by moorland burns, in bogs and on reseeded ground. Much of the Shetland plant is the form with widely spreading stems which are very gently spiralling, or merely curved, and which has recently been referred to var. *suberectus* D. M. Henderson.

J. conglomeratus L. **Compact rush**. Habitats similar to the preceding but less common and apparently not forming large stands.

Luzula pilosa (L.) Willd. **Hairy wood-rush**. Occasional to frequent among heather on dry heaths and moors. Scarce or overlooked in the North Isles.

L. sylvatica (Huds.) Gaudin. **Great wood-rush**. Common and often mat-forming on acid rocks (especially in ravines, on sea cliffs, holms in lochs, etc.), and locally on moorland slopes at high altitudes.

L. campestris (L.) DC. **Field wood-rush**. Common in dry grassland, chiefly on the better soils, but also in acid pastures and on heaths.

L. multiflora (Ehrh.) Lej. **Heath wood-rush**. Common on moors and heaths (as subsp. *multiflora*), and on heathy ground near the coast, including true maritime heaths (as subsp. *congesta* (Thuill.) Arcang.). The two subspecies are not always well defined, especially near the sea.

L. spicata (L.) DC. **Spiked wood-rush**. Known only, very sparingly, from the Ronas Hill summit plateau and slopes above *c.* 275 m.

Eriophorum angustifolium Honck. **Common cottongrass**. Abundant on wet or boggy moorland and (in the water) by the edges of peaty pools and lochs.

E. vaginatum L. **Hare's-tail cottongrass**. Common on damp moors and heaths; favouring drier ground than the preceding.

Trichophorum cespitosum (L.) Hartm. subsp. *germanicum* (Palla) Hegi. **Deergrass**. Very common on damp heaths and moors.

Eleocharis palustris (L.) Roem. & Schult. subsp. *vulgaris* Walters. **Common spike-rush**. Common in low-lying swampy areas, and in (and by the margins of) sandy or muddy lochs, often in eutrophic or brackish water.

E. uniglumis (Link) Schult. **Slender spike-rush**. A rare plant of grassy salt marshes and by brackish pools and lochs. Plants intermediate between this and the preceding have been collected in a few coastal sites.

E. multicaulis (Sm.) Desv. **Many-stalked spike-rush**. A frequent plant of boggy moorland (where it sometimes covers large areas in West and North Mainland) and the mossy edges of peaty lochs and pools.

E. quinqueflora (Hartmann) O. Schwarz. **Few-flowered spike-rush**. Frequent on base-rich marshy ground, stony flushes near lochs, moors, etc., also not uncommon in salt marsh turf.

E. acicularis (L.) Roem. & Schult. **Needle spike-rush**. Known only from the lochs of Spiggie and Brow where it occurs in both as a barren submerged form; flowering only when exposed, a rare occurrence noted only a few times by the former loch.

Bolboschoenus maritimus (L.) Palla. **Sea club-rush**. A large patch in the brackish, sluggish stream from The Wadill to the head of Ura Firth, near Hillswick. Found in 1997 by W. Scott.

Schoenoplectus lacustris (L.) Palla. **Common club-rush**. Rare. Scattered stations mainly in Central and West Mainland; particularly abundant in Sand Water, between Weisdale and South Nesting.

Isolepis setacea (L.) R.Br. **Bristle club-rush**. Apparently rare but easily overlooked. Base-rich muddy or boggy places (in ditches, by burnsides, etc.), mostly in Central Mainland.

Eleogiton fluitans (L.) Link. **Floating club-rush**. Peaty burns, lochs and pools, particularly on sandstone. Not uncommon in West Mainland and Fair Isle, very rare elsewhere.

Blysmus rufus (Huds.) Link. **Saltmarsh flat-sedge**. A local plant of salt-marsh turf, especially by sheltered voes.

Schoenus nigricans L. **Black bog-rush**. Frequent in wet stony flushes, marshes and bogs, and particularly characteristic of the serpentinite heathland of Unst and Fetlar.

Carex paniculata L. **Greater tussock-sedge**. Known only from peaty swamps and marshes in Foula, Fetlar and Unst.

C. diandra Schrank. **Lesser tussock-sedge**. Very rare. Known only from one station in Unst, a large base-rich marshy area near the Burn of Mailand, west of Mailand.

C. arenaria L. **Sand sedge**. A local plant of sand dunes and dune pasture except in southernmost South Mainland, where it is frequent.

C. maritima Gunnerus. **Curved sedge**. Rare. Damp hollows, etc., in dune pasture, very rarely in shell-sandy coastal turf. Most stations in South Mainland, very scattered elsewhere. Sometimes seen inland, as an introduction from the coast during building operations, as at the waterworks at Helliers Water, Unst, where R. C. Palmer (in 1989) found hundreds of plants.

C. ovalis Gooden. **Oval sedge**. Common in damp, rough meadows and pastures.

C. echinata Murray. **Star sedge**. Common on damp or wet heaths and moors, and in swampy and boggy places generally.

C. dioica L. **Dioecious sedge**. Frequent. Stony flushes, marshes and bogs, chiefly in the less peaty areas.

C. curta Gooden. **White sedge**. A rare sedge of mesotrophic swampy ground, at its best in parts of Unst and Fetlar.

C. rostrata Stokes. **Bottle sedge**. Frequent in and by peaty lochs, burns and swamps, and often forming large stands.

C. × involuta (Bab.) Syme (*C. rostrata* Stokes × *C. vesicaria* L.). Plants apparently of this origin, have been seen in a few places, mainly in West Mainland.

C. flacca Schreb. **Glaucous sedge**. A common sedge of base-rich places (flushes, damp undercliffs, etc.), and a feature of drier ground on limestone or serpentinite.

C. panicea L. **Carnation sedge**. Common in marshy, boggy and heathy ground.

C. binervis Sm. **Green-ribbed sedge**. Frequent in mainly dry heathy or moory places, on crags and by rocky streamsides.

C. hostiana DC. **Tawny sedge**. Widespread, but often in small numbers, in base-rich marshes and flushes.

C. × fulva Gooden. (*C. hostiana* DC. × *C. viridula* Michx.). Included here are hybrids of *C. hostiana* with *C. viridula* subsp. *brachyrrhyncha* and with *C. viridula* subsp. *oedocarpa*. Occasional or locally frequent, sometimes forming large populations and often with only one or neither parent present.

C. viridula Michx. **Yellow-sedge**. Subsp. *brachyrrhyncha* (Čelak.) B. Schmid is not uncommon on the Central Mainland limestone and other basic soils elsewhere. Subsp. *oedocarpa* (Andersson) B. Schmid is common in boggy or marshy places, stony lochsides, etc. Subsp. *viridula* is frequent and tends to replace subsp. *oedocarpa* near or by the coast (especially in cliff-top pasture); it also occurs occasionally on gravelly loch margins.

C. pilulifera L. **Pill sedge**. Frequent on dry heathy pastures and grassy moors.

C. limosa L. **Bog-sedge**. In watery swamps (often with *C. rostrata*) and in or by peaty pools. Rare in West Mainland, very rare elsewhere.

C. aquatilis Wahlenb. **Water sedge**. Known only from the mouth of the Burn of Northdale, Fetlar.

C. nigra (L.) Reichard. **Common sedge**. Very common and variable in many wet or damp habitats (marshes, bogs, sides of burns and lochs, damp heaths and moors, etc.).

C. bigelowii Torr. ex Schwein. **Stiff sedge**. Frequent on many of our higher hills in damp or dry moorland, on stony plateaux and ridges, and locally at lower levels on dry mossy heaths and moors.

C. pulicaris L. **Flea sedge**. Common in flushes and among wet rocks (notably on limestone or serpentinite), and on damp heaths, etc.

Nardus stricta L. **Mat-grass**. An abundant grass of damp heaths, moors, and poor acidic grassland.

Festuca pratensis Huds. **Meadow fescue**. Occasional as a colonist introduced with grass-seed or as a relict of past cultivation about crofts, by margins of hayfields, roadsides, etc.

F. arundinacea Schreb. **Tall fescue**. Of similar standing to *F. pratensis*. Very rare.

F. rubra L. **Red fescue**. Subsp. *rubra*. Very common in a variety of habitats: meadows, pastures, roadsides, rocks, etc. Subsp. *juncea* (Hack.) K. Richt. occurs locally on rocky sea cliffs, etc. (always as the pruinose form, subsp. *pruinosa* (Hack.) Piper). Subsp. *litoralis* (G. Meyer) Auq. has been recognized in grassy salt marshes at Whiteness, and may occur in this and other coastal habitats elsewhere. Subsp. *arctica* (Hack.) Govor. is frequent on the serpentinite (gravel and rock crevices) from Crussa Field to Muckle Heog, Unst. Subsp. *scotica* S. Cunn. ex Al-Bermani has been found on sea cliffs, Firths Voe, Mossbank, and probably occurs in similar places elsewhere. *Subsp. *commutata* Gaudin (Chewing's fescue) was found on a Hillswick roadside in 1979, probably as a grass-seed component. *Subsp. *megastachys* Gaudin, possibly of similar status, was found at Scalloway in 1966. Very similar plants were seen in 1996 in several reseeded areas elsewhere.

F. vivipara (L.) Sm. **Viviparous sheep's-fescue**. Common on the poorer, peatier soils (from wet bogs to dry, acid rocky outcrops).

× Festulolium loliaceum (Huds.) P. Fourn. (*Festuca pratensis* Hudson × *Lolium perenne* L.). **Hybrid fescue**. Apparently very rare (only twice collected) but perhaps overlooked.

Lolium perenne L. **Perennial rye-grass**. Possibly native in limestone grassland, etc., but much more commonly as an escape from, or relic of, cultivation.

L. multiflorum* Lam. **Italian rye-grass. Merely an occasional relic or waif of cultivation.

L. temulentum* L. **Darnel. A very rare casual once collected (in 1961) on the Scalloway rubbish-dump.

Vulpia bromoides* (L.) Gray. **Squirreltail fescue. A very rare casual with only three records, all in the early 1960s.

Cynosurus cristatus L. **Crested dog's-tail**. A common grass of usually dry pastures, etc., on the more fertile soils.

C. echinatus* L. **Rough dog's-tail. Casual, twice found in Bressay in the early 1840s; the first record for Scotland.

Puccinellia maritima (Huds.) Parl. **Common saltmarsh-grass**. Not uncommon in salt marshes and similar brackish situations, rarely among rocks, on beaches, etc.

P. distans (Jacq.) Parl. subsp. *borealis* (Holmb.) W. E. Hughes. **Reflexed saltmarsh-grass**. Common in many coastal habitats (especially on stacks and skerries), very rarely in salt-marsh turf.

Briza media L. **Quaking-grass**. Rare. Almost certainly native at Ollaberry (where it was discovered in abundance in natural pasture by R. C. Palmer in 1993). More likely a colonist in most or all of its other (mainly roadside) stations.

Poa annua L. **Annual meadow-grass**. A common colonist of artificial habitats (garden and arable ground, roadsides, walls, etc.), and on sea cliffs, holms in lochs, etc.

P. trivialis L. **Rough meadow-grass**. Common in damp grassy places, burns and ditches, arable and waste ground.

P. humilis Ehrh. ex Hoffm. **Spreading meadow-grass**. Common to abundant in mainly dry, often rocky, pastures, dune pastures and sandy shores, walls (especially of ruined crofts).

*P. pratensis L. **Smooth meadow-grass**. Included in grass mixtures for reseeding, etc., and thus a very rare escape from, or relic of, cultivation (perhaps sometimes overlooked).

*P. flabellata (Lam.) Raspail. **Tussac-grass**. Planted in enclosed or semi-enclosed situations about crofts and houses chiefly in South Mainland.

Dactylis glomerata L. **Cock's-foot**. A common colonist of rough grassy places (roadsides, churchyards, etc.), and on old walls and waste ground.

Catabrosa aquatica (L.) P. Beauv. **Whorl-grass**. A rare grass of rich, damp, sandy ground (shores of lochs, sandy-bottomed burns, watery hollows in dune pasture, etc.); in this century known only from southernmost South Mainland and the north of Yell, mainly in places near the coast.

Glyceria fluitans (L.) R.Br. **Floating sweet-grass**. Frequent in usually shallow water in lochs and pools, sluggish streams, ditches and swamps; prefers eutrophic conditions.

G. declinata Bréb. **Small sweet-grass**. An apparently very rare but probably native species collected on only two occasions, near Kergord (Weisdale), and by the Loch of Vatsetter, Yell; found (in 1994) at the latter site by R. C. Palmer.

*G. notata Chevall. **Plicate sweet-grass**. Casual. Once collected (in 1989) at the Baltasound Leisure Centre by R. C. Palmer.

Helictotrichon pubescens (Huds.) Pilg. **Downy oat-grass**. Occasional in dry (often rocky) grassland, by burns and on sea banks, notably on limestone or sandstone.

Arrhenatherum elatius (L.) P. Beauv. ex J. & C. Presl. **False oat-grass**. Probably colonist. Frequent in a variety of rough grassy places (including arable and waste ground) in inhabited areas (especially on limestone), low sea banks, burnsides, etc. The var. *bulbosum* (Willd.) St-Amans (**Onion couch**) is not uncommon.

*Avena strigosa Schreb. **Bristle oat**. Formerly the only oat in cultivation, before being almost entirely replaced by *A. sativa*. Bristle oat used to be a not uncommon relic or waif of cultivation but is now very rarely grown and equally rarely seen as a crofting stray.

*A. fatua L. **Wild oat**. A rare casual of arable ground, etc.

*A. sativa L. **Oat**. Formerly extensively grown in Shetland but now much less cultivated as oat acreage continues to fall. A mere outcast of cultivation.

*Trisetum flavescens (L.) P. Beauv. **Yellow oat-grass**. A very rare casual, most recently recorded from Hillswick in 1979.

Deschampsia cespitosa (L.) P. Beauv. subsp. *cespitosa*. **Tufted hair-grass**. Common in damp, rough, often heathy grassland, burnsides, etc.

D. setacea (Huds.) Hack. **Bog hair-grass**. Only in Northmavine where it occurs locally and sparingly on very watery, stony heathland and by boggy pools, on the plateau north of Ronas Hill.

D. flexuosa (L.) Trin. **Wavy hair-grass**. Common on heaths and moors (from wet and mossy slopes to stony summit plateaux), acid crags, etc.

Holcus lanatus L. **Yorkshire-fog**. Common, even abundant, in meadows and pastures, marshes, dune pastures, holms in lochs, etc.

H. mollis L. **Creeping soft-grass**. A local to occasional colonist of rough grassy roadsides, garden and arable ground, etc., mainly in Central Mainland.

Aira caryophyllea L. **Silver hair-grass**. Probably native, at least in the majority of cases. A local plant of dry, steep, grassy banks and short pastures.

A. praecox L. **Early hair-grass**. Common in dry turfy, heathy grassland, on bare peat on the moors, peat haggs, rocky outcrops, old croft walls, etc.

Anthoxanthum odoratum L. **Sweet vernal-grass**. Abundant on all soils (wet or dry), but especially dry heathy grassland, and in meadows and pastures.

Phalaris arundinacea L. **Reed canary-grass**. Common in the richer low-lying watery places (burnsides, ditches, wet meadows, etc.). Var. *picta* L., the cream and green striped ribbon grass of gardens, is occasionally seen as an outcast, sometimes persisting for a long time.

*P. canariensis L. **Canary-grass**. A rare casual of rubbish-dumps, foreshores, etc., in the more populous areas.

Agrostis capillaris L. **Common bent**. Common on heaths and moors.

A. × murbeckii Fouill. ex P. Fourn. (*A. capillaris* L. × *A. stolonifera* L.). Once collected (in 1956) in Foula.

A. gigantea Roth. **Black bent**. Very rare, probably a colonist. Sandy fields (in the only locality of which we have personal knowledge). Known only from the south of South Mainland.

A. stolonifera L. **Creeping bent**. Common in a very wide range of habitats, from salt-marsh turf and coastal sands, through marshy pastures and burns, to the serpentinite heaths of Unst and Fetlar.

A. vinealis Schreb. **Brown bent**. Common. Heathy pastures, grassy moorland, boggy and swampy places.

Ammophila arenaria (L.) Link. **Marram**. Frequent on sand dunes and associated sandy pastures in southern-most South Mainland (notably in the Quendale area), local elsewhere in Shetland. Occasionally seen away from beaches as an accidental or intentional introduction.

*Apera spica-venti (L.) P. Beauv. **Loose silky-bent**. Casual. Once collected (in 1989) at the Baltasound Leisure Centre by R. C. Palmer.

Alopecurus pratensis L. **Meadow foxtail**. Colonist. Frequent about houses and churchyards, by roadsides and fields, etc.

A. × brachystylus Peterm. (*A. pratensis* L. × *A. geniculatus* L.). Once collected (in 1979) at Gulberwick, near Lerwick.

A. geniculatus L. **Marsh foxtail**. A common grass of wet or damp places (ditches and burns, damp arable ground, muddy hollows, etc.).

*Alopecurus myosuroides Huds. **Black-grass**. Casual, once collected (in 1960) at Lerwick.

*Phleum pratense L. **Timothy**. A frequent relic of, or an outcast from, cultivation, being an important component of seed mixtures.

*Bromus commutatus Schrad. **Meadow brome**. A very rare casual, perhaps introduced in reseeding mixtures.

B. hordeaceus L. subsp. *hordeaceus*. **Soft-brome**. A frequent colonist of field borders, hayfields, etc., occasionally extending into natural pasture.

B. × pseudothominei P. M. Sm. (*B. hordeaceus* L. × *B. lepidus* Holmb.). **Lesser soft-brome**. A rare hybrid of hayfields, etc., now seldom seen.

B. lepidus Holmb. **Slender soft-brome**. A short-lived colonist which was once (from the mid-1950s, or earlier, to the mid-1960s) not uncommon, even abundant, in hayfields, etc. Last seen in 1968.

*B. pseudosecalinus P. M. Sm. **Smith's brome**. A very rare casual of sown meadows, twice collected in 1959.

*Anisantha sterilis (L.) Nevski. **Barren brome**. A very rare casual with new records from Scalloway (W. Scott, 1992) and Lerwick (I. Clark, 1994).

Elytrigia repens (L.) Desv. ex Nevski subsp. *repens*. **Common couch**. A common species, almost certainly a colonist, in arable and waste ground, by roadsides, on foreshores, etc.

E. × laxa (Fr.) Kerguélen (*E. repens* (L.) Desv. ex Nevski × *E. juncea* (L.) Nevski). A local hybrid of sandy (rarely shingly) beaches and adjacent sandy banks, in places supplanting one or other of the parents.

E. juncea (L.) Nevski subsp. *boreoatlantica* (Simonet & Guin.) Hyl. **Sand couch**. Local to occasional (sometimes in quantity) on sandy or sandy–shingly seashores, and on the seaward fringe of dunes.

Leymus arenarius (L.) Hochst. **Lyme-grass**. Locally plentiful on dunes and neighbouring sandy beaches; widespread but often sparingly on other beaches (sandy, shingly, or boulder) not associated with dunes, and on stacks, sides of *geos*, etc.

*Hordeum vulgare L. **Six-rowed barley**. A very rare relic or outcast of cultivation. Formerly a staple crop (along with *Avena strigosa*) but now grown in very limited quantity.

*H. distichon L. **Two-rowed barley**. A rare relic or outcast of cultivation.

*H. jubatum L. **Foxtail barley**. A very rare casual (introduced with seed mixtures) with records from Lerwick, Baltasound, and Hultness (near Wethersta).

*Triticum aestivum L. **Bread wheat**. A rare casual of rubbly places, etc.

*T. turgidum L. **Rivet wheat**. Casual, found once (in 1976) at Scalloway.

Danthonia decumbens (L.) DC. **Heath-grass**. Frequent in heathy grassland, by rocky burnsides, etc.

Molinia caerulea (L.) Moench. **Purple moor-grass**. Subsp. *caerulea* is common on rough heathy pastures (especially on the Unst and Fetlar serpentinite), and in marshes and watery base-rich places. Subsp. *arundinacea* (Schrank) K. Richt. was collected by R. C. Palmer (in 1986) on a holm in Sand Water, north of Hulma Water, West Mainland.

Phragmites australis (Cav.) Trin. ex Steud. **Common reed**. Rare. Marshy burnsides, small nutrient-rich lochs, swampy places, etc. The best site is near Clavel, South Mainland.

Sparganium erectum L. **Branched bur-reed**. Very rare and in grave danger of extinction in its only certainly recorded site, at the Ness of Sound, near Lerwick. Probably subsp. *neglectum* (Beeby) K. Richt.

S. angustifolium Michx. **Floating bur-reed**. Frequent. Peaty pools, lochs and burns.

S. natans L. **Least bur-reed**. Known only from a stretch of the Burn of Caldback, Unst.

Narthecium ossifragum (L.) Huds. **Bog asphodel**. Common on wet heaths and moors.

*Hosta cultivar or hybrid. **Plantain lily**. A very rare garden outcast.

*Colchicum autumnale L. **Meadow saffron**. Very rarely as a garden outcast or where planted.

*Lilium pyrenaicum Gouan. **Pyrenean lily**. A popular garden plant sometimes seen as an outcast or where planted.

*Ornithogalum angustifolium Boreau. **Star-of-Bethlehem**. A very rare garden outcast or straggler. Old quarry near Bakkasetter, South Mainland (L. A. Inkster, 1992), and more recently at Scalloway (W. Scott) and Clett, Whalsay (R. C. Palmer).

Scilla verna Huds. **Spring squill**. A common and characteristic species of dry heathy pastures and banks (especially by the coast), and on the serpentinite heath and associated debris of Unst and Fetlar.

Hyacinthoides non-scripta (L.) Chouard ex Rothm. × *H. hispanica* (Mill.) Rothm. **Bluebell**. An immensely popular garden plant occurring frequently as an outcast (usually persistent) or where planted.

Allium ursinum L. **Ramsons**. Garden relic at John Clunies-Ross's birthplace, Sound, Weisdale.

Narcissus. **Daffodil**. As popular as the bluebell in Shetland gardens and consequently planted about houses and crofts in many areas, and more recently by new roadside verges and embankments.

Alstroemeria aurea Graham. **Peruvian lily**. Sometimes seen as a garden escape or where planted, capable of persisting.

Iris pseudacorus L. **Yellow iris**. Common, often covering large areas, in marshy or boggy places, especially by burns.

I. latifolia (Mill.) Voss. **English iris**. A garden plant sometimes seen near houses where it has been planted, or as an outcast.

Crocosmia × *crocosmiiflora* (Lemoine) N.E. Br. (*C. pottsii* (Macnab ex Baker) N.E. Br. × *C. aurea* (Hook.) Planch.). **Montbretia**. A frequent garden escape or where planted. Burnsides, waste ground, etc., usually persistent.

Listera cordata (L.) R.Br. **Lesser twayblade**. Not uncommon. Typically among moss under heather on moors (and thus easily overlooked), less often in the open on short heathland.

Hammarbya paludosa (L.) O. Kuntze. **Bog orchid**. Very rare in mossy, boggy places. Four sites in Yell and one in Papa Stour, including its two most recent discoveries, at the Burn of Floga, North Sandwick, Yell, 1991 (M. Tickner) and at the east end of the Loch of Colvister, Yell, 1997 (A. D. D. Gear). It is still in good condition near North Brough, in the north of Yell, where it was first discovered as a Shetland plant in 1961.

[*Pseudorchis albida* (L.) Á. & D. Löve. **Small-white orchid**. Native, presumed extinct. Recorded from Bressay before 1845. No later record.]

Gymnadenia conopsea (L.) R.Br. subsp. *borealis* (Druce) F. Rose. **Fragrant orchid**. Now very rare and known only from dry serpentinite pasture north of Baltasound. Formerly at Skaw (Unst), North Roe and Boddam.

Coeloglossum viride (L.) Hartm. **Frog orchid**. An occasional species of dry coastal pasture (especially cliff-top sward), rocky limestone grassland, and serpentinite pasture and debris in Unst and Fetlar.

Dactylorhiza fuchsii (Druce) Soó. **Common spotted-orchid**. Rare. Lush marshes and sand-dune pastures, frequent to common where it occurs, especially in southernmost South Mainland. Also in marshy ground at Cunningsburgh, and in damp or even wet grassland between Ordale and Skeo Taing, Unst.

D. × *venusta* (T. & T. A. Stephenson) Soó (*D. fuchsii* (Druce) Soó × *D. purpurella* (T. & T. A. Stephenson) Soó). Usually with the parents in parts of southernmost South Mainland, and Cunningsburgh.

D. maculata (L.) Soó subsp. *ericetorum* (E. F. Linton) P. F. Hunt & Summerh. **Heath spotted-orchid**. Common on damp heathy pastures and moors.

D. × *formosa* (T. & T. A. Stephenson) Soó (*D. maculata* (L.) Soó × *D. purpurella* (T. & T.A. Stephenson) Soó). A not infrequent, showy hybrid growing with or near one or both parents and favouring the wetter places preferred by *D. purpurella*.

D. incarnata (L.) Soó. **Early marsh-orchid**. Subsp. *incarnata* is local in rich marshes and base-rich flushes. Subsp. *coccinea* (Pugsley) Soó inhabits damp, sandy dune pasture in southernmost South Mainland, while subsp. *pulchella* (Druce) Soó is known with certainty only from heathy serpentinite pasture north of Baltasound.

D. × *latirella* (P. M. Hall) Soó (*D. incarnata* (L.) Soó × *D. purpurella* (T. & T. A. Stephenson) Soó). First found, by the west side of the Loch of Tingwall, in 1993 by L. A. Inkster & W. Scott, with both parents.

D. purpurella (T. & T. A. Stephenson) Soó. **Northern marsh-orchid**. Frequent in marshy places and damp pastures, occasionally on much drier ground (serpentinite debris, road verges, etc.).

Orchis mascula (L.) L. **Early-purple orchid**. Scattered about on the serpentinite pastures and debris of Unst and Fetlar. Otherwise known only from Huney (Unst), on greenstone (1989, M. G. Pennington), and rocky limestone pasture on the White Ness peninsula.

INSECTS

by M. G. Pennington

The following lists of insects (compiled by M. G. Pennington; except Diptera, compiled by B. R. Laurence) include all species known to the authors to have been recorded in the islands up to 31 December 1996. The coverage is very patchy and even with best-known groups, Lepidoptera, Diptera and Coleoptera, there are gaps in our knowledge. There were over 40 species added to the Lepidoptera list in 1996 for example, the Diptera list is based mainly on short visits by one collector during the main season and the Coleoptera list is based largely on data from before 1980.

The lists should all be regarded as provisional, but they hopefully provide a useful baseline for future research. No attempt has been made to check collections, which would undoubtedly result in many more records.

For some species where enough data exists, status is given as either resident (R), immigrant (M) or vagrant

(V, a rare immigrant with fewer than 20 records), although several species still fall in a status uncertain (U) category. Errors and presumed errors (X) are placed in brackets. Accidental imports (AI) are species only known to have been imported by humans, and they are placed in brackets as they do not merit a place on the full list.

For some species a short statement on distribution and abundance (scarce, frequent, common or abundant) is also given. If a species is recorded from either Foula or Fair Isle this is specifically mentioned, unless the phrase 'throughout the islands' is used. This means that the species has been found wherever it has been looked for (including Foula and Fair Isle but usually excluding Yell, which is very poorly covered). The months in which the adults are most likely to be seen are given at the end of the account.

THYSANURA (bristletails)
An order of flightless insects. No studies have been carried out but there are only a few species which could occur.

Machilidae
Petrobius brevistylis Carpenter/*maritimus* (Leach) R

Lepismatidae
Lepisma saccharina **Silverfish** R

COLLEMBOLA (springtails)
An order of flightless insects. No studies have been carried out, although they certainly occur.

EPHEMEROPTERA (mayflies) (with thanks to Graeme Callender)
No detailed studies have been carried out on this group. The following species of mayflies have been recorded but there is not enough data to assess status. Some records are from King (1890) and Jones and Mortimer (1974).

Baetidae
Chloëon simile
Centropilium luteolum
Baetis tenax
B. rhodani

Caenidae
Caenis rivulorum

Siphlonuridae
Ameletus inopinatus

ODONATA (dragonflies and damselflies)
One species of damselfly is resident in Shetland and three species of dragonfly have occurred as vagrants (Pennington, 1995).

Coenagriidae
Enallagma cyathigerum (Charpentier). **Common blue damselfly** R: locally frequent in small, vegetated pools in North and Central Mainland and South Yell. May–August.

Aeshnidae
Aeshna juncea (Linn.). **Common hawker** V: one record, Fair Isle in July 1955.
Hemianix ephippiger (Burmeister). **Migrant emperor** V: one record, Fetlar in 1970; possibly another on Fair Isle in September 1995, but exact identity not determined.

Libellulidae
Libellula quadrimaculata (Linn.). **Four-spotted chaser** V: one record, Fair Isle in July 1958.

PLECOPTERA (stoneflies)
No detailed studies have been carried out on this group. The following species of stoneflies were recorded by King (1890) but other species have undoubtedly gone unrecorded.

Leuctridae
Leuctra fusciventris Ste.

Chloroperlidae
Chloroperla tripunctana Scop.

DERMAPTERA (earwigs)
Only one species of earwig has been recorded.

Forficulidae
Forficula auricularia Linn. **Common earwig** R: abundant throughout the islands. Mainly July–September.

DICTYOPTERA (cockroaches)
The usual domestic pest species of cockroaches, such as the common cockroach *Blatta orientalis* Linn., have been recorded occasionally, but there are no native species.

PSCOPTERA (booklice and barklice)
No detailed studies have been carried out on this group. The following species of booklice or dustlice were recorded by King (1890) but no doubt other species have gone unrecorded.

Pscodidae
Amphigerontia bifasciata (Latr.)

Mesopsocidae
Elipsocus westwoodii McLach.
Mesopsocus unipunctanus (Müll.)

Trogiidae
Trogium pulsatoria (Linn.)

PHTHIRAPTERA (biting lice) (with thanks to Jim Fowler)
Biting lice, formerly known as Mallophaga, are usually found on birds, and are often highly host-specific. The following list is largely derived from studies on petrels, but no doubt other species have gone unrecorded.

Menoponidae
Austromenopon pelagicum (Timmermann). Host: Storm petrel.

Philopteridae
Brueelia uncinosa (Burmeister). Host: hooded crow.
Halipeurus diversus (Kellogg). Host: Manx shearwater.
H. pelagicus (Denny). Host: Leach's and storm petrels.
Perineus nigrolimbatus (Giebel). Host: fulmar.
Philoceanus robertsi (Clay). Host: storm petrel.
Saemundssonia grylle (Fabr.). Host: black guillemot.
S. melanocephalus (Burmeister). Host: terns.
S. thalassidromae (Denny). Host: storm petrel.
S. occidentalis (Kellogg). Host: fulmar.
Trabeculus aviator (Evans). Host: Manx shearwater.

SIPHUNCULATA (sucking lice)
No detailed studies have been carried out on this group, also known as Anopleura. The following species of sucking lice, which are usually parasites of mammals, have been recorded but there are not enough data to assess status and no doubt other species have gone unrecorded.

Haematopinidae
Haematopinus vituli Linn.
H. ventricosus Denny

Pediculidae
Pediculus humanus. **Human louse**

Echinophthiriidae
Echinophthirius phocae Lucas

HEMIPTERA (true bugs) (with thanks to Thomas Huxley)
Only the aquatic Heteroptera have been researched, and there are not enough data to assess status. A number of terrestrial species, such as the heteropteran shieldbugs and ground bugs and homopteran froghoppers and aphids, also occur, but they have not been studied. Many other species undoubtedly occur.

Acanthosomatidae (shieldbugs)
[*Acanthosoma haemorrhoidale* (Linn.). **Hawthorn shieldbug** AI?]

Pentatomidae (shieldbugs)
[*Piezodorus lituratus*. **Gorse shieldbug** AI?]

Miridae (mirid bugs or capsids)
Calocoris norvegicus

Saldidae
Saldo morio

Corixidae (waterboatmen)
Arctocorisa carinata
A. germari
Callicorixa wollastoni
Corixa iberica
C. panzeri
C. punctata Illiger
Glaencorisa propinqua
Hesperocorixa castanea
Sigara distincta
S. dorsalis (Leach)
S. nigrolineata
S. scottii

Gerridae (pondskaters)
Gerris lateralis

Veliidae (water crickets)
Velia caprai Tamanini. **Common water cricket**
V. saulii

Aphrophoridae (froghoppers)
Neotholaenus lineatus
Streptanus sordidus

THYSANOPTERA (thrips)
Thrips, or thunderflies, certainly occur but have not been studied.

NEUROPTERA (lacewings) (with thanks to Colin Plant, Terry Rogers and Andrew Whittington)
Only six species of lacewings, the true Neuroptera, have been recorded, apparently all as immigrants. None of the small, allied orders, formerly included in the Neuroptera, have been recorded. Most records are unpublished but records from last century come from King (1890).

Hemerobiidae (brown lacewings)
Hemerobius humulinus Linn. V?: one at Eswick, Central Mainland, July 1994, several in conifers at Kergord in July and September 1996 and one at Baltasound, August 1996.
Hemerobius simulans Walker U: recorded on Unst in 1889; there are no conifers at the site so they could have been immigrants.
Hemerobius lutescens Fabr. M?: a few recorded at Eswick, Central Mainland in July 1994, July 1995 and June 1996.
Wesmaelius nervosus (Fabr.) M?: recorded on Unst in 1889 and at Eswick, Central Mainland and Baltasound, Unst in June–August 1994.
Wesmaelius subnebulosus (Steph.) M?: recorded at Baltasound, Unst in 1889, at Mid Yell in 1990, Unst in September 1995 and Eswick, Central Mainland in June and September 1996.

Chrysopidae (green lacewings)

Chrysoperla carnea (Steph.). **Common green lacewing** M: scarce to common, depending on suitable weather for immigration. Recorded throughout the islands, with immigrants May to October, commonest August–September. Frequently hibernates in the islands, although most unsuccessful.

TRICHOPTERA (caddisflies) (with thanks to Ross Andrew)

The following species of caddisflies have been recorded but there are not enough data to assess status. All are presumed resident. This list includes unpublished information and records from King (1890, 1896) and Kennedy (1996).

Rhyacophilidae

Rhyacophila dorsalis (Curtis)

Glossosomotidae

Agapetus fuscipes Curtis

Hydroptilidae

Hydroptila sparsa Curtis
H. tineoides Dalman
Oxyethira falcata Morton
O. flavicornis (Pictet)

Philopotamidae

Philopotamus montanus (Donovan)

Psychomyiidae

Tinodes waeneri (Linn.)

Polycentropodidae

Cyrnus trimaculatus (Curtis)
Plectrocnemia conspersa (Curtis)
Polycentropus flavomaculatus (Pictet)

Phryganeidae

Agrypnia picta Kolenati
A. varia (Fabr.)

Lepidostomatidae

Lepidostoma hirtum (Fabr.)

Limnephilidae

Drusus annulatus (Steph.)
Halesus radiatus (Curtis)
Mesophylax impunctatus McLachlan
Micropterna lateralis (Steph.)
M. sequax McLachlan
Potomophylax latipennis (Curtis)
Stenophylax permistus McLachlan
Grammotaulius nigropunctatus (Retzius)
Limnephilus affinis Curtis
L. auricula Curtis
L. griseus (Linn.)
L. ignavus McLachlan
L. incisus Curtis
L. lunatus Curtis
L. marmoratus Curtis
L. rhombicus (Linn.)
L. sparsus Curtis
L. stigma Curtis
L. vittatus (Fabr.)

Leptoceridae
Athripsodes cinereus (Curtis)
Ceraclea fulva (Rambur)
Mystacides azurea (Linn.)
Oecetis ochracea (Curtis)

LEPIDOPTERA (butterflies and moths) (with thanks to a great many but particularly Keith Bland, Svend Kaaber, the late Ian Lorimer, Frances Ratter, Nick Riddiford and Terry Rogers)
The best known of the insect orders in Shetland, but because of their strong powers of flight, immigration is frequent and species are regularly added to the list. The most important sources of information from last century are Weir (1880), Vaughan (1880), Briggs (1884), South (1888) and King *et al.* (1896). Other records come from Barrett (1895 *et seq.*), Meyrick (1928) and South (1961). This century's lists have been published by Beirne (1945) and Wolff (1971), although Kettlewell and Cadbury (1963), Goater (1969, 1973) and Bradley *et al.* (1973, 1979) add useful information. Recent work has been summarized by Riddiford and Harvey (1992), Pennington (1993), Pennington and Rogers (1994) and Pennington *et al.* (1997). However, this list includes information from a great many sources.

Eriocranidae
[*Eriocrania semipurpurella* (Steph.) X?: recorded by Meyrick but not known from any other source.]

Hepialidae
Hepialus humuli (Linn.). **Ghost moth** R: common in grassy areas throughout the islands, except Fair Isle. Shetland and Faroese specimens are subspecies *thulensis* Newman, with dark males, although pale specimens also occur. July.
[*Hepialus lupulinus* (Linn.). **Common swift** X?: probably misidentification of sandhill form of *H. fusconebulosa*.]
Hepialus fusconebulosa (Deg.). **Map-winged swift** R: common throughout the islands. The Shetland form ab. *zetlandicus* forms a small proportion of the population. June–August.

Nepticulidae
Stigmella sorbi (Stt.) R: larval mines found on a lone native rowan near Brae in 1973.

Zygaenidae
[*Zygaena exulans* (White). **Scotch burnet** X: specimens falsely labelled.]

Tineidae
Tineinae
Monopis laevigella ([D. & S.]). **Skin moth** R: locally frequent on Mainland, Unst and Fair Isle. June–August.
Tinea pallescentella (Stt.). **Large pale clothes moth** R: very locally common around outhouses on Fair Isle, Foula and Central Mainland. May–September.
Tinea trinotella (Thunb.) U: taken on Unst in 1895 but no recent records.

Ochsenheimeriidae
Ochsenheimeria urella (F.v.R.). **Cereal stem moth** U: taken on Unst in 1895 but no recent records.

Gracillariidae
Gracillariinae
Caloptilia elongella (Linn.) R: scarce, Eswick, Central Mainland. September–December.
Caloptilia syringella (Fabr.) R: scarce in established deciduous plantations in South and Central Mainland, also on Unst last century. July.
Aspilapteryx tringipennella (Zell.) R: old records on Mainland but recently only on Unst. June–July.

Sesiidae
[*Bembecia muscaeformis* (Esp.). **Thrift clearwing** X: larval mines reported on Unst in 1884 but no evidence that this species was really involved.]

Choreutidae
Anthophila fabriciana (Linn.). **Nettle-tap** R: abundant throughout the islands, even uninhabited islands such as Oxna. July–August.
[*Choreutis pariana* (Cl.). **Apple leaf skeletonizer** X?: listed by Meyrick but not known from any other source.]

Glyphipterigidae
Glyphipterix thrasonella (Scop.) R: frequent in damp areas on Mainland, Unst and Fair Isle. Always as the plain upland form *cladiella*. July.

Yponomeutidae
Argyresthiinae
Argyresthia conjugella Zell. **Apple fruit moth** R?: only record, several at Eswick, Central Mainland in July 1996.

Yponomeutinae
Yponomeuta evonymella (Linn.). **Bird-cherry ermine** M: six on Mainland and Bressay in July–August 1994 and 20 on Mainland and Unst in August 1996.
Yponomeuta cagnagella (Hb.). **Spindle ermine** V: at least four records from South and West Mainland and Foula in August 1996.

Plutellinae
Plutella xylostella (Linn.). **Diamond-back moth** M, possibly also R, at least temporarily: scarce to abundant depending on weather for immigration and recorded throughout the islands. May–October.
Rhigognostis senilella (Zett.) R: common throughout the islands. August–June.
Rhigognostis annulatella (Curt.) R: frequent throughout the islands. July–October.

Epermeniidae
Phaulernis fulviguttella (Zell.) R: only recent records from Fair Isle and Foula. July.

Coleophoridae
Coleophora mayrella (Hb.) R?: only record from Fair Isle in July 1994.
[*Coleophora lineola* (Haw.) X?: Listed by Meyrick but not known from any other source.]
Coleophora asteris (Mühl.) U: one record from Eswick, Central Mainland in August 1996.
Coleophora versurella Zell. R: singles collected from Eswick, Central Mainland in July and August 1994 and Baltasound, Unst in September 1995.
Coleophora vestianella (Linn.) R?: only record from Eswick, Central Mainland in July 1994.
Coleophora alticolella Zell. R: frequent on Foula but presumably overlooked elsewhere. July.

Elachistidae
Elachista kilmunella Stt. R?: only record, Foula, July 1996.
Elachista alpinella Stt. R: only record, several, Foula, July 1996.
Elachista apicipunctella Stt. R?: only record from Veensgarth, Central Mainland, July 1996.
Elachista argentella (Cl.) R?: only record, Norwick, Unst, June 1996.
[*Biselachista eleochariella* (Stt.) X: specimens are misidentifications of the next species.]
Biselachista albidella (Nyl.) R: scarce on Foula and Central Mainland, also Unst last century. July.

Oecophoridae
Oecophorinae
Hofmannophila pseudospretella (Stt.). **Brown house-moth** R: common indoors throughout the islands, scarce outdoors. Originally introduced into Britain last century. All year but commonest in July.
Endrosis sarcitrella (Linn.). **White-shouldered house-moth** R: abundant throughout the islands, mainly indoors, but often outdoors in summer. All year but commonest in June–July.

Depressarinae
Depressaria pastinacella (Dup.). **Parsnip moth** U: only record from Eswick, Central Mainland, August 1996.
Depressaria badiella (Hb.) R: frequent on Mainland, Foula and Unst. August–September.
Exaeretia allisella Stt. U: one record from Eswick, Central Mainland, August 1994.
Agonopterix heracliana (Linn.) R: locally common on Mainland and Unst. September–June.
Agonopterix ciliella (Stt.) U: collected from Shetland last century but no recent records.
Agonopterix subpropinquella (Stt.) U: one record from Eswick, Central Mainland in August 1996.
Agonopterix alstromeriana (Cl.) V?: one record from Veensgarth, Central Mainland in August 1996.
Agonopterix nervosa (Haw.) R: scarce in Central Mainland and Bressay, but one from Foula in 1994 is presumed immigrant. August.

Gelechiidae
Gelechiinae

Monochroa tenebrella (Hb.) R?: only recent record is from Eswick, Central Mainland but recorded on Unst last century. July.

[*Monochroa tetragonella* (Stt.) X?: recorded by Curzon on Unst last century but omitted from later lists.]

Bryotropha terrella ([D. & S.]) R: scarce on Mainland, Foula and Unst. July.

Bryotropha politella (Stt.) R?: only record from St Ninians Isle, South Mainland, July 1996.

Chionodes fumatella (Dougl.) U: one record from Ocraquoy, South Mainland, August 1996.

Neofaculta ericetella (Geyer) R: locally frequent on Muckle Roe and Unst, presumably also Mainland last century. June–July.

Scrobipalpa samadensis (Pfaff.) R: locally common on Mainland, Foula and Unst, as the British subspecies *plantaginella* (Stt.). July–August.

Scrobipalpa instabilella (Dougl.) V: one on Fair Isle in August 1994.

Scrobipalpa atriplicella (F.v.R.) U: one in Central Mainland in August 1994 and about 12 in Central Mainland, Foula and Unst in August 1996.

[*Scrobipalpa acuminatella* (Sirc.) X: misidentification of *Monopis laevigella*.]

[*Phthorimaea operculella* (Zell.). **Potato tuber moth** AI: several in imported bag of Cyprus potatoes on Foula in 1995.]

Momphidae
Momphinae

Mompha locupletella ([D. & S.]) U: common at one damp grassland site on Unst in 1895 but no other records.

Tortricidae
Cochylinae

Aethes cnicana (Westw.) R: frequent last century but only recent records in Central Mainland and Foula. July.

Aethes rubigana (Treit.) U: at least two records last century but none since.

Aethes smeathmanniana (Fabr.) U: two records in South and Central Mainland, August 1996.

Eupoecilia angustana (Hb.) R: common in grassy areas on Unst, scarce or overlooked on Mainland. The Shetland subspecies *thuleana* Vaugh. was originally described as a new species, but the nominate form also occurs rarely. June–July.

Falseuncaria ruficiliana (Haw.) R: scarce in Central Mainland. June

Tortricinae

Argyrotaenia ljungiana (Thunb.) R?: only record Hermaness, Unst in June 1995.

Syndemis musculana (Hb.) R: common on hills throughout the islands except Fair Isle. The Shetland subspecies *musculinana* Kennel is also found in Orkney and the Outer Hebrides. June–July.

Aphelia viburnana ([D. & S.]). **Bilberry tortrix** R: common on Fair Isle, but only one other record, on Foula in August 1995. June–July.

Aphelia paleana (Hb.). **Timothy tortrix** R: adults and larval spinnings recorded from North Mainland in July 1973.

Clepsis senecionana (Hb.) R: frequent on hills on Mainland, Foula and Unst. May–June.

Philedone gerningana ([D. & S.]) U: included in several lists but no records traced.

[*Philedonides lunana* (Thunb.) X?: listed by Meyrick but not known from any other source.]

Cnephasia stephensiana (Doubl.). **Grey tortrix** U: listed by Bradley *et al.* but original record not traced.

Eana osseana (Scop.) R: abundant in grassy areas and low heaths throughout the islands. July–September.

Eana penziana (Thunb.) R: frequent around coasts throughout the islands as the subspecies *colquhounana* Barr. which is found throughout Northern Britain. July–September.

Acleris sparsana ([D. & S.]) R: locally common in plantations in Central Mainland. September.

Acleris aspersana (Hb.) R: common throughout the islands. August–September.

Acleris notana (Don.) R?: only records from Central Mainland and Unst, September 1996.

Acleris variegana ([D. & S.]). **Garden rose tortrix** R: locally frequent in South and Central Mainland and Unst. September.

Acleris hastiana (Linn.) R: scarce in Central Mainland and Bressay. September–November.

Acleris hyemana (Haw.) R: frequent on moorland in Central Mainland, Muckle Roe and Unst. April–May.

Acleris maccana (Treit.) R?: only records from Eswick, Central Mainland and Baltasound, Unst in September 1996.

Acleris emargana (Fabr.) R: locally frequent in plantations in Central Mainland. August–September.

Olethreutinae

Olethreutes arbutella (Linn.) R: locally frequent in North Mainland and Muckle Roe. July.

Olethreutes schulziana (Fabr.) R: frequent on moorland on Mainland, Foula and Unst. July.

Olethreutes lacunana ([D. & S.]) R: common throughout the islands except Fair Isle. July–August.

Olethreutes obsoletana (Zett.) U: listed by Bradley *et al.* but original record not traced.

Hedya ochroleucana (Fröl.) U: one at Ocraquoy, South Mainland in August 1996. Another *Hedya* sp. on Foula in August 1994 could not be identified to species.

Endothenia ericetana (Humph. & Westw.) U: only record from Veensgarth, Central Mainland in August 1996.

Endothenia quadrimaculana (Haw.) R: scarce in Central and North Mainland. July.

Lobesia abscisana (Doubl.) M: one in Central Mainland in August 1994 and about 26 on Mainland, Bressay and Unst in August 1996.

Lobesia littoralis (Humph. & Westw.) R: frequent on Mainland, Unst, Foula and Fair Isle. June–September.

Bactra furfurana (Haw.) R?: only record from Eswick, Central Mainland, August 1994.

Bactra lancealana (Hb.) R: common in damp grassland and moors throughout the islands. June–August.

Ancylis unguicella (Linn.) R: frequent on drier moorland throughout the islands except Fair Isle. May–June.

Epinotia nisella (Cl.) V: eight recorded in South and Central Mainland and Unst in August 1996.

Epinotia mercuriana (Fröl.) R: common or abundant on hills throughout the islands. July–August.

Epinotia maculana (Fabr.) U: only record from Eswick, Central Mainland on unknown date in 1996.

Epinotia caprana (Fabr.) R: scarce in North and Central Mainland and Unst. August–September.

Rhopobota naevana (Hb.). **Holly tortrix** M: at least 23 on Mainland, Bressay and Unst in August 1996.

Rhopobota myrtillana (Humph. & Westw.) R?: only record from Nibon, North Mainland in June 1995.

Zeiraphera ratzeburgiana (Ratz.) R: scarce at Eswick, Central Mainland. August.

Zeiraphera rufimitrana (H.-S.) R?: recorded from South and Central Mainland and Unst in August 1996.

Zeiraphera isertana (Fabr.) U: only record from Eswick, Central Mainland in August 1996.

Zeiraphera diniana (Guin.). **Larch tortrix** R: locally common around conifer plantations in Mainland and Unst. August–September.

Epiblema foenella (Linn.) V: two records, i.e. singles on the same night at Easter Quarff, South Mainland and Veensgarth, Central Mainland in August 1996.

Eucosma lacteana (Treit.) V?: one record from Eswick, Central Mainland in August 1996.

Eucosma fulvana (Steph.) U: two singles in South Mainland July and August 1996.

Eucosma cana (Haw.) R: scarce in South and Central Mainland and Fair Isle. June–August.

Blastesthia posticana (Zett.) U: listed by Bradley *et al.* but original record not traced.

Cydia succedana ([D. & S.]) R: locally common on Unst but only old records from Mainland. June–July.

[*Cydia pomonella* (Linn.). **Codlin moth** AI: larva in imported apple in 1994.]

Dicrorampha plumbagana (Treit.) U: in several lists but no records traced

[*Dicrorampha acuminatana* (Lien. & Zell.) X?: listed by Meyrick but not known from any other source.]

[*Dicrorampha consortana* (Steph.) X?: found on Unst in 1895 but not known from any other record. Probably a misidentification of the next species.]

Dicrorampha montana (Dup.) R: locally common on Mainland, Bressay and Unst. July–August.

Pyralidae

Crambinae

Euchromius ocellea (Haw.) V: one record from Eswick, Central Mainland in September 1995.

Chrysoteuchia culmella (Linn.) R: scarce last century and only recent record from Easter Quarff, South Mainland in August 1996.

Crambus pascuella (Linn.) R, possibly extinct: locally common last century but no recent records.

Crambus lathoniellus (Zinck.) R: locally common in dry, grassy areas throughout the islands. June–July.

Crambus perlella (Scop.) U: recorded last century and two recent records in Central Mainland and Unst, possibly immigrants. July.

Agriphila selasella (Hb.) V: two records from Eswick, Central Mainland in August 1996.

Agriphila straminella ([D. & S.]) R: abundant in grassy areas throughout the islands. July–August.

Agriphila tristella ([D. & S.]) V: one on Fair Isle in August 1990 and about 10 in South and Central Mainland and Foula in August 1996.

Catoptria furcatellus (Zett.) R: locally common on Ronas Hill in North Mainland and Foula. July–August.

Pediasia aridella (Thunb.) V: one record from Eswick, Central Mainland, August 1996.

Platytes alpinella (Hb.) V: one record from Eswick, Central Mainland, August 1996.

Scopariinae

Scoparia subfusca (Haw.) R: only recent records from Fair Isle, North Mainland and Unst. July.

Scoparia ambigualis (Treit.) R: common throughout the islands. June–July.

Dipleurina lacustrata (Panz.) U: only record in 1880s, found in collection sent to Germany.

Eudonia pallida (Curt.) U: listed by South but only record since is unconfirmed.

Eudonia alpina (Curt.) R: locally common in South and Central Mainland, Foula and Unst. June.

Eudonia angustea (Curt.) R: common throughout the islands but possibly only migrant on Fair Isle. August–September.

[*Eudonia mercurella* (Linn.) X?: listed by Beirne but not known from any other source.]

Pyraustinae

Pyrausta cespitalis ([D. & S.]) R: locally frequent in dry heathery areas, Unst and Muckle Roe. May–June.

Margaritia sticticalis (Linn.) V: about 15 records, all in August 1996 from Central and South Mainland, Bressay, Fair Isle, Foula and Unst.

Udea lutealis (Hb.) R: common throughout the islands. July–August.

Udea ferrugalis (Hb.), **Rusty-dot pearl** M: annual in small numbers in South, Central Mainland and Foula in 1994–96.

Nomophila noctuella ([D. & S.]), **Rush veneer** M: just about annual in variable number, occasionally common. May–October, but most in autumn.

Pleuroptya ruralis (Scop.), **Mother of pearl** M: annual in small numbers in South, Central Mainland and Unst in 1994–96.

Phycitinae

Numonia advenella (Zinck.) V: one record from Eswick, Central Mainland in August 1994.

Pyla fusca (Haw.) R?: one at Sullom, North Mainland in July 1996.

Dioryctria abietella ([D. & S.]) M: singles on Fair Isle in August 1991 and Yell in August 1994, then over 30 on Mainland, Foula and Unst in August 1996.

Myelois cribrella (Hb.). **Thistle ermine** V: one record from Fair Isle in June 1992.

[*Ephestia elutella* (Hb.). **Cacao moth** probably AI in foodstuffs: three records from Fair Isle in July 1992 and Unst in July 1993 and May 1994.]

Pterophoridae
Platyptiliinae

Platyptilia gonodactyla ([D. & S.]) R: scarce in South Mainland and Unst. July–August.

Stenoptilia bipunctidactyla (Scop.) R: locally frequent on Mainland, Foula and Unst. July–August.

Pterophorinae

Emmelina monodactyla (Linn.) R?: scarce at Eswick, Central Mainland. September–December.

Hesperiidae
[*Erynnis tages* (Linn.). **Dingy skipper** X: specimens in the British Museum are presumed mislabelled.]

Papilionidae
Papilio machaon (Linn.). **Swallowtail** V: two records, from Voe, Central Mainland in August 1994 and Fair Isle in September 1995.

Pieridae
Coliadinae

Colias croceus (Geoff.). **Clouded yellow** V: three records, all on Fair Isle, July to August 1980, May and August 1992.

Pierinae

Pieris brassicae (Linn.). **Large white** R and M: rare until at least 1945, but a pest on *Brassica* by 1960 and breeding throughout the islands, except Fetlar and Fair Isle, in 1990s. Immigrants occur throughout the islands, May–September, local population flies June–August.

Pieris rapae (Linn.). **Small white** V: at least four records: Yell in 1970s and Fair Isle in June 1978, August 1989 and July 1992. Possibly other records not traced.

Pieris napi (Linn.). **Green-veined white** V: one record from Bressay in July 1994.

Lycaenidae
Lycaeninae

[*Aricia artaxerxes* (Fabr.). **Northern brown argus** X: one reported by the botanist Druce in the 1920s was presumably a female of the next species.]

Polyommatus icarus (Rott.). **Common blue**. Former resident, now extinct: locally common in South Mainland in 1960s and 1970s, possibly present before that and more widespread, but this is unconfirmed. Only records since 1980 are immigrants on Fair Isle in August 1980 and June 1990 and in South Mainland in July 1991.

Nymphalidae
Nymphalinae

Vanessa atalanta (Linn.). **Red admiral** M: annual in variable numbers, several hundred in good years when breeding also occurs, but they cannot overwinter. Recorded throughout the islands. May–October.

Cynthia cardui (Linn.). **Painted lady** M: annual in variable numbers, usually scarcer than the previous species, but can be much commoner, as in 1980 and 1996. Rarely breeds. Recorded throughout the islands May–September.

Aglais urticae (Linn.). **Small tortoiseshell** M: just about annual in small numbers, rarely double figures in a year. No known breeding. Recorded throughout the islands. May–September.

Nymphalis antiopa (Linn.). **Camberwell beauty** V: eight records: Foula and Scalloway last century, Unst in August 1901, Bressay in July 1976, Lerwick in August 1982, Foula in August 1995, Bressay in September 1995 and Exnaboe, South Mainland in August 1996.

Inachis io (Linn.). **Peacock** M: singles in 1961 and 1969, then nine in 1975–76 and another in 1983. Annual in 1990s including 14 in 1994 and 17 in 1995. Recorded throughout the islands. May–September with some records of hibernating insects in winter.

Satyrinae

Maniola jurtina (Linn.). **Meadow brown** V: one record from Fair Isle in June 1980.

Coenonympha pamphilus (Linn.). **Small heath** V: one record from Fair Isle in June 1980.

[*Coenonympha tullia* (Müll.). **Large heath** X: specimens reputedly taken last century erroneous or falsely labelled, as this species has never been recorded otherwise, despite most books until the 1970s stating this was Shetland's only resident butterfly.]

Danainae

Danaus plexippus (Linn.). **Monarch** V: one record from Bixter, West Mainland in September 1941.

Lasiocampidae

[*Lasiocampa quercus* (Linn.) *callunae* (Palmer). **Northern eggar** X: specimen seen by Beirne labelled Unst presumed mislabelled.]

Saturniidae

[*Pavonia pavonia* (Linn.). **Emperor moth** AI: one found on cruise ship released on Fair Isle in May 1992.]

Endromidae

[*Endromis versicolora* (Linn.). **Kentish glory** X: old specimens believed to be mislabelled.]

Thyatiridae

[*Tethea or* ([D. & S.]). **Poplar lutestring** X?: recorded by South but not known from any other source.]

[*Ochropacha duplaris* (Linn.). **Common lutestring** X?: recorded by South but not known from any other source.]

Geometridae
Sterrhinae

Timandra griseata (Peters.). **Blood-vein** V: four records, all in South and Central Mainland in August 1996.

Scopula imitaria (Hb.). **Small blood-vein** V: one record from Norwick, Unst in August 1994.

Idaea biselata (Hufn.). **Small fan-footed wave** V: one record from Fair Isle in July 1987.

Larentiinae

Orthanoma obstipata (Fabr.). **Gem** V: two records, both Eswick, Central Mainland, in October 1994 and August 1996.

Xanthorhoe munitata (Hb.). **Red carpet** R: common throughout the islands. The Shetland subspecies *hethlandica* Prout is distinct and restricted to the islands. July–August.

Xanthorhoe montanata ([D. & S.]). **Silver-ground carpet** R: common throughout the islands. The Shetland subspecies *shetlandica* Weir is distinct and restricted to the islands. June–July.

Xanthorhoe fluctuata (Linn.). **Garden carpet** R: frequent throughout the islands. The only Shetland macromoth with a regular second brood, albeit partial and not annual. The melanic ab. *thules* forms a small proportion of the population. May–September.

[*Epirrhoe tristata* (Linn.). **Small argent and sable** X?: recorded by South but not known from any other source.]

Epirrhoe alternata (Müll.). **Common carpet** V: one record from Eswick, Central Mainland in August 1996.

Camptogramma bilineata (Linn.). **Yellow shell** R: frequent but very local, recorded from Mainland, Muckle

Roe, Fair Isle and Unst. Most, but not all, specimens conform to the subspecies *atlantica* (Stdgr.) which may also occur in the Outer Hebrides. July–August.

Entephria caesiata ([D. & S.]). **Grey mountain carpet** R: locally frequent, recorded throughout the islands except Fair Isle. July–August.

Pelurga comitata (Linn.). **Dark spinach** V: one record from Fetlar in August 1991.

[*Lampropteryx suffumata* ([D. & S.]). **Water carpet** X?: recorded by the BRC in the 1960s but not known from any other source.]

[*Nebula salicata* (Hb.). **Striped twin-spot carpet** X?: recorded by Meyrick and on Fair Isle in the 1950s presumably in error for *P. didymata*.]

Eulithis testata (Linn.). **Chevron** R: common throughout the islands, except Fair Isle. August–September.

Eulithis populata (Linn.). **Northern spinach** R: common or locally abundant throughout the islands, except Fair Isle. July–August.

[*Chloroclysta siterata* (Hufn.). **Red-green carpet** X: all specimens have proved to be the next species.]

Chloroclysta miata (Linn.). **Autumn green carpet** R: scarce in Central Mainland, Fair Isle, Foula and Unst. September–October (no spring records yet).

Chloroclysta citrata (Linn.). **Dark marbled carpet** R: locally frequent in South and Central Mainland, Bressay and Foula with old records from Unst. Shetland specimens are the subspecies *pythonissata* Milliere, also found in Orkney. August.

[*Chloroclysta truncata* (Hufn.). **Common marbled carpet** X?: worn specimen reported in the 1960s presumed to be misidentification of the previous species.]

Thera cognata (Thunb.). **Chestnut-coloured carpet** R: bred from larvae collected on Collafirth Hill, North Mainland in 1996.

[*Thera juniperata* (Linn.). **Juniper carpet** X: recorded by South but disproved later.]

Hydriomena furcata (Thunb.). **July highflier** R: frequent and locally abundant, and recorded throughout the islands. August–September.

Rheumaptera hastata (Linn.). **Argent and sable** U: one record, Shetland specimen exhibited in London in 1891.

Operophtera brumata (Linn.). **Winter moth** R: common or locally abundant, throughout the islands except Fair Isle and Foula. December.

[*Perizoma bifaciata* (Haw.). **Barred rivulet** X?: records from North and Central Mainland in 1961 and 1962 later withdrawn by one of the observers.]

Perizoma blandiata ([D. & S.]). **Pretty pinion** R: scarce last century on Mainland but now rare and not seen since one on Bressay in 1985. July.

Perizoma albulata ([D. & S.]). **Grass rivulet** R: locally common on Mainland, Bressay, Fetlar, Unst and Foula. The Shetland population is separated as the subspecies *subfasciaria* Boheman. June–July.

Perizoma didymata (Linn.). **Twin-spot carpet** R: locally common throughout the islands, but possibly declining. August–September.

[*Eupithecia pulchellata* (Steph.). **Foxglove pug** X?: recorded by Barrett but not known from any other source.]

Eupithecia venosata (Fabr.). **Netted pug** R: locally frequent in the vicinity of beaches throughout the islands. The Shetland subspecies *fumosae* Gregson is also found in Orkney, along with other forms. June.

Eupithecia centaureata ([D. & S.]). **Lime-speck pug** U: three records: Foula and two at Eswick, Central Mainland in August 1996.

Eupithecia satyrata (Hb.). **Satyr pug** R: common on moorland throughout the islands. The Shetland subspecies *curzoni* Gregson is distinct and was originally described as a new species. May–July.

Eupithecia assimilata Doubl. **Currant pug** R: locally frequent at Eswick, Central Mainland. June–July.

[*Eupithecia vulgata* (Haw.). **Common pug** X?: two records from Fair Isle in August 1955 were presumably another species of pug.]

[*Eupithecia subfuscata* (Haw.). **Grey pug** X?: included in a list of BRC data but not known from any other source.]

Eupithecia nanata (Hb.). **Narrow-winged pug** R: only recent records from Fair Isle, but old records known to have been confused with *E. satyrata*.

Eupithecia pusillata ([D. & S.]). **Juniper pug** R and M: locally common on Fair Isle but singles on Unst in 1991, 1994 (two) and 1996 and Central Mainland in 1994 and 1996 are presumed immigrants. August.

Eupithecia lariciata (Freyer). **Larch pug** R: locally common at Kergord, Central Mainland. July.

[*Gymnoscelis rufifasciata* (Haw.). **Double-striped pug** X: misidentifications of species of *Eupithecia*.]

Carsia sororiata (Hb.). **Manchester treble-bar** R: locally frequent in South, Central and West Mainland and Foula with an old record from Unst. The Shetland population is the British subspecies *anglica* Prout. July–August.

Ennominae

Abraxas grossulariata (Linn.). **Magpie** V: two records: Baltasound, Unst in August 1991 and Eshaness, North Mainland in July 1996.

[*Lycia lapponaria* (Harr.). **Rannoch brindled beauty** X?: recorded by Wolff in his Faroese list but not known from any other source.]

Agriopos marginaria (Fabr.). **Dotted border** R: bred from larvae collected at Burn of Valayre, Central Mainland in 1996.

Erannis defoliaria (Linn.). **Mottled umber** R: locally abundant at Kergord, Central Mainland in 1996, presumably imported with trees. November.

[*Alcis repandata* (Linn.). **Mottled beauty** X?: recorded in BRC data in the 1960s but not known from any other source.]

Ematurga atomaria (Linn.). **Common heath** R: locally common in drier, heathery areas in Central Mainland and one site in South Mainland. May–June.

Bupalus piniaria (Linn.). **Bordered white** V: two records, male at Baltasound, Unst in June 1992 and female at Eswick, Central Mainland in June 1995.

Sphingidae
Sphinginae

Agrius convolvuli (Linn.). **Convolvulus hawkmoth** M: just about annual in small numbers, but occasionally 20 or more as in 1917, 1992 and 1996, recorded throughout the islands, except Foula. August–September (once in May).

Acherontia atropos (Linn.). **Death's-head hawkmoth** V: at least six records, but others almost certainly not traced: three in Lerwick in 1886, about 1960 on Yell and Central Mainland in June and September 1992.

Sphinx ligustri (Linn.). **Privet hawkmoth** V: one record from Brae, Central Mainland in August 1991.

Macroglossinae

Macroglossum stellatarum (Linn.). **Humming-bird hawkmoth** V: at least 17 records: at least two last century, two in 1924, six in 1992, four in 1994, three in 1996 from throughout the islands. May, July–September.

Hyles gallii (Rott.). **Bedstraw hawkmoth** M: less than annual, and apart from multiple records in 1934–35, usually rare, only nine since 1990, including a larva. Recorded from South and Central Mainland, Bressay, Fair Isle, Fetlar, Yell and Unst. June–August.

Hyles livornica (Esp.). **Striped hawkmoth** V: three records: Baltasound, Unst in May 1932, Whalsay and Lerwick in July 1952.

Lymantridae
Orygia antiqua (Linn.). **Vapourer** V: one record, male at Walls, West Mainland in September 1987.

Leucoma salicis (Linn.). **White satin moth** V: one record, male at Petester, Unst in July 1938.

Arctiidae
Parasemia plantaginis (Linn.). **Wood tiger** R: locally common in West, Central and North Mainland and Foula. Moths have been assigned to the northern Scottish subspecies *insularum* Seitz. June–July.

Arctia caja (Linn.). **Garden tiger** V: eight records: South Mainland in July 1995, seven in South and Central Mainland, Yell and Unst in August 1996.

Noctuidae
Noctuinae

Euxoa tritici (Linn.). **White-line dart** R: locally common around beaches in South Mainland and Burra. July–August.

Euxoa nigricans (Linn.). **Garden dart** U: included on several lists but no records traced.

Euxoa cursoria (Hufn.). **Coast dart** R: local around beaches on Unst and North Mainland but not recorded since 1974. August.

Agrotis segetum ([D. & S.]). **Turnip moth** V: nine records, all at Eswick, Central Mainland in July 1994, October 1994, four in September–October 1995, June 1996 and two in August 1996.

Agrotis exclamationis (Linn.). **Heart and dart** V: four records, Fair Isle in June 1992 and three in South and Central Mainland in June–July 1993.

Agrotis ipsilon (Hufn.). **Dark sword-grass** M: in variable numbers, occasionally hundreds, according to weather, recorded throughout the islands. April–October.

Ochropleura plecta (Linn.). **Flame shoulder** U: three records on Foula in June–July 1996.

Standfussiana lucernea (Linn.). **Northern rustic** R: locally common in rocky areas. July–September.

Rhyacia simulans (Hufn.). **Dotted rustic** U: old records only, details not traced.

Noctua pronuba (Linn.). **Large yellow underwing** R: probably also immigrant in some years, common throughout the islands. July–September.

Noctua orbona (Hufn.). **Lunar yellow underwing** U: two taken on Unst in July 1884, confirmation would be desirable.

Noctua comes Hb. **Lesser yellow underwing** U: recorded last century, but only recent records at Tingwall, Central Mainland in 1962, Eswick, Central Mainland in August 1994 and Fair Isle in September 1996.

Noctua fimbriata (Schreb.). **Broad-bordered yellow underwing** V: at least eight records: South Mainland in August 1994, Central Mainland in August 1995 and at least six in South and Central Mainland and Unst in August 1996.

Noctua janthe Borkh. **Lesser broad-bordered yellow underwing** V: eight, three in Lerwick in August 1993 then four in Central Mainland and another on Unst in August–September 1996.

Noctua interjecta Hb. **Least yellow underwing** V: one record from Eswick, Central Mainland in August 1996.

Paradiarsia glareosa (Esp.). **Autumnal rustic** R: common throughout the islands. The dark form *edda* increases from a small proportion in the south to over 95% of the population on Unst. August–September.

Lycophotia porphyrea ([D. & S.]). **True lover's knot** R: common throughout the islands. July–August.

Peridroma saucia (Hb.). **Pearly underwing** M: less than annual and in single figures when it occurs. June and September–October.

Diarsia mendica (Fabr.). **Ingrailed clay** R: abundant throughout the islands. The supposed Shetland subspecies *thulei* Staud. forms only a tiny part of the population. July–September.

[*Diarsia dahlii* (Hb.). **Barred chestnut** X?: recorded in BRC data in the 1960s but original source not traced.]

Diarsia brunnea ([D. & S.]). **Purple clay** U: only two records traced: Muckle Flugga, Unst in July 1914 and Norwick, Unst in August 1996.

Diarsia rubi (View.). **Small square spot** R: first recorded in South Mainland in 1959, now common throughout the islands, and apparently still increasing with first record on Foula in 1995. July–August.

Xestia alpicola (Zett.). **Northern dart** R: apparently common on Mainland and Unst last century, but not recorded since 1932, although most records in odd years. Shetland specimens are of the British subspecies *alpina* Humph. & Westw. (June–July?).

Xestia c-nigrum (Linn.). **Setaceous Hebrew character** M: just about annual in small numbers and possibly very small resident univoltine population in south of islands. June–September.

Xestia triangulum (Hufn.). **Double square-spot** V: one record from Eswick, Central Mainland, July 1995.

Xestia baja ([D. & S.]). **Dotted clay** U: two records: Unst in 1959 and Norwick, Unst in August 1996.

Xestia xanthographa ([D. & S.]). **Square-spot rustic** R: locally common throughout the islands. August–September.

Eurois occulta (Linn.). **Great brocade** M: less than annual, occasionally hundreds as in 1996. Only recorded from Mainland and Unst. July–August.

Hadeninae

Anarta melanopa (Thunb.). **Broad-bordered white underwing** R: apparently frequent on Unst and Mainland last century, but only one recent record, in North Mainland in 1992. (June–July?).

Anarta cordigera (Thunb.). **Small dark yellow underwing** U: apparently recorded last century but none since. (June–July?).

Discestra trifolii (Hufn.). **Nutmeg** M: first records on Unst in August 1974 and June 1992, but about 15 in 1994, five in 1995 and hundreds in 1996, on Mainland, Bressay, Foula and Unst. August.

Hada plebeja (Linn.) (= *H. nana* (Hufn.)). **Shears** R: common throughout the islands. May–June.

[*Polia trimaculosa* (Esp.). **Silvery arches** X?: recorded by Beirne but omitted from later lists.]

Mamestra brassicae (Linn.). **Cabbage moth** U: probably scarce immigrant which may breed, recorded last century, but only five captures, involving 33 individuals, since 1990, on Mainland and one on Unst. June–August.

Lacanobia thalassina (Hufn.). **Pale-shouldered brocade** R?: scarce, first record in 1960s, five records since 1990 from South and Central Mainland, Fetlar and Unst. June–July.

Lacanobia suasa ([D. & S.]). **Dog's tooth** V: about 12 records: one Unst in July 1996, and about 11 in South and Central Mainland and Unst in August 1996.

Lacanobia oleracea (Linn.). **Bright-line brown-eye** U: recorded last century, then nine records since 1990, in Central Mainland and Unst, often coinciding with immigration. July–August.

Papestra biren (Goeze). **Glaucous shears** R?: only record, about 12 at Eswick, Central Mainland, May–June 1995.

Ceramica pisi (Linn.). **Broom moth** V: four records: Baltasound, Unst in June 1992, two at Eswick, Central Mainland in June 1996 and Baltasound, Unst in August 1996.

Hadena confusa (Hufn.). **Marbled coronet** R: locally common around suitable beaches throughout the islands, except Foula. May–August.

Hadena bicrurus (Hufn.). **Lychnis** R: frequent throughout the islands, except Fair Isle. July.

Cerapteryx graminis (Linn.). **Antler moth** R: abundant throughout the islands. July–August.

[*Tholera cespitis* ([D. & S.]). **Hedge rustic** X?: in a list of BRC data but not known from any other source.]

Orthosia gothica (Linn.). **Hebrew character** R: common throughout the islands, but not Fair Isle or Foula. April–May.

Mythimna impura (Hb.). **Smoky wainscot** R: locally frequent around sandy beaches in South Mainland and Burra. July–August.

Mythimna pallens (Linn.). **Common wainscot** M: first record on Unst in August 1895, singles South Mainland in July 1992 and August 1994 and Unst in July 1994, but about 30 in Central and South Mainland, Fair Isle and Unst in August 1996.

Cuculliinae

[*Brachylomia viminalis* (Fabr.). **Minor shoulder-knot** X?: recorded by Barrett but not known from any other source]

Dasypolia templi (Thunb.). **Brindled ochre** R: frequent and locally common, throughout the islands. September–May.

Aporophyla nigra (Haw.). **Black rustic** V: four records: two on Fair Isle in September 1991, Fair Isle and Baltasound, Unst in September 1996.

Xylena vetusta (Hb.). **Red sword-grass** U: recorded by Curzon last century, then in variable numbers each year 1992–96, except 1993, mainly from Central Mainland, but also Bressay and Unst. Only spring records were in 1996. September–October and April.

Xylena exsoleta (Linn.). **Sword-grass** V: one record from Fair Isle in April 1992.

Dryobotodes eremita (Fabr.). **Brindled green** V: one record from Eswick, Central Mainland in September 1993.

Mniotype adusta (Esp.). **Dark brocade** R: common throughout the islands, except Fair Isle. June–July.

Eupsilia transversa (Hufn.). **Satellite** M: first records, Fair Isle in October 1991 and Unst in October 1992, then over 50 in Central Mainland, Bressay, Foula and Unst in September–October 1995 and 13 in 1996.

Agrochola circellaris (Hufn.). **Brick** M: recorded by Curzon last century, then annually in variable numbers 1992–96 and recorded throughout the islands. September–October.

Xanthia togata (Esp.). **Pink-barred sallow** V: one record from Eswick, Central Mainland in September 1993.

Xanthia icteritia (Hufn.). **Sallow** V: nine records: three in Central Mainland in August 1994, three in Central Mainland in August–September 1995, two in Central Mainland and one Unst in August 1996.

Amphipyrinae

[*Acronicta euphorbiae* ([D. & S.]). **Sweet-gale moth** X?: recorded by Wolff in his Icelandic list but not known from any other source.]

Amphipyra berbera (Linn.). **Svensson's copper underwing** V: one record from Eswick, Central Mainland in August 1996.

Amphipyra tragopoginis (Cl.). **Mouse moth** V: 19 records: six on Fair Isle in September 1991, Fair Isle and Noss in August 1994, Fair Isle, Foula, South and Central Mainland in September 1995, four each in Central Mainland and Fair Isle and one on Unst in August–September 1996. Possibly colonizing from south.

Phlogophora meticulosa (Linn.). **Angle shades** M, possibly temporarily R: scarce to common depending on weather, and recorded throughout the islands. May–October, but commonest in autumn.

Enargia paleacea (Hb.). **Angle-striped sallow** V: five records, all on the same date on Unst and Central Mainland in August 1996.

Parastichtis suspecta (Hb.). **Suspected** V: about 20 records, up to 18 in Central Mainland and three on Unst in August 1996.

Cosmia trapezina (Linn.). **Dun-bar** V: about 20 records, up to 17 on Unst and South and Central Mainland in August 1994, and five on Unst, Foula and Central Mainland in August 1996.

Apamea monoglypha (Hufn.). **Dark arches** R: scarce last century, now abundant throughout the islands. June–August.

Apamea zeta (Treit.). **Exile** R: locally common in North and Central Mainland and Unst, with single records from West Mainland and Yell. Originally thought to be endemic subspecies *exulis*, or even species, currently placed with Scandinavian subspecies *marmorata* Zett. July–August.

Apamea oblonga (Haw.). **Crescent striped** U: two records: recorded by Curzon on Unst in 1886 and at Norwick, Unst in August 1994.

Apamea crenata (Hufn.). **Clouded-bordered brindle** R: not recorded until 1959 but now locally abundant, throughout the islands except Fair Isle. June–August.

Apamea lateritia (Hufn.). **Scarce brindle** V: two records on consecutive nights at Norwick, Unst in August 1996.

Apamea furva ([D. & S.]). **Confused** R: frequent throughout the islands. August–September.

Apamea remissa (Hb.). **Dusky brocade** R: frequent throughout the islands, excluding Foula. June–August.

[*Apamea anceps* ([D. & S.]). **Large nutmeg** X?: recorded by South but not known from any other source.]

Apamea sordens (Hufn.). **Rustic shoulder-knot** U: several records last century, all apparently from Mainland, but one at Eswick, Central Mainland in July 1996 is only recent record.

Apamea ophiogramma (Esp.). **Double lobed** V: five records, on Unst and Central Mainland in August 1996.

Oligia fasciuncula (Haw.). **Middle-barred minor** R: common throughout the islands. July–August.

Mesoligia furuncula ([D. & S.]). **Cloaked minor** V: two records, singles on consecutive nights at Ocraquoy, South Mainland and Eswick, Central Mainland in August 1996.

Mesapamea secalis (Linn.). **Common rustic** R: scarce, recorded last century and recently from South and Central Mainland and Fair Isle. August.

Mesapamea didyma (Esp.). **Lesser common rustic** R?: one record, Eswick, Central Mainland in August 1996.

Photedes minima (Haw.). **Small dotted buff** U: five records at Eswick, Central Mainland in July–August of each year 1994–96 suggest a very small local population.

Photedes pygmina (Haw.). **Small wainscot** R: first recorded on Fair Isle in 1955 and Mainland in 1968, now common throughout the islands, but possibly only migrant on Fair Isle. August–September.

Luperina testacea ([D. & S.]). **Flounced rustic** U: one record from Norwick, Unst in August 1994.

Amphipoea lucens (Freyer). **Large ear** U: one on Fair Isle in 1991, then annual in small numbers 1994–96 with records throughout the islands. August.

Amphipoea fucosa (Freyer). **Saltern ear** V: at least 10 in Central Mainland, Muckle Roe and Unst in August 1994.

Amphipoea oculea (Linn.). **Ear moth** V: one record from Fair Isle in September 1991.

Hydraecia micacea (Esper). **Rosy rustic** R: recorded throughout the islands but only common in South Mainland, Fair Isle and Foula. August–September.

Celaena haworthii (Curt.). **Haworth's minor** R: scarce, but recorded throughout the islands except Fair Isle. August–October.

Celaena leucostigma (Hb.). **Crescent** M: usually scarce, and certainly less than annual, but hundreds in August 1996. August–September.

Rhizedra lutosa (Hb.). **Large wainscot** V: at least 15 records. Recorded by Curzon last century, then one North Mainland in September 1961. Recently another 13 in Central Mainland, Fair Isle, Foula and Unst. September–October.

[*Charanyca trigrammica* (Hufn.). **Treble lines** X: listed by Wolff in a list of Faroese Lepidoptera in 1929 but not in his Icelandic list of 1971.]

Spodoptera exigua (Hb.). **Small mottled willow** V: seven records, all in South and Central Mainland in August 1996.

Caradrina clavipalpis (Scop.). **Pale mottled willow** R: scarce on Mainland. Single records from Fetlar in July 1972 and Foula in June 1996 are probably immigrants. June–September.

Heliothinae

Heliothis armigera (Hb.). **Scarce bordered straw** V: two records: Hillswick, North Mainland in September 1961 and Baltasound, Unst in September 1996.

Heliothis peltigera ([D. & S.]). **Bordered straw** V: two records: Westing, Unst in 1948 and Eswick, Central Mainland in August 1996.

Plusiinae

Macdunnoughia confusa (Steph.). **Dewick's plusia** V: two records: different singles on consecutive nights at Eswick, Central Mainland in August 1996.

Plusia festucae (Linn.). **Gold spot** R: not recorded until 1959, now scarce but widespread on Mainland and Muckle Roe, also recorded on Unst in 1970s. July–August.

Autographa gamma (Linn.). **Silver Y** M: annual, sometimes in enormous numbers as in August 1996 when there were tens of millions or more. Breeds after large influxes but cannot overwinter. May–October.

Autographa pulchrina (Haw.). **Beautiful golden Y** R: not recorded until 1968, but now common throughout the islands, although not recorded on Fair Isle until 1996. July–August.

Autographa bractea ([D. & S.]). **Gold spangle** V: one record from Baltasound, Unst in August 1996.

Syngrapha interrogationis (Linn.). **Scarce silver Y** V: 16 records: one on Unst in August 1959, six in Central and North Mainland in August 1961 and nine in Central and South Mainland and Unst in August 1996.

Catocalinae

Catocala fraxini (Linn.). **Clifden nonpareil** V: at least three records: before 1945, early 1970s and Eswick, Central Mainland in September 1995.

Ophiderinae
Scoliopteryx libatrix (Linn.). **Herald** U: recorded by Curzon last century, then in Central Mainland, Bressay and Unst annually in 1994–96. Possibly colonizing from the south. August–June.

COLEOPTERA (beetles)

Very little work has been carried out on the beetles of Shetland since the list compiled by Bacchus and published in Berry and Johnston (1980). The list is included here with a few minor amendments; several species require confirmation. All are believed to resident unless otherwise indicated.

Carabidae (ground beetles)
Cychrus caraboides (Linn.)
Carabus nemoralis
C. problematicus Herbst
[*Leistus ferrugineus* (Linn.) X?]
L. rufescens
Pelophila borealis (Paykull)
Nebria gyllenhali (Schoenherr)
N. salina Fairmaire & Laboulbéne
Notiophilus aestuans (Motschulsky)
N. aquaticus (Linn.)
N. biguttatus (Fabr.)
N. germinyi Fauvel
N. palustris (Duftschmid)
Elaphrus cupreus Duftschmid
Loricera pilicornis (Fabr.)
Dyschirius globosus (Herbst)
D. politus (Dejean)
Clivinia fossor (Linn.)
Broscus cephalotes (Linn.)
Patrobus assimilis Chaudoir
P. atrorufus (Ström)
P. septentrionis (Dejean)
Trechus fulvus Dejean
T. obtusus Erichson
[*T. quadristriatus* (Schrank) X?]
T. rubens (Fabr.)
Bembidion atrocoeruleum Steph.
B. bruxellense Wesmael

B. tetracolum Say
B. unicolor Chaudoir
Pterostichus diligens (Sturm)
P. minor (Gyllenhal)
P. niger (Schaller)
P. nigrita (Paykull)
P. oblongopunctatus (Fabr.)
P. strenuus (Panzer)
Calathus fuscipes (Goeze)
C. melanocephalus (Linn.)
C. mollis (Marsham)
Laemostenus terricola (Herbst)
Olisthopus rotundatus (Paykull)
Agonum albipes (Fabr.)
A. ericeti (Panzer)
A. fuliginosum (Panzer)
Amara apricaria (Paykull)
A. aulica (Panzer)
A. bifrons (Gyllenhal)
A. familiaris (Duftschmid)
A. lunicollis (Schiodte)
Harpalus affinis (Schrank)
H. latus (Linn.)
Hapalus quadripunctatus Dejean
Dicheirotrichus gustavi Crotch
Trichocellus cognatus (Gyllenhal)
Bradycellus harpalinus Serville
Cymindis vaporariorum (Linn.)

Haliplidae (crawling water beetles)
Haliplus confinis Steph.
H. fulvus (Fabr.)

H. lineatocollis (Marsham)

Dytisticidae (water beetles)
Hydroporus erythrocephalus (Linn.)
H. gyllenhali Schiodte
H. longulus Mulsnat
H. memnonius Nicolai
H. morio Aubé
H. nigrita (Fabr.)
H. obscurus Sturm
H. obsoletus Aubé
H. palustris (Linn.)
H. pubescens (Gyllenhal)
H. tristis (Paykull)
H. umbrosus (Gyllenhal)
Potamonectes assimilis (Paykull)
P. griseostriatus (Deg.)

Oreodytes davisi (Curtis)
Agabus arcticus (Paykull)
A. bipustulatus (Linn.)
A. guttatus (Paykull)
A. melanocornis Zimmerman
A. nebulosus (Forster)
Ilybius fuliginosus (Fabr.)
Rhantus bistriatus (Bergstaesser)
R. frontalis (Marsham)
Colymbetes fuscus (Linn.)
Acilius sulcatus (Linn.)
Dytiscus lapponicus Gyllenhal
D. sulcatus (Linn.)

Gyrinidae (whirligig beetles)
Gyrinus opacus Sahlberg

G. substriatus Steph.

Hydrophilidae
Helophorus aquaticus (Linn.)
H. brevipalpis Bedel
H. flavipes (Fabr.)
H. grandis Illiger
H. granularis (Linn.)
Cercyon analis (Paykull)
C. depressus Steph.
C. haemorrhoidalis (Fabr.)

C. littoralis (Gyllenhal)
C. melanocephalus (Linn.)
Megasternum obscurum (Marsham)
Anacaena globulus (Paykull)
Laccobius bipunctatus (Fabr.)
Enochrus quadripunctatus (Herbst)
Chaetarthria seminulum (Herbst)

Hydraenidae
Ochthebius dilatatus Steph.
Hydraena gracilis Germar

Limnebius truncatellus (Thunb.)

Ptilidae
Ptenidium laevigatum Erichson
P. nitidum (Heer)

P. pusillum (Gyllenhal)
Acrotrichis danica Sundt

Leiodidae
Hydnobius punctatus (Sturm)
Anisotoma dubia (Kugelann)
A. obesa (Schmidt)
Agathidium laevigatum Erichson

Sciodrepa watsoni (Spence)
Catops fuscus (Panzer)
C. morio (Fabr.)

Silphidae (burying beetles)
Nicrophorus humator (Gleditsch) **Sexton beetle**
N. vespilloides

Thanatophilus rugosus (Linn.)
Aclypea opaca (Linn.)

Scydmaenidae
Stenichnus collaris (Müll. & Kunze)

Staphylinidae (rove beetles)
Magarthus denticollis (Beck)
Megarthus depressus (Paykull)
Olophrum piceum (Gyllenhal)
Arpedium brachypterum (Gravenhorst)
Acidota crenata (Fabr.)
Lestiva heeri Fauvel
L. longoelytrata (Goeze)
L. monticola Kiesenwetter
L. pubescens Mannerheim
Eusphalerum torquatum (Marsham)
Pyllodrepa floralis (Paykull)
Omalium excavatum Steph.
O. laeviusculum Gyllenhal
O. riparium Thomson
O. rivulare (Paykull)
Xylodromus concinnus (Marsham)
X. depressus (Gravenhorst)
Micralymma marinum (Ström)
Bledius subterraneus Erichson
Carpelimus pusillus (Gravenhorst)
Platystethus arenarius (Fourcroy)
Anotylus complanatus (Erichson)
A. maritimus Thomson
A. nitidulus (Gravenhorst)
A. rugosus (Fabr.)
A. sculpturatus (Gravenhorst)
Stenus brevipennis Thomson
S. brunnipes Steph.
S. clavicornis (Scop.)
S. geniculatus Gravenhorst

S. impressus Germar
S. juno (Paykull)
S. nitidiusculus Steph.
S. ossium Steph.
S. picipes Steph.
Lathobrium brunnipes (Fabr.)
L. fulvipenne (Gravenhorst)
Othius angustus (Steph.)
O. myrmecophilus Kiesenwetter
O. punctulatus (Goeze)
Gyrophypnus fracticornis (Müll.)
G. puctulatus (Paykull)
Xantholinus glabratus (Gravenhorst)
X. linearis (Olivier)
Philonthus cephalotes (Gravenhorst)
P. decorus (Gravenhorst)
P. fimetarius (Gravenhorst)
P. marginatus (Ström)
P. politus (Linn.)
P. sordidus (Gravenhorst)
P. varius (Gyllenhal)
Gabrius nigritulus (Gravenhorst)
G. trossulus (von Nordmann)
Cafius xantholoma (Gravenhorst)
Staphylinus aenocephalus Deg.
S. ater Gravenhorst
S. olens (Müll.). **Devil's coach horse**
Creophilus maxillosus (Linn.)
Quedius aridulus Jansson
Q. assimilis (von Nordman)

Q. boops (Gravenhorst)
Q. cinctus (Paykull)
Q. curtipennis Bernhauer
Q. fuliginosus (Gravenhorst)
Q. fulvicollis (Steph.)
Q. mesomelinus (Marsham)
Q. molochinus (Gravenhorst)
Q. nitipennis (Steph.)
Q. scintillans (Gravenhorst)
Q. semiaenus (Steph.)
Q. schatzmayri Gridelli
Q. tristis (Gravenhorst)
Q. umbrinus Erichson
Mycetoporus angularis (Mulsant & Ray)
M. splendidus (Gravenhorst)
Tachyporus atriceps Steph.
T. chrysomelinus (Linn.)
T. dispar (Paykull)
T. hypnorum (Fabr.)
T. nitidulus (Fabr.)
T. pusillus (Gravenhorst)
Tachinus laticollis Gravenhorst
T. signatus Gravenhorst
Cypha laeviusculus (Mannerheim)
Myllaena brevicornis (Matthews)
Autalia puncticollis Sharp
Boreophila islandica (Kraatz)
Aloconota gregaria (Erichson)
Amischa analis (Gravenhorst)
A. cavifrons Sharp
Lyprocorrhe anceps (Erichson)
Goestiba circellaris (Gravenhorst)
Liogluta longiuscula (Gravenhorst)
Atheta amicula (Steph.)
A. aterrima (Gravenhosrt)

Pselaphidae
Bryaxis bulbifer (Reichenbach)

Geotrupidae (dor beetles)
Geotrupes stercorarius (Linn.)

Scarabaeidae (scarab beetles)
Aphodius ater (Deg.)
A. borealis Gyllenhal
A. contaminatus (Herbst)
A. depressus (Kugelann)
A. fimetarius (Linn.)

Clambidae
Calyptomerus dubius (Marsham)

Scirtidae
Elodes marginata (Fabr.)

Byrrhidae

Simplocaria semistriata (Fabr.)
Cytilus sericeus (Forster)

Dryopidae
Dryops griseus (Erichson)

A. atramentaria (Gyllenhal)
A. atricolor (Sharp)
A. cadaverina (Brisout)
A. celata (Erichson)
A. debilis (Erichson)
A. elongatula (Gravenhorst)
A. excellens (Kraatz)
A. fallaciosa (Sharp)
A. fungi (Gravenhorst)
A. graminicola (Gravenhorst)
A. harwoodi Williams
A. hygrobia (Thomson)
A. ischnocera Thomson
A. longicornis (Gravenhorst)
A. melanocera (Thomson)
A. nigra (Kraatz)
A. nigripes (Thomson)
A. pertyi (Heer)
A. strandiella Brundin
A. tibialis (Heer)
A. trinotata (Kraatz)
A. vestita (Gravenhorst)
A. zosterae (Thomson)
Ocalea picata (Steph.)
Ocyusa hibernica (Rye)
Mniusa incrassata (Mulsant & Rey)
Oxypoda haemorrhoa (Mannerheim)
O. nigricornis Motchulsky
O. opaca (Gravenhorst)
O. umbrata (Gyllenhal)
Aleochara algarum Fauvel
A. grisea Kraatz
A. lanuginosa Gravenhorst
A. obscurella Gravenhorst
A. sparsa Heer

G. stercorosus (Scriba)

A. lapponum Gyllenhal
A. rufipes (Linn.)
A. rufus (Moll)
A. sphacelatus (Panzer)

Byrrhus fasciatus (Forster)
B. pilula (Linn.)

Elateridae (click beetles)
Hypnoidus riparius (Fabr.)
Athous subfuscus (Müll.)

Dalopius marginatus (Linn.)
Denticollis linearis (Linn.)

Cantharidae
Mathodes pumilis (Brébisson)

Anobiidae (wood-boring beetles)
Anobium punctatum (Deg.). **Furniture beetle**

Ptinidae (spider beetles)
[*Ptinus tectus* Boieldieu **Australian spider beetle** AI]

Nitidulidae
Brachypterus urticae (Fabr.)
Meligethes aenus (Fabr.)

Epuraea aestiva (Linn.)

Cryptophagidae
Cryptophagus acutanglus (Gyllenhal)
C. cellaris (Scop.)
C. dentatus (Herbst)
C. pilosus Gyllenhal
C. pseudodentatus Bruce
C. saginatus Sturm
C. scanicus (Linn.)
C. setulosus Sturm

Atomaria apicalis Erichson
A. atricapilla Steph.
A. berolinensis Kraatz
A. fuscipes (Gyellenhal)
A. lewisi Reitter
A. nitidula (Marsham)
A. ruficornis (Marsham)
Ephistemus globulus (Paykull)

Coccinellidae (ladybirds)
Nephus redtenbacheri (Mulsant)
Adonia variegata (Goeze)
Coccinella septempunctata Linn. **Seven-spot ladybird** M and AI

Adalia bipunctata (Linn.). **Two-spot ladybird** V and AI
[*Anatis ocellata* (Linn.). **Eyed ladybird** AI]

Lathridiidae
Aridius nodifer (Westwood)
Lathridius pseudominutus (Strand)
Enicmus histrio Joy & Tomlin

Corticarina elongata (Gyllenhal)
C. fuscula (Gyllenhal)
C. umbilicata (Beck)

Chrysolmelidae (leaf beetles)
Plateumaris discolor (Panzer)
Chrysolina hellieseni Silfverberg
C. staphylaea (Linn.)
Hydrothassa marginella (Linn.)

[*Leptinotarsa decemlineata* **Colorado beetle** AI]
Longitarsis luridus (Scop.)
Psylliodes marcida (Illiger)
P. picina (Marsham)

Apionidae (weevils)
Apion aethiops Herbst
A. cruentatum Walton
A. haematodes

A. loti Kirby
A. reyi Blackburn
A. violaceum Kirby

Curculionidae (weevils)
Otiorhynchus arcticus (Fabr.)
O. atroapterus (Deg.)
O. nodosus (Müll.)
O. porcatus (Herbst)
O. singularis (Linn.)
O. sulcatus (Fabr.). **Vine weevil**
Strophosomus melanogrammus (Forster)
Philopedon plagiatus (Schaller)
Barynotus schonherri
B. squamosus Germar
Tropiphorus elevatus (Herbst)

T. obtusus (Bonsdorff)
Sitona lepidus Gyllenhal
S. lineelus (Bonsdorff)
S. puncticollis Steph.
Hypera plantaginis (Deg.)
Leiosoma deflexum (Panzer)
Euophyrum confine (Broun)
Notaris acridulus (Linn.)
Micrelus ericae (Gyllenhal)
Cidnorhinus quadrimaculatus (Linn.)
C. assimilis (Paykull)

C. contractus (Marsham)
C. erisymi (Fabr.)
C. pollinarius (Forster)

Rhinoncus pericarpius (Linn.)
Phytobius quadrituberculatus (Fabr.)

HYMENOPTERA (bees, wasps, ants and allies)

Only the social Aculeata (bees, wasps and ants) have been studied. Several species of solitary wasps, sawflies and ichneumon flies also occur but no detailed studies have been carried out on these groups.

Siricidae (wood wasps)
[*Uroceros gigas* **Wood wasp** AI]

Tenthredinidae (sawflies)
Nematus ribesii **Gooseberry sawfly** R (AI?)

Ichneumonidae (ichneumon flies)
[*Rhyssa persuasororia* AI]
Ichneumon suspiciosus R

Formicidae (ants)
Myrmica ruginodis Nylander R: locally common on Mainland, Foula, Fair Isle and Unst. The only species of ant to occur in the islands.

Dryinidae
Lenchodryinus ruficornis

Vespidae (social wasps)
Dolichovespula norwegica Fabr. **Norwegian wasp** V: one record from Fair Isle in August 1991. Several other possible vagrants have not been identified.
[*Vespula germanica* (Fabr.). **German wasp** AI: one amongst fruit in a shop at Cunningsburgh in January 1993. Several other wasps in similar circumstances have not been identified.]
Vespula vulgaris (Linn.). **Common wasp** R: recent colonist, one nest in Lerwick probably of this species in 1989, then one in 1993 increasing to over 40 in Lerwick and Scalloway in 1995, but slight decline in 1996.

Apidae (social bees)
[*Apis mellifera*. **Honey bee** AI: not known to occur naturally, although there are several hives kept on Mainland.]
[*Bombus soroeensis* (Fabr.). **Broken-banded bumblebee** X?: a supposed old record from Yell has not been traced.]
Bombus magnus (Vogt). **Northern white-tailed bumblebee** R: common in gardens and crofting land throughout the islands except Fair Isle. April–September.
Bombus jonellus (Kirby). **Small heath bumblebee** R: scarce on moorland on Mainland, Muckle Roe and Unst at least. The subspecies *vogti* is restricted to Shetland. July–August.
Bombus hortorum (Linn.). **Garden bumblebee** R: scarce, usually around gardens or crops, but widespread on Mainland and Unst at least. June–August.
Bombus muscorum (Linn.). **'Shetland' bumblebee** R: common or very common throughout the islands. The Shetland subspecies *agricolae* Baker is also found in the Outer Hebrides. May–October.
Bombus distinguendus Morawitz **Great yellow bumblebee**. Presumed extinct: there is an old record from before 1960 but none since.

DIPTERA (true flies)   by B. Laurence

Flies have only been studied in any detail on brief visits by Brian Laurence. There is not enough information to assess status except for the hoverflies (Syrphidae), a section which includes information from other sources. In this list the asterisk indicates a species not recorded by B.R.L.

Visiting entomologists have made collections of flies and published lists of species in a variety of journals since 1873. Percy M. Grimshaw published the first comprehensive list of Diptera from Shetland in 1905, incorporating the earlier records. Notes on Shetland species have been published recently in the *Shetland Naturalist* (1992, 1994) and in the newsletter of the Shetland Entomological Group. At the present time, more than 200 species of Diptera have been found in Shetland (Laurence, 1997). The majority of these flies have a wide distribution and are found also in Orkney, the Hebrides and further south on the British mainland. Some of them, notably the hoverflies *Episyrphus balteatus* and *Metasyrphus corollae*, are known to be migratory and this family of flies, the Syrphidae, has attracted most attention on the islands.

Shetland is rich in other flies associated with damp peat moorland. These can be found down to sea level in Shetland, whereas species such as *Tipula alpium*, *Dolichopus rupestris* and *Phaonia consobrina* are to be found at altitude on mountains and moorlands further south. The empid *Rhamphomyia morio* is found on the seashore in Shetland but is regarded as a mountain species in Scotland. S. Kay found this empid as a frequent pollinator of Shetland's unique mouse-ear *Cerastium nigrescens* subsp. *nigrescens* on the Keen of Hamar in Unst and one suspects that the fly, as well as the plant, is a relict from the postglacial period. The nearest relatives of the fly are found mainly in the mountains of central Europe. Another boreo-arctic species is the blowfly *Calliphora uralensis*, common in Shetland but restricted to the north of Scotland and to offshore islands further south (Davies & Laurence 1992).

How the unique Shetland species of blackfly *Simulium zetlandense* (Davies, 1966) arrived and adapted to the different habitats in Shetland is not known. As it does not feed on human blood, it is left to the ubiquitous blood-sucking midge *Culicoides impunctatus*, which breeds in damp peat, to be the main nuisance on the islands.

These flies are representative of a series of invasions by different species of Diptera since postglacial times. Most species appear to be settled residents on Shetland, found regularly year by year, although there is evidence of annual amplification of populations by migrants, notably in certain of the hover flies, which is continuing today. Perhaps this mixture of boreo-arctic species and migratory species not yet fully established from further south is an ideal population to study for the future effects of global warming. Also Shetland is relatively unpolluted and one hopes that a unique species such as *Simulium zetlandense* will be allowed to continue to survive in the fast-flowing peaty streams..

Trichoceridae (winter gnats)
Trichocera annulata Mg.
T. hiemalis Deg.

* *T. regelationis* L.
* *T. saltator* Harris

Tipulidae (craneflies)
Prionocera turcica Fabr.
Tipula alpium Bergroth
T. grisescens Zett.
T. lateralis Mg.
T. marmorata Mg.
T. oleracea Linn.
T. paludosa Mg.
T. rufina Mg.
T. subnodicornis Zett.
T. varipennis Mg.
Limonia didyma Mg.
L. mitis Mg.

L. nubeculosa Mg.
L. tripunctata Fabr.
Pedicia immaculata Mg.
Limnophila ferruginea Mg.
L. meigeni Verrall
L. nemoralis Mg.
Gonomyia dentata De Meijere
Cheilotrichia cinerascens Mg.
Erioptera trivialis Mg.
Ormosia depilata Edwards
Molophilus obscurus Mg.
M. pleuralis De Meijere

Pyschodidae (mothflies and owl-midges)
Pericoma avicularia Tonnoir
P. nubila Mg.
P. pseudexquisita Tonnoir
Telmatoscopus labeculosus Eaton
T. maynei Tonnoir

Pyschoda grisescens Tonnoir
P. phalaenoides Linn.
P. severini Tonnoir
P. trinodulosa Tonnoir

Thaumaleidae
Thaumalea verralli Edwards

Ceratopogonidae (biting midges)
Culicoides impunctatus Goet.

Isohelea sociabilis Goet.

Chironomidae (non-biting midges)
Macropelopia nebulosa Mg.
Psectrotanypus varius Fabr.
Ablabesymia monilis Linn.
Cricotopus pulchripes Verrall
Eukiefferiella claripennis Lundbeck
Halocladius variabilis Staeg.
Synorthocladius semivirens Kieff.
Bryophaenocladius vernalis Goet.
Limnophyes exiguus Goet.
Metriocnemus gracei Edwards

M. ursinus Holmgren
M. 'picipes' Mg.
Parametriocnemus stylatus Kieff.
Pseudorthocladius curtistylus Goet.
Smittia aterrima Mg.
S. pratorum Goet.
Chironomus annularis Deg.
C. aprilinus Mg.
C. salinarius Kieff.
Cryptochironomus redekei Krusemann

Endochironomus lepidus Mg.
Limnochironomus pulsus Walker
Paracladopelma laminata Kieff.
Pentapedilum sordens Wulp
Stictochironomus sticticus Fabr.

Cladotanytarsus nigrovittatus Goet.
Micropsectra apposita Walker
M. aristata Pinder
M. fusca Mg.
Tanytarsus brundini Lindeberg

Dixidae
*Dixella martinii Pues

Simuliidae (blackflies)
Simulium aureum Fries

S. zetlandense Davies

Ansipodidae (window-midges)
Sylvicola fenestralis Scop.

S. punctatus Fabr.

Bibionidae
Bibio nigriventris Haliday

Dilophus femoratus Mg.

Mycetophilidae (fungus-gnats)
Mycomya fimbriata Mg.
Brevicornu fuscipenne Staeg.

B. sericoma Mg.

Sciaridae
Trichosia caudata Walker
T. glabra Mg.
T. pilosa Staeg.
Ctenosciaria hyalipennis Mg.
Bradysia confinis Winn. group
B. inusitata Frey

B. nitidicollis Mg.
B. subtilis Lengersdorf
B. triseriata Winn. group
Scatopsciaria nana Winn.
S. vitripennis Mg.
S. vivida Winn.

Scatopsidae
Scatopse notata Linn.

Cecidomyiidae (gall-midges)
Lestremia cinerea Macq.

Stratiomyidae (soldierflies)
Microchrysa polita Linn.

Empididae (danceflies)
Chersodromia arenaria Hal.
Tachypeza nubila Mg.
Platypalpus nigritarsis Fall.
P. pallidiventris Mg.
P. strigifrons Zett.
Hybos femoratus Müll.
Bicellaria sulcata Zett.
Rhamphomyia morio Zett.
R. simplex Zett.
R. stigmosa Macq.

Xanthempis trigramma Mg.
Empis tessellata Fabr.
E. verralli Collin
Hilara chorica Fall.
H. interstincta Fall. group
Dolichocephala guttata Haliday
Clinocera fontinalis Haliday
C. stagnalis Haliday
Wiedemannia bipunctata Haliday
W. lota Walker

Dolichopodidae
Dolichopus brevipennis Mg.
D. discifer Stannius
D. griseipennis Stannius
D. lepidus Staeg.
D. nubilus Mg.
D. plumipes Scop.
D. rupestris Haliday
D. urbanus Mg.

Hydrophorus albiceps Frey
Rhaphium brevicorne Curtis
Syntormon pallipes Fabr.
Argyra perplexa Becker
Campsicnemus armatus Zett.
C. loripes Haliday
C. scambus Fall.
Sympycnus desoutteri Parent

Lonchopteridae
Lonchoptera lutea Panz

Syrphidae (hoverflies)

Melanostoma mellinum (Linn.) R: not recorded until 1993, but frequent on Mainland, Unst and Foula. June–August.

*Melanostoma scalare (Fabr.) R: not recorded until 1995 but scarce on Unst, presumably overlooked elsewhere. July–August.

Platycheirus albimanus (Fabr.) R: frequent in lowland habitats and on moorland edges throughout the islands. June–September.

*Platycheirus clypeatus (Mg.) R: scarce in lush, damp areas in Central Mainland, Foula, Fair Isle and Unst. Recent records all of *P. clypeatus sensu stricto*. July.

Platycheirus manicatus (Mg.) R: common to abundant in lowland habitats throughout the islands. June–September.

Platycheirus nielseni Vockeroth R: several on the edge of moorland, Baltasound, Unst in July 1996. Records of *P. peltatus sensu lato* from Unst and Yell in the 1980s may relate to this recently separated species.

*Platycheirus ramsarensis Goeldlin de Tifenau, Maibach and Speight R: several in acidic grassland on Unst and Foula in July 1996.

*Platycheirus scutatus (Mg.) R?: one record, around conifers at Lerwick Observatory in June 1993.

Episyrphus balteatus (Deg.) M: annual in variable numbers, occasionally thousands as in July 1994, throughout the islands. June–September.

*Meliscaeva auricollis (Mg.) M: one in Lerwick, South Mainland in August 1993, then several in Central Mainland in August 1994 and July–August 1996.

Metasyrphus corollae (Fabr.) M: annual in variable numbers, usually scarcer than *E. balteatus*, throughout the islands. May–September.

*Metasyrphus luniger (Mg.) V: two records: Fair Isle in June 1993 and Norwick, Unst in September 1995.

*Metasyrphus lundbecki (Soot-Ryen) V: three records: Fair Isle in August 1984 and two on Foula in August 1996.

Parasyrphus punctulatus (Verrall) V: two records: Kergord, Central Mainland in June 1993 and Foula in May 1995.

Scaeva pyrastri (Linn.) M: just about annual in small numbers throughout the islands. July–August.

Scaeva selenitica (Mg.) M: less than annual and recorded West and Central Mainland, Fair Isle, Foula and Unst. June–October.

*Sphaerophoria ?scripta (Linn.) V: about a dozen recorded in Central Mainland, Foula and Unst in 1994–96 have all been females or evaded capture so the identity of the species is still uncertain. July–September.

Syrphus ribesii (Linn.)

Syrphus torvus Osten-Sacksen

*Syrphus vitripennis (Mg.) all M: these three species are annual in variable numbers, although they are inseparable in the field, *vitripennis* appears to be the commonest from specimens and *ribesii* the scarcest. Recorded throughout the islands. July–September.

Rhingia campestris Mg. R: common to abundant around crofting land throughout the islands. June–September.

Chrysogaster hirtella Loew R: common in damp lowland habitats throughout the islands except Fair Isle and Foula. June–July.

Lejogaster metallina (Fabr.) R: common in damp lowland habitats throughout the islands except Fair Isle. June–August.

*Neoascia podagrica (Fabr.) R: frequent around crofting land on Fair Isle but not elsewhere. July.

Neoascia tenur (Harris) R: scarce and very local in lush, damp habitats South and West Mainland and Foula. July.

[**Orthonevra splendens* (Mg.) X?: a record from Fetlar in July 1985 is considered unreliable in the absence of a specimen.]

Eristalis abusivus Collin R?: one record on Trondra in June 1987.

Eristalis arbustorum (Linn.) R: frequent in lowland habitats throughout the islands. June–September.

Eristalis intricarius (Linn.) R: common in lowland habitats throughout the islands. May–September.

[**Eristalis nemorum* (Linn.) X?: records from Burra and South Mainland in August 1993 are considered unreliable in the absence of specimens.]

Eristalis pertinax (Scop.) R and possible M: frequent in crofting land and gardens in South and Central Mainland and Bressay; singles on Unst in September 1995 and 1996 are presumed immigrants. May–September.

Eristalis tenax (Linn.) R and possible M: frequent in crofting land and gardens in South and Central Mainland; an old record from Fair Isle and one on Foula in September 1995 are presumed immigrants. June–September.

*Helophilus affinis Wahlberg V: one record from Fair Isle in August 1982. The only British record.

Helophilus pendulus (Linn.) R and possible M: common in lowland habitats throughout the islands; an increase in August 1996 may have indicated immigration. June–September.

*_Helophilus trivittatus_ (Fabr.) V: two records, from Foula in July 1994 and Unst in August 1995.
Sericomyia lappona (Linn.) R: scarce in Central Mainland, especially Kergord. June–July.
Sericomyia silentis (Harris) R: frequent in all habitats throughout the islands except Fair Isle and Foula. July–August.
Syritta pipiens (Linn.) R and possible M: scarce and local in South and Central Mainland, Foula, Fair Isle and Unst, some records coinciding with immigration. June–August.

Micropezidae (stilt-legged flies)
Calobata petronella Linn.

Psilidae
Loxocera fulviventris Mg.   _Psila humeralis_ Zett.

Lauxaniidae
Lyciella rorida Fall.

Coelopidae (kelp flies)
Coelopa frigida Fabr.

Heleomyzidae
Tephrochlamys rufiventris Mg.   _Heleomyza brachypterna_ Loew
Scoliocentra caesia Mg.   _H. modesta_ Mg. _s. czernyi_ Collart

Dryomyzidae
Heterocheila buccata Fall.

Sepsidae
Sepsis flavimana Mg.

Sciomyzidae
Tetanocera robusta Loew

Sphaeroceridae (lesser duny flies)
Alloborborus pallifrons Fall.   _M. vitripennis_ Zett.
Copromyza similis Collin   _Opacifrons septentrionalis_ Stenhammer
Crumomyia nitida Mg.   _Spelobia clunipes_ Mg.
Lotophila atra Mg.   _S. luteilabris_ Rond.
Ischiolepta vaporariorum Haliday   _S. palmata_ Richards
Leptocera caenosa Rond.   _S. rufilabris_ Stenhammer
L. fontinalis Fall.   _S. talparum_ Richards
L. nigra Olivier   _Telomerina flavipes_ Mg.
Minilimosina baculum Marshall   _Thoracochaeta zosterae_ Haliday
M. gemella Rohacek   _Trachyopella minuscula_ Collin

Piophildae
Piophila vulgaris Fall.

Pallopteridae
Palloptera umbellatarum Fabr.

Opomyzidae
Geomyza balachowskyi Mesnil   _Opomyza germinationis_ Linn.
G. tripunctata Fall.

Ephydridae
Notiphila cinerea Fall./_nigricornis_ Stenhammer   _Parydra pusilla_ Mg./_nigritarsis_ Strobl
Hydrellia griseola Fall.   _Limnellia quadrata_ Fall.
H. modesta Loew   _Scatella stagnalis_ Fall.

Drosophilidae (fruitflies or vinegarflies)
Scaptomyza graminum Fall.   _Drosophila andalusiaca_ Strobl
S. pallida Zett.   _D. funebris_ Fabr.

Agromyzidae
Phytomyza angelicae Kalten.
P. lonicerae

P. syngenesiae (Hardy)/*horticola* Gour.

Tachinidae
Siphona geniculata Deg.

Calliphoridae (blowflies)
Calliphora uralensis Vill.
C. vicina Rob. Des.
Bellardia viarum Rob. Des.

B. vulgaris Rob. Des.
Cynomya mortuorum Linn.
Protophormia terraenovae Rob. Des.

Scathophagidae (dungflies)
Scathophaga calida Curtis
S. furcata Say
S. litorea Fall.

S. stercoraria Linn. **Yellow dungfly**
Ceratinostoma ostiorum Curtis

Anthomyiidae
Anthomyia confusanea Michelson
Fucellia fucorum Fall.
F. maritima Haliday
Hydrophoria caudata Zett.
Delia echinata Seguy
D. nuda Strobl

Paregle cinerella Fall.
Nupedia aestiva Mg.
N. infirma Mg.
Pseudonupedia intersecta Mg.
Pegomya bicolor Hoffm.

Fanniidae (lesser houseflies)
Fannia canicularis Linn.
F. postica Stein

F. scalaris Fabr.
F. serena Fall.

Muscidae (houseflies)
Orthellia viridis Wied.
Morellia importuna Haliday
Thricops longipes Zett.
T. semicinerea Wied.
Hydrotaea basdeni Collin
H. cyrtoneurina Zett.
H. dentipes Fabr.
H. irritans Fall.
H. occulta Mg.
Phaonia consobrina Zett.
P. incana Wied.
P. palpata Stein
Helina duplicata Mg.
H. impuncta Fall.
H. laetifica Rob. Des.
Myospila meditabunda Fabr.

Graphomya picta Zett.
Spilogona falleni Pont
S. surda Zett.
S. trianguligera Zett.
Limnophora maculosa Mg.
L. uniseta Stein
Pseudocoenosia abnormis Stein
Schoenomyza litorella Fall.
Dexiopsis litoralis Zett.
Coenosia intermedia Fall.
C. means Mg.
C. mollicula Fall.
C. perpusilla Mg.
C. pumila Fall.
C. tigrina Fabr.

SIPHONAPTERA (fleas)
The following list of fleas, compiled by R. S. George, was published in Berry and Johnston (1980).

Pulicidae
Pulex irritans Linn. **Human flea**

Spilopsyllus cuniculi (Dale). **Rabbit flea**

Hystrichopysillidae (Field Mouse fleas)
Typhloceras poppei Wagner

Ctenophthalmus nobilis vulgaris Smit

Leptopysillidae (Mouse flea)
Leptopsylla segnis (Schonherr)

Ceratophyllidae (Bird flea)
Dasypsyllus gallinulae gallinulae (Dale)
Nosopsyllus fasciatus (Bosc)
Ceratophyllus gallinae (Schrank)
C. fringillae (Walker)

C. vagabundus insularis Rothschild
C. garei Rothschild
C. borealis Rothschild

SPIDERS

by J. E. D. Milner

The first collection of Shetland spiders was made, just over 60 years ago, by W. S. Bristowe (1931), when he made a short trip and identified some 30 species. A number of further records have been added by various authors but until P. Ashmole (1979), no concentrated and systematic study had been carried out. Edward Milner (1987, 1988 and with Nick Riddiford in press) has added many new species so that the species list now stands at 113. Almost all the species found in Shetland (and in Faroe and Iceland) are also present in both Scotland and Scandinavia. However, only two-thirds of the Faroe species and less than half of the Iceland species are also found in Shetland.

Amaurobidae
Amaurobius fenestralis (Stroem, 1768)

Pholcidae
Pholcus phalangioides (Fuesslin, 1775)

Gnaphosidae
Drassodes lapidosus (Walckenaer, 1802)   *Gnaphosa leporina* (L. Koch, 1866)
Haplodrassus signifer (C. L. Koch, 1839)

Clubionidae
Clubiona phragmitis (C. L. Koch, 1843)   *C. trivialis* (C. L. Koch, 1843)

Liocranidae
Agroeca proxima (O. P. Cambridge, 1871)

Thomisidae
Xysticus cristatus (Clerck, 1757)   *Ozyptila trux* (Blackwall, 1846)

Salticidae
Neon reticulatus (Blackwall, 1853)

Lycosidae
Pardosa palustris (Linnaeus, 1758)   *Trochosa terricola* (Thorell, 1856)
P. pullata (Clerck, 1757)   *Arctosa perita* (Latreille, 1799)
P. nigriceps (Thorell, 1856)   *Pirata piraticus* (Clerck, 1757)
Xerolycosa miniata (C. L. Koch, 1834)   *P. tenuitarsis* Simon, 1876
Alopecosa pulverulenta (Clerck, 1757)

Agelenidae
Textrix denticulata (Olivier, 1789)   *Cryphoeca silvicola* (C. L. Koch, 1834)
Tegenaria domestica (Clerck. 1757)

Hahniidae
Antistea elegans (Blackwall, 1841)   *H. nava* (Blackwall, 1841)
Hahnia montana (Blackwall, 1841)

Theridiidae
Robertus lividus (Blackwall, 1836)   *R. arundineti* (O. P. Cambridge, 1871)

Tetragnathidae
Tetragnatha extensa (Linnaeus, 1758)   *P. degeeri* Sundevall, 1830
Pachygnatha clercki Sundevall, 1823

Metidae
Metellina segmentata (Clerck, 1757)   *Zygiella x-notata* (Clerck, 1757)
M. merianae (Scopoli, 1763)

Araneidae
Araneus diadematus Clerk, 1757

Linyphiidae

Ceratinella brevipes (Westring, 1851)
Walckenaeria acuminata (Blackwall, 1833)
W. antica (Wider, 1834)
W. nodosa O. P. Cambridge, 1873
W. capito (Westring, 1871)
W. nudipalpis (Westring, 1851)
W. clavicornis (Emerton, 1882)
W. cuspidata Blackwall, 1833
W. vigilax (Blackwall, 1833)
Dicymbium brevisetosum Locket, 1962
Entelecara errata O. P. Cambridge, 1913
Dismodicus bifrons (Blackwall, 1841)
Hypomma bituberculatum (Wider, 1834)
Metopobactrus prominulus (O. P. Cambridge, 1872)
Gonatium rubens (Blackwall, 1833)
Pepanocranium ludicrum (O. P. Cambridge, 1861)
Pocadicnemis juncea (Locket Millidge, 1953)
Oedothorax fuscus (Blackwall, 1834)
O. retusus (Westring, 1851)
Trichopterna thorelli (Westring, 1861)
Pelecopsis nemoralis (Blackwall, 1841)
Silometopus elegans (O. P. Cambridge, 1872)
S. ambiguus (O. P. Cambridge, 1905)
Cnephalocotes obscurus (Blackwall, 1834)
Tiso vagans (Blackwall, 1834)
Monocephalus fuscipes (Blackwall, 1836)
M. castaneipes (Simon, 1884)
Lophomma punctatum (Blackwall, 1841)
Gongylidiellum vivum (O. P. Cambridge, 1875)
Erigonella hiemalis (Blackwall, 1841)
Savignia frontata (Blackwall, 1873)
Diplocephalus cristatus (Blackwall, 1833)
D. permixtus (O. P. Cambridge, 1871)
Araeoncus crassiceps (Westring, 1861)
Scotinotylus evansi (O. P. Cambridge, 1894)
Typhochrestus digitatus (O. P. Cambridge, 1872)
Erigone dentipalps (Wider, 1834)
E. atra (Blackwall, 1833)
E. promiscua (O. P. Cambridge, 1872)

E. arctica (White, 1852)
E. longipalpis (Sundevall, 1830)
E. capra Simon, 1884
Rhaebothorax morulus (O. P. Cambridge, 1873)
Latithorax faustus (O. P. Cambridge, 1900)
Leptorhoptrum robustum (Westring, 1851)
Drepanotylus uncatus (O. P. Cambridge, 1873)
Leptothrix hardyi (Blackwall, 1850)
Hilaira frigida (Thorell, 1872)
Haloratus reprobus (O. P. Cambridge, 1879)
Porrhomma egeria Simon, 1884
P. montanum Jackson, 1913
Agyneta subtilis (O. P. Cambridge, 1863)
Agyneta conigera (O. P. Cambridge, 1863)
Agyneta cauta (O. P. Cambridge, 1902)
A. decora (O. P. Cambridge, 1871)
Meioneta mossica (Schikora, 1993)
M. gulosa (L. Koch, 1869)
M. nigripes (Simon, 1884)
Centromerus prudens (O. P. Cambridge, 1873)
C. dilutus (O. P. Cambridge, 1875)
Centromerita bicolor (Blackwall, 1833)
C. concinna (Thorell, 1875)
Oreonetides vaginatus (Thorell, 1872)
Saaristoa abnormis (Blackwall, 1841)
Bathyphantes gracilis (Blackwall, 1841)
B. parvulus (Westring, 1851)
Diplostyla concolor (Wider, 1834)
Poeciloneta variegata (Blackwall, 1841)
Bolyphantes luteolus (Blackwall, 1833)
B. alticeps (Sundevall, 1833)
Lepthyphantes leprosus (Ohlert, 1865)
L. minutus (Blackwall, 1833)
L. obscurus (Blackwall, 1841)
L. tenuis (Blackwall, 1852)
L. zimmermanni Bertkau. 1890
L. mengei Kulczinski, 1887
L. ericaeus (Blackwall, 1853)
Allomengea scopigera (Grube, 1859)

NON-MARINE MOLLUSCA
by R. M. Tallack

As with many invertebrate groups the non-marine molluscan fauna of Shetland represents approximately one-third of the total for the British Isles, with several reaching the northern limits of their distribution. *Discus rotundatus*, ubiquitous throughout much of Britain, is known from only one site at Weisdale, where it could have been introduced. Likewise *Cepaea hortensi*, as its Latin name suggests, is associated with gardens; in Shetland it occurs only on limestone and dunes from Central Mainland southwards and lacks the interesting variations in banding characteristic of mainland specimens. Familiar garden 'pests' such as *Helix aspera* and *Trichia striolata* are absent. In all 65 species have been recorded: 3 brackish water, 17 freshwater and 45 terrestrial.

The main factor determining mollusc distribution in Shetland is lack of suitable habitat. The areas where molluscs are most successful are dunes, especially those on the west side between Sumburgh and Burra, and the narrow outcrops of limestone from Okraquoy through Tingwall and Whiteness up to Dury Voe, which provide a variety of habitats such as marsh, grassland and rocks. Elsewhere, gardens, walls, iris beds and the land around old crofts are the only locations where molluscs are likely to occur. The extensive areas of moorland are virtually devoid of molluscs apart from the occasional slug such as *Arion ater*. However some construction schemes have imported molluscs to comparatively inhospitable habitats; for instance the area in the immediate vicinity of the road bridge at Channerwick boasts a range of snails, including *Candidula intersecta*, which is found only on dunes elsewhere in Shetland.

Farming practices that involve disturbing the soil or decreasing vegetation cover have a detrimental effect on mollusc diversity, although increased grazing does not necessarily. However it may have been responsible for the demise of the large freshwater bivalve *Margaritifera margaritifera*, which was first recorded from the Burn of Setter, Walls in 1849 by Fleming and re-found by Oldham in 1928. In 1993–94 the same location was searched in vain on three occasions, and each time there was at least one dead sheep in the burn.

Most freshwater molluscs avoid very acid and peaty waters. The alkaline water of some lochs supports *Gyraulis laevis*, a species with a generally northern distribution. However, increased pollution, particularly seepage from silage, can have a potentially devastating effect on a small area. The best example is the well-documented pollution of the Loch of Hillwell. Here, in 1928, Oldham recorded five species of *Pisidium*, tiny freshwater bivalves known as 'pea-shells'. During 1993–94 two visits failed to produce any *Pisidium*, although freshwater gasteropods were numerous. As *Pisidium* siphon water for their food they would be more vulnerable to pollution than gasteropods which graze on the vegetation.

On balance, the impoverished fauna of Shetland is surviving remarkably well and recent discoveries have more than compensated for any losses.

Hydrobia ventrosa (Montagu): single record from Kergord, presumably Weisdale.
H. ulvae (Pennant): scattered records in *vadills*.
Potamopyrgus jenkinsi (Smith): common in fresh and brackish water.
Carychium minimum Müller seg.: local in marshes.
C. tridentatum (Risso): two known sites, Okraquoy and Spiggie.
Leucophytia bidentata (Montagu): single record from Whalsay.
Lymnaea truncatula (Müller): local in ditches, marshes, etc.
L. stagnalis (L.): introduced. Recently found in pond in Hamnavoe School.
L. peregra (Müller): widespread in most freshwater habitats.
Bathyomphalus contortus (L.): stony lochs.
Gyraulus laevis (Alder): stony lochs usually on limestone, mainly South Mainland.
Armiger crista (L.): widespread in lochs.
Oxyloma pfeifferi (Rossmässler): widespread in marshes.
Cochlicopa lubrica (Müller): widespread but local (South Mainland and Unst).
C. lubricella (Porro): confined to limestone and serpentinite.
Columella aspera (Walden): widespread but local in marshes and wet heath. Oldham's original specimen from Foula is for the aggregate *C. edentula* (Draparnaud). However all specimens found since have been *C. aspera*, although some from Quendale appear to have intermediate characteristics.
Vertigo substriata (Jeffreys): marshes. Two sites, Tingwall and Whiteness.
V. pygmaea (Draparnaud): found by Oldham at Tingwall. No recent records.
Pupilla muscorum (L.): dunes at Quendale and Scousburgh. Old record for Scalloway.
Lauria cylindracea (da Costa): widespread but local, mainly limestone.
Vallonia excentrica Sterki: single record from Scousburgh.
Punctum pygmaeum (Draparnaud): widespread but local in marshes and iris beds.
Discus rotundatus (Müller): despite old unlocalized records, currently known from a single site at Weisdale. Possibly introduced.
Arion ater (L.) agg.: widespread. Found in most habitats.
A. subfuscus (Draparnaud): widespread.
A. circumscriptus Johnston: scattered records.
A. sylvaticus Lohmander: scattered records.
A. fasciatus (Nilsson): mainly disturbed ground, e.g. around old crofts.
A. hortensis Férussac agg.: recently recognized as a species complex. All old records and juveniles are assigned to the aggregate.
A. distinctus Mabille: all segregates of *A. hortensis* agg. have been this species. Locally common.
A. intermedius Normand: widespread.
Vitrina pellucida (Müller): widespread.
Vitrea contracta (Westerlund): widespread. Old records refer to *V. crystallina* (Müller) agg. No specimens of the segregate *V. crystallina* have been found.
Nesovitrea hammonis (Ström): scattered records.
Aegopinella pura (Alder): limestone at Okraquoy and Whiteness.
A. nitidula (Draparnaud): widespread.
Oxychilus draparnaudi (Beck): widespread but local, often disturbed ground.
O. cellarius (Müller): widespread but local, often on disturbed ground.
O. alliarius (Miller): found in most terrestrial habitats.
Milax gagates (Draparnaud): very local.
Tandonia sowerbyi (Férussac): local.
T. budapestensis (Hazay): local, restricted to disturbed habitats.
Limax maximus L.: widespread.

L. cinereoniger Wolf: single record from Kurkigarth, Voe.

L. marginatus (Müller): widespread.

Deroceras laeve (Müller): in marshes. Widespread.

D. reticulatum (Müller): common in most habitats.

D. caruanae (Pollonera): confined to disturbed ground.

Euconulus fulvus (Müller) seg.: damp habitats. Widespread but local.

E. alderi (Gray): in wetter places than its congener.

Clausilia bidentata (Ström): currently known from one site, Whiteness. Old records from Out Skerries, Okraquoy and Tingwall.

Balea perversa (L.): not uncommon. Usually on limestone, rarely serpentinite.

Candidula intersecta (Poiret): dunes. Introduced elsewhere with extracted sand.

Arianta arbustorum (L.): dunes and limestone. Local.

Cepaea hortensis (Müller): confined to limestone and dunes.

Margaritifera margaritifera (L.): Burn of Setter, Walls. Last record 1929.

Sphaerium corneum (L.): lime-rich lochs.

Pisidium casertanum (Poli): widespread, often common.

P. personatum Malm: widespread in marshes, sometimes edges of lochs.

P. obtusale (Lamarck): due to misidentification distribution not clear. Generally marshes and ditches.

P. milium Held: local, often in small lochs.

P. subtruncatum Malm: local in lochs.

P. lilljeborgi Clessin: widespread in lochs.

P. hibernicum Westerlund: widespread in lochs.

P. nitidum Jenyns: widespread, often common in lochs.

BIRDS   by K. Osborn & Shetland Bird Club

The list below (compiled by K. Osborn and Shetland Bird Club) includes all records up to 31 December 1996 and includes all records from Fair Isle, which are assessed separately and published in the Fair Isle Bird Observatory annual reports produced by the Fair Isle Bird Observatory Trust (FIBOT).

Names follow the *Birding World Complete List of the Birds of the Western Palearctic*. English names used are those preferred and used by *Birding World* and the Shetland Bird Club. Known Shetland names are given below the standard name (see *Shetland Bird Report* 1992, pp. 101–106).

The following references were used for almost every species account and if mentioned in the text are referred to by the following abbreviations. Uncredited records will be from these sources.

B&J	Berry & Johnston (1980).
Davis	Davis (1965). Fair Isle records up to 1963.
Dymond	Dymond (1991). Fair Isle records up to 1990.
E&B	Evans & Buckley (1899). Records from a wider geographical area, although excluding Fair Isle.
Saxby	Saxby (1874). Records mainly from 1859 to 1871 with a heavy bias towards Unst.
Thom	Thom (1986).
Tulloch	Unpublished notes 1963–68 and annual reports compiled for 1969–72 by Bobby Tulloch.
V&V	Venables & Venables (1955). Records from all of Shetland except Fair Isle up to 1953.
BBRC	Annual reports of the British Birds Rarities Committee published in *British Birds*, 1958–96.
SBR	*Shetland Bird Report* published by the Shetland Bird Club, 1973–96.
FIBO	Fair Isle Bird Observatory reports published by FIBOT, 1948–96.
NMS	National Museum of Scotland.
NHM	Natural History Museum, Tring.

Species names marked with an asterisk are distinctly marked subspecies whose records are assessed separately. Species names in brackets are those whose origins are suspect, are considered to be escapes, are introduced or extinct species, probable subspecies, or records no longer considered acceptable.

The current national categorization of each species within the British and Irish list, as suggested by the British Ornithologists' Union Records Committee (BOURC), is included for those species where there is doubt as to their origins. The category key is as follows. Note that all species without a category key or labelled as escapes are included in category A.

A   Species that have been recorded in an apparently wild state in Britain or Ireland at least once since 1 January 1950.

B   Species that were recorded in an apparently wild state in Britain or Ireland at least once up to 31 December 1949 but have not been recorded subsequently.

C   Species that, although originally introduced by humans, have now established a regular feral breeding stock which apparently maintains itself without necessary recourse to further introduction.
D   Species that would otherwise appear in categories A or B except that there is reasonable doubt that they have ever occurred in a natural state. They do not form any part of the British list.
E   Species that have been recorded as introductions, transportees or escapes from captivity, and whose breeding populations (if any) are thought not to be self sustaining. They do not form any part of the British list.

The following abbreviations are used for references to some of the breeding population data: AONs, apparently occupied nests; AOTs, apparently occupied territories; SNH, Scottish Natural Heritage; SCR, Seabird Colony Register; RSPB, Royal Society for the Protection of Birds; SOTEAG, Shetland Oil Terminal Ecological Advisory Group.

Red-throated diver *Gavia stellata*
Shetland names: *raingoose, lum, loon*
Regarded largely as a breeding summer visitor, normally present from March through to September. A small number overwinter most years. The current breeding population is estimated at 430 pairs (RSPB 1993).

Black-throated diver *Gavia arctica*
Annual but scarce visitor, with usually less than 10 records in a year. Individuals have been recorded in all months of the year with the majority of records between November and May.

Great northern diver *Gavia immer*
Shetland names: *immer goose, immer gos*
Largely a winter visitor with most birds recorded from October to May, although a few sometimes remain to summer. The wintering population is estimated at between 200 and 400 birds.

White-billed diver *Gavia adamsii*
Rare migrant, recorded in all months of the year but especially in October and November and May and June. About 47 individuals have been recorded since 1973.

Little grebe *Tachybaptus ruficollis*
Uncommon passage migrant, mainly in October to November, but overwinters in small numbers. Usually less than 20 recorded in any year. A pair bred at Loch of Hillwell in 1967, successfully rearing three chicks, and this remains the only certain breeding record (*Scottish Birds* **4**: 563).

Great crested grebe *Podiceps cristatus*
Scarce migrant with at least 60 records all between October and June. One or two individuals are seen most years.

Red-necked grebe *Podiceps grisegena*
Scarce migrant with at least 72 records. Recorded during most years, the majority being seen from September to March, although there are records from all months except July.

Slavonian grebe *Podiceps auritus*
Winter visitor, mainly in October to April but recorded in all months. Records are regular at a few favoured localities, especially the voes around Weisdale and Tresta. The current wintering population is probably less than 75 birds, although as the total British wintering population is estimated at little more than 400 birds, the Shetland population is quite significant.

Black-necked grebe *Podiceps nigricollis*
Vagrant, five records, although the winter records are doubtful:
1966, Loch of Spiggie, 20 March (*Scottish Birds* **4**: 239)
1970, Weisdale Voe, 25 February
1976, Loch of Spiggie, 11 January
1977, Sand Water, Tingwall, 27 October
1984, off Burra, 29 May

Black-browed albatross *Diomedea melanophris*
Vagrant. An individual affectionately known as Albert Ross or just plain Albert became one of the ornithological attractions of Shetland. An unidentified albatross seen on three dates in 1970 (29 May, 10 & 12 July) was undoubtedly the same bird next seen again in July–August 1972. Although unrecorded in 1973, from 1974 to 1987 Albert spent most of the summer on a ledge amongst the gannets at Saito, Hermaness.

From 1976 the bird even built a nest. During this period the earliest recorded date was 14 February 1982, and the latest record was 7 October 1984. An unusually early departure on 2 July 1987 was followed by absences in 1988 and 1989, but the bird returned to the same ledge on 26 March 1990 and was seen intermittently in March to May 1990 and 1991, April to June 1992, April to June 1993, March to July 1995, and April to July 1995, although it was not seen in 1996. A single thought to be probably an immature of this species was also seen off Fair Isle on 14 May 1949.

Fulmar *Fulmarus glacialis*
Shetland name: *maalie*
Abundant breeding resident with some evidence of passage. Although fulmars were reported 'commonly seen out to sea' in the mid 1800s (Saxby), the first breeding record was not until 1878 on Foula when about 12 pairs were found nesting on the Kame on 4 June. This was only the second known breeding location of the species in Britain at the time, the other being at St Kilda. A stranded dead whale was said to have been the attraction to the island. In 1879 the number had increased to about 20 pairs with at least 16 pairs in 1887 and between 60 and 100 pairs in two groups about a mile apart in 1890. By 1898 there were 'multitudes' on The Kame, and on other cliffs on the island, the increase having been said as 'very remarkeable'. Since then the species has colonized almost every part of Shetland. SCR gave a whole Shetland count of 235 714 pairs in 1985–86, but this will have increased since then. Current estimates suggest at least 250 000 pairs, possibly as many as 300 000.

[Bulwer's petrel *Bulweria bulwerii*]
Sight records off Sumburgh Head on 7 September 1949 and off Fair Isle on 18 January 1952 were placed in brackets by V&V and are not considered acceptable by BOURC.

[*Soft-plumaged petrel (Madeiran/Cape Verde/soft-plumaged sp.) *Pterodroma madeira/P. feae/P. mollis*]
Vagrant, one record:
1996, approx. 130 km WNW of Unst at 60°56.56' N, 3°5.37' W, 25 June, Seabirds at Sea Team

Cory's shearwater *Calonectris diomedea*
Vagrant. Apart from 88 individuals seen off Fair Isle between 18 and 23 September 1965 (part of an exceptional movement of shearwaters at that time, *Scottish Birds* **4**: 218–222) there are only five other records:
1971, off Sumburgh Head, 22 June
1977, off Skerries, 24 September
1980, at sea, off Ramna Stacks, 20 June
1983, Banna Minn, Burra, dead on tideline, 20 November
1992, off Fair Isle, 9 October, possibly same 12 October

Great shearwater *Puffinus gravis*
Vagrant. V&V stated that a 'few' are seen from autumn until January every year from boats fishing in Shetland waters and Saxby apparently had one brought to him that had been shot at the *haaf* fishing in early June, although no further details are given. Off Fair Isle, three were seen in September and October 1936, and there was an exceptional single movement of about 180 individuals (seen both from the land and from the *Good Shepherd*) between 19 and 24 September 1965 (*Scottish Birds* **4**: 218–222), with about 12 records since then all between 22 August and 28 September. Away from Fair Isle there are only six records:
1965, at sea, between Scalloway and Foula, 13 April (*Scottish Birds*, **3**: 406)
1969, at sea, off Foula, 28 July
1983, at sea, 4.8–6.4 km off Fitful Head, 12 August
1990, at sea, off Foula, 22 August
1991, Wick of Breckon, Yell, long dead, 25 August
1995, at sea, 65 km NW of Ramna Stacks, 5 August

Sooty shearwater *Puffinus griseus*
Passage migrant in small numbers. Most records are in August to September with few seen in spring.

Manx shearwater *Puffinus puffinus*
Shetland names: *lyrie, leerie*
Uncommon summer visitor. Historically has bred at three colonies, on Foula, Yell and Fetlar, although is now probably restricted to one with less than 20 pairs breeding annually. Normally present from May to October, with some evidence of passage. Dunn (1837) said that 'considerable numbers' bred on Foula and Venables and Venables found quite an extensive colony on The Noup in 1938, although this was considerably smaller when they visited again in 1948.

Storm petrel *Hydrobates pelagicus*
Shetland names: *ala-mootie, alamutie*
Common summer visitor and breeding species, normally present from June to October.

Leach's petrel *Oceanodroma leucorrhoa*
Rare summer visitor, historically breeding in at least two known colonies, now only known to breed at one, where 20 occupied burrows were located in 1996. Very rare elsewhere with only about 60 confirmed records since the 1970s away from breeding colonies, usually on boat crossings, attracted to tape lures or associated with severe weather.

Wilson's petrel *Oceanites oceanicus*
Vagrant, one record:
1983, at sea, 50 km NW of Ramna Stacks (61°4′ N, 1°49′ W), 8 August

Gannet *Sula bassana*
Shetland name: *solan*
Locally abundant breeding resident, with the main colonies at Hermaness where 11 993 AONs were counted by SNH in 1994, and Noss where 7310 AONs were counted by SNH in 1994, and recently established colonies on Fair Isle where 1090 colonies were counted by FIBOT in 1996 and Foula where 600 pairs were counted in 1994.

Cormorant *Phalacrocorax carbo*
Shetland names: *skarf, lorin*
Common but local breeding resident. Bones of this species were found at the Jarlshof, Sumburgh settlement excavations dating from the ninth to tenth century. The breeding population appears to have undergone a slow decline over the last 25 years although counts during the last 5 years suggest this decline is slowing. The number of nests counted in 1996 at all colonies was 212 compared with 382 in 1987.

Shag *Phalacrocorax aristotelis*
Shetland names: *skarf*
Common breeding resident. The most recent estimate of the breeding population is from SCR where 6003 pairs were counted in 1985–86, a decline from the previous count in 1969–70 of 10 536 pairs.

Common bittern *Botaurus stellaris*
Vagrant. Eleven records, all of which were between October and May, and many involve dead or dying birds. This is one of the few species on the Shetland list with more than 10 records that has not been recorded on Fair Isle:
1843, Unst, spring (Edmondston 1844)
1871, Unst, March (Saxby)
1897, South Moustoft, Whiteness, moribund, late March (E&B)
1936, Skellister, found dead, February, specimen in the Anderson Institute (*Scottish Birds* 1937: 25–31)
1942, Mill Loch of Gorie, Bressay, later found dead, November (V&V)
1965, Papa, off Scalloway, 14–17 May, found dead on 19
1970, Loch of Tingwall, 27–28 March
1976, Lochend, 10 May
1978, Whalsay, male, found dead, 19 December
1985, Unifirth, 17 January, later found dead at Westerwick
1987, Clumlie, female, emaciated and captured, 19 October, later flown to England and released

Little bittern *Ixobrychus minutus*
Vagrant, four records.
1883, Whalsay, shot, mid August
1917, Burrafirth, Unst, adult female, killed, 29 May
1940, Fair Isle, shot, 10 April
1965, Scatness, female, 2–10 June
In addition, two or three others were reported to have been seen on Fair Isle in spring 1940, but these are regarded as unsubstantiated.

Night heron *Nycticorax nycticorax*
Vagrant, at least seven records:
1968, Loch of Spiggie, 26th May (not submitted to BBRC)
1981, Burrafirth, Unst, adult, 8–9 May, presumed same, Whalefirth, Yell, 1–3 June

1983, Norwick, Unst, adult, 25–28 April
1987, Seli Voe, Sandsting, first-summer, 18–30 April
　　　Loch of Brow, 27 April to 12 May, later found dead
　　　Haroldswick and Baltasound, Unst, possibly second-summer, 15–30 May,　　probably same Balta-
　　sound, adult, 31 May to 15 June
1993, North Roe, long dead adult, 20 June, body sent to NMS
1994, Fetlar, immature, 22 October

Little egret *Egretta garzetta*
Vagrant, six records:
1954, Loch of Spiggie, 15 May to 21 June
1961, Lochs of Spiggie and Brow, 11–13 June
1970, Easter, Sandness, dead, 2 May
1984, East Voe, Scalloway and Strand Loch, 1–2 June
1988, Loch of Spiggie, 6 April
1989, Lochs of Hillwell and Spiggie, 11–13 May

Great white egret *Egretta alba*
Vagrant, two records:
1985, Burrafirth, Unst, 5–6 June and Petta Water and Kirkabister, North Nesting, 27 June (given as different
　　birds in SBR 1985)
1994, Brow Marsh, 28 April
Another bird at Lochend on 26 March 1971, found dead the next day, was assigned to the south-west Asian
race *E. a. modesta* and was therefore presumed to be an escape from captivity. The specimen was retained in
the Shetland Museum.

Grey heron *Ardea cinerea*
Shetland names: *haigrie, hegri*
Regarded as a passage migrant with the majority of records in autumn, although recorded in all months of the
year. Apparently bred occasionally in the late 1800s and early 1900s.

Purple heron *Ardea purpurea*
Vagrant, five records:
1965, Fair Isle, immature, 17–22 June
1969, Fair Isle, immature, 2–31 May, trapped and had been ringed in The Netherlands in June 1967
1970, Fair Isle, second summer, 4–11 June
1977, Sinna Water, Northmavine, 14–15 May
1981, Weisdale, immature, 4 October; later found dead at Kergord, 17 October

Black stork *Ciconia nigra*
Vagrant, one record:
1977, Loch of Hillwell, 3–6 May

White stork *Ciconia ciconia*
Vagrant, five records:
pre 1844, Mainland, shot, sent to University of Edinburgh
1930, Fair Isle, 4–6 April
1975, Fair Isle, 25 May
1977, Turvister, Ollaberry, 14–15 May
1995, Fair Isle, adult, 28 April, presumed same, Northdale, Unst, 29 April to 11 May
It is assumed that the specimen shot on Mainland of Shetland last century and deposited at the University of
Edinburgh is the bird mentioned as being 'shot a few years ago' by Edmonston (1844).

Glossy ibis *Plegadis falcinellus*
Vagrant, two records:
1862, Stove, Haroldswick, shot, late October
1920, Unst, shot, 4 November

Spoonbill *Platalea leucorodia*
Vagrant, three records:
1871, Mid Yell Voe, two, 12 April
1975, Foula, three, flying west, 7 June

1992, North Roe, first winter female, moribund, 17 November, specimen now in NMS
Saxby stated that the species had several times been seen and killed previously but gave no details.

[Greater flamingo *Phoenicopterus ruber*]
Possible escape (Category D), one record:
1988, Virkie, adult, 27–31 May
This bird was of the nominate European race and was in immaculate condition with no apparent signs of recent captivity

Mute swan *Cygnus olor*
Formerly a rare migrant recorded mainly in April to June but with records in all months due to long-staying individuals. Failed introductions early in the century. One pair bred successfully on Loch of Tingwall in 1992, 1993 and 1994, with the progeny from 1992 breeding successfully on Loch of Asta in 1994 and subsequent progeny breeding elsewhere in the isles. The species is currently best regarded as an uncommon but increasing breeding resident.

Bewick's swan *Cygnus columbianus*
Vagrant, at least 15 records:
1910, Fair Isle, shot, 18 October
1911, Fair Isle, shot, 30 November
1922, Fair Isle, seven, 12 January
1925, Fair Isle, shot, 17 April
1964, Loch of Spiggie, two, 26 March to 23 April, possibly one of these, Loch of Hillwell, 5 May
1969, Skerries, two, 27 October
    Whalsay, from late October
1970, Whalsay, from 1969 to 5 January
    Whalsay, 1 October
1971, Fair Isle, two, 7–15 January
    Sandness, 22–24 March
1972, Loch of Spiggie, 19 January to at least end February, with seven there to 12 March
    Sand Water, two, 5–13 March
    Whalsay, two, at least 1–10 March
1985, Loch of Spiggie, adult, 6–28 April
1987, Loch of Spiggie and Scatness, adult, 14 November to 6 February 1988

Whooper swan *Cygnus cygnus*
Mainly a late autumn/winter migrant with numbers regularly exceeding more than 1% of the total international population of the species. A single injured pair bred irregularly between 1910 and 1918 and a 'wild' pair bred successfully in 1994–96. Injured birds often remain during the summer.

Bean goose *Anser fabalis fabalis*
Scarce migrant, recorded in small numbers in all months except June and August with most records in October. With recent developments in taxonomic study, research has indicated that two races of bean goose (the nominate form 'Taiga' bean goose *A. f. fabalis* and the smaller 'tundra' bean goose *A. f. rossicus*) may warrant specific status, and are likely to be split into two different species.

[*'Tundra' bean goose *Anser fabalis rossicus*]
Probably scarce migrant. Few subspecific identifications have been made on the previous bean goose records in Shetland, and the current status of this subspecies is under review.

Pink-footed goose *Anser brachyrhynchos*
Passage migrant in small numbers with most arrivals during September–October. One overwintered on Foula in 1955–56.

White-fronted goose *Anser albifrons*
Passage migrant and winter visitor in small numbers, with most arrivals during September and October. Birds of the Greenland race *A. a. flavirostris* are most regularly recorded.

Greylag goose *Anser anser*
Shetland names: *gro gøs*
Common passage migrant and winter visitor, with a small but increasing breeding population (currently less than 20 pairs), chiefly in the northern isles.

[**Bar-headed goose** *Anser indicus*]
Possible escape (category E), four records involving six individuals:
1967, Loch of Hillwell, pair, 24 May
1975, Eshaness, 20 June
1985, Scatness, two, 21 May
1990, Strand Loch, 9–18 May

Snow goose *Anser caerulescens*
Vagrant, six records:
1953, Delting area, blue phase, 20 September to February 1954 (*Scottish Naturalist* **66**: 13–14, photo)
1981, Lerwick, white phase, 13 October; presumed same, Levenwick, 10–20 November
1983, Foula, white phase, 29 June to 4 July
1984, Loch of Hillwell, white phase, 16–25 December
1988, Loch of Spiggie, blue phase, 21–26 October
1995, north over the Pool of Virkie, six, blue phase, 25 June

Canada goose *Branta canadensis*
Scarce migrant, recorded in all months because of long-staying birds, but with most arrivals in June.

Barnacle goose *Branta leucopsis*
Shetland name: *horra gøs*
Passage migrant, usually in small numbers although occasional influxes, mainly in September–October, occasional in winter and has overwintered. Large numbers were present in 1996 with approx. 600 on Fair Isle on 26 September and 520 at Scatness on the 16 October.

Brent goose *Branta bernicla*
Scarce migrant, recorded in all months but with most records in September to November. Two races occur in Shetland, the pale-bellied race *B. b. hrota* which is the more common, and the dark-bellied race *B. b. bernicla*.

[**Red-breasted goose** *Branta ruficollis*]
A record of a bird shot at Spiggie in about 1880 was placed in brackets by E&B and V&V as the specimen was not preserved. It seems unlikely that such a distinctive species could be misidentified but as the record is not acceptable to BOURC this species cannot be admitted to the Shetland list.

Shelduck *Tadorna tadorna*
Breeding resident in small numbers with some evidence of passage. The breeding population has declined during recent years.

[**Wood duck** *Aix sponsa*]
Possible escape (category E), two records:
1977, Sae Water, Laxo, male, shot, 30 October
1979, Fair Isle, male, shot, 27 November

[**Mandarin** *Aix galericulata*]
Vagrant or possible escape (category C), three records:
1942, Foula, male, 15–16 June
1985, Norwick, two males, 14 April
1989, Foula, pair, late May to early July
Included in category C of the British list as there is a feral breeding population, mainly in south-east England although there are small colonies in Scotland.

Wigeon *Anas penelope*
Regular passage migrant and winter visitor with a small number of pairs breeding successfully most years.

American wigeon *Anas americana*
Vagrant, 11 records:
1948, two, no details (B&J)
1966, Loch of Mails, Sumburgh, female, shot, 7 October; had been ringed in New Brunswick, Canada on 6 August 1966 (*British Birds* **60**: 314)
1967, Unst, pair, 22–23 May (*British Birds* **61**: 336)
1968, Norwick, Unst, pair, 20 January to 3 February (*British Birds* **62**: 464)
1973, Unst, male, 16–23 May
1983, Dam Loch, Unst, pair, 4 June

1986, Fair Isle, first-winter male, 21 September to 3 October, had been ringed as a duckling 4 weeks earlier in
    New Brunswick, Canada
1989, Melby and Loch of Collaster, two males, 17 January to 19 February
1992, Sae Water, Laxo, male, 9–12 June
1993, Gruiting, Fetlar, male, 13–14 February
1996, Gards Loch, Scatness, adult male, 1–10 October

Gadwall *Anas strepera*
Scarce migrant, recorded all months with most records in April and May.

[**Baikal teal** *Anas formosa*]
One record originally accepted by BOURC but now no longer considered acceptable:
1954, Hesti Geo, Fair Isle, juvenile female with two female teal, 24 September to 7 October

Teal *Anas crecca*
Regular passage migrant and winter visitor with a few pairs breeding successfully most years. Most records
are in late autumn/winter.

[***Green-winged teal** *Anas crecca carolinensis*]
Vagrant, at least 25 records, all males:
1970, Sinna Water, Northmavine, 5 April
1972, Lochs of Spiggie and Hillwell, 25 February to 23 March
    Papa Stour, 10 March
    Scatness, 11 October
1975, Unifirth, 15 November to 28 February 1976
1978, Scatness, 29 March to 17 April
    Voe, 13–15 May
1979, Hillswick, 25 May
1981, Sand Water, 14 March to 4 April, possibly same as Fetlar, male, 5 April
1983, Sand Water, 5 April to 11 May
1984, Sand Water, 20 March
1986, Loch of Hillwell, 16 February to 28 March
1987, Loch of Tingwall, 6–15 December
1989, Dalsetter, Boddam, 30 May
1990, Trondra, 12–17 March
    Scatness, 16 December to at least 3 March 1991
1991, Dale, 20 February
    Burn of Strand, 14 April
    Scatness, 20 November to at least 7 April 1992
1992, Burn of Kergord, 10 April, possibly same as above
    Scatness, 26 December to at least 9 March 1993
1993, Scatness, 9 November to at least 16 April 1994
1994, Scatness, 15 October to at least 16 May 1995
1995, Loch of Hillwell, 4 June
    Scatness, 15 November to at least 14 April 1996

Mallard *Anas platyrhynchos*
Shetland names: *stock deuk*
Common breeding resident, passage migrant and winter visitor.

American black duck *Anas rubripes*
Vagrant, one record:
1990, Loch of Spiggie, male, 4 February to 29 April

Pintail *Anas acuta*
Uncommon passage migrant, with most records in April to June and September although recorded in all
months. Has bred.

Garganey *Anas querquedula*
Scarce migrant, usually recorded in spring with most records in May. Rare in autumn.

Blue-winged teal *Anas discors*
Vagrant, at least six records:
1979, Scatness, pair, 8–12 September
1980, Skerries, female/immature, 29 September
1982, Skerries, probably immature male, 12–20 September
1983, Uyeasound, possibly immature male, 1–23 September
1995, Fetlar, first-winter male, 26 October, possibly same as Loch of Tingwall bird below
     Urafirth, first-winter male, 30 October to 3 November
     Loch of Tingwall, first-winter male, 2 November, same as bird below
     Grunna Water/Loch of Benston, first-winter male, 3–11 November

Shoveler *Anas clypeata*
Uncommon passage migrant, recorded in all months, but mainly in April to May and in August. Probably breeds most years.

Pochard *Aythya ferina*
Passage migrant and winter visitor, with most records in autumn.

Ring-necked duck *Aythya collaris*
Vagrant, at least 13 records:
1978, Loch of Snarravoe, male, 13–18 May
      Fair Isle, first-year male, 9–16 October
1979, Scatness area, immature male, 8 December to 7 January 1980
1980, lochs of Tingwall and Asta, male, 23 March to 16 May; second male present on 27–30 April
1981, Loch of Snarravoe, male, 12 February and 2 March; presumed same, Loch of Papil, Cullivoe, 13
      March, then Lochs of Tingwall and Asta and occasionally East Voe, Scalloway, 23–29 May, 9 and 19
      June
      Loch of Brow, immature male, 1 November to 6 December
1982, Loch of Brow, female, 21–25 October
1983, Loch of Norby, Sandness, male, 26 September to 1 November
1984, Loch of Norby, Sandness, male, 20 November into 1985; presumed same as 1983 individual
1985, Loch of Norby, Sandness, male, 13 March to 2 November; presumed same as 1983–84 individual
1986, Loch of Tingwall, male, 7 June
1988, Easter Loch, first-winter female, 2–6 November
1989, Loch of Collaster, female, 22 January to 13 February

Tufted duck *Aythya fuligula*
Mainly a regular passage migrant and winter visitor with a small number breeding successfully most years.

Scaup *Aythya marila*
Passage migrant and winter visitor with most records in late autumn/early winter. A few pairs usually linger into late spring and occasional non-breeding birds summer.

Lesser scaup *Athya affinis*
Vagrant, one record:
1993, Loch of Spiggie, first winter/summer male, 9–13 May

Eider *Somateria mollissima*
Shetland name: *dunter*
Common breeding resident. The population has declined significantly during recent years with counts of moult flocks in autumn (allowing for birds at Fair Isle and Foula and for scattered birds outwith the areas surveyed) indicating a current population of around 7000 birds, compared to 12 000 in 1984 and 16 500 in 1977.

King eider *Somateria spectabilis*
Rare migrant with at least 144 records. Most records are in October to March although individuals have been recorded in all months of the year. The majority of records are from the North Yell, Sumburgh, Tresta and Burra areas.

Steller's eider *Polysticta stelleri*
Vagrant, one record:
1971, Fair Isle, female, 9 May to 13 June
The left wing only of an adult male was also found on Tresta beach, Fetlar on 31 March 1996. A record published in the 1986 SBR was not accepted by BBRC.

Harlequin duck *Histrionicus histrionicus*
Vagrant, two records:
1965, Fair Isle, pair, 11 January to 2 February (*Scottish Birds* **4**: 83–86)
1987, Sullom Voe, first-winter male, 16 January to 25 February

Long-tailed duck *Clangula hyemalis*
Shetland names: *kallu, calloo*
Common winter visitor with a few non-breeding birds usually remaining throughout the summer. The current wintering population is estimated to be 3000 birds.

Common scoter *Melanitta nigra*
Passage migrant and winter visitor in small numbers, with most records in late winter/early spring. A small breeding population of up to four pairs are successful most years.

Surf scoter *Melanitta perspicillata*
Vagrant, at least seven records:
1975, Ronas Voe, first-winter male, 20–25 May
1986, Haroldswick and Norwick, male, 1–4 October
1987, Aith Voe, Bressay, first-winter male, 23 January to 27 May; presumed same Cat Firth, 29 May
1989, Noss Sound, first-summer male, 4–17 June
        off Trebister Ness, Gulberwick, pair, 24–25 August
1990, Voe of Cullingsburgh, Bressay, male, 31 May to 7 June; presumed same, Noss, 15 and 28 August
1992, off Houbie, Fetlar, first-summer male, 29 May to 2 July, and again on 12 August
In addition, four dated records exist from Fair Isle, one washed ashore in the winter of 1934, one at North Haven on 8 February 1936, an adult male offshore on 1 October 1936, and two in the North Haven in December 1940. Neither Williamson or Davis considered these to be acceptable records however (Dymond).

Velvet scoter *Melanitta fusca*
Uncommon late autumn and winter visitor.

[Barrow's goldeneye *Bucephala islandica*]
A record of two males shot in Scalloway in 1913 (*British Birds* **14**: 21–22) is not considered acceptable by BOURC.

Goldeneye *Bucephala clangula*
Winter visitor and passage migrant with a few non-breeding birds occurring throughout the summer.

[Hooded merganser *Lophdytes cucullatus*]
An adult male in Wick Museum had apparently been shot in Whalefirth, Yell in July 1884 (*Scottish Naturalist* 1951: 196–197). This record is not considered acceptable by BOURC.

Smew *Mergus albellus*
Vagrant with at least 43 records, all occurring between October and April.

Red-breasted merganser *Mergus serrator*
Shetland name: *herald deuk*
Winter visitor, passage migrant and breeding resident in small numbers.

Goosander *Mergus merganser*
Uncommon passage migrant and winter visitor, although rarely recorded overwintering. Recorded in all months with most records in December and January.

[Ruddy duck *Oxyura jamaciensis*]
Vagrant or possible escape (category C), 10 records involving at least 14 individuals, all but two in May:
1974, Norwick, male, 16 May

1986, lochs of Hillwell and Clumlie, female, 21–22 May
1987, Loch of Hillwell, male, 3–5 May
1989, lochs of Brow and Spiggie, two males and one female, 13–18 May, one male remaining to 21 May; presumed one of same, Loch of Tingwall, male, 19–27 May
1990, Loch of Norby, two males, 13 May
1991, Scatness, male, 1–3 May
1992, Loch of Hillwell, male, 18 May with presumed same on Loch of Spiggie, 26–27 May
1994, Loch of Hillwell, female/immature male, 11–20 November
1995, Funzie, Fetlar, male, 6–10 May
1996, Loch of Asta, Tingwall, two females, 1 June

Honey buzzard *Pernis apivorus*
Rare migrant with at least 80 records, all but one occurring between May and September (a late individual was on Fair Isle in mid-October). The majority of records are between late May and July.

Black kite *Milvus migrans*
Vagrant, two records:
1966, Sumburgh, 27 May to 2 June (*British Birds* **60**: 315)
1975, Unst, 11 June

Red kite *Milvus milvus*
Vagrant, at least 13 records:
1979, Fair Isle, 15 January
1983, Foula, 28 January to 1 February
1984, Quendale area, 13–19 October, presumed same as Fair Isle, 20–21 October
1988, Virkie, 14 February
    Fair Isle, 26 March to 10 April
    Quendale and Sumburgh area, 27–31 March
    Muckle Roe, 27 March
1991, North Unst, 19–27 March, presumed same, Weisdale 5 April, Quarff 6 April, presumed same as Fair Isle, record below
    Fair Isle, 13–17 April
1992, Tresta, 26–27 April and presumed same Cunningsburgh, 29, Tingwall Airport 2 May and Baltasound and Snarravoe, Unst, 5 May
1993, Effirth, Bixter, 21 August
    Fair Isle, 4–14 April
1996, Kergord, 22–23 March
    Skerries, 16–18 September, presumably same Kergord/Weisdale 30 September to 8 October

White-tailed eagle *Haliaeetus albicilla*
Shetland name: *erne*
Former rare breeding resident, at least in the 1800s and early 1900s with the last known breeding record in 1910. Currently a vagrant with 14 records (including wing-tagged birds released from Rum), assuming that all the 1983–84 records except the last refer to two individuals. A reintroduction scheme was initiated on Fair Isle in 1968 when four young birds were released there in September and October. One was thought to have left the island shortly after release, two left the following year and the remaining bird was found heavily fulmar-oiled and was thought to have died. No further reintroductions have since been attempted.
1935, Fair Isle, 18 September (Dymond)
1949, Hermaness, 11 June (V&V), possibly same as Fair Isle record below
        Fair Isle, 19 June (Dymond)
1981, Fair Isle, 6–7 April
        Vidlin area, immature, 5 December into 1982, regarded as originating from Rum
1982, Vidlin area, from 1981 to 7 February, presumed same, Unst 4 April, Yell 11 April and Fetlar 27 May (other unconfirmed reports from these islands in February and March)
1983, Skellister, 18 April, presumed same, north Unst, wing-tagged, 19 April to 1 May, and Gloup, Yell, 17 June
    Lunning, 4 November, presumed same, Spiggie, 23 November
    Fitful Head, two, unmarked male and wing-tagged female, from 15 December into 1984, presumably same as birds recorded earlier in year

1984, Fitful Head, two, from 1983 to 11 April, presumed same two, Trondra, 25 March and Scalloway, 26 March, and presumed same tagged female, Noss Hill, Dunrossness, 28 August and 14–21 October
 Hermaness and west Yell, second-summer female, 23–24 March
 Fair Isle, 2 April
 Fair Isle, 3 November (wing-tagged)
1986, Petta Dale, 28 February, presumed same there 1 March and Unst, 19 March to 10 April (unmarked)
 Fair Isle, 16 November
1988, Baltasound, late April, presumed same, Windhouse, Yell, 24 May
1989, Haroldswick, immature, 30 March
1994, Fair Isle, flying north, (wing-tagged), 27 April, same as individual below
 Sumburgh Head, first-summer (wing-tagged), 27 April
 Sobul, Unst, 30 April

Marsh harrier *Circus aeruginosus*
Rare migrant, at least 52 records with most in spring between April to June and by far the majority in May. Few autumn records.

Hen harrier *Circus cyaneus*
Scarce but annual migrant, recorded in all months with the majority in September and October.

Pallid harrier *Circus macrourus*
Vagrant, two records:
1931, Fair Isle, immature male, shot, 24 April to 8 May, specimen in British Museum
1993, Exnaboe/Quendale area, juvenile, 15–16 September
An adult male seen by G. Stout on Fair Isle for about a week from 6 May 1942 has not received general acceptance (Dymond).

[Montagu's harrier *Circus pygargus*]
Vagrant, three records:
1954, Spiggie, male, 5 May (*Scottish Naturalist* **68**: 4)
1982, Sumburgh, male, 6 May
1992, Fair Isle, juvenile (probably female), 31 August to 1 September
A male was seen by G. Stout on Fair Isle in May 1937, but details are lacking and the record is considered doubtful (Dymond).

Montagu's/pallid harrier
Birds thought to have been one or other of these species have been recorded on two occasions:
1949, Fair Isle, 'ring-tail', 20 October (Dymond)
1964, Quarsdale, juvenile, 7 August (*Scottish Birds* **3**: 364–365)

Goshawk *Accipter gentilis*
Vagrant, twelve records (a record in the 1992 SBR was subsequently rejected):
1859, Balta, April
1860, Skaw, Unst, female, shot, winter
1962, Fair Isle, 16–24 November
1967, Fair Isle, 21 May
1969, Kergord, 23 and 26 February
1971, Fair Isle, 24 November to 5 January 1972
1976, Kergord, 7–10 January
 Fair Isle, 6 May
 Saxa Vord, fulmar-oiled, 7 May, later died
1977, Dales Voe, Tingwall, 14 October
1991, East Burra, juvenile male, 31 October to 5 November
1996, Plantation/Ward Hill, Fair Isle, first-year male, trapped, 20 April, presumed same 27 April

Sparrowhawk *Accipter nisus*
Uncommon migrant, recorded in all months but mainly in April to May and October to November, with small numbers overwintering in most years. Breeding records from the last century are dubious.

Buzzard *Buteo buteo*
Rare but nearly annual migrant, recorded in all months although April is the month with the most records. A few have overwintered.

Rough-legged buzzard *Buteo lagopus*
Rare migrant with at least 80 records, almost annual in recent years. Recorded in all months except June with the majority in October and November. Few spring records although some birds have overwintered.

Golden eagle *Aquila chrysaetos*
Vagrant, ten records:
1961, Fair Isle, immature, 7–8 April
1963, Yell, immature, found dead, 27 November (FIBO BUL 5.4: 150)
1965, Unst, 8–14 May (FIBO BUL 5.6: 220)
1976, Foula, 14–21 November
1977, Gunnister, 6 and 12–13 March
1979, Noss, immature, at least 28–31 December
1981, Fetlar, immature, 17 April to 5 May, presumed same, Gloup, Yell, 17 May
1982, Unst, immature, 10 March
    Walls, 17 May
    Fetlar, immature, 1–18 June
In addition, a single flight feather in near perfect condition from an adult was found at the face of the Quendale Dunes on 30 January 1993. Unfortunately the rest of the bird was never seen.

Osprey *Pandion haliaetus*
Scarce migrant, usually recorded annually with the majority of records in spring.

Lesser kestrel *Falco naumanni*
Vagrant, one record:
1987, The Houll, Fair Isle, adult male, 23 June

Kestrel *Falco tinnunculus*
Regular spring and autumn migrant in small numbers with occasional birds overwintering and summering. There are breeding records from the last century and single pairs bred in 1905 and 1992.

American kestrel *Falco sparverius*
Vagrant, one record:
1976, Malcolm's Head/Setter area, Fair Isle, adult male, 25–27 May

Red-footed falcon *Falco vespertinus*
Vagrant, at least 33 records, all in late May/June except for singles in August and October. Individuals have occasionally remained throughout the summer.

Merlin *Falco columbarius*
Shetland names: *peerie hawk, smirl, maalin*
Breeding resident and passage migrant, although most locally bred birds are thought to leave Shetland in the winter. The current breeding population is estimated at 25–30 pairs (RSPB 1993).

Hobby *Falco subbuteo*
Vagrant. At least 45 records, almost all between 1 May and 28 July, with only nine autumn records between late August and early October.

[**Eleonora's falcon** *Falco eleonorae*]
The record in SBR 1985 was not accepted by BBRC.

[**Lanner falcon** *Falco biarmicus*]
A falconer's bird, complete with bells and jesses, was on Fair Isle on 7–15 June 1968, with probably the same bird picked up injured at Gruting on 9 June 1969 (it also had bells and jesses), which later died. The record in SBR 1981 was not submitted to BBRC.

[**Saker falcon** *Falco cherrug*]
Possible escape (category D), three records, one at Noness on 15–17 June 1979 was unsupported by a description:
1976, Skerries, 1–5 October
1977, Fetlar, 27–29 May
1986, Fair Isle, 23 October to 3 December

Gyr falcon *Falco rusticolus*
Vagrant, at least 32 records this century but apparently a regular winter visitor last century. All records are in October to April with almost half of these in April. Dark and light morph individuals have occurred about equally. In addition a bird captured aboard a fishing boat off the Hebrides was released at Gott on 2 March 1973, and was seen in that area on 11 March, and later at Voe on 18 March. Another was caught aboard a trawler in Shetland waters in February 1979.

Peregrine *Falco peregrinus*
Breeding resident and uncommon passage migrant in small numbers. Formerly several pairs bred annually but in recent years the number has declined to one to two pairs with none during 1991–92.

*Red grouse *Lagopus lagopus scoticus*
Widespread but uncommon introduced breeding resident, mainly in Central and South Mainland although a few are still present on Yell. Currently absent from all other islands. V & V reported that the species had been introduced several times in Shetland and was apparently 'abundant' in 1806, although this latter statement was anecdotal. Introductions were reported by V & V in the late 1800s and early 1900s on Yell (*c.* 40 birds), north-east Mainland (at least 600 birds which apparently spread to South Mainland), Vaila (a few in the early 1900s) and possibly Unst (small numbers seen there in 1885 and 1902), with the species also recorded on Bressay (a nest found in 1948) and Whalsay (one seen in about 1903). Since the mid-1900s the species has declined, probably through shooting, to its current level although it probably breeds successfully most years.

[Black grouse *Lyrurus tetrix*]
A bone of this species was found in the midden of House 2 at the Jarlshof excavations at Sumburgh dating from the ninth to tenth century.

[Grey partridge *Perdix perdix*]
Formerly introduced resident, now extinct. Small numbers were released at Delting in 1742 ('four brace', *Scottish Naturalist* 1937: 25–31) and Windhouse and Reafirth, Yell in 1882 for shooting, but their fate after this is unknown. In addition in one summer between 1906 and 1912 one was reported seen occasionally near the croft at Efrigarth, Bridge of Walls, with an adult and several eggs discovered when a crop was being cut. One was flushed between Scalloway and the south end of the Tingwall valley in an autumn in the late 1930s and occasional birds were seen 'in Mainland' during the 1930s (V & V).

Quail *Coturnix coturnix*
Uncommon passage migrant and currently a very rare breeding summer visitor. Formerly a regular breeding visitor until at least the 1960s but loss of suitable habitat has meant few records since.

[Pheasant *Phasianus colchicus*]
Formerly introduced resident, now extinct. At least five introductions of small numbers were reported from the early 1900s by V & V with four different locations involved. A 'few' were released on Vaila in the early 1900s with some remaining there and moving to the Walls area with small numbers surviving for a few years. Two males and six females were released at Brough Lodge on Fetlar in 1935 with the last remaining female shot in 1937. At Kergord in Central Mainland, small numbers were hatched from eggs a few years before 1914, but they were all shot during the First World War, a further small number were hatched from eggs there in about 1920 with most of these killed by vermin, and a small number of adults were released there in the mid-1920s, breeding successfully until the Second World War when poaching and machine-gun practice apparently killed most of them although one was seen at Sandwick sometime shortly after this date. A pair released at Burrastow in 1950 bred successfully in the following two years, although most were killed by 1953. Since then there have been occasional introductions of small numbers on Unst and Central Mainland, and although some of these have survived for a number of years they probably became extinct as a breeding species in the early 1980s with occasional birds being reported in Central Mainland until the late 1980s.

Water rail *Rallus aquaticus*
Irregular passage migrant and winter visitor in small numbers, with most records in autumn.

Spotted crake *Porzana porzana*
Rare migrant although formerly a breeding summer visitor in small numbers. Most records are in May and June and October and November.

Sora *Porzana carolina*
Vagrant, one record:
1982, Foula, adult, 30 October

Little crake *Porzana parva*
Vagrant, two records:
1959, Uyeasound, male, found dead, April, specimen in NMS (*British Birds* **58**: 417)
1970, Fair Isle, male, 11 May, found predated by a cat next day

Baillon's crake *Porzana pusilla*
Vagrant, two records, the record published in SBR 1982 was not accepted by BBRC:
1929, Fair Isle, female, shot, 11 May
1991, Fair Isle, juvenile, 28 September to 2 October when found dead, specimen in possession of D. Suddaby, Shetland

Corncrake *Crex crex*
Currently a rare passage migrant with a few records into early summer. Formerly a common breeding species until at least 1974. Loss of suitable habitat has meant the only breeding records since were single pairs in 1978, 1985 and 1986 with none recorded thereafter although it has been suspected in some years.

Moorhen *Gallinula chloropus*
Breeding resident and passage migrant in small numbers, first recorded breeding in 1890. The current breeding population of one to two pairs is not successful every year.

Coot *Fulica atra*
Passage migrant and winter visitor in small numbers although an influx of 200–300 was recorded in 1976. Formerly a regular breeding resident in small numbers until at least the 1960s, although small numbers occasionally still breed on Mainland.

Common crane *Grus grus*
Vagrant, at least 35 records. The majority of records are in late April to May and often involve groups of up to four birds. Only three singles have been recorded in autumn, one each in August, September and October.

Sandhill crane *Grus canadensis*
Vagrant, two records:
1981, Fair Isle, probably first-summer, 26–27 April
1991, Exnaboe and Sumburgh, first-summer, 17–26 September

Great bustard *Otis tarda*
Vagrant, two records:
1936, Hillswick, female, shot, 19 May (*Scottish Naturalist* 1937: 25–31)
1970, Fair Isle, female, 11 January, captured and taken into care 16 January, released 24 February but unable to fend for itself so recaptured 5 March and taken back into care. On 6 April flown south to join a reintroduction scheme for the species in Wiltshire

Little bustard *Tetrax tetrax*
Vagrant, one record:
1994, Fair Isle, male, 5–6 November

Oystercatcher *Haemotopus ostralegus*
Shetland names: *shalder, sjalder*
Common breeding summer visitor and passage migrant with a few birds overwintering. The most recent estimate of the breeding population (based on estimates during sample surveys) is about 3700 pairs (RSPB 1993).

Black-winged stilt *Himantopus himantopus*
Vagrant, two records:
c. 1840, Unst? (Saxby)
1934, Whalsay, September (V&V)
The nineteenth century record was apparently amongst golden plover, while the 1934 record is not included in Thom.

Avocet *Recurvirostra avosetta*
Vagrant, at least 15 individuals:
1871, Uyeasound, 4 March (Saxby)
1936, Whalsay, no date (V&V)

1947, Fair Isle, shot, 8 May (Dymond), specimen in Anderson High School, Lerwick
1952, Virkie, 12–18 May (V&V)
   Whalsay, 19 September
1964, Cullivoe, Yell, two, 22–25 March, one found dead on 28 March (FIBO BUL 5.5: 185)
   Unst, 26–29 March, possibly same as above
   Untabrake, Scalloway, 30 March, possibly same as above
   Unst, 28 May
1966, Whalsay, two, 16 May
1967, Kirkhouse Loch, Vidlin, 24 October
1974, Virkie, 27–28 April
1980, Virkie, 30 March to 2 April
1981, Loch of Snarravoe, Unst, 21 April
1992, Whalsay, 30 September, presumed same Skerries, 3 October
Saxby also refers to another old record, without date or locality.

Stone curlew *Burhinus oedicnemus*
Vagrant, 10 records:
1913, Fair Isle, shot by Eagle Clarke, 7 June
1930, Fair Isle, 'autumn' (Dymond)
1955, Loch of Spiggie area, 2 June (FIBO BUL 3.1: 23–24)
1963, Fair Isle, 23–25 May
1964, Fair Isle, 18–19 May
1974, Fair Isle, 23 May
1981, Scalloway, found injured, 6 December, later died
1985, Loch of Spiggie, 18 May
1992, Fair Isle, 9–16 June
1995, Fair Isle, 14 May

Collared pratincole *Glareola pratincola*
Vagrant, five records:
1812, Baltasound, Unst, shot, 16 August (Saxby) (September E&B)
1934, Fair Isle, 'May', seen by G. Stout (Dymond)
1935, Fair Isle, 'May' (Dymond)
1971, Leogh, Fair Isle, 2 June
1974, Unst, 2 July

Black-winged pratincole *Glareola nordmanni*
Vagrant, one record:
1927, Fair Isle, shot by J.H. Stenhouse, 18–19 May

[Pratincole sp.]
1987, Uyeasound, Unst, 25 May

Little ringed plover *Charadrius dubius*
Vagrant, eight records:
1965, Gully, Fair Isle, trapped, 4–7 September (*Scottish Birds* **4**: 224–225)
   Whalsay, first-winter, 17–19 September
1969, Muckle Uri Geo, Fair Isle, 20 July
1976, Fetlar, 19 May
1979, near South Harbour, Fair Isle, 20 May
1983, Virkie, 2 May
1989, Melby, juvenile, 6 September
1991, Sand Water, adult, 6 June

Ringed plover *Charadrius hiaticula*
Shetland names: *sandy loo, sandilu*
Common breeding summer visitor and passage migrant with a few birds overwintering. A few migrants in late May and early June have been seen showing characters of the high-arctic race *C. h. tundrae*. The most recent estimate of the breeding population (based on estimates during sample surveys) is about 800–1000 pairs (RSPB 1993).

Kentish plover *Charadrius alexandrinus*
Vagrant, one record:
1949, Skaddan, Fair Isle, male, 14 May

Killdeer *Charadrius vociferus*
Vagrant, one record, the record in SBR 1970 was not submitted to BBRC:
1983, Loch of Hillwell area, 13–20 March

Caspian plover *Charadrius asiaticus*
Vagrant, one record:
1996, Skelberry, Durossness, female, 3–4 June

Dotterel *Eudromia morinellus*
Rare migrant with at least 83 records involving at least 134 individuals. Spring records all fall between late April to mid July and autumn records between early August to October.

American golden plover *Pluvialis dominica*
Vagrant, fifteen records:
1956, Vaasetter, Fair Isle, adult, 14–15 September
1983, Rippack, Fair Isle, adult, 28–29 August
1984, Tarryfield, Fair Isle, juvenile, 17 October
1985, Rippack, Fair Isle, juvenile, 17–20 September
1987, Brecks o' Busta, Fair Isle, adult, 28 September to 11 October
1988, North Light, Fair Isle, juvenile, 21 September
    Brecks o' Busta, Fair Isle, different juvenile, 22 September
1989, Baltasound, adult, 24–25 September
    Ringasta, Dunrossness, adult, 19 October
1990, Fetlar, first-summer, 7–14 May
    Foula, adult, 1–2 September
    Scatness, juvenile, 20 September
1991, Kennaby, Fair Isle, adult, 15 August
    Virkie, juvenile, 9–14 October, and at Sumburgh Farm on 19 and Ringasta on 20 and 27 October
    Spiggie and Ringasta area, juvenile, 20 October to 3 November

Pacific golden plover *Pluvilias fulva*
Vagrant, two records:
1988, Uyeasound, adult, 6–13 November
1992, Fair Isle, adult, 2–3 July

Golden plover *Pluvialis apricaria*
Shetland names: *lu, plivver*
Common breeding summer visitor, passage migrant and winter visitor. The most recent estimate of the breeding population (based on estimates during sample surveys) is about 2000 pairs (RSPB 1993).

Grey plover *Pluvialis squatarola*
Scarce passage migrant, recorded in all months but mainly in September and October.

Lapwing *Vanellus vanellus*
Shetland name: *tieve's nacket*
Common summer visitor and breeding resident, passage migrant and winter visitor. The most recent estimate of the breeding population (based on estimates during sample surveys) is about 2200 pairs (RSPB 1993).

Great knot *Calidris tenuirostris*
Vagrant, one record:
1989, Scatness and Pool of Virkie, adult, 15 September

Knot *Calidris canutus*
Shetland name: *ebb cock*
Chiefly a passage migrant with a small overwintering population.

Sanderling *Calidris alba*
Passage migrant with most records in autumn and occasional non-breeding birds remaining throughout the summer.

Semipalmated sandpiper *Calidris pusilla*
Vagrant, two records:
1992, Field, Fair Isle, 13–15 May
1996, Pool of Virkie, juvenile, 11–22 September

Western sandpiper *Calidris mauri*
Vagrant, two records:
1956, Kirki Geo, Fair Isle, trapped, 27 May to 3 June
1988, Pool of Virkie, juvenile, 25 September

Red-necked stint *Calidris ruficollis*
Vagrant, one record:
1994, Fair Isle, juvenile, found freshly dead, 31 August, skin now in NMS

Little stint *Calidris minuta*
Uncommon passage migrant, recorded in May to October but mainly in late August to early October.

Temminck's stint *Calidris temminckii*
Rare migrant recorded in April to June and August to November. At least 58 records.

Least sandpiper *Calidris minutilla*
Vagrant, one record:
1955, Pool of Virkie, shot, 14 August, skin now in NMS (*Scottish Naturalist* 1957: 170)

White-rumped sandpiper *Calidris fuscicollis*
Vagrant, five records:
1972, Landberg, Fair Isle, 28 November to 2 December
1973, Grutness, 7–11 November
1980, Leestat, Fair Isle, 7–8 October
1981, Virkie, adult, 25–30 August
1993, Virkie, adult, 31 July to 2 August

Baird's sandpiper *Calidris bairdii*
Vagrant, five records:
1982, Sprittery Hole, Fair Isle, juvenile, 17–21 September
1989, Haroldswick, Unst, juvenile, 6–7 September, presumed same Pool of Virkie, 8–11 September
1991, North Haven/Buness, Fair Isle, juvenile, 5–16 September
1993, Scatness, juvenile, 19–22 September
1996, Malcolm's Head/Easter Lother Water, Fair Isle, juvenile, 1–2 October

Pectoral sandpiper *Calidris melanotos*
Rare migrant, at least 44 records. The majority of records are in September with extreme autumn dates of 4 August and the 16 October. The seven spring records were in mid May to 1 July.

Sharp-tailed sandpiper *Calidris acuminata*
Vagrant, one record:
1993, Scatness, adult, 13–15 September

Curlew sandpiper *Calidris ferruginea*
Scarce passage migrant, recorded from May to June and August to October with a single November record on Fair Isle on 3–9 1963. Occasional influxes of up to 50 individuals occur in autumn.

Purple sandpiper *Calidris maritima*
Shetland name: *ebb-sleeper*
Chiefly a winter visitor and passage migrant, although recorded during all months of the year.

Dunlin *Calidris alpina*
Shetland name: *plovers page, ebb-cock*
Common breeding summer visitor, passage migrant and winter visitor. The most recent estimate of the breeding population (based on estimates during sample surveys) is about 1700 pairs (RSPB 1993).

Broad-billed sandpiper *Limicola falcinellus*
Vagrant, four records:
1976, Whalsay, 3 November
1985, Virkie, 20–24 May
1987, Urafirth, 26 May
1988, Whalsay, 18–22 May

Stilt sandpiper *Micropalama himantopus*
Vagrant, one record.
1976, Scatness, 11–18 September

Buff-breasted sandpiper *Tryngites subruficollis*
Vagrant, 12 records:
1958, Buness, Fair Isle, 18 September
1972, Ward Hill, Fair Isle, trapped, 17–19 September
1973, Meoness, Fair Isle, 21 September
1974, Meoness, Fair Isle, 8 September
1975, Sumburgh, juvenile, 30 September
1977, Fair Isle, 11–12 September
1978, Breibister, Walls, 28 May
1980, Fair Isle, 17–20 September
1982, Skerries, juvenile, 17 September
1985, Scatness, juvenile, 23–24 September
1991, Fair Isle, juvenile, 26–28 September
1996, Twatt/Bixter area, juvenile, 12–22 September

Upland sandpiper *Bartramia longicauda*
Vagrant, four records:
1970, Fair Isle, 5 October
1975, Fair Isle, 25 September
1993, Foula, juvenile, 22 September to 6 October, found dead (not fresh) on 18 November
1996, Foula, 2–15 September

Ruff *Philomachus pugnax*
Irregular passage migrant with the majority of records in autumn. Occasional influxes of up to 60 individuls occur in autumn.

Jack snipe *Lymnocryptes minimus*
Passage migrant and winter visitor in small numbers.

Snipe *Gallinago gallinago*
Shetland names: *snippick, snippek*
Common breeding summer visitor, passage migrant and winter visitor. The most recent estimate of the breeding population (based on estimates during sample surveys) is about 4000 pairs (RSPB 1993).

Great snipe *Gallinago media*
Vagrant, at least 29 records since 1960 and at least a further 17 before then although some of these may be suspect. The majority of records are in September, particularly in the first few days of the month, with extreme dates in autumn of 26 August and 6 December. In spring there is a single record from March (found dead) and three records from the first half of May. Saxby shot 'large snipe' but only identified them retrospectively. E&B detail much circumstantial evidence but give just one record.

Long-billed dowitcher *Limnodromus scolopaceus*
Vagrant: five records:
1983, Easter Lother Water, Fair Isle, juvenile, 9–14 October
1988, Fetlar, juvenile, 18 October, presumed same Baltasound, Unst 6 December, remaining to 29 April 1989
1990, Golden Water, Fair Isle, juvenile, 14–15 September

1995, Loch of Houlland, South Nesting, 3–4 November
1996, Scatness, 17–18 May

[Dowitcher sp. (short or long-billed)]
1964, Westing, Unst, 23–24 May (*British Birds* **58**: 360)
1965, Symbister, Whalsay, 20 October and 7 November (*British Birds* **59**: 265)
1973, Field/Setter, Fair Isle, 20–21 September

Woodcock *Scolopax rusticola*
Chiefly a passage migrant and winter visitor, with occasional non-breeding birds during summer.

Black-tailed godwit *Limosa limosa*
Uncommon passage migrant with a small breeding population of up to three pairs.

Bar-tailed godwit *Limosa lapponicus*
Passage migrant in small numbers and uncommon winter visitor.

Whimbrel *Numenius phaeopus*
Shetland names: *peerie whaap, tang spui*
Breeding summer visitor and passage migrant. Individuals have overwintered. The most recent estimate of the breeding population (based on estimates during sample surveys) is about 480 pairs (RSPB 1993).

[*Hudsonian whimbrel *Numenius phaeopus hudsonicus*]
Vagrant, two records of this dark-rumped North American race of whimbrel:
1955, Fair Isle, 27–31 May
1974, Skerries, 24 July to 8 August

Curlew *Numenius arquata*
Shetland names: *whaap, spui*
Common breeding summer visitor, passage migrant and to a lesser degree winter visitor. The most recent estimate of the breeding population (based on estimates during sample surveys) is about 2800 pairs (RSPB 1993).

Spotted redshank *Tringa erythropus*
Uncommon passage migrant with most records in autumn, especially August.

Redshank *Tringa totanus*
Shetland name: *ebb-cock*
Common breeding resident, passage migrant and winter visitor. The most recent estimate of the breeding population (based on estimates during sample surveys) is about 500 pairs (RSPB 1993).

Marsh sandpiper *Tringa stagnatilis*
Vagrant, one record:
1969, Strand Loch, Tingwall, 4–6 May

Greenshank *Tringa nebularia*
Passage migrant with a small breeding population although this has declined in recent years. The most recent estimate of the breeding population (based on estimates during sample surveys) is about 5–10 pairs (RSPB 1993).

Greater yellowlegs *Tringa melanoleuca*
Vagrant, one record:
1953, Boddam, 26–27 May (*British Birds* **48**: 363)

Lesser yellowlegs *Tringa flavipes*
Vagrant, five records:
1910, Gilsetter, Fair Isle, shot, 24 September
1953, Field Pool, Fair Isle, 31 May
1976, Loch of Tingwall, 6–13 August
1980, Easter Loch, Uyeasound, 18 September
1984, Scatness, 20–21 May

Solitary sandpiper *Tringa solitaria*
Vagrant, one record:
1992, Field, Fair Isle, juvenile, 13–15 September

Green sandpiper *Tringa ochropus*
Uncommon spring and autumn passage migrant, recorded from April to October with most records in autumn.

Wood sandpiper *Tringa glareola*
Scarce and irregular spring and autumn passage migrant, recorded from April to October with most records in May and August.

Terek sandpiper *Xenus cinereus*
Vagrant, three records:
1975, Whalsay, 20–21 June
1991, Mid Yell Voe, 25 May
1995, Boddam Voe/Scatness, 11–13 June

Common sandpiper *Actitis hypoleucus*
Regular spring and autumn passage migrant with a small but widespread breeding population.

Spotted sandpiper *Actitis macularia*
Vagrant, three records:
1986, Leestat, south Harbour, Fair Isle, adult, 20 May
1991, Twageos, Lerwick, adult, 22–26 September
1996, Papil Water, Fetlar, adult, 17–18 May

Turnstone *Arenaria interpres*
Shetland names: *steynpecker, stenpikker, ebb pecker*
Common winter visitor and passage migrant, with a few non-breeding birds remaining throughout the summer during most years.

Wilson's phalarope *Phalaropus tricolor*
Vagrant, six records:
1973, Gremista, Lerwick, 2–21 September
1974, Loch of Hillwell, 27 September to 8 October
1975, Strand Loch, female, 9 May
1982, Fetlar, male, 27 May to 1 June
1988, Loch of Hillwell, 23–24 September
       Norwick, Unst, first-winter, 10–19 October

Red-necked phalarope *Phalaropus lobatus*
Uncommon passage migrant with a small breeding population of up to 40 pairs.

Grey phalarope *Phalaropus fulicarius*
Vagrant, at least 38 records. Most records are in September with one record in February, two in May and June, singles in July and November, and three in October.

Pomarine skua *Stercorarius pomarinus*
Uncommon passage migrant although occasionally observed on passage in large numbers off West Mainland coastline.

Arctic skua *Stercorarius parasiticus*
Shetland names: *skooty allan, sjui*
Common breeding summer visitor and passage migrant. The most recent estimate of the breeding population is 1423 AOTs in 1992 by the RSPB, compared with 1899 AOTs in 1985–87 by the SCR.

Long-tailed skua *Stercorarius longicaudus*
Scarce migrant recorded from April to November, occasionally observed on passage in large numbers off West Mainland coastline.

Great skua *Stercorarius skua*
Shetland names: *bonxie, skui*
Common breeding resident and passage migrant, occasionally recorded in winter. The most recent estimate of the breeding population is 5919 AOTs in 1992 by the RSPB, compared with 5647 AOTs in 1985–87 by SCR.

Mediterranean gull *Larus melanocephala*
Vagrant, three certain records and two doubtful records:
1957, [Hesti Geo, Fair Isle, first-summer, 31 August to 2 September, now considered uncertain]
    [Skaddan, Fair Isle, juvenile, 14 October, now considered uncertain]
1983, Lerwick, second-winter, 22 March
1992, Baltasound, adult, 26 April
1995, off Wirvie, Fair Isle, second-winter, 25 October, same as Virkie/Toab/Exnaboe area, second-winter, 26–28 October

Laughing gull *Larus atricilla*
Vagrant, four records:
1975, Easter Lother Water, Fair Isle, adult, 13 September
1983, Fetlar, adult, 15 June
1989, Gremista, Lerwick, second-summer, 31 August to 8 September
1996, Fetlar, first-summer moulting to second-winter, 24 July

Franklin's gull *Larus pipixcan*
Vagrant, three records:
1990, lochs of Hillwell and Spiggie, second-winter, 10–11 May
1991, Skellister, Nesting, adult, 27 May
1996, Foula, first-summer, 6–7 July

Little gull *Larus minuta*
Uncommon migrant, recorded most years with records from all months.

Sabine's gull *Larus sabini*
Vagrant, 14 records:
1909, Lerwick, late July (V&V)
1947, Whalsay, autumn (V&V)
1973, between Whalsay and Fetlar, two, 18 September
1974, Whalsay, immature, 12 October
1976, off Eshaness, 22 September
1977, North and South Haven, Fair Isle, juvenile, 5 September
1979, off South Lighthouse, Fair Isle, juvenile, 17 September
1982, off South Lighthouse, Fair Isle, juvenile, 11 September
1983, Sandness and Melby, juvenile, 27 September to 3 October
1987, Sumburgh Head, juvenile, 21 September
1988, Whalsay, juvenile, 23 September
1989, Gremista, Lerwick, juvenile, 30 August to 8 September
   Norwick, adult, 20 October
1993, Scatness, juvenile, 19–20 September
In addition to these records Saxby reports seeing a bird on Loch of Cliff on 1 January 1861, but this record is questioned by E&B, and the date and description are both dubious.

Bonaparte's gull *Larus philadelphia*
Vagrant, two records:
1982, Fetlar, adult, 25 June to 11 July
1987, Loch of Spiggie, first-summer, 23 May
Two unconfirmed sight records are also given by V&V.

Black-headed gull *Larus ridibundus*
Shetland name: *hoodie maa, peck maa*
Common breeding summer visitor, passage migrant and winter visitor. The most recent estimate of the breeding population is of 258 pairs in 1985–87 by SCR, a decline from the previous count in 1969–70 of 502 pairs.

Ring-billed gull *Larus delawarensis*

Vagrant, 12 records probably relating to eight individuals:

1981, Lerwick, second-winter, 29 December to 25 March 1982

1982, Scalloway, first-winter, 4 February to 12 April, presumed same as Scalloway, second-winter, December to 29 April 1983

1987, Loch of Hillwell, first-summer, 27 April to 9 May

1992, Fair Isle, second-winter, 12 August, possibly same as Virkie and Sumburgh Airport, second-winter, 8–13 October

   Sandy Loch, Lerwick, adult, 20 November and presumed same Lerwick, 24 November

1993, Boddam area and Virkie, first-summer, 17 April to 24 May, presumed same as Spiggie and South Mainland, second-winter, 6th September to 9 October

   Gremista, Lerwick, first-winter, 12 December

1994, Sound, Lerwick, first-winter moulting to first-summer, 22 March to 19 April, presumed same Strand Loch, 19 May

Common gull *Larus canus*

Shetland names: *peerie maa, pikka maa, tinna maa*

Common breeding summer visitor, passage migrant and winter visitor. The most recent estimate of the breeding population is of 2382 pairs in 1985–87 by SCR, an increase from the previous count in 1969–70 of 1336 pairs.

Lesser black-backed gull *Larus fuscus*

Shetland names: *peerie swaabie, sed ful*

Common breeding summer visitor and passage migrant, no overwintering records. The most recent estimate of the breeding population is of at least 464 pairs in 1985–87 by SCR, a similar number to the previous count in 1969–70 of 541 pairs.

Herring gull *Larus argentatus*

Shetland name: *maa*

Common breeding resident, passage migrant and winter visitor with birds of the larger northern subspecies *L. a. argentatus* common in winter. The most recent estimate of the breeding population is of 4392 pairs in 1985–87 by SCR, a decline from the previous count in 1969–70 of 9273 pairs.

Iceland gull *Larus glaucoides*

Uncommon winter visitor with occasional influxes of up to 50. Most records are in November to April but recorded in all months.

[*Kumlien's iceland gull *Larus glaucoides kumlieni*]

Vagrant, 13 records of this subspecies which breeds on Baffin Island in arctic Canada.

1869, Blacksness, Scalloway, 24 November, specimen in NHM Tring (*British Birds* **88**: 15–25), first for Britain

1983, Lerwick, adult, 3–10 February

1993, Scatness, fourth-winter female, moribund, 15 January, corpse sent to NMS

   Hillswick, fourth-winter or adult, 5–26 February

1994, Virkie, adult, 3 February (possibly same as bird below)

   St Ninian's Ayre, adult, found dead oiled, 6 February (skin now in NMS)

   Lerwick Harbour, second-winter, 25 January to 11 February

   Lerwick Harbour, adult, 8–14 February, presumed same as Scalloway Harbour, adult, 11 February

   Lerwick Harbour, first-winter, 10 February to 10 March

   Lerwick Harbour, different first-winter, 7–29 March

1995, Lerwick Harbour, first-winter, 23 March, presumed same there 28 April

   Lerwick Harbour, adult, 3–7 April

1996, Loch of Tingwall, possibly third-winter, 12 June

Glaucous gull *Larus hyperboreus*

Shetland name: *Iceland scorie*

Uncommon winter visitor, mainly in November to April but recorded in all months.

[Glaucous × herring gull hybrid]

A bird paired with a Herring Gull bred annually on Huney, Unst from 1975 to 1979. Hybrid chicks were reared in each of these years. This is the only breeding record for Britain. In addition there are the following records of birds showing characters of a hybrid between these two species, although others are alluded to:

1979, Fair Isle, 16–17 October

1988, Fair Isle, 26 May
1992, Sandy Loch, Lerwick, adult, 19 October
1993, Lerwick Harbour, adult, 25 October
1995, Lerwick Harbour, first-winter, 14 February

Great black-backed gull *Larus marinus*
Shetland names: *swaabie, swartback*
Common breeding resident, passage migrant and winter visitor. The most recent estimate of the breeding population is of 2156 pairs in 1985–87 by SCR, a decline from the previous count in 1969–70 of 2674 pairs.

Ross's gull *Rhodostethia rosea*
Vagrant, at least 13 records:
1935, off Whalsay, 16 April (*Scottish Naturalist* **65**: 50), not accepted by BOURC but probably reliable
1936, between Skerries and Whalsay, first-winter, moribund, 28 April (*Scottish Naturalist* **65**: 50)
1948, off Whalsay, 18 December (*Scottish Naturalist* **65**: 50), not accepted by BOURC but specimen retained
    on Whalsay
1969, near Mid Yell, 22 October
1972, Scalloway, 21 January
1975, Scalloway, first-winter, 19–29 January
1977, Lerwick, adult, 20–25 November
1979, Mid Yell, adult, 3 May
1981, Whalsay, adult, 14 January
  Baltasound, adult, 22–24 January
  Scalloway, 24 January to 5 February
  Quendale, 28–31 January
1982, Scalloway area, adult, 26 December to 31 January 1983, presumed same Lerwick, 3 February 1983
1983, Scatness, 22–23 January
1993, Skaw, Unst, adult, 21 September to 6 October
This species is mentioned by Saxby. V&V give two other sight records 1934–48, not accepted by BOURC.

Kittiwake *Rissa tridactyla*
Shetland names: *rippack maa, weg*
Common but declining breeding resident, passage migrant and, to a lesser degree, winter visitor. The latest breeding population estimates give a total of 36143 AONs for the whole of Shetland, comprising 17984 AONs on Shetland including Foula (counts by SOTEAG 1992–96) and 18159 on Fair Isle (counts by FIBOT 1992). This is a marked decrease from the whole Shetland total of 54264 AONs in 1975–81, and is probably due largely to predation.

Ivory gull *Pagophila eburnea*
Vagrant, at least 25 records:
1822, Baltasound (Saxby)
1861, Baltasound, adult, 16 January (Saxby)
c. 1885, Spiggie, shot, winter (E&B)
1890, 'from one of the islands', adult, February (E&B)
1892, Foula, 8 December, trapped with rod and line by Frank Traill (*Scottish Naturalist* **6**: 117–118)
1898, Scalloway, no date (E&B)
1933, Fair Isle, 28 December
1939, December, no other details (V&V)
1950, Whalsay, first-winter, 12 December (V&V)
  Lerwick, first-winter, 15–18 December (V&V)
1952, Meoness, Fair Isle, adult, exhausted and died, 9 February
1962, Scalloway, adult, 8–19 February (*British Birds* **56**: 401)
1964, 11 km SW of Burra, immature seen by Robert Duthie, 22 December (not submitted to BBRC)
1967, Whalsay, 10 December (*British Birds* **61**: 343)
1969, Ollaberry, 6 November
  Basta Voe, Yell, second-winter, 8 November
1979, Sullom Voe, first-winter, 29 December
1980, Unst, adult, dead, 27 April
  Unst, another, dead for several weeks, 29 June
  Virkie, Quendale and Sumburgh, first-winter, 13–19 November
  Whale Firth, Yell, adult, 7–10 December

1983, Muckle Flugga, first-summer, 6 June
    Whalsay, first-winter, 13 December
1989, Loch of East Yell and Otterswick, first-winter, 2–19 December
1990, Lerwick, first-winter, 10 and 18–20 December
1993, Collafirth, first-winter, 12 December, presumed same Symbister, Whalsay, 13 December, presumed
    same, Lerwick Harbour, 14–26 December
There are a number of other possible records last century: Edmondston mentions a bird shot sometime prior
to 1844; Saxby apparently recorded in the *Zoologist* for 1864 that he had 'only seen one Ivory Gull this winter';
E&B give a suspicious series of records at Muckle Flugga in 1888 with one on 1 February, three on 16
February and one on 3 October. B&J give a record for 1959–60, not given in BBRC reports. The 1822
sighting was apparently the first recorded in Britain.

Gull-billed tern *Gelochilodon niloctica*
Vagrant, two records:
1971, Fair Isle, 24–29 May
1995, Pool of Virkie, 25 June
A sight record at Skaw, Whalsay on 21 September 1938 was placed in brackets by V&V and is not considered
acceptable by BOURC.

Caspian tern *Sterna caspia*
Vagrant, four records:
1976, West Sandwick, Yell, long dead, early August
1978, south over Bird Observatory, Fair Isle, 29 May
1979, West Voe of Sumburgh, 8 October
1987, north over Bird Observatory, Fair Isle, 29 May
The 1976 bird had been ringed as a pullus near Stockholm, Sweden in 1975.

Sandwich tern *Sterna sandvicensis*
Scarce migrant, recorded March to October but mainly from May to September. Has bred at least twice, in
1955 (two pairs) and 1960 (six pairs).

Roseate tern *Sterna dougalli*
Vagrant, eight records:
1974, Whalsay, immature, 24–28 June
1978, Jarlshof, adult, 12 May
1983, Bressay, adult, 19 May
    Whalsay, adult, 16 June
1984, Burra, adult paired with arctic tern and incubating single egg, from 14 June, nest failed
1988, Fair Isle, adult, 12 May
1996, Tarryfield, Fair Isle, adult in arctic tern colony, 24–26 July
A record published in the 1993 FIBO report of an adult at the South Harbour, Fair Isle on 12 June was
subsequently rejected.

Common tern *Sterna hirundo*
Shetland name: *tirrick*
Passage migrant and breeding summer visitor, much scarcer than arctic tern. The current breeding
population is probably only around 100 pairs, although the actual figure may be between 50 and 250 (latest
estimate from SNH).

Arctic tern *Sterna paradisaea*
Shetland name: *tirrick*
Common passage migrant and breeding summer visitor. The latest estimate of the breeding population gives
a count of 16 400 incubating adults, which probably estimates to about 11 000 breeding pairs (RSPB). The
breeding population is increasing significantly on Fair Isle where 1250 pairs were counted in 1996, compared
to an estimated 400 pairs in 1990 (FIBOT).

Little tern *Sterna albifrons*
Vagrant, at least eight records, the 1900 records are considered dubious:
1900, Grutness, six, 20 September (V&V)
1906, Loch of Spiggie, 6 October (V&V)
1949, Bressay, June (V&V)
    Loch of Spiggie, two, 1 July (V&V)

1968, Whalsay, 28 May (*Scottish Birds* **5**: 333)
1975, Sound, Lerwick, 15 May
1990, West Voe of Sumburgh, adult, 3–5 May
1992, Sandwick, 26 April
      Quendale, 16 May

Black tern *Chlidonias niger*
Vagrant, at least 27 records:
1952, B&J
1954, Bay of Scousburgh, 18–21 June (*Scottish Naturalist* **68**: 6)
1962, Loch of Tingwall, 17 June, for several days (FIBO BUL 5.1: 29)
1963, B&J
1967, Unst, three, 5 May, six on 6 May, five on 7 May
  The Haa, Fair Isle, 6 May
  Cullivoe, Yell, three, 7 May
  Aywick, Yell, three, 7 May
  Loch of Clickhimin, Lerwick, two, 7 May
  Loch of Hillwell, two, 7 May
  Otterswick, Yell, *c*. 10, May
  Loch of Spiggie, *c*. six 8 May
  Unst/Hascosay, four, 8 May
  Whalsay, two, 9 May
  Fetlar, 9 May
  Loch of Spiggie, juvenile, 4 September
1971, Hillwell, 17 May
1980, Loch of Spiggie, two, 7 June
  Sinna Skerry, Yell Sound, 30 June
  Hillwell, 21 August
1981, Skerries, juvenile, 24–26 September
1986, Loch of Spiggie, juvenile, 18 August
1987, Skeld, 14 June
1988, Whalsay, 5 June
1990, Ness of Sound, Yell, adult, 6–7 August; presumed same, Mid Yell, 13 August
  Quendale Bay, juvenile, 6 September
1993, Virkie, adult, 12 June
1994, Loch of Tingwall, adult, 4–5 May
Saxby records one some years prior to 1844.

White-winged black tern *Chlidonias leucoptera*
Vagrant, five records:
1967, Burrafirth, Unst, 30 June to 6 July (*British Birds* **61**: 345)
1973, Fair Isle, adult, 10 June
1982, Easter Lother Water, Fair Isle, 9–12 May
  Loch of Flatpunds, Walls, at least 13–17 May
1994, lochs of Hillwell/Spiggie, adult, 7–15 June

Guillemot *Uria aalge*
Shetland names: *loom, longvi, lung wheeda*
Common breeding summer visitor and passage migrant although few are normally recorded inshore during winter. SCR estimate of the breeding population in 1985–87 gives 162 652 birds present. The most recent counts of individuals at the largest colonies are:
Noss, 45 696 (SNH 1996), 21% higher than 1986
Fair Isle, 37 563 (FIBOT 1994)
Foula, 37 500 (SCR 1987)
Hermaness, 20 185 (SNH 1996)
Sumburgh Head, 16 048 (SOTEAG 1994)
Saxavord, 8123 (SCR 1985)
Ramna Stack and Gruney, 4370 (SCR 1987)
Papa Stour, 2482 (SCR 1985)
Fetlar, 225 (SNH 1993)
This gives a figure of 172 192 individuals but excludes quite a few smaller colonies which when added would suggest about 180 000 individuals. This probably equates to about 120 000 pairs.

Brunnich's guillemot *Uria lomvia*

Vagrant, 10 records, but only four birds seen alive:

1968, Norwick, freshly dead on tideline, 20 March, specimen now in NMS (*British Birds* **62**: 473)

1977, Scord, Sumburgh, freshly dead on tideline, 18 December

1980, Burrafirth, dead for 2–3 weeks, 24 February

   North Haven/Furse, Fair Isle, adult, 16–17 October

1983, Banna Minn, Burra, freshly dead on tideline, 30 October, specimen now in NMS

1987, Hamnavoe, Burra, adult, 3–7 February

   Hamnavoe, Burra, different bird, freshly dead, 7 February, specimen now with D. Coutts, Shetland

1989, Sumburgh Head, adult in guillemot colony, 16 June to 12 July

1994, Wadbister Voe, freshly dead on tideline, 11 February

1995, Gulberwick, 4 January, exhausted and taken into care, released at Wadbister Voe 1 February remaining there until 2 February

Saxby reports that Captain Ross reputedly saw one off Unst last century while V&V believe they saw one in Weisdale on 15 May 1947.

Razorbill *Alca torda*

Shetland names: *sea craa, wolkie*

Common breeding summer visitor and passage migrant, although few are normally recorded inshore during winter. The most recent estimate of the breeding population is by SCR in 1985–87 which gives 13 159 individuals, although this is probably an underestimate.

[Great auk *Pinguinis impennis*]

Extinct (category B). Bones of this species have been found at the Jarlshof excavations at Sumburgh dating from the ninth to tenth century, and Eagle Clarke (1912) refers to a statement in Baikie and Hedle's *Historia Naturalis Orcadensis* (1848) that one was seen off Fair Isle in June 1798. The species bred at Papa Westray in Orkney, about 64 km away, at that time.

Black guillemot *Cepphus grylle*

Shetland names: *tystie, täisti*

Common breeding resident. The most recent count of the total breeding population is 12 008 pre-breeding individuals (birds counted just before the breeding season begins). More recent surveys have indicated there has been a considerable increase in numbers in some areas but not in others, with possibly a 25% overall increase. The actual figure may be around 15 000 pre-breeding adults, although this is only an estimate (SOTEAG).

Little auk *Alle alle*

Shetland name: *rotchie*

Winter visitor and passage migrant, usually in small numbers although with occasional large influxes.

Puffin *Fratercula arctica*

Shetland names: *tammy norie, lundi*

Common breeding summer visitor and passage migrant, with a few recorded inshore during the winter. The most recent estimates of the breeding population at the main colonies are as follows:

Foula, 48 000 pairs (SCR 1996)

Fair Isle, 21 000 (FIBOT 1995)

Hermaness, 22 000 (SNH 1995)

Noss, 1200 (SNH 1990)

Sumburgh, 1000 (SNH estimate)

Ramna Stacks and Gruney, 1000 (RSPB estimate)

This gives an estimate of 94 200 pairs and allowing for smaller colonies elsewhere this probably equates to about 100 000 pairs.

Pallas's sandgrouse *Syrrhaptes paradoxus*

Vagrant, recorded in two years last century with two records this century. A few were recorded in Shetland during two invasions into western Europe last century. Saxby saw one around Baltasound from 28 October to 4 November 1863, when it was shot, and singles were reported from Haroldswick and Balta Isle at around the same time. In 1888 there was a longer series of records involving about 100 birds: 20–30 in Dunrossness on 16 May, one at Baltasound on the 16 May, 14 in Haroldswick on 24 May, two on Unst on 5 June, one on Fetlar on 7 June, eight near Lerwick on 7 June, about 12 near Lerwick on the 27 June (E&B), while Eagle Clarke was informed by the Rev. H.A. MacPherson that a flock of 40 arrived on Fair

Isle at the beginning of June, but only five survived to the end of the month. Since then there have been two records:
1969, Foula, 26–31 May
1990, Quendale, adult male, 19 May to 4 June (*Birding World* **3**: 161–163)

Rock dove *Columba livia*
Shetland names: *doo, blo du*
Common breeding resident and partial migrant in small numbers.

Stock dove *Columba oenas*
Scarce migrant, recorded from February to December with most records in April/May and September/October.

Woodpigeon *Columba palumbus*
Breeding summer visitor and passage migrant in small numbers, with a few usually overwintering.

[**Barbary dove** *Streptopelia 'risoria'*]
Status unknown, one record:
1982, Virkie, in off the sea, 12 May, presumed same Dale of Walls, 7 June

Collared dove *Streptopelia decaocto*
Breeding summer visitor and passage migrant in small numbers with a few usually overwintering. The breeding population is mainly confined to the larger centres of population, e.g. Lerwick, Scalloway, Brae, etc. First recorded in Shetland on Fair Isle, with singles on 18 April and 18 June 1960, then on 12 and 24 May 1961, with records increasing annually thereafter (*Scottish Birds* **3**: 300). Away from Fair Isle, the first were singles at Hamnavoe, West Burra, on 31 May 1961 (L.A. Urquhart, *Scottish Birds* **1**: 488–489), none in 1962, one on Foula from 31 May to 2 June 1963 then at least 15 in 1964 throughout the isles including one or two on Unst in late May/June and September. The first breeding record was at least three pairs at Lerwick in 1965 (*Scottish Birds* **4**: 293).

Turtle dove *Streptopelia turtur*
Uncommon passage migrant with occasional non-breeding birds summering. Most records are in May, June and September. Has overwintered.

Rufous turtle dove *Streptopelia orientalis*
Vagrant, one record:
1974, Setter, Fair Isle, first-year, 31 October to 1 November

Cuckoo *Cuculus canorus*
Shetland name: *gok*
Passage migrant with occasional birds summering. Has bred occasionally.

Black-billed cuckoo *Coccyzus erythrophthalmus*
Vagrant, one record:
1953, Foula, moribund, 11 October, body sent to British Museum (*Scottish Naturalist* 1953: 196)

Yellow-billed cuckoo *Coccyzus americanus*
Vagrant, one record:
1952, Exnaboe, immature female, moribund, 1 November (V&V)

Barn owl *Tyto alba*
Vagrant, at least eleven records although individuals have been kept in captivity in Shetland and escaped:
1915, Baltasound, Unst, caught in shed, 5 November, dark-breasted (*Scottish Naturalist* **55/56**: 150)
1924, Fair Isle, pale-breasted, January to February, caught and collected at South Lighthouse
1928, Loch of Spiggie, pale-breasted, shot, November (V&V)
1940, Fair Isle, pale-breasted, October to November
1943, Fair Isle, dark-breasted, October to November
1944, Fair Isle, pale-breasted, 11 April
1951, Sumburgh, dark-breasted, shot, 16 October (V&V)
1958, Field, Fair Isle, pale-breasted, 25 November
1973, Skerries, pale-breasted, 3–5 June
1982, Sandwick, dark-breasted, 10 November, found dead next day
1989, Whalsay, pale-breasted, 10 October to 12 February 1990

V&V record up to four at Kergord in December 1945 but these are best regarded as unsubstantiated. Two captive birds at Bigton were allowed to fly free by their owner and were seen at various South Mainland localities in spring 1993.

Scops owl *Otus scops*
Vagrant, seven records:
1900, Foula, female, found dead, 10 May, specimen sent to RSM (*Scottish Naturalist* **159**: 68)
1901, Vaila, April (V&V)
1905, Muckle Flugga, about 20 August (V&V)
1926, Foula, 10 May (V&V)
1928, Cunningsburgh, female, 4 April (V&V)
1953, Jarlshot, Sumburgh, 6 June (FIBO BUL **11**: 18)
1988, Collafirth, Delting, 9 June

[**Eagle owl** *Bubo bubo*]
Presumed escape (category E), two records although both now considered unnaceptable:
1863, near Haroldswick, autumn (Saxby)
1871, Balta and Huney, Unst, March (Saxby)

Snowy owl *Nyctea scandiaca*
Formerly a rare breeding resident, successful in 1967–71, 1973–75 with an unsuccessful attempt in 1972, now regarded as a vagrant. Due to two long-staying females which frequented the Fetlar/Unst area throughout the 1980s and early 1990s, a true pattern of arriving birds is difficult to establish, with one or other of these being seen at various localities throughout the isles on an almost annual basis. Migrant individuals have occurred, however, probably on an almost annual basis, as indicated by 22 records from Fair Isle. Two individuals caught aboard vessels at sea were released on Fetlar in the hope of the species attempting to breed again but both departed soon after release.

Hawk owl *Surnia ulula*
Vagrant, two records:
1860–61, Skaw, Unst, winter (Saxby)
1983, Frakkafield, 12–13 September; presumed same, Bressay, 20–21 September

[**Little owl** *Athene noctua*]
E&B were informed that this species occurred in Shetland, but there is no evidence to support this unlikely statement.

[**Tawny owl** *Strix aluco*]
Claims given by E&B and V&V were bracketed by the authors as unacceptable.

Long-eared owl *Asio otus*
Mainly a scarce autumn migrant in October–November with small but regular numbers overwintering and a few spring migrants in April–May. Rare in summer in recent years but bred occasionally up to 1975.

Short-eared owl *Asio flammeus*
Uncommon migrant, recorded in all months but mainly in March to June and September to October. Possibly bred last century.

Tengmalm's owl *Aegolius funereus*
Vagrant, at least six records; these are the only dated records although others are alluded to:
1897, Scalloway, female, 14 March (V&V)
    Bressay, female, April (V&V)
1901, Sandsting, female, 5 November (V&V)
1908, Unst, female, 4 January (V&V)
1912, Unst, 23 January (V&V)
1917–18, Hillwell, dead, winter

Nightjar *Caprimulgus europaeus*
Formerly regarded as a scarce migrant, but since the 1960s only as a vagrant with about 30 records. Most records are in late May to August apart from one record in mid-April, four in September and one in late October.

Needle-tailed swift *Hirundapus caudacutus*
Vagrant, two, possibly three records:
1931, [Fair Isle, 6 August, discounted in recent literature but considered probably reliable by Dymond]
1984, Quendale, 25 May to 6 June
1991, Noup of Noss, 11 and 14 June

Swift *Apus apus*
Common although irregular passage migrant, recorded April to November with most records in late May to August. There is one dubious breeding record from the last century at Clickhimin Broch in 1890.

Little swift *Apus affinis*
Vagrant, one record:
1991, North Light, Fair Isle, 1 November

Alpine swift *Apus melba*
Vagrant, 10 records:
1962, Setter, Fair Isle, 20 June
   Hermaness, 12 July (*British Birds* **56**: 402)
1966, Shirva, Fair Isle, 25 April
   Compass Head, Sumburgh, 31 May (*British Birds* **60**: 322)
1967, Double Dyke, Fair Isle, 29 May
1972, Troila Geo, Fair Isle, 6 June
1977, Burra, 24 June
1981, Homisdale/Pund, Fair Isle, 18 April
   Fair Isle, 4–10 June
1994, Noup of Noss, 2–30 July
A record of one at Scalloway on 9 June 1972 was presumably not submitted to BBRC as there is no mention of the record in the rarities reports of the time.

Kingfisher *Alcedo atthis*
Vagrant, 12 records:
1936, Symbister, Whalsay, 18 August (*Scottish Naturalist* 1937: 25–31)
1945, West Voe of Sumburgh, early June (V&V)
1950, lochs of Asta and Tingwall, 6 November (V&V)
1971, Voe, 17 August to 1 September
1974, Skerries, 8 August
   Scalloway, 13 August
1980, Graven, 3 May
1982, Loch of Hillwell, 13–17 September
1986, Firth, 19 March
1988, Strand Loch, 13 August
1991, Sandsayre Pier, Sandwick, 23 August
1995, Fetlar, 28 May

Bee-eater *Merops apiaster*
Vagrant, 20 records involving at least 26 individuals:
1899, Whalsay, June, later found dead (V&V)
1915, Lerwick, 4–11 July (V&V)
1951, Lerwick, 4–5 October (*Scottish Naturalist* **64**: 117)
1955, Lerwick, 3 June (FIBO BUL **3.1**: 24)
1966, Springfield, Fair Isle, 13 June
1969, three Boini Mire, Fair Isle, 7–9 July, presumed same birds as below
   Stromfirth, three, 9–12 July
1970, Baltasound, two, 8 July to 5 August
   Pund, Fair Isle, 6–17 August
1971, Lerwick, 20–25 and 28–29 June, presumed same, Kergord, 26–27 June
   Hesti Geo, Fair Isle, 30 June to 18 August
   Lerwick, 31 August to 6 September
1972, Gloup, Yell, 25 May
1982, Furse, Fair Isle, 4–6 June
1989, Scalloway, two, 20–24 May, presumed same, Kergord, two, 24 May
   Scalloway, 21–22 July

1990, Vidlin, two, 9–21 May
1992, Sumburgh Hotel, 31 May
   Helendale, 6 June
1993, Noss, 23 May
1995, Vigga, West Yell, 6 June, same Whalsay 9 June, and Vidlin 10–11 June

Roller *Caracias garrulus*
Vagrant, seven records:
1930, Whalsay, shot, autumn (Waterston 1937)
1958, Mid Yell, 5 September (*Scottish Birds* **1**: 72)
1959, Northmavine, 20 July for 3–4 days (*British Birds* **53**: 421)
1971, Semblister, 4–5 June
1977, Yell, 17–22 July
1979, Whalsay, 5–7 June, later found dead and sexed as male
1981, Stackhoull, Fair Isle, 22 September, subsequently found dead

Hoopoe *Upupa epops*
Scarce migrant, recorded in April to June and August to November but mainly in April, May, September and October.

Wryneck *Jynx torquilla*
Uncommon migrant, recorded in April to June and August to October but mainly in May and September.

[Green woodpecker *Picus viridis*]
V&V give details of a series of as many as four claimed records in autumn on Whalsay between 1927 and 1930. All the records concern birds which were shot or found dead but destroyed before being seen by competent observers. Singles were also reported seen by Fred Hunter at Hay's Dock, Lerwick and by Robert Duthie at Westshore, Scalloway, both in the late 1950s. Given the circumstances and the confusion over the dates and numbers involved this species cannot be admitted to the Shetland List.

Great spotted woodpecker *Dendrocopos major*
Irruptive autumn visitor, recorded mainly August to October. Very rare attempting to overwinter or on spring passage but recorded in all months.

[Black woodpecker *Dryocopus martius*]
In a catalogue of the Birds of Shetland (*Zoologist*, 1861, p. 7431), it is stated that a specimen of this species had been killed at Belmont, Unst. Dr Laurence Edmondston believed the record acceptable but 'careful enquiry' by Saxby led him to believe it was a great-spotted woodpecker.

Calandra lark *Melanocorypha calandra*
Vagrant, one record:
1978, Field, Fair Isle, 28 April
A lark thought to be this species was shot at Setter by J.A. Stout in October about 1928, but apparently the specimen was lost in transit to the Paisley Museum.

Bimaculated lark *Melanocorypha bimaculata*
Vagrant, one record:
1976, Field, Fair Isle, 8 June

Short-toed lark *Calandrella brachydactyla*
Scarce migrant recorded mainly in autumn, especially in September and October but with a few spring records in April to June. The majority of records are of the southern race *C. b. brachydactyla* although at least 20 records, mainly in autumn, are of the 'grey' eastern race *C. b. longipennis*.

Crested lark *Galerida cristata*
Vagrant, one record:
1952, near the Chapel, Fair Isle, 2 November (seen by J.A. Stout)
A record for 1936 was given in brackets by V&V and is not acceptable to BOURC.

Woodlark *Lullula arborea*
Formerly a scarce migrant, now regarded as a rare migrant with about 60 records since the 1960s. Recorded in February to May and September to November with most records in October.

Skylark *Alauda arvensis*
Shetland names: *laverock, leverrek*
Common breeding summer visitor and passage migrant, most numerous in March to April and September to October, but scarce in winter.

Shore lark *Eromophila alpestris*
Scarce migrant, recorded in January to June and September to November with most records in May and October.

Sand martin *Riparia riparia*
Uncommon migrant, recorded in April to October with most records in May and early June. Possibly bred last century.

Swallow *Hirundo rustica*
Common migrant, recorded in April to November with most records in May–June and a much smaller autumn passage mainly in September. Annual but scarce breeder.

Red-rumped swallow *Hirundo daurica*
Vagrant, six records:
1905, three Fair Isle, 2 June (one shot)
1931, Fair Isle, 19 June
1971, Whalsay, 23–25 September
1972, Sumburgh Head, 29 May
1976, Skerryholm, Fair Isle, 9–11 May
   Skerryholm, Fair Isle, 3 June
1980, Loch of Clickimin, Lerwick, 15 May
1987, Wirvie, Fair Isle, 24 October
   Loch of Clickimin, Lerwick, 31 October
   Gremista, two, 3–7 November (presumably including the previous individual)
1990, Virkie and Sumburgh Head, 2–4 May

House martin *Delichon urbica*
Common migrant, recorded in April to November with the majority of records in May and June. Breeds occasionally.

Richard's pipit *Anthus novaseelandiae*
Scarce migrant, recorded in May and June and September to December with the majority of records in autumn between mid September and early October.

Blyth's pipit *Anthus godlewski*
Vagrant, two records:
1988, Quoy, Fair Isle, 13–22 October (not yet accepted by BBRC)
1993, South Harbour area, Fair Isle, 31 October to 10 November

Tawny pipit *Anthus campestris*
Vagrant, 23 records:
1933, Fair Isle, shot, spring
1935, Fair Isle, 8 October, shot
1943, Fair Isle, May
1951, Fair Isle, 15–17 September
1963, Meoness, Fair Isle, 6 June
1970, Wirvie, Fair Isle, 25–26 May
   Double Dyke, Fair Isle, trapped, 8–10 June
   Whalsay, 10–11 June
1971, Sumburgh, 29 September to 3 October
1973, Skerries, 22 September
1974, Skerries, 14–17 May
   Skerries, 26 May
1976, North Lighthouse, Fair Isle, 5–6 May
   west of Skerryholm, Fair Isle, 17 May, possibly same as bird below
   Golden Water, Fair Isle, 23 May
   Foula, 1 June

1977, Linni Geo/Malcolm's Head, Fair Isle, 26 May
1978, Hoini area, Fair Isle, 1–3 June
1982, South Lighthouse, Fair Isle, 22 May
1987, Fair Isle, 2–7 May
   Fair Isle, 29 October to 7 November
1990, Vaasetter, Fair Isle, 20–26 May
1993, South Light/South Reeva, Fair Isle, 22 October
1996, Skerries, first-winter, 20–30 September

Olive-backed pipit *Anthus hodgsoni*
Rare migrant, at least 84 records including at least 20 in 1993. Apart from one at Virkie on 3 January 1988 and one at the Plantation, Fair Isle on 24 April 1995, all other records have been from late September to the end of November, with by far the majority of these in October.

Tree pipit *Anthus trivialis*
Irregular passage migrant, sometimes in large numbers, recorded in April to November, with the majority of records in May and September.

Pechora pipit *Anthus gustavi*
Rare migrant with at least 50 records. One on Fair Isle on 23–24 September 1925 (shot) was the first British record. All records have occurred in September and October with the majority in October.

Meadow pipit *Anthus pratensis*
Shetland names: *hill sparrow, teetick, titek, titen*
Common breeding summer visitor and passage migrant with small numbers overwintering.

Red-throated pipit *Anthus cervinus*
Rare migrant with at least 76 records, more than half from Fair Isle. Approximately equal numbers have been recorded in spring, during May and June, and in autumn from late August to early November. Six were present on Fair Isle on 8 May 1936, at least six were also there between 24 May and 10 June 1975, and nine were recorded there in 1992.

Rock pipit *Anthus petrosus*
Shetland names: *banks sparrow, titek*
Common breeding resident, passage migrant and winter visitor.

Buff-bellied pipit *Anthus rubescens*
Vagrant, one record; a record in the 1981 SBR was not accepted by BBRC:
1953, Guidicum, Fair Isle, 17 September

[**Water pipit** *Anthus spinoletta*]
Vagrant, one record although this must now be considered doubtful:
1950, between lochs of Spiggie and Brow, 8–9 May (V&V)

Yellow wagtail *Motacilla flava*
Uncommon migrant, recorded in March to November, but mainly in May and more erratically in September. Three races occur regularly: *M. f. flavissima*, yellow wagtail; *M. f. thunbergi*, grey-headed wagtail; and *M. f. flava*, blue-headed wagtail; others possibly as vagrants. Has bred occasionally and a pair of grey-headed wagtails bred successfully on Fair Isle in 1996. Birds resembling black-headed wagtails *M. f. feldegg* were seen on Whalsay on 20 May 1936 (V&V), in 1960 (B&J), on Skerries on 8 May 1969, Fair Isle on 7–8 May 1970 and again there on 3–8 May 1974, and on Skerries on 5 June 1982. A male shot on Fair Isle on 18 May 1910 showed characteristics of Sykes wagtail *M. f. beema*. Birds resembling the Iberian form of the blue-headed wagtail *M. f. 'iberiae'* were seen on Skerries on 29 May 1969 and 17 May 1976, on Whalsay on 8 May 1977 and Fair Isle on 22–28 May 1980. Three birds in autumn 1988, two in autumn 1992 and 1993 and one in October 1994 were believed to belong to one of the eastern Siberian races, which in autumn can closely resemble the citrine wagtail *M. citreola*.

Citrine wagtail *Motacilla citreola*
Rare migrant, at least 47 records. All records are between the middle of August and end of October with the majority in September, apart from a single spring record on Fair Isle on 26 April 1996.

Grey wagtail *Motacilla cinerea*
Scarce migrant with similar numbers of records in spring and autumn, and a very rare breeding summer visitor. Recorded in all months except February but rare in December and January.

Pied/white wagtail *Motacilla alba*
Shetland name: *kirk sparrow*
Common passage migrant and summer visitor with a few pairs usually breeding annually. Most records are in autumn with occasional birds recorded in winter.

Waxwing *Bombycilla garrulus*
Irruptive migrant, with most records in October and November but records for all months except July and August.

Cedar waxwing
Vagrant, one record:
1985, Noss, 25–26 June

[Japanese waxwing *Bombycilla japonica*]
Presumed escape (category E), one record:
1996, Lerwick, 19–27 May

Dipper *Cinclus cinclus*
Vagrant, at least 37 records. The majority of records are in the first half of the year, from January to early May with smaller numbers recorded from October to December. Most records are of the nominate 'black-bellied' dipper *C. c. cinclus* from northern Europe, although brown-bellied birds of either the British race *C. c. gularis* or the central and west European race *C. c. aquaticus* have occurred.

Wren *Troglydytes troglodytes*
Shetland names: *sisti mus*, *Robbie Cuddie*, *stenkiw*
Common breeding resident, passage migrant and winter visitor. Native breeding birds are thought to be a possible subspecies *T. t. zetlandicus* on Mainland and *T. t. fridarensis* on Fair Isle, as they are larger and darker than British mainland birds.

Dunnock *Prunella modularis*
Common passage migrant, usually more numerous March to May than September to November, although recorded in all months. Occasionally overwinters but very rare in June to August. Two failed breeding attempts have been recorded.

Robin *Erithacus rubecula*
Common and sometimes abundant migrant, mainly in March to May and September to November but recorded in all months, with small numbers overwintering in most years. Has bred successfully on at least five occasions.

Alpine accentor *Prunella collaris*
Vagrant, two records:
1908, west cliffs, Fair Isle, 6 October (seen by Eagle Clarke)
1959, Wester Lother, Fair Isle, 27–28 June
In addition, singles are alleged to have been seen on Fair Isle on 14 September 1930 and 24 September 1933, but there are no further details.

Thrush nightingale *Luscinia luscinia*
Rare migrant, with at least 51 records. By far the majority of records are in May with seven in June, eight in August, and one in September and October.

Nightingale *Luscinia megarhynchos*
Rare migrant, at least 51 records. In spring, records are from mid-April to June with the majority in May, with only seven records in autumn, all between mid August and mid October. One on 30 October 1971 showed characteristics of the central and eastern Asian race *L. m. hafizi*.

Siberian rubythroat *Luscinia calliope*
Vagrant, one record:
1975, Plantation, Fair Isle, first-year male, 9 October.

Bluethroat *Luscinia svecica*
Uncommon migrant, although occasionally seen in large numbers in spring, recorded from April to July and August to November with by far the majority of records in May. Most are the red-spotted race *L. s. svevica* although there have been at least 13 records of the white-spotted bluethroat *L. s. cyanecula*.

Red-flanked bluetail *Tarsiger cyanurus*
Vagrant, five records:
1947, Whalsay, shot, 7 October, second British record, specimen sent to British Museum (*Scottish Naturalist* **60**:
    6–7, colour photograph)
1971, Fetlar, male, trapped, 31 May to 1 June
1981, Busta, Fair Isle, trapped, 29–30 September
1984, Hjukni Geo, Fair Isle, 21 September
1993, Easterhoull, Fair Isle, 16 September

Black redstart *Phoenicurus ochrurus*
Uncommon migrant, recorded in all months but mainly in March to May and October.

Redstart *Phoenicurus phoenicurus*
Common passage migrant, recorded in March to November but mainly in May and September to October. Has attempted to breed once.

Whinchat *Saxicola rubetra*
Common migrant, recorded in April to November, but mainly in May and September to October, more numerous in autumn.

Stonechat *Saxicola torquata*
Uncommon migrant, recorded in all months but mainly in March to May and September to November. Has bred successfully on at least five occasions although not in recent years, with a possible breeding record in one other year.

[*'**Siberian' stonechat** *Saxicola torquata maura/stejnegeri*]
Rare migrant, at least 54 records, all falling between 20 September and 20 November with the majority in October, apart from single males on Fair Isle on 28–30 April 1990 and 8–9 May 1994.

Wheatear *Oenanthe oenanthe*
Shetland names: *steynshekker, stenkall*
Common passage migrant and breeding summer visitor. Birds of the northern subspecies *O. o. leucorrhoa* are common on passage.

Isabelline wheatear *Oenanthe isabellinus*
Vagrant, one record:
1994, Skaw, Whalsay, 20 September to 10 October

Pied wheatear *Oenanthe pleschanka*
Vagrant, three records:
1989, Single Dyke, Fair Isle, first-winter male, 10 October
1991, Sumburgh, first-winter male, 9–13 October
    Lerwick, different first-winter male, 17 October

Black-eared wheatear *Oenanthe hispanica*
Vagrant, seven records:
1907, Fair Isle, male, shot by Eagle Clarke, 25 September
1951, Fair Isle, male, 8–13 November
1964, Huns Heilor, Fair Isle, female, trapped, 19 May
    North Grind, Fair Isle, first-winter female, trapped, 27 September
1979, Double Dyke, Fair Isle, adult female, trapped, 18 June, probably eastern race *O. h. melanoleuca*
1981, Skerries, 22–26 September
1983, Skerries, male, 5 October
1995, Fair Isle, 15 September, still under consideration by BBRC

Desert wheatear *Oenanthe deserti*
Vagrant, six records:

1928, Houll, Fair Isle, male, shot by J.A. Stout, 6 October
1929, Gunglesund, Fair Isle, male, shot by James Wilson, 26 October, eastern race *O. d. homochroa*
1940, Fair Isle, male, shot by L. Anderson, 18 November
1970, Millens Houllan, Fair Isle, male, 20 November
1988, Boddam, female, 2–3 November
1991, Skerryholm, Fair Isle, female, 26 October

[**Black wheatear** *Oenanthe leucura*]
Two records previously accepted by BOURC, neither now considered acceptable as the possibility of confusion with white-crowned black wheatear could not be ruled out.
1912, Fair Isle, male, seen by Eagle Clarke, 28–30 September
1953, Fair Isle, probably female, 19 October
A record of a black wheatear on Foula on 10 May (included in the 1970 SBR) was not submitted to BBRC.

Rock thrush *Monticola saxatilis*
Vagrant, three records:
1931, Fair Isle, 8 November
1936, Fair Isle, male, seen by L.S.V. Venables, 16 October
1970, Single Dyke trap (self caught), Fair Isle, male, 30 June, not seen again after release

White's thrush *Zoothera dauma*
Vagrant, 10 records:
1929, Fair Isle, male, shot by G. Stout, 19 October
1944, North Shirva, Fair Isle, male, shot by J.A. Stout, 18 October
1948, Burrashield, Fair Isle, mid-November
1958, Wirvie, Fair Isle, 6 November
1971, Setter, Fair Isle, 13 February
1973, Ward Hill, Fair Isle, first-winter, trapped, 24 September, kept overnight and released next day
1975, Whalsay, 11 October
1985, Catfirth, 10 October
1990, Sumburgh, 22 September
1993, Seafield, Lerwick, 1 October

Hermit thrush *Catharus guttatus*
Vagrant, two records:
1975, Field, Fair Isle, 2 June
1995, Observatory, Fair Isle, first-winter, trapped, 19 October

Swainson's thrush *Catharus ustulatus*
Vagrant, two records:
1980, Scatness, 25–29 October
1990, Hjukni Geo, Fair Isle, 30 September to 6 October

Grey-cheeked thrush *Catharus minimus*
Vagrant, three records:
1953, Observatory, Fair Isle, first-winter, 5 October, trapped and kept overnight, released next day
1958, Vaadal, Fair Isle, first-winter, trapped, 29 October
1982, Voe, 19–20 October

Ring ouzel *Turdus torquatus*
Uncommon passage migrant, recorded in all months except February, with most records in April–May and September–October. There are at least four breeding records.

Blackbird *Turdus merula*
Common breeding resident and sometimes abundant passage migrant with some migrants remaining to overwinter.

Eyebrowed thrush *Turdus obscurus*
Vagrant, two records:
1987, Gully/Observatory, Fair Isle, first-winter, 7–15 October
1992, Houll, Fair Isle, first-winter, 4 October

Dusky thrush *Turdus naumanni*
Vagrant, three records:
1961, The Haa, Fair Isle, first-winter female, 18–21 October
1968, Whalsay, 24 September (*British Birds* **62**: 476)
1975, Firth, 6–13 November

Black-throated thrush *Turdus ruficollis*
Vagrant, 13 records:
1957, Double Dyke, Fair Isle, adult male, trapped, 8 December to 22 January 1958
1974, Toab, adult female, 5–6 October
1977, Loch of Hillwell, female, 6–14 November
1978, Leogh, Fair Isle, male, 17 October
1981, Rova Head, Lerwick, first-winter, 7 December
1982, Utra, Fair Isle, male, 13 October
1987, Geosetter, male, 30 October
   Toab, first-winter male, 11 November
1993, Midway, Fair Isle, 11 October
   Brough, Whalsay, first-winter female, 19–23 October
1994, Upper Stoneybrake, Fair Isle, first-winter male, 16–17 October
   North Shirva, Fair Isle, first-winter male, different to above, 17 October
1995, Sumburgh Head, first-winter female, 1 October

American robin *Turdus migratorius*
Vagrant, two records:
1967, Foula, 11–16 November (*British Birds* **61**: 349)
1982, Foula, male, 3–16 November

Fieldfare *Turdus pilaris*
Common and sometimes abundant passage migrant most numerous in October, usually overwintering in small numbers. Has attempted breeding on at least 14 occasions.

Song thrush *Turdus philomelos*
Common passage migrant, most numerous in April and late September to October. Scarce in summer and winter but has attempted to breed on at least seven occasions.

Redwing *Turdus iliacus*
Common and sometimes abundant passage migrant most numerous in October, wintering in small numbers. Has attempted to breed on at least 13 occasions.

Mistle thrush *Turdus viscivorus*
Uncommon migrant recorded mainly in March to April and October but with records in all months.

Pallas's grasshopper warbler *Locustella certhiola*
Vagrant, 11 records:
1949, Leogh, Fair Isle, 8–9 October
1956, The Haa, Fair Isle, 2 October
1976, Kennaby, Fair Isle, 20–24 September
1981, North Grind, Fair Isle, first-winter, 21 September
1983, Skerries, first winter, 4–8 October
1986, Leogh, Fair Isle, first-winter, 26 September
1988, Utra, Fair Isle, 5 October
   Quoy, Fair Isle, 9 October
   Leogh, Fair Isle, 12 October
1994, North Leogh, Fair Isle, first-winter, trapped, 21–23 September, found dead on last date
1996, Quoy, Fair Isle, 17 September

Lanceolated warbler *Locustella lanceolata*
Rare migrant, 59 records, the majority on Fair Isle. All but one have occurred in autumn between early September and early November with the majority in the second half of September. The only spring record was on Fair Isle on 4 May 1953.

Grasshopper warbler *Locustella naevia*
Scarce passage migrant recorded in April to October but mainly in May. One probable breeding attempt in 1988.

River warbler *Locustella fluviatilis*
Vagrant, 12 records:
1961, Leogh, Fair Isle, trapped, 24–25 September
1969, Plantation, Fair Isle, trapped, 16 September
1981, Plantation, Fair Isle, trapped, 23 May, found dead next day
1982, Vaadal, Fair Isle, first-winter, trapped, 22 September
    Midway, Fair Isle, adult, trapped, 24–26 September
1984, South Reeva, Fair Isle, 7 June
1993, Fair Isle, trapped, 25–28 May
    Fair Isle, trapped, 26–27 September
    Skerries, trapped, 9–10 October
1995, Bull's Park, Fair Isle, 27 May
    Helendale, Lerwick, 14 September
    Sumburgh Head, trapped, 15–17 September

Savi's warbler *Locustella luscinioides*
Vagrant, six records involving seven birds:
1908, two, Fair Isle, one shot by Eagle Clarke, 14 May
1981, Gully, Fair Isle, trapped, 24 June
1986, Vaadal, Fair Isle, adult, 7 June
1993, Field, Fair Isle, trapped, 4–6 May
1995, Whalsay, 29–30 May
1996, Skerryholm, Fair Isle, 24–31 May

Aquatic warbler *Acrocephalus paludicola*
Rare migrant, at least 40 records, the majority on Fair Isle. All records have been in autumn, in August and September, with the majority in August.

Sedge warbler *Acrocephalus schoenobaenus*
Passage migrant in small numbers, recorded in April to November with the majority of records in May.

Paddyfield warbler *Acrocephalus agricola*
Vagrant, 15 records:
1925, Fair Isle, shot, 26 September to 1 October
1953, Brae of Restensgeo, Fair Isle, trapped, 16 September
1984, Gully, Fair Isle, trapped, 30 May
1986, Quoy, Fair Isle, first-winter, trapped, 26 September to 4 October
1987, Upper Stoneybrake, Fair Isle, first-winter, trapped, 22 September
1992, Charlie's Trees, Fair Isle, 9–10 June
1993, Schoolton, Fair Isle, 31 May
    Meadow Burn, Fair Isle, first-winter, trapped, 8–13 September
1994, Gully/Observatory, Fair Isle, first-winter, trapped, 22–26 September
    The Haa/Busta, Fair Isle, different to above bird, 24–25 September
    Quendale, 28 September to 1 October
    Lamba Ness, Unst, first-winter, trapped, 30 September to 2 October
1995, North Leogh, Fair Isle, first-winter, trapped, 9–17 September
1996, Fair Isle, first-winter, trapped, 19 September, had been previously ringed in Lithuania on 8 September 1996
    Feal Burn, Fetlar, 1 October, appeared to be ringed

Blyth's reed warbler *Acrocephalus dumetorum*
Vagrant, 16 records, involving at least 14 individuals:
1910, Fair Isle, shot, 29–30 September
1912, four or five, Fair Isle, 24, 26, 29, 30 September, 1 October, four birds shot
1928, Fair Isle, shot, 24 September
1985, Noss, 14 August
1987, Field, first-winter, trapped, 27–29 September
1993, Skerries, first-winter, trapped, 9–15 October

Gully, Fair Isle, trapped, 22 October, same as Sumburgh Hotel area, first-winter, 23–29 October, killed by
   cat and found on 31 October, trapped on 27, had previously been ringed on Fair Isle on 22 October
1994, Kergord, in song, trapped, 21–29 May
1996, Plantation, Fair Isle, trapped, 4–6 June
   Gully/Plantation, Fair Isle, trapped, 11–13 June
   Homisdale, Fair Isle, first-winter, trapped, 24 September

Marsh warbler *Acrocephalus palustris*
Rare passage migrant with most records in mid-May to July and especially in June, much scarcer in autumn
and recorded in August to October.

Reed warbler *Acrocephlaus scirpaceus*
Uncommon passage migrant recorded in April to November but mainly in August and September. Has bred
once.

Great reed warbler *Acrocephlus arundinaceus*
Vagrant, at least 22 records:
1958, Durigarth (Loch of Brow), 4–5 June (*British Birds* **53**: 168)
1964, Sompal/Hjukni Geo, Fair Isle, trapped, 8–11 June
1966, Gully/Quoy, Fair Isle, in song, trapped, 26–27 May
1970, Quoy, Fair Isle, trapped, 12–14 June
1971, The Haa, Fair Isle, 29 May
1974, Noss, 14 June
1975, Norwick, Unst, 8 June to 8 July
1976, Skerries, freshly dead, 21 May
1978, Meadow Burn, Fair Isle, trapped, 2–6 June
1979, Strand, Tingwall, 10–11 June
1985, Skerries, 28 May
1987, Frakkafield, 13–27 June
1988, Hjon Dyke, Fair Isle, trapped, 27 May to 10 June
   south of island, Fair Isle, 2–3 June
   Gully, Fair Isle, trapped, 3–4 June
1991, Norwick, Unst, 27 September
1992, Hill Dyke, Fair Isle, 9 June
1993, Geosetter, 22 May, trapped
1994, Eel Burn, Hillwell, 12–14 May, presumed same Quendale, 15 May, presumed same Geosetter, in song,
   22 May
1995, Quoy, Fair Isle, 30 September
1996, Field Ditch/Charlie's Trees, Fair Isle, 20 May
   Foula, 7–10 June

Thick-billed warbler *Acrocephalus aedon*
Vagrant, two records:
1955, Leogh, Fair Isle, trapped, 6 October
1971, Whalsay, 23 September, taken to Lerwick and killed by a cat there on 25 September

Olivaceous warbler *Hippolais pallida*
Vagrant, one record:
1995, Plantation, Fair Isle, first-winter, trapped, 5–13 June

Booted warbler *Hippolais caligata*
Vagrant, 17 records:
1936, Fair Isle, shot, 3 September
1959, Gully, Fair Isle, first-winter, trapped, 29–31 August
1966, Skerryholm, Fair Isle, first-winter, trapped, 28 August to 17 September
1968, Observatory, Fair Isle, first-winter, trapped, 8 September
1976, Quoy, Fair Isle, first-winter, trapped, 25 August to 2 September
1977, Observatory, Fair Isle, 20–27 August
   Whalsay, 26 September to 4 October
1981, Skerries, 11–17 September
1989, Schoolton, Fair Isle, first-winter, trapped, 22–27 September
1992, Upper Stoneybrake, Fair Isle, first-winter, 14–16 September

1993, Sumburgh Head, 20–21 September
  Seafield, Lerwick, 22 October to 9 November, trapped on 25, possibly eastern race *H. c. rama*
1994, Skerries, 27 August
  Furse, Fair Isle, 11 September
1995, Sumburgh Head, 7–10 September
  Fetlar, 11 September
1996, North Shirva, Fair Isle, 22–24 August

Icterine warbler *Hippolais icterina*
Scarce and irregular passage migrant, recorded from May to October, with most records at the end of May/ early June and from mid-August to mid-September.

Melodious warbler *Hippolais polyglotta*
Vagrant: 21 records:
1955, Fair Isle, trapped, 16 September
1964, Fair Isle, trapped, 12 June
1969, Fair Isle, trapped, 14–20 June
1972, Fair Isle, trapped, 29 August
  Fair Isle, trapped, 19–23 September
1973, Fair Isle, trapped, 15–17 June
1976, Whalsay, 28 May
  Foula, 4 July
  Scalloway, 30 August
1977, Fair Isle, trapped, 20 September
1980, Fair Isle, trapped, 22 September
1981, Fair Isle, trapped, 15 June
  Sumburgh, 10 September
1982, Skerries, 23 September
1983, Veensgarth, 13 September to 10 October
1986, Toab, 3–4 July
1987, Scatness, trapped, 23–24 September
1990, Fair Isle, trapped, 6 June
1992, Skerries, 28 May
  Double Dyke, Fair Isle, trapped, 8–10 August
1996, North Haven, Fair Isle, 20 August

Subalpine warbler *Sylvia cantillans*
Rare migrant, at least 93 records, with 80 of these in spring between late April and early July and the majority in May. Of the remaining autumn records three in mid-August were all trapped and found to be in heavy moult, making recent arrival unlikely, leaving three in late August, four in September and one in October as potentially the only genuine autumn arrivals. Males showing characteristics of the eastern race *S. c. albistriata* have been recorded in 1989, 1992, two in 1993, and 1994.

Rüppell's warbler *Sylvia rueppelli*
Vagrant, two records:
1977, Boddam, male in heavy moult, 13 August to 16 September, first record for Britain
1990, Whalsay, male, 3–19 October

Sardinian warbler *Sylvia melanocephala*
Vagrant, three records:
1967, Observatory, Fair Isle, male, trapped, 26–27 May
1992, Cunningsburgh, male, from at least 24 July to 11 November
1994, Shirva, Fair Isle, male, 26–28 June

Barred warbler *Sylvia nisoria*
Scarce passage migrant with all but two records from August to November, particularly in August–September. The only spring records were singles at Lerwick on the 14 June 1914 (*Scottish Naturalist* **42**: 143), on Foula on 1–8 June 1967, and a first-year at Scalloway from 31 May to 3 June 1990.

Lesser whitethroat *Sylvia curruca*
Passage migrant in small numbers in both spring and autumn with most records in May and September. Probably one breeding attempt recorded in 1993.

Whitethroat *Sylvia communis*
Passage migrant in small numbers in spring, with fewer records in autumn. Most records are in May and September and there have been at least three successful breeding attempts.

Garden warbler *Sylvia borin*
Common passage migrant in autumn, with fewer records in spring. Most records are in late May to mid-June and late August to mid-September.

Blackcap *Sylvia atricapilla*
Common and sometimes abundant passage migrant in autumn with most records from mid-September to mid-October. Scarcer in spring with most records in May. Has bred on at least four occasions and attempted on at least three.

Greenish warbler *Phylloscopus trochiloides*
Rare migrant, at least 57 records, by far the majority in autumn between July and early November, with most in August. There are only five certain spring records, one in late May and four in early June, with another four records in late June and July.

Arctic warbler *Phylloscopus borealis*
Rare migrant, at least 79 records, more than half from Fair Isle. All records apart from two in late June and one in early July were in August to October with the majority in mid to late September. Two were found together at the Plantation, Fair Isle on 12 September 1991.

Pallas's warbler *Phylloscopus proregulus*
Rare migrant, at least 74 records involving occasional influxes of up to 10, with all records in autumn between late September and early November, the majority in October. At least 12 were on Fair Isle in early October 1982.

Yellow-browed warbler *Phylloscopus inornatus*
Uncommon passage migrant, with occasional influxes of up to 30 at the same time. Only recorded in autumn from September to November with the majority of records from mid-September to mid-October. In recent years, annual totals for this species have been between 50 and 100.

Radde's warbler *Phylloscopus schwarzi*
Vagrant, 14 records:
1976, Whalsay, 3–4 October
1982, Catfirth, 10 October
1987, Setter, Fair Isle, first-winter, trapped, 2 October
    Scatness, 3 October
1988, Easter Lother, Fair Isle, 13 October
    Scatness, 27 October
1991, Meadow Burn, Fair Isle, first-winter, trapped, 10 October
    Skerries, 10 October, found dead on 11 October
    Kergord, first-winter, trapped, 11–19 October
1992, Sumburgh Head, first-winter, trapped, 29 September
    Sumburgh Hotel Garden, first-winter, trapped, 4 October
1996, Voe, 19 October
    Sandwick, 19–20 October
    Geosetter, 19–20 October

Dusky warbler *Phylloscopus fuscatus*
Vagrant, 24 records:
1961, Vaadal, Fair Isle, first-winter, trapped, 14 October
1974, Leogh/Busta, Fair Isle, first-winter, trapped, 13–14 October
1986, Gully, Fair Isle, first-winter, trapped, 14 November
    Kergord, first-winter, trapped, 15–19 November
1987, Meadow Burn, Fair Isle, first-winter, trapped, 14 October
    Dale of Walls, 30 October
    Midway, Fair Isle, 6 November
1988, Virkie, 27–28 October
1989, Hillwell, first-winter, trapped, 3 November
1990, Plantation/Leogh/Hesti Geo, Fair Isle, first-winter, trapped, 30 September

Utra, Fair Isle, 19 October
Frakkafield, 30 October to 1 November
1992, Scalloway, 1 October
Noness, 1–2 October
Whalsay, first-winter, trapped, 2–3 October
Whalsay, first-winter, trapped, 4 October
Dale of Walls, 4 October
1993, Voe, 3 October
The Haa/Skerryholm, Fair Isle, 10–11 October
Sumburgh Hotel Garden, 25–27 October
Exnaboe, 4 November
Sullom Plantation, first-winter, trapped, 5–15 November
1994, Noness, Sandwick, first-winter, trapped, 7–8 November
1995, Sumburgh Hotel Garden, 25–26 May

Bonelli's warbler *Phylloscopus bonelli*
Vagrant, six records:
1961, Shirva/Midway, Fair Isle, first-winter, trapped, 22 September
1974, Sumburgh, 5 September
1979, Whalsay, first-winter, 21–22 September
1981, Skerries, 22 September
1983, Helendale, Lerwick, 27 September to 3 October
1984, Fetlar, 19th September to 1 October
Whalsay, first-winter, 7 October
1992, Linni Geo, Fair Isle, 30 September
Exnaboe, adult, trapped, at least 11–15 October
1995, Sumburgh Head, first-winter, trapped, 13–18 September

Wood warbler *Phylloscopus sibalitrix*
Uncommon and irregular passage migrant, recorded from April to October with most records in May, August and September.

Chiffchaff *Phylloscopus collybita*
Common passage migrant, rare in mid-summer and winter. Both passage periods are prolonged with most spring records in April to May and most autumn records in late September to October. Birds showing characteristics of the eastern race *P. c. trisits* are annual in late autumn.

Willow warbler *Phylloscopus trochilus*
Common passage migrant in both spring and autumn, sometimes in large numbers, with most records in May and September. Has bred on at least six occasions and once overwintered.

Goldcrest *Regulus regulus*
Common and sometimes abundant passage migrant in autumn, mainly in October. Usually scarce in spring with most records in April. Has bred fairly regularly in the central Mainland in recent years and may be resident there.

Firecrest *Regulus igniacapillus*
Vagrant, at least 16 records:
1965, Seafield, Lerwick, male, 11 June to 11 July (*Scottish Birds* **4**: 291), same Seafield, 29 August to 27 September
1968, Seafield, Lerwick, 11th October (*Scottish Birds* **5**: 348)
1972, Sumburgh, 2–3 October
1976, Sumburgh Head, mid-October, later found dead
Whalsay, 17–21 October
1977, Seafield, Lerwick, 9 October
Sullom Plantation, 11 October
1981, Grutness, 22 September
Gully, Fair Isle, first-winter male, trapped, 7–8 November
1982, Whalsay, 14 November
1989, Pund, Fair Isle, 2 May
1992, Gully, Fair Isle, male, 15–17 May

1993, South Lochside, Lerwick, 23–25 September
  Fetlar, 6 October
1994, Whalsay, 24 October
  Helendale, Lerwick, 26 October

[**Brown flycatcher** *Muscicapa dauurica*]
Possible escape (category D), one record:
1992, Plantation, Fair Isle, trapped, 1–2 July

Spotted flycatcher *Muscicapa striata*
Regular passage migrant recorded in April to November, but mainly in May and September with most records in spring in late May and early June.

Red-breasted flycatcher *Ficedula parva*
Scarce migrant, recorded in May to June and August to November, with the majority of records in September and October.

Collared flycatcher *Ficedula albicollis*
Vagrant, six records:
1947, Skaw, Whalsay, adult male, shot, 11 May, specimen sent to Royal Scottish Museum, first for Scotland
  (*Scottish Naturalist* 1948: 51)
1975, Skerries, male, 13 May
1976, Skerries, female, 25 May
1979, Bressay, male, 23–24 May
1986, Double Dyke, Fair Isle, first-winter, trapped, 8 October
1995, Tresta House garden, male, 5 June

Pied flycatcher *Ficedula hypoleuca*
Common passage migrant, occasionally in large numbers in spring and autumn, recorded in April to November, with most records in May and September.

[**Bearded tit** *Panurus biarmicus*]
Listed in Tulloch and Hunter (1972) but the occurrence of this species in Shetland must be considered extremely remote.

Long-tailed tit *Aegithalos caudatus*
Vagrant, at least two records involving eight individuals:
1860, Halligarth, Baltasound, four, mid-April
1988, Helendale area, Lerwick, four, 12–13 November
A party of three or four is said to have also been on Fair Isle in about 1930, but no further details are known.

Willow tit *Parus Montanus*
Vagrant, one record:
1935, Fair Isle, seen by G. Stout with three blue tits, 3 November, thought to be of the north Eurasian race *P. m. borealis*

Coal tit *Parus ater*
Vagrant, eight records:
1936, west cliffs, Fair Isle, seen by L.S.V. Venables, 21 September
1965, Whalsay, two, 29 September (*Scottish Birds* **3**: 430)
  Setter, Fair Isle, 28 October
1965, Unst, 1 October (FIBO BUL **6.5**: 224)
1977, Lerwick, late October
  Sumburgh, 29 November
1981, Virkie, 2 April
1989, Vatstrass, Fair Isle, 26 September to 1 February 1990

Blue tit *Parus caeruleus*
Scarce autumn and winter visitor with about 115 records, occasionally irruptive. Recorded from October to March with most records in October and early November

Great tit *Parus major*
Rare, mainly autumn and winter visitor with about 137 records, occasionally irruptive. Recorded from September to May with the majority of records in October.

[**Nuthatch** *Sitta europaea*]
Singles were reported seen on Fair Isle by G. Stout on 29–30 May 1936 and at North Haven on 1 May 1939. In the absence of any descriptions and as the species is extremely unlikely to reach Shetland these records must be considered doubtful. E&B also quote Scot-Skirving (*Journal of Agriculture* 1868: 193) as saying that this species has been obtained in Bressay. However, no details were given and Saxby (p. 144) stated that it was really a wryneck!

Treecreeper *Certhia familiaris*
Vagrant, 34 records:
1859, Halligarth, Unst, September
1882, Bressay, 12 October
1906, Fair Isle, found exhausted after gale and collected, 27 December
1913, Fair Isle, shot, 14 April
1937, Lerwick, shot, 6 November
1959, The Haa, Fair Isle, trapped, 17–18 October
1961, B&J
1966, two (B&J)
1968, East Yell, 21 April, trapped, northern race *C. f. familiaris* (*Scottish Birds* **5**: 341)
1972, Kergord, 26 November to 11 March 1973, northern race *C. f. familiaris*
1975, Scalloway, 3 October
  Whalsay, about 25 October
1976, Whalsay, 2–4 October, found dead, 5 October, northern race *C. f. familiaris*
  Scalloway, 26 October
1979, Bixter, 11 October
1980, Lerwick, 29 September and 6 October
  Eshaness, 14 October
  Bressay, 27 October
  Taing, Fair Isle, found dead, 27 October
  Kergord, 8–22 November, northern race *C. f. familiaris*
1982, Kergord, 30 October into 1983
1983, Kergord, from 1982 into January
1987, North Reeva, Fair Isle, 30 October
1988, Cunningsburgh, 28 September
  West Voe of Sumburgh, 14–15 October
  Whalsay, 20 October
  South Collafirth, 21 October, northern race *C. f. familiaris*
1992, Sumburgh Farm, 14 September
  Sumburgh Head, 1 October
1993, Seafield, Lerwick, 27 September
  Double Dyke, Fair Isle, 30 September
  Whalsay, 2 October
  Legarth, Fetlar, 3 October

Golden oriole *Oriolus oriolus*
Scarce migrant with about 186 records. Most are recorded in spring, between May and early July with by far the majority in late May/early June. Very rare in autumn with only eight records, all between mid-August and early November.

Brown shrike *Lanius cristatus*
Vagrant, one record:
1985, Grutness, adult male, 30 September to 2 October (*British Birds* **86**: 600–604)
This is the only British and Western Palaearctic record of this species, which breeds in Siberia, northern China and Japan and winters in southern Asia.

Isabelline shrike *Lanius isabellinus*
Vagrant, six records:
1960, Gilsetter, Fair Isle, adult male, 12–13 May
1979, Dutfield, Fair Isle, juvenile/first-winter, 24 October

1981, North Shirva, Fair Isle, adult male, 9–12 October, showing characters of the eastern race *L. i. speculigerus*
1987, Eswick, intermediate between *L. i. isabellinus* and *L. i. phoenicuroides*, 23 October
1988, Catfirth, first-winter, 18–23 October
1994, Gully, Fair Isle, adult female, trapped, 23–24 August, probably *L. i. phoenicuroides*

Red-backed shrike *Lanius collurio*
Common passage migrant recorded in May to November but with most records in May and early June. Fewer are recorded in autumn, mainly in September. Successfully bred in 1990 and possibly in 1870.

Lesser grey shrike *Lanius minor*
Vagrant, at least 28 records with a further undocumented six records. Almost equal numbers have occurred in both spring and autumn with all spring records between 12 May and 28 June, and all autumn records between 8 August and 1 November:
pre-1950, six records, Fair Isle, undocumented sightings, all in spring
1929, Whalsay, shot, 14 September
1940, Fair Isle, 1 November
1944, Fair Isle, third week of October
1955, Fair Isle, trapped, 16–19 September
   Fair Isle, 19 September
   Fair Isle, trapped, 8 October
1956, Foula, 8–12 August
1958, Fair Isle, 30 May
1965, Sellafirth, Yell, 23–30 September
   Whalsay, adult, 17–24 October (*British Birds* **59**: 296)
1966, Fair Isle, 29 May
   Fair Isle, 19 June
   Foula, 20–28 June (*British Birds* **60**: 329)
   Fair Isle, 21 September
1967, Saxa Vord, 15 October (*British Birds* **61**: 354)
1970, Whalsay, 18–20 May
   Sumburgh, 26 September
   Catfirth, 7 October
1972, Fair Isle, 26 September to 5 October
1974, Fetlar, 14–15 June
   Unst, 19 June
   Fair Isle, 24–26 June
1977, Skerries, 20–21 May
1984, Fair Isle, 2–6 June
1990, Whalsay, adult female, 26th September to 20 October, trapped
1993, Fair Isle, 12–14 May
   Norwick/Skaw/Northdale, Unst, 30 September to 3 October
1994, Foula, 24–27 September

Great grey shrike *Lanius excubitor*
Uncommon migrant recorded from September to June but mainly in April and September to November.

Southern grey shrike *Lanius meridonalis*
Vagrant, three records:
1956, Fair Isle, trapped, 21 September (*British Birds* **50**: 246–249), first British record
1964, Taing, Fair Isle, 17–18 October
1994, Boddam, 7–10 November

Woodchat shrike *Lanius senator*
Vagrant, at least 37 records, the majority in spring between late April and early July and in autumn between mid-August and early October.

Jay *Garrulus glandarius*
Vagrant, recorded on three ocassions:
1861, Halligarth, Baltasound, 26 August (Saxby)
1890s, Belmont, Unst, three or four, autumn (V&V)
1940, North Haven, Fair Isle, seen by G. Stout, mid-May

Magpie *Pica pica*
Vagrant, one record:
1987, Bull's Park, Fair Isle, 22–25 April
One reported on Foula at the end of April 1987 was subsequently rejected by the Shetland Rarities Committee.

Nutcracker *Nucifraga caryocatactes*
Vagrant, one record:
1968, Lerwick, 22–23 August (*Scottish Birds* **5**: 290)

Chough *Pyrrhocorax pyrrhocorax*
Vagrant, two records:
1952, Exnaboe, Dunrossness, third week of March (*Scottish Naturalist* **69**: 42)
1984, Whalsay, 6–9 February

Jackdaw *Corvus monedula*
Scarce winter visitor and passage migrant although recorded in all months of the year. Most records are in January to May. Birds showing characters of the Baltic and Russian race *C. m. soemmerringii* were recorded in 1996, two at Westerwick 19 April and singles there on 8 May and 21 June, four at Strand on 13 October with three remaining to 20 October.

Rook *Corvus frugilegus*
Common but localized breeding resident, passage migrant and winter visitor.

Carrion crow *Corvus corone corone*
Uncommon passage migrant and winter visitor with most records in spring.

[***Hooded crow** *Corvus corone cornix*]
Shetland names: *craa, kroga*
Common and widespread breeding resident, with some evidence of passage.

Raven *Corvus corax*
Shetland names: *corbie, rafn*
Common and widespread breeding resident, and to a lesser degree passage migrant and winter visitor.

Starling *Sturnus vulgaris*
Shetland name: *stari*
Common and widespread breeding resident, passage migrant and winter visitor.

[**Daurian starling** *Sturnus sturninus*]
Possible escape (category D), one record:
1985, Observatory, Fair Isle, male, trapped, 7–28 May

[**White-shouldered starling** *Sturnus sinensis*]
Presumed escape (category E), two records:
1973, Fair Isle, 24–26 June
1980, Halligarth, Unst, 1–7 July, presumed same, Foula, 14 July

Rose-coloured starling *Sturnus roseus*
Vagrant, at least 54 records, excluding a record of five or six reported by V&V on Foula on 28 October 1906. All records are between late March and mid-November with the most records in August and September.

House sparrow *Passer domesticus*
Shetland names: *sparrow, kirk sparrow*
Common and widespread breeding resident.

Tree sparrow *Passer montanus*
Scarce passage migrant, recorded in all months of the year with most records in May and early June. There are confirmed breeding records in at least 20 years since the late 1800s.

[**Black-whiskered vireo** *Vireo altiloquus*]
Ship assisted, one record. The mummified corpse of an adult in very worn plumage was found on board a

tanker that arrived at Sullom Voe in June 1991. It was suspected that the corpse had been on board the ship since the autumn of 1990. The corpse was sent to the British Museum, London.

Chaffinch *Fringilla coelebs*
Common passage migrant with occasional large influxes, and small numbers overwintering. Recorded in all months of the year with most records in March–April and September–October. One or two pairs have bred successfully in at least 14 years since the early 1900s.

Brambling *Fringilla montifringilla*
Common migrant, recorded in all months of the year with most records in April to May and September to October. Rare from June to August.

Serin *Serinus serinus*
Vagrant, five records:
1914, Fair Isle, female, shot by Eagle Clarke, 22 May
1957, South Harbour, Fair Isle, singing male, 25 May
1964, South Reeva, Fair Isle, male, 29 May
1968, Easter Lother, Fair Isle, 1 October
     Scalloway, 17 November (*British Birds* **62**: 487)

Greenfinch *Carduelis chloris*
Uncommon migrant, recorded in all months except July and August with most records in March to April and October to November.

Goldfinch *Carduelis carduelis*
Rare migrant, recorded in all months except March and July, with most records in October to November.

Siskin *Carduelis spinus*
Common passage migrant recorded in all months of the year, with most records in April to early June and mid-September to early November. At least three successful breeding attempts in Central Mainland in recent years.

Linnet *Carduelis cannabina*
Uncommon migrant, recorded in all months of the year, with most records in April and May. Has summered but there are no confirmed breeding records.

Twite *Carduelis flavirostris*
Shetland name: *lintie*
Common and widespread breeding resident, with some evidence of passage.

Redpoll *Carduelis flammea*
Common migrant, recorded in all months with most records in September to November, and occasional large influxes. Sometimes overwinters and has bred twice. The mealy redpoll *C. f. flammea* is by far the commonest race recorded with one successful breeding attempt, the lesser redpoll *C. f. cabaret* is a scarce migrant with one successful breeding attempt, and the greater redpoll *C. f. rostrata* is a rare migrant.

Arctic redpoll *Carduelis hornemanni*
Rare migrant, at least 143 records, with the majority in late autumn/winter, occasionally in small influxes of up to 15. All autumn records have been between mid-September and December with one in February, the majority in late September and October. There have been only three spring records, two in late April and one in late May, and one in summer in mid-July. Most records are of the smaller race *C. h. exilipes* from northern Fenno-Scandia across to northern Russia, and North America, although the larger nominate race *C. h. hornemanni* from Greenland has occurred. The two races, however, can be very hard to differentiate.

Two-barred crossbill *Loxia leucoptera*
Vagrant, occasionally irruptive, at least 25 records involving a minimum of 39 individuals:
1859, Halligarth, Baltasound, two (female and immature), shot, 4 September (Saxby)
1908, Fair Isle, 13 June
1909, Fair Isle, 10 July
1927, Fair Isle, 2 and 5 September (possibly two birds)
1930, Fair Isle, three, 12 September, one 18 September
1939, Fair Isle, three, 29 September

1953, Fair Isle, 4 July
1959, Foula, female/immature male, 21 August
1962, Fair Isle, immature male, 29–31 July
1972, Observatory, Fair Isle, male, 8–9 July
  Whalsay, 19 July
1986, Skaddan, Fair Isle, male, trapped, 1 September
1987, Fetlar, adult female, killed by cat, 9 August
  Wester Quarff, juvenile, found dead, 10 August
  Bigton, juvenile, 11–19 August
  Basta, Yell, two juveniles, 11–13 August
  Foula, three juveniles, 11 August; six juveniles (probably 10), 15 August, two remaining to 16 August and
    one to 18 August
  Voe, four juveniles, 13–18 August
  Fair Isle, three juveniles, 15 August, two remaining to 16 August
1990, Fair Isle, pair, 25–31 July
  Fair Isle, juveniles, 16, 23 and 28 August
  Kergord, juvenile, 22 September
  Fair Isle, female, 20 October
Another, Kergord, 6–13 July 1972 was later rejected as a male crossbill with wing-bars. One on Skerries rejected in 1987.

Common crossbill *Loxia curvirostra*
Usually a scarce migrant, although occasionally irruptive in large numbers of up to several hundred. Recorded from April to January with most records in June to August.

Parrot crossbill *Loxia pytyopsittacus*
Rare migrant, occasionally irruptive, with at least 85 individuals recorded, and apart from two in March (probably remnants from a previous autumn invasion), with all records in September and October.
1962, Fair Isle, at least 20, 27 September, increasing to 33 by 4 October, decreasing to five on 6 October, increasing to 10–11 during 7–10 October, increasing to 25 on 12 October, falling to two on 23 and one on 29 October. Probably about 59 individuals, 34 of total trapped.
  Quendale, male, 7 October
  Spiggie, adult male, found dead, 12 October, sent to NMS
1963, Fair Isle, two, 20 March, birds from previous autumn influx, one trapped
1975, Grutness, male, killed by cat, 22 October
1982, Fair Isle, 7 October, with flocks of six and 22 there on 8 October, all departed by 9 October
  Fair Isle, 10 October, with five on 12 October, one remaining to 29 October. Probably about 35 individuals although only seven accepted by BBRC
    Catfirth, male, 12 October
  Voxter, seven: four (three males, one female) 16 October; six (three males, three females, two new) 18 October; six (four males, one new, two females) 19 October; and one male, 25 October
  Strand, female, 18–19 October
  Voe, female, 18 October
1990, Lower Shirva, Fair Isle, female, trapped, 23–24 September
  Whalsay, female, 14 October
1994, Kergord, female, 19–20 October
The 1962 record at Quendale is the only one accepted by BBRC but the bird was the only one trapped out of a flock of four, all of which were probably parrot crossbills. A male found dead at Spiggie on 12 October 1962 is also unaccepted by BBRC but was considered probably reliable by Catley & Hursthouse (*British Birds* **78**: 482–505).

Pine grosbeak *Pinicola enucleator*
Vagrant, one record:
1992, Lerwick, first-winter male, 25 March to at least 25 April

[Blue grosbeak *Guiraca caerulea*]
Possible escape (category D), one record:
1970, Skerries, male, 17–26 August

[Japanese grosbeak *Coccothraustes personatus*]
Presumed escape (category E), one record:

1992, Ollaberry, adult, 13 June, also Ronas Voe, 14 June, then at various North Mainland localities until Burravoe, Yell, 12 July, later taken into captivity, and died there in spring 1994

[Black-headed grosbeak *Pheuticus melanocephalus*]
Presumed escape (category E), one record:
1969, Setter, Fair Isle, male, trapped, 24 August

Common rosefinch *Carpodacus erythrinus*
Scarce but annual migrant since the late 1960s, recorded in April to October with most records in May–June and August–September. Increasing as a spring migrant with singing males often present in late June, but with most records in autumn.

[House finch *Carpodacus mexicanus*]
Presumed escape, one record:
1966, Fair Isle, female, trapped, 27–30 April, thought to be this species

Bullfinch *Pyrrhula pyrrhula*
Scarce migrant, occasionally irruptive, recorded from September to May with most records in October and November.

Hawfinch *Coccothraustes coccothraustes*
Scarce but almost annual migrant, recorded in all months except February, with most records in April and May.

Black-and-white warbler *Mniotilta varia*
Vagrant, one record:
1936, Scalloway, found dead, mid-October (*British Birds* **53**: 98)
Initially regarded as an escape from captivity, it is only relatively recently with the acceptance of the principle of unaided transatlantic vagrancy that this record has gained acceptance as the first record of this species for Britain and Ireland.

Yellow warbler *Dendroica petechia*
Vagrant, one record:
1990, Helendale, Lerwick, first-winter male/adult female, 3–4 November

Chestnut-sided warbler *Dendroica pensylvanica*
Vagrant, one record:
1985, Fetlar, first-winter, 20 September (*British Birds* **86**: 57–60)

Tennessee warbler *Vermivora peregrina*
Vagrant, two records:
1975, Double Dyke, Fair Isle, first-winter, trapped, 6–18 September
  Observatory, Fair Isle, first-winter, trapped, 24 September

[Magnolia warbler *Dendroica magnolia*]
Ship assisted, one record. The mummified corpse of a first-winter bird was found on board a tanker at Sullom Voe in mid-November. The tanker had left Delaware City, USA bound for Sullom Voe via Mexico and Venezuela (*Shetland Times*, 19 November 1993, p. 13).

Yellow-rumped warbler *Dendroica coronata*
Vagrant, one record:
1977, South Lighthouse, Fair Isle, male, 18 May

Blackburnian warbler *Dendroica fusca*
Vagrant, one record:
1988, Furse, Fair Isle, first-winter male, 7 October

Blackpoll warbler *Dendroica striata*
Vagrant, three records, and one ship assisted corpse:
1985, Whalsay, first-winter, 30 September to 3 October
1990, Sumburgh, first-winter, 6 October
1991, Fair Isle, 30 September

The mummified corpse of one of these American warblers was also found on board a tanker at Sullom Voe on 28 January 1992. The tanker had left Porto Bolivia on 24 December 1991 and arrived at Sullom Voe via Rotterdam. The specimen was sent to the British Museum

[American redstart *Setophaga ruticilla*]
Ship assisted, one record. The mummified corpse of a first-year male or adult female was found on board a tanker at Sullom Voe on 27 December 1992. The tanker had left Texas, USA on 4 November 1992 and arrived at Sullom Voe via Angola, West Africa (departed 6 December 1992). The specimen was sent to the NMS.

Ovenbird *Seiurus aurocapillus*
Vagrant, one record:
1973, Skerries, 7–8 October
What was probably the same bird was seen aboard a boat leaving Skerries on 11 October.

Common yellowthroat *Geothlypis trichas*
Vagrant, one record:
1984, Fetlar, male, 7–11 June

Savannah sparrow *Passerculus sandwichensis*
Vagrant, one record:
1987, Shirva, Fair Isle, 30 September to 1 October, nominate race *P. s. sandwichensis*

Song sparrow *Zonotrichia melodia*
Vagrant, at least three, possibly four records:
1959, Ward Hill/Observatory/Vatstrass, Fair Isle, trapped, 27 April to 10 May
1979, Setter, Fair Isle, trapped, 17 April to 7 May
        Sumburgh, 10 June
1989, Gully/North Haven, Fair Isle, trapped, 11–26 April
BBRC concluded that the Sumburgh record referred to the same bird present on Fair Isle in April and May 1979. However, the Fair Isle bird was ringed whereas the observers of the Sumburgh bird believed it to be unringed.

White-crowned sparrow *Zonotrichia leucophrys*
Vagrant, one record:
1977, Double Dyke/Shirva, Fair Isle, trapped, 15–16 May

White-throated sparrow *Zonotrichia albicollis*
Vagrant, eight records:
1966, Double Dyke, Fair Isle, trapped, 13 May
1971, Whalsay, 1 November
1973, Skerries, first-summer, 5–15 May
1978, Plantation, Fair Isle, first-year, trapped, 17 June
1987, Norwick, 13–15 May
   Kergord, 16 June
1989, Frakkafield, 27–28 May
1996, Voe, first-winter, 26 September to 7 October

Dark-eyed junco *Junco hyemalis*
Vagrant, three records:
1966, Foula, 1 May (*British Birds* **60**: 332)
1967, Foula, 10 May (*British Birds* **61**: 358)
1969, Skerries, 7 May

Lapland bunting *Calcarius lapponicus*
Passage migrant, scarce in spring and uncommon in autumn although recorded annually, with most records in September.

Snow bunting *Plectrophenax nivalis*
Shetland names: *snaa fool, sna ful*
Mainly a passage migrant, occasionally abundant in autumn (mainly in October to November), scarcer in spring. Small numbers overwinter during most years.

Pine bunting *Emberiza leucocephalos*
Vagrant, eight records:
1911, Fair Isle, male, shot by Jerome Wilson, 30 October
1980, Upper Stoneybrake, Fair Isle, first-winter, 14–16 October
  Quoy, Fair Isle, male, 3–8 November
1987, Upper Stoneybrake, Fair Isle, male, 11–20 October
  Utra Brecks, Fair Isle, female, 22 October to 13 November
1994, Skerries, first-winter female, 22–23 October
  Sumburgh Airport/Scord, male, 23 October
  The Haa, Fair Isle, male, 7 November
In addition, a male considered to be a pine bunting × yellowhammer hybrid was at Lower Stoneybrake/ Midway, Fair Isle on 29–30 November 1995 (*Birding World* **8**: 430–431).

Yellowhammer *Emberiza citrinella*
Uncommon although annual passage migrant in both spring and autumn. Recorded in all months of the year with most records in April and October to November.

Ortolan bunting *Emberiza hortulana*
Scarce migrant, recorded from April to June and August to October with most records in May and September.

Cretzschmar's bunting *Emberiza caesia*
Vagrant, two records:
1967, Gaila, Fair Isle, male, trapped, 10–20 June
1979, Bull's Park, Fair Isle, male, 9–10 June

Yellow-browed bunting *Emberiza chrysophrys*
Vagrant, one record:
1980, Setter, Fair Isle, probably male, trapped, 12–23 October

Rustic bunting *Emberiza rustica*
Rare migrant, recorded almost annually since the 1960s, about 164 records. Recorded from April to June and September to November with more records in autumn than spring, and most in May and late September/ early October.

Little bunting *Emberiza pusilla*
Scarce migrant, recorded annually since the 1960s, about 251 individuals with up to 20 in some years. Recorded from April to May and September to November with the majority in autumn and most in late September/early October.

[**Chestnut bunting** *Emberiza rutila*]
Possible escape (category D), three records:
1974, Foula, adult male, 9–14 July
1986, Observatory, Fair Isle, first-summer male, trapped, 15–16 June
1994, Skerries, adult female, trapped, 2–5 September

Yellow-breasted bunting *Emberiza aureola*
Rare migrant, recorded almost annually since the 1970s, at least 113 records, the majority from Fair Isle. Only one spring record a male at Sumburgh Airport on 20–22 May, two early July records, with the rest all between late August and early October, most in mid-September.

Reed bunting *Emberiza schoeniclus*
Uncommon breeding resident and passage migrant although recorded in all months of the year. Most migrants occur in May and late September/October.

Pallas's reed bunting *Emberiza pallasi*
Vagrant, two records:
1976, Skerryholm/Taing, Fair Isle, adult female, trapped, 29 September to 11 October
1981, Upper Stoneybrake, Fair Isle, first-winter female, trapped, 17–18 September

[**Red-headed bunting** *Emberiza bruniceps*]
Rare migrant or possible escape (Category D), at least 81 records. Almost annual in the 1970s with up to six in some years, only seven records since then. All records are between May and September, with the majority in May to July.

Black-headed bunting *Emberiza melanocephala*
Vagrant, 34 individuals recorded between May and October, with four in May, 14 in June, two in July, six in August, seven in September and one in October. A further record, from Skaw, Whalsay in March 1934, is placed in brackets by V&V, a decision which is still best considered as correct as there are no other March records for Britain.

Corn bunting *Miliaria calandra*
Shetland names: *cornbill, docken fool, docken laverock* (Muckle Roe), *docken sparrow, shurl, 'song thrush'* (Dunrossness), *titheree, trussy laverock*
Former breeding resident, apparently common in the first half of this century but now extinct and regarded as vagrant. The last breeding record was at Walls in 1983, since then there have been only seven records involving nine individuals.

[**Lazuli bunting** *Passerina amoena*]
Presumed escape (category E), three records:
1973, Fair Isle, male, 4–8 May
    Fair Isle, male, different bird, 7 June
1975, Foula, male, 12–23 June

[**Painted bunting** *Passerina ciris*]
Presumed escape (category E), four records:
1972, Voe, male, 28 May (described as wild and unfamiliar with a cage!)
1978, Hamnavoe, Yell, 9–27 July
1979, North Haven, Fair Isle, female, trapped, 19 June to 1 July
1981, Noss, male, 8 June

[**Indigo bunting** *Passerina cyanea*]
Possible escape (category D), two records:
1964, Fair Isle, male, 3–7 August
1974, Fair Isle, female, trapped, 20 May

[**Varied bunting** *Passerina versicolor*]
Presumed escape (category E), one record:
1974, Fair Isle, male, trapped, 8–17 October

Bobolink *Dolichonyx oryzivorus*
Vagrant, two records:
1975, Skerries, 18 September
1986, Upper Stoneybrake/Field, Fair Isle, 29 September to 2 October

[**Yellow-headed blackbird** *Xanthocephalus xanthocephalus*]
Presumed escape (category E), two records:
1987, Mid Yell, male, 13 May; presumed same seen previously Norwick, 10 May, and Burrafirth, 12–13 May, and Cullivoe, Yell 13 May
1990, Houll, Fair Isle, male, 26–30 April (*Birding World* **3**: 160)

Northern oriole *Icterus galbula*
Vagrant, two records:
[1889, Baltasound, Unst, caught alive, 26 September (E&B), specimen now in an Essex museum]
1974, Meoness, Fair Isle, first-winter, 19–20 September
The 1889 Unst record is currently under review by BOURC, the specimen having recently been discovered. There appears to be some confusion over the year of the Baltasound individual as the *Scottish Naturalist* **69**: 38 refer to the year as 1890.

TERRESTRIAL VERTEBRATES

by L. Johnston

Freshwater fish

Salmo trutta. **Brown** and **sea trout**. Ubiquitous. Sea trout much less common than formerly. Stocking of several lochs with non-indigenous fish in recent years.

Salmo salar. **Salmon**. Occasionally, and only at a few of the larger water systems with easy access to the sea.

Salmo gairdneri. **Rainbow trout**. Several lochs have been stocked, fish overwinter but no suggestion of breeding.

Salvelinus alpinus. **Char**. Confined to the Loch of Girlsta.

Anguilla anguilla. **Eel**. Widespread.

Gasterosteus aculeatus. **Three-spined stickleback**. Widespread except in the most acidic and peaty lochs.

Pingutius pingutius. **Ten-spined stickleback**. Recorded from the Loch of Cliff, requires confirmation.

Platichthys flesus. **Flounder**. In larger lochs with easy access to the sea.

Petromyzon marinus. **Lamprey**. Largest burns only, probably.

Reptiles (vagrants only)

Dermochelys coriacea. **Leathery turtle**. There are eight Shetland records of live individuals. All since 1955 and all recorded between August and October. The latest seen off north-west Yell by a fishing boat on 9 October 1995. The carapace or shell has also been occasionally recorded from the shore. This is the commonest turtle seen in British waters.

Caretta caretta. **Loggerhead turtle**. There is one Shetland record from the west side of Unst in June 1945.

Chelonia mydas. **Green turtle**. Fragments of a carapace of this tropical water vagrant were found on Burra Isle on 4 January 1956. There are only five British records, only one of which was alive.

Amphibians

Bufo bufo. **Common toad**. Introduced a number of times by adult and tadpole, but only one authentic record of spawning. Last known release in Lerwick in 1950. Not thought to have become naturalized.

Rana temporaria. **Common frog**. First record of introduction 1895 on Fetlar. Further introductions in 1920 at Lerwick and Scalloway. Now established throughout Mainland and most of the inhabited islands, including Foula and Fair Isle.

Mammals

Erinaceus europaeus. **Hedgehog**. Introduced about 1860 at Tingwall. Now widespread on Mainland and most inhabited islands, except Out Skerries.

Bats (vagrants only)

Vespertilio murinus. **Parti-coloured bat**. There are three records of this rare British vagrant which breeds in eastern Europe, in Whalsay 1927, Lerwick 1981 and Mid Yell 1984.

Eptesicus serotinus. **Serotine**. One record, Whalsay, 18 October 1991. The European breeding range only extends as far north as southern England and Denmark.

Nyctalus leisleri. **Leisler's bat**. Two records: Ollaberry 24 August 1978 and East Burrafirth, 16 October 1996. Predominantly an east European species with the nearest breeding colonies in Northern Ireland and Yorkshire.

Nyctalus noctula. **Noctule**. Three definite records: Burravoe (Yell), 25 July 1977; Asta, 20 August 1986; and Voe, 23 November 1987. There is also a record of a large bat emerging from the sails of a Swedish vessel in Scalloway Harbour in 1922 or 1923, and another large bat seen at Burrafirth, 29 March 1980. Most widespread of the larger European bats, absent from northern Scotland and most of Scandinavia.

Pipistrellus pipistrellus. **Pipistrelle**. There have been regular sightings of small bats in Shetland for many years, the majority thought to have been this species or the next. However of the eight small bats examined in the hand since 1980 only two, Sumburgh 3 October 1982 and Unst 26 October 1984, were pipistrelles. This is the commonest and most widespread bat in the British Isles.

Pipistrellus nathusii. **Nathusius' pipistrelle**. It is now thought that most of the small bats annually seen are this species. There are six definite records from bats examined in the hand, from 1980, 1987, 1989, 1992 (2), 1993, 1994 and 1996. Mainly eastern-Europe but a strong migrant.

Plecotus auritus. **Brown long-eared bat**. Three records: Lerwick, December 1947 (hibernating); Reafirth, 1972; and Sumburgh Airport, 12 March 1987. In addition one found alive on a North Sea oil rig in 1995 and flown to Shetland. Almost as widespread in the British Isles as the common pipistrelle, also the most widespread species in Scandinavia.

Lagomorphs

Oryctolagus cuniculus. **Rabbit**. Introduction date not known, but at least by the seventeenth century. Widespread on Mainland and most inhabited, and many uninhabited, islands.

[*Lepus capensis*. **Brown hare**. Introduced *c*. 1830 at Cunningsburgh. Appears to have survived on Mainland until 1937. Also introduced, but short-lived, on Yell in 1882.]

L. timidus. **Mountain hare**. Introduced *c*. 1907 at Kergord and separately to Vaila from Perthshire *c*. 1900. Now widespread on Mainland hills and still surviving on Vaila.

Rodents

Apodemus sylvaticus. **Field** or **hill mouse**. Introduced from Norway by Norse settlers. Ubiquitous, except Out Skerries. Separate races described. Separate races are described for Yell (*A. s. granti* Hinton), Foula (*A. s. thuleo* Hinton) and Fair isle (*A. s. fridariensis* Kinnear).

Mus musculus. **House mouse**. Presumably introduced by Norse settlers. Ubiquitous on Mainland and inhabited islands.

[*Rattus rattus*. **Black** or **ship rat**. Introduced from ships. Earliest record *c*. 1650. Known to be on some visiting vessels, e.g. klondykers, but no record ashore since 1990. Official records started by SIC Environmental Services.]

Rattus norvegicus. **Brown rat**. Introduced, but origin and date unknown. On all large inhabited islands except Yell (extinct within living memory) and Fetlar.

Carnivores

Vulpes vulpes. **Fox**. Apparently a single introduced in the 1860s but shot. From *c*. 1990 rumours have persisted of sightings of a fox in the Sullom, Voe and Delting areas. In August 1996 a dog fox was found dead on the road between Voe and Brae, apparently shot at close range. However rumours of others have persisted in the same area. It appears a very few animals have been brought and let loose deliberately, surviving possibly for some time. There are no records of breeding.

Mustela erminea. **Stoat**. Introduced in the seventeenth century. Widespread on Mainland.

M. putorius × *M. furo*. **Ferret-polecat**. Introduced through accidental or deliberate release in the early 1980s. Feral now throughout Mainland.

[*M. vison*. **Mink**. Accidentally released from Mink farms in the 1960s and 1970s. Individuals survived for a time, but now thought to be extinct.]

Lutra lutra. **Otter**. Once thought to be indigenous. Now presumed more likely to have been introduced, at least from Viking times, but origin and date unknown. Widespread, particularly on the coast, and very much a 'marine' animal in Shetland.

CETACEANS   by P. Harvey & Shetland Sea Mammal Group

Balaenidae

Eubalaena glacialis. **Northern right whale**. None have been sighted near Shetland since six were taken during the whaling between 1903 and 1914.

Balenopteridae

Megaptera novaeangliae. **Humpback whale**. Recorded annually since 1992. The same individual has returned to the Sumburgh/Fitful Head area each summer since 1993 and was accompanied by a second animal 1994–96. The handful of other records, from Eshaness, Fetlar, Mousa and Papa Stour, may relate to one or other of these two. During the whaling of 1903–14 and 1920–29, 51 of this species were taken off Shetland.

Balaenoptera physalis. **Fin whale**. Rarely recorded inshore, although one was seen off Noss in 1994. They are reported regularly along the continental shelf edge to the north-west of Shetland in June to August, and appear to be most common in July. The 1000-m contour appears to be favoured. The most commonly caught species during the whaling, when 4356 of this species were landed.

B. musculus. **Blue whale**. A rare deep-water species recorded off the continental shelf to the north-west of Shetland; 85 were taken during the whaling period.

B. borealis. **Sei whale**. Like the fin, rarely recorded inshore, but one was seen near Out Skerries on 27 August 1993. The status offshore is unclear, although it is likely to be regular along the shelf edge as 1839 were taken during the Shetland whaling early this century.

B. acutorostrata. **Minke whale**. The commonest baleen whale in Shetland waters. There has been a recent upsurge in sightings. Animals have been recorded in every month of the year but are most commonly seen from June to August. Although most sightings refer to single individuals, larger concentrations are occasionally reported, notably up to 12 feeding off Sumburgh Head in late June 1995 and 35 between Yell, Fetlar and Out Skerries on 8 July 1992. There have been a number of strandings, the most recent at Levenwick in 1997.

Physeteridae

Physeter macrocephalus. **Sperm whale**. There has been an increase in both strandings and sightings in recent years. There have been several strandings, the most recent in 1998, all of which have been male. The sperm whale is normally a deep-water species, but two recent individuals have approached very close inshore, one in Olnafirth on 20 February 1989 and one at the north mouth of Lerwick Harbour on 20 March 1995. During the whaling 19 were landed.

Monodontidae

Delphinapterus leucas. **Beluga**. A vagrant from the Arctic which has occurred in Shetland on 3 occasions, each a white adult. One record offshore by a Loganair pilot in the early 1970s, one in Hos Wick then Channer Wick on 4 September 1996, and one at Lund, Unst on 18 August 1997.

Monodon monoceros. **Narwhal**. Another arctic species occurring as a vagrant. One record driven ashore in 1808.

Ziphidae

Hyperoodon ampullatus. **Northern bottlenose whale**. A deep-water species recorded occasionally off the continental shelf edge. There have been a few strandings, the latest in 1983 and 1984; 25 Bottlenose whales were taken during the whaling between 1903 and 1929.

Ziphius cavirostris. **Cuvier's beaked whale**. An Atlantic species with only four recorded strandings in Shetland: August 1932; one on the east side of Fair Isle in late February/early March 1949; one stranded near Sandwick in April 1983; and the latest at Woodwick in Unst in May 1993.

Mesoplodon bidens. **Sowerby's beaked whale**. A North Atlantic species only recorded in Shetland from about 10 strandings in the last 100 years, the latest on the St Ninian's tombolo in December 1994.

Phocoenidae

Phocoena phocoena. **Harbour porpoise**. The commonest cetacean in Shetland waters. Seen very often throughout the year and often in pods of up to 70. Regularly stranded.

Delphinidae

Delphinus delphis. **Common dolphin**. A species of warmer waters seen irregularly as individuals mostly. Last record of three in Sullom Voe on 20 September 1993, with one remaining until 26 January 1994.

Tursiops truncatus. **Bottle-nosed dolphin**. Two in Uyeasound, Unst on 18–19 January 1998 represented the first confirmed record of this species for Shetland although there have been sightings of unidentified dolphins that may have been this species..

Lagenorhynchus acutus. **Atlantic white-sided dolphin**. An Atlantic species fairly regularly seen offshore and less regularly nearshore. Can occur in very large numbers as in 1926 and most recently when over 500 were seen off Sumburgh in 1994. There are a number of records of strandings.

L. albirostris. **White-beaked dolphin**. The commonest dolphin in Shetland waters, recorded in all months of the year, but most frequent in May–September. Small schools are the norm but concentrations of up to 100 have been reported in recent years.

Stenella coeruleoalba. **Striped dolphin**. A warm-water species recorded only three times in Shetland waters. One stranded alive in Tresta on 14 July 1993, and one dead at Muckle Roe on 1 January 1995 and another stranded alive at Whalefirth, Yell on 2 March 1998.

Orcinus orca. **Killer whale**. This species has become much more common in recent years. Pods, generally numbering up to 10, are most frequently recorded in May to August and it appears from photographic records that some of these pods are returning each year. Up to 100 were seen north of Muckle Flugga in June 1995.

Pseudorca crassidens. **False killer whale**. This pelagic species has only been recorded from Shetland as one stranding in 1944.

Globicephala melaena. **Long-finned pilot whale**. This pelagic species is probably quite common offshore, but records of animals inshore have decreased in recent years. Since 1913 there have been at least 28 strandings, the latest of 32 individuals at Urafirth, Hillswick in October 1983.

Grampus griseus. **Risso's dolphin**. A regular summer visitor to Shetland in small numbers. There have been at least seven strandings since 1913.

SEALS

by L. Johnston

Phocidae

Phoca vitulina. **Harbour seal**. A common resident breeding species with a population of *c*. 6200.

Halichoerus grypus. **Grey seal**. A common resident breeding species with a population of *c*. 3400.

The following species are seen as vagrants.

Phoca hispida. **Ringed seal**. A circumboreal species with a small population in the northern Baltic. One acceptable record (shot) in Whalsay in 1968. The species is difficult to separate from the harbour seal and other individuals were reputedly shot in the 1960s during hunting of harbour seals. An individual of this species taken into care in Northumberland was released from Shetland in May 1991.

P. groenlandica. **Harp Seal**. A species with a distribution off Newfoundland, Greenland and the White Sea, with seven Shetland records from 1830, the last at Hamnavoe on 7–9 February 1987 (which died) and Catfirth 31 January to 3 February. These last records coincided with an exceptional influx into southern Norway, apparently linked with food shortages.

Erignathus barbatus. **Bearded seal**. Another circumboreal species. Although normally non-migratory this has been the commonest vagrant seal recently, with eight records, all in the last 20 years.

Cystophora cristata. **Hooded seal**. Like the harp seal, a species of the pack-ice off Greenland and Newfoundland. There are five Shetland records, including two from last century. The last was a juvenile male at Norwick on 5 February 1993. In addition an individual of this species taken into care in Suffolk was released in Shetland in October 1989.

Odobenidae

Phoca rosmarus. **Walrus**. A species of the shallow arctic coasts with at least 12 Shetland records stretching back over 180 years; the last was an adult male seen off Fetlar, Lunna Ness and Papa Stour in June and July 1985. In addition walrus remains have been found in early Bronze Age levels at Jarlshof.

Glossary of Old Norse, Shetland and Scottish words and terms

Note that there are very many different spellings of dialect names. Where available, spellings and explanations have been taken from *The Shetland Dictionary* (Graham, 1993) or *Jamieson's Scottish Dictionary* (*Abridged*) (Johnstone, 1846).

ala-mootie/alamutie	storm petrel
aol	to squirt out
banks sparrow	rock pipit
bere	four-rowed barley
black-kyeppit maa	black-headed gull
blue-backit maa	herring gull
blu doo	rock dove
bonxie	great skua
boo-haid	stem
borg	fortified place
boucht	length
bruck	rubbish
brungawheedie	cormorant
bunksi	thick-set person
caa	to round up or drive
caain' whale	pilot whale
calloo	long-tailed duck
catyogle	snowy owl
chine	bevel at the top of the barrel where the lid sits
cottar	landless peasant
docken sparrow	corn bunting
draatsi	otter
dun	down
dunter	eider duck
ebb sleeper	purple sandpiper
eela	rod fishing (for *piltock*) from small open boat
erne	sea, or white-tailed eagle
feal	divot
flaa	piece of heather turf torn up by hand and used for thatching
floss	common rush
fourareen	four-oared boat
Fridarey	Fair Isle
fugl	bird
geo	narrow, sometimes deep, rock-bound coastal inlets

girse	grass
greff	bottom of a peat bank
grice	pig
grice-ingan	spring, or vernal squill
gronn	groan
haa	laird's house
haaf	deep-sea fishing in open boats 50–60 km offshore
haaf fish	grey seal
haaf-man	fisherman engaged at the *haaf*
heedie craa/hoodie maa	black-headed gull
herring hog	minke whale
hestr	horse
hill sparrow	meadow pipit
Hjaltland	Shetland
holm	islet
hoodie	hooded crow
houb	lagoon at the head of a voe
immer gos	great northern diver
innadaeks	inside the township (or hill) dyke
ingan	onion
laer	thigh
laverock	lark
lentens	lengthens
lintie	twite
lomr/lum/raingoose/regn gas	red-throated diver
loomieshun	small lock of the red-throated diver
looper dog	white-sided/white beaked dolphins
lorin/loren/muckle skarf	cormorant
longvi/longie	common guillemot
lyrie/leerie	Manx shearwater
maa	general term for seagull
maalie	fulmar petrel
mar	gull
marlie	eelgrass/sea grass
meldie	corn spurrey
moorit	brown
muckle	large
neesick	porpoise
noost	the place, usually a hollow at the edge of a beach, where a boat is drawn up
ootadaeks	outside the hill dyke
ootset	piece of ground in the *scattald* which lairds let to tenants upon which they had to build a house and bring the rough pasture into cultivation
Orkneyjar	Orkney islands
papae	priests/monks
peerie	small
peerie whaap	whimbrel
peewit	lapwing
Pettr	relating to the Picts
pikka/tinna/peerie maa	common gull
piltock	coal fish 2 to 3 years old
plantie crub/planticrub	a small circular dry-stone enclosure for growing cabbage plants
plivver	golden plover
plivver's page	dunlin
pone	a thin turf used as a shingle
ramn/rafn/corbie	raven
redd up	clean up
rig	plot of land
rivlin	shoe made from the untanned hide with the hair outermost
rivving	tearing
roo	to pluck the wool off a sheep
röyrr	reed
sandy loo/sandilu	ringed plover

scalp	remove divot, soil or thin peat
scattald	common grazings
skooty-aalin/scooty-aalin/ scuti-allan/sjui	arctic skua
scorie/skorie/skari	young gull in its speckled plumage
sea craa/wolkie	razorbill
sed ful/peerie swaabie	lesser black-backed gull
selkie/seli/selchie	seal
shaela	dark grey
shalder/shaldur/sjaldur	oystercatcher
shun	lochan
simmer din	twilight of a Shetland summer evening
sixern	six-oared boat
skarf/scarf	shag, and cormorant sometimes
skoot	excrement
smirl/smyril/peerie hawk	merlin
sna ful	snow bunting
snyrk	creak
solan/sula	gannet
souming	fixed share of cattle or sheep on a common grazing
spoot	razor-shell
steynpecker	turnstone
steynshekker/sten-shakker/ steinn-kalla	wheatear
stoaries	leather jackets
stock hawk	peregrine
strentens	strengthens
swaabie/swartback/svartbakv	great black-backed gull
swirten	flatten
taer	gnaw
Tammy Norie/lundi	puffin
tang fish	harbour seal
tirrick	tern
tjorn	tarn
tju	thief
toon	group of crofthouses
tre/timbr	tree
trows/peerie folk	mischievous fairies
tushkar	a spade with feathered blade for cutting peats
tussie girse	*Poa flabellata*, an introduced tussock-grass from South America
tystie	black guillemot
udal	land tenure system where inherited land divided between sons
Up-Helly-Aa	fire festival held in Lerwick on the last Tuesday in January
voar	spring
vadill/vaddel	sea-pool at the head of a voe which fills and empties with the tide
voe	inlet of the sea, generally long and narrow
wadmel	coarse woollen cloth
whaap	curlew
white maa	herring gull
whitrit	weasel, but in Shetland the stoat
yoal/yole	six-oared boat, slimmer, shallower and smaller than the *sixern*, usually rowed by three men

Index

Otter

499

ISBN 0-85661-105-0